Combating Terrorism in the 21st Century

Combating Terrorism in the 21st Century

American Laws, Strategies, and Agencies

Joseph R. Rudolph Jr. and William J. Lahneman, Editors

ABC-CLIO®

An Imprint of ABC-CLIO, LLC
Santa Barbara, California • Denver, Colorado

Library of Congress Cataloging-in-Publication Data

Names: Rudolph, Joseph R. (Joseph Russell), 1942- editor. | Lahneman, William J., 1952- editor. | Allison, Benjamin V., contributor.
Title: Combating terrorism in the 21st century : American laws, strategies, and agencies / Joseph R. Rudolph, Jr. and William J. Lahneman, editors ; contributors, Benjamin V. Allison [and others].
Other titles: Combating terrorism in the twenty first century
Description: Santa Barbara : ABC-CLIO, 2022. | Includes bibliographical references and index.
Identifiers: LCCN 2022012540 | ISBN 9781440855948 (hardcover) | ISBN 9781440855955 (ebook)
Subjects: LCSH: Terrorism—Law and legislation—United States. | Terrorism—Prevention—Law and legislation—United States. | Terrorism—Law and legislation—United States—Encyclopedias | BISAC: POLITICAL SCIENCE / Security (National & International) | POLITICAL SCIENCE / Terrorism
Classification: LCC KF9430 .C65 2022 | DDC 344.7305/325—dc23/eng/20220630
LC record available at https://lccn.loc.gov/2022012540

ISBN: 978-1-4408-5594-8 (print)
978-1-4408-5595-5 (ebook)

26 25 24 23 22 1 2 3 4 5

This book is also available as an eBook.

ABC-CLIO
An Imprint of ABC-CLIO, LLC

ABC-CLIO, LLC
147 Castilian Drive
Santa Barbara, California 93117
www.abc-clio.com

This book is printed on acid-free paper ∞

Manufactured in the United States of America

Dedicated to our longtime departmental chair, colleague, and friend,
Eric A. Belgrad (1934–2015)

—William J. Lahneman and Joseph R. Rudolph Jr.

Contents

List of Entries

Reader's Guide to Entries by Category

EXTREMIST GROUPS AND ORGANIZATIONS

INDIVIDUAL TERRORISTS

LAWS AND JUDICIAL BODIES AND RULINGS

SALIENT ISSUES

List of Documents

Preface

This book was written to serve as a single, authoritative source for information about America's experience with terrorist attacks and the responses to these attacks. It approaches these topics by using an encyclopedic format that not only permits readers to easily locate information on a particular issue or event that interests them but also allows them to both broaden and deepen their knowledge through associated readings. Terrorism in the United States and the American response to terrorism are topics of interest to all Americans, and, as a result, the book is designed to appeal to a wide audience and be a valuable addition to any public or school library. In particular, students of American history, politics, law enforcement, national security, homeland security, and related topics at all levels of instruction will find it a ready, easily understood source of detailed information. Scholars, researchers, and government officials will likewise find it to be a valuable resource.

The book contains nearly 150 entries, organized alphabetically, by more than fifty contributing authors, each an expert in their field of study. In addition to addressing their specific topics, many entries contain background history, current practices, and related information about the U.S. national security establishment, including the homeland security enterprise, the importance of civil liberties and civil rights in American life, the goals of terrorist groups, strategies and tactics that terrorist groups employ, and the kinds of targets that terrorist groups find attractive. Readers will appreciate that each entry provides the broader context for each topic by directing them to related articles within the volume as well as additional sources for further reading. The book also contains a helpful reader's guide that arranges entries in specific subject matter groupings to aid in research.

A separate primary document section follows the encyclopedia. This section contains important source documents such as federal laws, executive orders, speeches, and congressional testimony that provide insights into the effects of terrorist attacks and counterterrorism efforts on U.S. institutions and American society as a whole over the last century and a half.

Acknowledgments

The process of compiling and the quality of any edited volume depends entirely on the willingness of people to volunteer to assist and put aside their other responsibilities long enough to fulfill their promises. We thus owe special thanks to our more than fifty authors. Drawn from numerous disciplines and many with varied backgrounds in the national security field, they not only contributed outstanding work on the entries in this volume but also often answered our calls for assistance, multiple times. Most also labored to finish their entries by their deadlines despite the extra demands on their time caused by the need to adapt their courses and lives to the presence of a life-rearranging pandemic unknown at the time their commitments were made. First and foremost, we are deeply indebted to our contributors for joining us in this project and making this volume a reality.

Others also contributed their time in helping us to finalize our list of topics and in editing the primary documents to manageable size. In the latter instance, special thanks to Logan Danker, a local high school senior who sacrificed many hours of his summer vacation reading through congressional acts without succumbing.

Finally, our deepest gratitude to Kevin Hillstrom; his team of coworkers, particularly Saville Bloxham, who doggedly guided us through the last months; Kousalya Devi Krishnamoorthy, our editorial project manager; and, more broadly, ABC-CLIO, who stayed with us from inception to the conclusion of the project. Frankly, we would have given up on the volume ever making it into print without their encouragement and patience on so many occasions. Our grateful thanks.

William J. Lahneman and Joseph R. Rudolph Jr.

Introduction

On the first weekend in August 2019, the United States recorded its 249th and 250th mass shooting of the calendar year. On Sunday evening, August 4, in Dayton, Ohio, area resident Connor Betts took his assault rifle to the city's crowded restaurant and nightclub district and within one minute killed nine and wounded at least another twenty-six. A commitment to a cult of violence was the only motive investigators could find for the shooter's deadly attack. The previous day, in the heavily Hispanic city of El Paso, Texas, Patrick Wood Crusius opened fire with his own semiautomatic weapon in the parking lot of a Walmart Supercenter, killing twenty people and wounding another twenty-five in what he described as an effort to "save white America." Both of these shootings were horrific acts of violence against innocent people. But of the two shootings that weekend, only one was an act of terrorism.

FOUR DEFINING CHARACTERISTICS OF TERRORISM

Definitions of *terrorism* often vary in detail, depending on the specific criminal charges pursued by government security agencies, the altering nature of the terrorist threat over time, and the country confronting the threat. That noted, there is a general consensus across agencies, time, and space concerning unique characteristics of terrorism that set it apart from other forms of political violence.

First, terrorism is best understood within that world of political violence as a form of unconventional warfare distinguishable from other forms—for example, guerrilla warfare—by the fact that it explicitly and violently targets those who by any reasonable standard would be considered civilian noncombatants.

Second, like all warfare, terrorism is definable by a political content, whether employed by outsiders seeking to alter anything from specific government policies to regimes or by the state itself as a tool for controlling its citizens and ensuring the survival of the regime.

Third, terrorism is best seen as a tool of the weak, regardless of the user and whether terrorist acts are used as a means of achieving a specific goal or as a form of psychological warfare focused on instilling a sense of insecurity in a society as a whole. Outsiders with other instruments available to influence politics—for example, conventional military power, rare but vital natural resources, or great economic wealth—will usually eschew terrorism because of its unpredictability and its likelihood of being counterproductive (as well as on moral grounds). On the other hand, under certain circumstances, acts of terrorism can achieve short-term tactical success, as this volume's account of the 2004 bombings of Madrid's commuter trains documents. Likewise, albeit quite rarely, terrorist activities have *contributed* to the realization of strategic goals, for example, in the decolonization movements that ended the territorial empires of European states around the globe.

Fourth, as with other forms of warfare, terrorism is an ever-evolving threat against which counterterrorist agencies constantly run the risk of "fighting the last war." In other words, counterterrorist activities have to be prepared to not only defend against past iterations of terrorist activity but also guard against potential new types of attack. Moreover, the pace of change has considerably hastened in this century; for example, al-Qaeda quickly transitioned following the 2001 loss of its Afghan training camp—which it used to train its own operatives—to using Internet propaganda to radicalize homegrown terrorists. The recent resurgence of terrorist activity by hate groups and anti-government militias in the United States provides another example of the rapidly changing nature of terrorist threats.

But to return to that 2019 weekend in August, only Crusius's murders can be characterized as terrorism because investigators have been unable to discern any political motive behind Betts's action. Similarly, no political motive was ever found for the worst mass murder in recent U.S. history—the killing of sixty concertgoers in Las Vegas on October 1, 2017, by a single gunman.

HATE CRIMES AND TERRORISM AT HOME AND ABROAD

Unfortunately political motives are not always immediately apparent. Distinguishing a terrorist act from a hate crime often becomes a sticky matter given that the government's definition of a *terrorist act* often differs from that of Justice Oliver Wendell Holmes's "reasonable man." Happily this is less true in the case of an organization with an avowedly political agenda than with lone-wolf actors. Few would characterize action against racial or religious minorities by the Ku Klux Klan as anything other than terrorism, and federal authorities were quick to label the October 2020 plot by armed militias in Michigan to kidnap that state's governor as domestic terrorism.

On the other hand, in the case of an individual self-radicalized on the Internet, the federal government has often tended to draw a distinction between someone killing immigrants because he or she has been radicalized into hating them and someone doing so to advance an ideology (e.g., a call to arms to protect the supremacy of the white race). In choosing our case studies, we have chosen to take the reasonable person route and sidestep the line the government has drawn between advancing an ideology and acting on impulse. In our view, an act that involved murder in the name of jihad, white supremacy, or igniting a civil war warrants inclusion in this volume.

Another concern involved determining the extent of our coverage of terrorism on foreign soil, given this volume's primary focus on the United States. Some events in other countries were included simply because they galvanized public opinion in the United States concerning the threat of terrorism and necessary counterterrorism steps. In other instances, events in other countries received treatment because they involved American citizens, such as the hijacking of the *Achille Lauro* and explosion of the homeward bound Pan Am carrier over Lockerbie, Scotland. However, the greater number of entries that involve acts abroad were included because they either led to a reassessment of U.S. security measures (e.g., the 1972 Munich Olympics disaster) or affected the U.S. war on terror (e.g., the 2004 bombing of commuter trains in Madrid).

Finally, to illustrate both the persistence of the terrorist threat over time and especially in particular moments of American history, this work explores terrorist events that took place in the United States in the late nineteenth century as well as those of far more recent vintage, such as the infamous riot at the U.S. Capitol on January 6, 2021.

A

Abortion Facilities Attacks

Terrorism comes in many forms and with diverse ideology and effects. It has impacted our air travel, mass transit modes, workplace behaviors, and our kitchen table conversations. Terrorism has changed the way we worship and educate our children, especially when determining safety measures. That any one specific demographic or structure would be exempt from terrorism is simply wishful thinking. Even our most personal medical decisions have been affected, as in the long campaign against abortion facilities. Patients, employees, and medical facilities have been victimized and vandalized over the past few decades, often to a considerable degree.

The U.S. Supreme Court's landmark 1973 case *Roe v. Wade* delivered a moral and political blow to those opposing abortion. The controversial vote of 7-2 granted women the right to terminate a pregnancy without interference from the government. The pro-choice movement was now a force to be reckoned with. Countering this movement were pro-life advocates, mostly religious organizations that opposed the monumental legal decision. Pro-life advocates morally initially denounced any pro-choice groups or individuals through nonviolent means. Ultimately, in 1976, tensions between the two groups reached a boiling point, and the first abortion facility was attacked with arson and bombing—with many others to follow. This led to six years of death and destruction by terrorist groups such as the Army of God, also known as the Atlanta Bomb Squad and the Pensacola Pro-Life Hunt. Before 1983, twenty-nine bombings and arson attacks had occurred in New York, Virginia, and Florida. Over twenty-five additional terrorist attacks in Virginia and Florida were carried out in 1984 alone.

To extremists, no exceptions to abortion are acceptable; incest, rape, and proof of mental deformity or retardation of a fetus do not justify the "murder" of a fetus. The Army of God's manual still reads, "Those who have come to understand that the battle against abortion is a battle not against flesh and blood, but against the devil and all of the evil he can muster among flesh and blood to fight at his side" (Army of God Manual 1982).

Extremists did not differentiate between the women seeking abortions and the doctors, nurses, receptionists, and even law enforcement agents who were on the premises when the violent attacks were carried out. Since 1993, eleven people have been murdered by pro-life or antiabortion extremists. Of those murdered, four were health-care workers, along with a security guard, a police officer, and two bystanders. From 1977 to 2000, over 360 death threats were made against abortion facilities. Employees and patients fell victim to these violent acts. At least forty-one bombings, hundreds of anthrax threats, and kidnappings were among the tactics used by violent antiabortionists. The count of attempted murders and bombings is in the high hundreds. In 2015, a Planned Parenthood in Colorado Springs, Colorado, was attacked, leaving three dead and several injured. More recently, in 2016, a clinic was attacked in Columbus, Ohio. In addition to property damage, the offender left behind a written message: "Satan den of baby killers."

Recently, an article in *One News*, a Christian news source located in Ohio, addressed the labeling of an Ohio-based student group at Case Western Reserve University. Students for Life of America, a pro-life organization, was accused of terroristic behavior and directed to disband or be physically removed from campus. While these students, along with many other pro-life/antiabortion groups, may be peaceful and do not appear to advocate violence, their predecessors, like Operation Rescue and Army of God, most certainly did and continue to do so.

Pamela K. Mertens

See also: Army of God; Homegrown Terrorism; Rudolph, Eric Robert; Sociology of Terrorism.

FURTHER READING

Army of God Manual. 1982. https://www.armyofgod.com/AOGhistory.html

National Abortion Federation. 2020. "Convicted Murderer Released after 30 Years in Prison." July 30, 2020. https://prochoice.org/education-and-advocacy/violence/anti-abortion-extremists/

Roe v. Wade, 410 U.S. 113 (1973).

Turkewitz, J. A. 2015. "3 Are Dead in Colorado Springs Shootout at Planned Parenthood Center." *New York Times*, November 17, 2015.

Abu Ghraib Scandal

2004

The "Abu Ghraib scandal" refers to a U.S. military investigation into alleged abuses committed against Iraqi military prisoners and detainees early in the American military occupation of Iraq, from 2003 to 2011. Those accused of such abuse included uniformed U.S. military personnel as well as their civilian counterparts from various governmental agencies. The accusations became an international scandal in the spring of 2004 when the military investigation and its findings were released to the press.

Abu Ghraib was a notorious prison that was originally built in the 1950s and located in the town of Abu Ghraib, approximately twenty miles west of Baghdad, Iraq. During the regime of Saddam Hussein, the prison was internationally known for its overcrowding, unsanitary conditions, torture practices, and as a primary execution site for political prisoners. Following the American military invasion of Iraq in 2003, the prison was put in use by the U.S. military and other coalition forces as both a forward operating base and as a detention facility. Abu Ghraib housed detainees and military prisoners of interest, including insurgents accused of attacks against the U.S.-led coalition forces and Iraq's post-Hussein government. During the time the prison was run as a U.S.-led coalition detention facility, the detainee population increased to approximately 7,500 in the spring of 2004.

Shorty following the U.S.-led invasion, Amnesty International began publishing reports claiming human rights violations by the U.S. military of Iraqi prisoners, including torture and murder. In January 2004, in response to rising complaints from other international aid organizations about the deteriorating conditions at the prison, Lieutenant General Ricardo Sanchez, the commander of all coalition forces in Iraq, appointed Major General Antonio M. Taguba to investigate such claims. The *Taguba Report*, a fifty-three-page army investigation report completed in February 2004, was subsequently leaked to the *New Yorker* magazine, and the story soon became an international scandal after it was broadcast on the television news magazine *60 Minutes II*.

The report found that widespread and systemic abuse of Iraqi prisoners had occurred. It documented instances in which American soldiers from the U.S. Army's 372nd Military Police Company and contract employees hired to conduct interrogations had committed physical and sexual abuse, including torture and humiliation. The evidence contained within the report included not only eyewitness testimony but also numerous photographs and videos taken during the abuse. Some of these photos and videos were so graphic they have not been released to the public because of fears of reprisals against U.S. troops worldwide.

The fallout from the scandal led the U.S. Department of Defense to remove seventeen soldiers and officers from duty who were members of the 372nd Military Police Company. Eleven were later criminally charged under the Uniform Code of Military Justice for a variety of military crimes, including dereliction of duty, maltreatment of a prisoner, aggravated assault, and battery. Two of the soldiers found the most culpable were sentenced to terms of three and ten years, respectively, in a military prison. The highest-ranking officer implicated in the scandal was Brigadier General Janis Karpinski, the commanding officer of all detention facilities in Iraq. She was removed from duty, reprimanded, and demoted to the rank of colonel. In 2006, control of the Abu Ghraib prison was formally turned over to the Iraqi Ministry of Justice, which reopened the facility in 2009 as the Baghdad Central Prison.

John R. Capra

See also: War on Terror, The.

FURTHER READING

Cannon, Michael E., Jr. 2005. *Abu Ghraib.* Maitland, FL: Xulon Press.

Casteel, Joshua, and Joseph Clair. 2017. *Letters from Abu Ghraib.* 2nd ed. Eugene, OR: Cascade Books.

Clemens, Michael, and Christopher Graveline. 2010. *The Secrets of Abu Ghraib Revealed: American Soldiers on Trial.* Washington, DC: Potomac Books.

Danner, Mark. 2004. *Torture and Truth: America, Abu Ghraib, and the War on Terror.* New York: New York Review Books.

Funk, Deborah. 2004. "Environment, Attitudes Faulted at Abu Ghraib." *Air Force Times* 65 (16): 36. Supplemental Index, EBSCOhost.

Otterman, Michael. 2007. *American Torture: From the Cold War to Abu Ghraib and Beyond.* London: Pluto Press.

Achille Lauro Hijacking

1985

The basic facts pertaining to the *Achille Lauro* Italian cruise ship hijacking are straightforward. On October 7, 1985, four Palestinian terrorists seized the ship while it was on a twelve-day Mediterranean Sea cruise to Israel. Their demands were for the freedom of some of their brothers in arms imprisoned in Israel. An elderly American passenger confined to a wheel chair was killed and thrown overboard when he refused to immediately comply with instructions from his captors, and Israeli authorities refused to concede to the demands.

When their demands were not met, the terrorists were forced to surrender and were taken to Cairo, where they negotiated safe passage to Tunisia. The escape flight was intercepted by U.S. Navy fighter planes and forced to land at a NATO air base in Sigonella, Sicily. One year later, the captured terrorists were convicted in an Italian court for their crimes and sentenced to lengthy prison terms. Others, including Mohammed Abbas, the alleged mastermind, were convicted in abstentia.

Seizing a cruise ship at sea and demanding freedom for prisoners held in Israel was innovative as to location but not particularly original in terms of victims, anticipated media attention, and demands. The PLO attack, hostage holding, and subsequent flight from the country were what happened at the Munich Olympics in 1972.

This was not the first time that Abbas learned from history. According to N. C. Livingstone, he also attempted to use hang gliders to drop improvised explosive devices in Israel. Tactics such as this go back to at least the U.S. Civil War, when the North and the South used balloons that we might now recognize as recreational hot-air balloons for scouting.

Interestingly, about six months before the *Achille Lauro* hijacking, at the recommendation of the U.S. Coast Guard Captain of the Port, a wide-ranging tactical training operation was conducted jointly by the Coast Guard, the New York Police Department, and the FBI in New York City. A ship was seized in the harbor and the agencies had to collectively solve a waterborne terrorist hostage holding. The practical exercise had been about one year in planning.

An immediate reaction to the *Achille Lauro* experience was the formation of a multiagency and private sector task force to study the actual incident and consider plans to best react to a similar occurrence in the New York metropolitan area. Many recommendations were issued to enhance target hardening—undertaking a risk analysis for the protection of an asset and a cost benefit analysis of measures to protect such assets—for the cruise industry that sailed from New York and New Jersey. Changes in laws, rules, and regulations that impact numerous jurisdictions and entrepreneurs are known to take a long time. Some of the recommended changes were not adopted until after the terror attacks on September 11, 2001.

The historical examples noted here strengthen the dictum that students of terrorism must look back to better prepare for the future. Innovative professionals are also crucial to recognizing potential problems and planning reactions to them before we know that they exist.

Robert J. Louden

See also: Munich Olympics Terrorist Attack; Transportation Security.

FURTHER READING

Gooding, Gregory V. 1987. "Fighting Terrorism in the 1980's: The Interception of the *Achille Lauro* Hijackers." *Yale Journal of International Law* 12 (1): 158–179.

Halberstam, Malvina. 1988. "Terrorism on the High Seas: The Achille Lauro, Piracy and the IMO Convention on Maritime Safety." *American Journal of International Law* 82 (2): 269–310.

History.com editors. 2021. "US Navy Fighter Jets Intercept Italian Cruise Ship Hijackers." https://www.history.com/this-day-in-history/achille-lauro-hijacking-ends

Livingstone, Neil C. 1990. *Inside the PLO.* New York: Quill/William Morrow.

McCredie, Jeffrey A. 1986. "Contemporary Uses of Force against Terrorism: The United States Response to the *Achille Lauro*—Questions of Jurisdiction and Its Exercise." *Georgia Journal of International and Comparative Law* 16: 435f.

Active Shooter Scenarios

According to the Federal Bureau of Investigation (FBI), "An active shooter is an individual actively engaged in killing or attempting to kill people in a populated area." While it is difficult to accurately predict when or where incidents will occur and who will commit them, there are measures that can be taken to prevent and prepare for them.

FBI data suggest that active shooter incidents are most likely to occur in business workplaces, but they may also happen in primary and secondary schools, colleges and universities, government facilities, medical facilities, houses of worship, open areas, and other spaces. FBI data also indicate that the frequency of active shooter incidents has increased over time, as have the number of casualties.

While many psychological explanations have been offered, there is currently no predictive profile of a person who becomes an active shooter, nor a one single causal factor, or set of causal factors, that predicts with any certainty which individuals will carry out mass shootings. At the same time, research has determined that active shooter incidents rarely result from impulsive decisions occurring in the heat of a moment. Rather, shooters usually follow a pathway that builds from having a fantasy or desire to commit a shooting, to engaging in deliberate planning and preparations, to actually committing the incident. Threat assessment, in which trained teams review reports of behaviors of concern about individuals, has become an increasingly important preventive measure. These reports may come from a variety of sources, and the team triangulates them to determine level of risk and appropriate interventions.

Active shooter incidents may be committed by terrorists, but not all active shooter scenarios are terrorist events. Those motivated by actual or perceived grievances or by beliefs separate from ideology would likely not fall under the definition of terrorism. However, research has found that ideologically motivated shooters, generally in acts of lone-wolf terrorism, evince greater level of planning, utilize more weapons, and produce more casualties than nonideologically motivated actors (Capellan 2015).

"First response" agency policies and practices in regard to active shooter scenarios have changed over time. In the past, law enforcement agencies were trained to wait for special tactical teams (e.g., Special Weapons and Tactics, or SWAT) to arrive before entering a location where a shooting was occurring. Agencies are now trained for the first responding officers to join together in contact teams and to enter the shooting site quickly (or sometimes for individual officers to enter on their own), without waiting for special tactical teams. In the past, medical responders were trained to wait until a scene was cleared and declared fully safe before moving in to triage, treat, and transport the injured. Now, many agencies' rescue task forces are made up of police and medical responders who will enter a scene that is partially, but not fully, cleared so rescue work can begin. In doing so, they apply treatment principles learned from combat casualty care.

There are many models of public response, but they share in common the broad idea that, if possible, persons should leave the area where a threat is occurring. If leaving the area is not possible or practical, persons should secure themselves in locations that are protected and out of sight of the shooter. And in a worst-case scenario, as a last resort, persons should directly fight the attacker. Under Department of Homeland Security guidance, these steps are respectively known as "Run, Hide, or Fight."

Agencies, institutions, and individuals must recognize the risks of active shooter scenarios and plan and train to prepare for them.

Stephen Owen

See also: Charleston Church Massacre; Columbine Attack; Fort Hood Shooting; Orlando Pulse Nightclub Shooting.

FURTHER READING

Capellan, Joel A. 2015. "Lone Wolf Terrorist or Deranged Shooter? A Study of Ideological Active Shooter Events in the United States, 1970–2014." *Studies in Conflict and Terrorism* 38 (6): 395–413.

Federal Bureau of Investigation. n.d. "Active Shooter Resources." Accessed December 2, 2018.https://www.fbi.gov/about/partnerships/office-of-partner-engagement/active-shooter-resources

Fox, James Alan, and Monica DeLateur. 2014. "Mass Shootings in America: Moving beyond Newtown." *Homicide Studies* 18 (1): 125–145.

Sinai, Joshua. 2016. *Active Shooter: A Handbook on Prevention.* 2nd ed. Alexandria, VA: ASIS International.

al-Awlaki, Anwar

1971–2011

Anwar al-Awlaki, the so-called "bin Laden of the Internet," was an American-born member of al-Qaeda who rose into the upper ranks of the organization due to his abilities as a propagandist and recruiter. He was an important presence in—and often an architect of—much of al-Qaeda's global social media presence, maintaining accounts on Facebook, YouTube, a blog, and a magazine called *Inspire*. Eventually, al-Awlaki was targeted by the CIA on the orders of the U.S. government. Both his life and the manner of his demise highlight the challenges that anti-terrorism forces face in the complex environment mixing conventional and unconventional warfare (hybrid warfare) practiced by both state and non-state actors in the twenty-first century.

Born in New Mexico to parents of Yemeni extraction, al-Awlaki spent much of his childhood in Yemen. He traveled to Afghanistan in 1993 while he was a student at Colorado State University. He became increasingly interested in the study of Islam, and eventually became an *imam* (a Muslim cleric). By the late 1990s, he had cultivated a large and increasingly radical following that would eventually include two of the 9/11 hijackers and Nidal Malik Hassan, the perpetrator of the Fort Hood shooting.

Despite the investigation by the FBI into his alleged ties to various terrorist groups, al-Awlaki's rhetorical talents and ability to reach both English- and non-English-speaking audiences, as well as his perceived Islamic expertise, led George Washington University to hire him as its Muslim chaplain in 2001. Seen by a wide variety of news organizations as a brilliant moderate, he was highly sought for commentary in the wake of the September 11 terrorist attacks, greatly increasing his visibility and reputation. Such manipulations of the mass media would become a hallmark of al-Awlaki's career.

In 2002, al-Awlaki left the United States for the United Kingdom, where he preached increasingly radical and militant sermons. In 2004, he relocated to Yemen, where he was arrested in 2006 on charges of kidnapping and being party to an al-Qaeda plot to abduct an American officer.

After his release, allegedly following pressure by the CIA on the Yemeni government in the belief that al-Awlaki might be a useful asset for the United States, al-Awlaki went underground and became increasingly active in directing a wide variety of al-Qaeda's global social media activities. His sermons, broadcast over the Internet and spread via recordings, were successful in reaching a considerable audience among the radicalizing Muslims in Britain, Canada, and the United States. Al-Awlaki was seen as both an effective recruiter, enticing a considerable number of extremists into joining al-Qaeda overseas, and a spiritual inspiration for a number of attacks carried out by so-called homegrown terrorists within several Western countries.

Al-Awlaki's role in al-Qaeda prompted President Barak Obama to place his name on the list of individuals targeted for assassination, an extremely controversial decision due to al-Awlaki's American citizenship. After several unsuccessful attempts, al-Awlaki was successfully killed by a drone-fired missile on September 30, 2011.

Whereas his activities as al-Qaeda's propagandist underscore the multifaceted nature of modern asymmetrical warfare, the manner of al-Awlaki's execution heavily contributed to an ongoing debate over the use of drones for targeted assassinations. The potential extrajudicial assassinations of American citizens suspected of involvement in terrorist activities raised fears that such power could someday be used by the executive branch against *any* American. The manner of al-Awlaki's death also added heat to the ongoing debate about the impact of the U.S. war on terror on civil liberties.

Daniel Stotland

See also: al-Qaeda; Internet Surveillance; Recruiting Terrorists.

FURTHER READING

Ogun, Mehmet Nesip, ed. 2015. *Terrorist Use of Cyberspace and Cyber Terrorism: New Challenges and Responses.* Delft, Netherlands: Delft University Press.

Ramsden, Michael. 2011 "Targeted Killings and International Human Rights Law: The Case of Anwar Al-Awlaki." *Journal of Conflict and Security Law* 16 (2): 385–406.

Shane, Scott. 2015. *Objective Troy: A Terrorist, a President, and the Rise of the Drone.* New York: Tim Duggan Books.

al-Baghdadi, Abu Bakr

1971–2019

Abu Bakr al-Baghdadi was born Ibrahim Awwad Ibrahim Ali al-Badri in Samarra, Iraq, on or around July 28, 1971, one of four sons fathered by a teacher in a local Sunni mosque. At the age of thirty-two, having obtained a graduate degree in Islamic studies from Saddam University in Baghdad, he was fighting the U.S. forces that had invaded Iraq to topple Saddam's regime. A decade later, he founded the brutal Islamic State in Iraq and the Levant (ISIL), also known as the Islamic State in Iraq and Syria (ISIS), and became the most feared man in the region, with a $25 million bounty on him, dead or alive.

RADICALIZATION AND MILITARY SUCCESS

Al-Baghdadi's movement away from his father's moderate, conservative influence toward a more violent offshoot of the Islamic faith was well underway by the time he graduated from Saddam University. It was there that he embraced Salafism, an extremist branch of Sunni Islam whose followers are dedicated to preserving the purity of Islam as practiced during its early days following Muhammad's death, and are willing to kill Muslims deemed unfaithful to that true faith.

The U.S. invasion of Iraq in March 2003 moved al-Baghdadi's radicalization to the battlefield. Despite his 2004 capture and temporary incarceration by U.S. forces, he rapidly rose through the ranks of al-Qaeda jihadists to become the second leader (emir) of the Islamic State of Iraq (ISI) from April 18, 2010, to April 7, 2013. For al-Baghdadi, these were fruitful years. The withdrawal of U.S. forces from Iraq in 2011 enabled his followers to expand their territorial holdings in that country, and the growing chaos in Syria provided him with the opportunity to invade Syria and rename ISI as the Islamic State in Iraq and Syria (ISIS) in 2013.

One year later, al-Baghdadi captured the key city of Mosul, severed his remaining relations with al-Qaeda factions, and on June 29, 2014, declared ISIS as the new caliphate—a sovereign, political-religious state at the center of the Islamic faith for the global Muslim community—with himself as its chosen head.

THE CALIPHATE

At the peak of its influence under the leadership of Osama bin Laden, al-Qaeda only controlled a training camp in Afghanistan. Designating ISIS as a caliphate clothed it in Islamic history dating from the death of Muhammad and the rise of

Islamic empires under his successors (caliphs). Recognized Muslim leaders worldwide overwhelmingly rejected al-Baghdadi's declaration and his claim to be the new caliph; however, for his growing thousands of followers, that designation legitimized what soon became a bloody series of victories that brought Syrian and Iraqi Muslims under the control of a state built on conquest and sustained by terrorism directed against its own "citizens."

An even more important difference separated al-Baghdadi's caliphate from Osama bin Laden's al-Qaeda. Bin Laden appealed to the faithful to go to Afghanistan and elsewhere to support the community of believers. Al-Baghdadi, who expanded the ranks of his followers in 2012 by releasing Muslim prisoners in the areas he conquered, used the Internet to recruit volunteers with promises of blunder, spouses, and the opportunity to execute nonbelievers, driving the message home with videos of atrocities credited to ISIS. Indeed, al-Baghdadi actively involved himself in the instances of serial rape, brutal executions, and the spread of sexual slavery captured on ISIS videos.

By 2019, ISIS's desecration of religious sites (Muslim included), human rights violations, and savage cruelty had catapulted al-Baghdadi to the top of the U.S. most wanted list and made him the target of an international manhunt that ended on October 27, 2019. Then, on the verge of capture by U.S. Special Forces following leads supplied by his followers, al-Baghdadi's life as a terrorist caliph ended when he detonated a suicide vest, killing himself and two of his own children.

Joseph R. Rudolph Jr.

See also: Islamic State, The; Jihad; Psychology of Terrorists; Recruiting Terrorists; Returnees from Wars and Refugees as Terrorist Threats; Social Media and Terrorism; Sociology of Terrorism.

FURTHER READING

Callimachi, Rukmini, and Falih Hassan. 2019. "Abu Bakr al-Baghdadi, ISIS Leader Known for His Brutality, Is Dead at 48." *New York Times*, October 27, 2019. https://www.nytimes.com/2019/10/27/world/middleeast/al-baghdadi-dead.html

Griffin, Michael. 2016. *Islamic State: Rewriting History*. London: Pluto Press.

Steed, Brian L. 2019. *ISIS: The Essential Reference Guide*. Annotated ed. Santa Barbara, CA: ABC-CLIO.

Weiss, Michael, and Hassan. 2016. *ISIS: Inside the Army of Terror*. New York: Regan Arts.

"Alphabet Bomber," Muharem Kurbegovic

1943–

Muharem Kurbegovic was born in German-occupied Yugoslavia in 1943, immigrated to the United States after receiving an engineering education in Europe, and found work in the aerospace industry in California. He began his terrorist campaign in the early 1970s, when the United States was already regularly experiencing various forms of political violence committed by both the extreme left (e.g., the Weathermen, the Symbionese Liberation Army (SLA)) and the extreme right (e.g., anti-integration resistors in the American South). Unlike other lone-wolf terrorists at the time, however, he understood and exploited the *psychological* dimension of terrorism while practicing its destructive side.

Although Kurbegovic's knowledge of bomb construction was largely self-taught, his handiwork was notoriously impressive. His most lethal act, the August 6, 1972, bombing of the Pan Am Terminal at Los Angeles International Airport (LAX), tore hunks of the concrete from the wall anchoring the locker in which the bomb was sealed, killing three and injuring another thirty-six. Similarly, the Los Angeles policemen who defused the bomb he subsequently secreted in a Greyhound bus terminal locker reported it as the most destructive bomb they had encountered up to that time.

That bomb was only found because of the warnings Kurbegovic provided of its location. With phone calls and audiotapes in which he usually posed as "Isak Rasim"—alternately the voice of his group of one, Aliens of America, or the SLA—Kurbegovic co-opted the news media in his campaign to instill fear in the Los Angeles community in what counterterrorist personnel now label "information warfare." Among the first lone-wolf terrorists to do so, at one point, he threatened to escalate his campaign to include chemical warfare by employing sarin. Indeed, he went so far as to mail postcards purportedly containing sarin bombs under their stamps to the nine U.S. Supreme Court justices. The threat proved to be a hoax, but the publicity it reaped fed the sense of dread he was hoping to spread.

Reciprocally, it was the media who labeled him the "Alphabet Bomber" because his LAX and Greyhound targets fit the first two letters of his Aliens of America "group": *A* for airport and *L* for locker.

Less clear is Kurbegovic's mental state during his terrorist campaign. Though arrested within two weeks of the LAX bombing, competency hearings delayed his trial for nearly six years. On October 6, 1980, he was convicted of twenty-five felonies, including three murders, seven arsons, and the injury of eight (at LAX), and sentenced to multiple life terms without parole.

Kurbegovic's courtroom rantings during his trial aside, his arson convictions, in particular, indicated someone pursuing a quite rational design. Kurbegovic once saw his future as a successful operator of a string of taxi dance halls. However, his arrest for lewd activity at one of them, although dismissed, appeared to compromise that dream as well as the dream of becoming an American citizen. It was therefore not coincidental that the residencies he burned were owned by a municipal judge and two members of the Los Angeles Police Commission involved in the police and court system through which his arrest was processed. In fact, it was his personal connection to these earlier acts that facilitated his arrest so shortly after the LAX bombing.

The latter, in turn, also raises lingering questions about his agenda. The arc of Kurbegovic's spree ran from personal to political crimes. Hence, questions were raised as to the sincerity of his claim that his activity was intended to change laws regarding sex, immigration, and naturalization. Further muddying the issue was the fact that he only later said his goal was overly political: to destroy the Christian (Holy Bible) basis of Western civilization.

Motive and mental state aside, the "Alphabet Bomber" remains a troubling sign of the danger posed by intelligent, if unstable, lone wolves to homeland security.

Joseph R. Rudolph Jr.

See also: Pipe Bomber Attacks, Lucas John "Luke" Helder; Rudolph, Eric Robert; Unabomber Attacks, Theodore John "Ted" Kaczynski.

FURTHER READING

Newsweek Web Exclusive. 2003. "T Is for Terror." NBC News, July 9, 2003. Accessed June 22, 2020. http://www.nbcnews.com/id/3070093/t/t-terror/#.XTpJsLzYrnE

Rosenthal, Jason. 2015. "The Day LAX Was Bombed by the Alphabet Bomber." *Southern Californian*, July 24, 2015. https://thesoutherncalifornian.blogspot.com/2015/07/the-day-lax-was-bombed-by-alphabet.html

Simon, Jeffrey D. 2016. *Lone Wolf Terrorism: Understanding the Growing Threat.* Buffalo, NY: Prometheus.

al-Qaeda

Al-Qaeda (Arabic for "the base" or "base of operations") is a radical or extremist Sunni Islamic Salafist terrorist group approximately founded in 1988 by Osama bin Laden, Abdullah Azzam, and Ayman al-Zawahiri. It is most infamous as the organization responsible for the September 11, 2001, terrorist attacks on the United States that resulted in the collapse of the Twin Towers of the World Trade Center in New York City. Bin Laden was the emir, or leader, of al-Qaeda until his death in a raid by U.S. Navy SEALs on May 1, 2011. Following his death, al-Zawahiri became al-Qaeda's emir. The group promotes a violent and intolerant interpretation of Sunni Islam (the largest denomination of Islam). Moreover, as a Salafist movement, it purports to seek to purify Islam by emulating and returning to the example of *Salaf,* the pious predecessors who include the founder of Islam, the Prophet Muhammad; his family and companions; and the first four caliphs, or successors, to Muhammad following his death in AD 632.

ORIGINS OF AL-QAEDA

The origins of al-Qaeda date back to the Soviet-Afghan War. In 1979, the Soviet Union invaded Afghanistan to prevent the collapse of that country's Communist government and the regional instability this would cause. With Afghanistan being a majority Muslim nation and either bordering or in close proximity to five Muslim-majority republics of the Soviet Union, Moscow feared a Muslim government in Afghanistan would incite the political aspirations of the Soviet Union's oppressed Muslim populations, thereby undermining Soviet Communism. Earlier in 1979, the Soviet Union had witnessed the instability caused by the Iranian Islamic Revolution, the establishment of an Islamic government in that state bordering the Soviet Union, and the ensuing religious fervor this generated throughout the Middle East.

The invasion of Afghanistan by the Soviet Union—a non-Muslim state founded on the principle of atheism—rallied many Afghans to defend their country on religious grounds. They saw it as their duty as Muslims to wage *jihad*, or holy war, against a foreign occupier. At the same time, thousands of Muslims from throughout the Middle East, including bin Laden (who was from Saudi Arabia) and al-Zawahiri (from Egypt), also traveled to Afghanistan to wage jihad with their Afghan Muslim coreligionists. Other Muslim states, including Saudi Arabia (the birthplace of Islam) and Egypt, actively encouraged their citizens to travel to Afghanistan to fight the Soviet Union, although not always for religious reasons. The war in Afghanistan provided a convenient way for many Middle Eastern nations to export not only many of their unemployed, restless youth but also, most importantly, their dissidents, in the hope they would die in combat there. The latter were mainly Muslim extremists or fundamentalists.

When the Soviet occupation of Afghanistan became a deadly quagmire with no victory in sight, the United States saw an opportunity to inflict harm on its Cold War enemy by covertly arming what became known as the *mujahideen* (one engaged in jihad) fighting the Soviet Union. The United States channeled funds through Afghanistan's neighbor Pakistan to the mujahideen, who bought weapons, including shoulder-fired Stinger rockets, to destroy Soviet helicopters and tanks. The government of Saudi Arabia and wealthy Saudi citizens also funded the mujahideen as a way to bolster *their* religious credentials and legitimacy in the face of the Iranian Islamic Revolution and the 1979 uprising in Mecca, Saudi Arabia, when religious extremists seized the Grand Mosque and sought to overthrow the "House of Saud," the royal family that has long controlled the nation's government.

In 1981, after graduating from university, Osama bin Laden traveled from Saudi Arabia to Afghanistan to wage jihad against the Soviet Union. He used his considerable inheritance from his father to finance his own mujahideen group, recruit jihadists from all over the Middle East, and establish training camps for these jihadists. As both a fighter and financer, bin Laden earned considerable prestige and respect for his efforts. Seven year later, al-Qaeda was formally founded by Abdullah Azzam, a Palestinian Islamic scholar and university professor and a mentor to bin Laden at King Abdulaziz University in Jeddah, Saudi Arabia. Azzam formed the group by organizing a merger of bin Laden's mujahideen with Ayman al-Zawahiri's Egyptian Islamic Jihad terrorist group.

Following the Soviet withdrawal from Afghanistan in 1989—something bin Laden and the rest of the mujahideen interpreted as having occurred due to their devotion to God—a civil war erupted between the various Afghan mujahideen groups for control of the country, and bin Laden returned to his homeland of Saudi Arabia. Hailed at the time as a hero for his exploits in Afghanistan, he was expelled in 1992 for denouncing the Saudi government for inviting U.S. troops into Saudi Arabia. The Saudi government's invitation came after Iraqi dictator Saddam Hussein invaded neighboring Kuwait on August 2, 1990, and then deployed his army along the Saudi-Kuwait border. To bin Laden, it was an act of blasphemy to ask non-Muslim troops to defend Saudi Arabia, the birthplace of Islam. It was during this time that bin Laden's hatred for the United States and the West in general began to solidify into an ideology that would drive his actions as al-Qaeda's leader in the years to come.

Following his expulsion, bin Laden relocated to Sudan until May 1996, when the Sudanese government expelled him due to pressure from the United States. Bin Laden resettled in Afghanistan, almost certainly at the invitation of the Taliban government, which had emerged victorious from the Afghan Civil War and ruled from 1996 until 2001. The Taliban was a Sunni Islamic political group that promoted a fundamentalist and intolerant version of Islam that outlawed all music, sports, smoking, and Western clothing as allegedly un-Islamic. Women were forbidden to be educated and subjected to a wide range of laws that relegated them to a position of inferiority in Afghan society. In public, for example, women had to dress in a burka, a loose garment that covers the face and entire body.

OSAMA BIN LADEN ISSUES FATWA AGAINST UNITED STATES

On August 23, 1996, bin Laden issued a *fatwa*, or religious edict (despite lacking the credentials of an Islamic religious scholar), in which he declares war on the United States. In his edict, he criticizes what he calls the aggression and injustice caused by the "Jewish-Christian alliance and their collaborators," a reference to the states of Israel and the United States as well as their Middle East allies (i.e., Saudi Arabia, Egypt, Jordan, and Kuwait).

He identifies "the blood spilled" in Iraq and Palestine, a reference to what he regards as the Israeli occupation and oppression of Palestine since 1948, and the economic sanctions imposed on Iraq since 1990. He also identifies the "massacres of Muslims" in many places, including Bosnia, the Philippines, and Somalia, and blames the United States and its allies for using the United Nations as a cover for conspiring against Muslims. He accuses the United States of preventing Muslims in these conflict zones from acquiring weapons to defend themselves, presumably according to international bans on weapons sales. The fatwa also praises the terrorist attack of June 25, 1996, in Khobar, Saudi Arabia, which killed nineteen U.S. Air Force personnel. It ends with bin Laden calling for jihad by the mujahideen to "destroy, fight, and kill" the United States (and also Israel) to liberate and purify Saudi Arabia.

Two years later, on February 23, 1998, bin Laden issued another fatwa cosigned by, among others, Ayman al-Zawahiri. It reiterates the themes from bin Laden's 1996 fatwa, noting that "the ruling to kill the Americans and their allies—civilians and military—is an individual duty for every Muslim who can do it in any country in which it is possible to do it."

On August 7, 1998, al-Qaeda attacked two American embassies in East Africa, killing 12 Americans and 212 Africans. In retaliation, President Bill Clinton ordered a series of cruise missile strikes targeting al-Qaeda training camps in Afghanistan as well as a factory in Sudan with alleged ties to bin Laden that was suspected of making chemical weapons. The Afghan missile strikes caused minimal damage and inflicted few casualties (bin Laden and al-Zawahiri were not there at the time), as the camps had been evacuated earlier as a precaution. Some scholars believe that the limited nature of the strikes may have reinforced the belief among bin Laden and al-Zawahiri that the United States lacked the will to wage serious and sustained military attacks.

Two years later, on October 12, 2000, al-Qaeda suicide bombers steered a small boat up to side of the USS *Cole* and detonated explosives, blowing a massive hole in the hull of the destroyer anchored in Aden, Yemen, killing seventeen navy sailors and injuring another thirty-nine. Then came the attack on the U.S. homeland.

THE SEPTEMBER 11 ATTACKS

On September 11, 2001, al-Qaeda launched four coordinated attacks against the United States when nineteen terrorists hijacked four commercial airlines, all headed from either Boston or Newark to California, for the purpose of crashing them into specific targets. Two of the planes crashed into the 110-story North and South Towers of the World Trade Center in New York City. The collapse of both towers then destroyed and damaged dozens of nearby buildings. A third plane crashed into the Pentagon, the headquarters of the U.S. Department of Defense just across the Potomac River from Washington, DC. The fourth plane, headed toward Washington, crashed in a field near Shanksville, Pennsylvania, after the passengers, made aware of the other attacks from cell phone conversations with family, stormed the cockpit to thwart the terrorist hijackers. Altogether, 2,996 people died in the attacks, making them the deadliest terrorist attacks in history.

President George W. Bush responded to the September 11, 2001, attacks by declaring a "war on terror" directly targeting al-Qaeda. Less than a month later, on October 7, 2001, the United States, the United Kingdom, and Canada invaded Afghanistan with the stated purpose of overthrowing the Taliban government, which had given sanctuary in 1996 to bin Laden and al-Zawahiri, and destroying al-Qaeda.

Wielding a combination of U.S. Special Forces operations, anti-Taliban forces (called the Northern Alliance), and air strikes, the United States pounded both the Taliban and al-Qaeda. Although the Taliban and al-Qaeda suffered heavy casualties, bin Laden and al-Zawahiri, as well as Mullah Omar, the leader of the Taliban, disappeared. U.S. intelligence suspected that the three men had escaped into neighboring Pakistan. By 2003, the Taliban had regrouped and began attacking U.S. forces, its international allies, and Afghan security forces.

Meanwhile, the loss of its sanctuary in Afghanistan and the flight of its leadership into hiding turned al-Qaeda from a centrally organized and directed group to a franchise-like structure with affiliates in various countries urged to act on their own. Their subsequent handiwork includes lethal bombings in Bali (2002), attacks on Western compounds in Saudi Arabia (2003) that killed or wounded nearly 200, the 2004 detonation of bombs aboard Madrid commuter trains that killed 193, London transit attacks the following year that killed 52, and a series of lethal attacks on targets in France in 2015 and 2016. In between, the 2003 U.S. invasion of Iraq gave al-Qaeda an opportunity to establish an affiliate amid the violence and chaos that followed there, as it has done elsewhere in the Middle East, perhaps most notably in the civil war in Yemen. Success on that front, however, has been elusive. On occasion, al-Qaeda and the Islamic State in Iraq and Syria (ISIS and its remnants) have sometimes been on the same anti-Western page. But there have been tensions between the two terrorist groups as well, in part because of perceived competition for the same followers.

That dynamic did not change appreciably with bin Laden's death in 2011 at the hands of the U.S. Navy Seals who raided his compound in Abbottabad, Pakistan. Although killing bin Laden was a significant morale and public relations victory for the United States, by that time, bin Laden had become an increasingly irrelevant figure to al-Qaeda's operations. Unable to use email in his remote hideout, bin Laden had been limited to issuing audio- and videotape messages by courier to exhort his dwindling, scattered, and disunited followers to attack the United States and the West. Al-Qaeda, however, has continued to pose a challenge to the United States and its ongoing war on terror, in Afghanistan as well as other Muslim hot spots. The terrorist group has also used the Internet to recruit Americans to join its war on the United States.

Stefan Brooks

See also: bin Laden, Osama; Islamic State, The; Madrid Train Bombings and the War on Terror; September 11, 2001, Attack on America; War on Terror: Afghanistan and Pakistan.

FURTHER READING

al-Zawahiri, Ayman. 2005. "Letter from al-Zawahiri to al-Zarqawi: October 11, 2005." Office of the Director of National Intelligence, October 11, 2005. https://irp.fas.org/news/2005/10/dni101105.html

Holbrook, Donald. 2018. *Al-Qaeda 2.0: A Critical Reader.* Oxford: Oxford University Press.

Mendelsohn, Barak. 2016. *The al-Qaeda Franchise: The Expansion of al-Qaeda and Its Consequences.* Oxford: Oxford University Press.

Wright, Lawrence. 2007. *The Looming Tower: al-Qaeda and the Road to 9/11.* New York: Vintage.

Wright, Lawrence. 2017. *The Terror Years: From al-Qaeda to the Islamic State.* New York: Vintage.

Al-Suwaij, Zainab

1971–

In the world of political violence and terrorism, Zainab Al-Suwaij stands as a reconciliation figure, bridging the worlds of devout Islam, war and diplomacy, and social mediation. Her roadway to that destination, however, was not an easy one. At a minimum, she won no friends in Saddam Hussein's government when she refused to join a pro-Saddam youth group, and she later suffered a wound while participating in the unsuccessful rebellion against Saddam that was touched off inside Iraq following the global response that ousted and nearly decimated his army after its 1990 invasion of Kuwait.

Born in Basra in 1971 and raised in the home of her grandfather, the (Shi'ite) Ayatollah of Basra, Al-Suwaij was only twenty when she joined in that 1991 rebellion as an armed fighter and provider of medical assistance to the wounded. Then, when the rebellion was crushed, her flight ultimately brought her to the United States, where she found a position teaching Arabic at Yale University, aided the settlement of Sudanese refugees, and—after the September 11, 2001, attack on the World Trade Center and Pentagon—cofounded the American Islamic Congress (AIC), which is dedicated to defending and championing the interests of peace-loving Muslims in the United States. Eventually, its work would spread to Tunisia and Egypt as well.

Just as the Persian Gulf War led to Al-Suwaij's flight from Iraq, the Second Persian Gulf War brought her back with a new mission: to elevate the political standing of women in Iraq. A strong supporter of the 2003 American invasion of Iraq and the toppling of Saddam Hussein's regime, Al-Suwaij played a major role in lobbying for women's rights shortly after his fall from power. In particular, with the petition signatures of 45,000 Iraqi women, she was able to insert into the post-Saddam Iraqi Constitution a provision guaranteeing women 25 percent of the seats in the soon to be established Iraqi Assembly, despite strong opposition from the Governing Council. She also cofounded the Iraqi Women High Council in Iraq, and she played an active role in the USAID-funded Revitalization of Iraqi Schools and Stabilization of Education (RISE) program in postwar Iraq, which trained nearly 30,000 teachers and refurbished 600 or so schools from March 2003 to July 2004.

Then came the domestic backlash against the invasion, spearheaded by the Sunnis who had benefited from Saddam's rule, the rise of terrorist groups, the eventual drawdown of U.S. and allied forces, and the rise of the Islamic State in Iraqi power vacuum areas, undoing many of these gains. Nonetheless, as executive director of the AIC, and back in the United States, her work as a social activist on behalf of Islamic women has continuously garnered international acclaim and reaped honors such as her recognition in 2006 as International Person of the Year by Philadelphia's National Liberty Museum. Likewise, her testimony before congressional committees on domestic violence against women and her newspaper and television commentary on the right of Saudi women to drive remain widely viewed on the Internet.

Joseph R. Rudolph Jr.

See also: Anti-Muslim Attacks; Muslim American Community and Homeland Security; War on Terror, The.

FURTHER READING

Caballero, Maria Christina. 2004. "Dispatches from Iraq's Feminist Front: With Democratization Comes a Fierce Fight for Equality." *Harvard Gazette*, November 18, 2004. Accessed June 15, 2020. https://news.harvard.edu/gazette/story/2004/11/dispatches-from-iraqs-feminist-front/

Caballero, Maria Christina. 2005. "Women's Rights Put to Test in Iraq." *Boston Globe*, January 30, 2005. Accessed June 15, 2020. http://archive.boston.com/news/globe/editorial_opinion/oped/articles/2005/01/30/womens_rights_put_to_test_in_iraq/

Institute of Medicine and National Research Council. 2013. *Contagion of Violence: Workshop Summary.* Washington, DC. National Academies Press.

Anthrax Attacks of 2001

In the autumn of 2001, as the nation reeled from the unprecedented attacks of September 11, the U.S. Intelligence Community (USIC) turned its attention to the possibility of another attack. Al-Qaeda's responsibility for 9/11 created a focus on external adversaries. As the Federal Bureau of Investigation (FBI) and the rest of the USIC looked outward, another wave of attacks did come. Shortly after 9/11, letters containing spores of the bacteria *Bacillus anthracis* were received by prominent politicians and media outlets. They included Senators Tom Daschle and Patrick Leahy and NBC anchor Tom Brokaw. The targets of the letters were spared, but five innocent Americans died. Seventeen others were stricken but survived. Three of the deceased handled mail for a living, but the other two had no known connection to the targets or the letters.

Recovered letters included the words "Death to America; Death to Israel; Allah is Great," in an attempt to keep the attention on al-Qaeda. The tactic worked for a time. A "powder panic" swept through the country, causing many to see anthrax in their flour, talcum powder, and even their deodorant. The FBI and numerous other law enforcement agencies collaborated with fire departments, health departments, and emergency management officials on an unprecedented scale to manage the response and restore public calm.

The FBI also partnered with a variety of other agencies to further the "Amerithrax" investigation, including the U.S. Army. Fort Detrick, Maryland, is the home of the army's research into defense against biological warfare. Investigators needed the expertise of its scientists; however, it was readily apparent that the pool of experts who could advance the investigation might also include the person or persons responsible. Several scientists were interviewed and took polygraph examinations before being briefed on the case and reviewing the evidence. There were still many unknowns concerning the bacteria, and many assumptions were revealed to be inaccurate. For instance, it was initially believed a victim needed to inhale about 10,000 *B. anthracis* spores to receive a lethal dose. Yet, two of the deceased were so far removed from the contaminated letters, they may have only inhaled a few dozen spores. Groundbreaking microbiology and epidemiology techniques were developed during the investigation.

Investigators looked into the backgrounds of several individuals who were working, or had previously worked, at Fort Detrick. One former employee, Steven Hatfill, fell under suspicion, but after being subjected to intense scrutiny, he was exonerated. Eventually, after a seven-year investigation, the U.S. Department of Justice had amassed sufficient evidence to charge a Fort Detrick researcher, Dr. Bruce Ivins, with the anthrax attacks, but he committed suicide in 2008, before he could be arrested.

Some were skeptical regarding Ivins's guilt; however, prosecutors remained convinced he would have been convicted. Ivins had the knowledge and experience to produce the bacteria used in the letters, and he had been involved in an anthrax vaccine program. The FBI concluded he mailed the letters to reinvigorate interest in the vaccine program after funding was reduced. Evidence indicated Ivins acted alone.

Subsequently, the United States developed numerous new technologies and procedures to detect and respond to biological terrorism. New weapons of mass destruction (WMD) laws were enacted, and greater resources were dedicated to WMD matters.

*James T. Barry**

---

* Mr. Barry served the FBI for twenty-two years, retiring as a supervisory special agent with global assignments. Much of his career was spent in the WMD arena. Any opinions expressed in this article are those of the writer and not the official position of the FBI.

See also: Biological Weapons; Counterterrorism and the George W. Bush Administration.

FURTHER READING

Decker, R. Scott. 2018. *Recounting the Anthrax Attacks: Terror, the Amerithrax Task Force, and the Evolution of Forensics in the FBI.* Lanham, MD: Rowman & Littlefield.

FBI. 2016. "Amerithrax or Anthrax Investigation." May 17, 2016. https://www.fbi.gov/history/famous-cases/amerithrax-or-anthrax-investigation

Graysmith, Robert. 2004. *Amerithrax: The Hunt for the Anthrax Killer.* New York: Jove Books.

United States Department of Justice. 2008. "Transcript of Amerithrax Investigation Press Conference." August 6, 2008, #08-697. https://www.justice.gov/archive/opa/pr/2008/August/08-opa-697.html

United States Department of Justice. 2010. *Amerithrax Investigative Summary.* February 19, 2010. https://www.justice.gov/archive/amerithrax/docs/amx-investigative-summary.pdf

Antifa

Antifa, short for Anti-Fascist Action, is a movement of like-minded individuals committed to confronting extreme right-wing groups with racist, homophobic, and xenophobic agendas. Its historical roots can be traced to the interwar battles between radical leftists and fascist activists in Germany, Italy, and Spain, although perhaps the most famous incident was the Battle of Cable Street in London in October 1936.

The defeat of Nazi Germany and Fascist Italy in World War II produced a lull in the activity of anti-fascist groups on both sides of the Atlantic Ocean, but the resurgence of extreme right-wing (skinhead) activity in Europe breathed new life into the movement during the 1970s. Ten years later, local anti-fascist groups could be found, initially calling themselves Anti-Racist Action before adopting the broader anti-fascist focus and the Antifa name tag.

STRUCTURE

Antifa lacks a formal organizational structure, and even as a movement—some say negative ideology—it is a highly decentralized, nonhierarchical one that is best defined by its opposition to extreme right-wing views, especially those of white supremacists.

In its contemporary manifestation in the United States, Antifa is a movement that operates with little or no organizational structure. This lack of structure makes Antifa very difficult to infiltrate and track. Antifa is composed of autonomous regional and primarily local cells, most with small, tight-knit memberships of five to fifteen people. Members are bound together by mutual interests and trust and rely on social media for communication. Cells are nationwide, but most activity has recently been in the Northwest, with Portland in particular becoming a hub of anti-fascist activity.

Antifa is a negative coalition in nature, blending with its anti-fascist activists a grouping of anarchical anti-state, militant anti-capitalist, and antiauthoritarian protesters. They are sometimes also joined by goal-oriented leftists, such as environmentalists, at their protests. Analysts therefore generally distinguish between Antifa members and others joining Antifa gatherings, but differentiating individuals is difficult because Antifa membership itself is secretive, to the point of members wearing masks and nondescript clothing during demonstrations.

ACTIVITY AND THREAT LEVEL

Although a fringe group in the United States, within the first two years of the Trump presidency, Antifa achieved explosive growth and attracted expansive interest. Composed of anarchists, militant progressives, and Marxist revolutionaries, the contemporary Antifa movement in the United States seeks to proactively silence and intimidate perceived fascists and racists, often through violent means. To understand the motivations behind social movements such as Antifa, one must think critically about the inculcated views of reality, epistemological leanings, and differing intergenerational values. Here, the focus is thus on the ontological positions, epistemological leanings, and operational tactics demonstrated by the Antifa movement.

Antifa employs both violent and nonviolent tactics. Their most articulated goal is to deny fascists and white supremacists the opportunity to meet or otherwise disrupt their meetings by whatever means necessary. Physical confrontations have been common, as when protesters threw rocks and Molotov cocktails at police while successfully disrupting UC Berkeley's plans to host a speech by former Brietbart.com editor Milo Yiannopoulos. More tragic outcomes have also been a result, as in Antifa's presence in the 2017 Unite the Right rally in Charlottesville, Virginia, in which a young woman died and numerous injuries occurred when a rally supporter drove his car into the crowd of protesters. That said, Antifa itself limits its weapons to the nonlethal variety, as evident in the Clackamette Park (Oregon) violent but nonlethal clashes between the Proud Boys and Antifa activists in June 2021.

At the same time, Antifa activists also engage in nonviolent activity by monitoring right-wing organizations, exposing their memberships on websites, engaging in humanitarian relief efforts, following natural disasters, and supporting pro-immigrant groups in their activities.

Antifa often uses both violence and intimidation to attempt to silence perceived fascists and racists. Intimidation is often effective; for example, Antifa has succeeded in persuading right-wing speakers from honoring their speaking engagements or having them canceled to avoid a potentially violent gathering. The downside is that Antifa has often been a foil used by the right to justify its own activity or deflect from its own excess, for example, blaming the violence at the U.S. Capitol on January 6, 2021, on Antifa infiltrators. Antifa has also been criticized on the grounds that its militant activity has often undercut the effectiveness of groups on the left, such as Black Lives Matter, that attempt to get their messages across peacefully.

Ironically, Antifa has a symbiotic relationship with the supremacist and other right-wing groups it opposes, rising and falling in membership in correlation with the rise and decline of activity on the right. It is also inversely proportional to the perceived legitimacy of the government in Washington. For this reason, activity significantly increased during the Trump years as activity on the right grew more aggressive and the administration was portrayed as racist by its critics.

Though it may not be a terrorist organization, when Antifa aggressively confronts its opponents, however spontaneously, it can often be at the center of a violent moment.

Joseph R. Rudolph Jr.

See also: Domestic Terrorism, Anarchists; Psychology of Terrorists; Sociology of Terrorism.

FURTHER READING

Anti-Defamation League. 2021. "Who Are Antifa?" https://www.adl.org/antifa

Beinart, Peter. 2017. "The Rise of the Violent Left." *Atlantic* 320 (2): 13. https://www.theatlantic.com/magazine/archive/2017/09/the-rise-of-the-violent-left/534192/

Bray, Mark. 2017. *Antifa: The Anti-Fascist Handbook.* Brooklyn, NY: Melville House.

Kenny, Michael, and Colin Clarke. 2020. "What Antifa Is, What It Isn't, and Why It Matters." *Texas National Security Review*, June 23, 2020. https://warontherocks.com/2020/06/what-antifa-is-what-it-isnt-and-why-it-matters/

Vysotsky, Stanislav. 2020. *American Antifa: The Tactics, Culture, and Practice of Militant Antifascism.* Milton Park, Abingdon, England: Routledge Studies in Fascism and the Far Right.

Anti-Muslim Attacks

Prior to 9/11, Muslims in the United States went mostly unnoticed and appeared integrated into the fabric of society. The most significant change in the nationwide attitude toward Muslims came in the aftermath of the September 11, 2001, terrorist attacks orchestrated by Osama bin Laden, the leader of al-Qaeda. Resulting in nearly 3,000 deaths, the event shook the psyche of a nation that had not experienced a serious attack on its shores by foreigners since the Japanese attack on Pearl Harbor on December 7, 1941. The attack led to a foundational change in the way many Americans viewed and treated Muslims. Many began not only fearing Islam—the religion of Muslims—but the diversity of the religion. Like many religions, Islam draws followers and converts from every ethnicity and country across the world. It was this unknown of who was a Muslim that drove so much fear.

Pejorative stereotyping of Muslims through a belittling lens of caricatured Arabism painted many peoples and religions from the Middle East and North Africa (MENA) as turban-wearing, backward people who embodied terrorism. This broad-brush misunderstanding of Muslims, and those that looked like them, fueled a populist rise in Islamophobia. Anti-Muslim attacks ranged from acts of microaggressions to hate-driven murder, such as the execution-style killing of Deah Barakat, his wife, and her sister by Craig Stephen Hicks in February 2015.

In the United States, attacks by white supremacists against Muslim students saw a steady increase over the years as much of the white supremacist movement's focus shifted to anti-Muslim ideology. Fear of the rapid growth of Islam throughout the globe and record numbers of Muslim international students enrolled in universities in the United States caused growing concern over the erosion of American nationality as a Eurocentric Christian people. At the core of anti-Muslim rhetoric was an unspoken call for neo-crusaderism built on the dormant fears of Christians in the Middle Ages.

Attacks against perceived Muslims have included the targeting of people from other religions due to an ignorance of cultural awareness. A month after the 9/11 attacks, Balbir Singh Sodhi, a Sikh American, was killed in a hate crime by Frank Roque, who thought Sodhi's turban and beard identified him as an Arab Muslim. Anti-Muslim attitudes fostered the criminalization of people, customs, clothing, and language that differed from that of a predominantly Caucasian-based America. Movements such as burka bans targeted Muslim traditions, while the practices of covering heads and wearing long beads in Christian lifestyles were sanctioned.

Distrust of Muslims grew, as many saw the insular Muslim communities throughout the country as a threat. Repeated news coverage of Muslim communities' distrust of law enforcement and lack of cooperation, like that of many other minority groups, fueled the distrust and reinforced the notion that Muslims were not fully integrating into American culture.

Despite Muslims being part of the American experience since the Revolutionary War, entrenched centuries-old ideologies foster a continuing rise in Islamophobia in the United States. A poignant example of these strong anti-Muslim attitudes is that Hicks and Roque, though convicted of murder, avoided being labeled "terrorists." Had the circumstances been reversed, a Muslim American would have been identified as a terrorist, with general society denigrating the religion of Islam.

Ygnacio "Nash" Flores and Tarek Azmy

See also: Aryan Nations; Domestic Terrorism, Anti-Semitic; Domestic Terrorism, White Supremacists.

FURTHER READING

Barakat, Suzanne. 2016. *Islamophobia Killed My Brother. Let's End the Hate.* YouTube, TED. https://www.youtube.com/watch?v=XiEQmcZi8cM

Chappel, Bill. 2019. "N.C. Man Pleads Guilty to Killing 3 Muslim College Students; Video Is Played in Court." NPR, June 12, 2019. https://www.npr.org/2019/06/12/731981858/n-c-man-pleads-guilty-to-murdering-3-muslim-college-students

Corbin, Caroline Mala. 2017. "Terrorists Are Always Muslim but Never White: At the Intersection of Critical Race Theory and Propaganda." *Fordham Law Review* 86 (2): 455–485. https://ir.lawnet.fordham.edu/flr/vol86/iss2/5

Kang, Esther Yoon-Ji. 2019. "Study Shows Islamophobia Is Growing in the U.S. Some Say It's Rising in Chicago, Too." NPR, May 3, 2019. https://www.npr.org/local/309/2019/05/03/720057760/study-shows-islamophobia-is-growing-in-the-u-s-some-say-it-s-rising-in-chicago-too

Manseau, Peter. 2017. "What Happened to America's First Muslims?" *HuffPost*, December 6, 2017. https://www.huffpost.com/entry/what-happened-to-americas-first-muslims_b_6809326?ncid=txtlnkusaolp00000592

Armed Militias

Armed militias have a long history in the United States. During the colonial era, militias were local collectives separated by town, community, or perhaps colony. These militias were the fighting forces in conflicts such as the French and Indian War and were the basis for creating the Continental Army during the American Revolutionary War. The idea of armed citizens rising up against an oppressor is thus deeply entrenched in American ideology.

In the late twentieth and early twenty-first centuries, however, the armed militia movement became closely associated with aspects of far-right and anti-government extremism. Within white supremacist groups such as Christian Identity and neo-Nazi organizations, extreme racial and religious justifications combined with conspiracy theories have led to militia members committing many of the most notorious crimes of domestic terrorism in recent history.

The modern armed militia movement first emerged in the 1990s. Paramilitary groups began taking up arms and training to defend themselves against what they believed was an invasive government that had overstepped its constitutional authority. The main concern was the threat of firearms being confiscated by the federal government, backed by an anti-Semitic belief that a "New World Order" was controlling the U.S. government, leading businesses, and the American media. Militia groups claimed that this "shadow government" undermined American independence, threatened democracy, and wanted to crush constitutional rights—especially the Second Amendment guarantee of the right to bear firearms.

These groups typically have a central leader who is the heartbeat of the organization and a compound where they train in paramilitary tactics, survival skills, weapons instructions, and the movement's ideology. They tend to stockpile illegal weapons and ammunition, including illegal fully automatic weapons. In the most extreme instances, militias may buy or manufacture explosive devices. Members recruit new members and fundraise, often via websites and blogs, where like-minded thinkers can communicate, get information, or donate to their mission.

RUBY RIDGE AND WACO

Armed militia groups frequently reference two violent confrontations between federal law enforcement and private citizens in the early 1990s to explain their attitudes toward government authority. These episodes, which took place in Ruby Ridge, Idaho, and Waco, Texas, caused both growth in armed militia support and notoriety, and both were rooted in firearm violations.

In August 1992, Ruby Ridge resident Randy Weaver failed to appear in court on firearm-related charges. An unsuccessful mission to capture Weaver resulted in the killing of his fourteen-year-old son and a U.S. marshal, initiating an eleven-day standoff. During the course of that standoff, an FBI sniper killed Weaver's wife, and Weaver and a compatriot were shot and wounded and captured. Weaver was eventually sentenced to eighteen months in prison and a $10,000 fine. However, in 1995, he was awarded a $3.1 million settlement after suing the U.S. government for the wrongful deaths of his family members.

Then, in February 1993, a fifty-one-day standoff took place in Waco, Texas, between federal authorities and the Branch Davidian religious cult. The leader of the group, David Koresh, was wanted for federal firearms and explosives violations. An unsuccessful operation to arrest Koresh, led by the Bureau of Alcohol, Tobacco, Firearms and Explosives (ATF), resulted in four ATF agents and six Branch Davidians dying in a gunfight. A standoff ensued, and on April 19, federal agents took the offensive and breached the cult compound. The compound caught on fire, and at least seventy-five people died inside.

In the aftermath of Ruby Ridge and Waco, the militia movement briefly gained traction, as many Second Amendment advocates saw the events as evidence that the government would undermine, by force, their right to keep and bear arms. However, when Timothy McVeigh, a militia supporter, killed 168 people at the Alfred P. Murrah Federal Building in Oklahoma City in 1995 with a homemade truck bomb, the militia movement's growth halted, only to rise again in the twenty-first century.

Braden Eisenbeis and Tobias T. Gibson

See also: Domestic Terrorist Groups; Montana Freemen Siege; Oklahoma City Federal Building Bombing; Ruby Ridge Standoff.

FURTHER READING

Bjelopera, Jerome P. 2017. *Domestic Terrorism: An Overview.* Congressional Research Service, August 21, 2017. https://fas.org/sgp/crs/terror/R44921.pdf

Frontline. 2017. "American Patriot." PBS, May 16, 2017. https://www.pbs.org/video/american-patriot-b-eodf0p/

Gibson, Tobias T., and Richard Q. Sterns. 2017. "Extreme Right Wing Ideologues, Conservative Secession and Terrorism." In *Foundations of Homeland Security: Law and Policy.* 2nd ed., edited by Martin J. Alperen, 79–94. Hoboken, NJ: Wiley.

Huhn, Wilson. 1999. "Political Alienation in America and the Legal Premises of the Patriot Movement." *Gonzaga Law Review* 34: 417–444. https://heinonline.org/HOL/P?h=hein.journals/gonlr34&i=426

Loeser, Charles E. 2015. "From Paper Terrorists to Cop Killers: The Sovereign Citizen Threat." *North Carolina Law Review* 93 (4): 1106–1139. https://scholarship.law.unc.edu/nclr/vol93/iss4/4

Army of God

The Army of God (AOG) was the name adopted by the most militant of the Protestant antiabortion activists in the United States during late 1980s and 1990s. It had no formal organizational structure. One identified with the group by undertaking actions aimed at stopping abortion in the United States that went beyond clinic protests. Formed as a joke by antiabortion activists whose protests resulted in their incarceration, the AOG gradually became real as a "state of mind" organization with *The Army of God Manual* as its text.

The founders of the AOG were a small number of longtime pro-life activists who had long been part of the "rescue" movement. These activists broke with the latter's mandate to maintain nonviolence during clinic demonstrations. The most prominent rescue groups included the Protestant Operation Rescue, the Missionaries to the Preborn, and the Catholic Lambs of Christ, all of whom modeled their activism on the 1960s-era civil rights movement led by Martin Luther King Jr. as well as earlier nonviolent activists.

The turn to violence was gradual and largely imitative. Someone would take an action, and the loose network of rescuers who would later form the AOG would follow suit on a grander scale and with a national scope. For example, Melody Green began showing appalled pedestrians on Chicago street corners a jar with an aborted fetus, and Joe Scheidler published *99 Ways to Stop Abortion*, which urged actions ranging from destruction of property where abortion services were provided to "adopting an abortionist" by taking protests to doctors' homes.

Once formed, the core members of the AOG undertook a campaign of violence against property, including clinic burnings and the use of noxious chemicals to close clinics. *The Army of God Manual*, written by pseudonymous AOG members, provides recipes for these chemicals along with scriptural justifications for violence in defense of the unborn.

In 1993, Michael Griffin, who had no connection to either the rescue movement or the AOG, shot and killed Dr. David Gunn in Pensacola, Florida. The AOG took this as a sign that the time had come for more resolute action. Soon, Paul Hill and Shelley Shannon, among others, turned to lethal violence. This proved to be the core group's undoing. Many were imprisoned, and others, faced with civil suits under the Racketeer Influenced and Corrupt Organization Act (RICO), abandoned the movement lest their families face financial ruin.

The ghost of the AOG lives on through a website with its name and now defunct sites such as the Nuremberg Files, which offered the names and home addresses of abortion providers, drawing a bleeding line through their name if they were injured or killed. Lone-wolf antiabortion activists, such as Eric Rudolph, who combined bombings and shootings in the late 1990s on the basis of a mix of right-wing, antigay, and pro-life ideologies, were then free to adopt the title, as could anyone who undertook violence to stop abortion.

COUNTERTERRORISM PERSPECTIVE

Despite the best efforts of the FBI and a Justice Department–sponsored grand jury that (unsuccessfully) sought to indict activists for conspiracy, the AOG was for a considerable time impervious to detection or penetration. Activists were closely bonded, and outsiders were unequipped to infiltrate their churches or private lives. They were highly mobile, moving from city to city and staying at the homes of fellow activists. There was no central command structure, and individuals acted without formally notifying others for fear of implicating them should the activists be caught. Often jailed for demonstrating or other actions, they had no fear of prison.

The AOG was finally defeated in three ways. First, aggressive local law enforcement backed with federal support arrested the perpetrators of violence against property or people. The AOG members were so few in number that imprisoned activists could be supported but not replaced. Second, there was the threat of RICO suits. And, third, it was simple despair that doomed the AOG. Violence changed nothing. God did not act to punish America as they had expected Him to eventually do, and so many left activism altogether.

Jeffrey Kaplan

See also: Domestic Terrorist Groups; Single-Issue Terrorism.

FURTHER READING

Bader, Eleanor J., and Patricia Baird-Windle. 2015. *Targets of Hatred: Anti-Abortion Terrorism*. New York: St. Martin's Press.

Craig, Barbara Hinkson, and David M. O'Brien. 1993. *Abortion and American Politics*. Chatham, NJ: Chatham House.

Jefferis, Jennifer. 2011. *Armed for Life: The Army of God and Anti-Abortion Terror in the United States*. Santa Barbara, CA: ABC-CLIO.

Kaplan, Jeffrey. 1995. "Absolute Rescue: Absolutism, Defensive Action and the Resort to Force." *Terrorism and Political Violence* 7 (3): 128–163.

Aryan Nations

Mid-1970s–Early 2000s

Aryan Nations (AN) was a group of white separatists active from the mid-1970s to the early 2000s. AN was based in Idaho and led by Richard Butler. Although AN never claimed more than 300 followers locally and has never been directly involved in terrorist attacks, it was under the close scrutiny of law enforcement authorities and human rights groups due to its notoriety and its links with numerous violent neo-Nazi groups.

Richard Butler retired to Idaho in the early 1970s after having spent most of his life in California, where he had been close to various far-right organizations. He bought a twenty-two-acre compound outside of Hayden Lake, near Coeur d'Alene, where he founded his own church, the Church of Jesus Christ Christian, and its political arm, the Aryan Nations. As a Christian Identity group, AN promoted racism, anti-Semitism, and white separatism.

From 1980 to 2000, Butler hosted an annual Aryan World Congress (AWC) that attracted the far right's most prominent personalities. The AWC became the most attended event of the Christian Identity movement and of white separatism in the United States. Butler also regularly held an Aryan Youth Assembly in the 1980s. Through AWC, the AN compound became the center of a network of white supremacist and neo-Nazi groups, including the infamous group the Order.

The Order, also known as the Brüder Schweigen, a white supremacist group, was active between September 1983 and December 1984. Many of its members belonged to the AN or to the Church of Jesus Christ Christian. The Order's members carried out a variety of crimes (such as armed robbery and racketeering), and two of them (David Lane and Bruce Pierce) were convicted of the 1984 murder of Alan Berg, a liberal Denver radio talk show host. In 1986, the Brüder Schweigen Strike Force II was formed by other AN members, who committed various acts of violence (including bombings) against federal property, private individuals (e.g., a Jewish businessman, a Catholic priest), and private businesses near Coeur d'Alene during a six-month period before being arrested.

In 1985, David Tate, a member of the AN and the Order, shot and killed Jimmie Linegar, a state trooper in Missouri. That same year, the former security chief of AN's compound, Elden "Bud" Cutler, was arrested and later sentenced to twelve years in prison for hiring a hit man (who was actually an undercover FBI agent) to kill a former member of the Order who had become an FBI informant.

A decade of further violence attributed to AN followed until, in July 1998, security guards at the AN compound near Hayden Lake fired on Victoria Keenan and her son, who had stopped near the compound to retrieve a dropped wallet, striking their car several times. The Southern Poverty Law Center filed a civil lawsuit on behalf of the Keenans, and in September 2000, a jury issued a judgment of $6.3 million against the defendants. As a result, Butler was bankrupted, and the twenty-acre compound was sold. By that point, however, AN had steadily declined in influence since its mid-1980s peak. The group was on its way to dying even before the judgment. The loss of the compound and the death of Butler in September 2004 accelerated its disintegration. Subsequently, several factions have laid claim to the AN's legacy.

Gwenola Ricordeau

See also: Charleston Church Massacre; Domestic Terrorism, White Supremacists; Domestic Terrorist Groups.

FURTHER READING

Balch, Robert W. 2006. "The Rise and Fall of Aryan Nations: A Resource Mobilization Perspective." *Journal of Political and Military Sociology* 34 (1): 81–113.

Barkun, Michael. 1997. *Religion and the Racist Right: The Origins of the Christian Identity Movement.* Chapel Hill: University of North Carolina Press.

Simi, Pete, and Robert Futrell. 2010. *American Swastika: Inside the White Power Movement's Hidden Spaces of Hate.* Lanham, MD: Rowman & Littlefield.

Southern Poverty Law Center. n.d. "Aryan Nations." https://www.splcenter.org/fighting-hate/extremist-files/group/aryan-nations

Asymmetrical Warfare

The September 11, 2001, terrorist attacks against the United States and the subsequent U.S. wars in Afghanistan and Iraq are among the recent examples of *asymmetric warfare*, namely, conflicts between nations and armed non-state actors (ANSAs)—violent individuals and groups that are not part of official governments—that have disparate military capabilities and strategies.

ASPECTS OF ASYMMETRY

History is replete with examples of asymmetric war, like the guerrilla resistance to Alexander the Great in Sogdiana and Bactria. In addition, Francis Marion and other American commanders resorted to guerrilla warfare during the American Revolution. Furthermore, military historians referred to the same concept using different terms. China's Sun Tzu, for example, utilized the term "indirect approach" in urging readers of his book, *The Art of War*, to avoid an enemy's strength and attack him where he is unprepared.

The term *asymmetric warfare* first entered the American lexicon in the 1997 Quadrennial Defense Review (QDR), a Congress-mandated review of Department of Defense strategy and activities conducted every four years between 1997 and 2014. It then started to replace other terms (e.g., insurgency, guerilla warfare, low-intensity conflict). The Joint Chiefs of Staff have defined *asymmetric warfare* as "unanticipated or nontraditional approaches to undermine an adversary's strengths while exploiting his vulnerabilities through unexpected technologies or innovative means."

In the same vein, the North Atlantic Treaty Organization (NATO) defines *asymmetric warfare* as "a situation in which an opposing force uses dissimilar means, methods and/or rules to circumvent an opponent's strengths while exploiting his weakness to obtain a disproportionate result." The asymmetry, however, does not solely refer to the imbalance of military power between two actors, with one actor possessing a much larger relative share of power than the other. Asymmetry could also refer to asymmetry between two warring entities in their willingness to suffer casualties, or asymmetry in objectives or resolve to win.

Elsewhere, asymmetry can refer to organizational asymmetry, as when regular armies have a well-articulated hierarchical structure to increase effectiveness, but the ANSAs have a less formal command and control structure to provide greater flexibility and capacity to take action or change tactics quickly.

Still another area of asymmetry may fall in the realm of intelligence exploitation. Western forces, in particular, are predominantly oriented toward sophisticated systems optimized against rival countries that can be utilized in a conventional battlespace in terms of intelligence, surveillance, target acquisition, and reconnaissance (ISTAR). However, these capabilities may prove futile in the face of ANSAs, where human intelligence is a more useful tool in facing such groups. In contrast, unconventional forces often have a human intelligence advantage provided by local sympathizers. ANSAs can also obtain significant intelligence about Western armed forces from open sources.

TERRORISM AND ASYMMETRIC FORCES

Terrorist organizations cannot usually fight their government opponents on traditional battlefields because they have limited military resources. Therefore, the only option is to rely on asymmetric means in this conflict. The aim is to conduct continuous new attacks with the aim of gradually weakening the opponent's resolve to continue the conflict. In this context, Islamic terrorist groups think that they will have an advantage in the long term because Western nations, preoccupied with the well-being of their citizens, will not be capable of continuing the war indefinitely.

The following factors enable terrorist groups to successfully resort to asymmetric war:

1. Communication technology: Terrorism depends immensely on communications and information technology networks for planning and coordination, funding, intelligence, propaganda, recruiting, training, mobilization, and logistics.
2. Dual-use technology: Terrorist organizations utilize dual-use technology readily available for commercial uses. The Islamic State in Iraq and Syria (ISIS) has been one of the groups that utilized adjusted commercial drones in Iraq to conduct battlefield surveillance against the American-led military coalition, in addition to dropping bombs on U.S.-backed Iraqi and Kurdish forces or crashing into them. Thus, terrorist organizations were capable of utilizing air-based military resources for the first time in history.
3. External support: State support is considered vital in enhancing ANSAs' capabilities. Hezbollah, an anti-Israel Shia organization with considerable political and military influence in Lebanon, acquires advanced models of drones from Iran and is one of only ten entities that have fired missiles from a drone at targets on the ground. The other nine are all states. Also, Iran provided Houthis, an armed Shia Islamic movement in northern Yemen, with remote-controlled boat bombs, which they utilized to attack an Aramco oil distribution terminal in the Red Sea in 2017.

HYBRID WAR

To account for the increasing complexity of contemporary asymmetric wars, some scholars, led by Frank Hoffman, have suggested the term *hybrid war*. As Schroefl and Kaufman note in their essay on hybrid warfare, Hoffman defines hybrid wars as "wars that incorporate a range of different modes of warfare, including conventional capabilities, irregular tactics and formations, terrorist acts including indiscriminate violence and coercion, and criminal disorder" (2014, 866).

Cyberspace is another domain of conflict where insurgents and terrorists use the Internet for propaganda, recruitment, communications, and directing attacks, while their opponents are struggling to curtail these efforts.

Like asymmetric warfare, hybridity does not solely refer to combining regular and irregular forces on the same battlefields; it also refers to the range of actors involved and the goals being pursued. In hybrid warfare, a wide range of non-state actors are involved, including any grouping of insurgent or terrorist networks; organized crime groups; social groups such as clans, tribes, or ethnic groups; and ideologically or religiously motivated organizations.

The motivations of the armed groups are highly variable. Some conflicts may be primarily motivated by hopes for greater power and wealth, such as the wars over resources in West Africa, while others may be primarily nationalist or ideological in nature.

A prominent example in this context is ISIS, a violent Sunni jihadist group that has declared its religious authority over all Muslims. ISIS has adopted various tactics in battling its enemies. It first resorted to conventional tactics against the Iraqi army, which was incapable of utilizing air power effectively against the group. Later, ISIS shifted to guerilla tactics against the U.S.-led military coalition seeking to oust the group from Syria and Iraq. Concurrently, ISIS also utilized terrorist tactics, especially lone-wolf attacks to target Western countries. In addition, it used online propaganda to spread highly emotional narratives to defend its actions and recruit sympathizers. Other ANSAs in the Middle East utilizing similar tactics include the Lebanese Hezbollah, Yemeni Houthis, and Iraqi Popular Mobilization Forces, which are affiliated with Iran.

Finally, although hybrid war has been implicitly defined as a tactic of insurgent states or non-state actors, Russia's utilization of this type of war in Ukraine and Syria revealed that it is not just a "weapon of the weak" but can also be employed by the dominant side in a conflict.

COUNTERING ASYMMETRIC WARFARE

Several strategies have been employed to counter asymmetric warfare. The "hearts and minds" strategy seeks to garner social support by maintaining the rule of law, even under duress; addressing the feasible and legitimate opposition's grievances; and building an intelligence network capable of aiding armed forces to counter the insurgents. The final aim of this strategy is to realize a steady shift of popular support toward the government while isolating the insurgents from social support, thus increasing the difficulty of mounting operations. The British applied this strategy successfully in Malaysia against the Malaysian Communist Party insurgents from 1948 to 1950.

Another option pursued by states against insurgent groups is a so-called terror strategy. Roger Trinquier, a French veteran of colonial conflicts in both Asia and Africa, argued that "modern warfare" is essentially a war of ideology in which the will of insurgents is fundamentally beyond reach. According to him, the key to effective counterinsurgency was the utilization of terror to undermine social support for insurgents. Applying methods like torture would be the cornerstone of such a strategy.

A consistent theme of both the American and British counterterrorism campaigns since 2001 has been the systematic targeting of terrorist and insurgent leaders. However, this "decapitation" strategy has had mixed results. Moreover, while killing or capturing recognized leaders may reduce the operational effectiveness of these organizations in the short term, it could drive them to adopt more extreme positions and reduce the chances of any negotiated settlement. Despite these limitations, this strategy has enabled the United States to undermine the capacity of al-Qaeda in the Arabian Peninsula (AQPA) to carry out international terrorist attacks against American and Western interests.

Another option sometimes employed is to organize rival coalitions. The United States and other Western powers utilize a wide range of nongovernment capabilities, from soft power (e.g., press, communications) through harder options (e.g., cooperation by tech companies in eliminating terrorist accounts through the social media) to hard power (e.g., utilize local groups and train them to fight insurgency).

The United States utilized some of these approaches in Iraq starting in 2007, when the George W. Bush administration adopted the "surge" strategy to increase the number of American troops to undermine the Sunni insurgency. This strategy made use of the support of Iraqi tribes, and even other former Sunni insurgents, who worked with coalition forces and Shia police against al-Qaeda in Iraq. The terrorist organization responded by shifting its focus from targeting the Americans to instigating sectarian conflict between the Sunni and the Shia.

In addition, the United States promised the tribal and insurgent leaders that it would integrate them into the Iraqi security forces and the political process. However, the withdrawal of American forces in 2011 and the refusal of the Shia government in Baghdad to integrate them in state institutions paved the way for the rise of ISIS in that part of the world.

Shady Abdelwahab Mansour

See also: Foreign Terrorist Groups at War with the United States; Hezbollah; Islamic State, The; Unmanned Aerial Systems.

FURTHER READING

Arreguin-Toft. Ivan. 2012. "Contemporary Asymmetric Conflict Theory in Historical Perspective." *Terrorism & Political Violence* 24 (4): 635–657.

Blatt, Charlotte F. 2017. "Operational Success, Strategic Failure: Assessing the 2007 Iraq Troop Surge." *Parameters* 47 (1): 43–55.

Brüggemann, Ulf. 2017. "The Asymmetric War of ISIL Implications for Counter-Terrorism, Security Policy." Working Paper No. 13. https://bit.ly/2NaXa8U

Daley, Dan. 2000. *Asymmetric Warfare: The Only Thing New Is the Tactics.* Washington, DC: National Defense University National War College. https://bit.ly/2Mwcrou

Eaton, Wing Commander J. G., RAF. 2002. "The Beauty of Asymmetry: An Examination of the Context and Practice of Asymmetric and Unconventional Warfare from a Western/Centrist Perspective." *Defense Studies* 2 (1): 51–82.

Global Strategies. 2017. "Hybrid Warfare in the Middle East." London School of Economics, February 2017. https://bit.ly/2wkMq0p

Grossman, Nicholas. 2018. *Drones and Terrorism: Asymmetrical Warfare and the Threat to Global Security.* London: I. B. Tauris.

Lowther, Adam B. 2007. *Americans and Asymmetric Conflict Lebanon, Somalia, and Afghanistan.* Westport, CT: Praeger Security International.

Phelan, Colonel Pat. 2011. "Fourth Generation Warfare and Its Challenges for the Military and Society." *Defense Studies* 11 (1): 96–119.

Schroefl, Joseph, and Stuart J. Kaufman. 2014. "Hybrid Actors, Tactical Variety: Rethinking Asymmetric and Hybrid War." *Studies in Conflict & Terrorism* 37 (10): 862–880.

Attack on the U.S. Capitol, January 6, 2021

It is not always easy to determine the exact point at which efforts to influence become efforts to intimidate, nor when peaceful protests get out of hand and turn into riots or insurrections. The same is true in drawing a distinction between mass violence and terrorist activity explicitly targeting noncombatants to advance a political agenda. Yet, in the case of the January 6, 2021, assault on the U.S. Capitol and the elected officials and staff within as they set about the business of validating the electoral vote of several states and officially proclaiming the president-elect of the United States, no such determinations are necessary. Elements of all of the above were present and on camera.

THE ASSAULT

The group that gathered in Washington to protest/stop the electoral vote count had attended the Stop the Steal rally the night before and then assembled for an address by President Trump on January 6 before marching toward the U.S. Capitol. The crowd contained a diverse and volatile lot. Uniting them—despite more than a score of court cases dismissed for want of evidence, multiple recounts in contested states, and the certification of election results by state officials of Trump's own party—was a shared belief that the 2020 presidential election had been riddled with tabulation errors, fraud, possible outside interference, and other illegitimate factors that had denied President Trump the second term to which he was entitled. Many had journeyed great distances to protest peacefully but were swept up in the moment and became a part of the mob that stormed the Capitol.

Others, who journeyed to disrupt and prevent the count, arrived prepared for more violent action, following social media recommendations that they bring flags whose staffs could be used as clubs against Capitol defenders. The most militant were those from state militias and other extremist groups. They arrived—some in tactical body armor—with murderous intent; detailed plans for breaching the Capitol, which included rappelling down the side of the building; and cell phones for coordinating their assault.

By the time sufficient Washington, DC, police and National Guard reinforcements arrived hours later to restore order, casualties included four who had come to protest (one dying of a gunshot wound upon entering the Capitol through a smashed window, a second of a stroke related to heat exhaustion, a third of a heart attack, the fourth, weakened by a drug overdose, trampled to death by the crowd surging towards the Capital). Immediate fatalities also included a Capitol guard who died after being struck on the head by a fire extinguisher; however, a fair accounting of the casualties would include the hundreds among the crowd or working in the Capitol who were injured or traumatized by the events of that day, the 150 or more police and other responders who were injured, and the four members of the Capitol Police who took their own lives over the next six months following the insurrection.

Arrests, often initially only for trespassing, began on the Capitol grounds, and as they mounted, the numbers reflected the scope of the attack. Within four weeks, 211 individuals—nearly 90 percent men, representing forty-three of the fifty states and including at least a score of U.S. military veterans—had been charged, many for serious crimes carrying long sentences. By the spring of the following year that number had grown to over 700, with the leaders and members of such groups as the Proud Boys and Oath Keepers being indicted on more serious charges, including conspiracy to commit sedition.

CAUSES

Inquiries into the causes of and takeaways from the attack began almost immediately. Their findings will be spread over the years ahead, both in terms of the causal factors that will be identified and the relative priority attached to each. At this writing, only slightly over a month since the event, three elements stand out as most likely to be extensively cited in these studies.

First, there were the actions by those in government and the media who maintained the drum beat that the election of Joseph Biden as president was rigged and who urged the states to renounce the outcome of their votes and their citizens to protest the counts and certifications. The principal voice articulating such claims was President Trump himself, leading to his impeachment by the House of Representatives for "Incitement of Insurrection" by a vote of 232 in favor (with 10 Republicans joining the House majority Democrats) to 197 opposed (all Republicans and a majority of that party's embers holding seats in the House).

Abetting the president, and giving credibility to his charges, were not only conservative television and radio commentators but also those Republican members of the Senate and House of Representatives who had pledged to challenge Congress's certification of the electoral votes of six states—Pennsylvania, Michigan, Arizona, Nevada, Wisconsin, and Georgia. Indeed, one of the most chilling moments in the hours of footage covering the storming of the Capitol was the conversation between two men calmly discussing the murders of Vice President Mike Pence and House Speaker Nancy Pelosi, with one assuring the other that it would be okay because Senators Ted Cruz (Texas) and Josh Hawley (Missouri) would approve of their killings.

These assertions of electoral fraud and the urgings to disrupt the certification process might have found a less ready audience if not for two other factors shaping the 2020 political climate: the impact of the COVID-19 pandemic on American society and the "echo effect" resulting from the coupling of algorithm technology to social media and Internet communication outlets.

The arrival of COVID-19 contributed to the size and ferocity of the January 6 attack. Government-ordered lockdowns at the state and local levels idled and sometimes isolated tens of millions of Americans who would have ordinarily been at their jobs, in school, attending sporting events, dining out, and otherwise socially interacting. The crippling effect of the virus on the economy and closure of classroom schooling after the lockdowns ended similarly left a large number of people with hours to fill. The lockdowns also produced anger and intensified existing antigovernment sentiments across the country. Large crowds often gathered in open defiance of masking and social distancing orders, and a Michigan militia had weeks in which to plan the kidnapping and trial for treason of their state's governor, Gretchen Whitmer. By the end of the year, tens of thousands could plan to march on Washington to protest the January certification of the Electoral College vote without worrying about being at work or school the next day—or the next week.

Online self-radicalization also filled the idle hours of many. Those holding extremist thoughts found viewpoint reinforcement in Internet chat rooms and on the radical websites to which repeat browsers were algorithm steered. Conspiracy ideas like the Great Replacement theory found new devotees, and groups like the Proud Boys and movements like Antifa found new followers. Estimates suggest that QAnon "membership" increased two- to threefold in 2020 in the United States alone.

In short, in the aftermath of the November 3 presidential election, there was a sizable audience ready to accept the conspiracy theories of election fraud immediately spread by the White House, and many within it were ready to undertake political violence to overturn the "theft" of the presidency.

THREE IMMEDIATE OUTCOMES

Renewed Concern about Information Sharing within the Intelligence Community

The failure of security organizations to anticipate the severity of the January 6 attack despite the threatening nature of the information that many collected reawakened the concerns expressed by the 9/11 Commission about agency "siloing" of intelligence. In fact, as entries in this volume document, considerable progress has been made in information sharing within the federal government and between its agencies and state and local security forces since al-Qaeda's 2001 attack on the United States. Nonetheless, as the acting Capitol Police chief noted following the Capitol attack, there were multiple failings of various kinds by security and intelligence agencies both before and in the moment that the assault on the Capitol began. Collectively, these enabled the protesters to breach the security perimeter and roam dangerously free inside the building before sufficient reinforcements arrived to retake control of the premises.

Refocusing Domestic Counterterrorism Efforts

The 9/11 attack rechanneled domestic counterterrorism efforts from a prior concern with antiabortionists and militias on the right, radical leftist organizations, and lone-wolf terrorists like Ted Kaczynski and Eric Rudolph to countering the security threats posed by extremist Islamic operatives infiltrating the United States and domestic residents radicalized by the Internet propaganda of international terrorist organizations. The threat environment supported this action. The horror of the 1995 Oklahoma City Federal Building bombing had dampened the long run of domestic terrorism that began with the violent opposition to the civil rights movement. The images of the 9/11 carnage likewise worked against domestic groups urging violence. A decade and a half later, however, domestic violent extremism (DVE) was again claiming center stage, its uptick underscored by the 2015 massacre at the African American church in Charleston, South Carolina; the 2018 shootings at a Pittsburgh synagogue; and the Dallas area resident who drove 600 miles to kill Mexican immigrants at an El Paso Walmart in 2019.

Security services were consequently already focusing on domestic organizations as the graver threat to homeland security even before the October 2020 arrest of members of a Michigan militia for plotting to kidnap Whitmer. Nonetheless, the fact that the Department of Homeland Security found it necessary in the aftermath of the Capitol attack to release a rare Terrorism Advisory Bulletin urging domestic security agencies and citizens alike to be mindful of the DVE threat underscored where the government now saw the terrorist threat residing.

Trust

Finally, and the area least susceptible to easy cures, the attack on the Capitol opened a Pandora's box of trust issues, beginning with the problem that perhaps tens of millions of Trump supporters, believing that the election was stolen, are alienated from the current U.S. government. Trust issues also permeate those who voted for Biden but who have seen a large number of elected national and state officials place their political futures ahead of their oaths to uphold the Constitution of the United States. Theirs is no idle concern. The rule of the written law ultimately depends on respect for the unwritten rules of the game, perhaps the most important of which is that losers of fairly held democratic elections concede their loss in favor of an orderly transfer of power.

The wisdom of trusting security agencies to protect the homeland was also called into question. One of the elements of terrorism in the United States that set it apart from terrorist action in Western Europe had been the infrequency with which landmark political institutions had been targeted in the United States. In the aftermath of the January 6 rioting, the question was unavoidable. If the U.S. Capitol itself is vulnerable, what areas of life are safe?

Finally, by the time the last state's electoral vote was certified in the early morning of January 7, the trust of the members of the Congress in the integrity of one another had suffered a significant blow. The unwillingness of many Republicans to accept the new security protocols that were subsequently adopted and the insistence of some on their right to carry firearms into the Senate and House chambers only deepened those trust issues.

Joseph R. Rudolph Jr.

See also: Armed Militias; Director of National Intelligence; Domestic Terrorism, White Supremacists; Homegrown Terrorism; Information Sharing Environment; Intelligence Community, Adjustments to the Post-9/11 World; Michigan Governor Kidnapping Plot.

FURTHER READING

Bjelopera, Jerome P. 2017. "Domestic Terrorism: An Overview." Congressional Research Service, August 21, 2017. https://fas.org/sgp/crs/terror/R44921.pdf

Demirjian, Karoun, Aaron Davis, and Peter Hermann. 2021. "Acting Capitol Police Chief Apologizes to Lawmakers: Leader Cites Multiple 'Failings' That Contributed to Jan. 6 Breach." *Washington Post*, January 27, 2021: A6.

Department of Homeland Security. 2021. "National Terrorism Advisory System Bulletin." January 27, 2021. https://www.dhs.gov/ntas/advisory/national-terrorism-advisory-system-bulletin-january-27-2021

Frankel, Todd. "Majority of People Charged in Riot Have Had Money Woes." *Washington Post*, February 11, 2021: A7.

Itkowitz, Colby, and Mike DeBonis. 2021. "Animus Mounts Inside Capitol: 'Enemy from Within,' Pelosi Asserts, Fears of Violence from Trump Supporters Grow." *Washington Post*, January 29, 2021: A1.

Perez, Eva, Katelyn Polantz, and Mallory Simon. 2021. "New Charges Allege Proud Boys Prepped for Capitol Insurrection." CNN, February 4, 2021. https://www.cnn.com/2021/02/03/politics/proud-boys-indicted-capitol-riot/index.html

Rizzo, Melinda. 2021. "Capitol Riot Underscores Need to Set Standards for Employee Behavior." *Crisis Management Update*, January 24, 2021. https://crisismanagementupdate.com/capitol-riot-underscores-need-to-set-standards-for-employee-behavior/

Weiner, Rebecca Ulam. 2020. "The Growing White Supremacist Menace: COVID-19 Has Been a Boon for Far-Right Extremists." *Foreign Affairs*, June 23, 2020. https://www.foreignaffairs.com/articles/united-states/2020-06-23/growing-white-supremacist-menace

Axis of Evil

The *axis of evil* is a term used to describe maligned regimes in Iran, Iraq, and North Korea and their terrorist allies. It was used by President George W. Bush in his 2002 State of the Union (SOTU) address, the first SOTU after the terrorist attacks of September 11, 2001, against the United States. Bush cited intelligence estimates that concluded Iran was aggressively pursuing weapons and exporting terror, North Korea was arming itself with weapons of mass destruction while simultaneously starving its citizens, and Iraq was flaunting hostility toward the United States and supporting terror.

Bush speechwriters David Frum and Mike Gerson coined the term "axis of evil." It is an amalgamation of two dominant metonyms from twentieth-century American history. The first term, *axis*, is associated with the tripartite powers of World War II—German, Italy, and Japan—and represented the nefarious ideologies of fascism and Nazism. The second term, *evil*, hearkened to President Ronald Reagan's description of the Soviet Union and its authoritarian and repressive ideology as an "evil empire." The axis of evil represented the first major ideological threat facing the United States in the twenty-first century and was repeated by government officials and journalists throughout Bush's presidency.

Bush's 2002 SOTU and the axis of evil metaphor were partially intended to garner popular support from the American people against Saddam Hussein's regime in Iraq, which an American-led military coalition invaded the following year. While the metaphor served as a rhetorical device domestically, the aggressive tone degraded the previously constructive role Iranian officials had played in assisting U.S. efforts to counter the Taliban in Afghanistan. In North Korea, American foreign policy shifted from the "sunshine" strategy of engagement practiced under previous U.S. administrations toward more hawkish engagement and rhetoric.

Diane M. Zorri

See also: Counterterrorism and the George W. Bush Administration; War on Terror, The.

FURTHER READING

Cha, Victor. 2002. "Korea's Place in the Axis." *Foreign Affairs* 81 (3): 79–92.

Cummings, Bruce, et al., eds. 2004. *Inventing the Axis of Evil: The Truth about North Korea, Iran, and Syria.* New York: New Press.

Frum, David. 2005. *The Right Man: The Surprise Presidency of George W. Bush.* New York: Random House.

Gaddis, John L. 2002. "A Grand Strategy of Transformation." *Foreign Policy* 133 (Nov–Dec): 50–57.

Heradstveit, Daniel, and Matthew Bonham. 2007. "What the Axis of Evil Metaphor Did to Iran." *Middle East Journal* 61 (3): 421–440.

White House Archives. 2002. "President Delivers State of the Union Address." January 29, 2002. https://georgewbush-whitehouse.archives.gov/news/releases/2002/01/20020129-11.html

Woodward, Bob. 2004. *Plan of Attack.* New York: Simon and Schuster.

B

Bath School Bombing

May 18, 1927

The Bath School bombing was actually a series of attacks committed by Andrew Kehoe on May 18, 1927, in Bath Township, Michigan. Kehoe began the violence that day by killing his wife and firebombing his own farm. He then detonated an intricate explosive device he had planted earlier at the Bath Consolidated School. The attacks ended when Kehoe killed himself by detonating a final bomb in his truck. These violent events claimed the lives of thirty-eight children and six adults and injured an additional fifty-eight people.

Andrew Kehoe was born on February 1, 1872, in Tecumseh, Michigan. He married Ellen "Nellie" Price in 1912, and in 1919, they moved to a farm outside the unincorporated village of Bath, Michigan. The village is located in Bath Township, about ten miles northeast of Lansing, the state capital. In the early part of the twentieth century, Bath was primarily a rural farming community consisting of approximately 300 residents. In 1922, Bath Township voted for a property tax increase to create a new consolidated school district. When the new Bath Consolidated School first opened, it had 236 students enrolled in the first through twelfth grades.

In 1924, Kehoe was elected to a three-year term as a trustee on the school board and as its treasurer for one year. He repeatedly clashed with the other trustees and the school superintendent. Around this same time, Kehoe got into financial difficulties and began having trouble paying the mortgage on his farm. In 1925, Kehoe was appointed to temporarily fill a vacancy for the job of town clerk, but he was defeated in a 1926 election held to permanently fill that position. In June 1926, Kehoe was notified that the bank would soon foreclose on his farm. Additionally, by the time of the bombing, Nellie Kehoe was terminally ill from tuberculosis.

It has never been established when Kehoe began plotting his attacks, but it is clear that he began his meticulous planning many months before he acted. It was discovered later that Kehoe had cut all the wire fences at his farm and killed most of his trees and crops. Significantly, Kehoe had begun making several trips to nearby Lansing to purchase large quantities of dynamite and Pyrotol (an incendiary explosive used by farmers to clear land). He also had unrestricted access to the consolidated school building during this time, and no one thought to question why he was making so many trips into the school at night.

At approximately 8:45 a.m. on the morning of May 18, 1927, Kehoe detonated firebombs in his house and farm buildings. He had killed his wife sometime between May 16, when she was released from the hospital, and the morning of the bombing. Her heavily charred body was later recovered from inside a wheelbarrow behind the farm's chicken coop. Responders to the fiery scene found cases of unexploded dynamite and witnessed Kehoe leaving the farm in his Ford truck and heading toward the Bath School. Classes had already started there at 8:30 a.m., and Kehoe's homemade alarm clock detonator went off at approximately 8:45 a.m., igniting approximately 500 pounds of explosives that he had planted. The explosion destroyed the entire north wing of the school. During the search for survivors, an additional 500 pounds of dynamite that Kehoe had planted to obliterate the south wing of the building was discovered. Kehoe arrived at the school about an hour after the tragedy, and once there, he detonated the bomb he had placed in his truck, killing himself as well as three others.

John R. Capra

See also: Columbine Attack; Psychology of Terrorists.

FURTHER READING

Bernstein, Arnie. 2009. *Bath Massacre: America's First School Bombing.* Ann Arbor: University of Michigan Press.

Boissoneault, Lorraine. 2018. "The 1927 Bombing That Remains America's Deadliest School Massacre." *Smithsonian,* May 18, 2018. https://www.smithsonianmag.com/history/1927-bombing-remains-americas-deadliest-school-massacre-180963355/

Ellsworth, M. J. 1991. *The Bath School Disaster.* Bath, MI: Bath School Museum Committee.

Beirut Bombing of American Barracks

October 23, 1983

On the morning of October 23, 1983, vehicle-borne improvised explosive devices (VBIEDS) in trucks driven by suicide bombers exploded outside two buildings in Beirut, Lebanon, that served as barracks for U.S. Marines and French military personnel functioning as Multinational Force (MNF) peacekeepers during the Lebanese Civil War. The two bombings took the lives of 307 people and ultimately forced the withdrawal of the marines and other MNF peacekeepers from Lebanon.

The first explosion, outside the U.S. Marines barracks at Beirut International Airport, involved a stolen Mercedes-Benz truck laden with pentaerythritol tetranitrate (PETN) and butane gas canisters. Because rules of engagement prohibited them from having chambered rounds in their weapons, marine guards were unable to stop the truck before it reached the building. The explosion, equal in power to over 20,000 pounds of TNT, collapsed the building and resulted in 242 immediate deaths, including 220 U.S. Marines, 18 U.S. Navy sailors, 3 U.S. Army soldiers, and a Lebanese civilian. Another 128 Americans were wounded, and 13 subsequently died of their injuries.

Ten minutes later, a second truck bomb laden with a similar explosive detonated outside the building housing French peacekeepers. Alerted by the explosion at the marine barracks one kilometer away, French paratrooper guards fired at the truck, killing the driver and stopping the truck about fifty feet from the building.

Moments later, the truck exploded, apparently by remote control, collapsing the building and claiming the lives of fifty-eight French paratroopers and five French civilians. Fifteen French soldiers and twenty Lebanese civilians were injured.

Although a relatively unknown group, the Islamic Jihad initially claimed credit for the bombing, which was intended to force the U.S. and French peacekeepers to leave Lebanon. Subsequent investigations determined the attack was planned and carried out by Hezbollah operatives who were trained, equipped, and backed by Iran. Hezbollah formally announced its existence in 1985 but used the name Islamic Jihad to maintain secrecy and conceal ties to Iran. The National Security Council intercepted an Iranian diplomatic cable ordering an attack on U.S. Marines in Lebanon in September 1982, but it was not forwarded to the marines until after the barracks bombing.

The MNF, consisting of approximately 800 Marines, 800 Italians troops, and 400 French soldiers, was deployed in Lebanon in August 1982 following Israel's June 1982 invasion of southern Lebanon to establish a security buffer zone and to supervise the evacuation of Palestine Liberation Organization (PLO) forces from Lebanon. Following the September 1982 assassination of Lebanese president Bachir Gemayal and military action by Israeli and Lebanese Armed Forces (LAF) against Palestinian refugee camps, civil war erupted, pitting Lebanese Muslim, Maronite Christian, and various other factions against each other. Muslim factions believed the MNF, and the U.S. Marines in particular, were supporting the Maronite Christian groups and engaged in sniper and mortar attacks on MNF troops. With the consent of Syria, Iran established a military base in Lebanon's Beqaa Valley to train and arm the newly formed Shi'ite Hezbollah organization to serve as an Iranian proxy. In April 1983, a suicide truck bombing of U.S. embassy in Beirut, also planned, organized, and carried out by Iranian-backed Hezbollah operatives, claimed the lives of sixty-four people, including seventeen Americans.

Marine reinforcements arrived immediately from the United States. Two weeks later, a marine amphibious unit (MAU) consisting of a reinforced battalion and support troops relieved the marine garrison. Other than air strikes and naval artillery strikes on Syrian missile and artillery sites, the United States did not engage in robust retaliation for the barracks bombing, largely due to policy disagreements within the Reagan administration. In February 1984, President Ronald Reagan ordered the withdrawal of U.S. troops from Lebanon. It is widely believed that the failure to retaliate emboldened various terrorist groups to attack U.S. facilities and interests.

The subsequent investigation determined that Hezbollah planned and carried out the attacks under the direction of Imad Mughniyah (also known as Hajj Radwan), a founder of Islamic Jihad and Hezbollah, along with his cousin, Hezbollah military leader Mustafa Badr al-Din. A car bomb killed Imad Mughniyah in Damascus in February 2008.

Vincent E. Henry

See also: Hezbollah; Madrid Train Bombings and the War on Terror.

FURTHER READING

Burton, Fred, and Samuel Katz. 2018. *Beirut Rues: The Murder of a CIA Station Chief and Hezbollah's War against America.* New York: Berkley.

Frank, Benis M. 1987. *U.S. Marines in Lebanon, 1982–1984*. Washington, DC: History and Museums Division Headquarters, U.S. Marine Corps. https://www.marines.mil/Portals/1/Publications/US Marines In Lebanon 1982-1984 PCN 19000309800_1.pdf

U.S. Department of Defense. 1983. *Report of the DoD Commission on the Beirut International Airport Terrorist Act, October 23, 1983*. Washington, DC: Department of Defense. https://fas.org/irp/threat/beirut-1983.pdf

Beltway Sniper Attacks

October 2002

Occurring just a year after the September 11 terrorist attacks, the Beltway sniper attacks occurred over a three-week period, from October 2 to October 24, 2002. The arrest of the two shooters, John Allen Mohammed and John Lee Malvo, ended a shooting and crime spree that began on February 16, 2002, in Tacoma, Washington. The Beltway sniper shootings, coming as they did just a year after the Pentagon attack, set the whole of the National Capital Region (NCR) on edge. While the attacks were not initially connected to the global war on terrorism, the impact was the same, with widespread fear returning to the region.

The Tacoma shooting victim was the niece of a woman who had advised Mohammed's wife to seek a divorce from him, and she was killed at close range by Malvo. The second killing, which took place on March 19 in Tucson, Arizona, appeared to be a practice attack on a random victim, facilitated by the proximity of the home of Mohammed's sister to the golf course where the killing shot occurred.

As the pair crisscrossed the country toward the nation's capital, five deaths and seven injuries marked their path between February and September 23, 2002. None of the victims seemed to have any family or political relevance for the killers. Then, during the Beltway phase of the rampage, another ten people died and three more were critically wounded in the area between Ashland, Virginia, and Montgomery County, Maryland.

The pair utilized a 1990 Chevrolet Caprice that they had modified by cutting a hole in the hood just above the license plate to enable them to operate from cover and concealment. Their stated goal was to kill at least six people per day, but they never achieved it. An increasing number of witnesses reported the blue Caprice. Combined with an increasing number of clues left at the scenes of the killings (including a specific threat against children that caused chaos in local school systems) and phone messages left by Mohammed, these reports eventually led to the pair's capture at a Maryland rest stop as they slept in their car.

References to the sources of Mohammed's radicalization are few; however, his extremist views involving Black nationalism seem to date from approximately when he joined the Nation of Islam in 1987. Among his purported goals in the murder spree was to somehow regain custody of his children. He also sought to extort enough money to establish a Black nation in Canada separate from the United States. In his testimony, Malvo described a multipart plan by which Mohammed intended to raise money and recruits through his killings. Eventually, he intended to train a large murderous force to spread terror throughout the United

States, capitalizing on the fear engendered by the September 11 attacks. No evidence surfaced, however, of a connection between the pair and the broader network of radical Islamic terrorist groups.

Malvo, who was seventeen years old at the time of the shootings, appeared to have been radicalized through contact with Mohammed; however, he specifically cited a desire to engage in a jihad during his incarceration.

The pair faced trials in Virginia, a death penalty state, and Maryland, where the majority of the killings took place. Mohammed was sentenced to death in September 2003 and executed in November 2009.

Malvo claimed to have committed all of the killings in an effort to spare his mentor the death penalty. In the Maryland trials, however, he recanted to get the best deal for himself. He received six consecutive life sentences without possibility of parole. In 2017, two Virginia life sentences were vacated by the U.S. Fourth Circuit Court due to his age when the murders were committed. Reconsideration of his Virginia sentence was underway as of 2019. His Maryland sentences remain unchallenged.

John M. Callahan

See also: Columbine Attack; Homegrown Terrorism; Jihad.

FURTHER READING

Crime Museum. n.d. "The DC Beltway Sniper Attacks." Accessed November 20, 2019. https://www.crimemuseum.org/crime-library/mass-murder/the-washington-dc-sniper/

FBI. n.d. "Beltway Snipers." https://www.fbi.gov/history/famous-cases/beltway-snipers

Mataconis, Doug. "The Beltway Snipers Ten Years Later." Outside the Beltway, October 2, 2012. https://www.outsidethebeltway.com/the-beltway-snipers-ten-years-later/

Reichenbaugh, David. 2018. *In Pursuit: The Hunt for the Beltway Snipers*. Lebanon, NH: ForeEdge.

Benghazi

September 11, 2012

On the evening of September 11, 2012, the U.S. mission compound in Benghazi, Libya, came under rocket, mortar, and machine gun attack by members of Ansar al-Sharia, an extreme fundamentalist Islamist militia formed in 2011 during the Libyan Civil War. The attack resulted in the deaths by smoke inhalation of U.S. Ambassador Christopher Stevens and State Department communications specialist Sean Smith when the Ansar al-Sharia attackers breached the compound walls and set fire to the mission's residence, where Stevens and Smith had sought a safe haven from the attack.

Members of the CIA's Global Response Staff (GRS) security team stationed at a nearby CIA annex were notified of the attack after some delay, allegedly due to a "stand down" order issued by the top officer at the CIA annex. Six Diplomatic Security Service (DSS) officers and Libyan contract security guards from the 17th of February Brigade militia defending the mission located Smith's body in the burning residence but were unable to locate Stevens's body. As the attack continued, the defenders took Smith's body and evacuated thirty members of the mission's diplomatic staff to the nearby CIA annex, which then came under rocket, mortar, and machine gun attack from Ansar al-Sharia militants. A small team of CIA and Delta Force operators dispatched from Tripoli arrived at the annex, which was still under attack. Shortly after two of the defenders, former Navy SEALs Glen Doherty and Tyrone Woods, were killed by mortar fire, the annex was abandoned and all personnel evacuated to Benina International Airport in Benghazi.

Ambassador Stevens's body was located by Libyans in the mission compound and transported to a nearby hospital and thence to Benina International Airport. Shortly before 8:00 a.m. on September 12, the evacuation by air of all diplomatic personnel began. It ended around 10:00 a.m. when an aircraft containing the security team and the bodies of Stevens, Smith, Doherty, and Woods departed.

The terrorist attack on the mission, the sluggish military and inadequate diplomatic responses to it, and the allegedly negligent actions of President Obama, Secretary of State Hillary Clinton, and Secretary of Defense Leon Panetta prior to and during the attack generated substantial controversy and multiple congressional inquiries and reports. Members of the Obama administration initially attributed the attack to a spontaneous protest of a YouTube video offensive to Muslims, despite Ansar al-Sharia's claims of responsibility and other intelligence demonstrating the explanation was false. Anonymous officially unconfirmed reports claimed the mission and the secret CIA annex were engaged in the covert smuggling of weapons from Libya to anti-Assad rebel forces in Syria.

None of the ten inquiries or reports ultimately found direct misconduct or wrongdoing, but members of the administration were criticized for failing to mount a military response to the ongoing attack more quickly, failing to properly assess the threat of terrorist attacks on the Benghazi mission or other U.S. diplomatic facilities on the anniversary of the 9/11 attacks, falsely attributing the attack to the offensive video, and denying Ambassador Stevens's multiple earlier requests for additional security at the mission.

Vincent E. Henry

See also: Counterterrorism and the Obama Administration; United States Embassy and Consulate Attacks.

FURTHER READING

Murphy, Jack, and Brandon Webb. 2013. *Benghazi: The Definitive Report.* New York: HarperCollins.

New York Police Department. 2012. *NYPD SHIELD Assessment: U.S. Ambassador to Libya Killed in Attack on U.S. Consulate.* New York: New York Police Department Counterterrorism Bureau.

U.S. House of Representatives. 2016. *Final Report of the Select Committee on the Events Surrounding the 2012 Terrorist Attack in Benghazi.* Washington, DC: U.S. Government Printing Office. https://www.congress.gov/114/crpt/hrpt848/CRPT-114hrpt848.pdf

U.S. Senate Committee on Homeland Security and Governmental Affairs. 2012. *Flashing Red: A Special Report on the Terrorist Attack at Benghazi.* Washington, DC: Senate Committee on Homeland Security and Governmental Affairs.

U.S. State Department. 2012. *Accountability Review Board (ARB) for Benghazi*. Washington, DC: U.S. State Department. https://2009-2017.state.gov/documents/organization/202446.pdf

Zuckoff, Mitchell. 2014. *13 Hours: The Inside Account of What Really Happened in Benghazi*. New York: Twelve.

bin Laden, Osama

1957/8–2011

Osama bin Mohammad bin Laden, commonly known as Osama bin Laden (OBL) or Usama bin Laden, was a founder of the Islamic militant organization known as al-Qaeda. OBL was born in Riyadh, Saudi Arabia, in 1957 or 1958 and was the seventeenth child out of fifty-two fathered by Mohammed bin Laden, a Yemeni immigrant. His mother, Alia Ghanem, was from Syria. The senior bin Laden would eventually own one of the largest construction companies in Saudi Arabia. OBL was raised in a life of wealthy privilege and was a national citizen of Saudi Arabia until he was declared stateless in 1994 by that kingdom. The senior bin Laden was killed in a private plane crash, along with his American pilot, in 1967 in Saudi Arabia.

A devout follower of the Islamic religion, in the 1970s, while at college, OBL was deeply influenced by the Islamist scholar Abdullah Azzam, who taught that all Muslims should unite in jihad, or holy war, against decadent Western pressures and create a pan-Islamic national state. This merger of religion and anti-Western thinking led OBL to travel to Peshawar, Pakistan, on the border of Afghanistan, soon after Soviet troops invaded that country in 1979. Joining the anti-Soviet resistance, OBL used his wealth and extensive family contacts to raise money and international Islamic support for the Afghan resistance fighters, known as the *mujahideen*. The years financing and recruiting young Muslim men from all over the world to join the Afghan jihad convinced OBL that the possibility of establishing a pan-Islamic state was real.

In 1989, the Soviets withdrew from Afghanistan. OBL, buoyed by the success that he had found there in working for a united Islamic state, returned to the Saudi Kingdom and began organizing and fundraising for his newly formed Islamic militant group, al-Qaeda (AQ) or "the base." AQ would focus on committing acts of international terrorism to bring attention to its cause. A key tenet of AQ's ideology was the belief that civilians from enemy countries, including women and children, were legitimate targets for jihadists to put to death, whether as collateral damage or, more likely, as the target of the terror act itself. OBL also believed that only a complete embrace of Sharia law would save Islam from the crisis of secularism it was facing from the encroachment of the West. A core tenet of OBL's strategy to accomplish Islamic supremacy, in the face of superpower opposition like the United States', was to bait the West into a prolonged war of attrition that would gather large numbers of jihadist fighters from all over the Islamic world who would gladly give their lives for such a cause.

In the fall of 1990, military forces under Iraqi leader Saddam Hussein invaded the Kingdom of Kuwait and put thousands of Iraqi troops on the border of Saudi

Arabia, threatening the world's oil supply. In response, King Fahd asked for and received military support from the United States in the form of approximately 500,000 troops placed in Saudi territory in what would become known as Operation Desert Shield. OBL began a vocal campaign of criticism of the Saudi royal family for allowing American troops within the county that contained the two holiest religious sites in the Islamic world, Mecca and Medina, which OBL believed should only be defended by fellow Muslims. It was also at the end of 1990 that the first evidence of AQ's terror operation reached the United States, as a New Jersey FBI raid found evidence of an AQ plot to destroy New York City skyscrapers. In 1991, OBL was expelled from Saudi Arabia for his continued public criticism of that kingdom, and his Saudi citizenship was revoked in 1994.

By 1992, OBL and his followers had set up worldwide operational headquarters for AQ in the Northeast African desert nation of Sudan. In 1994, AQ was believed to be involved with the attempted assassination of Egyptian president Hosni Mubarak by the Egyptian Islamic Jihad. This led to intense pressure being put on Sudan by the United States, Saudi Arabia, and Egypt for that country to expel OBL and AQ. In 1996, Sudan expelled OBL and some 300 of his Arab followers, who chose to settle in Jalalabad, Afghanistan. It is estimated that OBL lost between $20 million and $200 million due to his assets and property being confiscated by the government of Sudan during his expulsion. In Afghanistan, OBL forged a close working relationship with Mullah Omar, who was a fellow Afghan mujahideen commander that now led the Taliban and who had founded the Islamic Emirate of Afghanistan in 1996.

Now in Afghanistan, in August 1996, OBL and AQ declared war on the United States. In issuing this *fatwa* (a formal decree under Islamic law), one of OBL's primary arguments was the unmet promises of President George H. W. Bush to remove military troops from Saudi Arabia, despite major combat operations ceasing in 1991. Citing the need to expel the "infidels" from the territory that housed the two most holy Islamic sites, OBL claimed that Saudi Arabia was allowing the Middle East to effectively become an American territory. One of AQ's early successes was the financing of the terror bombing at an archaeological site and major tourist attraction in Luxor, Egypt, in November 1997, killing sixty-two people, mostly foreign tourists.

In February 1998, OBL and Egyptian terrorist Ayman al-Zawahiri cosigned a fatwa declaring the killing of North Americans as the duty of all true Muslims. This was soon followed in August 1998 by bombings at the U.S. embassies in Dar es Salaam, Tanzania, and Nairobi, Kenya. Truck bombs were simultaneously detonated outside both major African cities, killing nearly 200. AQ publicly claimed responsibility for the terror acts. In retaliation, President Bill Clinton ordered bombing strikes on several OBL-related training camps in Sudan and Afghanistan two weeks later. Following an indictment in U.S. district court in late 1998 for his involvement in these attacks, OBL was placed on the FBI's Ten Most Wanted Fugitives list.

In further retaliation for the presence of U.S. military troops in the Saudi Kingdom and continued enforcement of sanctions on Iraq, OBL and AQ accomplished their most ambitious and successful plan on September 11, 2001, with attacks on the U.S. homeland. Nineteen members of AQ hijacked four airliners leaving out of the U.S. domestic terminals in Boston, Newark, and Washington, DC, all fully fueled for cross-country trips to the West Coast. American Airlines Flight 11 was intentionally flown into the north tower of the World Trade Center (WTC) located in downtown New York City. Less than twenty minutes later, United Airlines Flight 175 was flown into the south tower of the WTC. Approximately thirty minutes later, American Airlines Flight 77 slammed into the western side of the Pentagon in Arlington County, Virginia. A fourth plane, United Airlines Flight 93, crashed in a field near the town of Shanksville, Pennsylvania, as the passengers attempted to regain control of the aircraft. One of the original planners of the 9/11 attacks later admitted that the target for Flight 93 was the U.S. Capitol. In total, the 9/11 attacks killed 2,977 individuals and wounded over 25,000. It was the most deadly terror attack in world history. Immediately following the attacks, the United States identified OBL and AQ as the prime movers of the tragic events and offered a $25 million reward for OBL's capture, dead or alive.

The attacks were conceived by Khalid Sheikh Mohammed in 1996, who was later arrested by Pakistani security officials and turned over to the American CIA. Mohammed is currently being held at the U.S. military detention facility at Guantánamo Bay, Cuba. OBL initially denied any AQ involvement in the attacks. Later, however, in a 2004 video released by AQ, OBL admitted that he personally planned the attacks of 9/11 and that he was inspired to plan the destruction of the Twin Towers after watching towers be destroyed in Lebanon by Israel in the early 1980s during the Lebanon War.

On September 14, 2001, the U.S. Congress passed the Authorization for Use of Military Force against terrorists resolution, which gave the president the authority to use all necessary force against those determined to have been involved in the 9/11 attacks. On September 20, 2001, President George W. Bush addressed the nation and a joint session of Congress, expressing the nation's determination to bring the terrorists, and those who harbored them, to justice. Because AQ was operating out of Taliban-controlled Afghanistan at the time of the 9/11 attacks, the United States demanded that the Taliban extradite OBL, which they refused.

On October 7, 2001, the War in Afghanistan began with a military operation led by U.S. and British aerial forces bombing strategic locations throughout the country. In early December, U.S. CIA operatives and military Special Forces joined with the Afghanistan Northern Alliance, a group of local freedom fighters opposed to the Taliban's authoritative rule, and began a military ground operation in and around the mountains of the Tora Bora region along Afghanistan's eastern border with Pakistan. It was believed that AQ had its headquarters in the intricate cave complexes located there and that it was where OBL had taken refuge. Failure of the United States to commit adequate military ground troops to the operation, however, allowed OBL and many of AQ's senior leadership to avoid capture and escape into Pakistan. Amid years of conflicting reports about his whereabouts, and even occasional reports of his death, OBL remained at large and avoided capture for years—until his luck ran out.

Acting on specific intelligence, U.S. Navy SEALs killed OBL at the compound where he was hiding near Islamabad, Pakistan, on May 1, 2011. OBL had reportedly been hiding out in this specially built compound for five years prior to his death. The site was located less than a mile from the Pakistan Military Academy, the main training academy for Pakistani military officers. Although never officially charged for his involvement in the 9/11 attacks, OBL still had pending federal criminal indictments for the African embassy bombing in 1998 at the time of his death. On June 15, 2011, U.S. prosecutors officially dropped all criminal charges against him due to his death the previous month.

At the time of his death, OBL was believed to have at least five wives, possibly a sixth whose marriage was annulled shortly after it took place, and an estimated twenty to twenty-six children. Most of these children are believed to have fled to Iran following the September 11, 2001, attacks on the United States. Although OBL's death was a significant setback for the international AQ terror network, the group continues to thrive alongside other international terror groups.

John R. Capra

See also: al-Qaeda; Intelligence Community, Adjustments to the Post-9/11 World; September 11, 2001, Attack on America; United States Embassy and Consulate Attacks.

FURTHER READING

Atkinson, Rick. 1994. *Crusade: The Untold Story of the Persian Gulf War.* Boston, MA: Houghton Mifflin Harcourt.

Bergen, Peter L. 2013. *Manhunt: The Ten-Year Search for Bin Laden from 9/11 to Abbottabad.* New York: Broadway Books.

Coll, Steve. 2004. *Ghost Wars: The Secret History of the CIA, Afghanistan, and Bin Laden, from the Soviet Invasion to September 10, 2001.* London: Penguin Books.

Mangan, Dan. 2011. "Wanted: Dead—Not Alive!" *New York Post,* August 2, 2011.

Scheuer, Michael. 2011. *Osama Bin Laden.* Oxford, UK: Oxford University Press.

Wright, Lawrence. 2007. *The Looming Tower: Al-Qaeda and the Road to 9/11.* New York: First Vintage Books.

Biological Weapons

Since 1945, weapons of mass destruction (WMD) have included chemical, biological, and nuclear weapons. All have been used in wars, with casualties greatest for chemical, then nuclear, and the least from biological weapons, at least in the modern era. However, modern genetic engineering technologies designed to enhance antiviral defense mechanisms could change that dramatically.

Historical biological weapons typically involved infectious organisms from nature, such as smallpox, plague, and anthrax. They were used at least as early as circa 219 BC, when Hannibal tossed plague-infested corpses into Roman cities. Some white Americans gave smallpox-infected blankets to Indians during the nineteenth-century campaign to wrest the American West from its Indigenous peoples, and Japanese Unit 731, a secret wartime chemical and biological research unit, undertook similar and worse "experiments" on Chinese people during World War II. During the Cold

War, which endured from the late 1940s through the early 1990s, both the Soviet Union and the United States developed extensive biological warfare programs. However, near universal horror at the concept of breeding and weaponizing ancient plagues for use against human populations resulted in a United Nations–mediated treaty called the Biological Weapons Convention that banned all such activity by civilized nations in 1975. As of January 2018, this convention has been signed and ratified by 180 of the United Nations' 193 member nations.

Moral and legal constraints on biological weapons are challenged, however, by the relative ease and low cost of creating biological weapons compared with nuclear and even chemical weapons. Modern genetic engineering techniques raise fears that terrorists in basements using chemicals bought online could recreate ancient scourges like smallpox or even create new "designer diseases." These could be chimera organisms that combine lethal genes from multiple organisms, and they could even include genes for resistance to all known antibiotics.

One of the novel properties of biological weapons compared to other WMD is that they can reproduce themselves and spread far beyond any initial target. This helped military institutions to recognize that biologicals could turn on one's own troops and were not very useful against hardened military targets. Instead, they would mainly afflict vulnerable civilian populations and could spread worldwide. Biological weapons could also be used against food crops and animals, spreading famine as well as novel plagues. For all these reasons, even the most fierce warrior generals have generally agreed that biological weapons should not be created, much less used.

Some terrorist groups have expressed considerable interest in biological weapons. One Japanese death cult, Aum Shinrikyo, released the deadly chemical agent sarin on a Tokyo subway system in 1995, killing twelve people. The group also tried to make biological weapons to attack Japan's civilian population, but it was thwarted by Japanese police and counterterrorism forces. Another cult in Oregon, this one organized by Bhagwan Shree Rajneesh, put salmonella bacteria on salad bars in ten restaurants in November 1984 in an attempt to swing county elections against local officials bent on halting the expansion of their commune. More than 750 people were sickened, but no one died.

Assassinations are another area where biological weapons have been used. Biological toxins such as ricin have been used to kill selected individuals, like Bulgarian dissident writer Georgi Markov in London in September 1978. Several packages of weaponized anthrax were also sent to about a dozen targets shortly after 9/11, killing five people and infecting seventeen others. According to the FBI, the alleged culprit was not a "typical" terrorist but a veteran of the U.S. biological weapons program named Bruce Ivins. There remains controversy over that conclusion, but whomever sent the U.S. weapons-grade anthrax packages to several news media offices and two Democratic U.S. senators included notes with Islamic terminology hoping to arouse mass anger against Muslims. Therefore, better control of biological weapons before terrorists (or false flag operators posing as terrorists) can build or buy any is a top priority for counterterrorism around the world today.

Michael Andregg

See also: New Terrorism; Weapons of Mass Destruction.

FURTHER READING

Cirincione, Joseph, John B. Wolfsthal, and Miriam Rajkumar, 2005. *Deadly Arsenals: Nuclear, Biological and Chemical Threats.* 2nd ed. Washington, DC: Carnegie Endowment for International Peace.

Nuclear Threat Initiative. n.d. "Biological." https://www.nti.org/area/biological/

Osterholm, Michael T., and Mark Olshaker. 2017. *Deadliest Enemy: Our War against Killer Germs.* New York: Little, Brown and Company.

United Nations Office for Disarmament Affairs. n.d. "What are Biological Weapons?" https://www.un.org/disarmament/biological-weapons/about/what-are-biological-weapons/

Wright, Susan. 2002. *Biological Warfare and Disarmament: New Problems/New Perspectives.* Lanham, MD: Rowman & Littlefield.

Boston Marathon Bombing

April 15, 2013

The Boston Marathon bombing was a terrorist act carried out by two radicalized brothers on April 15, 2013, targeting the annual athletic event in Boston. The perpetrators' claim to have been unconnected to any organized terrorist group presented a troubling indicator of the growing potential of homegrown terrorism, the potential for disaffected individuals to embark on courses of self-radicalization, and the online proliferation of tools for learning the skills and tactics necessary to carry out terrorist attacks.

While born in Kalmyk Autonomous Soviet Socialist Republic and Kyrgyzstan, respectively, Tamerlan and Dzhokhar Tsarnaev were of Chechen ethnic descent. They were strongly influenced by the decades-long, ongoing insurgency raging in Chechnya against Russia. This insurgency, which started as a nationalist separatist conflict, gradually turned into an Islamist, religiously defined war by the late 1990s.

The Tsarnaevs immigrated to the United States in 2002, with Tamerlan, the older brother, eventually marrying an American. Dzhokhar, meanwhile, attended the University of Massachusetts, where he majored in marine biology and achieved U.S. citizenship in 2012. Yet, by that time, Tamerlan had steadily radicalized, perceiving Islam to be under attack by the United States in Iraq and Afghanistan. His views proved to be a model for his younger brother.

While not in direct contact with any known terrorist group, the brothers learned how to construct pressure cooker explosive devices from *Inspire*, an online journal published by the Yemen-based al-Qaeda branch (al-Qaeda in the Arabian Peninsula). *Inspire* is one of several English-language publications issued by al-Qaeda, providing both propaganda and practical instructions on weapons and tactics. Its creation is attributed to an American citizen, Samir Khan.

Having originally contemplated setting off the bombs on the Fourth of July, the brothers eventually decided to target the Boston Marathon instead. The bombs were set off on April 15, 2013, along the route of the marathon, with 5,700 participants still engaged in the event. There were 3 fatalities and 264 people wounded from the blasts. The injuries of 14 of the survivors were serious enough to result in amputation.

Early speculation placed the blame for the attack on North Korea, but the investigation, which was led by the FBI and included a wide array of other federal and local law enforcement organizations, focused on the Tsarnaev brothers as suspects within days. Photographs of the brothers were released to the public on April 18. With law enforcement closing in, the Tsarnaevs murdered a Massachusetts Institute of Technology (MIT) campus police officer, shooting him six times and unsuccessfully attempting to steal his firearm. They then carjacked an automobile, taking the owner hostage, with the purpose of driving to New York City to detonate additional bombs at Times Square.

The hostage, Dun Meng, managed to escape and alert the police, leading to a shootout between the brothers and the police in the Watertown district of Boston. Tamerlan was apprehended but was accidentally run over and killed by his brother during the latter's escape. Dzhokhar was apprehended after another gunfight one day later, after being discovered hiding in a moored boat. Thirty charges were brought against Tsarnaev, including the use of a weapon of mass destruction, and after standing trial, he was convicted on all counts on April 8, 2015, and sentenced on June 24 of that year to death by lethal injection.

While the president of Russia, Vladimir Putin, offered his condolences to the United States and urged closer cooperation between Russian and American counterterrorist organizations, the attack prompted a series of disagreements between the two countries. Russian intelligence services claimed that they had offered several warnings about the radical leanings of the brothers and their plans that were ignored by their American counterparts. Conversely, the FBI maintains that there was no proof of Russian claims at the time and that requests the agency made for additional information and details on the brothers had been ignored by Russian agencies.

Daniel Stotland

See also: Christmas Day "Underwear Bomber," Umar Farouk Abdulmutallab; War on Terror, The.

FURTHER READING

Gessen, Masha. 2015. *The Brothers: The Road to an American Tragedy.* New York: Riverhead Books.

Gunaratna, Rohan, and Cleo Haynal. 2013 "Current and Emerging Threats of Homegrown Terrorism: The Case of the Boston Bombings." *Perspectives on Terrorism* 7 (3): 44–63.

McPhee, Michele R. 2017. *Maximum Harm: The Tsarnaev Brothers, the FBI, and the Road to the Marathon Bombing.* Lebanon, NH: ForeEdge.

Postel, Thérèse. 2013. "The Young and the Normless: Al Qaeda's Ideological Recruitment of Western Extremists." *Connections* 12 (4): 99–118.

Speckhard, Anne. 2013. "The Boston Marathon Bombers: The Lethal Cocktail That Turned Troubled Youth to Terrorism." *Perspectives on Terrorism* 7 (3): 64–78.

C

Centennial Olympic Park Bombing

July 27, 1996

The Atlanta Committee for the Olympic Games had hoped that the newly built Centennial Park commemorating the one-hundredth anniversary of the renewed international competition would be a festive attraction and hangout spot for the 1996 Olympics. Instead, the explosion of a pipe bomb in the park on July 27, 1996, one week into the games, at approximately 1:20 a.m., made the lovely venue a symbol of domestic terrorism. The blast from the improvised device (consisting of nails, screws, a steel plate, and smokeless gunpowder hidden in a backpack) killed one person directly, injured over one hundred others, and caused a fatal heart attack in a journalist rushing to cover the incident.

Significant issues raised by this attack include the responsibilities of the media, particularly concerning ongoing investigations by law enforcement; the question of whether this constituted an act of "Christian" terrorism; and the impact the blast had on preparations for future events.

About twenty minutes prior to detonation, security guard Richard Jewell notified law enforcement that he had detected a suspicious pack. The bomb exploded only a few minutes after he and other officials began evacuating the park. An anonymous 911 call also alerted the police shortly before the blast. Although Jewell would eventually be cleared of all charges and never formally arrested, he was named a person of interest. Because of media coverage that presented his professional life as a failure and created a false story speculating that he might have planted the bomb himself to "discover" it and make himself a hero, Jewell sued a number of outlets for libel, including the *Atlanta-Journal Constitution* (*AJC*), NBC, and CNN. All of them settled out of court, except for the *AJC*, which fought successfully in court to defend its coverage as well as the right not to name journalistic sources.

The real bomber, Eric Rudolph, was not charged with this bombing until 1998 and not captured until 2003. His use of the same type of pipe bombs at abortion clinics as well as a gay bar in 1997 connected him to the attack at the park. Arrested in the mountains of North Carolina, where he had been hiding for several years, he confessed in 2005.

Rudolph's motives remain debated. On the one hand, he has been connected with the Christian Identity movement associated with both the idea of white supremacy and anti-Semitism. Similarly, the Army of God (a group of Christian antiabortion terrorists) maintains his confession on their website as a manifesto. In this text, he describes himself as pro-life and cites the Bible to defend his actions.

On the other hand, his motives, as presented in this formal statement on the bombings, could appear to be primarily political, albeit reinforced by religious beliefs. He condemned "the homosexual agenda" and "the ideals of global socialism," stating that the purpose of the bombing was "to confound, anger and embarrass the Washington government in the eyes of the world for its abominable sanctioning of abortion on demand." He also explicitly denied that he ever was an "Identity believing Christian," stating instead that "I was born a Catholic, and with forgiveness I hope to die one."

He continues to be studied by scholars and law enforcement authorities focused on assessing lone-wolf terrorists and developing profiles for preventing these kinds of attacks. More broadly, planners for the 2002 Salt Lake City Winter Olympic Games looked to events such as the Centennial Park bombing for their antiterrorism strategies. Although those games did not have a terrorist attack, subsequent incidents, such as the Boston Marathon bombing of 2013, have become a part of the history of terror at large public sports events.

David Keck

See also: Army of God; Homegrown Terrorism; Rudolph, Eric Robert.

FURTHER READING

Rudolph, Eric. 2005. "Full Text of Eric Rudolph's Confession." NPR, April 14, 2005. https://www.npr.org/templates/story/story.php?storyId=4600480

Schuster, Henry, with Charles Stone. 2005. *Hunting Eric Rudolph.* New York: Berkeley Books.

Seegmiller, Beau. 2007. "Radicalized Margins: Eric Rudolph and Religious Violence." *Terrorism and Political Violence* 19 (4): 511–528.

Vollers, Maryanne. 2006. *Lone Wolf: Eric Rudolph: Murder Myth, and the Pursuit of the American Outlaw.* New York: HarperCollins.

Central Intelligence Agency (CIA)

The United States established the Central Intelligence Agency (CIA) in 1947 to acquire a permanent peacetime intelligence capability for the first time in its history. The agency's mandate is to coordinate the government's collection and analysis of intelligence on foreign threats to the United States. While the agency has established a reputation for effective analytical capability and successful covert action over many decades, it has also suffered a number of setbacks, such as the Bay of Pigs invasion in April 1961, which failed to oust Fidel Castro's communist regime in Cuba. The scheme, which pivoted on providing secret aid to paramilitary rebels seeking to overthrow Castro, was a humiliating setback for both the agency and the Kennedy administration.

Despite its historical focus on state-centered problems, the CIA established a Counterterrorism Center within its Directorate of Operations in 1986, and the agency's focus on terrorism increased after the 1991 collapse of the Soviet Union brought an end to the Cold War and the radical Taliban rose to power in Afghanistan in the mid-1990s.

In the aftermath of the September 11, 2001, attacks, the CIA and other elements of the U.S. intelligence community were held responsible for their failure to connect the dots, infiltrate al-Qaeda's inner circle, and discover the September 11 hijacking plot before it could be launched. Critics particularly pointed to the CIA's overreliance on technical means to collect information, which many felt reflected a misplaced reliance on Cold War mentality and techniques.

In its counterterrorism efforts, the CIA focuses on external theaters. U.S. National Intelligence Estimates have repeatedly described Pashtun tribal areas of northwestern Pakistan as one of the greatest threats to American domestic security. The region harbored al-Qaeda agents who were actively plotting new attacks against the United States and who were able to operate with impunity until 2004, when the CIA began to utilize armed Predator drones to kill al-Qaeda militants.

From 2004 through 2009, estimates indicate that these CIA-directed drone strikes killed more than 600 people, including such high-profile al-Qaeda leaders as Baitullah Mehsud, the head of the Pakistani Taliban, and Abu Khabab al-Masri, the chief of al-Qaeda's weapons of mass destruction program. However, estimates also indicate that only two-thirds of those killed in these strikes have been terrorists. The remainder have been Pakistani civilians killed as "collateral damage."

Meanwhile, the CIA also played a decisive role in killing Osama bin Laden, the mastermind of the September 11 terrorist attacks on the United States. The agency maintained a safe house in the Pakistani city of Abbottabad and used this house as a base for collecting intelligence on the compound where Osama bin Laden was living in the months preceding the attack by U.S. Navy SEALs in May 2011.

Finally, in this short list of its counterterrorism activity, the CIA also utilized drone strikes in Syria in an attempt to target the senior members of the Islamic State in Iraq and Syria (ISIS) responsible for recruiting and planning attacks against the West.

Shady Abdelwahab Mansour

See also: al-Qaeda; bin Laden, Osama; Counterterrorism and the George W. Bush Administration; War on Terror: Afghanistan and Pakistan.

FURTHER READING

Byman, Daniel. 2014. "The Intelligence War on Terrorism." *Intelligence and National Security* 29 (6): 837–863.

Immerman, Richard H. 2014. *The Hidden Hand: A Brief History of the CIA*. New York: Wiley Blackwell.

Mayer, Jane. 2008. *The Dark Side: The Inside Story of How the War on Terror Turned into a War on American Ideals*. New York: Doubleday.

Miller, Greg. 2011. "CIA Spied on bin Laden from Safe House." *Washington Post*, May 6, 2011. https://wapo.st/2WTImj9

Williams, Brian Glyn. 2010. "The CIA's Covert Predator Drone War in Pakistan, 2004–2010: The History of an Assassination Campaign." *Studies in Conflict & Terrorism* 33 (10): 871–892.

Charleston Church Massacre

June 17, 2015

At 8:16 on the evening of June 17, 2015, after sitting among them for approximately fifteen minutes, twenty-one-year old Dylann Roof fired an estimated seventy rounds into a Bible study group as they prayed at the Emanuel African Methodist Episcopal Church in Charleston, South Carolina, killing nine and wounding three in the twelve-person gathering. A self-admitted white supremacist, Roof apparently saw himself as a soldier in the war against Black-on-white violence.

African American churches have long been a target of white supremacists, white segregationists before them, and other extremist groups, and not just because of the race of their congregations. From at least the days of Reconstruction, they have been meeting places for discussing social issues, and this was never truer than during the civil rights struggle and ongoing search for racial justice. Indeed, the number of arson attacks on predominantly Black churches during the 1990s prompted Congress to pass the Church Arson Prevention Act in 1996. Moreover, among those churches in Roof's region, his target stood out as a historic Black church at the center of the civil rights struggle since the slave era and as the oldest African Methodist Episcopal Church in the South, having been founded in 1816.

The church may have also been targeted for the pastor Roof murdered, Reverend Clementa Pinckney, a state senator and a strong advocate for police transparency who had drawn national attention over his remarks concerning the killing of Walter Scott by a police officer in North Charleston two months before.

Whatever his specific reasons for picking that church, Roof's flight from it was short lived. He was captured the following morning in Shelby, North Carolina, and returned to Charleston. After more than a year of tests to determine his ability to stand trial despite his social disorders, he was charged with thirty-three federal offenses and convicted in December 2016 on all charges. As frequently occurs in cases involving lone-wolf terrorists, Roof chose to defend himself.

Roof's crime was sufficiently heinous and his demeanor so unremorseful that even South Carolina's then governor, Nikki Haley, urged prosecutors to seek the death penalty, which was imposed on him in federal court on January 10, 2017, when, after only a two-hour deliberation, the jury unanimously recommended the death penalty. In a separate trial in state court, he pleaded guilty to all charges to escape a second death penalty. He currently awaits death by lethal injection in a federal prison.

Two side bars set Roof's case apart from most of those involving other lone-wolf killers. First, whereas most white supremacist radicalization occurs through social interaction with others sharing their beliefs, Roof substantially self-radicalized by immersing himself in extremist Internet websites focused on Black-on-white violence. Internet smart algorithms abetted him in the process by steering users to more of what they like to see and screening out content with which they would disagree.

Second, Roof's action led to public scrutiny of why murders by Muslims are invariably treated as terrorism, but white supremacist murders are normally described as mass killings, not terrorism, on the thin logic that somehow killing someone because of their race is not a political act.

Joseph R. Rudolph Jr.

See also: Aryan Nations; Domestic Terrorism, White Supremacists; Garden City, Long Island Rail Road Shooting.

FURTHER READING

Finley, Taryn. 2015. "The Charleston Shooting Was at Least the 91st Violent Attack on a Black Church since 1956." *HuffPost, Black Voices*, June 23, 2015. https://www.huffpost.com/entry/black-church-attacks_n_7618022

Ghansah, Rachael Kaadzi. 2017. "A Most American Terrorist: The Making of Dylann Roof." *GQ*, August 21, 2017. https://www.gq.com/story/dylann-roof-making-of-an-american-terrorist

Hawes, Jennifer Berry. 2019. *Grace Will Lead Us: The Charleston Church Massacre and the Hard, Inspiring Journey to Forgiveness*. New York: St. Martin's Press.

Southern Poverty Law Center. 2017. *The Miseducation of Dylann Roof.* YouTube, January 18, 2017. https://youtu.be/qB6A45tA6mE

Christmas Day "Underwear Bomber"

On December 25, 2009, as Northwest Flight 253 neared its Detroit destination, twenty-three-year-old Nigerian national Umar Farouk Abdulmutallab engaged a syringe to activate the plastic explosive secreted in his underwear. The bomb popped like a firecracker but misfired, literally causing a fire rather than a boom. After the resultant flames engulfing the terrorist's lower body were extinguished, the would-be suicide bomber was subdued by passengers and crew and surrendered to authorities following an emergency landing in Detroit.

The bomb's failure to detonate, attributed to cabin moisture, marked the end of Abdulmutallab's short life as a terrorist. The son of a Nigerian banker reputed to be one of richest men in Africa, Abdulmutallab's alienation from his profit-oriented family and his loss of self in Islam is generally dated from his years at the University College in London (2005–2008). There, he received a degree in mechanical engineering, was elected president of the school's Islamic Society, and first attracted the notice of Britain's MI5 unit due to his contacts with Islamic extremists.

Initially difficult when questioned by authorities following his hospitalization for his burns, once his parents were flown to the United States by the FBI and encouraged him to cooperate, Abdulmutallab spoke freely of his recruitment and training for the mission by U.S.-born cleric Anwar al-Awlaki while in a safe al-Qaeda location in Yemen. He also relayed al-Awlaki's explicit instruction that the bomb detonate over a U.S. target. His cooperation subsequently extended to dismissing his court-appointed counsel following his 2010 indictment on numerous counts, including intent to employ a weapon of mass destruction against the 290 passengers aboard his flight, and pleading guilty to all charges at his October 2011 civilian trial.

Sentenced in 2012 to serve four life sentences plus fifty years without parole in the "supermax" federal prison in Florence Colorado, Abdulmutallab's willingness to embrace his fate ended in 2017. At that time, he filed a federal lawsuit challenging his solitary confinement (i.e., no cellmate), the restrictions on his communications with relatives, and the force-feeding he suffered when engaging in a hunger strike in protest.

In the meantime, Abdulmutallab's success in almost completing his mission despite being on several intelligence agencies' lists of possible Islamic extremists produced a thorough administrative review of the shortcomings of the existing Flight Watch List System and of the human errors that almost resulted in tragedy.

Abdulmutallab's testimony placing al-Awlaki at the center of the plot is also widely seen as the catalyst that resulted in President Obama's April 6, 2010, order to eliminate al-Awlaki and his later authorization of the drone strike that killed him in Yemen on September 30, 2011.

Joseph R. Rudolph Jr.

See also: al-Awlaki, Anwar; Recruiting Terrorists; Transportation Security.

FURTHER READING

Ariosto, David, and Deborah Feyerick. 2012. "Christmas Day Bomber Sentenced to Life in Prison." CNN, February 17, 2012. Accessed June 3, 2002. https://www.cnn.com/2012/02/16/justice/michigan-underwear-bomber-sentencing/index.html

Meleagrou-Hitchens, Alexander. 2020. *Incitement: Anwar al-Awlaki's Western Jihad.* Cambridge, MA: Harvard University Press.

Scott, Shane. "Inside Al Qaeda's Plot to Blow Up an American Airliner." *New York Times,* February 22, 2017. Accessed June 3, 2020. https://www.nytimes.com/2017/02/22/us/politics/anwar-awlaki-underwear-bomber-abdulmutallab.html

White House, Office of the Press Secretary. 2010. "White House Review Summary Regarding 12/25/2009 Attempted Terrorist Attack." January 7, 2010. Accessed June 3, 2020. https://obamawhitehouse.archives.gov/realitycheck/the-press-office/white-house-review-summary-regarding-12252009-attempted-terrorist-attack

Columbine Attack

April 20, 1999

Shortly after 11:00 a.m. on Tuesday, April 20, 1999, Eric Harris and Dylan Klebold began shooting students outside of their south Denver school, Columbine High School, when the homemade bombs they had placed inside just minutes before failed to detonate. Once they entered the school, they headed for the library, where they killed most of their victims. In just over fifteen minutes, they had slayed twelve students and one teacher and wounded twenty-three others. Within a half hour, Harris and Klebold were dead, having taken their own lives.

In the following months, many investigations were initiated and analyses offered to not only answer the "why" question but also to consider whether the massacre could have been prevented. Rumors and misinformation made it harder to sift through the mountain of evidence, testimony, and opinion. After many years, however, an explanatory analysis emerged.

Early theories focused on such causes as bullying, music, and video games. Inherent in the argument that any of these factors played a major role was the assumption that anyone could become a mass killer. What many experts now believe about the Columbine attack suggests a more individualized explanation.

Peter Langman, author of *Why Kids Kill,* concluded after thousands of research hours that both shooters were mentally disturbed far beyond what even intensive peer bullying or the bloodiest video games could produce. What he uncovered was a pattern of anger and depression almost impossible for those closest to Harris and Klebold to detect. The signs in their schoolwork, personal journals, and online posts played themselves out over the year prior to the attack, not the week or month before. The evidence was widespread, but it is perhaps only in retrospect that the path to the massacre becomes clear. Both boys were deeply disturbed in a time when American culture was not on constant alert for mass killing threats, and worrisome reports made to both school and law enforcement authorities were treated lightly or ignored.

One piece of evidence that was closely examined in a 2001 CBS inquiry into what was known before the attack was Harris's violent website. As early as March 1998, investigators were surveilling threats made on his website that suggested a number of terrorist bombing targets in the Denver area. Another piece was a pipe bomb found in a field near his house that matched the bomb types discussed on his website, and essays written for school assignments revealed the dark sides of both troubled teens. Yet, no one entity had access to all of these pieces to see their connection. Prevention, while theoretically possible, did not happen, but Columbine has helped shape the profiling and active shooter measures employed today, arguably saving lives in subsequent shooting tragedies.

One of the biggest criticisms was the length of time it took before police entered the school. By the time SWAT forces arrived, dozens of police officers had been outside the building for over forty-five minutes, immobilized by both conflicting information on the number and location of shooters and the procedural requirement at the time that local law enforcement should await the arrival of specially trained SWAT teams.

SWAT building clearance and evacuation procedures also jeopardized the lives of those inside. They began clearing the building areas farthest from the shootings, delaying life-saving medical care to the wounded, while unaware for three hours that within five minutes of the SWAT team's entry, both assailants had committed suicide.

The attack on Columbine thus marks a turning point in the tragic history of U.S. mass shootings. While causes and prevention are still hotly debated, early alert systems and tragedy response plans have become standard across the country. As a result, lives are now saved that might otherwise have been lost.

Stacy Kowtko

See also: Active Shooter Scenarios; Sociology of Terrorism.

FURTHER READING

Brown, Brooks, and Rob Merritt. 2002. *No Easy Answers: The Truth behind Death at Columbine High School.* Seattle, WA: Lantern Press.

Kass, Jeff. 2014. *Columbine: A True Crime Story.* 2nd ed. Crested Butte, CO: Conundrum Press.

MediaNews Group. n.d. "Columbine: 20 Years Later." *Denver Post.* Accessed October 4, 2019. https://www.denverpost.com/news/columbine-20/

Muschert, Glenn, and Ralph Larkin. 2007. "The Columbine High School Shootings." In *Crimes of the Century*, edited by Glenn W. Muschert and Ralph W. Larkin, 47–76. Santa Barbara, CA: Praeger Publishers.

Counterterrorism, the Courts, and the Constitution

Following the September 11, 2001, terrorist attacks, the executive and legislative branches of the U.S. government enacted sweeping legislative and policy reforms aimed at protecting the public from future terrorist violence on American soil. One of the most significant of these reforms was the USA PATRIOT Act (or Patriot Act). More than 300 pages long and enacted seven weeks after the 9/11 attacks, the Patriot Act radically transformed existing laws by vastly expanding the government's surveillance powers. Additionally, the Patriot Act expanded the scope of existing criminal laws, including statutes proscribing the provision of material support for terrorist organizations. Rarely used prior to the 9/11 attacks, material support laws have been among the most frequently prosecuted federal counterterrorism statutes over the past two decades.

While it is generally accepted that no right is beyond the reach of government regulation, the government's expansive and aggressive counterterrorism framework raises important questions regarding whether the government has struck the proper balance between national security on the one hand, and respecting Americans' civil liberties on the other. Because it is the courts that ultimately determine where the proper balance lies, judicial rulings on challenges to government counterterrorism efforts have and will continue to indelibly shape the landscape of U.S. counterterrorism law and policy.

MASS SURVEILLANCE AND PRIVACY

Disputes over the legality of the expansive surveillance powers granted to the government under the Patriot Act reflect the complexity of balancing security interests with privacy interests in the digital era, in which surveillance capabilities are constantly evolving. Among other things, the Patriot Act expanded the government's ability to view records on an individual's activity in the possession of third parties, such as telephone companies and banks; to conduct surreptitious physical searches; and to wiretap American citizens without probable cause. Expiring provisions of the Patriot Act were reauthorized by the USA PATRIOT Act Improvement and Reauthorization Act of 2005 and by subsequent legislation.

Several civil liberties organizations, including the American Civil Liberties Union (ACLU) and the Brennan Center for Justice, have voiced concerns regarding the far-reaching authority granted to the government under the Patriot Act and related legislation and argued that various provisions of the act violate Americans' civil liberties. Of particular concern was Section 215, which permitted the FBI to obtain secret court orders compelling third parties to produce information the government argued was relevant to terrorism investigations.

Civil liberties advocates have brought several cases in federal courts challenging various provisions of the Patriot Act. In a 2004 case brought by the ACLU, a lower federal court struck down a provision of the act that allowed the government unchecked authority to issue letters to obtain sensitive customer records from Internet service providers and other businesses without judicial oversight and imposed an automatic and broad gag provision on persons who received such letters. The court held that the challenged provision violated the Fourth Amendment's right to be free from unreasonable searches and seizures and free speech rights guaranteed by the First Amendment. In 2015, the ACLU brought suit challenging the National Security Agency's (NSA) bulk collection program. Revealed by Edward Snowden in 2013, this program relied on provisions of the Patriot Act to indiscriminately and surreptitiously collect cell phone records of millions of Americans held by several U.S. phone companies. A federal appeals court held that the NSA's bulk collection program was illegal on the basis that it exceeded the authority granted to the government under Section 215 of the Patriot Act.

When Section 215 came up for reauthorization in 2015, Congress passed the USA FREEDOM Act (or Freedom Act) with the aim of prohibiting the heavily contested bulk collection program. Notwithstanding these changes, the large-scale collection of the private information of American citizens continued under other provisions of the Patriot Act. At the time of this writing, the future of mass surveillance in the United States remains unclear. Some of the Patriot Act's most controversial provisions, including Section 215, expired in March 2020. On May 15, 2020, the Senate passed the USA FREEDOM Reauthorization Act of 2020 that would, among other things, reauthorize Section 215 as amended by the Freedom Act. The Senate's version of the 2020 act is currently (July 31, 2020) being considered by the House of Representatives, and it remains unclear whether it will become law and, if so, in what form. Civil liberties advocates remain concerned that the reforms contained in the Senate version of the 2020 act are insufficient to protect Americans' privacy rights. Thus, while there is uncertainty regarding the legal landscape of surveillance in the United States, it is clear that disputes regarding the proper balance between privacy and security will continue to be litigated, both in the court of public opinion as well as in federal courts.

MATERIAL SUPPORT LAWS AND FREE SPEECH

The federal criminal laws prohibiting the provision of material support to foreign organizations designated as being involved in terrorism by the secretary of state are another significant part of the U.S. counterterrorism framework. These laws criminalize the provision of support to designated organizations in the form of expert advice or assistance, personnel, service, and training. An important question related to material support statutes is the extent to which they implicate the free speech protections afforded under the First Amendment. Unlike other liberal democracies, including many European countries, Canada, and Australia, the United States provides expansive protection to virulent and dangerous speech. For example, in the case of *Brandenburg v. Ohio*, the U.S. Supreme Court held that the First Amendment does not permit the government to forbid or proscribe advocacy of violence except where such advocacy is directed to inciting or producing imminent lawless action and is likely to incite such action.

The Supreme Court addressed the question of whether laws criminalizing material support for terrorism violate the First Amendment in the 2010 case of *Holder v. Humanitarian Law Project* (*HLP*). In this case, U.S, citizens and domestic organizations interested in providing support for the lawful activities of two designated foreign terrorist organizations sought an injunction to prohibit enforcement of the criminal ban on providing material support to such organizations. The desired support included training members of these organizations on how to use international law to resolve disputes peacefully and how to petition the United Nations and other representative bodies for relief.

The plaintiffs in this case argued that the material support statute violated their freedom of speech and freedom of association under the First Amendment because it criminalized their providing material support to particular organizations without requiring the government to prove that the plaintiffs had a specific intent to further the unlawful ends of those organizations.

The case ultimately reached the U.S. Supreme Court, which held that the government could prohibit the plaintiffs' proposed activities without violating the First Amendment. The court rejected the plaintiffs' argument that the statute restricted pure political speech on the grounds that only material support was targeted, emphasizing that independent advocacy or membership in international terrorist organizations is not prohibited and that the statute was drawn to cover only a narrow category of speech under the direction of, or in coordination with, foreign groups that are known to be terrorist organizations.

Notwithstanding the peaceful nature of the plaintiffs' proposed activities, the Supreme Court accepted the government's conclusion that all contributions to foreign terrorist organizations, even for ostensibly benign purposes, further terrorist activities. Highlighting the sensitive interests in national security and foreign affairs at stake, the court held that the government met its burden of demonstrating that the statute served the interest of preventing terrorism, even if those providing support intended to promote an organization's nonviolent ends. The court emphasized that its holding did not suggest that a regulation of independent speech would pass constitutional muster, even if the government were to show that such speech benefited foreign terrorist organizations. The court also noted that its decision was limited to the particular activities that the plaintiffs in the case wished to pursue and that it was not addressing the resolution of more difficult cases that could arise under the statute in the future.

While the court thus stressed the narrowness of its holding in *HLP*, civil liberties defenders have expressed concerns regarding the potential scope of the decision. For example, the ACLU argues that the Supreme Court's decision represents a retreat from the precedents and principles that have served as the cornerstone of First Amendment doctrine since the 1950s, including the incitement principle espoused by the Supreme Court in the *Brandenburg* case. The ACLU also cautions that the *HLP* holding expands government authority to suppress political expression and association on the grounds of national security. These concerns appear to be well founded, as recent arguments by the government in cases involving material support statutes suggest that it is applying an extremely broad interpretation of the Supreme Court's holding in *HLP*. For example, in a 2014 case, the government argued that an individual who translated terrorist propaganda for a website, following a general call from al-Qaeda for such work, violated the material support statute, notwithstanding the fact that the government presented no evidence that the individual had ever been in contact with al-Qaeda, that he translated or spoke under al-Qaeda's direction, or that he acted at al-Qaeda's request. The government's argument in this case appears to come close to collapsing the distinction between free-standing advocacy and support coordinated with a proscribed group on which the Supreme Court's holding in *HLP* rests.

While there is broad consensus in the United States that terrorism poses a significant threat to national security, the extent to which the government's efforts to protect the public from the threat of terrorist violence have resulted in violations of Americans' civil liberties remains heavily contested. Moreover, debates over the constitutionality of provisions of the Patriot Act and the material support statutes reflect the inherent challenges of government efforts to ensure the safety and security of Americans while respecting their rights. Disputes regarding whether the government has overstepped its authority are ultimately resolved by judges, who are tasked with the responsibility of making determinations regarding whether the government has violated civil liberties in its counterterrorism efforts. It is for this reason that courts have shaped and will continue to shape the landscape of counterterrorism law and policy in the United States.

Eliza Bechtold

See also: Holder v. Humanitarian Law Project; Internet Surveillance; USA PATRIOT Act of 2001.

FURTHER READING

ACLU v. Clapper, 785 F.3d 787 (2nd Cir. 2015).

Cole, David. 2016. "The First Amendment's Borders: The Place of *Holder v. Humanitarian Law Project* in First Amendment Doctrine." *Harvard Law & Policy Review* 6: 148–177. Georgetown Public Law Research Paper No. 12-047. https://ssrn.com/abstract=2023436

Doe v. Ashcroft, 334 F.Supp.2d 471 (S.D.N.Y. 2004) and related cases.

Etzioni, Amitai. 2005. *How Patriotic Is the Patriot Act? Freedom versus Security in the Age of Terrorism*. Abingdon-on-Thames, England: Routledge.

Holder v. Humanitarian Law Project, 561 U.S. 1 (2010).

Howell, Beryl. 2004. "Seven Weeks: The Making of the USA PATRIOT Act." *George Washington Law Review* 72: 1145–1207.

United States v. Mehanna, 734 F.3d 32 (1st Cir. 2013).

Weinstein, James, and Ashutosh Bhagwat. 2019. "Bad Law: How the United States Supreme Court Mishandled the Free Speech Issue in *Holder v. Humanitarian Law Project*." In *Extremism, Free Speech, and Counter-Terrorism Law and Policy*, edited by Ian Cram, 158–171. Abingdon-on-Thames, England: Routledge.

Counterterrorism and the Clinton Administration

Political violence has been persistent throughout U.S. history, but over the last fifty years, the threat of domestic and foreign terrorism has significantly evolved, challenging administrations in varying severity. The twenty years prior to the events of September 11, 2001, and the creation of the Department of Homeland Security saw inconsistent prioritization of terrorism, leaving a significant lack of counterterrorism continuity between administrations. It was not until the 1990s that the threat and frequency of terrorism became so prominent that its acknowledgment became unavoidable and, thus, a priority of each subsequent administration.

CHALLENGES

William Jefferson "Bill" Clinton took office in 1993 and was elected for a second term in 1997, extending his presidency to January 2001. While Clinton was not the first president to be confronted with threats or acts of terrorism against U.S. citizens, both at home and abroad, one can arguably claim that his presidency was confronted with terrorism at a higher magnitude than his predecessors and during a period of significantly increased anti-American sentiment in the Middle East. There is an inherent challenge associated with combating a problem without a history of successes and failures on which to base decisions, and this challenge was further compounded by a history of inconsistent prioritizations of terrorism and a lack of strategic continuity between administrations.

The start of Clinton's presidency was marked by the first World Trade Center bombing in New York City in 1993, perpetrated by a small group of Islamic fundamentalist terrorists. Two years later, the Oklahoma City bombing was carried out by Timothy McVeigh. It was the deadliest domestic terror incident in U.S. history and had been motivated by the federal response to the Waco siege in 1993. While these two acts certainly highlighted the importance of developing counterterrorism strategies, Clinton and his administration were also significantly challenged by domestic lone-wolf terrorism as well as the rise of Islamic terrorism in the Middle East. As the United States had up to this point, the Clinton administration had mostly relied on law enforcement to prevent and investigate terrorist acts; however, these largely consisted of outdated laws that did not wholly account for the unique needs of law enforcement and the justice system in terms of preventing, investigating, and punishing acts of terrorism.

With respect to foreign terrorist threats, the Clinton administration was challenged on several fronts. First, throughout the 1990s, the U.S. government was widely uninformed on the threat posed and the players involved, and it was naive concerning the sophistication of such terrorist groups as al-Qaeda. Osama bin Laden, for example, was viewed as not much more than a financier in the earlier parts of the 1990s, and al-Qaeda was relatively unknown in both name and capability.

Second, historical rivalries and a lack of information exchange between government agencies created distinct gaps in knowledge and a siloed approach to extinguishing the threat posed by bin Laden and al-Qaeda. A task force in the CIA assigned to monitor bin Laden in the early to mid-1990s was likely the most informed group in the government as to the threat posed by bin Laden, yet much of the administration remained ill-informed on the subject. The siloed approach by various agencies was evidenced by the fact that the FBI's plan to indict bin Laden on criminal charges for planning to destroy U.S. military bases overlapped with the CIA's plan for Afghan tribes to capture and remove bin Laden from Afghanistan. Meanwhile, the State Department was almost entirely aloof from the bin Laden threat and focused instead on the increased tensions between India and Pakistan and potential for nuclear war between the two countries.

Third, throughout the various CIA attempts at targeting or capturing bin Laden, the Clinton administration was consistently challenged by the credibility of its intelligence. This was a persistent theme throughout the later 1990s and resulted in several canceled plots to assassinate bin Laden. Indeed, claims of faulty intelligence were hardly unfounded. When the United States responded to the U.S. embassy bombings in Nairobi and Tanzania, air strikes were targeted toward bin Laden's camp in Afghanistan as well as a pharmaceutical plant in Sudan believed to be processing the VX nerve agent; however, the aftermath of the strike showed no indications that the plant was actually processing the nerve agent, the Sudanese government vehemently disputed the claim, and neither bin Laden nor any other al-Qaeda leaders were at the camp in Afghanistan during the time of the strikes. The lack of confidence in intelligence gathered by the Afghan tribes and the inability of the United States to gather intelligence independently would continue to plague the CIA's ability to execute missions.

Fourth, pertaining to the U.S. efforts to target or capture bin Laden specifically, the United States was unable to overcome significant relationship challenges with critical allies in the Middle East, such as Saudi Arabia, Pakistan, and the United Arab Emirates (UAE). Saudi Arabia, for its part, was helpful to a degree in disrupting al-Qaeda cells in Saudi Arabia, and it attempted to persuade the Taliban to turn over bin Laden. But the Saudis did not fully engage in the U.S. request for intelligence sharing, nor did they provide access to detainees linked to al-Qaeda. Moreover, the CIA was aware that Pakistan was leaking intelligence and selling weapons to the Taliban and cautious of the significant Islamic Jihadist movement within the county.

Likewise, although the UAE threatened to impose sanctions on the Taliban if they did not release bin Laden, the Taliban did not take these threats seriously. Driven largely by the sectarian division in Islam between Shia and Sunni Muslims, the UAE and the Taliban had a shared enemy in Iran, and the UAE benefited from the Taliban's Sunni extremists, who provided a certain level of counterbalance to threats from Iran—a security service in the region that the United States was simply unable to provide.

Fifth, it is important to consider the geopolitical landscape at the time and its effects on counterterrorism policy development and terrorism response strategies. Within Afghanistan, a civil war was underway. The Taliban had overthrown the government, and the Northern Alliance had been created in opposition. The Taliban, however, was only recognized as the official government of Afghanistan by the UAE, Saudi Arabia, and Pakistan. Official recognition of a government is significant on many fronts, but it particularly challenged the Clinton administration in deciding whether to designate the Taliban as a state sponsor of terrorism. The Afghan Civil War and the human rights violations committed by the Taliban were occupying much of the State Department's attention, furthering the divide between U.S. agencies.

Tensions in South Asia between India and Pakistan were also drawing significant attention in the State Department and presented obstacles in the CIA's approach in targeting bin Laden in Afghanistan. On one hand, the CIA was wary of alerting Pakistanis of their plans for air strikes, knowing that they leaked intelligence to the Taliban; on the other hand, it was hesitant to launch air strikes over Pakistan out of fear that Pakistan would mistake it for an assault by India and ignite a potential nuclear war. Meanwhile, the 1999 NATO bombing of Kosovo coupled with the failed missile strikes the United States launched in Afghanistan and Sudan the year prior caused the Clinton administration to hesitate in carrying out future strikes against bin Laden lest the public conclude that the United States was engaging in indiscriminate bombing campaigns. And it is not irrelevant to note that as all of this was occurring on an international scale, President Clinton was fully engaged in his own personal scandal and eventual impeachment trial.

Lastly, in retrospect, it is possible to see that during the Clinton years, the threat environment was evolving to what culminated in 9/11; yet, at the time, an attack on U.S. soil of that magnitude was unimaginable. The event of 9/11 itself solidified for all future presidents the severity of the foreign terrorist threat, and while there were attacks on U.S. soil during the Clinton administration, none ratified the immediate need for and public approval of action like 9/11. In this sense, the lack of a precedent-setting 9/11-type event, for lack of a better analogy, was a challenge unique to presidents predating the Bush administration in 2001.

RESPONSE

Although not much may have come to fruition, the Clinton administration was active in its response to terrorism both domestically and internationally. After the 1995 Oklahoma City bombing, Clinton issued Presidential Decision Directive 39 (PDD-39), which spoke to the unconventional tactics used by terrorists and the need to protect critical infrastructure through a broader national security approach, as opposed to solely relying on law enforcement. PDD-39 addressed the roles of various agencies, such as the Federal Emergency Management Agency (FEMA), the Environmental Protection Agency (EPA), the Department of Energy (DOE), the Department of Justice (DOJ), and the Department of Defense (DoD), among others. This directive was reaffirmed and strengthened in 1998 via PDD-62, in which Clinton identified terrorism among the top national security priorities. Additionally, in 1996, the Antiterrorism and Effective Death Penalty Act was signed into law. The act sought to increase investigative tools for law enforcement, prevent the raising of money within the United States to support terrorist acts, provide for an effective death penalty through the limitation of appeals, and provide assistance to victims of terrorism. Similarly, in 1998, when intelligence suggested a planned attack at New York City airports, the FBI and the Federal Aviation Administration (FAA) worked together to issue an advisory alert and implement additional security measures at all city airports. By early 1999, however, there was no new intelligence on the attacks; the advisory eventually expired, and some of the implemented security measures were reduced.

Developing a response to the threat of bin Laden was ongoing throughout the Clinton administration. Beginning in the early 1990s, the CIA established a bin Laden team that was responsible for bringing to light bin Laden's role as al-Qaeda's leader and the complex nature of the terrorist organization. Spanning the remainder of Clinton's presidency, the CIA team engaged Afghan tribes for intelligence gathering, and by 1997, it had developed a plan alongside the tribes to capture bin Laden, although the plan was eventually called off, even though Clinton had signed two memorandums of notice for plans to capture bin Laden. The CIA team also experienced similar scenarios of called-off plots throughout the remainder of the 1990s as a result of perceived untrustworthy intelligence, the risk of civilian casualties, concern of public perception, fear of retaliation, and lack of belief that bin Laden could be captured alive. The one exception to this was the 1998 air strikes against the al-Qaeda camp in Afghanistan and the pharmaceutical lab in Sudan, which were both perceived as ultimately unsuccessful.

Finally, throughout his presidency, Clinton leveraged various leaders and the United Nations in his response tactics. In an attempt to reduce the challenges posed by complicated relationships in the Middle East, Clinton and CIA Director Tenet worked closely with Saudi Arabia. The Pakistani prime minister was brought to Washington in an effort to strengthen the U.S.-Pakistan relationship and to push for more involvement with bin Laden's capture. Clinton spoke directly with the president of the UAE to request increased pressure on the Taliban. In 1999, Clinton designated the Taliban as a state sponsor of terrorism, and UN Security Resolution 1267 was adopted, designating bin Laden and his associates as terrorists and imposing economic and travel restrictions in Afghanistan. By the following year, the United States had successfully championed Resolution 1333, which called for an embargo on weapon sales to Afghanistan.

EFFECTIVENESS

Although the World Trade Center and Oklahoma City bombings were not prevented, the FBI was successful in its intervention of the "Day of Terror" plot, a follow-up to the World Trade Center attack, that was targeted at several New York and New Jersey landmarks. Additionally, the FBI was successful in the monitoring and arrest of known extremist Omar Abdel Rahman, who had come to be regarded as a godfather of the radical Islamic movement, had ties with bin Laden, and regularly preached to several of the "Day of Terror" terrorists. Abdel Rahman was eventually convicted of several charges, including conspiracy to conduct bombings and soliciting an attack on a U.S. military installation.

Similarly, though the 1996 AEDPA was criticized for tightening habeas corpus requirements, the bill passed through the Congress with overwhelming support and was generally viewed by the public as a positive step forward in the aftermath of the World Trade Center and Oklahoma City bombings. Additionally, Clinton's Presidential Directives 39 and 62 were a step in the right direction, although work still needed to be done to improve the interagency approach to terrorism and, more broadly, national security.

The CIA's bin Laden team, however, was largely unsuccessful in its attempts to produce actionable intelligence. The intel on the Sudan pharmaceutical plant was questionable, and, again, bin Laden and his principal lieutenants were not present at the camp in Afghanistan during the air strikes in 1998. Additionally, over the following three years, the CIA identified multiple opportunities to target bin Laden but was unable to demonstrate a plan based on reliable intelligence that promised a significant rate of success with reasonable risks. By 2000, the team was transitioning away from its reliance on the Afghan tribes and toward an internal intelligence structure, but this plan was put into action too late to produce a return.

Likewise, Clinton's engagement efforts with Saudi Arabia, Pakistan, and the UAE, while not in vain, were unsuccessful in pressuring the Taliban to forgo a pro–bin Laden policy. As noted, the Taliban did not take the threat of sanctions from the UAE seriously and was generally unconcerned about the UN Security Council resolutions because Pakistan continued to arm them in their defense against the Northern Alliance.

Even with the dedicated bin Laden team within the CIA, the Clinton administration failed to prevent the USS *Cole* bombing, which took place in October 2000 and was perpetrated by al-Qaeda, resulting in the deaths of seventeen American sailors. And, lastly, the most unfortunate measure of success came on September 11, 2001, just nine months after the conclusion of Clinton's administration.

Diana LaBoy

See also: Oklahoma City Federal Building Bombing; USS *Cole* Attack; World Trade Center Attack.

FURTHER READING

C-SPAN. "Anti-Terrorist Bill Signing." April 24, 1996. https://www.c-span.org/video/?71430-1/anti-terrorism-bill-signing

National Security Council and National Security Council Records Management Office. 1995. "PDD-39—U.S. Policy on Counterterrorism, 6/21/1995." Clinton Digital Library. Accessed March 16, 2022. https://clinton.presidentiallibraries.us/items/show/12755

Thrall, A. Trevor, and Erik Goepner. 2017. "Lessons for U.S. Foreign Policy from the Failed War on Terror." CATO Institute Policy Analysis No. 814, June 26, 2017. https://www.cato.org/publications/policy-analysis/step-back-lessons-us-foreign-policy-failed-war-terror

United Nations Security Council. 2020. "Resolution 1333: The Situation in Afghanistan." Adopted December 19, 2000. http://unscr.com/en/resolutions/1333

Watson, Dale L. 2002. Testimony before the Senate Select Subcommittee on Intelligence, February 6, 2002. https://archives.fbi.gov/archives/news/testimony/the-terrorist-threat-confronting-the-united-states

Counterterrorism and the George W. Bush Administration

The September 11, 2001, attacks on the United States by the transnational terrorist group al-Qaeda meant that counterterrorism would be a major feature of the new George W. Bush administration, which had only been in office eight months at the time of the attacks. Bush came to the presidency espousing a neoconservative ("neocon") philosophy of foreign policy that believed that the power of the United States should be used to promote American interests, which included the development of democratic states. This belief system can be readily seen in many of his administration's policies.

In fact, countering the threat of terrorism became the predominant and defining feature of George W. Bush's presidency. It is very difficult for people who are too young to remember the attacks to appreciate the sense of uncertainty, insecurity, fear, and anger that gripped the American people in the wake of the attacks. What is al-Qaeda? Hardly any Americans had ever heard of the organization. What drove them to murder so many innocent people? How many al-Qaeda "sleeper cells" and "hit squads" had infiltrated American society, and when would the next attacks occur? Why had U.S. military forces failed to successfully engage the hijacked airliners before they completed their attacks? Why had the U.S. intelligence community (IC) and law enforcement organizations at all levels of American government failed to detect plans for the 9/11 attacks? What is the Taliban, and why do they support al-Qaeda?

In this tense environment, the Bush administration needed to formulate policy responses to many security issues both rapidly and simultaneously. With regard to counterterrorism (CT), these responses can be categorized into two broad categories. First, activities in the newly prominent emerging field of "homeland security" dealt with both offensive and defensive actions to protect against terrorist attacks on the U.S. homeland. Second, the government adopted policies to attack and eliminate terrorists in their home bases in foreign countries to destroy the ability of al-Qaeda and other transnational terrorist groups to attack the U.S. homeland. Action in both areas was swift.

On October 8, 2001, the White House issued Executive Order (EO) 13228 that established the Office of Homeland Security and announced that the purpose of its efforts was to keep the United States safe from terrorist attacks by detecting terrorist attack plans; developing plans to prepare to protect against attacks; preventing attacks before they could start; protecting targets when attacks were not prevented; responding in the aftermath of a successful attack; and restoring from terrorist attacks (returning conditions to as close to preattack conditions as possible). These major functions became the guiding principles for the Bush administration's efforts to establish and guide the development of homeland security as a new element of national security.

A largely united Congress passed several major pieces of homeland security legislation in rapid succession. These included the Uniting and Strengthening America by Providing Appropriate Tools Required to Intercept and Obstruct Terrorism Act (or USA PATRIOT Act, October 26, 2001); the Homeland Security Act (November 25, 2002); and the Intelligence Reform and Terrorism Prevention Act (December 6, 2004). The latter two acts constituted the largest restructuring of the U.S. government's security and intelligence apparatus since the National Security Act of 1947.

The Bush administration managed the strategic direction and development of its homeland security enterprise through a series of presidential decision directives labeled Homeland Security Presidential Directives (HSPDs). Other presidential directives were labeled as National Security Presidential Directives (NSPDs). This distinction highlights the Bush administration's practice of separating homeland security from other national security issues and seemed to help identify and prioritize the development of different homeland security mission areas.

Several of the twenty-five HSPDs issued have had major and lasting impacts on the nation's security. These include HSPD-1 Organization and Operation of the Homeland Security Council; HSPD-4 National Strategy to Combat Weapons of Mass Destruction; HSPD-5 Management of Domestic Incidents; HSPD-7 Critical Infrastructure Identification, Prioritization, and Protection; HSPD-8 National Preparedness; HSPD-9 Defense of United States Agriculture and Food; HSPD-10 Biodefense for the 21st Century; HSPD-13 Maritime Security Policy; HSPD-16 Aviation Security Policy; HSPD-18 Medical Countermeasures against Weapons of Mass Destruction; HSPD-19 Combating Terrorist Use of Explosives in the United States; HSPD-21 Public Health and Medical Preparedness; and HSPD-23 Cybersecurity Policy.

As the homeland security enterprise developed, the administration became embroiled in several legal battles, primarily concerning Americans' privacy rights, such as surveillance and freedom from unreasonable searches and seizures, and certain First Amendment rights, such as the legality of gag orders in certain situations. Civil liberties groups challenged many new programs and practices in court, including DHS's Computer-Assisted Passenger Prescreening System, the Defense Department's Total Information Awareness System, the FBI's Carnivore Project, the FBI's use of national security letters, and the use of warrantless and "sneak and peek" searches. In many cases, the courts ruled that changes to the programs were required.

Other areas of the Bush administration's homeland security efforts also drew criticism. For example, applying risk analysis to the nation's critical infrastructure proved difficult. Terrorism watch lists and aviation security efforts repeatedly displayed weakness when tested. Achieving satisfactory border security remained an elusive goal. Achieving maritime cargo container security remained challenging. However, despite these and other shortcomings, a terrorist attack on the scale of the 9/11 attacks did not recur, and the government successfully prevented many plans for terrorist attacks on the homeland.

With regard to actions abroad, on September 14, 2001, Congress passed legislation authorizing the president to "use all necessary and appropriate force against those nations, organizations, or persons responsible for the 9/11 attacks." The president signed this legislation into law on September 18, 2001 (P.L. 107-40, 115 Stat. 224). Prior to this event, the president had declared a "war on terrorism" (soon changed to "war on terror"), which referred to the administration's global efforts to eliminate transnational terrorism by using the full range of U.S. military, diplomatic, and economic power in cooperation with other states. Critics decried this term as not only needlessly inflammatory and aggressive but also inaccurate, as it would not be possible to "defeat" illusive terrorist groups that utilized evasion and concealment as a principal tactic.

Afghanistan was the first obvious target because an Afghani political faction known as the Taliban controlled most of Afghanistan's territory and had provided a safe haven for al-Qaeda to train and equip its terrorists. On September 20, President Bush demanded that the Taliban turn over Osama bin Laden and all al-Qaeda leaders in Afghanistan to the U.S. government or face U.S. attack. The Taliban refused. On September 26, members of the Central Intelligence Agency, later augmented by U.S. and British special operations personnel, initiated a covert operation to defeat the Taliban using Northern Alliance (the Taliban's main adversary for control of Afghanistan) forces as the principal fighters. On October 7, a U.S.-led coalition began bombing attacks on Taliban-controlled areas of Afghanistan. December 6 marked the end of the Taliban's power, and the U.S installed the Afghan Interim Authority as the provisional government. On December 20, the United Nations (UN) Security Council unanimously passed Resolution 1386, which authorized "the establishment for 6 months of an International Security Assistance Force to assist the Afghan Interim Authority in the maintenance of security in Kabul and its surrounding areas" and imparted legitimacy to U.S. and coalition activities.

Throughout these months, U.S. public opinion had supported military action against al-Qaeda. Patriotic enthusiasm ran high, and many Americans volunteered for service in the armed forces. The United States also enjoyed virtually universal international support, including UN endorsement, for invading Afghanistan to remove the threat of al-Qaeda. President Bush's domestic public approval ratings, at 51 percent on the eve of the 9/11 attacks, soared to 90 percent in late September. His average public approval rating for his first term was 62 percent. (In contrast, by October 2008, his ratings had plummeted to 25 percent, partly due to problems resulting from setbacks in Afghanistan and Iraq discussed below, but also due to the onset of the Great Recession, which was not related to the war on terror and homeland security matters.)

Unfortunately, Osama bin Laden and many al-Qaeda members had evaded coalition efforts to capture or kill them in the final days of this campaign, which meant that al-Qaeda remained an active threat. The Taliban also remained an effective force that continued to threaten coalition occupation forces, infiltrate many parts of the new Afghan government, and destabilize Afghanistan by reasserting control of various sections of the country. These actions degraded the Bush administration's efforts to stabilize, democratize, and develop Afghanistan's economy. The presence of rampant corruption at all levels of the Afghan government and society further impeded these initiatives.

A decisive moment in the Bush presidency came in late 2002 when the issue of Iraq's alleged possession of weapons of mass destruction (WMDs) became an issue of great concern. The United States had opposed Saddam Hussein's Iraqi regime since Hussein invaded Kuwait in 1990, sparking the Persian Gulf War in early 1991. Iraq had been under UN sanctions of various types ever since, and the United States maintained no-fly zones that severely restricted Iraq's use of its northern and southern airspace. Intelligence estimates indicated that Iraq might possess WMDs, including nuclear weapons. The Bush administration argued that this posed a grave threat to the U.S. homeland because Hussein would give the weapons to terrorists who would use them to attack the United States. The accuracy of this estimate was hotly debated both within the United States and around the world. Unlike after the 9/11 attacks, UN members were divided concerning the existence of Iraqi WMDs and thus over whether an existential threat to the

United States existed. The Bush administration sought UN support, but the Security Council would not endorse an American invasion of Iraq to neutralize a questionable WMD threat.

As a result, the Bush administration formed a "coalition of the willing" composed of states that supported the American position and launched an invasion of Iraq in March 2003. While this coalition rapidly defeated Hussein's regime, the collapse of the Iraqi government created an extremely destabilizing power vacuum that occupied the administration's attention and military resources for the remainder of the Bush presidency and diverted its attention and resources from ongoing operations in Afghanistan. Following the invasion, searches failed to discover Iraqi WMDs, which, in addition to the lack of UN endorsement, weakened the invasion's legitimacy and harmed the international standing of the United States.

Domestically, the IC once again found itself the subject of major investigations into why its intelligence on Iraq and Iraqi WMD programs was incorrect, and investigations concluded that the IC had practiced poor tradecraft in both intelligence collection and analysis. In addition, the subject of whether intelligence had been "politicized"—purposely manipulated to strengthen the case that Iraq possessed WMDs—became a major issue. With the benefit of hindsight, it appears likely that politicization did occur. Supporters of this conclusion point to the actions of Vice President Dick Cheney, Secretary of Defense Donald Rumsfeld, Undersecretary of Defense for Policy Douglas Feith, and Undersecretary of Defense for Intelligence Stephen Cambone, all advocates of the invasion, to support this view. A third reason offered for the Iraqi WMD intelligence failure is the assertion that, having been accused of a lack of imagination in failing to detect the 9/11 attacks, the IC exercised too much imagination when analyzing the case for Iraqi WMDs.

In conclusion, the George W. Bush administration reacted to the 9/11 attacks and the threats posed by transnational terrorism with expansive defensive and offensive counterterrorism policies and actions. Bush presided over the largest restructuring of the U.S. government since the National Security Act of 1947. His administration transformed what had been a group of separate agencies and bureaus that performed various roles and missions that are now identified as homeland security functions into a standardized and coordinated homeland security enterprise consisting of many government and private sector partners. His administration's invasions of Afghanistan and Iraq led to a continuous U.S. military presence until all U.S. forces were withdrawn from Afghanistan in August 2021, incurred large costs, and produced both stabilizing and destabilizing effects throughout the Middle East. However, they were instrumental in breaking the power of al-Qaeda and, with other U.S. initiatives, have greatly expanded and improved worldwide efforts to suppress transnational terrorism.

William J. Lahneman

See also: Abu Ghraib Scandal; Anthrax Attacks of 2001; Critical Infrastructure as a Terrorist Target; Department of Homeland Security; Homeland Security Act of 2002; Intelligence Reform and Terrorism Prevention Act of 2004; National Security Letters Controversy; Transportation Security; USS *Cole* Attack; War on Terror, The; War on Terror: Afghanistan and Pakistan.

FURTHER READING

Dagger, Richard, and Terence Ball. 2016. "Neoconservatism." *Encyclopedia Britannica*, May 3, 2016. Accessed October 16, 2020. https://www.britannica.com/topic/neoconservatism

Gates, Robert M. 2014. *Duty: Memoirs of a Secretary at War*. New York: Vintage Books.

Hayden, Michael V. 2016. *Playing to the Edge: American Intelligence in the Age of Terror*. New York: Penguin Press.

Jones, Seth G. 2012. *Hunting in the Shadows*. New York: W. W. Norton and Company.

Schoenfeld, Gabriel. 2010. *Necessary Secrets: National Security, the Media, and the Rule of Law*. New York: W. W. Norton & Company.

Select Committee on Intelligence, U.S. Senate. 2004. *Report on the U.S. Intelligence Community's Prewar Intelligence Assessments on Iraq*. July 7, 2004. Accessed October 18, 2020. https://fas.org/irp/congress/2004_rpt/ssci_iraq.pdf

Counterterrorism and the Obama Administration

Before the September 11, 2001, attack on the Twin Towers of the World Trade Center and the Pentagon, the term *counterterrorism* customarily referred to efforts *in* the homeland to protect the homeland as opposed to confronting the enemy in the broader world outside a country's borders. Different agencies were usually tasked with the two jobs, separated by invisible walls of sometimes jealously guarded agency jurisdictions. In the United States, it was the Federal Bureau of Investigation (FBI) that loomed large over domestic security; in Britain, it was MI5. Likewise, action against potential threats abroad was given to MI6 in Britain and divided among a variety of U.S. agencies, some—like the Central Intelligence Agency (CIA)—statutorily forbidden from operating on American soil or targeting American citizens.

The events of 9/11 destroyed many of these walls; indeed, the 9/11 Commission blamed them as one of the reasons for the country's vulnerability on that September morning. Institutional boundaries hindered the information sharing that might have enabled the intelligence community to connect the dots before the hijacked airliners struck their targets.

Consequently, by the time President Obama first took the oath of office in January 2009, counterterrorism meant fighting terrorism on all fronts, at home and abroad, albeit with the heaviest commitment of resources at the time still abroad. Eight years later, despite having reduced troop numbers overseas, the inherited war in Afghanistan and obligations to Iraq's security still weighed heavily on Obama's administration, but so too did new challenges—abroad with the rise of the Islamic State in Iraq and Syria (ISIS) and at home with sharp increases in both domestic and foreign-instigated homegrown lone-wolf extremism.

2009–2013: FIRST-TERM COUNTERTERRORISM STRATEGY ABROAD

During his presidential campaign, Barack Obama promised to withdraw troops from Iraq and increase stabilization efforts in Afghanistan as part of an overall goal of attaining a strong defense against terrorism without a significant troop presence overseas. Foreign engagements were thus woven into the 2010 *National Security Strategy*, stressing a "whole government" approach that included transparency, bolstering military defense and homeland security, responsible diplomacy, economic stability, countering radicalization, improving intelligence gathering, securing cyberspace, collaborative foreign policy, and protecting the nation's borders and critical infrastructure. Still, dealing with the two wars that President Obama inherited from his predecessor dominated much of his counterterrorism policy during his first term in office.

Afghanistan and Iraq

Now America's longest war, albeit with far fewer American deaths than in the shorter war in Vietnam (as of August 2019, 2,372 and 58,193, respectively), the war in Afghanistan gave the Obama administration no easy option. The war had begun as the closest thing to a "just war." It was in response to an unprovoked attack on the homeland, remedies short of war were explored, it was sanctioned by an international body, and it was conducted with an effort to minimize civilian casualties. At the same time, there was no end in sight in 2009. At best, the post-Taliban government in Kabul had only passive support in a hinterland often controlled by warlords.

The administration's chosen strategy was to disrupt and dismantle al-Qaeda by reinforcing aviation security and denying extremists safe havens. Troops were to remain, and their numbers soon increased when Obama sent an additional 21,000 troops to Afghanistan in 2009 and approved another surge of 33,000 soon after. The number of American troops peaked in 2011 at 97,000.

Meanwhile, by the time President Obama took the oath of office, regime change and capacity building in Iraq were faring little better than in Afghanistan despite the apparent conflict stabilization resulting from the surge in American troop presence the last years of the Bush administration. Obama's policy choice was to honor his campaign pledge despite warnings that a sharp pull down of U.S. forces might undo the benefits of that stabilizing military action. In February 2009, there were 160,000 U.S. troops in Iraq. By 2012, there were only 150.

Human Rights and Regime Change Elsewhere

President Obama had also pledged to abandon many of the controversial parts of the Bush administration's war on terror, including extreme interrogation measures, abuse of prisoners abroad, and the closing of the prison facilities at the Guantánamo Bay Naval Base in Cuba. Most of these pledges were honored; however, the Guantánamo Bay prison remains open, though with fewer detainees.

Obama had also championed fostering human rights abroad, a sometimes hazardous pledge given the frequent need to rely on less than perfect political allies. It was a pledge that was also complicated by the use of drones, with their inevitable collateral damage, to assassinate targeted enemies rather than risk the lives of American forces.

Against this backdrop, when the seductive Arab Spring that occurred early in his administration seemed to be spreading to Libya and Egypt in 2011, Obama supported regime change in both. In Libya, that support came via the "leading from behind" collaborative strategy of encouraging NATO to give air support to the anti-Gaddafi rebels on the ground; in Egypt, it was the visible withdrawal of support for the Mubarak government that had long supported U.S. policy in the Middle East. Neither policy was directly linked to the war on terror but rather to the creation of democratic regimes that might be helpful in that war. Neither policy yielded the intended dividends. Egypt is currently stable, but under a less democratic regime than Mubarak's, and at this writing, Libya remains a jumble of terrorist and other groups vying for territory; it is also the country where an American ambassador was killed during Obama's second term in office.

Finally, also growing out of the Arab Spring of 2011, the anti-government protests in Syria that developed into a civil war presented yet another foreign policy counterterrorism challenge to Obama's first term of presidency. Beyond offering to settle refugees, the administration took a hard position on regime change, maintaining that no settlement was possible as long as Assad remained in office, which—with Assad bent on staying—tabled any possibility for a diplomatic settlement of that ongoing war. The administration did threaten retaliation if Assad continued to use biological weapons on his own people; however, when that "red line in the sand" was flagrantly crossed, administrative hesitancy gave Russia a diplomatic opportunity in the area. Syria's steady disintegration, in turn, resurfaced as a major counterterrorist test in Obama's second term.

2013–2017: SECOND-TERM COUNTERTERRORISM STRATEGY ABROAD

In addition to seeing Iraq as sufficiently stable for the United States to draw down its forces there, in its first year in office, the administration also viewed the many autocratic leaders in the Middle East to be malevolent but stable. Both assumptions were debunked by the rise of ISIS in 2011 as well as during the Arab Spring of 2010–2012.

The 2015 *National Security Strategy* had some similarities to the 2010 strategy in encouraging resiliency, hardening national critical infrastructure, preventing the spread of nuclear weapons, and building alliances to combat terrorism. Climate change was also included as a national security issue, but by then, ISIS had become the most imminent terrorist threat. A U.S. military campaign ensued to arrest its advance and the spread of its ideology, and targeted counterterrorism missions and drone attacks were to continue.

The Rise of ISIS

The response to ISIS was the defining counterterrorist success of the Obama administration. Critics argue that the administration's quick decision to withdraw troops from Iraq directly contributed to the rise of ISIS. Even if so, the same administration can be credited with implementing a successful strategy to combat

ISIS, enabling the successor Trump administration to neutralize it and destroy its "caliphate."

ISIS began as an affiliate of al-Qaeda and heavily participated in the insurgency following the 2003 invasion of Iraq. The 2010 troop withdrawal from Iraq corresponded with the start of the Arab Spring, creating an especially volatile environment in the Middle East. When Syria became embroiled in civil war, ISIS took advantage of the volatility in the region to spread extremism in Iraq and Syria.

At the height of its power, ISIS controlled large swaths of territory in both states, livestreaming beheadings and desecrating ancient archaeological heritage sites. In response, the Obama administration was forced to rededicate significant resources to combating Islamic terrorism in the Middle East, and on September 10, 2014, President Obama announced the formation of an international coalition to combat the spread of ISIS.

Operation Inherent Resolve was created by the Department of Defense (DoD) to spearhead this counteroffensive, which eventually involved cooperation among seventy-three countries who either contributed to warfighting or stabilization activities. Also, U.S. defense advisers were tasked with retraining the Iraqi army for the new fight, and the administration gave the U.S. military more freedom in combating ISIS by loosening rules of battlefield engagement and placing more special operators in the theater. In all, approximately 16,000 air strikes were conducted against ISIS and its affiliates. By the end of Obama's presidency in 2017, ISIS had lost 10,000 square miles of controlled territory, and its membership had shrunk from 35,000 to 3,000.

Containing al-Qaeda and the Hunt for bin Laden

In 2015, the Obama administration was key in negotiating a nuclear deal with Iran in which Iran agreed to significantly diminish its nuclear capability, a deal that the Obama administration viewed as a significant step in preventing terrorist organizations from gaining nuclear weapons. Nevertheless, instability was again increasing in the north.

By 2014, most U.S. troops had been withdrawn from Afghanistan, and if future historians credit the Obama administration with having contributed successfully to the fight against al-Qaeda, it will be because it then decided to reverse course. The administration increased U.S. troops to maintain a presence in Afghanistan and continued drone strikes and special operations in Pakistan and beyond.

Meanwhile, the U.S. intelligence community was targeting al-Qaeda across the globe—an operation that culminated with the killing of Osama bin Laden, the al-Qaeda leader behind the 9/11 attacks, on May 2, 2011. His elimination brought an end to a nine-year manhunt; however, for the remainder of Obama's presidency, the military continued to kill al-Qaeda leaders, including Faruq al-Qatani on October 23, 2016, by a precision air strike in Afghanistan's Kunar region.

The Use of Drones and Special Forces

President Obama oversaw more drone strikes in the first year of his presidency than were used in the entirety of the Bush presidency. Their use aligned well with his goal to continually engage al-Qaeda by using strategic targeted killings while withdrawing U.S. troops from costly wars. A total of 563 drone strikes targeted Pakistan, Afghanistan, Somalia, and Yemen during his presidency. Yet, drone usage proved controversial and was not without political consequences.

As civilian collateral damage caused by Obama-approved drone strikes increased, many human rights groups questioned the morality of drone attacks. Because the drones occupied foreign air space, many Middle Eastern nations also opposed them as a breach of their sovereign rights and international laws of warfare. Still other critics condemned indiscriminate drone attacks for terrorizing local populations and fueling the spread of extremism. In response, the Obama administration made some efforts to provide transparency in its drone usage and argued that they are so exceptionally surgical and precise that they avoid civilian casualties at a much higher rate than traditional warfare.

To supplement drone attacks, the administration deployed special operations forces on secret missions around the globe at an unprecedented rate. In 2016 alone, U.S. special force units were deployed to 138 countries, gathering intelligence and engaging in targeted killings. Their use, under the U.S. Special Forces Command (SOCOM), met Obama's goal of keeping the traditional military at home while highly trained career commandos engaged in counterterrorist operations. The bonus was that special operations are classified, allowing White House deniability of SOCOM missions, albeit at the cost of criticism for the lack of transparency in their operations and difficulty of congressional oversight.

COUNTERTERRORISM, HOMELAND SECURITY, AND INTELLIGENCE GATHERING

Surveillance and Counterterrorism

Unwanted controversy also surrounded the administration's heightened use of surveillance tactics to further national security. In 2011, Obama signed a four-year renewal of the Patriot Act, which contained provisions that allowed roving wiretaps. Two years later, former National Security Agency (NSA) contractor Edward Snowden revealed that the NSA had implemented a global system of surveillance that was collecting massive amounts of data on American and foreign citizens, including phone logs. It was later found that President Obama was made aware of the program, which was created to store data that could potentially identify terrorists, in 2009. Although Obama claimed that the program was under review when its existence was leaked in 2013, it was roundly criticized by civil rights organizations and the American public as a violation of privacy rights.

Snowden's revelations forced the administration to redress the ever-challenging balance between freedom (here, the right to privacy) and security, most notably in the 2015 Freedom Act, which extended the life of the Patriot Act for another four years but curtailed the government's ability to collect bulk electronic data. In 2014, Obama proposed requiring the NSA to obtain a warrant signed by a federal judge before collecting phone data; however, the administration continued to apply for secret Foreign Intelligence Surveillance Act (FISA) court orders requiring phone companies to turn all of their phone records over to NSA, and critics contend that Obama's administration never made any meaningful change to NSA surveillance policies during his presidency.

Protecting the Homeland and Lone-Wolf Terrorism

The administration's second-term success in fighting terrorist organizations abroad was not matched by success in combating terrorism at home, with the possible exception of complicating the entry of terrorists into the homeland. Even as presidential candidate Donald Trump was talking about building a wall along the border with Mexico, the Obama administration was doubling the number of Border Patrol agents there to 17,000 and increasing border fencing to 700 miles, nine times over what existed in 2009, by the end of his term.

Internet extremism, however, cannot be fenced off, and especially during Obama's last term, the United States experienced a sharp rise in terrorist acts linked to Internet radicalization of Muslim residents (e.g., the violence at Fort Hood in 2009, in San Bernardino in 2015, and in Orlando in 2016) as well as lone-wolf terrorist attacks by men frequenting the sites of white supremacists (e.g., the attack on the Charleston church in 2015).

By the end of Obama's tenure in office, the threat of homegrown lone-wolf extremism had become the primary focus of domestic anti-terrorist policy. Given the country's success in stopping elaborate terrorist plans, many terrorist organizations were publicly encouraging inexpensive lone-wolf, self-radicalized, small-scale attacks. These require less planning and fewer resources, which significantly reduces the footprint of the perpetrators while still inflicting significant economic impact and instilling fear in the American public.

In response, Obama promoted a twofold response focused on blunting the Internet spread of radical ideologies that lead to terrorist attacks. This included a Twitter campaign to combat ISIS propaganda on social media domestically and the creation by executive order in March 2016 of an interagency Global Engagement Center to oversee the government's counterterrorist messages aimed at foreign audiences.

Kyle Feeley with the Editors

See also: al-Qaeda; Charleston Church Massacre; Homegrown Terrorism; Islamic State, The; Orlando Pulse Nightclub Shooting; San Bernardino Attack.

FURTHER READING

Bergen, Peter, and David Sterman. 2018. *Jihadist Terrorism 17 Years after 9/11: A Threat Assessment*. New America, September 2018. https://d1y8sb8igg2f8e.cloudfront.net/documents/ISP_17_Years_DIGITAL_Final.pdf

Jenkins, Brian. 2017. "Bush, Obama, and Trump: The Evolution of U.S. Counterterrorist Policy since 9/11." International Institute for Counterterrorism, September 24, 2017. https://www.ict.org.il/Article/2079/BUSH-OBAMA-AND-TRUMP

Masters, Jonathan. 2013. "Targeted Killings." Council on Foreign Relations, May 23, 2013. https://www.cfr.org/backgrounder/targeted-killings

Stern, Jessica. 2015. "Obama and Terrorism: Like It or Not, the War Goes On." *Foreign Affairs*, September/October 2015. https://www.foreignaffairs.com/articles/obama-and-terrorism

Valella, Andrew. 2016. "A Critique of the Obama Administration's Approach to Counterterrorism, as Outlined in the 2015 *National Security Strategy*." *Small Wars Journal*, April 21, 2016.

White House. 2010. *The National Security Strategy of the United States of America*. May 27, 2010.

White House. 2015. *The National Security Strategy of the United States of America*. February 6, 2015.

Counterterrorism and the Trump Administration

Similar to his predecessor, Barack Obama, who had promised to withdraw American troops from Iraq and close the detentions center at Guantánamo Bay while running for office, President Donald Trump's campaign rhetoric and promises heavily influenced his approach to foreign policy and, in particular, his counterterrorism agenda.

The heart of Trump's message to "Make America Great Again" was the promise to scale back commitments and international contacts. The Iran deal, which Obama had seen as a step toward preventing terrorists from acquiring weapons of mass destruction, and the Paris Accords on climate fell into the category of commitments that the United States did not need. Moreover, because they were the products of executive action, they could easily be undone by executive orders. Accordingly, early in his tenure in office, President Trump withdrew the United States from both agreements.

THE WALL

Candidate Trump often stressed the criminal problems resulting from the slippage of a large number of illegal aliens across the U.S. southern border with Mexico, and he promised that he would construct a wall the full length of that 1,954-mile border if elected. He also vowed that Mexico would pay for it, and from the moment he entered office until the 2020 arrival of both COVID-19 and a new round of presidential campaigning, he labored hard to make that happen. Contractors competed with prototype walls to gain the contracts, and funds were moved from other security projects and the budgets of other departments to fund it—the idea of Mexico doing so having been a nonstarter.

By the middle of 2020, and a confidence game scandal involving the bilking of millions of dollars from private donors to finance the wall's construction, a total of 307 miles of border fencing and walls had been erected during the Trump presidency, of which only 5 miles covered an area previously lacking some form of barrier. In contrast, by the end of President Obama's eight years in office, approximately 700 miles of fencing had been completed under the Secure Fence Act of 2006 signed into law by President George W. Bush.

LIMITING TRAVELERS FROM DANGEROUS STATES

More successful, eventually, were President Trump's efforts to fulfill his promise to close U.S. borders to would-be terrorists from foreign continents by executive proclamation. The pledge was secondary to Trump's focus on a border wall, but it increasingly became a part of his campaign after the attack by Syed Farook and his Pakistan-born wife, Tashfeen Malik, in San Bernardino on December 2, 2015, left fourteen dead and more than a score injured. Once in the White House, however, President Trump ran into constitutional difficulties in following up on his promise.

The problem was in part self-made. The first list of states from which visitors were to be barred was exclusively composed of Muslim countries (Iraq, Iran, Libya, Somalia, Sudan, Syria, and Yemen) and was successfully challenged on constitutional grounds in lower federal courts as a violation of the free exercise of religion provision of the First Amendment. The second effort fared no better constitutionally. It was not until the third attempt—framed carefully to indicate that admissions to the United States would only be blocked on the basis of nonsectarian national security considerations—that the U.S. Supreme Court upheld the president's action, albeit by a narrow 5–4 majority, in the June 2018 case of *Trump, President of the United States, et al. v. Hawaii, et al.*

NATIONAL SECURITY STRATEGY—CONTINUING THE FIGHT ABROAD

Beyond these areas, even allowing for the "America First" rhetoric, much of President Trump's counterterrorist activity was not unlike that of his predecessors, if only because the broad outlines of the U.S. *National Security Strategy* documents have varied little since 9/11 in stressing a mix of isolating terrorists abroad, countering terrorist radicalization and recruitment at home and abroad, modernizing counterterrorist tools, protecting and enhancing the resiliency of vital infrastructure, and working with international partners.

Within this framework, the Trump administration not only continued the fight against ISIS in Iraq and Syria but relaxed the Obama-imposed rules for engagements involving drone strikes and commando raids by American military personnel. Likewise, following the January 2020 strike on a Kenyan military base that left three Americans dead, the administration was receptive to expanding U.S. drone strikes into Somalia, where the al-Qaeda-linked al-Shabaab fighters who launched the attack had fled for cover.

The promised international cooperation, however, occurred less frequently given the America First approach of Trump's foreign policy. In particular, a temporary cooling of U.S.-U.K. exchanges followed Trump's criticism of British leaders, including the Muslim mayor of London, following the 2017 terrorist attacks in Britain. Sharp criticism also followed when the White House signaled that it had no objection to Turkey expanding its war against Kurdish separatists across the border into Syria and establishing a Kurd-free zone, even though Syrian Kurds had been the backbone of the resistance against ISIS fighters in northwestern Syria.

NATIONAL SECURITY STRATEGY—THE HOME FRONT

On the front, there was also a mixed bag of policy pluses and minuses measured against administration and *National Security Strategy* goals. An early (January

2018) executive order addressing the contentious Guantánamo Bay detention facility, for example, continued the administration's hardline policy against foreign terrorists in eschewing any closing date and extending the prison's operations for an indefinite period. Figures from May of that year showed 40 still being detained out of the approximately 780 once incarcerated there, down from the 55 being detained when Trump took the presidential oath of office in January 2017.

Positive steps to secure the country's critical infrastructure (CI) also occurred during Trump's presidency, especially in the case of protecting the U.S. electrical grid—and everything dependent on it—from destructive energy surges caused by electromagnetic impulses (EMIs). With several agencies and cabinet departments already at work on assisting CI providers with guidelines for surviving an EMI assault, in January 2019, President Trump issued an executive order aimed at coordinating "national resilience" efforts vis-à-vis the threat posed.

On the downside of the ledger is the administration's record in combating terrorism at home. Internet communication, like bacteria and international diseases, cannot be easily stopped at the border. And the terrorist threat confronting the homeland has never been limited to foreign state-sponsored terrorists or global terrorist organizations. Thus, despite a continuation of the Obama administration's efforts to combat outside groups using the Internet to inspire American citizens and residents to terrorist action, the Trump administration found itself increasingly challenged on the home front. The source was a spike in terrorist action by radical domestic organizations, in particular right-wing white supremacy groups and individuals. Indeed, by mid-2019, the FBI was routinely tracing the majority of domestic terrorist acts to this sector; a year later, the acting secretary of the Department of Homeland Security, Kevin McAleenan, acknowledged that domestic terrorism was becoming the priority area for national counterintelligence. He also acknowledged in the same September 2020 *Meet the Press* interview that border and international issues had received the most consideration despite the high-visibility violence attributed to the radical right in Charlottesville, Virginia; El Paso, Texas; Pittsburgh, Pennsylvania; and elsewhere.

The latter can generally be credited to President Trump's influence and his focus on the threats of Islamic terrorism abroad and left-wing radicalism at home. In office, he initially proposed that the program created under Obama for Countering Violent Extremism (CVE) be renamed "Countering Radical Islamic Extremism" (CRIE), and shortly after the attack on a Pittsburgh synagogue by a right-wing extremist in 2018, he diverted funds from a CVE grant program to tighten border security against the immigrant caravans arriving through Mexico. The administration also urged adding the left-wing Antifa movement to the list of officially designated terrorist organizations, which was a nonstarter as a suggestion because that list is only for foreign terrorist groups.

On the upside, as was the case during the tenure of the post-9/11 George W. Bush administration and the presidencies that followed, no major terrorist attack occurred during the Trump administration. Furthermore, although increasing in number, the terrorist instances that took place during the Trump presidency were overwhelming by homegrown lone-wolf terrorists on soft targets, by nature the most difficult events to foresee and prevent.

Joseph R. Rudolph Jr.

See also: Antifa; Domestic Terrorism, White Supremacists; El Paso Walmart Shooting; Electromagnetic Pulse; Islamic State, The; Pittsburgh Synagogue Shooting; San Bernardino Attack.

FURTHER READING

Alexander, Dean C. 2017. "Terrorism Challenges Facing the Trump Administration." *SecurityMagazine*, January 1, 2017. https://www.securitymagazine.com/articles/87681-terrorism-challenges-facing-the-trump-administration

Benner, Katie. 2019. "Inside the Government, Addressing Domestic Terrorism Has Been Fraught." *New York Times*, August 11, 2019. https://www.nytimes.com/2019/08/11/us/politics/domestic-terrorism.html

Chalfant, Morgan. 2019. "FBI's Wray Says Most Domestic Terrorist Arrests This Year Involve White Supremacy." The Hill, July 23, 2019. https://thehill.com/homenews/administration/454338-fbis-wray-says-majority-of-domestic-terrorism-arrests-this-year

Davis, John. 2019. *Trump's World: Peril and Opportunity in US Foreign Policy after Obama*. Lanham, MD: Lexington Books.

Savage, Charlie, and Eric Schmitt. 2017. "Trump Poised to Drop Some Limits on Drone Strikes and Commando Raids." *New York Times*, September 21, 2017. https://www.nytimes.com/2017/09/21/us/politics/trump-drone-strikes-commando-raids-rules.html

Criminal Organization Terrorism

As terminology, *terrorism* and *terrorists* commonly evoke images of indiscriminant acts of violence directed against specific policies (e.g., racial integration) or political processes (e.g., 9/11 attack on the Pentagon and, more broadly, the United States). Less frequently receiving media coverage, but often much more successful in terms of goal realization, is the use of violence by states to maintain control over their territory and citizenry.

Likewise, images of criminal organizations and gang warfare tend to alternately produce visions of Prohibition and Al Capone's Chicago or Mexican/Latin American drug cartels, decapitation by machete, and civilians caught up in the violence. Seeing gang warfare in the United States as more than vicious gang-on-gang economic competition or the dance routine between the Jets and Sharks in a production of *West Side Story* is a rarity. Yet, like the most repressive regimes, these gangs frequently use terrorist tactics to protect their control of their neighborhood territories and silence resistance from those living there.

As a case study, consider Baltimore, which in 2020 held the ignominious honor of being the United States' most violent city in terms of murders (58) per 100,000 inhabitants. A quarter century ago, there was little in the way of criminal organizations capitalizing on this relatively poor city's drug problem, and its mayor, Kurt Schmoke, hoped to keep it that way by advocating decriminalization of some prohibited substances. The proposal brought him national notoriety and failed locally. Soon afterward, organized criminal gangs began to arrive.

The year 2002, again ignominiously, marked a watershed year in the city's battle to control increasing drug-related violence and gain citizen support for their efforts. Tired of watching her neighborhood honeycombed with street criminals, Angela Dawson repeatedly notified police of the drug dealing and other crimes visibly and daily occurring around her. On October 16 of that year, her house was firebombed, killing her, her husband, and five children trapped in the inferno. Subsequently, Baltimore police have for nearly two decades found it nearly impossible to obtain information from citizens who most likely know the names of those committing violence in their streets.

Meanwhile, the analogy between organized gangs using terrorist tactics to control their blocks and states doing the same has become eerily closer. In April 2015, following the accidental death of a Black male being transported in police custody, Baltimore underwent several nights of violence before deployed National Guard units exerted their tranquilizing effect. In between, respected political leaders like Baltimore congressman Elijah Cummings and members of the City Council took to the streets nightly to calm the citizenry. Pointedly, they were joined by two other groups: leaders of churches in the affected neighborhoods and gang leaders who had their own stake in preventing random amateur lawlessness.

Baltimore is a relative newcomer to the list of American cities whose gangs have long been studied, like Detroit and Los Angeles. Across the country, however, the pattern in medium-sized cities such as Baltimore and St. Louis has become much the same. Dominance-prolonging gang intimidation and excessive responses toward disobedient citizens have often become as certain as a painful death was for those opposing dictators like Stalin and Saddam Hussein.

Joseph R. Rudolph Jr.

See also: Reign of Terror; State Terrorism.

FURTHER READING

Cairns, Kathleen. 2017. "Dawson Family Relatives Re-Live the Horror after News of Baltimore Firebombing." WBFF news story, March 20, 2017. Accessed February 17, 2020. https://foxbaltimore.com/news/local/after-baltimore-firebombing-dawson-family-relatives-re-live-the-horror

Kennedy, Sean. 2020. "'The Wire' Is Finished, but Baltimore Still Bleeds." *Wall Street Journal*, February 7, 2020.

Knox, George W. 2018. *Gangs and Organized Crime*. New York: Routledge.

Critical Infrastructure as a Terrorist Target

The U.S. government defines *critical infrastructure* (CI) as "systems and assets, whether physical or virtual, so vital to the United States that the incapacity or destruction of such systems and assets would have a debilitating impact on security, national economic security, national public health or safety, or any combination of those matters" (U.S. Department of Homeland Security 2013). CI provides the essential services that underpin American society. Approximately 80 percent of U.S. CI is owned and operated by the private sector. This fact often places government entities in the roles of adviser and facilitator rather than director of how the owners of critical infrastructure should practice CI security and resilience. This fact has led to the creative development of many public-private partnerships since the 9/11 attacks. All CI has three broad components: physical (buildings, highways, chemical factories), human (operating CI often requires specialized skills), and cyberspace (all CI is dependent on the proper functioning of cyber operations and cybersecurity).

HISTORY OF CI SECURITY

The owners of CI and the U.S. government have traditionally protected certain elements of infrastructure that are critically important for maintaining essential public services, for national security reasons and for supporting the country's economic growth and vitality. For example, during World War II, the U.S. government posted troops to guard major dams against sabotage by hostile agents, and commercial nuclear power plants have maintained strong protective measures to deter and prevent unauthorized access.

The Clinton administration was the first to apply a unified national approach to CI protection when it issued Presidential Decision Directive (PDD)-63, Critical Infrastructure Protection, on May 29, 1998. This document states,

> No later than the year 2000, the United States shall have achieved an initial operating capability and no later than five years from today the United States shall have achieved and shall maintain the ability to protect the nation's critical infrastructures from intentional acts that would significantly diminish the abilities of the Federal Government to perform essential national security missions and to ensure the general public health and safety; state and local governments to maintain order and to deliver minimum essential public services; [and] the private sector to ensure the orderly functioning of the economy and the delivery of essential telecommunications, energy, financial and transportation services.

Following the 9/11 attacks, the Bush administration issued Homeland Security Policy Directive (HSPD)-7, Critical Infrastructure Identification, Prioritization, and Protection, on June 27, 2008. This directive established sixteen CI sectors and two key resource (KR) sectors. As HSPD-7's title implies, the Bush administration focused on identifying and attempting to prioritize the country's critical assets and develop ways to improve their protection from terrorist attacks. The administration also established *risk management* as the underlying concept for Department of Homeland Security (DHS) programs to improve CI protection. On February 12, 2018, the Obama administration replaced HSPD-7 with Presidential Policy Directive (PPD)-21, Critical Infrastructure Security and Resilience. This document established sixteen CI sectors by incorporating the two KR sectors—Postal and Shipping and National Icons and Monuments—into the Transportation and Government Facilities Sectors, respectively.

PPD-21 identified the Energy and Communications Sectors as particularly critical because all other sectors depended on them for continued operations. The Obama administration also replaced the Bush administration's emphasis on CI *protection* with the more holistic concept of CI *security*, where the term *security* embodied not only CI protection but also the mitigation of damage after an event as well as the need to improve the resilience of CI. *Resilience* refers to the ability of CI assets, networks, and systems to rapidly restore their functions following an event. The Obama administration also made the need to improve CI cybersecurity a primary CI security concern.

The Trump administration continued to use the guidance in PPD-21. However, the Cybersecurity and Infrastructure Security Agency Act of 2018 established a new agency within DHS, the Cybersecurity and Infrastructure Agency (CISA), to further improve cybersecurity across all CI sectors. Additionally, CISA's 2019 *Guide to Critical Infrastructure Security and Resilience* expanded the list of the most important critical infrastructure sectors from two to four (Energy, Communications, Water, and Transportation) and relabeled them "lifeline functions."

Since the Bush administration's emphasis on the terrorist threat to CI, CI security and resilience has expanded its focus to include risks from five main sources: terrorist attacks, extreme weather events, accidents/technical failures, cyber threats, and pandemic diseases.

CRITICAL INFRASTRUCTURE DETAILS

The size of U.S. CI is immense, and the responsibility for its security is spread over many public and private actors. The sixteen CI sectors are described below. The Emergency Services and the Government Facilities sectors are the only two CI sectors that are substantially owned and operated by government.

1. Chemical—Chemical plants and related facilities
2. Commercial Facilities—Entertainment and media (TV, newspapers, radio), gaming (casinos), lodging (hotels), outdoor events (fairs, parades), public assembly (concerts, cinema), real estate (offices, houses), retail (malls, supermarkets), sports leagues (NFL, NBA)
3. Communications—Broadcast, cable, satellite, wireless, and wireline communications systems
4. Critical Manufacturing—Manufacturers of primary metals, heavy machinery, electrical equipment and appliances, and transportation equipment
5. Dams—Dams (including hydroelectric power facilities), levees, canal locks, and industrial waste impoundments
6. Defense Industrial Base—Government and private organizations that support military operations, conduct research, and develop, design, and manufacture military weapons, systems, and components for the U.S. Armed Forces
7. Emergency Services—Police departments, sheriff's offices, fire departments, municipal public works departments, private security organizations, and private emergency medical services (EMS) providers
8. Energy—Facilities that produce, refine, store, and distribute oil, natural gas, and electricity (including coal-fired plants but excluding hydroelectric and nuclear power plants)
9. Financial Services—Banks and other depository institutions, providers of investment products, insurance companies, and other financing and credit organizations

10. Food and Agriculture—Farms, restaurants and other food service establishments, supermarkets/grocery stores, food processing facilities
11. Government Facilities—Offices and office buildings; housing for government employees; correctional facilities; embassies, consulates, and border facilities; education facilities; courthouses; libraries and archives; military bases; monuments
12. Healthcare and Public Health—Entities engaged in direct patient care, health information technology providers, health plans and payers, mass fatality management services, medical materials, laboratories, blood banks, and pharmaceutical manufacturing
13. Information Technology—Providers of products and services that support the efficient operation of today's information-based society
14. Nuclear Reactors, Materials, and Waste—Nuclear power plants; non-power reactors used for research, training, and radioisotope production; fuel cycle facilities; licensed users of radioactive sources; transportation, storage, and disposal of nuclear material and radioactive waste
15. Transportation Systems—Aviation, maritime, freight rail, highway and motor carrier, pipeline, postal and shipping, and mass transit activities
16. Water and Wastewater Systems—Water treatment and wastewater treatment facilities and associated systems

MANAGING AND COORDINATING CRITICAL INFRASTRUCTURE SECURITY

The DHS is responsible for guiding the development of CI security and resilience for all CI sectors, but achieving CI security involves a major interagency effort. The DHS's *National Infrastructure Protection Plan* (NIPP) designates a federal department or agency as the lead coordinator, or sector-specific agency (SSA), for each CI sector. Each SSA issues a *Sector Specific Plan* for its assigned CI sector. This approach is dictated by the great diversity of the country's CI, which requires different approaches for each sector. The DHS continues to refine its recommended risk analysis and management techniques and develops and distributes best practices guidelines to assist private CI stakeholders and federal, state, local, tribal, and territorial governments to improve their CI security measures. A series of DHS-developed counsels coordinate the security practices of the vast array of CI owners and operators. These include the following:

- Sector Coordinating Councils (SCCs)—Sector-specific private sector councils consisting of CI owners and operators. SCCs serve as principal collaboration points between the government and private sector owners and operators to enhance CI security and resilience.
- Government Coordinating Councils (GCCs)—Sector-specific councils that consist of representatives from across various levels of government. GCCs enable intergovernmental coordination within and across sectors and partner with SCCs on public-private efforts.

- Critical Infrastructure Cross-Sector Councils—Councils that consist of the chairs and vice chairs of the SCCs and coordinate cross-sector issues.
- Federal Senior Leadership Council (FSLC)—Council that consists of senior officials from the SSAs and other federal CI security stakeholders. It facilitates coordination of CI security and resilience efforts across the federal government.

TERRORIST THREATS TO CRITICAL INFRASTRUCTURE

When terrorists plan an attack, they want to produce the maximum political effect for a given expenditure of resources. Their goal is to spread as much terror as possible into the hearts and minds of their target audience to advance the terrorist group's political agenda. CI constitutes the perfect target given this goal because it is possible for a properly coordinated and executed limited attack to produce large-scale cascading effects.

Terrorists can choose from an array of potential CI targets and strike when and how they choose. In contrast, CI stakeholders not only must provide security for the physical, cyber, and human components of individual CI assets but also for the systems and networks in which these assets are embedded. It is neither practical nor affordable to protect all CI assets, systems, and networks at a level of security that either makes them impregnable to attack or deters terrorists from trying to attack them. This fact is why DHS's definition of CI security includes mitigation and resilience considerations as well as protective measures. This is also why DHS's emphasis on risk management is so important. This approach combines information about the threat of an attack, an asset's vulnerability to attack, and the consequence should an attack be successful to calculate the overall risk of an attack.

Determination of risk allows CI stakeholders to optimize their CI security efforts by concentrating security measures on high-risk assets. The interdependencies among the sixteen CI sectors are many and varied, which presents the potential for cascading casualties if terrorists can disable a small number of important CI assets, systems, or networks. The 9/11 attacks—perpetrated by nineteen terrorists at a relatively low cost—starkly demonstrate these relationships. Al-Qaeda terrorists hijacked four commercial aircraft (Aviation subsector of the Transportation Sector) and used them as weapons of mass destruction to attack the World Trade Center (Commercial Facilities Sector) and the Pentagon (Government Facilities Sector). Many first responders were killed (Emergency Services Sector). Moreover, in addition to these immediate destructive effects, the attacks also produced several cascading effects. All activity in the Aviation subsector was halted for several days. Significant strains were placed on local hospitals (Healthcare and Public Health Sector). The Communications, Information Technology, and Financial Services Sectors were all affected to some degree. The 9/11 attacks also showcase the desire by terrorist groups to conduct attacks with symbolic significance. This is why National Monuments and Icons are included in the Government Facilities Sector.

William J. Lahneman

See also: Cybersecurity; Department of Homeland Security; September 11, 2001, Attack on America; Transportation Security.

FURTHER READING

Cybersecurity & Infrastructure Security Agency. 2020a. *Guidance on the Essential Critical Infrastructure Workforce: Ensuring Community and National Resilience in COVID-19 Response.* March 19, 2020. https://www.cisa.gov/sites/default/files/publications/CISA-Guidance-on-Essential-Critical-Infrastructure-Workers-1-20-508c.pdf

Cybersecurity & Infrastructure Security Agency. 2020b. "Infrastructure Security." July 2020. https://www.dhs.gov/topic/critical-infrastructure-security

Cybersecurity & Infrastructure Security Agency, U.S. Department of Homeland Security, and U.S. Department of State. 2019. *A Guide to Critical Infrastructure Security and Resilience.* Washington, DC: Cybersecurity and Infrastructure Security Agency, Department of Homeland Security.

U.S. Department of Homeland Security. 2013. *NIPP 2013: Partnering for Critical Infrastructure Security and Resilience.* https://www.cisa.gov/sites/default/files/publications/national-infrastructure-protection-plan-2013-508.pdf

U.S. Department of Homeland Security. 2014. *Joint National Priorities for Critical Infrastructure Security and Resilience.* November 14, 2014. https://www.cisa.gov/sites/default/files/publications/Joint-National-Priorities-Fact-Sheet-20180928-508.pdf

Cyberattacks

Most people think of *cyberspace* as referring to computing devices, communications networks, and information that encompasses the Internet. The U.S. Department of Defense (DoD), however, provides a more comprehensive definition of the term. It defines *cyberspace* as the convergence of all networks of information technology infrastructures and information, including telecommunications networks, computer systems, and embedded processors and controllers, which includes the internet and more. As the world has become reliant on this cyberinfrastructure, there has been an attendant increase in the number of cyberattacks. A *cyberattack* is typically interpreted to be where both the source and the immediate target of the attack are cyber based.

There are several terms used to classify cyberattacks, including *cyberterrorism*, *cyberwarfare*, *cybercrime*, *cyberespionage*, and *hacktivism*. There is limited consensus on the definitions of these terms. To complicate matters, the characteristics of a cyberattack may align, more or less, with one or more of the definitions of these terms; for example, incidents classified as *cyberespionage* are likely to also align with the definition of *cybercrime*.

One characteristic that affects classification is the attribution of the source of the attack, which may range from a single malicious actor to nation-states. It is (arguably) more straightforward to assign attribution to the source of a physical (kinetic) attack; there are obstacles in attributing, with certainty, the source of a cyberattack. Here is a simple example: A malicious actor in country A compromises computers in countries B, C, and D, hopping from one compromised computer to the next—a common technique employed to hide their identity—until they attack a target computer in country E. Resolving from target E back through computers in countries D, C, and B to the source A is a difficult undertaking. In this example, investigators might erroneously conclude that the source of the attack resided in country D.

Attribution affects the classification of many cyberattacks, as attribution is tenuous at best: the classification of a cyberattack, whether cyberterrorism, cyberwarfare, or something else, may depend on whether the source is an independent malicious actor, a group of actors, third-party groups influenced or controlled by a nation-state, or a nation-state alone.

CYBERTERRORISM

Cyberterrorism is a marriage of the terms *cyberspace* and *terrorism*. Accordingly, the definition of the former term is entwined with the definitions of the latter terms. The term *terrorism*, however, has no widely accepted definition; definitions of *cyberterrorism*, then, are as varied as the definitions of *terrorism*. The Code of Federal Regulations defines *terrorism* as "the unlawful use of force and violence against persons or property to intimidate or coerce a government, the civilian population, or any segment thereof, in furtherance of political or social objectives" (Code of Federal Regulations 2001, 51). Therefore, *cyberterrorism* could integrate the above definition with the qualification that both the attack source and immediate target are cyber based.

The Federal Bureau of Investigation (FBI) defines *cyberterrorism* as "the use of cyber tools to shut down critical national infrastructures for the purpose of coercing or intimidating a government or civilian population" (Federal Bureau of Investigation 2006, 46). This is a somewhat narrow definition, as it limits the classification of cyberterrorism to cyberattacks on a nation's critical infrastructure. Although not specifically mentioned in these definitions, there is some consensus that the source of a cyberterrorism attack is any source other than a nation-state; cyberattacks controlled by nation-states are more likely to be classified as cyberwarfare (described below).

There have been several incidents that are (tenuously) consistent with the FBI's definition of *cyberterrorism* but have, nevertheless, been used as examples of cyberterrorism. In 2008, alleged Russian actors used malware to attack a Turkish oil pipeline, infecting the industrial controls systems that regulate the pipeline's operations, resulting in massive explosions and fire damage. In 2016, alleged Russian actors used sophisticated malware to infect the Ukrainian electrical grid, leaving 230,000 residents without power. There were no reported injuries or deaths in either attack. The extent to which these incidents were classified as cyberterrorism is based on the inability to attribute with certainty that a nation-state controlled the attacks. If the Russian government either directly or indirectly influenced these attacks, they could just as well be classified as acts of cyberwarfare.

CYBERWARFARE

Currently there is no legal or military-doctrinal definition of *cyberwarfare*. The *Department of Defense Law of War Manual* (U.S. Department of Defense 2016) includes a section on "Cyber Operations," along with definitions of "cyberspace" and "cyber operations"; yet, there is no definition of *cyberwarfare*, nor are the terms *cyber war* or *cyberwarfare* ever used. Some experts contend that, like warfare, cyberwarfare must result in kinetic effects: destruction of physical objects or death. Others support a broader definition to include cyber operations used as preludes or in support of kinetic attacks, such as the exfiltration (i.e., theft) or adulteration of information, or disruption of services. Nevertheless, scholars have suggested that the term *cyberwarfare* is typically construed as "state-on-state action equivalent to an armed attack or use of force in cyberspace that may trigger a military response with a proportional kinetic use of force" (Theohary and Rollins 2015, 4). As such, a cyberattack would be classified as cyberwarfare if its resulting effects were proportionate to the effects of a kinetic attack deemed an act of war. As of 2022, no nation-state has publicly claimed that a cyberattack has escalated to this level of kinetic force.

An incident used as an example of cyberwarfare, rightly or wrongly, was the discovery of Stuxnet malware in 2010. Stuxnet was a sophisticated worm—malware with the ability to self-replicate across a network—that was able to identify and infect Windows computers with the control software of a specific model of centrifuge known to be used in Iranian uranium enrichment facilities, a capability not seen previously. Stuxnet forced centrifuges to exceed their working tolerances, resulting in physical (kinetic) damage to the centrifuges and controllers. Stuxnet also acquired control of the human-machine interfaces used to manage operations, making it appear that the centrifuges were working normally while, in reality, the centrifuges were spinning out of control to destruction. The damage was widespread and required the replacement of thousands of units, but there were no reported deaths or injuries from the attack.

Some experts have called Stuxnet the first true cyberweapon. Based on the sophistication of the software, there was conjecture that the U.S. and Israeli governments were involved in its development; both governments have neither confirmed nor denied the claim. Another lesson of Stuxnet is that only 59 percent of its damage occurred in Iran; unlike a weapon is physical space, it is difficult to control where a cyberweapon will attack (Vigiliarolo 2017).

CYBERCRIME

Cybercrime is the use of computers and networks to engage in unlawful activities. Although many acts of cybercrime are financially motivated, they can also be rooted in revenge, entertainment, and curiosity. Examples of cybercrimes include malware infections, computer and network intrusions, distribution of child pornography, fraud, theft of intellectual property, industrial espionage, distributed denial-of-service attacks (DDoS), and identity theft. It has been estimated that cybercrime worldwide will result in damages and losses of $10.5 trillion through 2025 (Morgan 2020).

The FBI has cited ransomware as the fastest-growing and most significant cybercrime threat. *Ransomware* is malware that encrypts information stored on a computer, rendering it unreadable. The malicious actor subsequently requests a monetary ransom, typically in a form of cryptocurrency. If the ransom is paid, the malicious actor releases the decryption key, which is then used to decrypt the information, making the information readable. A seminal outbreak of ransomware, dubbed "WannaCry," first occurred in 2017. It infected hundreds of thousands of computers around the world, with extensive infections occurring in Russia, Taiwan, Ukraine, India, Spain, Germany, Indonesia, China, Japan, and the United Kingdom.

The United Kingdom's National Health Services (NHS) took a particularly hard hit, as the ransomware affected at least 81 out of 236 trusts across England. A further 603 primary care and other NHS organizations were infected, including 595 general practitioners' offices, resulting in the cancellations of 19,000 appointments and operations. The attack was ostensibly financially motivated, as the malicious actors requested a payment of $300 in ransom per infected computer. Security experts identified code in the malware that was similar to code used by a known North Korean hacking group. The extent to which this group is controlled or influenced by the government of North Korea is unknown.

CYBERESPIONAGE

Cyberespionage is an act of a nation-state, corporation, or other party designed to unlawfully obtain intellectual property, critical technologies, sensitive government or military information, or other data through the use of computers, networks, and software. Some acts of cyberespionage are economically motivated: theft of intellectual property obviates the need to spend millions or billions in research and development. Additionally, cyberespionage has been used in the exfiltration of sensitive government and military information as well as for gathering intelligence on potential criminals, terrorists, and other threats. Note that acts of cyberespionage can most likely be classified as acts of cybercrime. Most cyberespionage campaigns are prolonged, involving multiple well-planned stages of gaining and maintaining access over time to effectuate the exfiltration of information. Such campaigns are often called *advanced persistent threats* (APT).

One of the largest incidents of cyberespionage was precipitated by a software update supply chain attack. In late 2020, the U.S. government and enterprise software development company SolarWinds disclosed a breach into the latter's software development network. SolarWinds Orion is software deployed to manage large and complex networks and is commonly used by governments and private companies. In early 2020, malicious actors breached SolarWinds' software development network and installed malware into the software updates for Orion. When companies updated their installation of Orion, the malware-infected version of Orion allowed malicious actors to steal information from their networks and install additional malware. Reports indicated that at least nine U.S. government agencies, including the Departments of Homeland Security, Treasury, State, and Energy and the Pentagon, and up to 18,000 private companies were affected by the attack (Jibilian and Canales 2021).

Another incident of cyberespionage was identified in 2018, when security experts identified sophisticated malware, dubbed "Slingshot," that targeted Latvian-made routers used in the Middle East, Africa, and Southeast Asia. The purpose of the malware was to steal large amounts of sensitive information. Over a period of six years, the malware targeted internet cafés known to be used by radical Islamic groups for communicating among members. It was reported that unnamed U.S. intelligence officials suggested that the malware was part of an anti-terrorism operation run by the U.S. Joint Special Operations Command. According to published sources, an analysis of the malware indicated that it shared code with malware known to have been developed by the National Security Agency (NSA) and the Central Intelligence Agency (CIA).

HACKTIVISM

Hacktivism—also called *cyberactivism*—is a marriage of the terms *hacking* and *activism* and describes acts involving the use of computers and networks to achieve a social or political agenda for the purpose of effectuating change. Note that many acts of hactivism have also been classified as acts of cyberterrorism or cybercrime. Hacktivists have been around since the advent of the internet, and their activities run the gamut from website defacement to computer and network intrusions. Recent acts of hacktivism include doxing and DDoS attacks. *Doxing*—a derivative of *documents*—involves the theft of sensitive information on an individual, group, or organization and then publishing that information on the internet for the purpose of humiliation or intimidation.

Anonymous is an antiauthoritarian group closely associated with hacktivism and arguably the best-known hacktivist group. Anonymous is a decentralized collection of individuals with no identifiable leader, no formal membership, and no central road map of activities; members presumably perform hacktivist activities for the "common good."

In 2010, Anonymous performed a series of DDoS attacks against PayPal, Visa, and MasterCard after the three financial-based companies began refusing transactions involving donations to the media organization WikiLeaks. Later in 2010, the CEO of HBGary Federal, a cybersecurity firm whose clients included government and intelligence agencies, insinuated that his company had infiltrated Anonymous and intended to release information on the members' identities (an activity that would itself be considered doxing). In retaliation, Anonymous subsequently penetrated HBGary Federal's network and siphoned thousands of sensitive business emails, which were subsequently posted online. In 2013, Anonymous went after a town in Ohio that was "covering up" the sexual assault of a woman by members of the local high school football team. Other Anonymous targets have included Israeli government and Palestinian Authority websites, the Church of Scientology, Westboro Baptist Church, the FBI, and other varied sites, demonstrating that, as a "group," Anonymous does not have a specific ideology.

J. Philip Craiger and Gary C. Kessler

See also: Critical Infrastructure as a Terrorist Target; Cybersecurity.

FURTHER READING

Bing, Chris, and Howard O'Neill. 2018. "Kaspersky's 'Slingshot' Report Burned an ISIS-Focused Intelligence Operation." Cyberscoop, March 21, 2018. https://www.cyberscoop.com/kaspersky-slingshot-isis-operation-socom-five-eyes/

Code of Federal Regulations. 2001. "28 CFR. Section 0.85 on Judicial Administration." July 2001.

Federal Bureau of Investigation. 2006. "Terrorism: 2002–2005." https://www.fbi.gov/file-repository/stats-services-publications-terrorism-2002-2005-terror02_05.pdf

Jarvis, Lee, and Stuart Macdonald. 2014. "What Is Cyberterrorism? Findings from a Survey of Researchers." *Terrorism and Political Violence* 27 (4): 657–678. https://doi.org/10.1080/09546553.2013.847827

Jibilian, Isabella, and Katie Canales. 2021. "The US Is Readying Sanctions against Russia over the SolarWinds Cyber Attack." Business Insider, April 15, 2021. https://www.businessinsider.com/solarwinds-hack-explained-government-agencies-cyber-security-2020-12

Morgan, Steve. 2020. "Cybercrime to Cost the World $10.5 Trillion Annually by 2025." Cybercrime Magazine, November 3, 2020. https://cybersecurityventures.com/cybercrime-damages-6-trillion-by-2021/

Sanger, David E. 2012. "Obama Order Sped Up Wave of Cyberattacks against Iran." *New York Times*, June 1, 2012. https://www.nytimes.com/2012/06/01/world/middleeast/obama-ordered-wave-of-cyberattacks-against-iran.html

Theohary, Catherine. 2021. "Defense Primer: Cyberspace Operations." Congressional Research Service, December 1, 2021. https://crsreports.congress.gov/product/pdf/IF/IF10537

Theohary, Catherine, and Anne Harrington. 2015. "Cyber Operations in DOD Policy and Plans: Issues for Congress." Congressional Research Service, January 5, 2015. https://fas.org/sgp/crs/natsec/R43848.pdf

Theohary, Catherine, and John Rollins. 2015. "Cyberwarfare and Cyberterrorism: In Brief." Congressional Research Service, March 27, 2015. https://fas.org/sgp/crs/natsec/R43955.pdf

U.S. Department of Defense. 2016. "Law and War Manual." July. https://dod.defense.gov/Portals/1/Documents/law_war_manual15.pdf

Vigiliarolo, Brandon. 2017. "Stuxnet: The Smart Person's Guide." Tech Republic, August 15, 2017. https://www.techrepublic.com/article/stuxnet-the-smart-persons-guide/

Cybersecurity

Cybersecurity—the common term today for the practice of *information security*—refers to the protection of information and information systems from any unauthorized or unintended access or modification. Information systems consist of hardware, software, communications networks, and the people who are authorized to use them (i.e., users). Information is to be protected while being stored, processed, or transmitted over a communications network.

Confidentiality, integrity, and availability are three of the most important attributes of information to be protected. *Confidentiality* refers to protecting information from unauthorized access or disclosure by individuals or systems. An example of an attack on confidentiality is the 2017 data breach of the credit reporting bureau Equifax that resulted in the loss of nearly 150 million credit records containing extensive personal information. *Integrity* refers to ensuring that the information is complete, uncorrupted, and authentic; that is, the data that arrives is identical to the data that was sent. The principle of integrity has been extended to the integrity of information systems themselves, requiring that systems perform their intended functions free from deliberate or inadvertent unauthorized manipulation. *Availability* means to ensure that authorized users can access information when needed. Recent examples of attacks on availability involve *malware* (i.e., malicious software) known as *ransomware*, which encrypts information stored on a computer, making the information unreadable. The malicious actor subsequently requests a monetary ransom, typically via a form of cryptocurrency; if the ransom is paid, the attacker releases the decryption key, which is then used to decrypt the information.

Three concepts related to accessing information and information systems are identification, authentication, and authorization. *Identification* is when a user asserts his or her identity (e.g., a username) during the process of logging into an information system. *Authentication* is when the user provides proof of his or her identity (e.g., a password). Successful identification and authentication only provide a user access to the use of the information system; access to applications and specific files is controlled through authorization. *Authorization* is a process by which an information system determines whether the user has permission to use a resource or access a file or other resource on the system or network. The principle of *least privilege* is often applied in granting access: users should only have permission to resources or files necessary to do their job. As an example, for a home computer with multiple users, a single user should not have access to other users' files or resources, nor should a single user have access to critical operating system files that could damage the operating system if destroyed or altered, resulting in lack of access to resources or files on the system by any user.

THREATS TO CYBERSECURITY

Hacking is a catchall term that is defined as the act of acquiring unauthorized access to a computer or network. Unauthorized access is typically gained when malicious actors exploit vulnerabilities in an operating system, application, hardware, or software or through the psychological manipulation of authorized users. Hackers vary in their technical expertise, from novices who simply download premade scripts or software from the Internet to those who have the capability of creating their own customized software and hardware for use as cyberweapons.

Threats to cybersecurity can be categorized as technical, nontechnical, or a combination of the two. A common nontechnical attack involves *social engineering*: gaining unauthorized access to information by exploiting human psychology. To illustrate, a young man in a suit approaches the receptionist at the lobby desk of a large business. Nervously, he shows her a copy of a résumé with a coffee stain, telling her that he has an interview upstairs in ten minutes and he just spilled coffee on the only copy of his résumé. Could she please plug in a thumb drive that he has containing the résumé and print him a fresh copy? Unbeknownst to the receptionist, the thumb drive also has malware that infects her computer in order to access other computers on the corporate network.

An example of a threat combining technical elements and social engineering is *phishing*. Phishing involves an email that attempts to convince a user to reveal personal information or perform a behavior, such as clicking on a link to a malicious website or an email attachment masquerading as an innocuous file (e.g., a word processing document) when in reality it contains malware. Phishing emails are written to appeal to a user's greed or vanity, to promote fear, or to appeal to authority as a means of persuasion.

Most purely technical attacks involve malware that is used to gain unauthorized access to an information system, destroy or alter information, or prevent an information system from functioning properly. *Malware* is an umbrella term for many forms of malicious software, a inexhaustive list that includes viruses, worms, Trojan horses, bots, adware, spyware, and ransomware.

As of 2021, two of the more vicious forms of malware involved bots and ransomware. A *bot*, short for "Internet robot," is a small program that carries out an automated task. A *botnet* is a collection of many bots under the command and control of a malicious actor and can be used to perform massive attacks on computers and networks. For instance, a *distributed denial-of-service* (DDoS) attack botnet involves implanting bots on thousands, tens of thousands, or hundreds of thousands of computers that are then used to attack an Internet resource, such as a web server or Internet service provider, with a barrage of requests; a successful DDoS attack overwhelms the bandwidth or computer processing resource of the victim to the point that the site can no longer function. Bots are surreptitiously implanted through phishing campaigns (e.g., via email attachments) or by implanting them on smart devices connected to the Internet (i.e., Internet of Things devices, such as smart TVs, security cameras, digital video recorders, etc.) that have known, hard-coded login credentials. The largest DDoS attack to date occurred in 2020, when Amazon Web Services (AWS) received a barrage of data at a rate of 2.3 terabits (trillions of bits, or 10^{12} bits) per second. The attack used a broadcast amplification technique so that the amount of data being sent to the victim sites increased by a factor of 56 to 70. The attack lasted for three days, costing an undisclosed amount of revenue for AWS.

STRATEGIES FOR CYBERSECURITY

Perfect security can never be achieved, as both technology and users are fallible. *Defense in depth* is a guiding principle in cybersecurity that deals with the eventuality of imperfect security. The purpose of defense in depth is to manage risk using multiple and independent layers of protection: if one layer is compromised, there are additional barriers in place to prevent, or at least impede, unauthorized users from gaining further access. This follows the model of a castle—the community is surrounded by a high wall with few doors, surrounded in turn by a moat, surrounded in turn by flat, open land. Each protective element is independent of the other and, in fact, deters a different type of attack. In the case of cybersecurity, defenses that may include routers, firewalls, anti-malware software, and intrusion detection/prevention systems can all be employed. Layers of defense in cybersecurity can be classified as either nontechnical or technical.

NONTECHNICAL LAYERS OF DEFENSE

Policies, Standards, and Practices

Organizations must be proactive to threats by creating policies, standards, and practices. Policies provide a high-level explanation as to how security issues are to be resolved and how information is to be protected. Standards and procedures specifically address the current security technologies used and specific steps to be taken to protect information. An enterprise cybersecurity policy should include a business continuity plan, disaster recovery plan, and incident response plan to guide the organization when disaster strikes.

Education, Training, and Awareness Programs

Users are an important part of information systems, yet they are the weakest link in security, as users are the (possibly inadvertent) source or target of most attacks. Education, training, and awareness programs provide users with an understanding of how to secure information; the need to be vigilant; and the importance of policies, standards, and practices that support the financial health of the organization.

Physical Security

There is a saying in cybersecurity that if a hacker has physical access to a computer, then they own it. There are various physical security measures to prevent unauthorized physical access, including alarms, door locks, security guards, walls/fencing/gates, and ID cards and badges. Additional forms of physical security protect systems from hazards, such fire, water, power spikes, or other potential sources of physical damage.

TECHNICAL LAYERS OF DEFENSE

Backups

Backups are copies of information. Backups should be made on a frequent basis, and, ideally, multiple backups should be made, with at least one backup source kept off-site in case an organization's physical facilities are destroyed (e.g., through fire or natural hazards such as a tornado, hurricane, or earthquake).

Operating System and Application Updates

Operating systems and applications are highly complex software and are likely to contain vulnerabilities (i.e., flaws) that can be exploited by malicious actors. Most large software companies provide updates on a regular basis to remove known vulnerabilities. Users should schedule automatic updates for all software products that support it.

Anti-Virus Software

Although usually referred to as *anti-virus software*, a better term is *anti-malware* (AM), as these programs have the capability of identifying many different forms of malware, including viruses, worms, Trojan horses, adware, and even ransomware. AM software uses several techniques to identify malicious programs. When threats are identified, the software quarantines the malicious program so that it is unable to harm the system. Users should configure the AM software to update its database of malware signatures on a regular (and automatic) basis to keep abreast of current forms and versions of malware.

Firewalls

A firewall is software or hardware that inspects network traffic and either allows or denies that traffic based on firewall security policies. All major operating systems include a firewall. Users should verify that their firewall is turned on and verify that their firewall security policies only allow necessary traffic to pass through the firewall.

Network Intrusion Detection Systems (NIDS)

Network intrusion detection systems (NIDS) are a second layer of defense on a network and are typically placed after a firewall. The purpose of the NIDS is to identify malicious network traffic that has passed through the firewall. NIDS are commonly employed in larger organizations as another layer of network defense and less likely to be encountered on a home or small business network.

Two-Factor Authentication (2FA)

There are three means to verify a user's identity: something the user knows (e.g., a password), something the user has (e.g., a token, smart card, or smartphone), or something the user *is* (e.g., a physical attribute such as a fingerprint, voice print, or facial scan). Two-factor authentication (2FA) is a concept by which two or more of these mechanisms are combined to provide a more secure means of verifying a user's identity. A common 2FA scheme is a combination of password and a smartphone. With this scheme, a user logs into a computer or website with a username and password (first factor), and they subsequently receive a onetime token sent to their smartphone (second factor), which is used in the final step of authentication. By combining two forms of authentication, there is a higher probability that the user has been accurately verified. Many large e-commerce and financial institution websites require 2FA.

Encryption

Encryption involves encoding information so that only authorized users can view it. More generically, encryption is used to ensure data confidentiality, data integrity, nonrepudiation, and user authentication. There are several forms of encryption, but all require an encryption algorithm and one or more keys used to encrypt the information and then decrypt it into a readable form. Common uses of encryption include encrypting the contents of a hard drive or network communications. Encrypting network communications—whether browsing the web, accessing an online banking service, or sending/receiving emails—is particularly important because unencrypted information traveling over networks has the potential to be read by malicious actors. The current standard of web-based encryption is the hypertext transfer protocol over the secure sockets layer (HTTPS), which is replacing the unencrypted version, HTTP; you know that you are at an HTTPS site because of the lock icon in the browser's address bar. The encryption and decryption occurs transparently at these sites, without the need for manual intervention by users.

J. Philip Craiger and Gary C. Kessler

See also: Critical Infrastructure as a Terrorist Target; Cyberattacks.

FURTHER READING

Anderson, Ross. 2008. *Security Engineering: A Guide to Building Dependable Distributed Systems*. Hoboken, NJ: Wiley.

Clarke, Richard, and Robert Knake. 2012. *Cyber War: The Next Threat to National Security and What to Do about It*. New York: Ecco.

Schneider, Bruce. 2004. *Secrets and Lies: Digital Security in a Networked World*. Hoboken, NJ: Wiley.

Stoll, Cliff. 2005. *The Cuckoo's Egg: Tracking a Spy through the Maze of Computer Espionage*. New York: Pocket Books.

D

Defense Intelligence Agency (DIA)

The Defense Intelligence Agency (DIA) was established in 1961 by Secretary of Defense Robert McNamara as the central intelligence manager for the Department of Defense (DoD). This move was an attempt to resolve the Soviet missile gap controversy of the time, as each branch of the U.S. armed services had its own estimate of Soviet missile strength that varied widely from those of the other branches.

The DIA's main objective is to assess military-related issues and coordinate the work of military intelligence branches within the DoD, that is, the intelligence units of the army, navy, air force, and marines, which are mainly preoccupied with gathering and analyzing tactical intelligence from the battlefields where American military personnel serve. Additionally, the DIA is one of the U.S. intelligence community's (IC) three all-source analytic agencies and, as such, has the mission of analyzing intelligence from all IC agencies on important military issues and issuing strategic intelligence products.

U.S. military intelligence as an activity dates from the colonial period of American history, when the collection and analysis of intelligence helped to compensate for the British numerical and operational superiority during the War of Independence (1775–1783). Nevertheless, after the war, successive presidential administrations and Congress undermined the military intelligence organizations. It was not until the aftermath of the surprise December 1941 Japanese attack on a U.S. naval base at Pearl Harbor, Hawaii, that U.S. policy makers accepted the need to develop a centralized peacetime military intelligence organization.

During the 1960s, the DIA focused on China's detonation of an atomic bomb; the increasing instability among African nations; and the fighting in Malaysia, Cyprus, and Kashmir. The agency's reputation was significantly enhanced by the mid-1970s, as its information-gathering activities and analysis were perceived as valuable to national security decision-making.

The DIA's focus on terrorism dates from the mid-1980s, when the world experienced a large number of terrorist attacks that included hijackings, bombings, kidnappings, and murders. The DIA proved valuable during these attacks, in countering incidents like the hijacking of TWA Flight 847 and unrest in the Philippines; and in supporting Operation El Dorado Canyon against Libya, which was intended as a retaliation to Libyan-sponsored terrorist attacks in Berlin.

In the aftermath of a deadly attack by the terrorist organization al-Qaeda on the USS *Cole* during a scheduled refueling stop in the Yemeni port of Aden on

October 12, 2000, the DIA sought to enhance its counterterrorism mission. The DoD issued a report that concluded that not enough resources were being directed to fight terrorist groups. It recommended increasing the resources devoted to combating terrorism. In response, the DIA experienced structural changes. Its counterterrorism office was transformed into the Joint Terrorism Analysis Center (JTAC). JTAC's mission was expanded, and it became the Joint Intelligence Task Force–Combating Terrorism (JITF-CT), which produced daily assessments of possible terrorist threats to DoD personnel, facilities, and interests. In 2012, the JITF-CT became the Defense Counterterrorism Center (DCTC), which consolidates national-level terrorism-related intelligence from all agencies and sources.

Shady Abdelwahab Mansour

See also: USS *Cole* Attack.

FURTHER READING

Defense Intelligence Agency. n.d. *A History of the Defense Intelligence Agency.* DIA Office of Historical Research. https://bit.ly/2VTXZqR

Federation of American Scientists. 1996. *A Brief History: Defense Intelligence Agency.* https://fas.org/irp/dia/dia_history.pdf

Johnson. Loch K., ed. 2010. *The Oxford Handbook of National Security Intelligence.* Oxford, UK: Oxford University Press.

Richeslon, Jeffrey T. 2016. *The US Intelligence Community.* 7th ed. Denver, CO: Westview Press.

West, Nigel. 2015. *Historical Dictionary of International Intelligence.* 2nd ed. Lanham, MD: Rowman & Littlefield.

Department of Homeland Security (DHS)

President George W. Bush signed the Homeland Security Act of 2002 into law on November 25, 2002. The Act was a direct response to the 9/11 attacks on the United States. The centerpiece of the law was the creation of a new Department of Homeland Security (DHS), which became operational on March 1, 2003. It consolidated twenty-two diverse federal government agencies and bureaus with a combined total of 163,000 employees into a single cabinet department directed by a secretary of homeland security, who is appointed by the president with the advice and consent of the Senate. By 2022, DHS had grown to over 240,000 employees. It is the third-largest cabinet department after the Departments of Defense and Veterans Affairs.

SECRETARIES OF HOMELAND SECURITY

2003–2005

Thomas "Tom" Ridge was formerly the governor of Pennsylvania (1995–2001) and a U.S congressman (1982–1994). Ridge served as the first director of homeland security in the Executive Office of the President, beginning on September 22,

2001, and he became the first secretary of homeland security on January 24, 2003. He was faced with the difficult leadership challenge of forging personnel from many disparate government agencies—many with strong institutional heritage and organizational identification, widely varying missions, and, in many cases, former status as independent agencies and bureaus—into an effective and unified whole dedicated to the newly important "homeland security" mission.

2005–2009

Michael Chertoff was a former federal judge and prosecutor. Chertoff is best known for restructuring the DHS's directorate structure, including its intelligence organization, along more functional lines; for formally adopting the risk analysis and management methodology that has become the foundation of DHS's programs for strengthening the country's critical infrastructure (CI); and for formally changing the department's mission from one that emphasized counterterrorism to an "all-hazards" approach. An all-hazards approach includes measures to prevent, protect against, respond to, and recover from not only terrorist attacks but also disasters (both natural and human induced) and criminal activities.

2009–2013

Janet Napolitano was formerly a two-term governor of Arizona, the attorney general of Arizona, and a U.S. attorney for the District of Arizona. Napolitano presided over the creation of programs such as TSA PreCheck and Global Entry and worked to make DHS a more efficient, effective, and cohesive organization. She increased the priority that DHS placed on cybersecurity and resilience. She also created the Deferred Action for Childhood Arrivals (DACA) initiative and improved immigration enforcement and border security.

2013–2017

Jeh Johnson was formerly the general counsel of the Department of Defense (2009–2012), where he was one of the architects of the U.S. military's counterterrorism mission, and former General Counsel for the Department of the Air Force. Johnson led DHS's response to a large wave of undocumented immigrants, many of whom were children, along the southern border in 2014. He also directed DHS's measures to identify travelers entering the United States who might have been infected with the Ebola virus as a result of exposure to the epidemic raging in West Africa.

2017–2017

John F. Kelly was a retired four-star general in the U.S. Marine Corps and commander of U.S. Southern Command (2012–2016). General Kelly's tenure at DHS was cut short after approximately six months when he was selected in July 2017 to serve as President Trump's White House chief of staff.

2017–2019

Kirstjen M. Nielsen was the former chief of staff to DHS secretary John Kelly, a White House deputy chief of staff, and a special assistant to President George W. Bush on the White House Homeland Security Council.

2019–2021

Chad F. Wolf was designated as the acting secretary of homeland security on November 13, 2019. He formerly served as the first undersecretary of DHS's Office of Strategy, Policy, and Plans; as chief of staff for the Transportation Security Administration (TSA); and as DHS chief of staff.

2021–Present

Alejandro Mayorkas was formerly the deputy secretary of the U.S. Department of Homeland Security and director of U.S. Citizenship and Immigration Services. He is the first Latino and immigrant confirmed to serve as secretary of homeland security. During his initial months in office, his department needed to respond to another wave of undocumented immigrants at the southern border, including many unaccompanied children, which posed unique problems for their care and processing.

MISSIONS AND RISK ANALYSIS METHODOLOGY

DHS has six overarching missions that encompass the department's all-hazards approach to homeland security and reflect the seven missions mandated for DHS by the Homeland Security Act of 2002. To achieve these missions, DHS employs a risk analysis methodology to identify homeland security threats, assess vulnerabilities, and calculate the consequences should a particular hazard occur, and it uses these factors to estimate the risk posed by different hazards under various scenarios. DHS and other homeland security stakeholders from the private sector as well as federal, state, local, tribal, and territorial (FSLTT) governments use this information to prioritize risk-reduction measures. The goal is to achieve the greatest risk reduction in the most cost-effective way by directing limited funding, technology, and personnel to the highest-risk assets, systems, and networks across physical, human, and cyber domains.

The six missions include the following:

1. Counterterrorism and Homeland Security Threats. Activities in this mission area focus on collecting, analyzing, and sharing actionable intelligence; detecting and disrupting threats; protecting designated leadership, events, and "soft" (relatively unprotected) targets; and countering weapons of mass destruction and emerging threats.
2. Securing Cyberspace and Critical Infrastructure. DHS considers cyberspace to be the most active threat domain in the world and the most dynamic threat to the homeland. Cybercrime damages are likely to exceed $6 trillion per year by 2021. All critical infrastructure sectors depend on the cyber domain to run effectively. Cyberattacks to critical infrastructure can cause devastating cascading destruction with heavy economic impacts.

3. Securing U.S. Borders and Approaches. Border security responsibilities focus on securing and managing air, land, and maritime borders; extending the reach of U.S. border security; enforcing U.S. immigration laws; and administering immigration benefits to advance the security and prosperity of the nation.
4. Preserving and Upholding the Nation's Prosperity and Economic Security. Responsibilities in this area include enforcing U.S. trade laws and facilitating lawful international trade and travel, safeguarding the U.S. transportation system, maintaining U.S. waterways and maritime resources, and safeguarding U.S. financial systems.
5. Strengthening Preparedness and Resilience. These responsibilities include developing a national culture of preparedness, incident response, support for community recovery, and training and exercising first responders.
6. Championing the DHS Workforce and Strengthening the Department. Goals in these areas involve steps to strengthen DHS management functions, increase integration, clarify roles and responsibilities, champion its workforce, advance risk-based decision-making, and promote transparency and accountability.

DHS STRUCTURE

The publicly available organizational chart of the DHS shows a department that consists of twenty-four separate offices, agencies, and administrations in addition to headquarters staff consisting of the Offices of the Chief of Staff, Chief Financial Officer, Chief Information Officer, Executive Secretary, and Military Adviser. Several of the important elements of the department are listed below to illustrate the range of the department's activities, including its missions that do not pertain to detecting, protecting against, responding to, and recovering from terrorist attacks:

Countering Weapons of Mass Destruction Office (CWMD). CWMD works to prevent attacks against the United States by actors using a weapon of mass destruction (WMD) through close cooperation with operational partners.

Cybersecurity and Infrastructure Security Agency (CISA). CISA works with partners to defend against today's threats and collaborates to build more secure and resilient infrastructure.

Federal Emergency Management Agency (FEMA). FEMA's mission statement is "to help people before, during, and after disasters." In addition to its direct role in support of disaster response, FEMA seeks to unify and further professionalize emergency management across the United States.

Federal Law Enforcement Training Centers (FLETC). The FLETC provides career-long training to law enforcement professionals to help them fulfill their responsibilities safely and proficiently.

Office for Civil Rights and Civil Liberties (CRCL). The CRCL supports DHS's mission to secure the nation while preserving individual liberty, fairness, and equality under the law.

Office of Intelligence and Analysis (I&A). I&A is DHS's dedicated intelligence office with the primary mission of equipping DHS with the intelligence and information it needs to keep the homeland safe, secure, and resilient. I&A is a member of the U.S. intelligence community (IC) and the only member charged with providing intelligence to state, local, tribal, and territorial (SLTT) governments as well as private sector actors.

Science and Technology Directorate (S&T). S&T's mission is "to enable effective, efficient, and secure operations across all homeland security missions by applying scientific, engineering, analytic, and innovative approaches to deliver timely solutions and support departmental acquisitions."

Transportation Security Administration (TSA). TSA's mission is to "protect the nation's transportation systems to ensure freedom of movement for people and commerce."

U.S. Citizenship and Immigration Services (USCIS). USCIS's mission is "to administer the nation's lawful immigration system, safeguarding its integrity and promise by efficiently and fairly adjudicating requests for immigration benefits while protecting Americans, securing the homeland, and honoring our values."

U.S. Coast Guard (USCG). The USCG's missions include ports, waterways, and coastal security; drug interdiction; migrant interdiction; marine safety; search and rescue; aids to navigation; living marine resources; marine environmental protection; and U.S. Immigration and Customs Enforcement (ICE) operations. The USCG is also a member of the IC.

U.S. Customs and Border Protection (CBP). CBP's mission statement is "to safeguard America's borders thereby protecting the public from dangerous people and materials while enhancing the Nation's global economic competitiveness by enabling legitimate trade and travel."

U.S. Immigration and Customs Enforcement (ICE). ICE's primary mission is "to promote homeland security and public safety through the criminal and civil enforcement of federal laws governing border control, customs, trade and immigration." These activities include the detection and dismantling of transnational criminal networks in the United States as well as ongoing U.S. government efforts to combat terrorism.

U.S. Secret Service. The Secret Service ensures the security of the president, vice president, their families, the White House, the vice president's residence, national and visiting world leaders, former presidents, and events of national significance. It also protects the integrity of the U.S. currency and investigates crimes against the U.S. financial system.

DHS CHALLENGES

DHS has wrestled with several difficult problems since its inception. While the department has made progress in these areas, there is still room for improvement. First, many of the agencies incorporated into DHS have missions not directly related to homeland security except under the broadest definition of the term. For example, the USCG conducts search and rescue at sea, marine safety, and ICE operations, and the U.S. Secret Service investigates cases of currency counterfeiting. DHS must allocate resources to effectively carry out these activities as well as those that align more directly with homeland security.

Second, merging twenty-two separate organizations into a new organizational structure and culture proved challenging. The sheer size of this undertaking was daunting. Many of the entities incorporated into DHS had existed for many years, were accustomed to operating autonomously, and had strong organizational cultures and illustrious histories. Many employees of these agencies did not welcome being part of a new and very large cabinet department, and forging a common DHS identity while preserving each organization's unique identities was difficult.

Third, many members of the IC did not welcome new DHS intelligence entities into the community but rather tried to protect and strengthen their own identities as the suppliers of homeland security intelligence. This caused delays in organizing an effective DHS intelligence capability.

Fourth, the new department required that existing sources of information be combined in new ways to provide homeland security–related intelligence. This blurred the then existing "wall" between domestic and foreign intelligence. In addition to being a difficult problem to sort out, civil liberties advocates criticized that this effort was being carried out in a way that violated American civil liberties, particularly in the area of privacy rights.

Additionally, developing effective risk analysis and management programs has proven very difficult. An initial effort to prioritize the nation's CI foundered on the extreme size of the endeavor and the fact that different states possessed very different CI and prioritized their CI differently. Later, it was found that trying to assess vulnerability was very difficult because it depended on the kinds of threats under consideration. This awareness meant that an effective risk assessment system needed to analyze many threats for each vulnerable asset. Furthermore, the fact that terrorists often change their attack plans meant that threat probabilities were subject to rapid change. The vast number of CI stakeholders also further complicated attempts to develop an effective risk analysis and management structure.

William J. Lahneman

See also: Critical Infrastructure as a Terrorist Target; Cyberattacks; Cybersecurity; Homeland Security Act of 2002; Intelligence Fusion Centers; Transportation Security; Weapons of Mass Destruction.

FURTHER READING

Department of Homeland Security. n.d.-a. "About DHS." Accessed October 11, 2020. https://www.dhs.gov/about-dhs

Department of Homeland Security. n.d.-b. "U.S. Department of Homeland Security Organizational Chart." Accessed April 18, 2022. https://www.dhs.gov/sites/default/files/publications/21_0402_dhs-organizational-chart.pdf

Edwards, Chris. 2014. "Make America Safer: Shut Down the Department of Homeland Security." CATO Institute, October 27, 2014. Accessed October 5, 2020. https://www.cato.org/publications/commentary/make-america-safer-shut-down-department-homeland-security

[Redacted]. 2005. *Homeland Security: Department Organization and Management—Implementation Phase*. CRS Report for Congress, January 3, 2005. Congressional Research Service. Accessed on October 11, 2020. https://www.everycrsreport.com/files/20050103_RL31751_4aad21b3861d88ec225804fc7d1d61c3932563ac.pdf

Department of State Bureau of Intelligence and Research (INR)

The collection and analysis of intelligence has always been one of the functions of the U.S. State Department, the cabinet department of the federal government charged with conducting diplomacy in support of U.S. foreign policy. U.S. embassies around the world continue to be important sources of intelligence about foreign affairs, including the intentions and plans of other states. Secretary of State George Marshall established the State Department Bureau of Intelligence and Research (INR) in 1947. INR is a direct descendant of the Office of Strategic Services (OSS) Research Department, making it the oldest civilian intelligence element in the U.S. government. It is one of the original members of the U.S. intelligence community (IC), which was established by the National Security Act of 1947. INR's primary mission is to harness intelligence to serve U.S. diplomacy.

INR performs three key activities. First, it is one of the IC's three "all-source" intelligence agencies, along with the Central Intelligence Agency (CIA) and the Defense Intelligence Agency (DIA). These agencies fuse self-produced intelligence with intelligence from other IC agencies as well as domestic and international partners to develop all-source, or "fusion," intelligence in response to intelligence requirements from the State Department and the National Intelligence Council (NIC) in the Office of the Director of National Intelligence (ODNI). The goal of fusing intelligence from as many collection sources as possible is to produce intelligence that compensates for the intelligence gaps and organizational biases that each IC agency may possess while capitalizing on the strengths of all IC members.

Second, INR is tasked with the important mission of coordinating between the State Department and IC members to ensure that U.S. intelligence, counterintelligence, and law enforcement activities are consistent with U.S. foreign policy interests.

Third, INR leads the IC in analytic outreach. INR's Analytic Exchange Program connects government analysts and policy makers with hundreds of outside experts from the private sector, academia, and other organizations to facilitate the exchange of information and perspectives on challenging foreign policy and intelligence issues.

Structurally, INR's analytic functions are divided into a number of regional and functional offices. Regional offices include the Offices of Analysis for African Affairs, East Asia and the Pacific, Europe, Near Eastern Affairs, Russia and Eurasia, South Asia, and the Western Hemisphere. Functional offices include offices devoted to Economic Analysis; Geography and Global Issues; Opinion Research; Strategic, Proliferation, and Military Issues; and Terrorism, Narcotics, and Crime.

INR is an important source of open-source intelligence on a number of global issues. Its intelligence products contribute to a number of the State Department's well-known and authoritative recurring reports that are available in the public domain. These include *Country Reports on Human Rights Practices*; *Country Reports on Terrorism*; *International Religious Freedom Reports*; *Trafficking in Persons Reports*; *Investment Climate Statements*; and *To Walk the Earth in Safety* (dealing with conventional weapons destruction programs).

William J. Lahneman

See also: Central Intelligence Agency; Defense Intelligence Agency; Director of National Intelligence; Homeland Security Act of 2002; Intelligence Fusion Centers; National Security Act of 1947.

FURTHER READING

Lowenthal, Mark M. 2017. *Intelligence: From Secrets to Policy.* 7th ed. Los Angeles: CQ Press.

U.S. Department of State. 2020a. "About Us—Bureau of Intelligence and Research." Accessed September 13, 2020. https://www.state.gov/about-us-bureau-of-intelli-gence-and-research/

U.S. Department of State. 2020b. "Department Reports and Publications." Accessed September 13, 2020. https://www.state.gov/department-reports/

Director of National Intelligence (DNI)

The director of national intelligence (DNI) serves as the head of the U.S. intelligence community (IC) by overseeing and directing the implementation of the National Intelligence Program (NIP) and acting as the principal adviser to the president for intelligence matters related to national and homeland security. The DNI also directly controls the Office of the Director of National Intelligence (ODNI). DNI candidates are nominated by the president and confirmed by the Senate.

The National Commission on Terrorist Attacks upon the United States, more commonly known as the 9/11 Commission, recommended that the position of DNI be created; the Intelligence Reform and Terrorism Prevention Act of 2004 (IRTPA) authorized this new position; and the first DNI, Ambassador John Negroponte, assumed duties in 2005. Prior to this time, a director of central intelligence (DCI) coordinated the IC, acted as the president's principal intelligence adviser, and served as director of the Central Intelligence Agency (CIA). IRTPA replaced the DCI with two positions: the DNI, who would perform the coordination and advisory functions, and a director of the CIA (DCIA), who would be responsible for running the CIA. The rationale behind these actions was that the DCI's duties were too extensive and diluted his ability to perform all three functions well. Dividing the DCI's duties between the DNI with enhanced powers and the DCIA was intended to correct this problem.

The DNI's ability to oversee and direct the IC stems from three main sources. First, the DNI's control of NIP budgetary allocations is an important lever of power for coordinating the activities of the seventeen agencies that currently comprise the IC. The U.S. intelligence budget is divided into two categories, the NIP and the Military Intelligence Program (MIP). The DNI is only responsible for the NIP, which includes programs that either affect more than one agency or are nondefense in nature. In 2016, the NIP ($53.3 billion) was about three times larger than the MIP ($16.8 billion).

Second, the DNI's role as principal intelligence adviser to the president and the National Security Council imparts authority to coordinate the IC to the degree that the president empowers the DNI and relies on its products.

Third, the DNI has direct authority over the following organizations that contribute to the independence and power of the position: the Office of the Director of National Intelligence (ODNI); the National Counterterrorism Center (NCTC); the National Counterproliferation Center (NCPC); the Cyber Threat Intelligence Coordination Center (CTIIC); the National Counterintelligence and Security Center(NCSC); the Intelligence Advanced Research Projects Activity (IARPA); and the National Intelligence Council (NIC). All of these entities are staffed by analysts and other specialists from various IC agencies.

Both IRTPA and the National Security Act of 1947 provide the DNI with a number of authorities and duties, including requirements to

- Provide timely and objective national intelligence to the president, senior managers of the executive branch, the chairman of the Joint Chiefs of Staff and senior military commanders, and the Congress.
- Establish objectives and priorities for collection, analysis, production, and dissemination of national intelligence.
- Ensure maximum availability of and access to intelligence information within the IC.
- Develop and ensure the execution of the NIP based on budget proposals provided by IC component organizations.
- Oversee coordination of relationships with the intelligence or security services of foreign governments and international organizations.
- Ensure the use of all sources of intelligence to develop the most accurate analysis of intelligence to support national security needs.
- Develop personnel policies and programs to enhance the capacity for joint operations and to facilitate staffing of community management functions.
- Oversee the development and implementation of a program management plan for acquisition of major intelligence systems.

William J. Lahneman

See also: Defense Intelligence Agency; Intelligence Reform and Terrorism Prevention Act of 2004; National Security Act of 1947.

FURTHER READING

DeVine, Michael E. 2019. *The Director of National Intelligence (DNI).* Washington, DC: Congressional Research Service.

Lowenthal, Mark M. 2019. *Intelligence: From Secrets to Policy*. 8th ed. Washington, DC: CQ Press.
National Commission on Terrorist Attacks upon the United States. 2004. *The 9/11 Commission Report: Final Report of the National Commission on Terrorist Attacks upon the United States*. New York: W. W. Norton and Company.
Office of the Director of National Intelligence website. www.dni.gov

Dirty Bombs

The term *dirty bomb* (also known as a radiological dispersal device, or RDD) refers to the use of nuclear waste or fissile material to cause mass casualties in cases where it is impossible or impractical to use a fully functional nuclear weapon. Dirty bombs became a watchword for terrorism and homeland security experts most directly after the September 11 attacks, particularly when Jose Padilla, an al-Qaeda operative, was apprehended in Chicago and convicted for plotting an attack involving the use of radioactive material.

The end of the Cold War raised concerns about the disposition of the former Soviet nuclear arsenal, which appeared to be both poorly secured and spread across the former Soviet territories. One stream of thought was that a terrorist group might acquire one or more of these weapons for use against the United States. However what if the group lacked the technical proficiency to operate such a weapon or only had access to radioactive materials with a refinement level too low to make a traditional atomic bomb? It is from those questions that the concept of the dirty bomb arose.

A dirty bomb is any device that has as its intent the spread of radiological material against a target without enacting a complete nuclear ignition process or the achievement of a critical mass nuclear explosion. Whereas a nuclear or thermonuclear device relies on the blast and heat released by the explosion for its primary effects (with the spread of radiation as a secondary and often redundant effect), RDDs have as their primary impact the health-damaging spread of radioactive material. While both types of devices utilize conventional triggers, the similarity ends there. RDDs are considered much easier to make than nuclear weapons because of this distinction. Rather than a Manhattan Project, all that is needed to create a dirty bomb is industrial- or even medical-level radioactive particles married to a conventional explosive device.

The fundamental purposes of an RDD are the denial of access to the area of the detonation and the creation of terror; because radiation is invisible, RDDs are the perfect weapons for this. They are most effective when used against unprotected civilian targets, as any conceivable military target could mitigate the impact of an RDD through retiring to a vehicle or location with proper ventilation systems or by donning protective gear. For this reason, RDDs are sometimes classified as *weapons of mass disruption*—rather than weapons of mass destruction, or WMDs—focusing on the public's fear of the prompt (radiation sickness) and enduring (increase in cancers) effects of exposure to high doses of ionizing radiation. The panic that would ensue could meet the goals of terrorists in numerous ways, both in denying access to key areas and in spreading anxiety and panic.

Dirty bombs have never been utilized; however, the possibility of their use remains one of the chief threats considered by the U.S. Department of Homeland

Security. DHS looks at a particular isotope, cesium-137. Easy to spread, cesium-137 mimics potassium in the body and causes significant burns, while also binding well to stone and concrete. These factors make it a likely isotope for an RDD, and it is used in the National Planning Scenarios by which DHS plans for exercise funding. Dirty bombs rank with the use of improvised or military-grade nuclear weapons as the most powerful potential tools in the hands of terrorists and remain a grave concern to U.S. counterterrorist and intelligence institutions.

John M. Callahan

See also: Internet as a Virtual School for Terrorism; Weapons of Mass Destruction.

FURTHER READING

Federal Emergency Management Agency. 2006. *National Planning Scenarios: Created for Use in National, Federal, State, and Local Homeland Security Preparedness Activities.* Accessed December 1, 2019. https://info.publicintelligence.net/DHS%20-%20National%20Planning%20Scenarios%20March%202006.pdf

Lichtblau, Eric, Bob Drogin, and Josh Meyer. 2002. "U.S. Citizen Accused of Planning an Attack Using a 'Dirty' Bomb." *Los Angeles Times*, June 11, 2002.

RANE/Stratfor. 2006. "Dirty Bombs: Weapons of Mass Disruption." Accessed on December 3, 2019. https://worldview.stratfor.com/article/dirty-bombs-weapons-mass-disruption

U.S. Nuclear Regulatory Commission. 2018. "Backgrounder on Dirty Bombs." Accessed on December 5, 2019. https://www.nrc.gov/reading-rm/doc-collections/fact-sheets/fs-dirty-bombs.html

Domestic Terrorism, Anarchists

Anarchism is a political philosophy that supports the idea of a stateless society composed of voluntary institutions and absent the hierarchy found in other political models of governance. The many theoretical forms of anarchy occupy a spectrum from extreme individualism to complete collectivism. The use of violence to overthrow a government or change people's perspective of the need for government falls in the anarchist political sphere, as is the promotion of chaos. Hence, a popular symbol of anarchist groups is the letter *A* (for anarchy) inside a circle. Those proponents of anarchism who challenge the ruling government in an established society with the use of violence are domestic terrorists. Due to the etymology of anarchy, there is a belief that anarchism is a system that has no formal rules.

Pierre-Joseph Proudhon, a French political philosopher who lived in the nineteenth century, is the father of modern anarchy, having influenced movements around Europe. France and Russia experienced numerous attacks by anarchists in the late nineteenth and early twentieth centuries, including the assassinations of Czar Alexander II of Russia, President Sadi Carnot of France, Empress Elisabeth of Austria, King Umberto I of Italy, King Carlos I of Portugal, and King George I of Greece.

In the United States, Leon Czolgosz, an anarchist sympathizer, assassinated President William McKinley in 1901. At approximately the same time, Luigi Galleani, an Italian American, and his followers (Galleanists) sought to disrupt American democracy by conducting a series of bomb attacks in the early twentieth century. Modern scholars of terrorism have referred to nineteenth-century anarchists as the first global terrorists.

During the counterculture era in the United States, in 1971, William Powell promoted violence in his infamous book *The Anarchist Cookbook*. Written as part of his active protest of the U.S. military activity in Vietnam, *The Anarchist Cookbook* provided guidance on how to manufacture explosives, weapons, and controlled substances. Powell later tried, unsuccessfully, to have his book removed from publication. Over the years, many jurisdictions have examined the legality of selling the book. Despite the popularity of the book, many anarchists distanced themselves from it, claiming it did not align with anarchist political philosophy.

Although the use of violence is not an essential element of anarchism (Tolstoy called for the promotion of anarchism through pacifism), the crossroads of anarchism and violence result in a phenomenon referred to as the *propaganda of the deed*, and execution of the "deed" often involves terrorist acts and the assassination of political leaders.

Today, the use of violence by anarchists is considered a form of domestic terrorism by the Federal Bureau of Investigation (FBI). Included in the FBI's definition of *anarchist extremism* are individuals and groups that promote the ideologies of anti-capitalism, anti-globalization, anti-urbanization, and green anarchism—an element of anarchism that works in conjunction with environmental extremism. The *anarchist*, therefore, is a person that uses criminal tactics to promote his or her ideology of fighting against the established political order.

The success of contemporary anarchist activity is often measured against the actions of the extremists who disrupted the 1999 World Trade Organization meetings in Seattle, Washington. The event was the first significant mobilization of protestors using the Internet to attract and broadcast their disagreement with perceived human rights failures due to free trade and globalization. Anarchists view the injuries to law enforcement personnel, damage to property, and the protest's negative impact on the economy as significant political statements.

The surge in populist movements throughout the globe in the early twenty-first century has seen subsets of anarchy grow in the United States. The use of social media has facilitated the footprint of anti-fascist groups like Antifa that use violence against far-right extremists.

Don Mason, Ygnacio "Nash" Flores, and Tracy E. Rickman

See also: Antifa; Sociology of Terrorism; Wall Street Bombing.

FURTHER READING

Falk, Gerhard. 2012. *Assassination, Anarchy, And Terrorism*. Boulder, CO: University Press of America.

FBI. 2010. "Domestic Terrorism: Anarchist Extremism: A Primer." https://archives.fbi.gov/archives/news/stories/2010/november/anarchist_111610/anarchist_111610

Murphy, Philip. 2017. *Anarchist Extremists; Antifa*. State of New Jersey Office of Homeland Security and Preparedness. https://www.njhomelandsecurity.gov/analysis/anarchist-extremists-antifa

Powell, W. 1971/2002. *The Anarchist Cookbook*. El Dorado: Ozark Press.

Woodcock, G. 2004/2009. *Anarchism*. Toronto: University of Toronto Press.

Domestic Terrorism, Anti-Semitic

The Anti-Defamation League (ADL), a Jewish civil rights and human relations organization, defines *anti-Semitism* as beliefs and behaviors that are hostile toward Jews simply because they are Jewish. As the ADL states on its website, anti-Semitism "may take the form of religious teachings that proclaim the inferiority of Jews, for instance, or political efforts to isolate, oppress, or otherwise injure them. It may also include prejudiced or stereotyped views about Jews."

Historical themes asserting anti-Semitism have fallen into three pejorative narratives. The first is the belief that Jews were responsible for killing Jesus Christ. Complementing this theme is that Jews followed the medieval practice of blood libel, which purported that Jews used the blood of non-Jewish children to make Passover bread. Another pernicious falsehood embraced by some anti-Semites is that Jews maintain a secret society that is intent on ruling the world. This conspiracy is captured most famously in *The Protocols of the Elders of Zion*, a book first published in 1903 in Russia that offers a fraudulent account of a Jewish plan for global domination. The final theme of anti-Semitism is that Jews exploit the Holocaust to gain concessions not afforded to other religions, races, or cultures. These themes continue to serve as catalysts for anti-Semitic views and actions that have led to hate and violence against people of Jewish faith and heritage.

Anti-Semitic activities fall under the category of hate crimes. The United States Code defines *hate crimes* as "offenses involving actual or perceived race, color, religion, or national origin." A hate crime goes beyond the definitions of traditional offenses by having the additional element of bias as part of the criminal act. Currently, forty-five states impose a penalty enhancement for crimes motivated by religious ideology.

By most estimates, hate crimes are increasing in the United States. Some reports, like that of the ADL, indicate the incidents of anti-Semitism have increased each year in the twenty-first century. On October 27, 2018, the deadliest attack against an American synagogue took place in Pittsburgh, Pennsylvania, killing eleven people and wounding six others. Authorities arrested and charged the attacker, Robert D. Bowers, with forty-four federal counts in the massacre at the Tree of Life Synagogue as well as thirty-six counts in state court. Bowers's murder spree was designated a hate crime.

Lost in the reporting methodologies of law enforcement agencies is that many hate activities go unreported as crimes. Mirroring this social practice is coverage in the media that downplays many anti-Semitic activities as perceived by the Jewish Telegraphic Agency.

Many white supremacist groups find shelter in the U.S. Constitution's First Amendment that guarantees the right to freedom of speech to promote their ideology, including that of anti-Semitism. In the United States, anti-Semitism is a significant part of racist conspiracies that shape white supremacist extremists, in particular, the belief that a secretive Zionist Occupied Government (ZOG) controls the United States. This viewpoint extends to other state governments in the claim that there is an international effort to promote Jewish interests.

After President Donald Trump took office in 2017, some political observers and many Jewish groups expressed concern that some of his rhetoric included anti-Semitic elements. These critics worry that such statements may encourage white supremacists to act on their anti-Semitic beliefs with acts of violence and terror.

Tracy E. Rickman, Ygnacio "Nash" Flores, and Don Mason

See also: Domestic Terrorism, White Supremacists; Domestic Terrorist Groups; Ku Klux Klan.

FURTHER READING

Anti-Defamation League. n.d. "Anti-Semitism." https://www.adl.org/anti-semitism

Anti-Defamation League. 2018. *Audit of Anti-Semitic Incidents: Year in Review 2017.* New York: ADL.

Cohen, Richard. 2017. "SPLC to Homeland Security Committee: Focus on Domestic Terrorism from the Radical Right." Southern Poverty Law Center, November 30, 2017. https://www.splcenter.org/news/2017/11/30/splc-homeland-security-committee-focus-domestic-terrorism-radical-right

The Economist. 2018. "Anti-Semitism in the West: Jew-Hatred Keeps Mutating to Survive: Lessons from the Pittsburgh Massacre." November 1, 2018.

FBI. "What We Investigate: Hate Crimes." https://www.fbi.gov/investigate/civil-rights/hate-crimes

Lipstadt, Deborah E. 2019. *Anti-Semitism: Here and Now.* New York: Schocken Books.

Nilus, Sergei. 1906/2015. *Protocols of the Elders of Zion.* Princeton, NJ: Eulenspiegel Press.

Sales, Ben. 2021. *The IHRA Definition of Anti-Semitism and Why People Are Fighting over It, Explained.* Jewish Telegraphic Agency, January 15, 2021. https://www.jta.org/2021/01/15/global/the-ihra-definition-of-anti-semitism-and-why-people-are-fighting-over-it-explained

Domestic Terrorism, Pre-1950 Activity

Long before the attacks of September 11, 2001, created a broad social awareness of terrorism as a security threat, the violence associated with the civil rights struggle of the 1950s and 1960s, radical opponents of the Vietnam War, lone-wolf terrorists like Ted Kaczynski, and the bombing of the Oklahoma City Federal Building had alerted the country to the menace within.

Before 1950, however, instances that likely would be described as at least borderline terrorism today were often dismissed as simply lamentable criminal acts, even though gang warfare during the Prohibition era did not spare civilians caught in the crossfire any more so than today's gangs bent on controlling the drug trade in their sectors of American cities. Likewise, it was a "disgruntled" failed office seeker angered by a township property tax increase, not a terrorist, who committed what is still the worst attack on a school in U.S. history, the 1927 bombing of the Bath Consolidated School in Michigan that killed forty-four and injured another fifty-eight.

In retrospect, though, three categories of pre-1950 violence clearly qualify for being characterized as politically motivated terrorism: the murders and bombings committed by anarchists seeking to destroy the political order; anti-Semitic, anti-Catholic, and racist violence against American citizens; and state violence in support of capitalists facing union activists.

Anarchism's origins are European, but by the late nineteenth century, it had a transatlantic presence, anarchists having successfully assassinated a Russian czar, two Spanish premiers, a French president, an Italian king, and President William McKinley over three decades, beginning in 1880. The person who shot McKinley on September 6, 1901, and was executed a month later offered little justification except that McKinley was an "enemy of the people." McKinley's assassination, however, was consistent with the ultimate goal of anarchism: to disrupt politics in general and democracy in particular.

Anarchists' major foothold in the United States involved infiltrating the unionist movement emerging at that time. The appeal of anarchists to those seeking to organize labor in the late nineteenth and early twentieth centuries in the United States can partly be traced to the violent reception they often encountered from elected officials willing to use force to defend their capitalist backers. For example, President Cleveland had used federal troops to end the Pullman Strike in 1894, with resultant violence breaking out in several American cities. Most infamously, twenty years later, the governor of Colorado called out the National Guard to assist his company guards in ending the strike by coal miners in Ludlow. When the confrontation ended, twenty-five miners and family members, including eleven children, were dead. Twenty years later, the American labor movement's legitimacy was established when the leader of the coal miners' union brought organized labor into the Democratic Party coalition supporting President Franklin Roosevelt.

Meanwhile, from the time of its founding in 1865 until World War II, the Ku Klux Klan, a self-defined white Christian organization, was actively using political violence against outsiders. The only exception was the brief period between the U.S. Supreme Court's decision in the 1896 *Plessy* case that provided a constitutional basis for segregating the races until World War I, when the violent intimidation of Black Americans seemed less necessary. The influx of immigrant Jews and Catholics into the country as well as the Great Migration of Black southerners to the Midwest after World War I, however, spurred a second wave of growing KKK influence, which included the election of numerous local and state officials with Klan backing. By World War II, however, internal scandals had undermined its image and influence, and its activities faded until being reborn in the civil rights movement of the 1950s.

Joseph R. Rudolph Jr.

See also: Bath School Bombing; Haymarket Affair; Ku Klux Klan; Domestic Terrorism, Anarchists; Domestic Terrorism, White Supremacists; State Terrorism.

FURTHER READING

Cornell, Andrew. 2016. *Unruly Equality: U.S. Anarchism in the Twentieth Century.* Berkeley: University of California Press.

Gage, Beverly. 2009. *The Day Wall Street Exploded: A Story of America in It First Age of Terror.* New York: Oxford University Press.

Gordon, Linda. 2018. *The Second Coming of the KKK: The Ku Klux Klan of the 1920s and the American Political Tradition.* New York: Liveright Publishing.

Taity, Stephen. 2017. *The Black Hand: The Epic War between a Brilliant Detective and the Deadliest Secret Society in American History.* Boston: Mariner Books Reprint.
Zimmer, Kenyon. 2015. *Immigrants against the State: Yiddish and Italian Anarchism in America.* Champaign: University of Illinois Press.

Domestic Terrorism, the Civil Rights Era

The civil rights movement, which swept across the United States in the 1950s and 1960s, was an exceptionally transformative force in American domestic politics, pushing the nation to confront its racist past and laws and work toward building a society marked by greater racial equality. This volatile political climate, however, ignited fanaticism among white supremacist groups like the Ku Klux Klan (KKK), which used violence to intimidate civil right activists and impede progress toward legal, social, and political equality. While white supremacist terrorism was prevalent throughout the era, the years leading up to and immediately following the enactment of the Civil Rights Act of 1964 marked the period of its greatest intensity. Examining key cases of domestic terrorism during those years provides insight into how responses to acts of racially motivated terrorism changed over time and how they relate to counterterrorism strategies today.

MURDER OF MEDGAR EVERS (JACKSON, MISSISSIPPI)

One of the first high-profile cases of civil rights terrorism was the murder of Medgar Evers, a distinguished civil rights activist serving as the field secretary at the Mississippi office of the National Association for the Advancement of Colored People (NAACP) at the time of his death. During his career, Evers had investigated several high-profile cases, including that of Emmett Till, a fourteen-year-old African American teen who was tortured and murdered in Mississippi in 1955 for allegedly being flirtatious with a white woman (the identities of Till's killers were well known, but they were acquitted by an all-white jury). Consequently, Evers had received numerous death threats before his murder early in the morning of June 12, 1963, upon returning home from a long day at the NAACP office advocating for repeal of Jim Crow laws.

The local police department leading the investigation quickly found the rifle used in the killing and submitted the fingerprints on it to the Federal Bureau of Investigation (FBI) for analysis. The FBI matched the prints to those of Bryson De La Beckwith, a fervent white supremacist and member of the KKK. Due to Evers's prominence in the civil rights movement, his murder was politically symbolic and designed to instill fear in the broader community of civil rights activists. In 1964, Beckwith was tried twice for Evers's murder; each trial resulted in a mistrial by an all-white, all-male hung jury.

Although the federal government's involvement in the investigation was minimal, this case provides context for examining its response to later acts of terrorism during the civil rights era. For one, the case of Medgar Evers signaled the effectiveness of the FBI in identifying suspects, but it also highlighted the corruption of local law enforcement and bias in local judicial processes across the Jim Crow South.

In 1994, the case was reopened after documents from the Mississippi State Sovereignty Commission were uncovered, indicating that the defendant's lawyers had illegally screened the jurors in Beckwith's previous trials. In the 1994 trial, the original evidence was used along with testimony from new witnesses who testified that Beckwith had since bragged about killing Evers. This time, a more gender- and race-diverse jury convicted Beckwith of murder, and he was sentenced to life in prison.

The 1994 retrial of Beckwith demonstrated the value of revisiting cases of race-motivated terrorism to hold perpetrators accountable. The success of the justice system in the Evers case contributed to the enactment of the Emmitt Till Act of 2008, which provided for reopening cases of civil rights era terrorism that had been derailed by racist authorities and juries when they had first been investigated or tried in court.

SIXTEENTH STREET BAPTIST CHURCH BOMBING (BIRMINGHAM, ALABAMA)

Three months after Evers's death, on September 15, 1963, the Sixteenth Street Baptist Church in Birmingham, Alabama, was hosting Sunday school when twenty sticks of dynamite laid against its walls exploded. Four young African American girls died in the explosion, and twenty-three other members of the African American church were injured. The church was targeted because it was a landmark of Birmingham's civil rights movement and had been a meeting place for many of the city's civil rights protests and demonstrations. Four suspects were identified as having planned and executed the attacks: Bobby Frank Cherry, Thomas Blanton, Robert Chambliss, and Herman Frank Cash, each of whom was affiliated with the KKK. However, due to a lack of witnesses willing to testify, no charges were filed against them at the time.

Following the bombing, protests erupted in the city that produced violent clashes between citizens and police officers and ultimately resulted in the deaths of two African American men. Despite the lack of attention given to the case by the local and federal governments, the attack intensified the push for racial equality by civil rights workers in the southern United States.

It was later discovered that the FBI had intelligence related to the identity of the perpetrators but never acted on the information. As a result, the case was reopened in 1977, and Robert Chambliss was convicted for participating in the attack. Two other suspects, Thomas Blanton and Bobby Frank Cherry, were convicted in 2001 and 2002, respectively, for their roles in the crime. All received life sentences. The fourth suspect, Herman Frank Cash, died before he could be brought to trial.

MISSISSIPPI BURNING (PHILADELPHIA, MISSISSIPPI)

One of the infamous and pivotal domestic terrorism events of the civil rights era was the 1964 murder in Philadelphia, Mississippi, of activists James Chaney,

Michael Schwerner, and Andrew Goodman by white supremacists. This dark event came to be known as the Mississippi Burning murders. In the summer of 1964, the three victims were working as civil rights activists for the Congress of Racial Equality (CORE) to improve access to voter registration for African Americans. This work was violently opposed by white supremacist groups, particularly the KKK in Mississippi, which included several members of local law enforcement. Shortly after the CORE workers visited Mount Zion Methodist Church in June 1964, Sam Bowers, the leader of the Mississippi chapter of the KKK, ordered the murder of Michael Schwerner. Following Bower's speech, Klan members ambushed a meeting at Mount Zion Methodist Church, assaulted members of the congregation, and set the church on fire.

When Chaney and Schwerner heard the news, they decided to travel back to Mississippi, along with their colleague Andrew Goodman, to meet with members of the congregation. After visiting the church, as the three men were driving back to CORE headquarters in Meridian, Mississippi, their vehicle was pulled over by Neshoba County Deputy Cecil Price, and all three men were arrested. They were reportedly released from the Philadelphia jail after being detained six hours; however, they were never seen alive again. The later confessions of Klan members Horace Doyle Barnette and James Jordan revealed that while the three were in custody, Deputy Price called Edgar Killen, a Baptist minister and member of the local Klan, and asked him to organize a group of Klansmen to ambush the activists. After Deputy Price released the three men, two cars of Klansmen chased them down, murdered them, and buried their bodies in a dam on Old Jolly Farm.

In stark contrast to the prior cases, the disappearance of the three civil rights workers attracted major national media coverage, and the response of the federal government to the attack was much more extensive. Researchers and commentators on the case have heavily implied that one of the reasons for the elevated concern was that two of the three victims were white.

After hearing of the disappearance of the three men, the federal government immediately launched a formal investigation. Attorney General Robert F. Kennedy announced that the case would be treated as a kidnapping, thereby guaranteeing a federal presence in the investigation. Shortly thereafter, the Department of Justice requested the assistance of the FBI, which subsequently led the investigation. Over 200 FBI agents traveled to Mississippi to work on the case. During the investigation, President Lyndon Johnson ordered the establishment of an FBI field office in Jackson, Mississippi, which opened on July 10, 1964.

On August 4, 1964, the bodies were found buried on Old Jolly Farm. Despite the abundance of evidence uncovered by the FBI, the State of Mississippi declined to bring murder charges against the men who committed the crime. The federal government, however, charged eighteen Klan members involved in the crime with having conspired to violate the activists' civil rights.

The murders of Chaney, Schwerner, and Goodman also caused the FBI to expand the scope of its Counterintelligence Program (COINTELPRO). Initiated in 1956, the program's original purpose was to gather information and disrupt the activities of the Communist Party of the United States of America. Following the Mississippi Burning murders, however, the FBI expanded its directive on

September 2, 1964, to include "white hate groups" and listed seventeen white supremacist groups for counterintelligence action, including two groups based in Mississippi: the White Knights of the KKK of Mississippi and the Mississippi Knights of the KKK.

PROTESTS IN SELMA, ALABAMA

Although the Mississippi Burning murders are often considered the landmark terrorism case of civil rights era, attacks against African American civil rights leaders intensified after the signing of the Civil Rights Act of 1964. The murder of Jimmie Lee Jackson in 1965 was a galvanizing moment for the civil rights movement and became a driving force behind the famous March 1965 civil rights marches in Alabama from Selma to Montgomery.

In February 1965, in Marion, Alabama, twenty-six-year-old African American activist Jimmie Lee Jackson was participating in a peaceful protest along with his mother and grandfather at Zion Methodist Church when white Alabama state troopers violently disrupted the protest by beating participants with clubs and nightsticks. Trying to escape the violence, Jackson ran with his grandfather and mother into a nearby café. However, two state troopers followed them and attacked Jackson's mother. When Jackson attempted to shield his mother from the officers, they threw him against the wall, and Officer Bonard Fowler shot him twice. He then staggered into the street, where the two troopers continued to beat him. He died eight days later.

The State of Alabama initially investigated the case with assistance from the FBI. In September 1965, a grand jury declined to indict Officer Fowler. The case was reopened in 2007 pursuant to the Department of Justice's Cold Case Initiative, which later became known as the Emmett Till Unsolved Civil Rights Crime Act of 2008. In his testimony, Fowler asserted that he acted in self-defense and claimed that Jackson had attacked him with a glass bottle. However, none of the civilian witnesses of the event corroborated this account. In 2010, Fowler pleaded guilty to misdemeanor manslaughter and was sentenced to six months in jail.

FIREBOMBING IN HATTIESBURG, MISSISSIPPI

One final case that demonstrates the evolution of government responses to terrorism in the civil rights era is the firebombing of civil rights activist Vernon Dahmer's house on January 10, 1966. Dahmer was the former president of the Forrest County chapter of the NAACP in Hattiesburg, Mississippi, and a public advocate for African American voting rights.

In the days preceding the attack, the local radio station announced that Dahmer's grocery store would be one of the few places in the area that African Americans could register to vote and pay poll taxes. Late on the night of January 10, while Dahmer and his family were asleep, members of the White Knights—a KKK organization founded in Mississippi and Louisiana in the early 1960s—poured gasoline on Dahmer's house, ignited it, and shot rounds of gunfire into the house to prevent the family from escaping. Dahmer returned fire using a shotgun while his wife and daughter ran out of the back of the house. While Vernon Dahmer was also able to escape the fire, he died later that day due to severe burns.

The FBI field office in Meridian, Mississippi, which had been installed by the federal government in response to the Mississippi Burning murders, immediately launched a thorough investigation. As in the case of the Mississippi Burning murders, the level of attention given to the Dahmer case is often attributed to the fact that Dahmer was white. The FBI's expeditious investigation resulted in thirteen members of the Mississippi White Knights being arrested within twenty-four hours, and Sam Bowers, the leader of the white supremacists that committed the Mississippi Burning murders, turned himself in for his role in Dahmer's murder several days later. However, out of the fourteen individuals charged for participating in Dahmer's murder, only four were found guilty. Other trials resulted in hung juries or acquittals, largely due to acts of jury tampering and bribery carried out by the Mississippi White Knights. Likewise, Bowers was tried three times in the 1960s for his involvement in Dahmer's murder, with each trial ending with a hung jury. However, in the 1990s, the case was reopened, and in 1996, Bowers was convicted of having ordered and organized Dahmer's killing. He received a life sentence.

CONCLUSION

The response of government officials, law enforcement, and the media to instances of white supremacist terrorism during the civil rights era of the 1950s and 1960s was often muted and inconsistent. These cases, however, highlight two primary legal responses that took shape over this period. One of the most significant was the growing involvement of the FBI, underscored by the expansion of COINTELPRO following the Mississippi Burning murders. A second official government response came decades later with the enactment of the Emmett Till Unsolved Civil Rights Crime Act of 2008, previously known as the Department of Justice's Cold Case Initiative, which reopened cases from the civil rights era in which there was an unfair or biased trial. The tendency to increase avenues of federal government involvement in response to acts of terrorism is also prevalent today and continues to be controversial.

Mackenzie Rice

See also: Aryan Nations; Charleston Church Massacre; Domestic Terrorism, White Supremacists; Domestic Terrorist Groups; Ku Klux Klan.

FURTHER READING

Anderson, S. Willoughby. 2007. "The Past on Trial: Birmingham, the Bombing, and Restorative Justice." *California Law Review* 96 (2): 471–504. http://www.jstor.org/stable/20439181

Department of Justice. 2016. "Trial Transcripts in the Case *United States v. Price, et al.* (Also Known as the 'Mississippi Burning' Incident)." Accessed July 29, 2018. https://www.justice.gov/crt/trial-transcripts-caseunited-states-v-price-et-al-also-known-mississippi-burning-incident-1967

FBI. 1964. *Freedom of Information and Privacy Acts, Subject: COINTELPRO.* Accessed July 28, 2018. https://vault.fbi.gov/cointel-pro/White%20Hate%20Groups/white-hate-groups-part-01-of-14/view

FBI. 2007. "A Byte Out of History: Mississippi Burning." Accessed July 25, 2018. https://archives.fbi.gov/archives/news/stories/2007/february/miburn_022607

Richardson, Christopher M. 2014. *Historical Dictionary of Civil Rights Movement.* Lanham, MD: Rowman & Littlefield.

Swanson, Craig. 2014. *The Selma Campaign: Martin Luther King Jr., Jimmie Lee Jackson, and the Defining Struggle of the Civil Rights Era.* Bloomington, IN: Archway Publishing.

Domestic Terrorism, the Vietnam Era

The Federal Bureau of Investigation (FBI) defines *domestic terrorism* as "violent, criminal acts committed by individuals and/or groups to further ideological goals stemming from domestic influences, such as those of a political, religious, social, racial, or environmental nature." The acutely controversial Vietnam War created a ripe social and political environment within the United States for domestic terrorism. Political violence in the Vietnam era grew out of the antiwar, Marxist-Leninist–inspired social movement in the United States termed the "New Left," which was not fundamentally violent in nature but from which violent factions arose. Prominent New Left organizations included the Black Panther Party for Self-Defense, the Students for a Democratic Society (SDS), the Weather Underground Organization (WUO) (originally known as the Weathermen), and the Symbionese Liberation Army (SLA).

The Black Panther Party (BPP) was formed in Oakland, California, in 1966 as the Black power movement began to take shape in response to violent reactions against the peaceful civil rights movement. By 1968, the organization boasted more than 2,000 members and forty chapters nationwide and had become the face of the Black power movement. The Black Panthers became notable in their early years for their militant street demonstrations and anti-police rhetoric and were active through the late 1970s. By the mid-1970s the organization had dialed down the militancy as a result of a severe FBI crackdown against its leadership. Former members organized the Black Liberation Army in 1970, which was responsible for numerous bombings, bank robberies, and the murders of at least thirteen police officers. It is worth noting, however, that in the ensuing decades, many scholars and journalists have come to dispute the BPP as terrorist narrative and have noted that the FBI and local police departments may have framed BPP members.

The Students for a Democratic Society (SDS) was founded in June 1962 at a small convention in Port Huron, Michigan. The organization's primary function eventually became protesting U.S. involvement in Vietnam and supporting the Black power movement. By 1968, the SDS had become more militant and was responsible for dozens of disturbances on college campuses, including a seizure of Columbia University that ended in a riot and hundreds of arrests and a later strike that closed the university. In 1969, the SDS split into three factions, the most prominent of which was the WUO.

The Weathermen openly advocated bombings and assassinations and participated in jailbreaks, vandalism, and street fights with the Chicago police in their "Days of Rage." In March 1970, an explosion in a townhouse bomb factory in New York City killed three Weathermen. The rest of the organization went underground and renamed themselves the WUO. Members of the WUO were responsible for at least forty bombings, with targets including the Pentagon, police stations, and ROTC buildings, among others.

The Symbionese Liberation Army (SLA) was active from 1973 to 1975 outside San Francisco, California. Under the leadership of Donald DeFreeze, the SLA was a violent group that advocated against racism, colonialism, and capitalism, among other leftist issues. The SLA took credit for the 1973 assassination of the Oakland school superintendent, and in February 1974, the group kidnapped Patricia "Patty" Hearst, who two months later participated in an SLA bank robbery. The SLA was also responsible for several bombings in California in 1975.

In addition to the anti-war protests and related domestic terror organizations, the era also saw the assassination of President John F. Kennedy, his brother and presidential candidate Robert F. Kennedy, and civil rights icon Martin Luther King Jr. There was violent pushback across the country toward civil rights activists. The Vietnam era, especially when coupled with burgeoning civil rights movements based on race, gender, and sexual preferences, was among the most contentious and violent in U.S. history.

Brooke Thompson and Tobias T. Gibson

See also: Domestic Terrorism, the Civil Rights Era; Domestic Terrorist Groups; Police Officers as Terrorist Targets.

FURTHER READING

FBI. n.d. "Terrorism." https://www.fbi.gov/investigate/terrorism

Loadenthal, Michael. 2018. "Leftist Political Violence: From Terrorism to Social Protest." In *Terrorism in America*, edited by Robin Maria Valeri and Kevin Borgeson, 36–74. Abingdon, England: Routledge.

Martin, G. 2018. *Understanding Terrorism: Challenges, Perspectives, and Issues*. 6th ed. Los Angeles: SAGE Publications.

Williams, Yohuru R. 1998. "In the Name of the Law: The 1967 Shooting of Huey Newton and Law Enforcement's Permissive Environment." *Negro History Bulletin* 61 (2): 6–18.

Domestic Terrorism, White Supremacists

Right-wing terrorism is driven by white supremacist ideologies that include neo-Nazism, neofascism, anti-communism, nationalism, anti-Semitism, and Islamophobia. While the Federal Bureau of Investigation (FBI) does not list domestic terrorist organizations, it has identified white supremacy as an ideology that is related to criminal activity.

White supremacy, as a political ideology, holds that traditional practices of institutionalizing white hegemony in Western society be maintained and strengthened.

Declared confirmation of the supremacy of white people draws from a history of European expansion, colonialization, the slave trade in America, and apartheid in South Africa. These historical patterns promote the political and socioeconomic privileges that lead to institutionalized structural advantages for white people over minorities.

While ideological approaches to white supremacy differ, the core of the philosophy is based on the Nordic and Aryan races being superior to all other races. White supremacists often fuse narrow views from the religious beliefs of Christianity and Odinism as justification of their supremacy as a master race.

White supremacy has long been a dominant feature in Western culture. Colonialization of the United States, Australia, parts of Africa, the Indian Subcontinent, parts of Asia, and other colonial states was based on the domination of Indigenous people by white people, who would come to structure the colonies and their later nation-states in social, political, economic, and cultural infrastructures that disenfranchised minorities.

The dominant ideology of white supremacism in the United States has disenfranchised many people who were not of European descent. Practices of segregation were institutionalized as minority people experienced social, political, economic, and cultural exclusion. These practices sparked mid-twentieth-century movements based on attaining civil rights. The goal of the civil rights movements grew from wanting constitutional rights for African Americans to inclusion of all minorities in the United States.

Many organizations support the ideas of white supremacy. Notable among them is the Ku Klux Klan (KKK). Often referred to as the Klan, it is an organization that promotes white supremacy, white nationalism, and anti-immigration. The history of the Klan consists of acts of terrorism, including acts of murder. Operating in secrecy, Klansmen often wear regalia that is designed to hide the identity of the wearer and instill fear among nonmembers. The contemporary Klan, now in its third iteration, is considered a hate group by the Southern Poverty Law Center (SPLC) and the Anti-Defamation League (ADL). The Klan, in its efforts against civil rights movements, has continued to use violence in pursuit of its aims.

Prisons have been a recruiting ground for many violent extremists and white supremacists. The Aryan Brotherhood, also known as AB, the Brand, Alice Baker, and One-Two, is the oldest of the significant white supremacist prison gangs. The gang was originally formed for protection in prison from other rival gangs, such as the Black Guerilla Family and El Eme. The AB has members inside and outside of prison. The AB operates a major criminal enterprise and uses extreme violence, including murder, in pursuit of its goals.

GLOBAL PERSPECTIVES ON WHITE SUPREMACY

Colonialism of the nineteenth and twentieth centuries has begun to be viewed through the lens of white supremacy. This lens reveals the extreme violence of state-sponsored genocide. Early perspectives of white superiority were present in the expansion of the Spanish Empire in the Americas, the British Empire in the

Americas and the Indian subcontinent, and the United States as the nation grew from the original thirteen colonies. Leaders during this era used violence and terror to ensure white people were superior to nonwhite races and cultures.

In the twentieth century, Adolf Hitler built his Third Reich on the idea of a superior Aryan race. Hitler's view of Aryan supremacy focused on the use of institutionalized extreme violence against Jews, Slavs, and Gypsies in Europe. The white supremacy touted by Hitler and his followers survived the Second World War.

In the mid-twentieth century, South Africa was a holdout in the era of colonialization, as it had entrenched its social and political institutions in apartheid—the legal segregation of people based on race. South Africans had four distinct racial groups: white, Black, colored, and Indian. Apartheid was officially abolished in 1991, though racism continued to be practiced by people from many racial groups in South Africa and other democratic countries.

The twenty-first century has seen white supremacy in the form of the rise of nationalism and a call for anti-immigration as war, drought, and lack of government have caused migration across national and international borders. Among the countries that have people and organizations supporting forms of white supremacy as a grand strategy are the United States, Britain, France, Germany, Hungary, and many other nations with democratic governments.

INFLUENTIAL LITERATURE IN WHITE SUPREMACY

The Turner Diaries is the 1978 novel by William Luther Pierce, under the pseudonym Andrew Macdonald, that has been designated the bible of the racist-right movement by the SPLC. The novel tells of a violent nuclear race war that took place in the United States. At the center of the plot is the protagonist Earl Turner, who plays a significant role in the violent overthrow of the federal government. The story is told one hundred years after the revolution to empower white rule in the United States. Turner is a member of the Order, a racist group that eventually gains control over society and sets the stage for an eventual worldwide rebellion that ends in all nonwhite people being exterminated as a means of establishing a utopian white world.

Timothy McVeigh, convicted and executed for his role in the Oklahoma City bombing in 1995, carried pages of *The Turner Diaries* with him. *The Turner Diaries* has influenced many white supremacist and far-right movements in the United States and Europe.

The Protocols of the Elders of Zion is a fabricated plan that centers on a Jewish plot to dominate the world. Written in the early twentieth century, the book details how Jewish leaders will establish control of the world by undermining the morals of non-Jewish people and gaining control of the world economy and the media. Henry Ford printed 500,000 copies of the book in support of his fear of a Jewish threat to American values. Though *The Protocols of the Elders of Zion* has been declared a hoax, many people and organizations continue to treat the book as factual.

The Camp of Saints is a French novel (*Le Camp des Saints*) that depicts the events that lead to white genocide in Europe because of mass immigration by people from the third world. While it has been denounced as racist or xenophobic literature, white supremacists have used the novel as a prophetic predictor of contemporary immigration issues being the precursor to the destruction of Western civilization and culture. The English version was published by the Social Contract Press, an organization the SPLC has labeled as promoting anti-immigration ideology. *The Camp of Saints* had a resurgence of popularity in France in the second decade of the twenty-first century. Steve Bannon, a controversial member of the early Trump administration, has referred to the novel as an illustration of immigration challenges in the United States and Europe.

WHITE SUPREMACISM AND LONE WOLVES

Lone-wolf terrorists are people that use acts of extreme violence to perform terrorist attacks. The lone-wolf terrorist is supposed to carry out violent acts outside the construct of a command structure of an organization. The isolation of a lone-wolf terrorist does not mean that the person is not motivated by the ideology or beliefs of another person or organization. Lone-wolf terrorists have been influenced by external organizations, as exemplified by many of the attacks committed by people sympathetic with Islamic jihadism.

Though the term *lone wolf* came to be associated with Islamic jihadism in the wake of the September 11, 2001, terrorist attacks against the United States, the idiom became a terrorist neologism when white supremacist Tom Metzger used the expression in the 1990s, calling on fellow white supremacists to attack the U.S. government in small groups.

POPULISM, ANTI-IMMIGRATION, AND FREE SPEECH

The twenty-first century has seen a rise in populist, national, and anti-immigration movements in the United States and across Europe as historically Eurocentric countries have experienced what is perceived as record immigration flows by non-Europeans. In the United States, white supremacist groups have relied on the Constitution's First Amendment to speak openly about their ideology and beliefs. A significant result of this constitutional right is that labeling white supremacist activities as "terrorism" is legally difficult.

EXCLUSIONARY NATIONALISM, THE NEW NOMENCLATURE FOR WHITE SUPREMACY?

For many in the United States, the term *nationalism*, including those white supremacists who have co-opted an exclusionary (white Protestants only) version of it, has recently become increasingly associated with white supremacy. Although nationalism is, historically, a political ideology rooted in the drive for self-determination and ultimately a sovereign state by people(s) sharing a sense of national identity, the term has also been viewed as synonymous with Fascism and Nazism and the racist policies pursued by Mussolini's Italy and Hitler's Germany.

The current discussions of nationalism are ubiquitous and frequently phrased in pejorative terms. In its self-consciously exclusionary form, it is analogous with xenophobia, populism, authoritarianism, and illiberalism. French president Emmanuel Macron blamed excessive nationalism for fueling the passions of World War I and warned that "old demons" threatened a return to "chaos and death."

More broadly, contemporary global challenges ensuring the security of people across social, economic, and political dimensions is not conducive to the goals of nationalism, exclusionary or otherwise. The challenge with nationalism is not to frame it as a dog whistle for white supremacy or the primacy of one ethnic group or nation-state over others—actions that guarantee to produce negative residual effects. Countries and individuals that embrace the supremacy brand of nationalism create unwarranted conflict and destabilize the possibility of international, cultural, and religious collaboration. While nationalism can foster solidarity in government efforts to address localized social challenges, fight social and economic inequalities, and take care of social groups that have been left behind, it is done with a narrow focus. Indeed, nationalism is inherently exclusive. The dangers come from how exclusive nationalism is exercised, as supremacist movements founded on it have too often resulted in the use of violence and terrorism.

Ygnacio "Nash" Flores, Don Mason, and Tracy E. Rickman

See also: Aryan Nations; Charleston Church Massacre; Domestic Terrorism, Anti-Semitic; Domestic Terrorism, the Civil Rights Era.

FURTHER READING

Bjelopera, Jerome P. 2013. *The Domestic Terrorist Threat: Background and Issues for Congress*. Washington, DC: Congressional Research Service.

Bjelopera, Jerome P. 2017. *Domestic Terrorism: An Overview*. Washington, DC: Congressional Research Service, August 21, 2017. https://fas.org/sgp/crs/terror/R44921.pdf

Blumenthal, Paul, and J. M. Rieger. 2017. "The Stunningly Racist French Novel Is How Steve Bannon Explains the World." *HuffPost*, March 6, 2017. https://www.huffingtonpost.com/entry/steve-bannon-camp-of-the-saints-immigration_us_58b75206e4b0-284854b3dc03

Harari, Yuval, N. 2018. *21 Lessons for the 21st Century*. New York: Penguin Random House.

Jenkins, Brian M. 2011. *Stray Dogs and Virtual Armies: Radicalization and Recruitment to Jihadist Terrorism in the United States Since 9/11*. Santa Monica, CA: RAND. https://www.rand.org/pubs/occasional_papers/OP343.html

Nilus, Sergei. 1906/2015. *Protocols of the Elders of Zion*. Princeton, NJ: Eulenspiegel Press.

Pierce, William L. (MacDonald, Andrew [pseud.]). 1978/1999. *The Turner Diaries*. 2nd ed. Hillsboro: National Vanguard Books.

Reilly, Ryan J. 2018. "There's a Good Reason Feds Don't Call White Guys Terrorists, Says DOJ Domestic Terror Chief." *HuffPost*, January 11, 2018. https://www.huffingtonpost.com/entry/white-terrorists-domestic-extremists_us_5a550158e4b00-3133ecceb74

Tamir, Yael Y. 2018. "In Defense of Nationalism." Project Syndicate, December 19, 2018. https://www.project-syndicate.org/commentary/nationalism-often-beneficial-by-yael-yuli-tamir-2018-12

Domestic Terrorist Groups

Viewed comparably, extremist groups in the United States have exhibited two distinct characteristics that have tended to set them apart from their counterparts in European democracies. First, most American extremist groups, and their lone-wolf subspecies, have tended to focus on a nominal set of objectives and have been organizationally small. Only the Ku Klux Klan (KKK) had a large following at its outset and again in its early twentieth-century revival. Moreover, although its active persecution of minorities did extend beyond the Black community to the immigrant Jews and Catholics arriving in the post–Civil War South, it had no real social or political agenda beyond repressing these minorities in the name of white supremacy. This characterization largely holds today, whether you are discussing state militias or the various groups with a white supremacist agenda, whose combined number of activists, according the respected Southern Poverty Law Center (SPLC), is only around 8,000 in a country of 330 million.

In contrast, other movements of comparable or greater scale have tended to be peaceful, from the Depression-era groups erecting a tent city on the Potomac to the civil rights, anti-war, and environmental movements of the 1950s–1970s. Demonstrations have gotten out of hand, often on both or all sides, and individuals spoiling for a fight and sometimes exercising their state-conferred right to bear arms are increasingly showing up at political demonstrations. Consequently, though still rare, shootings have recently occurred.

Second, explicitly anti-government violence, and especially that threatening the institutions of the federal government, has been the exception to the rule in terms of domestic extremist activity. Those with an ideological agenda have tended to go the party route (e.g., Gus Hall's mid-twentieth-century Communist Party) rather than engage in violent protests in the street. Even those with an anti-government agenda have tended to engage in tax evasion, fraud, and other forms of "paper warfare" against Uncle Sam, not the killing of federal officials.

To the extent that casualties have historically ensued, it has more often been the product of individual excess (e.g., McVeigh and Nichols, the Oklahoma City Federal Building bombers) or groups driven by their agendas to attack nongovernmental entities operating legitimately in terms of public policy. For example, antiabortion extremists have not attacked the surgeon general but they have targeted clinics carrying out abortions and killed doctors who perform them. The Earth Liberation Front (ELF) has not gone after the Department of Commerce or the Department of Energy because of their permissive development policies, but they have attacked logging camps—and so forth.

That noted, the categories of terrorist activity in Western European democracies do, or have had, their parallels in the United States.

SEPARATIST VIOLENCE

The continental United States is a broadly multicultural, multiracial, and increasingly multilingual country, but its diverse peoples have long been spatially intermixed. Consequently, it has been spared political violence by groups engaging in territorial separatist activity since the end of the resistance by Native American tribes and their subsequent relocation or the confinement to reservation systems of those tribal members desiring to protect and continue their Native heritage. Black power groups embraced the goal of independence for African Americans at the time of the Vietnam War; however, without a territorial base, that realization was never a possibility.

Even Puerto Rican separatists, who have lost all twenty-first-century independence referendums on their island have pursued little violent activity since the 1980s. In the thirty years prior to that time, however, matters were different. On October 30, 1950, Puerto Rico received Commonwealth status and the right to self-government (under congressional oversight), not the statehood desired by its militant nationalistic organizations. The result was a quarter century of separatist violence on both the island and the mainland. Inside Puerto Rico, shootouts immediately occurred between security personnel and various pro-independence groups violently protesting the Commonwealth decision; two days later, Puerto Rican nationalists attempted to assassinate President Harry S. Truman in Washington.

Only after a direct, island-wide popular vote (plebiscite) supported by President Truman recorded 82 percent of the voters in favor of the island's Commonwealth status did armed resistance to the new constitution abate. Even so, in 1952, four nationalists gained admission to the U.S. Capitol and fired on the floor of the House of Representatives, wounding five. A decade later, an armed quest for independence again gained momentum, most notably pursued by the *Fuerzas Armadas de Liberacion Nacional* (FALN), officially founded in 1974. The latter dramatically announced its arrival in October of that year by detonating bombs in Rockefeller Center and Manhattan's Wall Street and Park Avenue sections. No casualties ensued from that action, but the following year, it took credit for an explosion on Wall Street that killed four and injured more than fifty and for nine almost simultaneous explosions in New York, Washington, and Chicago. Its members were aggressively hunted thereafter, and its activities diminished over the rest of the decade. The arrest of a majority of its activists in 1980 marked the end of its violent campaign and essentially the end of separatist violence by other Puerto Rican nationalist organizations as well.

SINGLE-ISSUE POLITICAL EXTREMISTS

Hate Groups and Supremacists

The emergence of single-interest organizations is common in the advanced democratic world, where citizens have resources to pursue a wide variety of interests, such as abolishing capital punishment, protecting a pro-choice right to an abortion, withdrawing from foreign wars, securing civil rights for homosexuals, or advancing pro-environment agendas. The nature of such groups varies with the political interests of people from country to country, as does the tendency of those organizations to employ political violence.

In the United States, since the Civil War (1860–1865), the most political violence in general and acts of terrorism in particular have been the work of individuals and organizations committed to ideas of Christian white supremacy. Their hate campaigns have targeted and often continue to target African Americans, Jews, Catholics, and, most recently, the "mud races" from South America, Asia, and the Middle East. Fueled by fears of losing their majority status in the population, and energized by the waves of immigrants journeying to the U.S. border with Mexico during the Trump administration, these groups have experienced a significant increase in the level of their activity and in their association with the acts of lone-wolf terrorists since 2015. Moreover, although groups like the Aryan Nation attract the most attention, these organizations are exceedingly numerous in nature; indeed, the SPLC tabulated approximately 750 individual hate groups operating in the country, even during the early years of this century.

Antiabortionists

Second only to the hate groups in terms of involvement in violent activity during the last half century have been antiabortion organizations such as the Army of God and individuals like Eric Rudolph. Believing that abortion during any stage of pregnancy constitutes murder, the most extreme elements drawn to this cause have had little difficulty in setting their pro-life placards aside long enough to murder doctors, assault nurses, and bomb clinics that perform abortions. By 1996, the violence associated with their blockades of abortion facilities had become so pervasive that Congress was persuaded to pass the Freedom of Access to Clinic Entrances Act (FACE), curbing future activities of that nature with penalties ranging up to $100,000 in fines and a year in jail for even first-time offenders. Clinic bombings and other acts of political violence against those counseling and performing abortions continued almost immediately thereafter when Eric Rudolph bombed family planning and abortion facilities in Georgia (1997) and Alabama (1998).

Anti-Government Citizens Movements and Armed Militias

As in the case of the hate groups and antiabortionist bodies, right-wing organizations like the Posse Comitatus (which believed supreme power remains with the people under the leadership of their local sheriffs) and the sovereign citizen movement developed across the nation during the 1960s and 1970s, initially in protest to the federal surtax imposed during the 1960s to finance the Vietnam War.

Engaging primarily in nonviolent activities such as filing bogus lawsuits in their paper war against the federal government, these pro-gun, anti-government movements and state militias became most notable two decades later. They were animated by the federal standoff with armed Weaver family in 1992 at Ruby Ridge and especially the 1993 fatal fire that ended the fifty-one-day standoff at Waco between the Bureau of Alcohol, Tobacco, and Firearms (ATF) and the Branch Davidian religious cult at the cost of eighty lives, including twenty-five children. Both were interpreted as examples of a government bent on erasing the nonconforming by any means. And as in the case of the hate groups and antiabortionists, the terrorist activity associated with this end of the political spectrum emanated not from the organizations per se but those inspired by their message, most notably the two bombers of the Oklahoma City Federal Building on the second anniversary of the bloody end of the siege at Waco, the four federal judges murdered since 1979, and the gunman who fired shots in 2017 at Republican congressmen practicing for the annual Congressional Baseball Game between Republicans and Democrats.

Ecoterrorism and Animal Rights Extremists

Overshadowed more recently by white supremacist violence, the majority of terrorist "instances" in the United States before 2005 resulted from the activities of such militant environmental groups as the ELF and animal rights groups such as People for the Ethical Treatment of Animals (PETA) and the underground Animal Liberation Front (ALF). Though nonlethal in nature, their crimes against logging camps, housing developments they deemed environmentally destructive, and animal testing labs have caused hundreds of millions of dollars of damage. As in the case of the violence committed by antiabortionists, the activities of these groups has only affected a small number of the population at large and is therefore easy to overlook; however, for those who were targeted, the damage has not been inconsequential. Moreover, on more than one occasion, only good luck spared night watchmen and others unexpectedly on-site at the time of the groups' raids.

LONE-WOLF TERRORISTS

Perhaps the most defining characteristic of terrorism in the United States has been the lone-wolf nature of those committing most contemporary terrorist acts, albeit often with advice from and after radicalization by Internet and social media messaging. There are exceptions to this rule, of course, such as groups formed with the explicit intent of engaging in political violence in opposition to the Vietnam War, such as the Weathermen and its spinoff organizations. Others at the same or different times notably include the Symbionese Liberation Army (SLA), the various anarchist groups still active a century ago (the Wall Street bombings of 1920, for example), and the KKK, perhaps the oldest terrorist organization in the Western democratic world. Nonetheless, the most notable terrorist acts in the United States since the Vietnam War concluded in the mid-1970s are attributable to the acts of one or—as in the case of the Oklahoma City Federal Building and Boston Marathon bombings—two individuals.

The lone-wolf designation, for its part, covers actors ranging across a wide political spectrum, and some are not easy to place within it. Among those terrorists and terrorist acts treated in separate entries in this volume can be found lone-wolf terrorists animated by leftist causes (e.g., the early twentieth-century anarchists, the Beltway snipers) and, dominating these early days of the twenty-first century, those on the right identified with a variety of political agendas. Chief among these have been Islamic extremism (e.g., the San Bernardino shooters, the Orlando Pulse Club shooter, the Fort Hood attacker), militant Christianity (e.g., the Army of God), white supremacist groups like the Aryan Nation (e.g., the Charleston church massacre, the El Paso shootings, the Pittsburgh synagogue shooting), and state "militias" (e.g., the Oklahoma City Federal Building bombing).

To these can also be added the lone-wolf terrorist acts committed by individuals feeling personally aggrieved (e.g., the "Alphabet" bomber, the Boston Marathon bombers, the "Black rage" Garden City, Long Island Rail Road shooter, the LAX bomber), those harboring personal beliefs (e.g., Luke Helder, Eric Rudolph), and those with personally constructed ideologies (e.g., Ted Kaczynski). In many cases, the trials of these latter terrorists have been long delayed by defense attorneys requesting psychiatric examinations and by court-ordered competency hearings.

Joseph R. Rudolph Jr.

See also: Abortion Facilities Attacks; Armed Militias; Army of God; Aryan Nations; Beltway Sniper Attacks; Domestic Terrorism, Anti-Semitic; Domestic Terrorism, the Civil Rights Era; Domestic Terrorism, the Vietnam Era; Domestic Terrorism, White Supremacists; Rudolph, Eric Robert.

FURTHER READING

Anti-Defamation League Center on Extremism. n.d. "Extremism, Terrorism, and Bigotry." https://www.adl.org/what-we-do/combat-hate/extremism-terrorism-bigotry

Clarkson, Frederick. 2009. "Anti-Abortion Strategy in the Age of Obama." Political Research Associates, December 1, 2009. https://www.politicalresearch.org/2009/12/01/anti-abortion-strategy-in-the-age-of-obama-2

Herb, Jeremy, Evan Perez, Donie O'Sullivan, and Mark Morales. 2020. "What We Do and Don't Know about the Extremists Taking Part in Riots Across the United States." CNN, May 31, 2020. https://www.cnn.com/2020/05/31/politics/outside-influence-extremists-riots-us/index.html

Lewis, John. 2004. "Animal Rights Extremism and Ecoterrorism." Testimony before the Senate Judiciary Committee, May 18, 2004. FBI website. https://archives.fbi.gov/archives/news/testimony/animal-rights-extremism-and-ecoterrorism

Martin, Gus. 2018. *Understanding Terrorism: Challenges, Perspectives, and Issues.* 6th ed. Los Angeles: SAGE.

Perliger, Arie. 2020. *American Zealots: Inside Right-Wing Domestic Terrorism.* New York: Routledge.

E

Earth Liberation Front (ELF)

A historically major actor in ecoterrorism activities, the Earth Liberation Front (ELF) is a movement composed of a network of clandestine, autonomous cells organized around a radical ideology in collective defense of the environment. Since 1996, ELF attacks have caused over $100 million in damage and resulted in over 180 investigations by the federal government. In the late 1990s, federal officials considered ELF one of the most active terrorist threats in the United States. Despite a reduction in activities since the early 2000s, ELF remains a group that law enforcement and private industry must continue to assess.

ELF is rooted in the radical ideology of *deep ecology* based on environmental concerns that justify violent acts or attacks against profit-driven entities that damage the environment. Violent ecoterrorism traces back to the environmental movements of the 1970s, when radical individuals began to insist that violent means were necessary to defend nature against destruction and to aid the overall environmental movement. Ultimately, ELF emerged in the United Kingdom and the United States in the early to mid-1990s.

ELF is not a traditional organization, as it utilizes a *leaderless resistance* model of autonomous cells. These cells are self-contained, operate without external support, and are self-sufficient in terms of logistics, funding, intelligence, and weapons. The result is a loosely bound network of radical actors who persist over time and across vast geographical areas while carrying out attacks in support of the global ELF campaign. This organizational structure poses tremendous challenges to federal, state, and local law enforcement in terms of investigating and infiltrating individual cells.

Since U.S.-based activity began in 1996, twenty-six states have experienced at least one ELF attack. ELF utilizes *direct action* as its standard operating procedure due to the perception that the indirect system of representative democracy is corrupt and cannot produce satisfactory results in a timely manner. Hence, ELF utilizes *monkeywrenching*, which involves sabotaging and destroying the equipment and property of industries and other entities perceived to be damaging to the environment. Examples include tree spiking, arson, sabotage of logging and construction equipment, and other types of property destruction. ELF defines these acts as nonviolent because property, corporations, and governments are considered nonliving things. ELF does not target individuals, and to date no human injuries have been associated with an ELF attack.

ELF attacks tend to be well planned and involve significant preattack surveillance, focusing clandestinely on unguarded properties (typically within thirty miles of where the cell is located) with low-tech tactics. Therefore, ELF commonly selects targets based on their vulnerability, attractiveness, and lack of security measures, which are core principles of situational crime prevention. This is in addition to ELF's demonstrated organizational and operational security as well as knowledge of forensics, signals intelligence, computer security, cryptography, intelligence gathering, target surveillance, countersurveillance, and improvised incendiary devices.

The government's crackdown on ecoterrorists via Operation Backfire, the application of the terrorist definition in the USA PATRIOT Act of 2001 to ecoterrorists, and the aging of ELF members resulted in a drastic decline in ELF activity in the early 2000s. Despite this reduction, ELF remains a group that all levels of law enforcement and private industry must continue to monitor, especially as individuals are now self-radicalizing via the Internet. For example, there are concerns within the counterterrorism and law enforcement community that ELF may change tactics in the future. Cyberattacks, for example, are appealing to the ELF due to the nonviolent nature of the attack, increased reliance on networked and connected infrastructure by targeted entities, and the ability to expand attacks from the local scale to the national and global scales.

Brian K. Simpkins

See also: Domestic Terrorist Groups; Homegrown Terrorism.

FURTHER READING

Carson, Jennifer Varriale, Gary LaFree, and Laura Dugan. 2012. "Terrorist and Non-Terrorist Criminal Attacks by Radical Environmental and Animal Rights Groups in the United States, 1970–2007." *Terrorism and Political Violence* 24 (2): 295–319.

Deshpande, Nick, and Howard Ernst. 2012. *Countering Eco-Terrorism in the United States: The Case of Operation "Backfire."* Final Report to Human Factors/Behavioral Sciences Division, Science and Technology Directorate, U.S. Department of Homeland Security. College Park, MD: START.

Hirsch-Hoefler, Sivan, and Cas Mudde. 2014. "'Ecoterrorism': Terrorist Threat or Political Ploy?" *Studies in Conflict & Terrorism* 37 (7): 586–603.

Jarboe, James F. 2002. "The Threat of Eco-Terrorism." Testimony before the House Resources Committee, Subcommittee on Forests and Forest Health, February 12, 2002. FBI website. https://archives.fbi.gov/archives/news/testimony/the-threat-of-eco-terrorism

Joosse, Paul. 2007. "Leaderless Resistance and Ideological Inclusion: The Case of the Earth Liberation Front." *Terrorism and Political Violence* 19: 351–368.

Joosse, Paul. 2012. "Elves, Environmentalism, and Eco-Terror: Leaderless Resistance and Media Coverage of the Earth Liberation Front." *Crime Media Culture* 8 (1): 75–93.

Loadenthal, Michael. 2013. "The Earth Liberation Front: A Social Movement Analysis." *Radical Criminology* 2: 15–45.

Economic Costs of Terrorism

Terrorist organizations seek to achieve political objectives by striking against economic targets of the targeted government to inflict harm to force it to make concessions or to discredit it. Successful attacks can reduce the economic resources available to the government or increase public frustration, thus providing terrorist groups opportunities to gain at the expense of the state. As CNN noted in 2004,

Osama bin Laden claimed such success for al-Qaeda as a result of the 9/11 attack: "We are continuing this policy in bleeding America to the point of bankruptcy." He also claimed that the mujahideen fighters did the same thing to the Soviet Union in Afghanistan in the 1980s.

Certainly, the 9/11 attacks increased interest in assessing the costs of terrorism and generated studies focused on assessing its economic effect on individual countries. Most of these studies agree that the losses are both direct and indirect. Direct costs entail the value of tangibles damaged or destroyed in the attack and the resulting disruption in the economic activity, like lost wages, in addition to the value of the human lives lost. Calculating the indirect costs is always more problematic insofar as there is no consensus as to the list of factors that should be taken in consideration. Some studies include the losses in the travel and tourism industry and in the stock markets in the aftermath of an attack, while others add the treatment and suffering of the victims and their relatives. Still other studies add the diversion of funds from sectors such as health or education to counterterrorism.

In the 9/11 attacks, the direct cost involved the private property destruction (including the value of the four airplanes used in the attacks), which was estimated to be $14 billion, in addition to the losses governmental organizations incurred, which is considered around $2.2 billion. Finally, the lost wages and salaries resulting from the attacks were $2.5 billion, and the cleanup costs were approximately $10 billion.

According to a Rand study, terrorist attacks between 2004 and 2016 produced similar results, costing states in the European Union around €180 billion in GDP. This estimate included lost lifetime earnings and the cost of medical treatments, the wider psychological effects of terrorism on the behavior of people and companies, and the negative impact of terrorism on some sectors, like the tourism sector.

Elsewhere, rather than analyzing the cost of terrorism, studies assessed the relationship between the duration of terrorist attacks and economic consequences. These studies found that the effects of a terrorist campaign are much more severe than the impact of isolated incidents. A case in point is the impact of the terrorist activities of the Basque Euskadi Ta Askatasuna (ETA) separatist organization on this Spanish region, which resulted in a loss in GDP growth by about 10 percent during the 1980s and 1990s.

Comparative studies exploring terrorism's negative economic growth in developed and developing countries produce unsurprising findings. A 2009 study by Khusrav Gaibulloev and Todd Sandler, for example, investigating seven developed and thirty-five developing Asian countries, found that while the economic growth of the developed countries was not affected by transnational terrorism, the growth rate in developing states declined by around 1.4 percent.

Shady Abdelwahab Mansour

See also: New Terrorism; September 11, 2001, Attack on America.

FURTHER READING

Bandyopadhyay, Subhayu, and Javed Younas. 2017. "Trade and Terror: The Impact of Terrorism on Developing Countries." *Regional Economist* 25 (4): 12–13.

CNN. 2004. "Bin Laden: Goal Is to Bankrupt U.S." November 2, 2004. https://cnn.it/2cV56O1

Enders, Walter, and Eric Olson. 2012. "Measuring the Economic Costs of Terrorism." In *The Oxford Handbook of the Economics of Peace and Conflict*, edited by Michelle R. Garfinkel and Stergios Skaperdas. Oxford, UK: Oxford University Press.

Gaibulloev, Khusrav, and Todd Sandler. 2009. "The Impact of Terrorism and Conflicts on Growth in Asia." *Economics and Politics* 21 (3): 359–383.

Lutz, Brenda J., and James M. Lutz. 2017. *Globalization and the Economic Consequences of Terrorism*. London: Palgrave Macmillan.

Martin, Gus, ed. 2011. *The SAGE Encyclopedia of Terrorism*. Thousand Oaks, CA: SAGE Publications.

Rand Corporation. n.d. "The Cost of Terrorism in Europe." https://bit.ly/2RAvKQ5

El Paso Walmart Shooting

August 3, 2019

On August 3, 2019, in the largely Hispanic city of El Paso, Texas, Patrick Wood Crusius fired a semiautomatic assault rifle into crowds outside and inside a Walmart superstore with the intent, by his own words, of killing Mexicans and thereby contributing his part to saving white America from a "replacement" invasion by nonwhite immigrants. Before he finished and drove away, only to surrender to authorities shortly thereafter, he had killed twenty-one, including eight Mexicans, and injured as many more, two of whom would eventually die.

Casualties could have been higher had the Walmart store manager, upon hearing gunfire, not warned employees of an active shooter outside and Walmart workers not helped many shoppers escape or take shelter before the shooter entered the building. The manager also dialed 911, and within six minutes, local, state, and federal law enforcement personnel were at the scene. Nonetheless, the shooting remains the deadliest attack on Latinos in recent U.S. history.

Like Robert Bowers, who attacked the refugee-assisting Tree of Life Synagogue in Pittsburgh (2018), and Dylann Roof, who killed nine at an African American church in Charleston, South Carolina (2015), Crusius was a homegrown terrorist. He was not, however, a *hometown* terrorist. Having driven some 650 miles from his Dallas area home, Crusius had more in common with the growing category of right-wing extremists who travel to faraway killing grounds, such as James Alex Fields Jr., whose trip from Ohio to a white supremacist rally in Charlottesville Virginia, ended when he drove his car into a crowd of counter protestors (2017), and Brenton Tarrant, who traveled from Australia to kill fifty-one and injure as many more at two mosques in Christchurch, New Zealand (2019).

Linking many of these killers is the acceptance, echoed in a 2,500-word manifesto believed to have been posted by Crusius before initiating his attack, of the "Great Replacement" (or "white genocide") theory that maintains an international cabal of Jews and ultraliberals is conspiring to replace the white majorities in Western democracies with third world immigrants. The theory's origin is attributed to Renaud Camus, who in 2011 published a book of that name foreseeing Europe's doom as a result of the Black and brown immigrants "invading" it. Procreation as well as immigration trends in most Western states, however, had long before raised warnings of a coming "majority of minorities" in countries where urbanized white couples average less than two children per household and hence are not replacing themselves in the population.

To this argument, Crusius's motives included a partisan element: a fear that Texas's growing Hispanic population would make Texas a stronghold of the Democratic Party, given its greater success than Republicans in wooing immigrants, and thereby lock in the replacement of pro-white America by peoples from the Southern Hemisphere.

Indicted on multiple murder, hate crime, and other charges by both state and federal authorities between September 2019 and February 2020, Crusius waived his *Miranda* rights when interrogated but subsequently entered not guilty pleas at both levels. On July 14, 2020, citing the difficulty of interviewing the necessary neurological and related experts to build a mitigating "red flag" defense given state responses to the COVID-19 pandemic, his attorneys won a motion that delayed the filing of capital murder charges by federal authorities.

Joseph R. Rudolph Jr.

See also: Charleston Church Massacre; Pittsburgh Synagogue Shooting; Psychology of Terrorists.

FURTHER READING

Andone, Dakin, Hollie Silverman, and Nicole Chavez. 2019. "20 People Killed in El Paso Shooting, Texas Governor Says." CNN, August 4, 2019. https://www.cnn.com/2019/08/03/us/el-paso-shooting/index.html

Long, Trish. 2020. "El Paso Walmart Shooting Anniversary: A Timeline of Tragedy." *El Paso Times*, July 30, 2020. https://www.elpasotimes.com/in-depth/news/2020/07/29/el-paso-shooting-victims-timeline-walmart-gun-violence-texas/5475951002/

Razek, Raja, and Hollie Silverman. 2020. "El Paso Walmart Shooter Has Mental Disabilities and Was in a Psychotic State after the Shooting, Defense Counsel Says." CNN, July 14, 2020. https://www.cnn.com/2020/07/14/us/el-paso-shooter-psychotic-state/index.html

Stengle, Jamie, and Cedar Attanasio. 2020. "El Paso Marks Walmart Shooting Anniversary Amid Pandemic." ABC News, August 2, 2020. https://abcnews.go.com/US/wireStory/el-paso-marks-walmart-shooting-anniversary-amid-pandemic-72131324

Electromagnetic Pulse (EMP)

An electromagnetic pulse (EMP) is a pulse of radiofrequency electromagnetic radiation produced during a nuclear explosion or occurring naturally due to heightened solar flare activity on the sun. An EMP's intense electric and magnetic fields produce near-instantaneous voltage surges in electricity-conducting materials. These surges are capable of damaging unprotected electronic and electrical equipment. EMPs pose no direct health threat; however, by destroying critical infrastructure (CI), EMPs can produce cascading casualties that can cause crippling economic disruption and associated human suffering and death.

While all nuclear explosions produce EMPs, other effects of nuclear explosions, such as blast effects, overshadow EMP effects for explosions near the earth's surface. An EMP is, however, a major effect for large-yield bursts at very high altitude (25–250 miles above the earth's surface). An EMP is similar to the electrical signal from lightning, but the rise in voltage is typically a hundred times faster. This means that most equipment designed to protect electrical facilities from lightning works too slowly to be effective against an EMP. EMP effects were observed during U.S. and Soviet nuclear weapon atmospheric test programs in 1962. A U.S. detonation 250 miles above Johnson Atoll in the Pacific Ocean and Soviet high-altitude detonations over South Central Asia damaged electrical and electronic equipment up to 900 miles away. Estimates indicate that the EMP produced by a high-yield nuclear explosion of approximately ten megatons detonated 200 miles above the center of the continental United States would affect almost the entire country as well as parts of Mexico and Canada.

The widespread use of electronics in modern CI has increased the damage that an EMP can cause. The most technically advanced societies are the most vulnerable because they are the most dependent on electronic and electrical technologies. In these societies, an EMP will not only damage electrical grids and associated power generating and distribution equipment; it will also disable vehicles; destroy the electronics in communications, health-care, financial services, and information technology equipment; and damage control and safety devices in virtually all CI sectors. Damaged safety systems can subsequently destroy equipment by failing to prevent an unsafe condition.

Following an EMP event, equipment brought in from unaffected areas will function normally, and affected vehicles such as automobiles will operate once damaged parts are replaced. It is possible to protect (or harden) equipment and systems against the effects of an EMP.

The Commission to Assess the Threat to the United States from Electromagnetic Pulse (EMP Commission) issued its 2004 report at the same time that the National Commission on Terrorist Attacks upon the United States issued the 9/11 report, and American political reaction subsequently focused on actions to prevent terrorist attacks rather than on strengthening the country's ability to survive EMP effects. In 2008, the EMP Commission issued a follow-up report on U.S. vulnerabilities to an EMP attack. Since then, the Department of Defense has hardened some of its most vulnerable systems, and key federal agencies have taken actions to address EMP risks to the electric grid. In addition, the Department of Homeland Security, the Department of Energy, and the Federal Energy Regulatory Commission have established industry standards and federal guidelines to help CI owners improve CI survivability to an EMP event. In 2019, President Trump signed an Executive Order on Coordinating National Resilience to Electromagnetic Pulses, which many observers see as an important step in confronting an unconventional threat with the potential to wreak havoc on the United States.

William J. Lahneman

See also: Critical Infrastructure as a Terrorist Target; Weapons of Mass Destruction.

FURTHER READING

Cochran, Thomas B., and Robert S. Norris. 2017. "Nuclear Electromagnetic Pulse." *Encyclopedia Britannica*, November 20, 2017. Accessed August 12, 2020. https://www.britannica.com/science/nuclear-electromagnetic-pulse

Commission to Assess the Threat to the United States from Electromagnetic Pulse Attack. 2004. *Report of the Commission to Assess the Threat to the United States from Electromagnetic Pulse (EMP): Volume 1: Executive Report.* Accessed August 10, 2020. http://www.empcommission.org/docs/empc_exec_rpt.pdf

Commission to Assess the Threat to the United States from Electromagnetic Pulse Attack. 2008. *Report of the Commission to Assess the Threat to the United States from Electromagnetic Pulse (EMP) Attack: Critical National Infrastructures.* Accessed August 10, 2020. http://www.empcommission.org/docs/A2473-EMP_Commission-7MB.pdf

Executive Order 13865—Coordinating National Resilience to Electromagnetic Pulses. White House, March 26, 2019. Accessed August 10, 2020. https://www.govinfo.gov/content/pkg/DCPD-201900176/pdf/DCPD-201900176.pdf

U.S. Government Accountability Office. 2016. *Critical Infrastructure Protection: Federal Agencies Have Taken Actions to Address Electromagnetic Risks, but Opportunities Exist to Further Assess Risks and Strengthen Collaboration.* Washington, DC: U.S. Government Accountability Office. Accessed August 10, 2020. https://www.gao.gov/products/GAO-16-243

Enhanced Interrogation Debate

In the wake of the terrorist attacks of September 11, 2001, the U.S. government created enhanced interrogation policies, including most infamously a technique of simulated drowning called *waterboarding*, as a means of preventing further attacks. Used on detainees, these tools were employed by the Central Intelligence Agency (CIA), Defense Intelligence Agency (DIA), and some components of the U.S. Armed Forces to glean information regarding anti-American terrorist organizations and future attacks against the United States or its allies and citizens. The enhanced interrogation program at the Guantánamo Bay detainment facility is the most well known, but there were other sites, including Abu Ghraib and so-called black sites in several locations around the world.

Vice President Dick Cheney was one of the most vociferous proponents of enhanced interrogation in President George W. Bush's administration, and he has stated on numerous occasions that the interrogation program prevented further attacks on the United States. Numerous government officials, human rights advocates, and international bodies such as the European Court of Human Rights, however, have decried these techniques as acts of torture. Though the techniques were officially ended in 2005, the matter of their legality and morality remains important. As a presidential candidate and in his first interview as president, Donald J. Trump advocated a return to enhanced interrogations.

Abu Zubaydah provides a case study. He was among the most prominent subjects of the enhanced interrogation program after his capture in March 2002, when officials believed more attacks on American sites by al-Qaeda were likely. Considered to be a high-value source of information, Zubaydah refused to cooperate with interrogators. In response, the CIA sought permission to use enhanced interrogation techniques to obtain information.

The proposed techniques were largely adapted from U.S. military training designed to prepare its members for capture and interrogation by enemy actors. The Office of Legal Counsel approved these techniques, including sleep deprivation, exposure to extreme temperatures, confinement in either "small" or "big" boxes, and waterboarding.

Some policy makers and others, including former president Trump and former vice president Cheney, believe that an exception to existing doctrine is needed to provide interrogators with greater flexibility when questioning subjects with information pertaining to upcoming terrorist attacks or agendas. Others, including the Senate Select Committee on Intelligence, argue that "the use of brutal interrogation techniques [violates] U.S. law, treaty obligations, and our values" (2014). Evidence also suggests that popular entertainment, such as the TV show *24*, which depicts the use of torture techniques as successful means of preventing a terrorist plot, may increase popular support for enhanced interrogation.

There is evidence that suggests that techniques such as waterboarding do not work. Khalid Sheikh Mohammed was reportedly waterboarded 183 times. Moreover, there is evidence that noncoercive interrogation methods are more effective. Zubaydah himself, in fact, ultimately revealed valuable information, not as a result of the enhanced interrogation techniques but through noncoercive methods. Indeed, many law enforcement agencies, including the FBI, have said that applying more rigorous methods can reduce the veracity of the information obtained.

Jakob R. Gibson and Tobias T. Gibson

See also: Abu Ghraib Scandal; Counterterrorism and the George W. Bush Administration; Guantánamo Bay Detention Camp.

FURTHER READING

Abrams, Norman, and Christopher Slobogin. 2012. "Interrogations." In *Patriots Debate: Contemporary Issues in National Security Law*, edited by Harvey Rishikof, Stewart Baker, and Bernard Horowitz, 41–70. Chicago: American Bar Association.

Goldsmith, Jack. 2012. *Power and Constraint: The Accountable President after 9/11.* New York: W. W. Norton.

Harlow, George, ed. 2015. *Rebuttal: The CIA Responds to the Senate Intelligence Committee's Study of Its Detention and Interrogation Program.* Annapolis, MD: Naval Institute Press.

Senate Select Committee on Intelligence. 2014. "Senate Intelligence Committee Study on CIA Detention and Interrogation Program." December 9, 2014. Accessed June 9, 2020. https://www.feinstein.senate.gov/public/index.cfm/senate-intelligence-committee-study-on-cia-detention-and-interrogation-program

Entebbe Rescue Operation

The "Raid on Entebbe" refers to a 1976 hostage rescue operation conducted by the Israeli Defense Forces (IDF) at Entebbe International Airport, Uganda. During the operation, the IDF successfully rescued 102 of 106 hostages held on a parked airplane by hijackers affiliated with the Popular Front for the Liberation of Palestine (PFLP) and an East German Revolutionary Cell.

On Sunday, June 27, 1976, Air France Flight 139 took off from Tel Aviv bound for Paris via Athens. During the layover in Athens, two members of the PFLP and two members of an East German Revolutionary Cell boarded the flight, and shortly after taking off, the four individuals hijacked the aircraft. The hijackers subsequently diverted the plane to Benghazi, Libya, where it landed and refueled. After more than seven hours in Libya, the aircraft departed for Khartoum, Sudan. The hijackers' request to land in Khartoum was denied, and at 3:15 a.m. on Monday, June 28, 1976, the aircraft landed at Entebbe International Airport in Uganda. Upon arrival, the aircraft held 252 passengers, 12 crewmembers, and the 4 hijackers, for a total of 268 individuals.

The president of Uganda, Idi Amin Dada, expressed sympathy for the cause of the PFLP and welcomed the hijackers. Through the Ugandan government and the Somali ambassador to Uganda, the PFLP and the East German Revolutionary Cell demanded $5 million and the release of fifty-three Palestinian or pro-Palestinian militants held in Israel, West Germany, France, Switzerland, and Kenya.

Over the next two days, the hijackers released non-Israeli, sick, young, and elderly hostages. On June 30, the PFLP sent 48 hostages to Paris, and on July 1, the PFLP released another 100 hostages. All 12 members of the Air France crew refused to leave the remaining hostages, the majority of whom were Israeli citizens or of Jewish heritage.

Acting on information from the Israeli intelligence services, the Israeli cabinet authorized Operation Thunderbolt, an IDF plan to rescue the remaining hostages, on July 3. The IDF operation in Uganda included a combined force of two C-130 cargo aircraft, one Boeing 707, light infantry, reconnaissance, paratroopers, and a commando assault team. The operation culminated in the early hours of Sunday, July 4, 1976, when all three IDF aircraft and the rescue team landed at Ben Gurion International Airport in Tel Aviv with the rescued hostages.

During the operation, Israeli commandos killed twenty Ugandan guards. Three hostages and the ranking officer on the IDF commando team, Yonatan Netanyahu, died in the crossfire, and one wounded hostage was murdered by Ugandan security services at a hospital in the Ugandan capital of Kampala. Yonatan Netanyahu was the older brother of Israeli prime minister Benjamin Netanyahu, who served as Israel's prime minister from 2009 to 2019. The Raid on Entebbe is also referred to as "Operation Yonatan" in his honor.

Although many military experts have hailed the Raid on Entebbe as a daring and successful hostage rescue operation, critics of the event have criticized the aggression of the Israeli commandos and the high body count that resulted. The Ugandan foreign minister appealed to the United Nations Security Council, stating that the raid violated Uganda's sovereignty and territorial integrity.

Diane M. Zorri

See also: Munich Olympics Terrorist Attack; State Terrorism.

FURTHER READING

Dunstan, Simon. 2012. *Israel's Lightning Strike: The Raid on Entebbe, 1976*. Oxford, UK: Osprey Publishing.

Jewish Telegraphic Agency. 1976. "Mission Incredible: Operation of Redemption of Hostages." July 6, 1976. Accessed September 15, 2018. http://pdfs.jta.org/1976/1976-07-06_129.pdf

Salter, Leonard. 1977. "Commando Coup at Entebbe: Humanitarian Intervention or Barbaric Aggression?" *International Lawyer* 11 (2): 331–338.

Umozurike, Von U. O. 1979. "The Israelis in Entebbe—Rescue or Aggression?" *Law and Politics in Africa, Asia and Latin America* 12 (4): 383–392.

United Nations Security Council. 1976. "Official Records, 31st Year, 1939th Meeting, 9 July 1976." Accessed September 18, 2018. https://digitallibrary.un.org/record/86947

Evolution of Terrorism

Terrorism is one of the most contested concepts that has evaded a widely agreed upon definition, which could be attributed to a host of factors, prominent among which is the fact that many find it difficult to draw a clear distinction between terrorism and other forms of political violence, like resistance or guerrilla warfare. In addition, ascribing terrorism to some criminal activities, such as air piracy or assassinations, often depends on the motivations of the perpetrators.

Despite these inherent difficulties, most the definitions of *terrorism* approximate that of Roxana Simus, a PhD student at the Police Academy in Romania: "Premeditated, politically motivated violence perpetrated against noncombatant targets by subnational groups or clandestine agents, usually intended to influence an audience" (Simus 2016).

THE FOUR PRIOR WAVES OF TERRORISM

David Rapoport, professor emeritus at the University of California Los Angeles and a founding editor of the journal *Terrorism & Political Violence*, coined the concept of "waves of terrorism" to describe and distinguish between terrorism's different historical phases. He argued that modern global terrorism (starting from 1880) falls into four different periods, each of which has its own domestic and international features, theater of operation, ideological character, and activists. Others, such as Jeffrey Kaplan, the director of the Institute for the Study of Religion, Violence and Memory at the University of Wisconsin Oshkosh, and Jeffrey Simon, president of Political Risk Assessment Co., would add a fifth contemporary wave to this list, albeit differing among themselves as to its main characteristics and driving ideology.

Critics have noted that such typologies are inherently selective in nature, emphasizing certain phenomena while ignoring others, such as right-wing terrorism and organized crime terrorism. Furthermore, Rapoport's assertion that each wave disappears to birth a new one is problematic, given, as many note, that there is very little evidence that the activities associated with any of his four waves have actually disappeared. Despite these drawbacks, the typology remains useful in depicting the central aspects of differing eras of modern terrorism, in each of which, according to Rapoport, terrorist organizations were able to avail themselves of the changing nature of international communications to spread their doctrines elsewhere.

The Anarchist Wave (1880s–1890s)

The first wave started with the Russian populist group Narodnaya Volya (the "People's Will") when Vera Zasulich, an anarchist, shot and wounded a police commander in St. Petersburg, Russia, on January 24, 1878, who was accused of torturing political prisoners. This wave continued until the early decades of the twentieth century, spreading quickly from Russia to Western Europe, the United States, and even Japan and China. Utilizing assassination as their principal tool of attack, committed anarchists murdered a large number of government leaders, senior politicians, and military officers during this period, including President William McKinley in 1901.

The Anti-Colonial Wave (1920s–Mid-1960s)

The second wave began with the conclusion of World War I, when several significant European colonies began to feel that political independence was at hand, given the emphasis accorded to the principle of national self-determination by President Woodrow Wilson. The Versailles Treaty officially ending the war, however, dashed such hopes by, among other things expanding colonial control over new areas, thereby triggering the second wave of terrorism, spearheaded by the postwar activity of the Irish Republican Army (IRA), one of the first national liberation terrorist movements and one that has outlived most other second-wave groups.

During this wave, foreign governments played a vital role in providing support to these liberation groups. As colonial-backed local police forces became primary targets, guerrilla tactics became increasingly important. Whereas anarchist violence had been primarily urban, the second wave was heavily influenced by Maoist thought, in that it was focused primarily on the countryside and accentuated the local struggle against colonial rule.

The New Left Wave (1975–1980s)

The Vietnam War produced the psychological requisites for the third wave, as the effectiveness of the Viet Cong's guerrilla war tactics against the American army revealed the vulnerability of the Western heartland. Indeed, many groups in the developed world were themselves the primary actors during this wave; notably, the American Weather Underground, Italian Red Brigades, and Japanese Red Army. At the same time, outsiders like the Soviets encouraged these groups in many ways.

The main international feature of this age was airline hijacking, and over a hundred occurred during the 1970s as planes were taken to get hostages to gain political leverage and raise funds for the perpetrating terrorist organization. The most memorable domestic event was the 1979 kidnapping of Italian prime minister Aldo Moro by the Red Brigades. Attacks on foreign embassies also began during this wave, notably the attack of the Peruvian "Shining Path" on the Japanese embassy in 1996, where it held seventy-two hostages for more than four months.

The Religious Wave (1980s–2000s)

Although religious identity played a role in the early waves insofar as it overlapped with ethnic identities, the main goal of those terrorist organizations was to create secular sovereign states. To the contrary, the role that religion played in the fourth wave was central, supplying the justification and organizing principles for the New World to be established.

All religious communities produced terrorists. Sikhs sought a religious state in the Punjab. Jewish terrorists attempted to blow up Islam's most sacred shrine in Jerusalem and waged an assassination campaign against Palestinian mayors in the 1990s. Aum Shinrikyo, a group that combined Buddhist, Christian, and Hindu religious themes, released nerve gas on the Tokyo subway, killing 12 and injuring 3,000. The Iranians, after a 1979 revolution, inspired and helped Shiite terror movements in Iraq, Saudi Arabia, Kuwait, and Lebanon.

Suicide bombing was the deadly tactical innovation most heavily utilized during this wave, with the Tamil Tigers in Sri Lanka using more "suicide bombers" than all Islamic groups combined. Fourth-wave groups have also launched massive attacks against military and government installations, such as al-Qaeda's attack on the American embassies in Kenya and Tanzania.

FIFTH WAVE CONCEPTUALIZATIONS

Theorizing about a fifth wave movement began in 2007, with Jeffrey Kaplan's article in *Terrorism and Political Violence*, "The Fifth Wave: The New Tribalism?" Building on Rapoport's four waves theory, and drawing on an analysis of terrorist groups like the Khmer Rouge in Cambodia and the Lord's Resistance Army in Uganda, Kaplan contends that a new wave has emerged whose defining characteristic is the desire of terrorist organizations to create a new world. This would-be utopian society is to be created in this lifetime by means of harsh tactics such as killing on a massive scale or genocide to wipe out existing ethnic or religious minorities deemed undesirable in their world. Future children are to be produced through rape and isolated from existing society at an early age. It is their greater radicalization, Kaplan argues, that separates the terrorist organizations in this era from their counterparts in, mainly, the second and fourth waves.

Anthony N. Celso, in his 2015 article "The Islamic State and Boko Haram: Fifth Wave Jihadist Terror Groups," extended Kaplan's theoretical framework to various jihadist groups, namely, Boko Haram in Nigeria, al-Qaeda in Iraq, and al-Qaeda in Islamic Maghreb, thereby contradicting Kaplan's argument that fifth-wave terrorism does not include terrorist Islamic groups. Rejecting the existing political and social order, according to Celso, these jihadist groups are in search of a mythic past and seek to establish a new Islamic state. Their recruitment strategy relies on enslaving women and children through kidnappings and forced marriages.

In the same vein, Or Honig and Ido Yahel used the fifth wave designation to refer to what they label "terrorist semi-states" (TSSs) in the Middle East and North Africa, where terrorist groups have achieved relatively exclusive territorial control. These groups and territories include al-Shabaab in south Somalia since 2009, the Islamic State's West Africa Province (ISWAP), Boko Haram's control of northeast Nigeria since 2014, Hezbollah since 2000, the Taliban state in Pakistan (TTP) since 2007, al-Qaeda in the Arabian Peninsula (AQAP) in South Yemen since 2015, and the Houthis in Northern Yemen since 2015.

Both Honig and Yahel acknowledge that the new TSS phenomenon will not completely replace the old terrorist groups or lone-wolf terrorists; however, they assume that TSS will remain the dominant form of terrorism in the foreseeable future. On the other hand, they were also cautious enough in this prediction to acknowledge that the destruction of the Islamic State in Iraq and Syria (ISIS) by Western military action could reduce the appeal of this wave of terrorism elsewhere around the world.

Meanwhile, Jeffrey Simon provides a completely different conception of the fifth wave in arguing that technology, not ideology, will be the dominant feature of this wave, given that innovations in weapons, communications, information systems, and the like are readily available for all groups to take advantage of, including terrorists. More specifically, he predicts that lone operators will become the significant players by using the Internet to learn about weapons, targets, and techniques, and he rejects the proposition that religious terrorism will be the sole player. Rather, other forms of terrorism will persist, such as narcoterrorism in Colombia, Mexico, and Afghanistan, among other countries, and ethnic separatist terrorism, which continues unabated in Kashmir.

Despite these different conceptions of fifth-wave terrorism, Islamic terrorist groups seeking to establish TSSs arguably fall under the initial Kaplan conception of fifth-wave terrorism. Simon, however, clearly deviated from Kaplan's, Celso's, and Honig's conceptions insofar as they agree that the coming wave is tribal or semi-state terrorism in nature, whereas Simon argues that it will be lone-wolf terrorism with no dominant ideology.

Finally, this fifth wave may be a hybrid form of TSS and lone-wolf terrorism, especially in the light of the increasing lone-wolf attacks directed by ISIS against Western countries. And although ISIS's terrorist state in Syria and Iraq was dismantled by an American-led coalition, its affiliated terrorist groups did not face a similar fate, especially Boko Haram in Nigeria and Islamic State in Libya, which means that both forms will prevail in the terrorist landscape, with Islamic ideology as the dominant ideology.

Shady Abdelwahab Mansour

See also: Haymarket Affair; Islamic State, The; New Terrorism; Recruiting Terrorists; War on Terror: Afghanistan and Pakistan.

FURTHER READING

Celso, Anthony N. 2015. "The Islamic State and Boko Haram: Fifth Wave Jihadist Terror Group." *Orbis* 59 (2): 251–252.

Honiga, Or, and Ido Yahelb. 2019. "A Fifth Wave of Terrorism? The Emergence of Terrorist Semi-States." *Terrorism and Political Violence* 31 (6): 1210–1228. https://doi.org/10.1080/09546553.2017.1330201

Kaplan, Jeffrey. 2007. "The Fifth Wave: The New Tribalism?" *Terrorism and Political Violence* 19 (4): 545–546.

Kaplan, Jeffrey. 2016. "Waves of Political Terrorism." In *Oxford Research Encyclopedia of Politics*, edited by William R. Thompson. n.p.: Oxford University Press. EPUB edition.

Rapoport, David. C. 2002. "The Four Waves of Rebel Terror and September 11." *Anthropoetics* 8 (1). https://goo.gl/Q5wRpP

Sánchez de Rojas Díaz, Emilio. 2016. "Are We Facing the Fifth Wave of International Terrorism?" *Spanish Institute for Strategic Studies (IEEE).* January 19, 2016. https://goo.gl/DXSPeL

Simon, Jeffrey D. 2011. "Technological and Lone Operator Terrorism: Prospects for a Fifth Wave of Global Terrorism." In *Terrorism, Identity and Legitimacy: The Four Waves Theory and Political Violence*, edited by Jean E. Rosenfeld, 44–65. New York: Routledge.

Simus, Roxana. 2016. "The Evolution of Terrorism." *Acta Universitatis George Bacovia* 5 (2). https://bit.ly/2OT4OVQ

Weinberg, Leonard, Ami Pedahzur, and Sivan Hirsch-Hoefler. 2004. "The Challenges of Conceptualizing Terrorism." *Terrorism and Political Violence* 16 (44): 777–794.

F

Federal Bureau of Investigation (FBI)

The Federal Bureau of Investigation (FBI), established in 1908, is the nation's premier law enforcement organization, with broad authority in federal law enforcement and in national security. It is also a member of the U.S. intelligence community.

From its inception, the FBI has been a major domestic and international force in the war against terrorism. The first counterterrorism raid performed by the FBI came on February 14, 1920, when the bureau arrested seventeen members of an Italian anarchist gang called L'Era Nuova.

In its efforts to thwart future terrorist attacks, the FBI's authority has gradually grown. The Foreign Intelligence Surveillance Act (FISA) of 1978 enabled the FBI to utilize electronic surveillance within the United States in foreign counterintelligence and counterterrorism cases and established a court to process and review requests for electronic intercepts in those cases.

Following the World Trade Center bombing in 1993, the FBI increased the number of special agents deployed abroad at foreign embassies to cope with the growing globalization of crime and the rising threat of terrorism and to enforce U.S. extraterritoriality laws.

The terrorist attacks of September 11, 2001, represented another catalyst for changing the priorities of the FBI—especially after being criticized for "failing to face the domestic terrorist threat; collect useful intelligence; and to share intelligence internally and with other members of the Intelligence Community" by the Congressional Joint Inquiry into the Terrorist Attacks of September 11, 2001. The Joint Inquiry also found the FBI was extremely deficient in recognizing, reporting on, and defending against the foreign terrorist organizations operating against the United States. Accordingly, counterterrorism became the FBI's number one priority starting from May 29, 2002. Other major priorities now included countering foreign intelligence activity directed against the United States, countering cybercrime, and working against public corruption. In addition, the FBI has adopted new procedures to enhance intelligence sharing.

In addition, following Congress' findings, the FBI significantly reorganized to enhance its domestic intelligence collection and analytic capabilities. In particular, it implemented a National Security Branch with a deputy director as its head with the aim of increasing the FBI's domestic intelligence and counterintelligence capabilities. It also modernized its data management systems to facilitate information sharing both within the FBI and among its intelligence community (IC) partners. Nonetheless, some experts continue to argue that American security institutions are still engaged in a "zero-sum battle for autonomy and power" in which narrow bureaucratic interest hinders intelligence sharing between intelligence and law enforcement organizations.

On the plus side, the FBI has successfully infiltrated many terrorist cells and defeated many terrorist attacks within the United States, including the successful infiltration of a local terrorist cell by an Arabic-speaking Muslim American. This successful undercover operation thwarted an al-Qaeda plot to derail the New York City to Toronto train in 2013.

Shady Abdelwahab Mansour

See also: Foreign Intelligence Surveillance Act of 1978; Homeland Security; Intelligence Community, Adjustments to the Post-9/11 World.

FURTHER READING

Cumming, Alfred, and Todd Masse. 2004. "FBI Intelligence Reform since September 11, 2001: Issues and Options for Congress." *Congressional Research Service Reports*, no. RL32336, August 4, 2004. https://bit.ly/2uTbhrZ

El Noury, Tamer, and Kevin Maurer. 2017. *American Radical: Inside the World of an Undercover Muslim FBI Agent.* New York: Dutton.

Foley, Frank. 2016. "Why Inter-Agency Operations Break Down: US Counterterrorism in Comparative Perspective." *European Journal of International Security* 1 (part 2): 150–175.

Masse, Todd, and William Krouse. 2003. "The FBI: Past, Present, and Future." *Congressional Research Service Reports*, no. RL32095, October 2, 2003. https://bit.ly/2D1mdrS

Weiner, Tim. 2012. *Enemies: A History of the FBI.* New York: Random House.

Federal Bureau of Investigation, Directorate of Intelligence

The Federal Bureau of Investigation's (FBI) Directorate of Intelligence (DI) was established in 2005. The DI was intended to unify the FBI's intelligence functions, improve its intelligence capabilities, and increase the status and role of its intelligence analyst workforce. In 2014, the DI was incorporated into a newly created Intelligence Branch (IB) headed by an executive assistant director, which served to further emphasize the important role played by intelligence in achieving the FBI's mission. The DI coordinates and provides intelligence support to all of the FBI's other branches and directorates.

Like all law enforcement organizations, the FBI has always used intelligence to investigate and solve crimes. In addition to its core domestic law enforcement role, its missions include counterterrorism, counterintelligence, detection and prevention of weapon of mass destruction (WMD) threats to the U.S. homeland, and cybersecurity, all of which depend on a steady supply of high-quality intelligence from many sources to be effective. For this reason, the FBI is a long-standing member of the U.S. intelligence community.

Following the September 11, 2001, attacks, *The Final Report of the National Commission on Terrorist Attacks upon the United States* (*The 9/11 Commission Report*) criticized the FBI's intelligence functions for two main reasons. First, the FBI used outdated technology to support its intelligence functions. This fact not only reduced the quality of intelligence overall but also made it difficult for analysts in one field office to access intelligence produced at other field offices. This latter condition inhibited the fusion of intelligence that is so important in areas such as counterterrorism. Second, the FBI viewed itself as a law enforcement agency, and its sworn law enforcement agents, with the power to make arrests, dominated its organizational culture. The commission recommended and the Intelligence Reform and Terrorism Prevention Act of 2004 (IRPTA) required that the FBI create the DI to focus on ways to give its intelligence analysts more status in the organization, to manage them and intelligence functions better, and to create meaningful career paths for them within the organization to both retain good analysts and attract talented new analysts.

The FBI was directed to create the DI through a provision in the IRPTA and a 2004 presidential memorandum entitled "Further Strengthening Federal Bureau of Investigation Capabilities." It was initially funded through the Consolidated Appropriations Act of 2005. The DI's central mission is "to optimally position the FBI to meet current and emerging national security and criminal threats." Achieving this mission requires close cooperation and information sharing with partner intelligence organizations as well as with other directorates and branches of the FBI. The DI has authority and responsibility for all FBI intelligence functions, which includes the intelligence functions of the Criminal, Cyber, Response, and Services Branch (CCRSB) as well as the National Security Branch (NSB). The NSB was established in 2005 to improve the effectiveness of the FBI's national security elements, including counterintelligence, counterterrorism, and detection of WMD threats. The 2014 creation of the IB has improved the DI's organizational clout by placing it in an organizational entity headed by an executive assistant director, the same as the FBI's other five branches.

William J. Lahneman

See also: Federal Bureau of Investigation; Intelligence Community, Adjustments to the Post-9/11 World; Intelligence Fusion Centers; Intelligence Reform and Terrorism Prevention Act of 2004.

FURTHER READING

FBI. 2020a. "Intelligence." https://www.fbi.gov/about/leadership-and-structure/intelligence-branch

FBI. 2020b. "Leadership & Structure." https://www.fbi.gov/about/leadership-and-structure

FBI. 2020c. "National Security Branch." https://www.fbi.gov/about/leadership-and-structure/national-security-branch

Lowenthal, Mark M. 2017. *Intelligence: From Secrets to Policy.* 7th ed. Los Angeles: CQ Press.

National Commission on Terrorist Attacks upon the United States. 2004. *The 9/11 Commission Report: Final Report of the National Commission on Terrorist Attacks upon the United States.* Authorized ed. New York: W. W. Norton & Company. https://9-11commission.gov/report/

Female Terrorists, Ideology and Logistics

Women have played an active and important role in terrorist groups throughout modern history. Indeed, in the modern era, women have been understood to participate and even lead acts of terrorism and mass violence. Like most human experiences, terrorism is a gendered construct, in that people of different genders have different relationships with terrorism, both as perpetrators and victims.

The focus here is on women in jihadist terrorist organizations, whose mandates fall largely within the post-9/11 Western understanding of radical Islamic terrorism. Research suggests that terrorist organizations utilize women for five primary reasons: (1) through a desire for increased media attention; (2) to differentiate themselves from other similar groups; (3) tactically, to reach targets impenetrable by male actors; (4) because of limited male recruits or to use male recruits for other purposes; and (5) under pressure from female organizations to include women. The focus here is on the ideological and logistical roles of women in their operations.

By unpacking the ideological role of women in terrorist groups, we gain an understanding of how the groups themselves perceive women's roles and capabilities. The best-known document outlining such policies is *Women in the Islamic State: Manifesto and Case Study* (2015), which was circulated on a jihadist forum used by the Islamic State (IS). The major purpose of the treatise was to recruit women by providing an organized framework for describing the ideal role for women in a state governed by IS as homemakers and mothers. There is heavy emphasis on religious motifs that promise the fulfillment of life as a religious individual and that justify legal limitations placed on women by IS, such as restricting the woman's ability to leave the home unless going to pray, being employed as a doctor or teacher, or participating, in extreme need, in the fighting of the organization. Limiting a woman to the home is justified by such statements as "verily God has ordained this sedentary existence for women, and it cannot be better in any way, for He is the Creator and He knows what works and what does not in religion" (Winter 2015). Women are also frequently idealized as the future of jihad by sending sons to fight against the West.

One of the many ironies of this document is that the Al-Khansaa Brigade, a specifically all-female security force with the mandate to go out armed and act as police, authored it. However, in IS and other jihadist organizations, women are in no way perceived as equal to men within terrorist organizations. Nonetheless, women do elect to participate in terrorist organizations as providers of logistical support, and groups such as Hezbollah, Palestinian terrorist groups, and others operationalize women as fundraisers, demonstrators, and recruiters. Women are rarely included in the political operations of terrorist groups, but this has occurred; researchers frequently point to Rima Fakhry, the only female member of Hezbollah's political bureau.

In short, most recent research now shows that the inclusion of women into terrorist groups is part of a pragmatic and institutional choice with distinct organizational advantages for those groups. Including women does not give women equal rights or access to power within the organization, but they are generally used for roles supporting a male-dominated agency. Sometimes this includes participating in tactical operations such as suicide bombings, while other organizations keep women in more logistical roles.

Elisabeth Hope Murray

See also: Female Terrorists, Suicide Bombers; Islamic State, The; New Terrorism.

FURTHER READING

Blee, Kathleen. 2009. *Women of the Klan: Racism and Gender in the 1920s*. 2nd ed. Berkeley: University of California Press.

Bloom, Mia. 2017. "Women and Terrorism." *Oxford Research Encyclopedia of Politics* 1 (1): 1–17. https://doi.org/10.1093/acrefore/9780190228637.013.124

Davis, Jessica. 2017. *Women in Modern Terrorism: From Liberation Wars to Global Jihad and the Islamic State*. London: Rowman & Littlefield.

McCoole, Sinead. 2003. *No Ordinary Women: Irish Female Activists in the Revolutionary Years, 1900–23*. Madison: University of Wisconsin Press.

Oriola, Temitope. 2017. "'Unwilling Cocoons': Boko Haram's War against Women." *Studies in Conflict & Terrorism* 40 (2): 99–121. https://doi.org/10.1080/1057610X.2016.1177998

Siljak, Ana. 2008. *Angel of Vengeance: The Girl Who Shot the Governor of St. Petersburg and Sparked the Age of Assassination*. New York: St. Martin's Press.

Warner, Jason, and Hilary Matfess. 2017. *Exploding Stereotypes: The Unexpected Operational and Demographic Characteristics of Boko Haram's Suicide Bombers*. West Point, NY: Combating Terrorism Center at West Point.

Winter, Charlie. 2015. *Women of the Islamic State: A Manifesto on Women by the Al-Khanssaa Brigade*. London: Quilliam.

Female Terrorists, Suicide Bombers

Compared to male actors, fewer women have carried out suicide bombing attacks; however, research suggests that women have increasingly played key roles in most jihadist terrorist organizations as female suicide bombers.

Recent scholarship suggests that approximately one out of every five terrorist attacks are carried out by women (approximately 23%). This number is far from negligible. In fact, most terrorist organizations have utilized women in these roles, with Hezbollah and al-Qaeda in Afghanistan being the least likely to do so, and Boko Haram, the Islamic State, the Kurdish Workers' Party (PKK), and Fatah most likely to do so. Women are also more likely than men to participate in terrorist operations through social connections and organizations. Only a few women have acted as lone-wolf terrorists; as of the writing of this piece, all women suicide bombers have been part of terrorist organizations, in stark contrast to the male experience with jihadist terrorism.

Although a number of women identify as acting voluntarily on their own accord, research highlighting the inclusion of women in terrorist organizations underscores the fact that many women do so under coercive duress. Boko Haram is understood to have one of the highest percentages of female actors, many of whom are victimized and coerced into supporting the organization despite institutionalized sexual violence against them. Between January 1 and June 30, 2017, women executed 64.5 percent of Boko Haram suicide bombings, suggesting that the use of women in this role is on the rise. The majority of women's bombings were against civilian targets, whereas bombings carried out by male actors were more likely to be against military targets. Children, and particularly girls, are not immune to systematic violence; in fact, the youngest bombers noted in the above report were three seven-year-old girls whose attacks resulted in the deaths of six at different market venues in Nigeria. Children are the most easily coerced into action, particularly if they are orphans or born into the organization itself.

Nonetheless, many women profess to join foreign terrorist organizations and perform acts of terror of their own choice. Using women as suicide bombers can have tactical and strategic benefits, most notably because women are less likely to be perceived as a security threat, they can obscure incendiary devices under clothing more easily than men, and the deaths of women in terrorist attacks frees men to fight in other ways. Despite these facts, many reporting agencies, including datasets, mainstream media, policy makers, and politicians, consistently marginalize the actions of women in terrorist organizations, thereby perpetuating the ideal of women as victims rather than actors and limiting effective prevention and response measures. Scholars and activists alike agree that more research in this field is necessary, particularly on the motivation of women as suicide bombers.

Elisabeth Hope Murray

See also: Female Terrorists, Ideology and Logistics; Profiling; Sociology of Terrorism.

FURTHER READING

Alakoc, Burcu Pinar. 2018. "Femme Fatale: The Lethality of Female Suicide Bombers." *Studies in Conflict & Terrorism* 43 (9): 1–19. https://doi.org/10.1080/1057610X.2018.1505685

Bloom, Mia. 2007. "Female Suicide Bombers: A Global Trend." *Daedalus* 136 (1): 94–102. https://doi.org/10.1162/daed.2007.136.1.94

Davis, Jessica. 2013. "Evolution of the Global *Jihad*: Female Suicide Bombers in Iraq." *Studies in Conflict and Terrorism* 36 (4): 279–291. https://doi.org/10.1080/1057610X.2013.763598

Narozhna, Tanya, and W. Andy Knight. 2016. *Female Suicide Bombings: A Critical Gender Approach.* Toronto: University of Toronto Press.

Oriola, Temitope. 2017. "'Unwilling Cocoons': Boko Haram's War against Women." *Studies in Conflict & Terrorism* 40 (2): 99–121. https://doi.org/10.1080/1057610X.2016.1177998

Salem, Edmar. 2015. "Attitudes towards Female Suicide Bombers in Palestine and Tamil Sri Lanka." *Behavioral Sciences of Terrorism and Political Aggression* 7 (3): 200–209. https://doi.org/10.1080/19434472.2015.1009482

Turner, Kathleen. 2016. "The Rise of Female Suicide Bombers." *Counter Terrorist Trends and Analyses* 8 (3): 15–19.

Vogel, Lauren, Louise Porter, and Mark Kebbell. 2014. "The Roles of Women in Contemporary Political and Revolutionary Conflict: A Thematic Model." *Studies in Conflict & Terrorism* 37 (1): 91–114. https://doi.org/10.1080/1057610X.2014.853606

Warner, Jason, and Hilary Matfess. 2017. *Exploding Stereotypes: The Unexpected Operational and Demographic Characteristics of Boko Haram's Suicide Bombers.* West Point, NY: Combating Terrorism Center at West Point.

Note: The University of Chicago's Project on Security and Terrorism (CPOST) maintains a searchable database on all suicide attacks from 1974 through 2021, including information about the location of the attack, the target type, the weapon used, and systematic information on the demographic and general biographical characteristics of suicide attackers, including gender. At the time of this writing, the dataset can be found at https://cpost.uchicago.edu/research/suicide_attacks/database_on_suicide_attacks/.

Foreign Intelligence Surveillance Act of 1978 (FISA)

HISTORY

The Foreign Intelligence Surveillance Act (FISA) was signed into law by President Jimmy Carter on October 25, 1978. The catalyst for the act was a series of revelations starting in the 1950s and continuing through the 1970s regarding various warrantless surveillance activities of federal and state law enforcement agencies, national security organizations, and military intelligence. The multiple disclosures of abuses led to congressional hearings, often referred to as the Church Committee hearings, named after Senator Frank Church, who headed one of the Senate committees conducting the investigations. Also, the U.S. Supreme Court weighed in on domestic counterterrorist activity in *United States v. U.S. District Court*, 407 U.S. 297 (1972). This case is often referred to as the Keith case, after Judge Damon Keith, the federal district judge in the lower court. It remains an important case that addresses the extent to which the president, acting in the interest of national security, may authorize warrantless electronic surveillance of persons within the United States.

THE CODE

FISA is codified, as amended, at 50 U.S.C. §§ 1801-1885c. The act is composed of seven subchapters, each addressing a particular aspect of foreign intelligence surveillance. The subchapters include electronic surveillance (§§ 1801-1813); physical searches (§§ 1821-1829); pen registers and trap and trace devices for foreign intelligence purposes (§§ 1841-1846); access to certain business records for foreign intelligence purposes (§§ 1861-1864); oversight (§§ 1871-1874); additional procedures regarding certain persons outside the United States (§§ 1881-1881g); and protection of persons assisting the government (1885-1885c). Additionally, the act created the Foreign Intelligence Surveillance Court (FISC) and the Foreign Intelligence Surveillance Court of Review (FISCR) to oversee requests for surveillance warrants by federal law enforcement and intelligence agencies.

The intent underpinning FISA was to allow the continued collection of national security intelligence while preserving the civil liberties granted by the U.S. Constitution. Congress recognized the need to distinguish foreign intelligence gathering from surveillance for law enforcement purposes. As related to this act, the term *foreign* generally refers to the target rather than the location. Electronic surveillance and physical searches of an entity that does not fall within the definition of a *foreign power* or an *agent of a foreign power* are governed by Title III and Federal Rule of Criminal Procedure 41.

In broad terms, the act gives each branch of our national government some role in regulating foreign intelligence. It establishes the process for the executive branch to obtain surveillance warrants for gathering intelligence within the United States for foreign intelligence and foreign counterintelligence and creates the court system (judicial branch) with judicial review of the process. Additional oversight rests with Congress (legislative branch).

AMENDMENTS

The act has been amended numerous times since its enactment. Significant amendments include the USA PATRIOT Act of 2001, the Terrorist Surveillance Act of 2006, the Protect America Act of 2007, the FISA Amendments Act of 2008, the FISA Amendments Act Reauthorization Act of 2012, the USA FREEDOM Act of 2015, and FISA Amendments Reauthorization Act of 2017. The USA FREEDOM Reauthorization Act of 2020 was passed in both chambers of Congress albeit in non-identical forms. Since the versions were not reconciled, the bill died in Congress.

Ann Phillips

See also: Counterterrorism, the Courts, and the Constitution; Foreign Intelligence Surveillance Court; USA PATRIOT Act of 2001.

FURTHER READING

Bureau of Justice Assistance, U.S. Department of Justice. n.d. "The Foreign Intelligence Surveillance Act of 1978 (FISA): Justice Information Sharing." https://it.ojp.gov/PrivacyLiberty/authorities/statutes/1286

Foreign Intelligence Surveillance Act of 1978, 50 U.S.C. 36. https://fas.org/irp/agency/doj/fisa/

Tallman, Richard C., and Culbertson, Tania M. 2019. "2019 James R. Browning Distinguished Lecture in Law, 'Holding the Delicate Balance Steady and True': The History of FISA's Grand Bargain." *Montana Law Review* 80 (2): 137.

United States v. U.S. District Court, 407 U.S. 297 (1972).

Foreign Intelligence Surveillance Court (FISC)

The Foreign Intelligence Surveillance Court (FISC) was established in 1978 with the enactment of the Foreign Intelligence Surveillance Act (FISA). The original act has been amended many times since its original enactment. The makeup of the court and the many rules by which it operates are codified in the U.S. Code at 50 U.S.C. §§ 1801-1885c. This specialized Article III court reviews government applications to conduct electronic surveillance for domestic foreign intelligence purposes, including counterterrorism operations.

STRUCTURE OF THE COURT

The court itself is seated in Washington, DC, and is currently composed of eleven federal district court judges who have been designated by the chief justice of the U.S. Supreme Court for this additional assignment. No Senate confirmation for this additional duty assignment is required. Each judge on the FISC serves for a maximum of seven years and may not be redesignated. The terms of the judges are staggered to ensure the continuity of the court; one judge is designated by the chief justice as the "presiding judge," and this judge handles the various administrative duties of the court, such as assigning matters to the judges of the court. Pursuant to federal statute, the judges must, at all times, represent at least seven of the U.S. judicial circuits. Additionally, three of the judges must reside within twenty miles of the District of Columbia. Typically, each week, one of the designated judges sits on the FISC in Washington, on a rotating basis. Most of the court's work is handled by that duty judge and the support of attorneys and the personnel from the clerk's office. The more complex or time-consuming matters are assigned outside the duty-week system by the presiding judge.

SECRECY

The FISC is unique in that, contrary to typical courts of law, much of this court's work is conducted in secret. As the name indicates, this court is responsible for reviewing government applications for surveillance and other investigative activities related to foreign intelligence collection. In addition, orders of the court, including those which entail the court's legal analysis, often contain highly sensitive information. The release of such information could be damaging to national security. Documents that do not contain classified material and those that the FISC has deemed safe for dissemination can be found on the FISC's website (http://www.fisc.uscourts.gov/).

For security reasons, the FISC has its own clerk of court who is responsible for the record keeping, filings, and conventional duties of a court's clerk. All of the FISC's staff must possess and maintain security clearances commensurate with their individual responsibilities.

PRACTICE BEFORE THE COURT

Attorneys must be licensed and members, in good standing, of a U.S. district or circuit court. An exception is made in that an attorney who is employed by and representing the United States or any of its agencies in a FISC matter may appear before the court regardless of federal bar membership. All attorneys appearing before the FISC must have security clearances appropriate to the case and information involved. Parties other than the government must provide information regarding their security clearances in their initial submissions to the court. The nongovernment litigants who have the right to challenge a FISC order are individuals and companies who have been ordered to turn over information regarding a particular target.

In June 2015, both FISC and its court of review were mandated by statute to jointly designate no fewer than five individuals to be eligible to serve as amicus curiae, also known as friends of the court. The duty of the amicus curiae is to assist the court in the consideration of any filing that, in the opinion of the court, presents a novel or significant interpretation of the law. Additionally, amicus curiae may be appointed to provide technical expertise. To be considered eligible for designation, a person must possess expertise in privacy and civil liberties, intelligence collection, communications technology, or any other area that may lend legal or technical expertise to either the FISC or the FISC court of review. Like the attorneys who appear before the courts, amicus curiae must be eligible for access to classified information necessary to participate in matters before the courts, if such access is necessary to participate in the matters in which they may be appointed.

MATTERS PRESENTED TO THE COURT

All FISA orders are reviewed by this special court. There are four means of requesting relief from the FISC: by application, by certification, by petition, and by motion. An application is the most commonly used filing document when the government seeks to conduct domestic foreign surveillance pursuant to federal statutes. The government may also, when targeting non-U.S. persons reasonably believed to be located outside the United States, file a certification. Parties may file petitions with the court when seeking to review a production or nondisclosure order issued by the court or for review of enforcement of a directive. For example, an electronic communications service provider who has received a directive may file a petition to modify or set aside the directive; the government could file a petition to compel compliance with a directive where such compliance has not been forthcoming in accordance with the directive. A party seeking another type of relief must do so by filing a motion. The FISC has jurisdiction to hear applications for, and issue orders authorizing, four traditional FISA activities: electronic surveillance, physical searches, pen/trap surveillance, and compelled production of tangible things. In addition, the FISC has jurisdiction to review the government's targeting and minimization procedures related to programmatic surveillance certified under Section 702 of the FISA Amendments Act of 2008.

Pursuant to statutory authority, the FISC entertains applications submitted by the U.S. government and its agencies for approval of electronic surveillance, physical searches, and other investigative actions conducted for foreign intelligence purposes. In most circumstances, the government submits a proposed application, sometimes referred to as a "read copy," to the FISC no later than seven days prior to the government seeking to have the matter entertained; applications for bulk collection are typically filed more than one week in advance to allow for more exacting review using this same process. Upon receipt, someone from the court's legal staff reviews the application to evaluate whether it meets the legal requirements under the statute. After discussion with the government about the application, a written assessment is prepared by the court's attorney. This assessment is given to the duty judge for the week. The judge will review both the application and the legal staff's evaluation. A preliminary decision will be made by the judge regarding the course of action to be taken. Possible actions include approval without a hearing, imposing conditions on the approval, seeking additional information, or deciding a hearing is required prior to ruling. The judge's preliminary decision is conveyed to the government, which can proceed by providing additional information, filing a final application, or filing a final application with amendments; the government could also decide not to file a final application after learning the judge intends to deny it.

If the judge decides to deny the application, the judge must immediately prepare a written order denoting each of the reasons for the denial. In practice, the methodology of the process of application and review is similar to that utilized by other federal courts in their consideration of applications for wiretap orders under Title III of the Omnibus Crime Control and Safe Streets Act, codified at 18 U.S.C. §§ 2510-2522.

The process for addressing what is commonly referred to as Section 702 applications (see 50 U.S.C. § 1881a) differs but is based in large part on the statutory requirements set forth in the U.S. Code. The statute requires that, prior to implementation of such an authorization, both the attorney general and the director of national intelligence (DNI) must provide the FISC with a written certification. The court then reviews the certification not later than thirty days after the date upon which the certification was submitted. Similar to the other process, a read copy is submitted and reviewed by court staff, and recommendations for changes are made.

EX PARTE COMMUNICATIONS

In addition to being conducted in secret, most of the court's work is also conducted ex parte, meaning with only one side presenting information to the court. This aspect of the court is both required by statute and based on the need to protect classified national security information. As part of the review process, the court's attorney will often have multiple conversations with the government's attorney to seek additional information or discuss concerns with the application. As stated above, this is similar to the process employed in the federal courts when addressing applications for wiretap orders. A typical interaction would include telephone conversations on secure lines wherein the court staff ask the government questions regarding the legal and factual elements of the application or submission.

Additionally, the FISC, pursuant to statute and the procedural rules, holds hearings in which the judge assesses the information needed to make a fair determination on the matter at hand. Hearings are attended by, at a minimum, the attorney from the Department of Justice who prepared the application and a fact witness from the agency seeking the authorization of the court. Topics of the hearings will generally include the court seeking additional information on facts to justify the government's belief that the application is warranted, additional information on minimization procedures, any prior implementation of a court order, or information about a novel issue of law or new technology. It is standard procedure for the court to seek such information in a fair majority of cases.

COURT ORDERS

If the FISC judge determines that the final application has met all the statutory requirements and should be granted, the judge must issue an order approving the surveillance or search. Pursuant to statute, the order must describe the target, the information sought, the means of acquiring the information, and the period of time the order covers.

If a judge denied a final application of the government, that judge must provide a written statement providing the reasons for its ruling. The author of an opinion, order, or other decision may, either on their own or pursuant to a party, request the publication of the document. Upon such a request, the other judges are consulted. Prior to publication, the FISC may direct the executive branch to review the document and redact it as necessary to ensure that properly classified material is protected. Since the enactment of the FREEDOM Act, the DNI is responsible for reviewing each FISC order or opinion to determine whether it "includes a significant construction or interpretation of any provision of law." If so, it must be made public "to greatest extent practicable." When necessary to protect national security, however, the Office of the Director of National Intelligence (ODNI) may release a summary of the order or opinion.

EN BANC PROCEEDINGS

Pursuant to statute, the FISC may sit en banc, wherein the entire FISC membership sits to hear a case. The court only orders or grants such a determination where it deems it necessary to secure or maintain the uniformity of the court's decisions or where the case presents an issue of exceptional importance.

FOREIGN INTELLIGENCE SURVEILLANCE COURT OF REVIEW

The Foreign Intelligence Surveillance Court of Review (FISCR) was established in 1978 in the same bill that created the FISC. The review court also sits in Washington, DC. It is composed of three federal district court or appeals court judges who are designated to sit in that capacity by the chief justice of the U.S. Supreme Court. The purpose of this court is to review the decisions of the FISC, much in the same way the federal circuit courts of appeal review decisions of the federal district court.

The clerk that handles the matters of the FISC also takes care of the review court's filings and docket. To appeal a FISC decision to the review court, a party must file a petition of review with the clerk no later than thirty days after the entry of the decision or order for which review is sought. If necessary, the U.S. Supreme Court can, in certain circumstances, review FISCR decisions.

Ann Phillips

See also: Counterterrorism, the Courts, and the Constitution; Foreign Intelligence Surveillance Act of 1978; Homeland Security.

FURTHER READING

Federation of American Scientists. n.d. "Foreign Intelligence Surveillance Act." https://fas.org/irp/agency/doj/fisa/#rept

Foreign Intelligence Surveillance Court website. http://www.fisc.uscourts.gov/

Nolan, Andrew, and Richard M. Thompson II. 2014. Reform of the Foreign Intelligence Surveillance Courts: Procedural and Operational Changes. *CRS Report* R43362, August 26, 2014. https://sgp.fas.org/crs/intel/R43362.pdf

Reagan, Robert Timothy. 2016. "Foreign Intelligence Surveillance Act Litigation." Jurisdiction of the Federal Courts, Federal Judicial Center, September 26, 2016. www.fjc.gov/content/305810/foreign-intelligence-surveillance-act-litigation

Foreign Terrorist Groups at War with the United States

At this writing, the U.S. Department of State's Bureau of Counterterrorism lists fifty-six groups as foreign terrorist organizations (FTOs) with interests hostile to U.S. national security. Some are hostile due to U.S. support of their home regimes, some because of the footprint of Western culture on their homeland, some because of a belief that their resources have been exploited by neocolonial U.S. corporations, some because they want to topple the world order with the United States at its center, some because of a perceived arrogance of American foreign policy behavior in the postcommunist order, and some for reasons impossible to detect. The further reading section contains a link to that list, and the interests of those upon it vary. It is not so much the individual groups that are of importance here as the list itself.

Geographically, those listed encompass groups from around the globe, although the heaviest concentration originates in the Middle East. What unites them is that they must, by law, be *foreign* organizations. Nonetheless, the procedure for being placed and remaining on the list incorporates a level of due process. Once a group has been identified as a possible candidate for inclusion, an investigation ensues, with the report going to the secretary of state for action. In consultation with the secretary of the treasury and the attorney general, a final determination is made, albeit with Congress being notified and having seven days to block official action, which involves the group's name being published in the Federal Register. Periodic review is then required for the group to remain on the list. Hence, of the sixty-nine organizations designated as FTOs since 1997, the year following Osama bin Laden's first declaration of war against the United States, thirteen have subsequently been removed from the listed.

Once listed, sanctions take hold, which is the official list's real significance. Among the most serious penalties of being designated an FTO is that no U.S. citizen or resident can provide material support to the group, not even, given the 2010 ruling in the *Holder v. Humanitarian Law Project* case, to the nonviolent endeavors of any group. Banks holding their accounts must freeze the funds and notify the Office of Foreign Assets Control of the Treasury Department of their action. Noncitizen members of the groups are inadmissible to the United States and, if present, can be deported under certain conditions.

The action also puts the states containing them on notice that the continued harboring of an FTO may result in the state itself being placed on the State Department's State Sponsors of Terrorism list, with its own list of parallel sanctions. These include a ban on purchasing even defensive arms, limits on its exports to the United States, and a bar on receiving economic aid, including the United States opposing World Bank loans to the listed state. In short, states so designated often make numerous efforts to remove themselves from the list, like Sudan, even to the point of ousting organizations with local support. North Korea, Iran, Sudan, and Syria make up the current roster of State Sponsors of Terrorism.

Joseph R. Rudolph Jr.

See also: al-Qaeda; Hamas; Hezbollah; *Holder v. Humanitarian Law Project*; Islamic State, The; War on Terror: Somalia and Sudan.

FURTHER READING

U.S. Department of State, Bureau of Counterterrorism. n.d. "Foreign Terrorist Organizations." https://www.state.gov/foreign-terrorist-organizations/

U.S. Government Accountability Office. 2019. *Combating Terrorism: Foreign Terrorist Organization Designation Process and U.S. Agency Enforcement Actions*. Washington, DC: Government Printing Office.

Weesjes, Elke, with Phil Nerges. 2016. "100 Years of Terror." Natural Hazards Center, October 31, 2016. https://hazards.colorado.edu/article/100-years-of-terror-the-black-tom-explosion-and-the-birth-of-u-s-intelligence-services-1

Wright, Lawrence. 2017. *The Terror Years: From al-Qaeda to the Islamic State*. Visalia, CA: Vintage Reprint.

Fort Hood Shooting

November 5, 2009

Fort Hood was established in 1942 near Killeen, Texas, as Camp Hood and was later made a permanent military installation and renamed as Fort Hood. It is currently the largest active duty armored post in the U.S. Armed Forces, supporting almost 40,000 soldiers serving as infantrymen, cavalrymen, and tankers as well as units of engineers, mechanics, and health-care professionals. Home to III Corps, Fort Hood has a rich history of fulfilling defense missions dating back to the Second World War. However, it is also known as the site of one of the most deadly acts of domestic terrorism in American history.

2009 MASS SHOOTING

On November 5, 2009, Major Nidal Hasan, MD, a psychiatrist stationed at Fort Hood, entered the Soldier Readiness Processing Center, a facility where soldiers receive routine medical treatment before and after a deployment. Hasan had visited this facility as part of his preparations for deployment to Afghanistan. From a position behind a service desk, Hasan shouted, "*Allahu Akbar*!" (meaning "God is greater") and opened fire on the soldiers present. Witnesses said Hasan took care not to shoot civilians. Hasan was armed with an FN Five-seveN semiautomatic pistol and a Smith & Wesson .357 Magnum revolver, though he did not use the revolver in the shootings.

Wounded by a base civilian police officer, Hasan was captured as he moved through the center and was subsequently court-martialed in August 2013. He was found guilty of thirteen counts of premeditated murder and thirty-two counts of attempted murder. Hasan represented himself at the trial, claiming he had switched sides to fight as a Mujahideen against the United States. Hasan was unanimously sentenced to dismissal from the army and death.

Hasan's trial revealed that he had a relationship with the imam Anwar al-Awlaki, a major political voice for al-Qaeda. In prison he wrote a letter to Abu Bakr al-Baghdadi, the self-proclaimed caliph of the Islamic State, requesting to be made a citizen of his nation.

At the time of this writing, Hasan is incarcerated at Fort Leavenworth, Kansas, awaiting appellate review of his death sentence.

Despite the urgings of many survivors and families of the victims that the attack be classified as an act of terrorism, the Department of Defense classified Hasan's action as a case of workplace violence. The Federal Bureau of Investigation (FBI), in investigating the relationship between Hasan and al-Awlaki by reviewing emails between the two, had concluded that the communications were within Hasan's sphere of professional research. As investigators built a profile of Hasan, however, there were many signs of his claiming to be a soldier of Allah, holding anti-American views, and having contacts with people being tracked by the FBI.

Ygnacio "Nash" Flores

See also: al-Awlaki, Anwar; al-Qaeda.

FURTHER READING

Lieberman, Joseph I., and Susan M. Collins. 2011. *A Ticking Time Bomb: Counterterrorism Lessons from the U.S. Government's Failure to Prevent the Fort Hood Attack.* February 3, 2011. Washington, DC: U.S. Senate Committee on Homeland Security and Government Affairs. https://www.hsgac.senate.gov/imo/media/doc/Fort_Hood/FortHoodReport.pdf

McHugh, John M. 2014. *Approval of Report of Investigation into the Facts and Circumstances Pertinent to the Shooting Incident at Fort Hood, Texas, on 2 April 2014.* September 4. 2014. Washington, DC: Department of the Army. https://www.hsdl.org/?view&did=761564

William H. Webster Commission. 2012. *Final Report of the William H. Webster Commission on the Federal Bureau of Investigation, Counterterrorism Intelligence, and the Events at Fort Hood, Texas, on November 5, 2009.* July 19, 2012. Washington, DC: Federal Bureau of Investigation. https://www.hsdl.org/?view&did=717443

Zegart, Amy. 2015. "Insider Threats and Organizational Root Causes: The 2009 Fort Hood Terrorist Attack." *Parameters* 45 (2): 35–46. https://doi.org/10.55540/0031-1723.2907

G

Gaddafi (Qaddafi), Muammar

1943–2011

Muammar Mohammed Abu Minyar Gaddafi, commonly known as Colonel Gaddafi, was an Arab nationalist leader who ruled the North African country of Libya from 1969 until his 2011 death at the hands of insurgents. A military officer, Gaddafi orchestrated a coup d'état against the Western-backed monarchy that ruled Libya and instituted a period of over four decades of personal authoritative rule in its place.

Muammar Gaddafi was born into a family of Bedouin goat herders in western Libya in either 1942 or 1943. Gaddafi's father insisted that his son be educated, which was unusual for a poor family of Bedouin heritage. This primary education exposed Gaddafi to anti-colonial teachings and the pro-Arab nationalist movement spreading throughout the Middle East during the years following World War II. He briefly studied at the University of Libya but dropped out, choosing a military career instead. After attending the Royal Military Academy in Benghazi, Gaddafi organized a military coup in 1969 and formed the Revolutionary Command Council, whereby he ruled the new Libyan Arab Republic by personal decree. Advocating a pan-Arab political union, he strengthened ties with other Arab nationalist states, in particular Gamal Abdel Nasser's Egypt.

Following this bloodless revolutionary coup, Gaddafi, as chairman of the Revolutionary Command Council of the new Libyan Arab Republic, worked to consolidate his personal power. He appointed himself to the rank of colonel, assumed the title of commander in chief of the Libyan armed forces, and introduced several economic and social reforms in his goal toward socialism for Libya, including the nationalization of oil production starting in 1971.

In 1973, Gaddafi proclaimed as his political ideology the Third International Theory, which rejected both Western imperialism and Soviet-style communist atheism in favor of a form of progressive nationalism that he summarized and published collectively as *The Green Book* in 1975. In 1977 Gaddafi orchestrated the dissolution of the Libyan Arab Republic and formed the Great Socialist People's Libyan Arab Jamahiriya, naming himself general secretary and later the "leader of the revolution." However, Gaddafi effectively still ruled Libya through his force of personality and as its military commander.

Gaddafi's continued move toward socialism and pan-Arab nationalism put him on a collision course with the West. During the 1980s, Libya increasingly turned to the Soviet Union for support as its economy faded, further straining his relationship with the United States. Several incidents, including the Libyan government's possible involvement in the 1986 Berlin discotheque bombing that killed two American servicemen, resulted in a U.S. military air strike against Libya. Investigators once believed that in retaliation for that air strike, Gaddafi was behind the 1988 bombing of New York–bound Pan Am Flight 103. Gaddafi denied ordering it, but in 2003, he accepted responsibility for the bombing that took 259 lives and provided compensation to survivors of its victims.

Meanwhile, following the September 11, 2001, attacks on the U.S. homeland, Gaddafi condemned militant Islam and sought to normalize Libya's relations with the international community. In December 2003, after the U.S. invasion of Iraq, Libya agreed to dismantle its chemical and nuclear weapons programs under international supervision.

During the events of the Arab Spring in 2011, massive protests broke out against government corruption that soon spread into civil war. In March 2011, the United Nations Security Council declared a no-fly zone over parts of Libya, and on April 30, NATO announced it would enforce it. On October 20, 2011, Colonel Gaddafi was killed by rebel forces after he and his party were captured as his convoy was attacked by NATO warplanes.

John R. Capra

See also: Pan Am Flight 103 (Lockerbie) Bombing; State Terrorism; Transportation Security.

FURTHER READING

Cojean, Annick. 2013. *Gaddafi's Harem: The Story of a Young Woman and the Abuses of Power in Libya.* New York: Grove/Atlantic.

Crawford, Alex. 2012. *Colonel Gaddafi's Hat Hardcover.* New York: Collins.

Gaddafi, Muammar al-. 1975. *The Green Book.* Scotts Valley, CA: CreateSpace Independent Publishing Platform.

Kawczynski, Daniel. 2011. *Seeking Gaddafi: Libya, the West and the Arab Spring.* London: Biteback Publishing.

Little, Douglas. 2013. "To the Shores of Tripoli: America, Qaddafi, and Libyan Revolution 1969–89." *International History Review* 35 (1): 70–99. https://doi.org/10.1080/07075332.2012.742448

Ugongene, Lucky Emeka. 2018. *Face to Face with Gaddafi's Secret Security Forces.* London: Olympia Publishers.

Garden City, Long Island Rail Road Shooting

December 7, 1993

On the evening of December 7, 1993, a mentally unstable Jamaican American immigrant, Colin Ferguson, began shooting passengers on an eastbound Long Island Rail Road commuter train as it entered the Merillon Avenue station in Garden City, New York. Firing a Ruger 9 mm semiautomatic pistol, Ferguson shot twenty-five passengers, killing six and wounding nineteen others over the course of three minutes before he was subdued by other passengers. Statements Ferguson made following his arrest and notes found in his pockets indicated the shootings were racially motivated.

Ferguson was born in Kingston, Jamaica, in 1958 and immigrated to the United States in 1982, becoming a permanent resident when he married an American citizen in 1986. The marriage ended in divorce in 1988, and Ferguson held a succession of menial jobs; attended several colleges (including Adelphi University in Garden City), where he encountered academic difficulties; and increasingly experienced interpersonal conflicts due to his irrational and aggressive behavior. Ferguson's mental condition continued to deteriorate as he became obsessed with race and blamed his academic and employment problems as well as his interpersonal conflicts on racial discrimination. He regularly accused those around him of racism and racial discrimination.

On December 7, Ferguson boarded the 5:33 eastbound Long Island Rail Road train from New York's Penn Station to Hicksville. Witnesses stated that as the train entered the Merillon Avenue station in predominantly white Garden City, Ferguson rose from his seat and began calmly and methodically shooting passengers on both sides of the car's aisle. After firing thirty rounds, Ferguson paused to reload his gun, and several passengers tackled and held him for police.

Pretrial psychiatric examinations found that Ferguson was competent to stand trial. The trial itself was noteworthy because his attorneys raised a unique "Black rage" defense, arguing that after years of living in a discriminatory society, Ferguson was driven temporarily insane and therefore was not responsible for his actions.

Ferguson retained and subsequently fired a series of defense counsel and ultimately represented himself, denying that he had engaged in any shootings and conducting bizarre cross-examinations of victims and witnesses. He denied being at the scene of the murders and claimed they were carried out by another person. Found guilty of six counts of murder and nineteen counts of attempted murder, he received a sentence of 315 years and 8 months to life in prison. He remains in prison in upstate New York.

Carolyn McCarthy, whose husband was killed by Ferguson and whose son was severely injured in the attack, successfully campaigned for the U.S. House of Representatives on a gun control platform and served in Congress from 2013 to 2015.

Vincent E. Henry

See also: Beltway Sniper Attacks; Homegrown Terrorism; Psychology of Terrorists.

FURTHER READING

Barron, James. 1993. "Death on the L.I.R.R.: The Overview; Portrait of Suspect Emerges in Shooting on L.I. Train." *New York Times, December 9, 1993.*

McCoy, Kevin. 1993. "Ferguson Was 'Bomb Waiting to Explode.'" *Newsday*, December 9. 1993.

McFadden, Robert D. 1993. "A Tormented Life—A Special Report; A Long Slide from Privilege Ends in Slaughter on a Train." *New York Times, December 12, 1993.*

McQuiston, John T. 1995. "Jury Finds Ferguson Guilty of Slayings on the L.I.R.R." *New York Times, February 18, 1995.*

Guantánamo Bay Detention Camp

The Guantánamo Bay detention camp, often called Gitmo, is a U.S. military prison built within the confines of Guantánamo Bay Naval Base and opened in April 2002. The detention camp was established by President George W. Bush, and construction finished in January 2007.

Secretary of Defense Donald Rumsfeld had originally said that Guantánamo Bay was established for the long-term detention of "unlawful combatants" apprehended in Afghanistan, Pakistan, and further afield, to interrogate the detainees in an optimal setting and to prosecute them for war crimes in the U.S. "war on terror." Initial detainees were suspected al-Qaeda members as well as Taliban fighters, the Sunni fundamentalist political and military organization that ruled Afghanistan (1996–2001). The largest number of detainees were from Afghanistan, followed by Saudi Arabia and Yemen. Eventually, 779 prisoners from fifty countries would be held at the Guantánamo Bay detention camp without formal charges. It has been reported that most of the detainees were low-level operatives who were not affiliated with either al-Qaeda or the Taliban but captured by Afghans or Pakistanis and then sold for bounty payments.

Since the detention facility was outside of U.S. territory, the United States was neither required to grant constitutional protections nor required to observe the Geneva Conventions regarding the treatment of prisoners of war and civilians during wartime. In 2006, the U.S. Supreme Court ruled that the system of military commissions used to try detainees held at Guantánamo was in violation of the Geneva Conventions and the Uniform Code of Military Justice. The legality of the military commissions was addressed by the Military Commission Act of 2006. The ruling also denied the federal court's jurisdiction to hear habeas corpus petitions. This provision was overturned in 2008 with *Boumediene v. Bush*, 553 U.S. 723. The ruling held that aliens detained as military combatants in Guantánamo were entitled to a writ of habeas corpus protected in Article I, Section 9 of the U.S. Constitution. On October 28, 2009, President Barack Obama signed the Military Commissions Act of 2009, which amended the Military Commissions Act of 2006 and provided new rules for handling commission trials as well as defendant rights.

By May 2011, over 600 detainees had been released from Guantánamo. Most had been repatriated to facilities in their home countries with little chance for release. As of June 2013, the U.S. government has identified 46 detainees who were to be held indefinitely. In January 2018, President Donald Trump signed an executive order to keep the Guantánamo Bay detention camp open indefinitely. Currently, there are 40 detainees being held, nearly all without formal charges or trial.

Keith A. Leitich

See also: Counterterrorism and the George W. Bush Administration; Enhanced Interrogation Debate; War on Terror: Afghanistan and Pakistan.

FURTHER READING

Aradau, Claudia. 2007. "Law Transformed: Guantánamo and the 'Other' Exception." *Third World Quarterly* 28 (3): 489–501.

Fletcher, Laurel, and Eric Stover. 2009. *The Guantánamo Effect: Exposing the Consequences of U.S. Detention and Interrogation Practices*. Berkeley: University of California Press.

Johns, Fleur. 2005. "Guantánamo Bay and the Annihilation of the Exception." *European Journal of International Law* 16 (4): 613–635.
Rose, David. 2004. *Guantánamo: The War on Human Rights*. New York: New Press.
Steyn, Johan. 2004. "Guantánamo Bay: The Legal Black Hole." *International & Comparative Law Quarterly* 53 (1): 1–15.

H

Hamas

Hamas is a Sunni-Islamist Palestinian resistance movement. Its name is an acronym for *Harakat al-Muqāwamah al-Islāmiyyah*, which translates from Arabic to "Islamic Resistance Movement." The word *Hamas* itself literally translates to "zeal" in Arabic. The organization formed in 1987 as an offshoot of the Sunni-dominant Muslim Brotherhood in Palestine. Hamas opposes the recognition of Israel as a nation-state and promotes the Palestinian desire for nationhood and legitimacy. The movement consists of two main branches: a military branch known as the Izz al-Din al-Qassam Brigades, and a social service branch called Dawah.

Notable founders include Sheikh Ahmed Yassin, Abdel Aziz al-Rantisi, and Mahmoud Zahar. Hamas's headquarters and base of operations is located in the Gaza Strip, a narrow piece of land on the western Mediterranean Sea bordering Israel to the north and east and Egypt's Sinai Peninsula to the south.

Hamas defines Israeli and Western colonialism as the enemy of the Palestinian people. Its charter, approved in 1988, rejects involvement in peaceful solutions, initiatives, or international conferences related to the Israeli-Palestinian conflict. Hamas first came to be identified as a terrorist organization during its participation in the First Intifada, a wave of civil disobedience, violence, and mass protest by Palestinians against the Israeli state from 1987 to 1993. Hamas leadership opposed the 1993 Oslo peace process, a diplomatic bid for the Palestine Liberation Organization (PLO), led by Yasser Arafat, to recognize Israel's right to exist and for the Israeli government to recognize the PLO as the official representation of the Palestinian people.

In the years following the 1993 Oslo Accords, Hamas has conducted assassinations, kidnappings, shootings, suicide bombings, arson, and property damage as well as mortar and rocket attacks against Israeli citizens. The organization has been on the U.S. State Department's foreign terrorist organizations (FTO) list since its founding in October 1997 and the European Union's list of designated terrorist organizations. In a 2017 Hamas policy document, the organization stated its goals included the rejection of "Zionism," or the return of Jewish people to the region, and the liberation of Palestinian territories.

Hamas's strategy involves co-opting social organizations, mosques, and educational institutions to offer extensive social services to the Palestinian people. Hamas receives most of its funding from Palestinian expatriates, foreign officials, and wealthy benefactors outside the Levant, the geographical area that includes Israeli and Palestinian territories, Syria, Lebanon, and much of Jordan. Yet, Hamas's constituency is also actively involved in garnering financial support through charitable organizations, mosques, social institutions, and criminal organizations within Palestinian territories and the Levant region.

During the al-Aqsa Intifada, a second wave of Palestinian resistance against Israel from 2000 to 2006, Hamas offered medical support and financial assistance to Palestinian noncombatants. Campaigning under the Change and Reform Party, Hamas earned 74 of 132 seats during the 2006 Palestinian National Authority's (PA) parliamentary elections, gaining the majority of the seats in the Palestinian Legislative Council. Meanwhile, the incumbent party, Fatah, won only 45 seats.

After the 2006 elections, Hamas designated Ismail Haniyeh as its nominee for prime minister, establishing a unity government with the incumbent Fatah. The next year, after disputes between Fatah and Hamas leadership, PA president Mahmoud Abbas dismissed Haniyeh from the prime minister's office. In return, Hamas leadership forcibly removed all Fatah officials from the Gaza Strip. From 2007 onward, Fatah controlled the PA from the West Bank, while Hamas remained in power over the Gaza Strip and its nearly two million inhabitants, effectively splitting Palestine's governing factions.

Both Israeli and Egyptian diplomats have urged Hamas to release control of the Gaza Strip to the PA. From the time of Hamas's seizure of Gaza's governmental institutions, both Israel and Egypt have enforced an ongoing blockade of the Gaza Strip, cutting access by land, sea, and air. The blockade prompted tensions between Hamas and Israel, resulting in the three-week Gaza War in December 2008 and January 2009. In May 2018, representatives of the Fatah-led PA and Hamas met in Cairo to discuss reconciliation and cessation of the Gaza Strip to PA control, but talks were inconclusive.

Diane M. Zorri

See also: Female Terrorists, Suicide Bombers; War on Terror, The.

FURTHER READING

Baumgarten, Helga. 2005. "The Three Faces/Phases of Palestinian Nationalism, 1948–2005." *Journal of Palestine Studies* 34 (3): 25–48.

"The Covenant of the Islamic Resistance Movement HAMAS." *Oxford Islamic Studies Online*. Accessed August 31, 2018. http://www.oxfordislamicstudies.com/article/book/islam-9780195174304/islam-9780195174304-chapter-66

Levitt, Matthew. 2006. *Hamas: Politics, Charity and Terrorism in the Service of Jihad.* New Haven, CT: Yale University Press.

Pina, Aaron D. 2006. "Fatah and Hamas: The New Palestinian Fractional Reality." CRS Report for Congress, March 3, 2006. https://sgp.fas.org/crs/mideast/RS22395.pdf

U.S. State Department. n.d. "Foreign Terrorist Organizations." Accessed August 30, 2018. https://www.state.gov/j/ct/rls/other/des/123085.htm

Hard and Soft Targets

TARGETING AS A TERRORIST STRATEGY

Targeting by combatants has long been part of the strategy and tactics used against an adversary. Sun Tzu, the Chinese strategist who lived between 544 and 469

BCE, devoted significant sections on *The Art of War* to understanding the vulnerabilities and methods of mitigating points of attack against the enemy as well as one's own forces. Likewise, strategists since Sun Tzu have directly or indirectly referred to targeting as a strategy.

Terrorists and revolutionaries understand the importance of target selection. Sophia Perovskaya, a Russian revolutionary member of Narodnaya Volya, understood the assassination of Czar Alexander II to be both a social and political victory. Early seminal "how-to books" on revolutionary action discuss strategic targeting. The *Minimanual of the Urban Guerrilla* by Carols Marighella, a Brazilian guerrilla fighter; *Guerrilla Warfare* by Ernesto Che Guevara, an Argentine Marxist revolutionary; and *On Guerrilla Warfare* by Mao Zedong, a Marxist revolutionary all devoted space to target selection.

Islamist mentors also stress the importance of selecting targets for maximum impact with minimal resources. Sayyid Qutb, a founding leader in Islamist ideology and member of the Muslim Brotherhood, called for an offensive jihad when targeting the ignorant (*jahiliyah*) in his quest to establish Sharia in the Muslim world. His seminal book, *Ma'alim fi al-Tariq* (*Milestones*), established a pattern followed by contemporary Islamists. Muhammad Abd al-Salam Faraj discusses the concept of selecting targets from the perspective of the near and far enemy in his *Al-Farīḍah al-ghā'ibah* (1981; *The Neglected Duty*). Calls for homegrown terrorists to attack soft targets is a hallmark of communications from Osama bin Laden, Ayman al-Zawahiri, and Anwar al-Awlaki.

TARGETS

Targets are the points of concentration where combatants direct their efforts to control, disrupt, or destroy. A target can be a specific individual, illustrated in the assassination of President William McKinley by Leon Czolgosz, an anarchist, in 1901. A target can be a place, as seen in the attacks on abortion clinics in the twentieth and twenty-first centuries. A target can also be an idea or a symbol as exemplified by the September 11, 2001, terrorist attacks by al-Qaeda, a global Islamist group. A target can also serve as a hybrid of targeting for control, disruption, and destruction, as seen in the 2008 Mumbai terrorist attacks by Lashkar-e-Taiba, an Islamist terrorist group from Pakistan.

Hard Targets

Targets that are difficult to attack are hard targets. Hard targets have robust security in place. This includes layered physical security measures that may include perimeter barriers covered by one or more technologies to recognize intrusion or to ward off intruders. Security can include roving patrols that are human, animal, or technological. People entering a hardened facility use credentials in a system that controls access based on function within the organization. Hardened targets also have a visitor control system in place that monitors and controls access within the organization.

Examples of hard targets are military bases, federal buildings, courts, nuclear facilities, critical infrastructure, armories, banks, and other places or people that require security above the pedestrian concerns. The goal of hardening a target is to reduce the likelihood of a successful attack.

Soft Targets

Targets lacking layered and robust security measures are defined as soft targets. The lack of security in soft targets forms part of the culture of openness in democratic societies. Values based on access and openness of public spaces create parallel vulnerabilities that can be exploited by terrorists and violent extremists. Schools, colleges, universities, parks, national landmarks, malls, and concerts are examples of soft targets.

Ygnacio "Nash" Flores, Tracy E. Rickman, and Don Mason

See also: Fort Hood Shooting; Oklahoma City Federal Building Bombing; Targeted Assassinations; USS *Cole* Attack; World Trade Center Attack.

FURTHER READING

Asal, Victor H., R. Karl Rethemeyer, Ian Anderson, Allyson Stein, and Jeffrey Rizzo. 2009. "The Softest of Targets: A Study on Terrorist Target Selection." *Journal of Applied Security Research* 4 (3): 258–278. https://doi.org/10.1080/19361610902929990

Hammock, Dan W. 2020. "Terrorist Target Selection: Why Would They Come Here?" *IACP Police Chief*, June 2020. https://www.policechiefmagazine.org/terrorist-target-selection-why-would-they-come-here/

Nilsson, M. 2018. "Hard and Soft Targets: The Lethality of Suicide Terrorism." *Journal of International Relations and Development* 21: 101–117. https://doi.org/10.1057/jird.2015.25

Haymarket Affair

May 4, 1886

On May 4, 1886, Haymarket Square in Chicago was the site of a major labor rally organized to protest Chicago police violence and to demand the standardized eight-hour workday that was the subject of a strike on May 3 at McCormick Reaper Works. While eight hours had been the limit for workdays for some time, the federal government generally failed to enforce the applicable laws. In Illinois, evasion took the form of forcing job applicants to waive this right as a condition of employment. Chicago's mayor, Carter Harrison, who was a prolabor politician, had declared the May 4 protest to be peaceful and, therefore, allowed. Toward the rally's end, however, a still anonymous individual threw a bomb at the police line that had formed to disperse the protestors, protect strikebreakers, and intimidate the strikers. Almost immediately, the rally became a riot in which at least ten people, both police and civilian, died, and dozens were injured.

In the aftermath, and despite an overwhelming lack of evidence, eight labor activists who had not been present at the rally were convicted as accessories to the bombing. The then growing labor movement soon came to see them as martyrs; however, the riot itself was a major setback for labor concerns in the eyes of American business and society.

THE BROADER CONTEXT

By the late 1800s, the U.S. Industrial Revolution was in full swing, but it had evolved with little oversight, regulation, or control over either the factories or the companies that owned them. Working conditions were abysmal, wages were too low to live on, and workdays were unhealthily long. Labor unions fought to correct the barbarities that characterized working life in nineteenth-century factories. There was, however, significant opposition to the labor movement as a whole, in part because within the American labor movement, a radical faction pushed the idea that the capitalist system should be destroyed because it inherently abused workers and fueled class conflict.

In the context of this countrywide opposition to unions and the violence at Haymarket Square, law enforcement across the country began rounding up labor leaders, especially those born in other countries, in an effort to crack down on the perceived international threat. Of the eight men tried in connection with the Haymarket bombing, in what became a high-profile, controversial trial, seven were sentenced to death and one to fifteen years in prison. In the heated atmosphere of the time, this occurred despite the absence of concrete evidence and inconsistent testimony. Four were eventually hanged, one committed suicide the night before his execution, and two had their sentences reduced to life.

THE AFTERMATH

In 1893, public questioning of the trial's validity led Governor John Altgeld to reexamine the trial and conclude that the prosecution packed the jury, the judge was biased, and much of the evidence was unreliable. He thus pardoned the three activists still alive.

More broadly, there is a long social and economic legacy attached to this seminal labor event. The Knights of Labor, the country's largest and most successful union at the time, was blamed for the bombing. While their involvement was never proven, public distrust pushed many to leave the Knights for the more conservative American Federation of Labor (AFL), helping solidify AFL's place in labor history. Moreover, generations of activists were born of the Haymarket event, and their activism permanently changed the status of unions in the United States.

Finally, on the international stage, an AFL delegate attending a Paris labor conference recommended May 1 be designated International Labor Day in recognition of those injured and killed in the Haymarket Affair, and in almost every industrialized nation, May Day is now Labor Day. The United States, which celebrates Labor Day in September, is a notable exception to this custom. There are two reasons for this practice. First, President Grover Cleveland, the president when Congress passed legislation in 1894 to make Labor Day a federal holiday, opposed the May date specifically because it would remind Americans of the

Haymarket Affair. Second, the widely celebrated International Labor Day in May came to be associated with the political far left.

In the United States, there are visual reminders of the Haymarket Affair. A statue erected in 1889 to the police who died there stands in Haymarket Square, and a monument to the convicted stands in Forest Park, Illinois, in the cemetery that houses their graves.

Stacy Kowtko

See also: Domestic Terrorism, Anarchists; Domestic Terrorism, Pre-1950 Activity.

FURTHER READING

Adelman, William J. n.d. "The Haymarket Affair." Illinois Labor History Society. Accessed October 4, 2019. http://www.illinoislaborhistory.org/the-haymarket-affair

Green, James. 2007. *Death in the Haymarket: A Story of Chicago, the First Labor Movement and the Bombing That Divided Gilded Age America.* New York: Anchor Press.

Library of Congress. n.d. "Topics in Chronicling America: The Haymarket Affair." Library of Congress Newspaper & Current Periodical Reading Room. Accessed October 4, 2019. https://www.loc.gov/rr/news/topics/haymarket.html

Hezbollah

Hezbollah, meaning "Party of God," originated in the early 1980s, largely in response to the decades of conflict in Lebanon and the religious engagement of many clerics embracing the teachings of Iran's supreme leader, Ayatollah Khomeini. As a Shia Islamist group, Hezbollah has had a widespread impact over the last forty years in terms of its military and political involvement in multiple conflicts, including those involving Israel, Bosnia, and most recently Syria. Often listed as a terrorist organization by many Western governments, Hezbollah has been championed at home in Lebanon for providing social programs, hospitals, etc. when the Lebanese government could not due to poor fiscal management.

HISTORICAL CONTEXT

Hezbollah was created in Lebanon in response to the 1982 Israeli invasion of that country. With the logistical and financial support of Iran, and by embracing the Iranian leadership's religious rhetoric, the group gained momentum with its altercations with Israel and began carrying out terrorist attacks (primarily against Westerners) and other acts that were condemned by the global community. Some of the most infamous of these attacks were the 1983 bombing of the U.S. embassy (sixty-nine dead), the 1994 AMIA bombing (eighty-five dead), and the United Nations–investigated assassination of Rafic Hariri in 2005.

Although the acts of terror and atrocities continue under Hezbollah's organizational umbrella, during the 1990s, Hezbollah entered the political arena, shifting from seeking an official Islamic state to promoting policies that would support Lebanon as a whole. In addition, a marketing campaign was incorporated into Hezbollah's official television station, Al-Manar TV, showcasing the social service programs Hezbollah created or funded to assist the Lebanese people.

Globally, Hezbollah has been defined by its direct engagement in anti-Israeli and anti-Western action, by its forces in Syria allied with the Ba'ath government led by Bashar al-Assad's family, and by its global presence, which ranges from direct engagement in the Balkans and increasing activity in Latin America to the 2019 exposure of its sleeper cell in New York City. The latter is particularly troubling given that the Lebanese government, which includes Hezbollah representatives with access to funding, receives $10,000,000 each year from the United States via USAID.

EMBEDDED IN SOCIETY—WHEN THE LEBANESE GOVERNMENT FAILS ITS PEOPLE, HEZBOLLAH APPEARS TO FILL A VOID

Hezbollah's survival—despite its casualties in Syria—is largely due to the role it plays in a multitude of areas that are traditionally filled by global or local nongovernmental organizations (NGOs) or the government itself. It not only funds a multitude of projects; it also provides jobs, media, and health-care services, many of which are superior to those of Middle Eastern states.

There is also the organization's reach beyond the Lebanese people themselves. In addition to the displaced Syrian refugees in Lebanon, there is a large population of Palestinians who have been migrating to Lebanon for over half a century. Due to the Palestinian uprising in Lebanon in the 1970s, these refugees live in camps or often on the streets in the Hamra red light district. They have separate, poorly funded hospitals; are not allowed to own property; and face other highly restrictive policies unless a Lebanese man marries a displaced female. (There are no exceptions for males.) This in turn provides a perfect recruiting ground for Hezbollah, which often seems like a beacon of light in a very dark situation. The majority of camps in Lebanon have "stations" next to the camps that are recruiting posts either for Hezbollah or another familiar group, Hamas.

Although affected by the U.S. 2019 sanctions against Iran, Hezbollah continues to appear as an intricate component of every aspect of Lebanese life—education, health, government, media, and so on. Is there a possibility for change? According to recent activity in terms of public outcry against the government in October 2019 and again in August 2020, Hezbollah's influence may *possibly* be coming to an end. This has become even more apparent after the August 30, 2020, bombing of the Port of Beirut. Protests calling for change, including Hezbollah's role in governmental decisions, have only escalated since the bombing. Hezbollah's role in Lebanon is no longer guaranteed.

Rachel E. McGinnis

See also: Hamas; Recruiting Terrorists; Sociology of Terrorism.

FURTHER READING

Ali, Mohanad H. 2019. *Power Points Defining the Syria-Hezbollah Relationship.* Carnegie Middle East Center Series on Political Islam. Washington, DC: Carnegie Endowment for International Peace.

Flanigan, Shawn, and Mounah Abdel-Samad. 2009. "Hezbollah's Social Jihad: Nonprofits as Resistance Organizations." *Middle East Policy* 16 (2): 122–137. https://doi.org/10.1111/j.1475-4967.2009.00396.x
Mapping Militant Project. 2019. "Hezbollah." Stanford University. Last modified July 2019. https://cisac.fsi.stanford.edu/mappingmilitants/profiles/hezbollah
Norton, Augustus R. 2007. *Hezbollah: A Short History*, 34–45. Princeton, NJ: Princeton University Press.
USAID. 2020. *Lebanon: Country Development Cooperation Strategy: December 31, 2014–December 31, 2020.* https://www.usaid.gov/sites/default/files/documents/1883/Lebanon_CDCS_Dec_2020.pdf

Holder v. Humanitarian Law Project

2010

Holder v. Humanitarian Law Project, 561 U.S. 1 (2010), is a U.S. Supreme Court decision concerning the "material support" provision of the Anti-Terrorism and Effective Death Penalty Act of 1996 (AEDPA), 18 U.S.C. §2339(B)(a)(1). This statute made it a crime to provide "material support or resources" to groups designated as "foreign terrorist organizations" by the secretary of state. As part of the USA PATRIOT Act (or Patriot Act), Congress amended the definition of "material support or resources" to include "expert advice or assistance." The plaintiffs wished to aid groups that had been designated foreign terrorist organizations to enable them to, among other things, train to resolve disputes peacefully through humanitarian and international law. The plaintiffs claimed the statute was unconstitutionally vague and violated their First Amendment free speech and free association rights. The Supreme Court held that §2339(B) was not unconstitutional as applied to the plaintiffs.

More specifically, the Humanitarian Law Project and other plaintiffs wished to provide support, including legal advice and training, and political advocacy, for the *nonviolent* activities of the Kurdistan Workers' Party (PKK) and the Liberation Tigers of Tamil Eelam (LTTE). Under an older version of the law, they won a permanent injunction that prevented the government from prosecuting them for providing personnel and training on the grounds that the statute was unconstitutionally vague.

Congress amended the definition of "material support or resources" in §2339(B) as part of the Patriot Act in 2001. The amended definition included "expert advice or assistance," and the plaintiffs were concerned they would again be subject to prosecution. They wished to train PKK members on the use of humanitarian and international law to resolve disputes without violence, to engage in political advocacy for Kurds living in Turkey, and to teach PKK members how to apply for relief from the United Nations and other international organizations. They filed a pre-enforcement challenge to the constitutionality of the amended statute, challenging it on both vagueness and First Amendment grounds.

When the plaintiffs' second case reached the Supreme Court, the justices addressed four substantive legal issues:

1. Does the statute, when applied to speech, require proof that a defendant intended to further a foreign terrorist organization's illegal activities?

2. Is the material support statute unconstitutionally vague as applied to the plaintiffs?
3. Does the statute violate the plaintiffs' First Amendment right to free speech?
4. Does the statute violate the plaintiffs' First Amendment right to freedom of association?

The court answered "no" to each of the questions, holding on the first issue that the statute does not require the government to prove a defendant's intent to further a foreign terrorist organization's illegal activities. The statute defines "knowingly" as having knowledge about the organization's terrorist activities, not an intent to further those activities.

The court also held that the material support statute was not unconstitutionally vague as applied to the plaintiff, who argued the statute was so vague as to violate the Fifth Amendment's due process guarantee because it did not provide fair notice of what it prohibits. The court disagreed, stating that narrowing definitions in the statute clarified the relevant terms "training," "expert advice or assistance," and "personnel" so that plaintiffs could reasonably determine whether the activities they wanted to engage in were prohibited.

The court further held that the statute did not violate the plaintiffs' First Amendment rights to freedom of speech or freedom of association. While the statute did infringe on plaintiffs' speech rights, combating terrorism was a sufficiently compelling interest to justify this infringement. The court's opinion invoked precedents that applied "strict scrutiny" but never explicitly said they were applying this standard. Strict scrutiny applies when a statute burdens freedom of speech. It requires that the government demonstrate a compelling interest and that the statute be narrowly tailored to achieve that interest. In finding that the government met its burden, the court cited findings of Congress and the executive branch that terrorist groups are so tainted by criminality that even contributing to their legal nonviolent activities also facilitates their terrorist activities.

The court also held that the plaintiffs' freedom of association was not violated, as the statute only prohibits specific activities defined in the material support statute. It does not prohibit someone from simply joining a foreign terrorist group or from supporting a group's political goals.

The decision could have important repercussions for the work of some nongovernmental organizations. David Cole, a law professor and the attorney who represented the Humanitarian Law Project, noted that "nongovernmental organizations working to resolve conflict or to provide humanitarian assistance may well be unable to operate where designated 'terrorist organizations' are involved, because any advice or assistance they provide could be criminally prohibited" (Cole 2012, 149). As one example, Cole noted that the law would criminalize the Carter Center's election monitors meeting with Hezbollah in Lebanon to explain their criteria for a free and fair election.

In analyzing material support prosecutions before and after *Holder v. Humanitarian Law Project*, Benjamin Bricker found that the case did not represent a major change from existing material support jurisprudence. Prior to this case, three federal circuits had all reached similar conclusions that the statute did not violate the First Amendment. In this respect, the court only solidified already existing doctrine.

The court's most important legal contributions in this case were to clarify that the material support statute burdens speech and must therefore be analyzed with strict scrutiny and that the government's justification for the statute passes the strict scrutiny test. This is a significant development, as many statutes judged by the strict scrutiny standard are overturned by the court.

Jonathan B. Hensley

See also: Foreign Intelligence Surveillance Act of 1978; Intelligence Community, Adjustments to the Post-9/11 World; USA PATRIOT Act of 2001.

FURTHER READING

Bricker, Benjamin. 2017. "Material Support for Terror and *Holder v. Humanitarian Law Project*: An Empirical Examination." *Southern Illinois University Law Journal* 42 (1): 1–40.

Cole, David. 2012. "The First Amendment's Border: The Place of *Holder v. Humanitarian Law Project* in First Amendment Doctrine." *Harvard Law and Policy Review* 6: 147–177.

Homegrown Terrorism

Homegrown terrorism is a common term used to describe acts of domestic terrorism carried out by citizens against the nation of which they are a part. Examples of groups and individuals in the United States who have committed acts of homegrown terrorism over the last half century include the Weathermen, the Symbionese Liberation Army (SLA), "Unabomber" Ted Kaczynski, and Timothy McVeigh and Terry Nichols, who carried out the Oklahoma City bombing.

The acts of violence carried out by these individuals and groups have been treated by some people as criminal acts rather than as the more repugnant act of terrorism, in large part because few can agree on what exactly *terrorism* is despite the ubiquitous nature of the term. This paradox still fuels social, political, economic, and cultural arguments concerning the management and mitigation of acts and people related to homegrown terrorism. What can be noted clearly is that although homegrown terrorism was considered rare in the past, there has been an increase in the use of extreme acts of violence carried out for political and ideological reasons by citizens against their own countries in the twenty-first century.

LONE WOLVES

Associated with the violence of homegrown terrorism is the idea of the perpetrator acting alone as a non-state actor. The label associated with an individual homegrown terrorist is *lone wolf.* This term was initially coined in the 1990s by self-professed white supremacist Alex Curtis. Curtis encouraged fellow white supremacists to carry out individual acts of terrorism in what he called "Operation Lone Wolf" as a form of activism. Curtis pictured numerous lone wolves acting in a noble fashion to further the ideology of white supremacy.

Some people and organizations that study terrorism or are engaged in counterterrorism activities have sought to replace the term *wolf,* which connotes fierceness and independence, with animals that have more negative connotations. Brian Michael Jenkins, a scholar of terrorism, called them "stray dogs," and Ygnacio Flores, a professor of homeland security studies, referred to them as "hyenas," portraying homegrown terrorists as lesser entities in the greater animal kingdom.

HOMEGROWN VIOLENT EXTREMISM

A subset of homegrown terrorism is homegrown violent extremism (HVE). HVE is on the rise as seen in attacks in the United States and around the world in incidents involving guns, knives, vehicles, and bombs—all used with the intention of inflicting mass casualties. Motivation for these attacks is an extreme ideology acted out through intense violence. Erroll Southers (2013), a terrorism expert, posits that HVE stands apart from terrorism in that the extremist both goes beyond the protections of the First Amendment of the U.S. Constitution in using extreme violence and is often motivated by revenge or altruism. Comparably, Flores views violent extremism through a lens that involves the dynamic relationship between an oppressor and the oppressed and the use of violence as a means for either regime annihilation or regime continuity.

Similar to the predisposition to couple perceptions of terrorism with the Islamic faith, HVE is often perceived as the result of individuals influenced by al-Qaeda and the Islamic State (IS) to use violence in their global jihad. There are corresponding reports of white supremacists and national movements using the same tactics to influence followers and would-be followers.

Also associated with HVE is the use of social media and the Internet to influence people to engage in extreme violence. Al-Qaeda, IS, and many white supremacist groups have used the virtual environment to radicalize people against their own countries. White supremacists have also targeted college campuses for venues to recruit people to their cause.

CONTROVERSY OF HOMEGROWN TERRORISM

Adding to the quandary surrounding the definition of terrorism is that the primary viewpoints of terrorism are based on culturally Western political perspectives. There is a marked emphasis in the United States on linking homegrown terrorists with the Islamic faith. Contemporary political views of the Trump administration alluded to a corresponding perspective on homegrown terrorism being an Islamic-related issue. Scholars point out, however, that many acts of homegrown terrorism in the United States in the twenty-first century have been carried out by right-wing or white supremacist groups that have no Muslim component to them (in fact, these groups are notably hostile to followers of the Islamic faith). Political currents in reframing violence were notable in the decoupling of the term *domestic terrorism* from the 2009 Fort Hood mass shooting by Major Nidal Hasan. Instead, the deaths and injury caused by Hasan were categorized as "workplace violence."

The rise of HVE has led to the passage of new laws authorizing federal law enforcement and national security agencies to conduct surveillance of citizens and people in the United States. This trend has led both liberals and conservatives to express concerns that those actions have eroded privacy rights and other constitutional liberties.

INFAMOUS ACTS OF HOMEGROWN TERRORISM

One of the earliest examples of homegrown terrorism cited by scholars was the Milwaukee Police Department bombing. On November 24, 1917, a janitor took a bomb originally intended to explode at an evangelical church in the city's Third Ward to a Milwaukee police station, where it exploded, killing nine officers and one civilian. Investigators believed the perpetrators were Galleanist anarchists; however, no arrests occurred.

Other notorious instances of homegrown terrorism in American history include the 1886 Haymarket Affair, in which rioting broke out in the streets after a bomb exploded during a labor union meeting in Chicago; the 1920 Wall Street bombing that killed 38 and injured over 400; the 1995 bombing of the Oklahoma City Federal Building, which killed 168 people and wounded 680 others; the letter bombs sent by "Unabomber" Theodore "Ted" Kaczynski to members of the academic community between 1978 and 1995; and Eric Robert Rudolph's detonation of bombs during the 1996 Summer Olympics in Atlanta.

Since 9/11, instances of homegrown terrorism in the United States have not only multiplied but also involved an expanding universe of actors. Many of these horrible events, like the Wisconsin Sikh temple shooting of August 5, 2012, in which Wade Michael Page shot and killed six people from the Gurdwara Sikh Temple in Oak Creek before committing suicide, involve self-proclaimed white nationalists. The shooter who killed twenty-two and wounded twenty-four others at a Walmart in El Paso in August 2018 was motivated by anti-immigrant hatred, while the 2015 Charleston church shooting in which a white man killed nine African American worshippers stemmed from virulent racist beliefs.

Self-proclaimed and suspected Islamic jihadists offer a second set of actors, most notably present in the San Bernardino shooting in December 2015 and the Orlando Pulse nightclub shooting the following year. In the first instance, Syed Farook, a Pakistani American, and his wife, Tashfeen Malik, a Pakistani immigrant, killed 14 people and wounded 24 others at a San Bernardino County Department of Public Health holiday party. In the latter case, Omar Martin, who pledged allegiance to IS before the attack, entered the Pulse nightclub, an LGBT venue, and killed 49 people and wounded another 58 before police killed him. The 2015 Boston Marathon bombing, meanwhile, was carried out by two Kyrgyz American brothers who had fallen under the influence of radical Islamic beliefs. They detonated two pressure cooker bombs near the finish line during the Boston Marathon, killing 3 people and wounding at least 264 others.

Then there are the cases in which motivations are almost impossible to discern, such as the October 1, 2017, Las Vegas shooting in which Stephen Paddock shot people attending the Route 91 Harvest Musical Festival from his Mandalay Bay Hotel room on the thirty-second floor. He killed 58 concertgoers, and his attack resulted in injuries to more than 850 others. Paddock killed himself as police officers began to breach his hotel room. His motivation for the attacks is still undetermined, although the terrorist group ISIS later tried to take credit for Paddock's killing spree.

Finally, the sheer volume of mass shooting incidents in the United States often complicates ascertaining motives and separating terrorist acts from the pack. Between 1949 and 2018, there was over twenty-six mass shooting attacks that resulted in the deaths of more than ten people, perpetrators included. When incidents with fewer than ten deaths are included, the total jumps into the hundreds. School shootings, however, constitute many of these incidents, and analysts infrequently classify these horrific events as acts of homegrown terrorism.

Ygnacio "Nash" Flores

See also: Active Shooter Scenarios; Aryan Nations; Boston Marathon Bombing; Centennial Olympic Park Bombing; Charleston Church Massacre; Christmas Day "Underwear Bomber," Umar Farouk Abdulmutallab; Columbine Attack; Domestic Terrorism, Anarchists; Domestic Terrorism, Anti-Semitic; Domestic Terrorism, the Civil Rights Era; Domestic Terrorism, White Supremacists; Fort Hood Shooting; Haymarket Affair; Oklahoma City Federal Building Bombing; Orlando Pulse Nightclub Shooting; Rudolph, Eric Robert; San Bernardino Attack; Unabomber Attacks, Theodore John "Ted" Kaczynski; Wall Street Bombing.

FURTHER READING

ADL Center on Extremism. 2017. *Murder and Extremism in the United States in 2017.* New York: Anti-Defamation League. https://www.adl.org/media/10827/download

Bjelopera, Jerome P. 2013. *American Jihadist Terrorism: Combating a Complex Threat.* January 23, 2013. Washington, DC: Congressional Research Service. https://fas.org/sgp/crs/terror/R41416.pdf

Bjelopera, Jerome P. 2017. *Domestic Terrorism: An Overview.* Washington, DC: Congressional Research Service, August 21. https://fas.org/sgp/crs/terror/R44921.pdf

Brooks, Risa A. 2011. "Muslim 'Homegrown' Terrorism in the United States: How Serious Is the Threat." *International Security* 36 (2): 7–47. http://www.jstor.org/stable/41289697

CNN. n.d. *Deadliest Mass Shootings in Modern US History Fast Facts.* CNN Library webpage. Accessed September 22, 2018. https://edition.cnn.com/2013/09/16/us/20-deadliest-mass-shootings-in-u-s-history-fast-facts/index.html

Flores, Ygnacio. 2017. *The Pedagogy of Violent Extremism.* New York: Peter Lang.

Flores, Ygnacio. 2018. "Mismanaging America's Demographic Shift, the Rise of Violent Extremism, and Responding to a Culture of Fear." In *Homeland Security Cultures: Enhancing Values while Fostering Resilience*, edited by Alexander Siedschlag and Andrea Jerkovic, 65–78. New York: Rowman & Littlefield.

Jenkins, Brian M. 2011. *Stray Dogs and Virtual Armies: Radicalization and Recruitment to Jihadist Terrorism in the United States Since 9/11.* Santa Monica, CA: RAND. https://www.rand.org/pubs/occasional_papers/OP343.html

Reilly, Ryan J. 2018. "There's a Good Reason Feds Don't Call White Guys Terrorists, Says DOJ Domestic Terror Chief." *HuffPost*, January 11, 2018. https://www.huffingtonpost.com/entry/white-terrorists-domestic-extremists_us_5a550158e4b00-3133ecceb74

Southers, Erroll. 2013. *Homegrown Violent Extremism.* New York: Elsevier.

University of Maryland. n.d. *Global Terrorism Database.* Accessed September 23, 2018. https://www.start.umd.edu/gtd/

Homeland Defense and the Department of Defense

The U.S. Department of Defense (DoD) is responsible for two principal missions in the U.S. homeland: homeland defense and defense support of civil authorities.

HOMELAND DEFENSE (HD)

The DoD's Joint Publication 3-27 defines *homeland defense* (HD) as "the protection of US sovereignty, territory, domestic population, and critical infrastructure against external threats and aggression or other threats, as directed by the President of the U.S." HD is thus a very specific part of the overall U.S. homeland security enterprise. For example, during the 9/11 attacks, the DoD was responsible for being prepared to shoot down the hijacked aircraft before the terrorists could complete their attacks. HD is the only homeland security–related mission for which the DoD is the primary lead federal agency, which means that it bears primary responsibility for accomplishing this mission.

HD is not a new role for the DoD. Since 1957, the North American Aerospace Defense Command (NORAD) has been a joint U.S.-Canadian military command charged with defending the airspace of North America. In 2006, NORAD's mission was expanded to include maritime warning. NORAD monitors North America's airspace and maritime approaches to warn of attacks by aircraft, missiles, and spacecraft. The investigation into the failure of NORAD's airborne-alert fighters to intercept the commercial aircraft hijacked by al-Qaeda terrorists on September 11, 2001, resulted in the creation of a new DoD joint combatant command designated U.S. Northern Command (USNORTHCOM). USNORTHCOM's mission is to detect, deter, and defeat threats to the United States; to conduct security cooperation activities with allies and partners; and to support civil authorities. The commander of USNORTHCOM also commands NORAD. As a joint command, USNORTHCOM commands forces from all service branches to accomplish its HD mission.

DEFENSE SUPPORT OF CIVIL AUTHORITIES (DSCA)

USNORTHCOM is also responsible for accomplishing the DoD's *defense support of civil authorities* (DSCA) mission by providing military forces from all branches to provide assistance to civil authorities during disasters. The Stafford Act of 1998 provides the authority for the domestic use of U.S. military forces in this support capacity. DSCA includes support to prepare, prevent, protect, respond to, and recover from domestic incidents and is provided in response to approved requests from civil authorities. The DoD possesses a wide range of capabilities that are valuable during a disaster, such as air, sea, and land transport of supplies; provision of emergency electrical power; operation of mobile military hospitals; and extensive portable communications capabilities. DoD's DSCA activities follow the procedures described in the *National Response Framework* (NRF) and the *National Incident Management System* (NIMS). The DoD always plays a supporting role in DSCA missions. It is never the lead federal agency, which is usually the Federal Emergency Management Agency (FEMA).

ADDITIONAL DOD CONTRIBUTIONS TO HOMELAND SECURITY

The DoD continuously shares relevant intelligence from its considerable intelligence assets to support the intelligence community's efforts to detect threats to the homeland. When authorized by the president pursuant to the Insurrection Act of 1807 (as amended), the DoD can employ the U.S. Armed Forces to reestablish law and order in areas where local and state governments either cannot or will not do so. Otherwise, uses of the U.S. Armed Forces to perform domestic policing functions are limited by the Posse Comitatus Act of 1878 (as amended). Prohibiting direct military involvement in law enforcement is in keeping with long-standing U.S. law and policy limiting the military's role in domestic affairs.

William J. Lahneman

See also: Defense Intelligence Agency; Department of Homeland Security; Director of National Intelligence; Information Sharing Environment; September 11, 2001, Attack on America.

FURTHER READING

Defense Support of Civil Authorities. 2015. "Interagency Partner Guide for Disasters and Emergencies." January 2015. https://policy.defense.gov/Portals/11/Documents/hdasa/DSCAInteragencyPartnerGuide.pdf

Joint Chiefs of Staff. 2018a. *Joint Publication 3-27: Homeland Defense: 10 April 2018*. Washington, DC: U.S. Department of Defense. https://www.jcs.mil/Portals/36/Documents/Doctrine/pubs/jp3_27.pdf

Joint Chiefs of Staff. 2018b. *Joint Publication 3-28: Defense Support of Civil Authorities: 29 October 2018*. Washington, DC: U.S. Department of Defense. https://www.jcs.mil/Portals/36/Documents/Doctrine/pubs/jp3_28.pdf

U.S. Department of Homeland Security and FEMA. 2017. *National Incident Management System*. 3rd ed. October 10, 2017. Washington, DC: DHS and FEMA. https://www.fema.gov/sites/default/files/2020-07/fema_nims_doctrine-2017.pdf

U.S. Department of Homeland Security and FEMA. 2019. *National Response Framework*. 4th ed. October 28, 2019. Washington, DC: DHS and FEMA. https://www.fema.gov/sites/default/files/2020-04/NRF_FINALApproved_2011028.pdf

U.S. Northern Command website. https://www.northcom.mil/

Homeland Security

Homeland security is an overarching concept that includes the national effort to keep the United States safe from threats and hazards caused by manmade or natural disasters. The characterization of the homeland, as a point of reference for security, came into the American lexicon after the September 11, 2001, al-Qaeda terrorist attacks on New York City and Washington, DC, and in response to the Homeland Security Act of 2002. With the creation of the cabinet-level Department of Homeland Security, defending the United States from acts of terrorism became a leading national security issue and policy priority.

HOMELAND SECURITY AS A DEPARTMENT

The Department of Homeland Security (DHS) was created by bringing together twenty-two separate federal agencies under the newly created cabinet-level department to safeguard the United States against terrorism. Some of the federal agencies that joined the DHS included the U.S. Coast Guard, the Federal Emergency Management Agency (FEMA), the U.S. Customs and Border Protection, U.S. Citizenship and Immigration Services, Federal Protective Service, Transportation Security Administration (TSA), and the U.S. Secret Service.

Driving the initial efforts and direction of homeland security was the *9/11 Commission Report*, which explored the national vulnerabilities that precipitated the September 11, 2001, terrorist attacks by al-Qaeda. With an emphasis on terrorism, the 9/11 report helped shape the first *National Strategy for Homeland Security* in 2002. Subsequent national strategies have been inclusive of all hazards and have balanced terrorism and emergency management.

The emphasis on countering terrorism as a primary mission area of the DHS was expanded to include disasters and the discipline of emergency management after Hurricane Katrina caused over $125 billion in damage when it struck the Gulf Coast of the United States in August 2005. The heavily criticized federal response during Hurricane Katrina prompted Congress to pass the Post-Katrina Emergency Management Reform Act of 2006, elevating emergency management as a priority for DHS.

HOMELAND SECURITY VERSUS HOMELAND DEFENSE

While often used interchangeably, there is a distinct difference between the term *homeland security*—the national effort to prevent and respond to hazards domestically—and *homeland defense*, which is the protection of national sovereignty from external threats. Homeland defense is a responsibility of the Department of Defense (DoD), while homeland security is a responsibility of DHS.

Of particular importance in these two mission areas is the use of the National Guard by DHS and the DoD. The orders calling the National Guard to duty are authorized under the United States Code. Normally when the National Guard is used to support the actions of the DHS, the authority over the forces falls under Title 32, which is authorized by a state governor. When the National Guard is called to service under the authority of the DoD, Title 10 is enacted.

HOMELAND SECURITY ENTERPRISE

As the DHS refined its mission areas, a term was developed that encompassed the growing public-private partnerships that became known as the *homeland security enterprise*. Composed of various institutions, agencies, and businesses, the collective efforts address the various mission areas of homeland security.

Critical infrastructure (CI) protection, part of the homeland security enterprise, includes sixteen sectors: chemical; commercial facilities; communications; critical manufacturing; dams; defense industrial base; emergency services; energy; financial services; food and agricultural; government facilities; healthcare and public health; information technology; nuclear reactors, materials, and wastewater; transportation systems; and water and wastewater systems.

In addition to the *National Strategy for Homeland Security* series, the next federal-level document that guides homeland security strategy and priorities is the *Quadrennial Homeland Security Review*. Published by the secretary of homeland security, the *Quadrennial Homeland Security Review* is a legal requirement that is dynamic and takes over three years to develop. This document is developed in concert with a wide range of stakeholders from within and outside the government.

Ygnacio "Nash" Flores

See also: Counterterrorism and the George W. Bush Administration; Critical Infrastructure as a Terrorist Target; Department of Homeland Security; Homeland Defense and the Department of Defense; Homeland Security Act of 2002.

FURTHER READING

Bullock, J. A., G. D. Hassow, and D. P. Coppola. 2016. *Introduction to Homeland Security*. 5th ed. New York: Elsevier.

Bush, G. W. 2002. *National Strategy for Homeland Security*. Washington, DC: Office of Homeland Security.

9/11 Commission. 2004. *The 9/11 Commission Report*. New York: W. W. Norton & Company.

109th Congress. 2006. *Post-Katrina Emergency Management Reform Act of 2006 (Pub.L. 109-295)*. Washington, DC: Government Printing Office.

107th Congress. 2002. *An Act to Establish the Department of Homeland Security and for Other Purposes (Pub.L. 107-296)*. Washington, DC: Government Printing Office.

Homeland Security Act of 2002

President George W. Bush signed the Homeland Security Act of 2002 into law on November 25, 2002. The centerpiece of the law was the creation of a new Department of Homeland Security (DHS). The Bush administration initially opposed the creation of this new department, preferring instead to conduct the federal government's homeland security responsibilities by coordinating various executive branch agencies through the October 2001 creation of an Office of Homeland Security in the Executive Office of the President and a Homeland Security Council. However, President Bush reversed his position on June 6, 2002, when evidence began to accumulate that the person charged with coordinating and directing the actions of the many disparate government departments and agencies charged with homeland security responsibilities required an official with cabinet-level status. Passage of the Homeland Security Act of 2002 mandated the largest reorganization of the federal government since the National Security Act of 1947. Highlights from the 2002 act's seventeen major sections, or titles, are explained below. In general, it is important to note that the original system of directorates established by the act has been substantially modified by subsequent legislation when original structures proved unwieldy or ineffective.

Title I of the act established a new Department of Homeland Security that consolidated twenty-two diverse federal government agencies and bureaus with a combined total of 163,000 employees into a single cabinet department directed by a secretary of homeland security who is appointed by the president with the advice and consent of the Senate. The new department's missions are to (1) prevent terrorist attacks within the United States; (2) reduce the vulnerability of the United States to terrorism; (3) minimize the damage and assist in the recovery from terrorist attacks that occur within the United States; (4) carry out all functions of entities transferred to DHS; (5) ensure that the functions of the agencies and subdivisions within DHS that are not directly related to securing the homeland are not diminished or neglected except by a specific act of Congress; (6) ensure that the overall economic security of the United States is not diminished by efforts, activities, and programs aimed at securing the homeland; and (7) monitor connections between illegal drug trafficking and terrorism, coordinate efforts to sever such connections, and otherwise contribute to efforts to interdict illegal drug trafficking. The act thus clearly established counterterrorism as DHS's primary mission. However, DHS's mission was subsequently expanded to include an all-hazards approach that included fighting terrorism.

Title II of the act established an Office of Information Analysis and Infrastructure Protection. This combination of missions proved unsuccessful, and while both functions remained DHS responsibilities, the intelligence function and the critical infrastructure protection function were subsequently placed in their own offices. Title II also established information security requirements for homeland security–related information and established an Office of Science and Technology within the Department of Justice (DOJ).

Title III established a Directorate of Science and Technology within DHS to support research, development, and procurement of technologies to further the department's missions.

Title IV established the Directorate of Border and Transportation Security. While this directorate was subsequently reorganized into a number of more specialized offices, Title IV provided the authorization to transfer the following organizations to the DHS: the U.S. Customs Service, the Transportation Security Administration (TSA), the Federal Protective Service of the General Services Administration (GSA), the Federal Law Enforcement Training Center of the Department of the Treasury, and the Office for Domestic Preparedness of the Office of Justice Programs of the DOJ. Title IV also directed the transfer to DHS of programs from the Immigration and Naturalization Service (INS) and abolished the INS following these transfers.

Title V deals with the important DHS function of emergency preparedness and response. It made the secretary of homeland security responsible for functions such as helping to ensure the effectiveness of emergency response providers to terrorist attacks, major disasters, and other emergencies; providing the federal government's response to terrorist attacks and major disasters; aiding recovery from terrorist attacks and major disasters; building a comprehensive national incident management system with federal, state, and local governments to respond to such attacks and disasters; consolidating existing federal government emergency response plans into a single, coordinated national response plan; and developing comprehensive programs for developing interoperative communications technology and helping to ensure that emergency response providers acquire such technology. Title V also transferred the Federal Emergency Management Agency (FEMA) to the DHS as well as a number of offices in other federal organizations dealing with emergency preparedness.

Title VIII established a DHS Office of Inspector General and transferred the U.S Secret Service and U.S. Coast Guard to the DHS.

Title IX established a Homeland Security Council (HSC) within the Executive Office of the President to advise the president on homeland security matters. The Obama administration subsequently merged the HSC with the preexisting National Security Council.

The act incorporated a number of previously proposed legislative bills. These included the Federal Information Security Management Act (Title X), the Safe Explosives Act (Title XI), and the Arming Pilot's against Terrorism Act (Title XIV).

William J. Lahneman

See also: Department of Homeland Security.

FURTHER READING

Destler, I. M., and Ivo H. Daalder. 2002. "Promise and Problems: President Bush's Homeland Security Department." Brookings Institution, June 1, 2002. Accessed October 2, 2020. https://www.brookings.edu/articles/promise-and-problems-president-bushs-homeland-security-department/

Edwards, Chris. 2014. "Make America Safer: Shut Down the Department of Homeland Security." CATO Institute, October 27, 2014. Accessed October 5, 2020. https://www.cato.org/publications/commentary/make-america-safer-shut-down-department-homeland-security

Gressle, Sharon S. 2003. *Homeland Security Act of 2002: Legislative History and Pagination Key.* CRS Report for Congress, April 11, 2003. Washington, DC: Congressional Research Service. Accessed October 2, 2020. https://www.everycrsreport.com/files/20030411_RL31645_b48b3674f0cd2fe0b1d4200bfb92ec1eecba5cb3.pdf

Homeland Security Act of 2002, H.R. 5005, 107th Cong. (2001–2002). Accessed October 2, 2020. https://www.congress.gov/bill/107th-congress/house-bill/5005

Hostage Negotiation

Hostage and crisis negotiation was formally developed as a police role in the United States by the New York City Police Department (NYPD) in 1972–1973. The practice has saved countless lives during the ensuing forty-seven years. The original hostage recovery plan was developed as part of a broader counterterrorism strategy and was largely influenced by the terrorist hostage event at the Munich Olympics in 1972.

Negotiation is a transaction between two parties, representing themselves or others, which is designed to arrive at a mutually agreeable resolution. Negotiation does not automatically presuppose equality between parties, but it does recognize the relative strength or power of each side. Implied in the negotiation process is that each side has something that the other wants, that there is no better mutually acceptable solution immediately available, and that there is a willingness to communicate and to discuss compromise.

According to criminology scholars Ronald Crelinsten and Denis Szabo, "Hostage-taking is a very ancient form of criminal activity. In fact, it was even an accepted tool of diplomacy when used by legitimate authority" (1979). *Hostage-taking* is defined by the United Nations as the involuntary restraint of and threat of bodily harm to a person or persons in order to force a third party to undertake or abandon action in order to free the hostage(s). Hostage and crisis negotiation is a police strategy that consists of responding to a situation that involves imminent danger to the life or limb of a person or persons being held against their will. There is not necessarily an immediately apparent connection between captor and victim. As University of Missouri–Rolla history professor Russell D. Buhite noted, individuals are often "taken hostage [only] because they were available and vulnerable" (1995).

Terrorism scholar H. H. A. Cooper noted that there was a shift in official responses to hostage situations following the 1972 Munich Olympics incident. In the Munich Olympics hostage situation, two members of the Israeli Olympic team were killed in the original takeover. Additionally, one West German police officer, five PLO terrorists, and eight Israeli hostages died during an attempt to free the hostages by force. The Munich event alerted the NYPD that their jurisdiction could provide a similar opportunity for some group to engage in terroristic diplomacy. The fact that the hostage holding occurred during the international Olympics; involved American allies, Israel and West Germany; and was broadcast live by the media was enough to prompt an immediate study of the issues.

During the NYPD's post-Munich policy study period, an internal report titled *Recommended Guidelines: Incidents Involving Hostages* was developed. The contingency plans in the report stressed that the primary goal in hostage situations is to vouchsafe the safety of all involved, including not just the hostages but responding officers, bystanders, and even the hostage takers. An American journalist Stephen Gettinger noted that "shortly after the Munich incident, Patrick Murphy, then NYPD Commissioner, gave the order that New York should prepare itself for terrorist hostage-taking" (1983).

Negotiation came to be appreciated as a viable strategy for dealing with terrorist hostage holding. Responders were trained to "meet the problem of hostage negotiating and rescue" under the direction of an incident commander, according to a 1979 NYPD document titled *Terrorism Control in New York City.* The original plan to deal with terror-related hostage holders expanded over the years to also include criminal- and domestic violence–related crisis situations, persons barricaded without hostages, and emotionally disturbed and mentally ill individuals. Additionally prestaging for high-risk raid and warrant execution often includes a hostage negotiation component as part of the preparation for dignitary protection.

One additional type of event that is worthy of reflection involves groups of individuals, not in a correctional setting, that may or may not be "willing" hostages or a combination of willing participants and innocent victims. The Branch Davidian incident near Waco, Texas, in 1993 is a good example. What started as an execution of search and arrest warrants for firearms violations by the federal Bureau of Alcohol, Tobacco, and Firearms (ATF) of the U.S. Department of the Treasury very quickly deteriorated into an exchange of gunfire, initially resulting in death and serious injury on both sides of the perimeter. The ensuing standoff ended fifty-one days later with the Davidian compound in flames and the deaths of more than seventy-five individuals.

After the initial ill-fated encounter at Waco on February 28, the FBI assumed command of the situation and engaged in a variety of negotiation and tactical strategies until the April 19 conclusion. Numerous U.S. government reports, academic and popular press books, movies, and TV shows have told the story of this unparalleled siege. (See, for example, *Recommendations of Experts for Improvement in Federal Law Enforcement after Waco.*)

Another manifestation of hostage negotiation is in incidents involving extortion and kidnapping. As with the more traditional hostage and crisis negotiation, both local and federal law enforcement responders are involved, sometimes cooperatively and at other times when the negotiation is primarily the responsibility of a given agency.

Not all negotiation to secure the release of hostages from terrorists is conducted by police agencies or well publicized. One must recognize the exceptional work accomplished by the military in war zones and by diplomats worldwide. For an excellent account of the breadth and depth of one diplomat's activities on behalf of innocent victims, see Giandomenico Pico's autobiography, *Man without a Gun.*

Robert J. Louden

See also: Munich Olympics Terrorist Attack; Ruby Ridge Standoff.

FURTHER READING

Auerbach, Ann Hagedorn. 1998. *Ransom: the Untold Story of International Kidnapping.* New York: Henry Holt.

Buhite, Russell D. 1995. *Lives at Risk: Hostages and Victims in American Foreign Policy.* Wilmington: Scholarly Resources.

Cooper, H. H. A. 1985. "Hostage Rights: Law and Practice in Throes of Evolution." *Journal of International Law* 15 (1): 7–10.

Crelinsten, Ronald D., and Denis Szabo. 1979. *Hostage-Taking.* Lexington, MA: D.C. Heath and Company.

Gettinger, S. 1983. "Hostage Negotiators Bring Them Out Alive." *Police Magazine* 6 (1):10–28.

Louden, Robert J. 1999. *The Structure and Procedures of Hostage/Crisis Negotiation Units in U.S. Police Organizations.* Unpublished doctoral dissertation, City University of New York.

Louden, Robert J. 2007. "Local Law Enforcement Hostage/Crisis Negotiation: An Essay on Continued Viability in the Aftermath of the Attacks of 9/11." In *Understanding and Responding to the Terrorism Phenomenon: A Multi-Dimensional Perspective,* edited by Ozgur Nikbay and Suleyman Hancerli, 167–179. NATO Science for Peace and Security Series, vol. 21. Amsterdam, Netherlands: IOS Press.

National Institute of Justice. 1993. *Recommendations of Experts for Improvement in Federal Law Enforcement after Waco.* Washington, DC: U.S. Department of Justice.

New York City Police Department. 1979. *Terrorism Control in New York City.* Unpublished document.

NYPD Departmental Manual, Patrol Guide.

Pico, Giandomenico. 1999. *Man without a Gun: One Diplomat's Secret Struggle to Free Hostages, Fight Terrorism, and End a War.* New York: Random House.

I

Information Sharing Environment (ISE)

The September 11, 2001, terrorist attacks on the United States prompted a wave of inquiries into the reasons why the law enforcement and intelligence communities failed to provide warning of al-Qaeda's attack plans. There was wide agreement that one reason for this intelligence failure was that the various organizations of the U.S. intelligence community (IC) had failed to effectively share intelligence. The authors of *The 9/11 Commission Report: Final Report of the National Commission on Terrorist Attacks upon the United States* expressed this lack of cooperation by stating that the IC had "failed to connect the dots," where the "dots" referred to individual pieces of intelligence held by different IC agencies that, if they had been combined (or *fused*) and analyzed properly, may have provided indications and warning of the impending attacks. As a result, the Intelligence Reform and Terrorism Prevention Act of 2004 (IRTPA) contained a provision tasking the executive branch to develop and implement an "information sharing environment" (ISE) to foster improved information sharing among the various public and private actors involved and thus improve intelligence fusion. The Office of the Program Manager for the ISE (PM-ISE) is within the Office of the Director of National Intelligence (ODNI), but the PM-ISE also maintains close contact with the Office of Management and Budget (OMB) and the Executive Office of the President.

The ISE has three principal missions. First, it fosters responsible information sharing to further the government's counterterrorism, homeland security, and weapons of mass destruction (WMD) counterproliferation missions. Second, it works to change IC and law enforcement (LE) organizational cultures from one that looks upon information as a source of power to be "owned" and guarded to one that views information as a resource to be used to accomplish the larger IC and LE missions. This latter viewpoint, expressed as "stewardship," emphasizes that sharing relevant information to achieve common goals is more important than retaining important information to enhance one's organizational status and objectives. Third, the ISE promotes partnerships across federal, state, local, tribal, and territorial government actors; the private sector; and internationally. These actors are collectively known as the "IC Enterprise."

In its efforts to expand the sharing of appropriate information, the ISE must devise ways to not only share information but also protect it from access by unauthorized actors. Accordingly, information sharing must be balanced by appropriate security and counterintelligence measures. Additionally, the ISE must use appropriate procedures to guard "protected information." The ISE defines protected information as information about U.S. citizens and legal permanent residents that is subject to information privacy, civil rights, and civil liberties protections under the U.S. Constitution and federal laws.

Section 1016(h) of IRTPA requires the ISE to provide an annual status report to Congress. The 2017 report states that "federal departments and agencies have continued to make significant progress to strengthen the sharing of terrorism-related information among federal, state, local, tribal, and private sector (FSLTT/PS) partners."

William J. Lahneman

See also: Director of National Intelligence; Intelligence Fusion Centers; Intelligence Reform and Terrorism Prevention Act of 2004; Weapons of Mass Destruction.

FURTHER READING

Department of Homeland Security. 2009. *Department of Homeland Security Federal Information Sharing Environment Privacy and Civil Liberties Policy.* June 5, 2009. Washington, DC: Department of Homeland Security. https://www.dhs.gov/publication/department-homeland-security-federal-information-sharing-environment-privacy-and-civil

National Commission on Terrorist Attacks upon the United States. 2004. *The 9/11 Commission Report: Final Report of the National Commission on Terrorist Attacks upon the United States.* New York: W. W. Norton and Company. Accessed September 13, 2020. https://9-11commission.gov/report/

Office of the Director of National Intelligence. 2015. *Brief History of the Information Sharing Environment.* Version 2.0. Washington, DC: Office of the Director of National Intelligence.

Office of the Director of National Intelligence. 2017. *Information Sharing Environment 2017 Annual Report to Congress.* Washington, DC: Office of the Director of National Intelligence. Accessed September 13, 2020. https://www.dni.gov/files/documents/FOIA/2017_Information_Sharing_Environment_Annual_Report.pdf

Office of the Director of National Intelligence. n.d. "About the ISE." Accessed September 13, 2020. https://www.dni.gov/index.php/who-we-are/organizations/national-security-partnerships/ise/about-the-ise

Intelligence Community, Adjustments to the Post-9/11 World

During the initial months of the George W. Bush presidency, George Tenet, the director of Central Intelligence (DCI), informed Bush about Osama bin Laden's danger to American interests on numerous occasions. In addition, CIA reports referred to the fact that bin Laden's plans to launch terrorist attacks against the United States were ongoing, despite some delays. These warning did not prevent the CIA from bearing the brunt of blame for its failure to monitor al-Qaeda's network or to trace its operatives as they carried out preparations for the attack.

One of the reasons why the CIA was held responsible for this general failure lies in its specific failure to zero in on one of the perpetrators of the attack, Khalid al-Mihdhar, who spent nearly twenty months in the United States before September 11, 2001, and took flying lessons during this period. Yet, the CIA did not put him on the State Department's watch list until nineteen days before the terrorist attacks.

Similarly, although in August 2001 the FBI failed to share information with other intelligence agencies, especially the CIA, about the potential arrival of Khalid al-Mihdhar and Nawaf al-Hazmi, another al-Qaeda operative who participated in the attacks, and did not itself assign resources, or give sufficient priority to the search for them, the FBI subsequently blamed the CIA for not sharing its information about these terrorists and argued that sharing such information would have possibly assisted it in thwarting the 9/11 attacks.

Nonetheless, George Tenet, before and after 9/11, strongly rebuffed using the term *intelligence failure* to describe 9/11 events and preferred the term *deficiency*. The debate over the proper term to describe the incapability of the intelligence community to foresee and thwart these attacks aside, this tragic event triggered a major reform of the intelligence community to better enable it to confront such threats. One of the early adjustments was the issuance of the Intelligence Reform and Terrorism Prevention Act of 2004 (IRTPA).

The National Commission on Terrorist Attacks upon the United States, or 9/11 Commission, and several other studies attributed the overall failure to prevent the 9/11 attacks to a lack of a coherent leadership in the intelligence community insofar as the CIA director then had the dual roles of heading his agency and another fourteen major agencies despite the fact that, in reality, he had no real authority over any agency other than the CIA. A second important problem identified was a lack of guidelines for the intelligence agencies because policy makers had not established priorities for their work.

Pertinently, the 9/11 Commission underscored the importance and necessity of integrating information derived from multiple sources, thus acknowledging that the pre-9/11 failure to "connect the dots" was one of the main problems facing American intelligence agencies that needed to be addressed.

Finally, the lack of *human* intelligence was considered another deficiency affecting the CIA with respect to terrorist organizations, more specifically, the CIA's failure to cultivate spies in the innermost circle of al-Qaeda leadership. In fact, the CIA did direct part of its efforts to doing so, but it failed due to the "inherent challenges" of infiltrating terrorist organizations.

ENHANCING INFORMATION SHARING

As noted, one of the identified failures of the American intelligence community in preventing the 9/11 attacks was a lack of coordination due to the competitive nature of the intelligence agencies, which obstructed interagency collaboration, as evident in the FBI's failure to inform the CIA that suspected Islamic radicals were taking flying lessons in the United States.

To overcome this drawback, organizational reforms were initiated, and a new office was established, the Office of the Director of National Intelligence (ODNI), whose head replaced the director of the CIA as an independent leader of the intelligence community. Thus, the CIA director lost his role as the overseer of American intelligence. The main responsibilities of the ODNI are to provide strategic warnings, set priorities, enhance coordination among the agencies, and delegate the conduct of operations to the agencies in the intelligence community. IRTPA also, provided the ODNI with some supervisory and financial powers, including certain prerogatives to transfer personnel and to reallocate funds from one agency to another.

Another attempt to induce cooperation was the establishment of interagency coordination centers that focus on a certain threat. For this purpose, two agencies were established: the National Counterterrorism Center (NCTC) and the National Counterproliferation Center (NCPC). The principal goal in establishing the NCTC was to ensure that all information about terrorist activities would be available to the center from different intelligence agencies, whether operating inside or outside the United States. IRTPA charged its director with undertaking strategic operational planning for counterterrorism operations. Conducting assessments of terrorist threats to the United States and establishing requirements for other intelligence agencies to gather information about terrorist activities also lie within the realm of the NCTC.

In addition, a partnership termed "information sharing environment" (ISE) was established among all levels of American government, including state and local law enforcement agencies, and it also included a commitment to establish partnerships with private sector actors and friendly foreign governments. This partnership works through state and local fusion centers, that is, points for cooperative efforts between two or more agencies, as they pool together resources, expertise, and information with the purpose of maximizing their ability to detect, thwart, investigate, and respond to criminal or terrorist activity. Stated otherwise, this "fusion" turns information and intelligence into *actionable* knowledge. Finally, a classified online application system was established similar to encyclopedia-style web pages that are accessible to any person with clearance.

REVITALIZING THE FBI

Part of the reforms were specifically directed at the FBI, which was ordered to transform itself from a law enforcement agency, with the mandate to fight crime and prosecute criminals, to a national security agency authorized to preemptively prevent future terrorist attacks, which compelled the agency to develop domestic intelligence capability. Thus, the FBI had to integrate two mandates: its traditional law enforcement responsibility and an intelligence gathering mission. Accordingly, the FBI's powers are no longer confined to arrests and prosecutions but now take many forms, including recruiting potential intelligence sources, developing new collection requirements, and supporting our federal, state, and local law enforcement agencies' efforts to disrupt plots before they cause harm.

Such a change required a shift in the knowledge, skills, and expertise required of agents and opened the way for hiring new personnel with the required abilities. By 2003, the FBI had hired 112 analysts in the intelligence field, 45 information technology people, and 94 administrative personnel.

Elsewhere in reform action, the FBI is enhancing its cooperation with other intelligence institutions within the United States to increase its analytic capabilities. One example of this collaboration is allowing a number of distinguished FBI personnel with intelligence expertise to receive a master of science of strategic intelligence from the Joint Military Intelligence College.

Finally, the FBI, also received more investigative powers from the USA PATRIOT Act aimed at monitoring public events and enabling it to conduct investigations beyond the confines of an ongoing investigation. These powers, too, may assist the FBI in countering terrorist threats.

A CONTESTED REFORM LEGACY

The debate over the effectiveness of these reforms is still ongoing. Some sources within the American intelligence community confirm that the reform process was successful, especially regarding the sharing of information. Others still assert that after a decade of reforms, there is still internal fighting between the ODNI and CIA chiefs. Others argue that personal ties with the president still play an important role in deciding who gets the prominent role within the intelligence community.

Still others argue that the reform process was misguided because the CIA did alert the Bush administration of the gravity of the threat posed by terrorist organizations; however, these warnings were systematically ignored. Likewise, many experts who analyzed fusion centers were critical of the system, citing issues related to the quality of the intelligence produced from these centers. Rather than producing accurate and timely actionable intelligence, experts argue that the product was rarely timely and that some of the reports were taken from open sources, some of which were not even related to terrorism.

Meanwhile, other critics focus on the structural deficiencies in the reforms. Because the different fusion centers follow different structural patterns, there is a lack of coherent procedures for sharing the information that they receive from federal agencies with other partner agencies.

Despite such criticism, it can be argued that the intelligence community within the United States today is nonetheless far more capable at confronting and foiling terrorist attacks before they occur, which can be considered as evidence that the reform process was effective, even if some pieces are still missing.

Shady Abdelwahab Mansour

See also: Enhanced Interrogation Debate; Federal Bureau of Investigation; USA PATRIOT Act of 2001.

FURTHER READING

Alotaibi, Yasmine B. 2010. "Revitalizing the CIA: Intelligence Reform in the Post–Cold War World." *Chancellor's Honors Program Projects.* University of Tennessee honors thesis. https://bit.ly/3cXhWoo

Best, Richard A., Jr. 2010. *Intelligence Reform after Five Years: The Role of the Director of National Intelligence (DNI).* No. R41295, June 22, 2010. Washington, DC: Congressional Research Service. https://bit.ly/2MTpr5h

Best, Richard A., Jr. 2011. *The National Counterterrorism Center (NCTC)—Responsibilities and Potential Congressional Concerns.* No. R41022, December 19, 2011. Washington, DC: Congressional Research Service. https://bit.ly/2AmEuC0

Davis, Lois M., et al. 2010. *Long-Term Effects of Law Enforcement's Post-9/11 Focus on Counterterrorism and Homeland Security.* Washington, DC: RAND Corporation.

Fernando Celaya. 2009. "To What Extent Was Western Intelligence at Fault in Failing to Identify the Nature of the Terrorist Threat before 9/11 and Its Aftermath?" *Athena Intelligence Journal* 4 (1): 155–187.

Gulati, Ranjay, Ryan Raffaelli, and Jan Rivkin. 2016. "Does 'What We Do' Make Us 'Who We Are'? Organizational Design and Identity Change at the Federal Bureau of Investigation." Working Paper No. 16-084. Harvard Business School, January 12, 2016. https://bit.ly/2AVZHm1

Immerman, Richard H. 2014. *The Hidden Hand: A Brief History of the CIA.* New York: John Wiley & Sons.

Intelligence Reform and Terrorism Prevention Act of 2004. Pub. L. No. 108-458, 118 STAT. 3638. (2004). https://bit.ly/3eLy5yG

National Commission on Terrorist Attacks upon the United States. 2004. "How to Do It? A Different Way of Organizing the Government." In *The 9/11 Commission Report,* 399–428. https://bit.ly/3dKEWIE

Rosenbach, Eric, and Aki J. Peritz. 2009. *Confrontation or Collaboration? Congress and the Intelligence Community.* Cambridge, MA: John F. Kennedy School of Government, Harvard University. https://bit.ly/2XylhpE

Salvatore, Shane A. 2018. "Fusion Center Challenges: Why Fusion Centers Have Failed to Meet Intelligence Sharing Expectations." Master's thesis, Naval Postgraduate School, March 2018. https://apps.dtic.mil/sti/pdfs/AD1052869.pdf

Walker, David M. 2003. *FBI Reorganization: Progress Made in Efforts to Transform, but Major Challenges Continue.* June 18, 2003. Washington, DC: U.S. General Accounting Office. https://bit.ly/2YrTGFN

Warner, Michael, and J. Kenneth McDonald. 2005. *US Intelligence Community Reform Studies since 1947.* April 2005. Washington, DC: Center for the Study of Intelligence. https://www.cia.gov/static/b62f5dec88ecc1051861aec57cfd470f/Community-Reform-Studies-1947.pdf

Zakaria, Tabassum. 2011. "Post-9/11 U.S. Intelligence Reforms Take Root, Problems Remain." Reuters, September 7, 2011. https://reut.rs/2A7BN74

Zegart, Amy B. 2005. "September 11 and the Adaptation Failure of U.S. Intelligence Agencies." *International Security* 29 (4): 78–111.

Zegart, Amy B. 2007. "'CNN with Secrets': 9/11, the CIA, and the Organizational Roots of Failure." *International Journal of Intelligence and CounterIntelligence* 20 (1):18–49.

Intelligence Fusion Centers

The term *intelligence fusion center* refers to an organizational entity that combines intelligence from various sources, *fuses* this information to produce finished intelligence products, and distributes these products to various intelligence consumers. In the United States, the term is most commonly used to refer to the network of U.S. fusion centers at city, state, and regional levels that has rapidly developed following the 9/11 terrorist attacks on the United States. Most of these centers originally had a counterterrorism mission, but most have now expanded their focus to either an "all-crimes" (terrorism is a crime, and the same resources devoted to detecting criminal activity can be applied to detecting terrorist plans) or "all-hazards" approach (to align with the Department of Homeland Security's (DHS) mission). Fusion centers are staffed by analysts from diverse agencies, which fosters information sharing as fusion center members become accustomed to working in an interagency setting.

Intelligence fusion centers existed prior to the September 11, 2001, terrorist attacks, but their numbers were small. At the federal government level, both the Central Intelligence Agency (CIA) and the Federal Bureau of Investigation (FBI) maintained fusion centers focused on detecting terrorist and nuclear proliferation threats prior to the 9/11 attacks, and only two U.S. major urban areas—New York and Orange County (Los Angeles)—maintained fusion centers. The number of state and major urban area intelligence fusion centers has now risen to seventy-nine, a growth rate that has led to their incorporation into a National Network of Fusion Centers and the creation of several umbrella organizations to monitor their activities, recommend best practices, and help them to obtain funding and support. DHS and other federal agencies provide substantial support for state and major urban area fusion centers in the form of deployed personnel, training, technical assistance, exercise support, provision of security clearances, connectivity to intelligence from the intelligence community (IC) and other federal systems, technological expertise and systems, and grant funding.

The number of fusion centers has grown so rapidly because they are focused on providing intelligence about terrorist threats to specific cities and states by fusing intelligence from federal, state, and local assets, including local police forces and the owners of critical infrastructure, such as power plants, port facilities, railroads, and pipelines. Additionally, the National Network of Fusion Centers shares information to produce intelligence about threats that operate at a regional level. In contrast, the IC lacked the assets to provide focused, continuous intelligence on terrorist threats in every area of the country.

The rapid and ad hoc development of today's fusion center network has produced two principal criticisms. First, fusion centers have displayed a wide range of designs and have often suffered from a lack of trained analysts. The DHS has led an effort to provide strategic guidance and has provided standardized guidelines to improve fusion center performance based on best practices. Second, fusion centers' combination of personnel from local, state, federal, and private organizations has resulted in access to a number of databases whose contents had not previously been fused. Critics argued that combining information from these diverse databases violated Americans' civil liberties. Congress responded by providing enhanced public oversight, which produced a number of recommendations to improve fusion centers' performance while respecting civil liberties.

William J. Lahneman

See also: Central Intelligence Agency; Department of Homeland Security; Director of National Intelligence; Information Sharing Environment; Intelligence Reform and Terrorism Prevention Act of 2004.

FURTHER READING

American Civil Liberties Union. 2012. "ACLU Calls for Hearings on Fusion Centers Following Senate Report." ACLU, October 3, 2012. https://www.aclu.org/press-releases/aclu-calls-hearings-fusion-centers-following-senate-report

American Civil Liberties Union. 2020. "More about Fusion Centers." ACLU. https://www.aclu.org/other/more-about-fusion-centers

National Fusion Center Association et al. 2014. *2014–2017 National Strategy for the National Network of Fusion Centers.* July 2014. Public Intelligence. https://info.publicintelligence.net/NationalFusionCenterStrategy-2014-2017.pdf

Ozer, Nicole. "Twitter Cuts Off Fusion Spy Centers' Access to Social Media Surveillance Tool." ACLU, December 15, 2016. https://www.aclu.org/blog/privacy-technology/internet-privacy/twitter-cuts-fusion-spy-centers-access-social-media

U.S. Department of Homeland Security. 2019. "National Network of Fusion Centers Fact Sheet." https://www.dhs.gov/national-network-fusion-centers-fact-sheet

U.S. Department of Justice and the U.S. Department of Homeland Security. 2008. *Fusion Center Guidelines: Developing and Sharing Information and Intelligence in a New Era.* September 2008. Washington, DC: Global Justice Information Sharing Initiative. https://it.ojp.gov/documents/d/fusion_center_guidelines.pdf

Intelligence Reform and Terrorism Prevention Act of 2004

President George W. Bush signed the Intelligence Reform and Terrorism Prevention Act of 2004 (IRTPA) on December 6, 2004. The act mandated the most sweeping revisions to the U.S. intelligence community since the National Security Act of 1947. Many of the act's provisions had appeared in *The 9/11 Commission Report: Final Report of the National Commission on Terrorist Attacks upon the United States*. The act's main feature was the creation of two new positions—a director of national intelligence (DNI), who would coordinate the activities of the U.S. intelligence community's (IC) agencies funded by the National Intelligence Program (NIP) budget, and a director of the Central Intelligence Agency (DCIA), who would be the chief executive of the Central Intelligence Agency (CIA)—to replace the single position of director of central intelligence (DCI). The DCI had also served as the president's senior intelligence adviser, and IRTPA did not specify which of the new positions would fill this role. President Bush decided that the DNI would serve in this capacity, and successive presidents have maintained this practice.

The rationale for these changes derived from the 9/11 Commission's recommendations that these three jobs were too much for one person (the DCI) to carry out effectively for two main reasons. First, it was generally believed that previous DCIs had spent too much time directing the CIA and not enough time coordinating the actions of the IC. Second, many felt that being the CIA director biased DCIs to favor the intelligence products of the CIA over other IC agencies. Since a principal conclusion of the 9/11 Commission was that the IC had failed to connect the dots—to fuse all available intelligence information effectively—the change would fix this problem by making the DNI primarily responsible for IC coordination and intelligence fusion and the DCIA in charge of running the CIA. The DNI, freed from managing the CIA, would also be more objective about the strengths and weaknesses of the different IC agencies.

The wisdom of creating the DNI position was hotly debated prior to IRPTA's passage. In fact, the idea of a DNI had already arisen several times when different commissions and reports on the IC's effectiveness noted problems with IC agency coordination and information sharing under the DCI system. However, critics of the DNI concept warned that a DNI/DCIA model would prove ineffective. They argued that the new model would amount to little more than the establishment of a new level of bureaucracy over existing IC structures unless the DNI was granted significant executive authority over IC agencies. In the absence of such authority, they argued that the additional layer of bureaucracy would degrade IC performance rather than improve it.

Second, critics pointed out that the DNI's authority depended on giving the new position decisive budgetary authority over IC agencies. Otherwise, the DNI would be a coordinator who could recommend but not command cooperation. However, giving the DNI such strong budgetary authority would limit the ability of cabinet secretaries to fully control and utilize their intelligence services, such as the State Department's Bureau of Intelligence and Research (INR), and many Department of Defense intelligence agencies, such as the National Security Agency (NSA) and the Defense Intelligence Agency (DIA). Cabinet secretaries objected to the idea of needing to negotiate with the DNI for intelligence support from intelligence organizations within their own departments.

The passage of IRTPA was made possible by the incorporation of several compromises that reduced the power of the new DNI to below what proponents of the new position had advocated. However, without such compromises, the Defense Department would not have supported IRTPA, and its congressional allies would have voted against passage. An important compromise was to give the DNI control over the NIP but leave the Military Intelligence Budget (MIP) under the control of the secretary of defense. IRTPA requires the DNI to ensure effective execution of the NIP but provides cabinet secretaries the ability to challenge certain DNI actions to redirect funds within the NIP. In the years since IRTPA was signed into law, the DNI has become a coordinating force in the IC not only by control of the NIP but also by other provisions of IRTPA that were not controversial at the time. For example, the DNI's Office of the Director of National Intelligence (ODNI) has worked to standardize IC enterprise architecture, vision, and missions; to professionalize the intelligence workforce by promulgating standards of conduct and training; and to improve IC information sharing through the ODNI's Office of the Program Manager for the Information Sharing Environment. The DNI's ability to establish national intelligence fusion centers has also fostered information sharing and has created useful interagency relationships and informal professional networks.

Other highlights of IRTPA related to intelligence include the following:

- The DNI is responsible for IC information security, including counterintelligence efforts.
- The DNI oversees the coordination of relationships with the intelligence and security services of foreign governments and international organizations.
- The DNI recommends to the president nominees for principal deputy DNI and for CIA director. The DNI has the right to concur in the appointment or the recommendation for nomination of the heads of IC agencies funded by the NIP.
- The DNI appoints a civil liberties protection officer to oversee related aspects of IC operations.
- IRTPA provides guidance for conducting intelligence analysis to maintain objectivity and other professional standards.

- IRTPA established a Joint Intelligence Community Council (JICC), chaired by the DNI, composed of the secretaries of state, treasury, defense, energy, and homeland security and the attorney general to advise the DNI on budget and other matters and to ensure the timely execution of the DNI's programs, policies, and directives.
- IRTPA directed the Federal Bureau of Investigation (FBI) to establish a national intelligence workforce. The FBI's Office of Intelligence was redesignated the Directorate of Intelligence.
- IRTPA established a single entity to streamline and standardize the security clearance process across the U.S. government.

Beginning with Title IV, IRTPA shifted its focus to actions aimed to reduce the threat of terrorism to the United States. The following topics are addressed:

- Aviation and maritime security:
    - Recommends various measures to improve passenger prescreening systems, explosives detection, and air cargo security
    - Recommends steps to improve maritime passenger screening
- Border protection security:
    - Recommends development of advanced technology for border protection security; an increase in Border Patrol and Customs Enforcement agents; an increase in detention bed space; enhanced visa requirements; and changes to immigration laws affecting deportation and special treatment for aliens who have committed acts of torture or extrajudicial killings abroad
- Terrorism prevention measures:
    - Clarifies legal status of foreign lone-wolf terrorists; funds improvements of the Treasury Department's Financial Crimes Enforcement Network; authorizes a pilot program for enhancing criminal history background checks
- Material support to terrorism measures:
    - Makes it illegal to knowingly receive military-type training from a designated foreign terrorist organization; clarifies definitions of several types of material support; clarifies current law's requirement that the defendant knowingly provided material support to a designated foreign terrorist organization
    - Strengthens and clarifies criminal penalties for hoaxes related to terrorism or the death or disappearance of a member of the armed services during a war and for crimes involving weapons of mass destruction and other military weapons systems
    - Expands the list of offenses and penalties for crimes that can be considered terrorism
    - Implements 9/11 Commission recommendations regarding the importance of using all elements of national power to win the war on terrorism
    - Requires development of a strategy to intercept terrorists, find terrorist travel facilitators, and constrain terrorist mobility domestically and internationally

- Recommends the adoption of a unified incident command system and significant enhancing of communications connectivity between and among all levels of government and emergency response providers

William J. Lahneman

See also: Director of National Intelligence; Federal Bureau of Investigation, Directorate of Intelligence; Information Sharing Environment; Intelligence Community, Adjustments to the Post-9/11 World; Intelligence Fusion Centers; National Security Act of 1947.

FURTHER READING

Intelligence Reform and Terrorism Prevention Act of 2004. Pub. L. No. 108-458, 118 STAT. 3638 (2004). Accessed October 4, 2020. https://www.intelligence.senate.gov/laws/intelligence-reform-and-terrorism-prevention-act-2004

Lowenthal, Mark M. 2017. *Intelligence: From Secrets to Policy.* 7th ed. Los Angeles: CQ Press.

National Commission on Terrorist Attacks upon the United States. 2004. *The 9/11 Commission Report: Final Report of the National Commission on Terrorist Attacks upon the United States.* Authorized ed. New York: W. W. Norton & Company. https://9-11commission.gov/report/

United States Senate Committee on Governmental Affairs. 2004. *Summary of Intelligence Reform and Terrorism Prevention Act of 2004.* December 6, 2004. Accessed October 4, 2020. https://www.hsdl.org/?view&did=812947

Intelligence-Led Policing

One of the main factors leading to the evolution of intelligence-led policing (ILP) was the terrorist attacks of September 11, 2001, against the United States. These attacks triggered widespread advocacy among law enforcement agencies to adopt "proactive" styles of policing, to thwart terrorist attacks, and to rectify the limitations associated with traditional reactive approaches to maintaining security and social order.

There is no universally agreed upon definition for ILP. This could be attributed to two factors. First, this concept is a relatively new and evolving concept. Second, there are different applications of ILP that vary from country to country. For instance, the United States emphasizes the creation of actionable intelligence products, which can prevent or mitigate threats. The United Kingdom's model of ILP, on the other hand, places more emphasis on generating and analyzing situational crime and habitual offender data to make more informed decisions regarding police resources and the targeting of specific crime problems.

Despite these differences, one of the most common definitions is from Petter Gottschalk's 2019 title *Policing Organized Crime: Intelligence Strategy Implementation.* He defines ILP as "a systematic approach to collecting information with the purpose of tracking and predicting crime to improve law enforcement operations."

Historically, ILP originated in Great Britain in the early 1990s, when the Kent Constabulary coined the concept in response to sharp increases in property-related crimes at a time when police budgets were being cut. The success of this model led to its evolution as a template for ILP across Britain.

Similarly, the Global Intelligence Working Group, whose members are law enforcement representatives from the federal, state, local, and tribal levels in the United States, developed an initiative called the *National Criminal Intelligence Sharing Plan* (NCISP), which urged all U.S. law enforcement agencies to develop an ILP model. This initiative has been adopted by the U.S. Department of Justice (DOJ) and every key professional law enforcement association in the United States since 2004. Furthermore, law enforcement agencies in the United States believe that they have achieved success in combating terrorism and crime by applying this approach, which in turn legitimized and accelerated its adoption.

Several factors have contributed to reinvigorating the utilization of intelligence by the police in combating terrorism. First, police agencies are more able to access information within communities that cannot be obtained by more remote specialized intelligence agents. Second, they are aware of the facilities or criminal groups that might provide resources to terrorists, such as providers of fertilizers that can be used as ingredients in making explosives. Finally, their routine activities put them in a position to monitor local radical groups and people acting suspiciously near critical infrastructure.

Shady Abdelwahab Mansour

See also: Active Shooter Scenarios; Information Sharing Environment; Intelligence Fusion Centers.

FURTHER READING

Bacon, Matthew. 2016. *Taking Care of Business: Police Detectives, Drug Law Enforcement and Proactive Investigation.* Oxford, UK: Oxford University Press.

Bayley, David H., and David Weisburd. 2009. "Cops and Spooks: The Role of the Police in Counterterrorism." In *To Protect and to Serve: Policing in an Age of Terrorism*, edited by David Weisburd et al., 81–100. New York: Springer.

Carter, Jeremy G., and Scott W. Phillips. 2015. "Intelligence-Led Policing and Forces of Organisational Change in the USA." *Policing and Society* 25 (4): 333–357.

Gottschalk, Petter. 2010. *Policing Organized Crime Intelligence Strategy Implementation.* UK: Routledge.

James, Adrian. 2013. *Examining Intelligence-Led Policing: Developments in Research, Policy and Practice.* London: Palgrave Macmillan.

McGarrell, Edmund F., Joshua D. Freilich, and Steven Chermak. 2007. "Intelligence-Led Policing as a Framework for Responding to Terrorism." *Journal of Contemporary Criminal Justice* 23 (2): 142–158.

Organization for Security and Co-Operation in Europe. 2017. *OSCE Guidebook: Intelligence-Led Policing.* Vienna, Austria: OSCE. https://goo.gl/6sLQ4M

Peterson, Marilyn. 2005. *Intelligence-Led Policing: The New Intelligence Architecture.* Washington, DC: Bureau of Justice Assistance. http://bit.ly/2f5kd5C

International Criminal Court (ICC)

The International Criminal Court (ICC) is the first permanent international criminal court set up to investigate and try individuals accused of the gravest crimes: genocide, crimes against humanity, war crimes, and the crime of aggression, which is one state using armed force against another state. In 1998, 120 states adopted the Rome Statute, the international treaty that established the ICC, to bring perpetrators of such actions to justice. Supporters of the ICC also argued that it would act as a deterrent against such crimes in the future. The court would serve as an international justice mechanism for cases in which states did not have the capacity or the will to prosecute individuals accused of these crimes in national courts. The ICC is located in The Hague, the Netherlands.

The Rome Statute entered into force on July 1, 2002, with its ratification by sixty countries, establishing the court's jurisdiction over crimes committed on or after that date within the territory of a state party or by individuals who are nationals of a state party. The UN Security Council can also refer a case to the ICC, even if the case involves a state that has not ratified the statute. As of 2021, 123 countries are state parties to the ICC, with notable exceptions including the United States, Russia, and China. President Bill Clinton signed the Rome Statute on December 31, 2000, but did not submit it to the U.S. Senate for ratification and suggested his successor also wait until American concerns about the treaty were addressed. President George W. Bush nullified the U.S. signature in 2002. American concerns about the ICC related to the court's jurisdiction—and specifically that it had the potential to result in the prosecution of American citizens over the objections of the U.S. government.

The court has an independent Office of the Prosecutor who can investigate evidence of alleged crimes and ask the court to issue arrest warrants for individuals. Investigations are opened in a number of ways: a state party can make a request, a non-state party can agree to give the ICC jurisdiction and make a request, the UN Security Council can refer a situation, or the prosecutor can independently decide to carry out an investigation that involves a state party. As of this writing, the ICC has launched fourteen investigations of situations, leading to thirty cases before the court (including some with multiple defendants). Those cases have so far resulted in ten convictions and four acquittals. Preliminary examinations are also ongoing in seven countries; those will result in a decision to either close the examination or proceed to an investigation.

One of the significant questions that has arisen with the establishment of the ICC is whether the distinct crime of terrorism should be included in the court's purview. The crime of terrorism was considered in a provision during the Rome Conference that produced the treaty creating the ICC, but it was not approved for several reasons, including the absence of an internationally accepted definition of *terrorism* and related concerns that adding terrorism to its purview would politicize the court. While the Rome Statute recommended reconsidering the inclusion of terrorism at a future review conference, the 2010 Review Conference did not discuss the issue, and there has been no major push by state parties to reexamine its inclusion. Nonetheless, international legal scholars suggest it may be possible to prosecute terrorist acts under the four crimes currently dealt with by the ICC, although there are challenges. Examples of these challenges include how fittingly the four crimes can be applied to specific terrorist acts, questions over the ICC's jurisdiction in the territory of a non-state party and when nationals of a state party are involved, and practical issues such as attaining state cooperation for evidence collection and other elements of an investigation.

Amy E. Grubb

See also: Enhanced Interrogation Debate; State Terrorism.

FURTHER READING

Clinton, William J. 2000. "Statement on the Rome Treaty on the International Criminal Court." *37 Weekly Compilation of Presidential Documents 4* (December 31, 2000). https://www.govinfo.gov/content/pkg/WCPD-2001-01-08/pdf/WCPD-2001-01-08-Pg4.pdf

Coalition for the International Criminal Court. Accessed September 18, 2021. http://www.coalitionfortheicc.org

Cohen, Aviv. 2012. "Prosecuting Terrorists at the International Criminal Court: Reevaluating an Unused Legal Tool to Combat Terrorism." *Michigan State International Law Review* 20 (2): 219–257.

Cóman, Kenny. 2017. "Prosecuting Crimes of International Concern: Islamic State at the ICC?" *Utrecht Journal of International and European Law* 33 (84): 120–145.

International Criminal Court. Accessed September 18, 2021. https://www.icc-cpi.int

McKay, Fiona. 2004. "U.S. Unilateralism and International Crimes: The International Criminal Court and Terrorism." *Cornell International Law Journal* 36 (3): 455–471.

Sadat, Leila N., and Mark A. Drumbl. 2016. "The United States and the International Criminal Court: A Complicated, Uneasy, yet at Times Engaging Relationship." Washington University in St. Louis Legal Studies Research Paper Series.

Stahn, Carsten, ed. 2015. *The Law and Practice of the International Criminal Court.* Oxford, UK: Oxford University Press.

Internet as a Virtual School for Terrorism

Terrorists have used the Internet since the 1990s and are increasingly doing so to spread radical ideology and recruit new members. Modern technology, including the advent of the smartphone in 2007; proliferating social media; and the like have further allowed terrorists to communicate freely, anonymously, and in real time. Terrorists use these technologies for multiple purposes, including research, communication, fundraising, training, media operations, publicity, radicalization, and recruitment of new members.

Terrorists can easily build and run a website or microblog that serves as a virtual school of terrorism. Content can include tutorials on constructing improvised explosive devices, firing surface-to-air missiles, making car bombs, assassinating foreign soldiers, or sneaking into Iraq. These websites can host chat rooms and message boards for anonymous communications, videos serving as propaganda for recruitment, how-to training videos, or publicity videos depicting the beheadings of journalists. Thousands of websites currently deemed as "terrorist-related" exist around the world and serve the same essential purpose for educating terrorists as the distance-based learning portals used by colleges and universities for educating students online.

Terrorist recruiting has increased with the advent of social media, which provides numerous advantages for communication, being free, vast in scope, and available to anyone with an Internet connection. A tweet on Twitter or post on Facebook can be seen globally by millions of users instantaneously. Additionally, the social media company provides the infrastructure and maintenance of the platform, permitting terrorists and terrorist organizations to move swiftly toward achieving their goals, unhampered with the costs and time delays that establishing their own internet structure would take.

Identifying terrorists on the Internet is increasingly difficult. End-to-end encryption allows terrorists to communicate without fear of their conversations being read even if intercepted. There is a growing list of free smartphone apps that provide such encryption, including Silent Phone, Signal, Facebook's WhatsApp, and Apple Facetime, all of which allow terrorists to communicate in real time. Terrorists also use chat rooms and message boards on the dark web for asynchronous communications: the dark web is a part of the deep web, the latter of which is the part of the Internet that is not indexed by search engines and cannot be directly accessed. The dark web includes content that is intentionally hidden for illegal or illicit purposes. Accessing the dark web requires easily obtainable special software that provides anonymity. Terrorists also use steganography, which is the practice of secretly encoding a message or file in another file.

All these technologies, the Internet, encrypted smartphone apps, and the dark web, combine to enhance terrorist organizations to rapidly recruit, radicalize, train, and direct terrorist incidents in an unprecedented way.

J. Philip Craiger

See also: Internet Surveillance; New Terrorism; Recruiting Terrorists.

FURTHER READING

Conway, Maura. 2016. "Determining the Role of the Internet in Violent Extremism and Terrorism: Six Suggestions for Progressing Research." *Studies in Conflict and Terrorism* 40 (1): 77–98. https://doi.org/10.1080/1057610x.2016.1157408

Mantel, Barbara. 2009. "Terrorism and the Internet: Should Web Sites That Promote Terrorism Be Shut Down?" *GC Researcher* 3 (11): 129–153.

United Nations Office on Drugs and Crime. 2012. *The Use of the Internet for Terrorist Purposes*. Vienna, Austria: United Nations. Accessed April 4, 2020. https://www.unodc.org/documents/frontpage/Use_of_Internet_for_Terrorist_Purposes.pdf

Weimann, Gabriel. 2016. "Terrorist Migration to the Dark Web." *Perspectives on Terrorism* 10 (3): 40–44. Accessed April 6, 2020. https://www.jstor.org/stable/26297596

Wu, Paulina. 2015. "Impossible to Regulate: Social Media, Terrorists, and the Role for the U.N." *Chicago Journal of International Law* 16 (1): Article 11.

Internet Surveillance

As communications technology advances, making communication between distant persons easier, terrorists, like others, can communicate across the globe quickly, cheaply, and efficiently. Because of widespread communication using websites such as YouTube and social media sites such as Facebook, governments are increasingly dependent on Internet surveillance to counter terrorist activity.

In the United States, the legal foundation for Internet surveillance rests on the third-party doctrine. During the 1970s, the U.S. Supreme Court ruled that individuals who provide third parties with data about their communication do not have a reasonable basis to assume that their communication is private. Using that precedent, current use of Internet surveillance argues that when one purchases Internet or smartphone technologies or purposefully accesses websites where histories are logged, such as Google, or social media, that party no longer has an assumption of privacy for purchases, contacts, messages sent, videos watched, and the like.

After the terrorist attacks of September 11, 2001, Congress swiftly passed the USA PATRIOT Act, which increased the surveillance powers of the federal government, including the intelligence agencies such as the National Security Agency (NSA). These surveillance programs became extremely controversial in the wake of former NSA contractor Edward Snowden's 2013 leaks about the breadth and depth of the programs. Political fallout was swift, with many in Congress looking to pass new privacy protection laws. Heads of intelligence agencies explained that the surveillance programs successfully prevented terrorist acts, while critics accused the government and, importantly, private companies such as Yahoo! and Facebook of failing to protect the privacy of their customers.

There is no doubt that the Internet is used extensively to aid terrorists and terrorist organizations. American radical cleric Anwar al-Awlaki successfully used YouTube and other sites to radicalize potential terrorists across the globe, including Nidal Hasan, the 2009 Fort Hood shooter. More recently, the Islamic State in Iraq and Syria (ISIS) used videos and websites to inspire thousands, including dozens from the United States, to join ISIS or to participate in terrorist activities closer to their homes. Domestic threats, including radical right groups also spread their messages of hate using websites and social media outlets. Importantly, terrorist groups also use the Internet to raise or collect funds, which makes monitoring electronic money transfers an important counterterrorism tool as well.

Internet surveillance is thus one of the most important controversies of our time. Given the prevalence of online communication and the threat of online activity by terrorists, both critics and supporters have strong arguments. Do Americans, with their long history of limiting government, want a government that can listen to or read every electronic communication they have? Do customers want companies to use their purchasing habits, Internet search interests, and seemingly private communications to collect data for sale or future use? On the other hand, the threat of terrorism is palpable. Should not government, whose duties include national security protections, use every means to effectively protect its citizens and assets from terror attack?

In short, Internet surveillance is an effective counterterrorism tool; however, its size and scope in the United States, whether conducted by government or private companies, remains an important debate. In the wake of the Snowden leaks, individual states reinforced a right to privacy, and Facebook, a popular social media site, is consistently in the news at the time of this writing defending itself from claims that it collects and distributes user data without permission.

Brett M. Gould and Tobias T. Gibson

See also: al-Awlaki, Anwar; Internet as a Virtual School for Terrorism; Social Media and Terrorism.

FURTHER READING

Anti-Defamation League. 2016. *The ISIS Impact on the Domestic Islamic Extremist Threat: Homegrown Islamic Extremism 2009–2015*. New York: ADL. https://www.adl.org

/sites/default/files/documents/assets/pdf/combating-hate/CR_4473_HomegrownExtremismReport-2009-2015_web2.pdf

Donohue, Laura K. 2016. *The Future of Foreign Intelligence: Privacy and Surveillance in a Digital Age*. New York: Oxford University Press.

Goedman, Menno. "The New Tools of Counterterrorism: Combating Illicit Finance and Imposing Sanctions." *National Security Journal*, February 22, 2013. http://harvardnsj.org/2013/02/the-new-tools-of-counterterrorism-combating-illicit-finance-and-imposing-sanctions/

Greenwald, Glenn. 2015. *No Place to Hide: Edward Snowden, the NSA and the U.S. Surveillance State*. New York: Picador.

Holyan, Anna E., and Tobias T. Gibson. 2013. "Surveillance, Law and Policy in the 21st Century." *Law and Courts* 23 (1): 41–46.

Islamic State, The

ORIGINS

The Islamic State (IS), previously called the Islamic State in Iraq and Syria (ISIS) or the Islamic State in Syria and the Levant (ISIL), is an extremist Sunni Islamic Salafist terrorist group that from 2004 to 2006 was known as al-Qaeda in Iraq (AQI) and from 2006 to 2013 as the Islamic State of Iraq (ISI). IS promotes a violent and intolerant misinterpretation of Sunni Islam (the largest denomination of Islam) and, as a Salafist movement, seeks to reform Islam by returning to the example of *Salaf* (the pious predecessors) who founded the faith. IS has become infamous for its brutality, which eclipsed even that of al-Qaeda.

The origins of IS trace back to Jordanian terrorist Abu Musab al-Zarqawi's Monotheism and Jihad terrorist group, which he founded in 1999. By 2003, he had arrived in Iraq, and in 2004, one year after the American invasion of Iraq, he pledged loyalty to al-Qaeda leader Osama bin Laden, renamed his group al-Qaeda in Iraq (AQI), and began capitalizing on the chaos and instability that followed the overthrow of Saddam Hussein's government and American occupation of Iraq.

Determined to make the American occupation of Iraq a failure, during the summer of 2003, al-Zarqawi directed several car bombings of foreign embassies in Baghdad, thereby isolating the U.S. presence in post-Saddam Iraq. He also directed the August 19, 2003, bombing of the United Nations' Baghdad headquarters that killed twenty-three people and effectively ended all UN work in an Iraq facing a growing insurgency that al-Zarqawi eagerly participated in and gave direction to.

The insurgency stalled U.S. efforts to turn over control of the country to Iraqis, making it clear to most that the United States would need to remain in Iraq indefinitely despite the growing loss of American lives. Moreover, and to the surprise of the United States, members of Iraq's minority Sunni population also began attacking U.S. troops in May 2003, after the administration of President George W. Bush ordered the firing of the entire Sunni-dominated Iraqi military, the police, and all members of Saddam Hussein's Ba'ath political party (which included teachers, engineers, nurses, and doctors). After decades of Sunni-dominated government, the formerly oppressed majority Shia Muslims were to become the new ruling class.

For its part, al-Zarqawi's terrorist group not only eagerly joined the growing insurgency but also targeted Iraq's Shia, thereby provoking a religious war between Sunnis and Shia from 2003 to 2009 that killed tens of thousands. In turn, these assaults against the Shia provoked retaliatory violence against Sunnis, and armed Shia groups also started attacking U.S forces to expel them from Iraq.

The attacks on Shia religious clerics, bombings of Shia mosques, and killings of ordinary Shia citizens were unexpected and troubled bin Laden, who correctly perceived that most Muslims did not care about the theological differences between the Sunnis and Shia. Furthermore, attacking Iraq's Shia was a distraction from the goal of forcing the United States to withdraw from Iraq.

In 2005, al-Qaeda deputy leader Ayman al-Zawahiri wrote a letter urging al-Zarqawi to stop releasing videotaped beheadings of hostages, including Americans, and to stop attacking Shia; however, Zarqawi ignored the order. With bin Laden and al-Zawahiri in hiding after al-Qaeda lost its sanctuary in Afghanistan following the U.S. occupation of that country in response to the September 11, 2001, attacks, al-Zarqawi was disinclined even to compromise with other Sunni groups fighting the United States. A year later, on June 7, 2006, al-Zarqawi was killed in the U.S. bombing of a safe house.

By 2009, the anti-AQI revolt of Sunni tribes in Anbar Province along with the co-optation of approximately 100,000 tribesmen paid to fight against AQI, the deployment of an additional 30,000 troops to Iraq, and a new U.S. counterinsurgency strategy by General Petraeus called "clear and hold" (U.S. forces, along with the Iraqi military, would now clear areas infested with insurgents and then hold the territory) had destroyed AQI. By then, in October 2006, it had been renamed the Islamic State of Iraq (ISI) without any effect on its continued decline. Indeed, in June 2010, it was reported that 80 percent of ISI's top forty-two leaders had been killed or captured.

Meanwhile, Abu Bakr al-Baghdadi became the new leader of ISI on May 16, 2010. The U.S. forces had detained him for most of 2004 on suspicion of terrorism but released him at the end of the year for lack of evidence. As the new leader of ISI, al-Baghdadi replenished its decimated ranks by recruiting former members of Saddam's military and intelligence agencies. In so doing, ISI developed tactics more associated with an army than a terrorist group, namely, the ability to organize and coordinate the combat operations of even thousands of fighters. These tactics would prove instrumental in enabling ISI to conquer large parts of Iraq in 2014 and 2015. In the short term, however, with Iraq a largely inhospitable place for ISI, neighboring Syria proved to be a blessing for its survival and resurrection.

EVOLUTION: THE BIRTH OF THE CALIPHATE

In March 2011, protests erupted in Syria against the dictator Bashar al-Assad. The ensuing crackdown by the Assad government sparked a civil war. Taking advantage of the growing chaos and lawlessness in Syria, al-Baghdadi dispatched fighters from Iraq to establish a presence in eastern Syria that Assad forces had abandoned. ISI then began occupying large parts of the region that included significant oil production that IS sold on the black market, earning millions of dollars in revenue a month.

On January 23, 2012, the ISI affiliate in Syria announced its existence as Jabhat al-Nusra (or the Nusra Front), led by the Syrian Abu Mohammad al-Julani. After the March 2003 American invasion of Iraq, he traveled to Iraq and joined AQI to fight the United States. Subsequently, Jabhat al-Nusra became a major group fighting Assad, with the goal of establishing an Islamic government in Syria.

Developments in Iraq also favored ISI's influence. In campaigning for the presidency in 2008, Senator Barack Obama promised to end the Iraq War and withdraw all U.S. forces from Iraq before the end of his first term. With the security situation in Iraq stabilized and AQI decimated, on August 19, 2010, all U.S. combat forces withdrew from Iraq, with the remaining 50,000 U.S. troops engaged in counterterrorism operations and the training and advising of Iraqi forces. The warnings that such a move might end the stabilizing presence they had provided soon proved to be true. Both the Sunni insurgency and the violence between Iraq's Sunnis and Shia began increasing again in 2012.

The situation worsened when Iraq's Shia prime minister, Nouri al-Maliki, adopted policies that consolidated the power of the Shia and marginalized the Sunnis, thereby providing ISI with a situation ripe for exploitation. Another followed when Maliki refused to honor his commitment to continue paying the Sunni tribes who had been instrumental in helping the United States defeat AQI during 2006–2008. More broadly, Maliki purged most Sunni officers and soldiers from the Iraqi military, turning it into arguably an exclusively Shia force, even as Sunnis complained that Iraq's Shia were disproportionately benefiting from the country's oil wealth and reconstruction contracts.

During this time, ISI resumed its attacks on Iraq's government and the Shia population, which caused the Sunni population to experience the brunt of the government's counterterrorism crackdown and encouraged armed Shia group to retaliate by killing Sunnis. ISI also attacked prisons, liberating hundreds of AQI fighters. Finally, the Syrian Civil War fueled even more tensions between Iraq's Sunnis and Shia, as the Sunnis supported the various Sunni groups fighting the Assad government while the Shia supported the Assad government, which belonged to an offshoot of the Shia called the Alawite.

Starting in December 2012, massive protests erupted in the Sunni Anbar Province, quickly spreading to other Sunni regions of Iraq, sparked by the government's raids on the homes of Sunni politicians. On April 23, 2013, the government's aggressive efforts to end the protests led to violent clashes that killed dozens of Sunnis and a handful of Iraqi soldiers. The violence continued to rise throughout May between Sunnis and the Iraqi army, producing a cycle of retaliatory killings by Sunnis against the Shia and vice versa. In short, Iraq's descent into a new state of civil warfare was already well underway when the Sunni tribes of Anbar Province rose up in revolt against the Maliki government in April 2013 and, along with ISI, seized control of the city of Fallujah.

That same month, ISI leader Abu Bakr al-Baghdadi announced that ISI had created and financed the Jabhat al-Nusra group in Syria, and the two groups were merging under the name of the Islamic State in Iraq and Syria (ISIS; or the Islamic State in Iraq and the Levant (ISIL)). Al-Julani denounced the merger, declaring his loyalty remained with Ayman al-Zawahiri, the leader of al-Qaeda. Al-Zawahiri also denounced the merger, but al-Baghdadi rejected al-Zawahiri's ruling, announcing his loyalty was to God. During this public feud, clashes in Syria between Jabhat al-Nusra and ISIS erupted throughout 2013 and into 2014, with ISIS prevailing in this jihadist civil war after Jabhat al-Nusra suffered major defections to ISIS and the loss of much of the territory it controlled.

In February 2014, after months of repeated mediation efforts that failed to rein in ISIS, al-Qaeda formally disassociated itself from its affiliate in Iraq, exposing the dwindling influence al-Qaeda had on a new and younger generation of jihadists. Following the capture of Fallujah, ISIS's invading armies from Syria also gained control of Mosul, the second-largest city in Iraq (June 2014) and Ramada (May 2015).

ISIS's rapid conquest of large parts of Iraq; the collapse of the Iraqi army, which fled in panic in the face of these conquests; and the brutality of ISIS that became public knowledge as ISIS publicized its video recordings compelled the United States to respond. On August 7, 2014, President Obama ordered the U.S. military to begin bombing ISIS targets in Iraq to protect the American consulate in Erbil and stop ISIS's advance toward the capital of Baghdad, and the following month, the United States expanded its air campaign against ISIS to Syria. Australia, Belgium, France, Jordan, and the United Kingdom soon joined the air campaign against ISIS in Iraq and Syria.

In response to the air campaign, ISIS publicly broadcast the beheadings of captured American journalists, British and American aid workers, and citizens of other nations. During the same time and into 2015, ISIS also broadcast the drowning, crushing by tanks, and burning of hundreds of other people of various nationalities—executions representing but a small fraction of the tens of thousands murdered by ISIS. Still, the air campaign quickly stalled ISIS's advance in Iraq and Syria, and ISIS casualties soared.

In the meantime, after seizing Mosul, on June 29, 2014, al-Baghdadi declared the establishment of a caliphate, or Muslim government, designating himself the caliph, its religious leader, and announcing that ISIS was now the Islamic State (IS). By declaring a caliphate, the IS claimed authority over all Muslims worldwide, yet the violent means by which IS created and governed the caliphate made it illegitimate according to Islam. Less grandly, IS actually *ruled* large parts of western and northern Iraq and eastern Syria, which contain several million people.

LIFE IN IS CALIPHATE

As IS captured large swathes of territory, it used social media and its own media organization—including a magazine called *Dabiq*—to publicize its success and recruit men and women. Aided by an international press that reported extensively on IS's territorial conquests, its declaration of a caliphate prompted tens of thousands of mostly foreign males from throughout the world to travel to Syria and Iraq to join IS and be part of what they saw as history in the making.

Their motives for joining varied. Many wanted to be part of history; others joined out of a sense of adventure and boredom with their lives back home, which often included unemployment or underemployment. Regardless of motives, it is questionable how many of these foreign fighters, or IS fighters from Iraq and Syria, had any understanding of Islam, and once recruits arrived, they were subjected to extreme indoctrination. Dissent or leaving was prohibited and risked death. Additionally, the phenomena of groupthink and the pressure to conform instilled a high degree of cognitive dissonance among recruits and IS fighters—such that they blindly accepted the propaganda from IS about its Islamic credentials and legitimacy.

In addition to male recruits, perhaps thousands of women, principally from Europe and the Middle East, also joined IS, seduced by offers to become brides of jihadist fighters and thus guaranteed the life of purpose and esteem that they presumably lacked back home. Finally, IS also recruited children, calling them the "Cubs of the Caliphate" and using them to murder prisoners.

In reality, IS rule was anything but what its propaganda portrayed. Its capture of territory was never based on the consent of its residents. IS captured territory by force or the threat of force, which regularly included the murder of captured Iraqi, Kurdish, and Syrian soldiers. Elsewhere, people of many different religions suffered persecution, including murder, enslavement, and the rape of women of different faiths, especially those deemed to be heretics, such as the Yazidi people.

Within its territory, IS's armies destroyed non-Muslim places of worship, something forbidden in Islam, and all people, regardless of their faith, were required to obey IS's radical and intolerant interpretation of Islam. Punishments for things such as doing business during prayer times, dancing, listening to music, and women not dressing modestly could result in beatings and whippings, jail, and perhaps even execution.

IS also radically transformed education to conform to its brutal misinterpretation of Islam. Subjects deemed un-Islamic, such as art, history (other than that of Islam), and evolution, were banned. In their place, IS developed its own textbooks and curricula, while religious police enforced its interpretation of Islamic law and customs. In sum, despite its propaganda extolling the caliphate as a divinely sanctioned paradise on earth, the caliphate was a religious dictatorship ruled by violent extremists who falsely justified their brutality according to Islam.

The speed with which IS captured large parts of Iraq in 2014 belied its strength. The flight in panic of tens of thousands of Iraqi soldiers and officers in the face of at most a few thousand IS fighters speaks more to the corruption and dysfunction of the Iraqi military than the power of IS. Still, because IS *seemed* invincible, many existing Sunni jihadist terrorist groups—some previously associated with al-Qaeda—pledged loyalty to IS. Moreover, affiliates of IS quickly developed in Algeria, Afghanistan, the Russian Caucasus, Egyptian Sinai, Philippines, and West Africa. When IS started suffering heavy casualties from American and allied air strikes and began losing territory, those groups pledging loyalty to IS reacted by launching a series of deadly terrorist attacks worldwide.

THE CALIPHATE ENDS

Despite its seeming invincibility, IS was unable to continue its expansion and eventually suffered heavy casualties. Apart from conducting bombing campaigns, the United States began arming Kurdish groups in Syria and Iraq. At approximately the same time, the Iraqi army used the allied air campaign against ISIS that began in August 2014 to regroup, and the Iraqi government encouraged various Shia militia—known as the Popular Mobilization Forces (PMF)—to join in the fight against IS.

In June 2015, the U.S. government reported that allied airstrikes had killed more than 10,000 IS fighters over the previous nine months. By 2016, this number may have doubled, and the number of recruits once flocking to join IS was in the midst of a three-year decline. More importantly, by 2017, IS was losing much of its territory, and for all of its claims of representing Sunni Muslims, those in the territories it ruled did not jump to defend the caliphate as it came under attack. Thus, in July of that year, Mosul fell after a nine-month battle, and in October, IS lost its de facto capital of Raqqa in Syria. The following month, it lost control of its last cities in Syria and Iraq.

IS has now entirely lost its caliphate, and from a force of tens of thousands, it may have no more than a few hundred fighters, scattered mostly along the Iraq and Syrian border. Iraqi intelligence reports that Baghdadi ordered the execution of 320 of his followers for their "betrayal" and "recklessness," sending some IS militants into hiding in unknown locations in fear for their lives. On October 27, 2019, al-Baghdadi killed himself by detonating a suicide vest during a U.S. Special Operations forces raid in Barisha, Syria.

With the loss of its caliphate and with insufficient fighters to seize and rule territory, in 2017, IS returned to launching car and suicide bombings and guerrilla-style terrorist attacks inside Iraq and Syria. Its future largely depends on its ability to exploit the political situation in Iraq. If the Iraqi government can govern in a noncorrupt manner, representing Shia *and* Sunnis, the rebirth or resurrection of ISIS is unlikely. Nevertheless, it would be a mistake to underestimate IS, including its ability to wait patiently for an opportunity to regenerate. Moreover, were it to collapse, there is no reason to assume that another Sunni jihadist terrorist group would not take its place. After all, terrorism thrives owing to the existence of grievances or the appeal of an idea, ideology, or vision.

Stefan Brooks

See also: al-Baghdadi, Abu Bakr; al-Qaeda; Recruiting Terrorists; State Terrorism; War on Terror, The.

FURTHER READING

Gerges, Fawaz. 2017. *ISIS: A History*. Princeton, NJ: Princeton University Press.

McCants, William. 2016. *The ISIS Apocalypse: The History, Strategy, and Doomsday Vision of the Islamic State*. New York: Picador Press.

Warrick, Joby. 2016. *Black Flags: The Rise of ISIS*. New York: Anchor Press.

Wright, Lawrence. 2017. *The Terror Years: From al-Qaeda to the Islamic State*. New York: Vintage Press.

J

Jihad

Jihad is an Arabic word that is often translated literally to English as "striving" or "struggle," and it describes a central concept in Islamic theology and Islamic life. Depending on the context in which it is used, *jihad* has a number of complex meanings and religious connotations within Islam. *Jihad* is often used in a religious context to denote the Islamic obligation to conform one's thought and actions to those prescribed by the Quran and by the Islamic faith, but it may also refer to an armed or violent struggle against those who are nonbelievers or who threaten either the Islamic faith or the *Ummah*—the Muslim community at large. Thus, the term may, according to the context in which it is used, have a moral or spiritual meaning or a military or martial meaning.

The term and the concept of *jihad* in both contexts can be found throughout Islamic theology in the Quran, the Hadith, and the various schools or traditions of Islamic jurisprudence, and the concept has evolved over time through various interpretations of Islam's sacred texts. Notwithstanding the complexity of the concept and its various interpretations, Islamic theology considers two general types or classifications of jihad: the "greater jihad" and the "lesser jihad."

The internally focused concept of *greater jihad* is concerned with the spiritual and moral aspects and obligations of the Islamic faith and with the individual's personal struggle to live a life that is consonant with those obligations. The externally focused concept of the *lesser jihad* concerns the religious obligation of every Muslim to extend Islam through proselytizing and peaceful conversion of nonbelievers as well as to defend Islam and the Ummah from enemies. Because this defensive conceptualization of the lesser jihad may, in some cases and under certain conditions, necessitate violence or military action, it is often characterized as a form of unrestricted "holy war." That blanket characterization is not entirely accurate.

The externally focused concept of the lesser jihad is further delineated into a "jihad of the heart" (faith), "jihad of the pen" (knowledge of Islam), "jihad of the hand" (good works), and "jihad of the tongue" (promoting the growth of Islam through dialogue leading to conversion) as well as a more aggressive and violent "jihad of the sword" (military activities aimed at defending Islam from those who threaten it or vanquishing the enemies of Islam and the Ummah).

While an understanding of the overall concept and the several meanings of jihad is essential to an understanding of the Islamic faith and the Islamic world, the aggressive and violent jihad of the sword is of primary importance to an understanding of Islamic terrorism and the Islamist ideology that supports it.

Although the practice of violent jihad of the sword is typically associated with Islamist extremism and Islamist terrorism, it is important to recognize that legitimate jihad of the sword does not permit unrestricted warfare or indiscriminate violence. Rather, Muslims may not legitimately engage in jihad to force conversion to Islam, to settle disputes, or to conquer, colonize, or economically exploit a nation or territory. Legitimate jihad requires that the opponent must have initiated the conflict and must pose a real threat; that women, children, and noncombatant civilians may not be killed or injured; and, importantly, that the jihad must be sanctioned by a legitimate religious authority.

Thus, for example, Osama bin Laden's 1998 *fatwah* (a legal opinion by an Islamic scholar) entitled "Jihad against the Jews and Crusaders" attempted to justify jihad of the sword against Israel and the United States and its allies. Although the fatwah spelled out various perceived grievances, bin Laden was not a bona fide religious scholar; therefore his call to jihad was not theologically valid.

Vincent E. Henry

See also: bin Laden, Osama; Islamic State, The.

FURTHER READING

Bonney, Richard. 2004. *Jihād: From Qur'ān to bin Lāden.* New York: Palgrave-Macmillan.

Gerges, Fawaz A. 2009. *The Far Enemy: Why Jihad Went Global.* New York: Cambridge University Press.

Knapp, Michael G. 2003. "The Concept and Practice of Jihad in Islam." *Parameters* (Spring): 82–94. https://www.hsdl.org/?view&did=1867

Morag, Nadav. 2015. *The Global Jihadi Threat: Module 2, The Role of Jihad in Islam.* Naval Postgraduate School, Center for Homeland Defense and Security, Monterey, CA. Video, 22:12. https://calhoun.nps.edu/handle/10945/48381

Pelicano, Stephen M. 2011. "The Legality of al-Qaeda's Jihad." Fort Leavenworth, KS: US Army Command and General Staff College, School of Advanced Military Studies. https://www.hsdl.org/?view&did=683124

Justice against Sponsors of Terrorism Act (JASTA)

2016

Civil efforts by victims to receive compensation for their 9/11 losses began as early as August 2002, when Motley Rice, one of the country's largest plaintiff litigation firms, filed a claim against Saudi Arabia on behalf of approximately 500 survivors of the terrorist attacks of September 11, 2001, and the family members of those who did not survive. In the years following, the number of plaintiffs, now organized for litigation purposes as the "9/11 Families and Survivors United for Justice against Terrorism," increased to more than 6,600. Yet, until the 2016 passage of the Justice against Sponsors of Terrorism Act (JASTA), from which the organization took its name, the litigation floundered in the lower federal courts hearing the case.

The most significant obstacle faced by the action was the long-standing legal doctrine of foreign sovereign immunity, as codified in the Foreign Sovereignty

Immunities Act of 1976 (FSIA), which limits judicial action by all American courts against a foreign sovereign state or its political agencies, subdivisions, or instrumentalities, such as its banks. Prior to JASTA's passage, the foreign state essentially had to be on the U.S. Department of State's official State Sponsors of Terrorism list. Saudi Arabia had not, and still has not, been so designated.

JASTA, passed unanimously by both houses of Congress by voice vote, eased that restriction by amending FSIA and the Anti-Terrorism and Effective Death Penalty Act (which addresses claims involving death, injury and destruction resulting from international terrorist acts). Under JASTA, the foreign state need no longer be on the State Sponsors of Terrorism list; to be liable, it need only be proven to have supported an act of terrorism against a U.S. national or U.S. property.

Two weeks following JASTA's passage by Congress, President Barack Obama vetoed it on the following grounds:

- "JASTA departs from longstanding standards and practice . . . and threatens to strip all foreign governments of immunity . . . based solely upon allegations by private litigants that a foreign government's overseas conduct had some role or connection to a group or person that carried out a terrorist attack inside the United States."
- "The United States has a larger international presence, by far, than any other country, and sovereign immunity principles protect our Nation and its Armed Forces, officials, and assistance professionals, from foreign court proceedings. . . . This could lead to [retaliatory] suits against the United States or U.S. officials for actions taken by members of an armed group that received U.S. assistance . . . or abuses committed by police units that received U.S. training even if the allegations at issue ultimately would be without merit."
- "JASTA threatens to create complications in our relationships with even our closest partners. . . . By exposing these allies and partners to this sort of litigation in U.S. courts, JASTA threatens to limit their cooperation on key national security issues, including terrorism." (White House 2016)

Within five days, the Senate and House of Representatives overwhelmingly overrode Obama's veto, and litigation against Saudi Arabia resumed, currently in the case *In re: Terrorist Attacks of September 11, 2001.* That case contends that the kingdom, named princes, a Saudi banker, and a Saudi charity played a critical role in the 9/11 attack by funding Muslim groups who supported al-Qaeda's attack on the United States.

As of October 2020, the case is still proceeding, having won a major federal district court victory in March 2018 when the judge ruled against the Kingdom of Saudi Arabia's motion to dismiss the case on the grounds that the allegations met required standards for the case to move forward *and* granted the plaintiffs' request for permission to conduct targeted discovering proceedings. Whether the plaintiffs' case will ultimately succeed, however, is still being debated, even within the legal community. Ingrid Wuerth, the director of legal studies at Vanderbilt University's School of Law and a frequent Department of State consultant on matters of international law, has noted that capitalizing on any judgment may be difficult because some parts of FSIA conferring sovereign immunity were not amended by JASTA. Moreover, although Congress might then authorize new enforcement measures should the plaintiffs win their case, it might also take a renewed look at the possible harm to the foreign relations of such action and choose not to do so.

Joseph R. Rudolph Jr.

See also: Counterterrorism, the Courts, and the Constitution; Counterterrorism and the Obama Administration; Foreign Terrorist Groups at War with the United States; September 11, 2001, Attack on America.

FURTHER READING

George Washington University. 2014. "Fighting Terrorism in Court: Peter Raven-Hansen Answers Questions about Cases Brought under the Anti-Terrorism Act." GW Law, October 17, 2014. https://www.law.gwu.edu/fighting-terrorism-in-court

Vladeck, Steve. 2016. "The 9/11 Civil Litigation and the Justice against Sponsors of Terrorism Act (JASTA)." Just Security, April 18, 2016. https://www.justsecurity.org/30633/911-civil-litigation-justice-sponsors-terrorism-act-jasta/

White House, Office of the Press Secretary. 2016. "Veto Message from the President—S.2040." September 23, 2016. https://obamawhitehouse.archives.gov/the-press-office/2016/09/23/veto-message-president-s2040

Wuerth, Ingrid. 2016. "Justice against Terrorism Act: Initial Analysis." Lawfare, September 29, 2016. https://www.lawfareblog.com/justice-against-sponsors-terrorism-act-initial-analysis

K

Ku Klux Klan

Formed in December 1865 in Pulaski, Tennessee, by six Confederate veterans, the Ku Klux Klan (KKK), or the Klan, is often referred to as America's first terrorist organization. The name was derived from the Greek *kuklos*, meaning "circle," and the English word *clan*. Adopting secret initiation rituals and white robes and hoods, by 1866, the KKK had evolved into an organization dedicated to intimidation and violence against former slaves in the wake of the U.S. Civil War.

In March 1867, Congress overrode President Johnson's veto and passed the Reconstruction Acts, which abolished the ex-Confederate state governments and divided them into a series of military districts. The Klan's reaction was to organize into an "invisible empire" throughout the South under the official philosophy of white supremacy while steadily increasing its campaign of violence and terror against newly freed persons. In 1871, Congress passed strict anti-Klan legislation that allowed the president to declare martial law and suspend the writ of habeas corpus over citizens in the South. Night riding and the wearing of masks were expressly prohibited. With the 1896 U.S. Supreme Court decision in *Plessy v. Ferguson*, which permitted the introduction of an official system of segregation based on "separate but equal" facilities throughout the South, the violent intimidation tactics of the KKK became less tolerated, and the group eventually faded into the background of history.

Reborn during a 1915 cross burning in Stone Mountain, Georgia, the same year the pro-Klan motion picture *Birth of a Nation* was released, the group's ranks swelled following World War I. The KKK now recruited those who were not only rabidly anti-Black but also anti-Jewish and anti-Catholic. The Klan launched a campaign of terrorism in the early and mid-1920s, with lynching, shooting, and whippings being favorite tactics used against Blacks, Jews, Catholics, Mexicans, and other immigrant groups. By the mid-1920s, nearly three million dues-paying members had enrolled in the organization, and numerous local, state, and federal officials were elected with Klan support, giving the organization political legitimacy and power. Internal power struggles and high-profile scandals eventually brought this new reiteration of the KKK into disgrace, and its membership again dwindled.

During the civil rights movement of the 1950s and 1960s, the KKK saw a brief resurgence as many whites throughout the South were determined to oppose the law and maintain segregation following the U.S. Supreme Court's 1954 *Brown v. Board of Education* decision to strike down the separate but equal doctrine and order school integration. During this period, the Klan was responsible for several acts of terror, including the bombing and burning of Black-owned homes, churches, and businesses. Klan members were implicated in the murders of three civil rights workers in Mississippi in the summer of 1964. Starting in the mid-1960s, following intense pressure from the FBI, civil and criminal lawsuits, and congressional investigations, the KKK has continually seen its membership and influence wane. Although still active, the modern KKK has been subjugated by more racial paramilitary hate groups, such as the neo-Nazis and other white supremacy organizations.

John R. Capra

See also: Domestic Terrorism, Anti-Semitic; Domestic Terrorism, the Civil Rights Era; Domestic Terrorism, White Supremacists.

FURTHER READING

Chernow, Ron. 2017. *Grant.* London: Penguin Press.

Fischer, William Harvey. 1980. *The Invisible Empire.* Metuchen, NJ: Scarecrow Press.

Katz, William Loren. 1986. *The Invisible Empire: The Ku Klux Klan Impact on History.* Seattle, WA: Open Hand Publishing.

Ridgeway, James. 1991. *Blood in the Face: The Ku Klux Klan, Aryan Nations, Nazi Skinheads, and the Rise of the New White Culture.* New York: Thunder's Mouth Press.

Trelease, Allen W. 1971. *White Terror: The Ku Klux Klan Conspiracy and Southern Reconstruction.* Baton Rouge: Louisiana State University Press.

L

London Terrorist Attacks

March–June 2017

Three separate pedestrian-vehicle terrorist attacks occurred in London during 2017. The first attack occurred on March 22 on Westminster Bridge. Khalid Masood (52) drove a rented SUV into pedestrians, killing four and injuring over fifty. Masood then exited the SUV and fatally stabbed a police officer. Responding officers fatally shot Masood to end the attack.

Masood, born Adrian Russell Ajao in southeastern England, had an extensive criminal record with prior convictions for shoplifting, possession of weapons, and assault. Masood converted to Islam in prison while serving a two-year sentence for assault. He was the subject of an MI5 investigation between 2010 and 2012 as a result of his connections to a terrorist network plotting to use homemade explosives against targets in the United Kingdom (UK) and individuals seeking to travel outside the UK for terrorist training. Authorities closed Masood's investigation after it failed to produce intelligence suggesting Masood was planning attacks, and they deemed he was not a threat to national security. Although not a member himself, Masood maintained contacts with members of al-Muhajiroun (ALM) and expressed support for violent terrorist actions.

The Westminster Bridge investigation indicated Masood began planning the attack in 2016. Minutes prior to the attack, Masood digitally shared with contacts a document with quotes supportive of jihad and martyrdom. While the Islamic State (IS) claimed responsibility for the attack, investigators concluded Masood acted alone, and no formal connection was established to the group.

The second attack occurred on June 3 on London Bridge. Khuram Butt (27), Rachid Redouane (30), and Youssef Zaghba (22) drove a rented van into pedestrians, killing two immediately. The attackers then exited the van wearing fake suicide vests and used ceramic knives to attack pedestrians in the nearby Borough Market, killing six and injuring at least another forty-five victims. Responding officers fatally shot the attackers to end the eight-minute attack for which the IS claimed responsibility.

MI5 had Pakistan-born British citizen Butt under investigation at the time of the attack based on his connection to ALM and expression of extremist views. Moroccan-citizen Redouane did not have a criminal record but had previously falsely claimed asylum as a Libyan citizen. The family of Moroccan/Italian citizen Zaghba claimed he had been radicalized through the Internet and attempted to travel to Syria to join IS. On his way to Syria, Italian law enforcement stopped

Zaghba. His confiscated phone contained IS propaganda, prompting law enforcement to enter Zaghba in a European database of suspected terrorists.

The final attack occurred on June 19 at the Finsbury Park Islamic Centre. Singapore-born British citizen Darren Osborne (47) drove a rented van into worshippers outside the Islamic center, killing one and injuring twelve others. A jury convicted Osborne, who acted alone, and he was sentenced to life in prison for the attack. While Osborne had an extensive criminal history, he was previously unknown to MI5. The judge indicated at sentencing that Osborne had been radicalized in less than a month by anti-Islamic radical ideology viewed on the Internet.

In the wake of these attacks, Prime Minister Theresa May ordered a public review of British counterterrorism, which resulted in a new policy introduced in 2018 focused on coordination across the public sector to address terrorism.

Dawn M. Wozneak

See also: Homegrown Terrorism; London Transit Terrorist Attacks; Madrid Train Bombings and the War on Terror.

FURTHER READING

Anderson, David. 2017. *Attacks in London and Manchester: March–June 2017: Independent Assessment of MI5 and Police Internal Reviews: Unclassified.* Report prepared for the Home Office, December 2017. https://assets.publishing.service.gov.uk/government/uploads/system/uploads/attachment_data/file/664682/Attacks_in_London_and_Manchester_Open_Report.pdf

Cheema-Grubb, Parmjit Kaur. 2018. R v. Darren Osborne, Sentencing Remarks. Woolrich Crown Court, February 2, 2018. https://www.judiciary.uk/wp-content/uploads/2018/02/r-v-osborne-sentencing-remarks.pdf

London Transit Terrorist Attacks

July 7, 2005

The July 7, 2005, bombings—often referred to as the 7/7 bombings—were a series of coordinated attacks by four British-resident suicide bombers, wearing backpacks filled with explosives, that killed 52 commuters on London's transport system. Nearly simultaneous explosions tore through three London Underground trains in three locations at approximately 8:50 a.m. Altogether, over 700 passengers were injured, and many more were traumatized by the experience. An hour later, a fourth bomb was detonated aboard a double-decker bus at the junction of Upper Woburn Place and Tavistock Square, killing 13 people and damaging nearby cars.

On July 16, Mohammed Sidique Khan, Hasib Hussein, Shehzad Tanweer, and Germaine Lindsey were identified by the London Metropolitan Police as the Muslim perpetrators of the attack. Khan, Hussein, and Tanweer were British-born sons of Pakistani immigrants, while Lindsey was a convert born in Jamaica. None of the bombers were known to British intelligence services, according to Home Secretary Charles Clarke.

On the morning of the attacks, CCTV captured the movements of all four suicide bombers. Three traveled from Leeds to Luton, where they all boarded a train to London's King's Cross station. Shortly thereafter, explosions ripped through the three London Underground trains. Response to the bombings was immediate. London Underground stations in Central London were closed while forensic investigators began their search for evidence.

A group claiming affiliation with al-Qaeda took responsibility for the attacks on a website; however, those claims were quickly debunked by British intelligence services. The investigation then turned to uncovering other possible accomplices and motives. Theories of a fifth bomber and links to foreign terrorist organizations were investigated and dismissed by police, and the British Home Office produced a report that laid the blame for the bombings on the four men, operating with a budget of only a few hundred pounds. Tapes would subsequently surface in which two of the bombers described themselves as Islamic soldiers in the war with the West.

The response by London's emergency services is considered the city's most comprehensive and complex to a terrorist attack. Following the September 11 attacks in the United States, the London police had been rehearsing emergency procedures and followed prearranged measures after the blasts.

Keith A. Leitich

See also: Boston Marathon Bombing; Homegrown Terrorism; Madrid Train Bombings and the War on Terror.

FURTHER READING

Bean, Hamilton, Lisa Keränen, and Margaret Durfy. 2011. "'This Is London': Cosmopolitan Nationalism and the Discourse of Resilience in the Case of the 7/7 Terrorist Attacks." *Rhetoric & Public Affairs* 14 (3): 427–464.

Cottey, Andrew, and Ian Davis. 2005. "After the London Suicide Bombings: Facing Difficult Choices on Homegrown Terrorism." *Occasional Papers on International Security Policy*, British American Security Information Council: 4. Unpublished report.

Kirby, Aidan. 2007. "The London Bombers as 'Self-Starters': A Case Study in Indigenous Radicalization and the Emergence of Autonomous Cliques." *Studies in Conflict & Terrorism* 30 (5): 415–428.

Lieberman, Charles A., and Serguei Cheloukhine. 2009. "2005 London Bombings." In *A New Understanding of Terrorism: Case Studies, Trajectories and Lessons Learned*, edited by M. R. Haberfeld and Agostino Hassell, 233–248. New York: Springer.

London Assembly. 2006. *Report on the 7 July Review Committee.* London: Greater London Authority.

M

Madrid Train Bombings and the War on Terror

March 11, 2004

On Thursday morning, March 11, 2004, between 7:30 and 7:40, ten bombs exploded nearly simultaneously aboard four commuter trains at or near three different train stations in Madrid, Spain. The blasts killed 193 people and injured nearly another 2,000. They also significantly affected the outcome of Spain's imminent parliamentary election and had an impact on anti-terrorist politics as far away as Iraq.

In the attacks' immediate aftermath, speculation regarding the perpetrators quickly took a partisan turn. The then ruling People's Party, the favorite to win reelection and a contributor to the "Coalition of the Willing" that joined American forces in post-invasion Iraq, blamed the Basque Euskadi Ta Askatasuna (ETA), the separatist group whose fight for the independence of Spain's Basque provinces often involved terrorist activity. The main opposition party, the Socialists, blamed the attack on opponents of the deployment of Spanish troops in Iraq, including al-Qaeda itself or its cells in Spain and North Africa.

The majority of voters apparently agreed with the Socialists' interpretation and voted the People's Party out of office when the election took place three days after the bombings. By the end of May, the Socialist leader, Premier José Luis Rodríguez Zapatero, fulfilled his campaign promise and withdrew Spain's forces from Iraq. However, more than a decade and a half since the bombings, a definitive judgment of guilt remains elusive.

Investigations following the attacks, and the 2007 trial of nearly thirty people for being involved in the plot to bomb the commuter trains, essentially cleared the ETA of any involvement and found no *direct* connection between the event and al-Qaeda, which had claimed credit almost immediately after the attack. As for the perpetrators, three of the eight initially sought for having purchased the explosives used in the blasts blew themselves up on April 3, 2004, when surrounded by police in their suspected base of operations. The other five managed to escape the country, and the 2007 trial focused on the alleged masterminds, who were acquitted, and a second tier of suspects who sold the alleged explosives to the terrorists or otherwise abetted them. Two received multiple life sentences for committing murder.

Meanwhile, the bombing of the commuter trains reminded the world that terrorism can be effective, at least at the tactical level. Timed to coincide with Spain's parliamentary elections, the event shaped the election's outcome and led to the subsequent removal of the Spanish forces supporting U.S. troops in Iraq. Just as important, it proved that high-impact terrorism can be achieved economically and without outside financing. The 9/11 attack on the World Trade Center and Pentagon cost at least a half million dollars and the lives of nearly a score of carefully selected and trained al-Qaeda soldiers. The Madrid bombings cost less than $40,000, and were self-financed by the perpetrators by selling drugs.

Joseph R. Rudolph Jr.

See also: Counterterrorism and the George W. Bush Administration; London Transit Terrorist Attacks; War on Terror, The.

FURTHER READING

Fredrik. 2016. "The 2004 Madrid Train Bombings." Crime Scene Database, May 14, 2016. Accessed January 24, 2020. http://crimescenedb.com/the-2004-madrid-train-bombings/

Reinares, Fernando. 2017. *Al-Qaeda's Revenge: The 2004 Madrid Train Bombings.* New York: Columbia University Press.

Soufan Center. 2019. "IntelBrief: 15 Years after Madrid Train Bombings, What Have We Learned." March 11, 2019. Accessed January 24, 2020. https://thesoufancenter.org/intelbrief-the-15th-anniversary-of-the-madrid-train-bombings/

Manhattan, New York City Bombing

September 17, 2016

At approximately 8:30 p.m. on September 17, 2016, a shrapnel-filled pressure cooker bomb exploded on West Twenty-Third Street between Avenue of the Americas and Seventh Avenue in New York City. The explosion was powerful enough to destroy and move a sidewalk dumpster more than 120 feet, damage nearby buildings, and shatter windows throughout the neighborhood. Thirty-one people were injured, only one of them seriously.

Police searching the area for secondary devices discovered another pressure cooker bomb under a mailbox several blocks away. That device also contained shrapnel and had a cell phone–activated remote control detonator attached. After rendering the bomb safe, NYPD Bomb Squad officers recovered the cell phone, fingerprints, and DNA evidence. Both pressure cooker bombs utilized cell phones and Christmas tree lights to ignite hexamethylene triperoxide diamine (HMTD), itself an explosive, to detonate the secondary explosive.

The NYPD; the FBI; the Bureau of Alcohol, Tobacco, Firearms, and Explosives (ATF); and the NYPD-FBI Joint Terrorism Task Force collectively investigated the incidents, and by September 19, they had linked them to similar incidents that occurred in New Jersey on September 17 and 18. The former involved a pipe bomb exploding in a trash can near the starting point of a 5 km run in Seaside Park sponsored by a Marine Corps veterans' organization. Then, on the evening of the following day, two homeless men discovered a backpack containing six pipe bombs outside a train station in Elizabeth, New Jersey. Investigations revealed that the pipe bombs were similar in appearance and construction to the pipe bombs discovered in Seaside Park and the Manhattan bombs.

Forensic examination of the fingerprints and cell phones recovered in New York led authorities to thirty-one-year old Ahmad Khan Rahimi, who immigrated to the United States from Afghanistan in 1995 and became a naturalized citizen in 2011. Surveillance video near the Chelsea Manhattan bombing site showed Rahimi placing the pressure cooker bomb. The investigation revealed that Rahimi was an unaffiliated, aspirational, or lone-wolf, Islamist terrorist inspired by Osama bin Laden and the rhetoric of al-Qaeda propagandist and cleric Anwar al-Awlaki. Rahimi had returned to Afghanistan several times and visited Pakistan for extended periods, presumably becoming radicalized on the trips. Investigators also determined that Rahimi purchased the bomb components online during the summer of 2016.

Law enforcement officials broadcast alarms for Rahimi on the morning of September 19, and he was quickly located sleeping in a doorway in Linden, New Jersey. He engaged in a gun battle with police officers attempting to arrest him, shooting two officers and receiving nine gunshot wounds. He was in possession of a handwritten journal with entries praising bin Laden, al-Awlaki, and Fort Hood mass shooter Major Nidal Hasan.

Following a two-week federal district trial in New York, on October 16, 2017, Rahimi was convicted of eight felony counts related to the New York City bombing incidents and sentenced to life in prison on February 13, 2018.

A November 2016 issue of the al-Qaeda magazine *Inspire* praised Rahimi and speculated that the September 17 and 18 bombings were originally scheduled for the anniversary of the 9/11 attacks but may have been delayed by the time necessary to construct multiple devices.

Vincent E. Henry

See also: al-Awlaki, Anwar; Homegrown Terrorism; Internet as a Virtual School for Terrorism.

FURTHER READING

New York Police Department. 2016. *NYPD SHIELD Assessment: Explosion in New York City: Currently No Known Links to Other Violent Events*. September 18, 2016. New York: New York Police Department Counterterrorism Bureau.

Santora, Marc, William K. Rashbaum, Al Baker, and Adam Goldman. 2016. "Ahmad Khan Rahami Is Arrested in Manhattan and New Jersey Bombings." *New York Times*, September 18, 2016.

U.S. Department of Justice. 2017. "Chelsea Bomber Ahmad Khan Rahimi Convicted for Executing September 2016 Bombing in New York City." October 16, 2017. https://www.justice.gov/opa/pr/chelsea-bomber-ahmad-khan-rahimi-convicted-executing-september-2016-bombing-new-york-city

Media, Changing Roles in the Terrorist Era

1960–Present

Our direct relationship with the media is more complex than ever. It serves as our main source of news and information, allowing us to learn about events that we are often unable to directly witness. It has also allowed us to see significant historical events, such as the fall of the Berlin Wall, and somber moments, such as 9/11.

Traditionally, we have trusted the media—watching the news first thing in the morning and again in the evening as part of our daily ritual. That has significantly changed over the last few decades with the need for a news station to be first to report becoming more important than the information being true or valid. This, coupled with the constant flow of information via social media, has created an additional dynamic that has the potential to be beneficial as well as problematic.

A component that is also critical in understanding this topic is the fiscal funding by a handful of conglomerate companies that have a built-in platform and bias that impacts what information is delivered and how. This is especially true when reporting on terrorism. Simply put, where you live in the world often has a high impact on how a story is reported. This, coupled with political and extremist groups with open access, provides a difficult and complex landscape for people to navigate to get to the truth, whether we are looking at current events in the United States or around the globe.

THEMATIC AND HISTORICAL CONTEXT

A foundational tool of the media's reporting style is the use of *framing*, which is how information or an event is fit into simple context. This allows the audience to interpret events according to their own existing knowledge and value system. It is necessary for the general audience, but it can also be potentially problematic, especially when the goal becomes viewership and not the dissemination of accurate information. For example, during the Syrian conflict, the government-controlled news station, Syrian Arab News Agency (SANA), reported events that supported the pro-Ba'ath/Assad narrative of protecting the Syrian people against terrorists. During this time, Daesh (an acronym for the Islamic State) created the Al Hayat Media Center, which provided information via a lens that would lead many to believe that the Islamic State in Iraq and Syria (ISIS) was an organized group of freedom fighters sent to liberate and support the Syrian people. Both media sites repeatedly failed to provide a historical, economic, or humanitarian context to allow understanding of the bigger picture. In addition, the media outlets often presented event response retaliation when confronted about the impact on the country. Citizens became increasingly confused and suspicious of the role media was playing in the conflict. This created a difficult environment to disseminate important information when it was greatly needed.

Unfortunately, Syria is just one of many examples where dissemination of information has become secondary to the crafted message of the media's platform. Since the 1960s, the world has seen a significant shift, especially in relation to terrorism involving both state and non-state actors. When reviewing the last several decades, we see the beginning of televised single lens narratives. In Africa, the West refused to support the liberation of South Africa and originally labeled Nelson Mandela as a terrorist. Media outlets reported on post-Cold War Africa as a continent, not a multitude of states being labeled as primitive, inferior, prone to war, and so on—a framing hangover from colonial rule that still has ramifications in current times. This is done repeatedly simply because it is easier to frame it in a familiar construct than address the complex political, economic, and other factors that are involved. With the funding cuts after the Cold War, strategic communication has significantly faltered, particularly in the United States.

This continues today in the United States as we continue our war against terrorism. The media long ago realized that "if it bleeds, it leads"—often leaving fact-checking, historical context, and well-rounded reporting almost nonexistent. Even more discerning is the integration and utilization of the media by many terrorist organizations. With the use of Twitter, YouTube, and aesthetically pleasing recruiting tools, terrorist organizations have capitalized on a multitude of platforms. The social media accounts are often banned or blocked, but they sometimes pop up again with new accounts within minutes.

In addition, the traditional media's failure to report events within a proper context (e.g., historical, political) has left a vast space for terrorist groups to create their own narratives, often appearing to validate the very propaganda they are using to recruit new members. How can the U.S. government and other sovereign states approach this issue? Traditional kinetic campaigns of the past are not enough to combat it. Currently, social media is working very hard to be part of the solution by fact-checking and documenting dated articles, among other efforts. This has been met with resistance from some groups who feel this is another form of censorship and control. What it clearly demonstrates is that although the U.S. government should be vigilant, engaged, and using cutting-edge technology, it still requires a timely, consistent, and multifaceted approach to the relationship between media, terrorism, and the future of mass communication.

Rachel E. McGinnis

See also: Internet as a Virtual School for Terrorism; Social Media and Terrorism.

FURTHER READING

Asongu, Simplice A., Stella-Maris I. Orim, and Rexon T. Nting. 2019. "Terrorism and Social Media: Global Evidence." *Journal of Global Information Technology Management* 22 (3): 208–228. https://doi.org/10.1080/1097198X.2019.1642023

Besova, Asya A., and Skye Chance Cooley. 2009. "Foreign News and Public Opinion: Attribute Agenda-Setting Theory Revisited." *African Journalism Studies* 30 (2): 219–242. https://doi.org/10.1080/02560054.2009.9653403

Harley, Williamson, Suzanna Fay, and Toby Miles-Johnson. 2019. "Fear of Terrorism: Media Exposure and Subjective Fear of Attack." *Global Crime* 20 (1): 1–25. https://doi.org/10.1080/17440572.2019.1569519

Huey, L. 2015. "This is Not Your Mother's Terrorism: Social Media, Online Radicalization and the Practice of Political Jamming." *Journal of Terrorism Research* 6 (2): 1–16.

Office of the Director of National Intelligence. 2016. *Applying Private Sector Media Strategies to Fight* Terrorism. https://www.odni.gov/files/PE/Documents/Media-Strategies.pdf

Michigan Governor Kidnapping Plot

On Wednesday, October 7, 2020, federal, state, and local authorities concluded a successful counterterrorist operation with the arrests of thirteen men, six of whom were charged by federal authorities with conspiring to kidnap Gretchen Whitmer, the governor of Michigan, at her vacation home. The remainder were arrested on state charges, reportedly involving weapons violations.

Inferred in all the arrests was the willingness of those charged to murder the governor's security detail and others around her. Explicit was their intent to transport her out of state to Wisconsin and to try her there for treason because of the strict COVID-19 regulations she had ordered. Broader plans included storming the capitol buildings of several states, seizing hostages and perhaps somehow igniting a civil war less than a month before the country was to vote in the acrimonious 2020 presidential race.

Those federally charged—Adam Fox, Barry Croft, Ty Garbin, Kaleb Franks, Daniel Harris, and Brandon Caserta—were all linked to a central militia group, the Wolverine Watchmen, as were the other seven arrested. Michigan had recently become a key venue for both gun-bearing protests against the COVID-19 restrictions placed on business operations and militia training exercises. Discussions involving the kidnapping operation began as early as June among those arrested, followed by three days of firearms and combat training in July. Communication among those involved was often encoded; however, from the outset, the many moving parts of the plot(s) facilitated detection, and the amassed evidence was sufficient for the men's arrest.

Apart from their newsworthiness, the arrests were significant on several counts. First, they underscored the warning issued only two days previously in the Department of Homeland Security's Threat Assessment Report that the country's greatest terrorist threat is now posed by both ideologically motivated lone wolves and *small groups of extremists*, largely concentrated on the right. The most notable instances of political violence had previously been of the lone-wolf variety.

Second, the arrests also underscored what many had been observing: since 2015, unofficial armed groupings, calling themselves state militias, had experienced a renaissance after being chastened following the 1995 bombing of the Oklahoma City Federal Building by someone with militia leanings. Likewise, they were overshadowed during the first decade and a half of the twenty-first century by the threats posed at home and abroad by international terrorist organizations.

Like white supremacists, their activity was spurred by the combination of (1) the sense of peril within portions of white America's dwindling majority in the U.S. population, (2) the perceived success of progressive groups like Black Lives Matter in achieving their goals, and (3) what they perceived to be the illegitimate growth of state authority. In 2020, the latter in particular gained center stage as states adopted policies restricting activities at the moment when efforts to combat the COVID-19 pandemic had closed universities, bars, and businesses, leaving millions temporarily idle for public protesting and thousands free to follow their extremist interests for months at a time.

Finally, whereas late twentieth-century anti-government groups had largely waged a "paper war" of bogus suits and counterfeit deeds against public authorities, the Michigan plot denoted a sharp turn toward employing deadly force against government officials and the institutions of governance.

Joseph R. Rudolph Jr.

See also: Armed Militias; Domestic Terrorist Groups; Montana Freemen Siege; Oklahoma City Federal Building Bombing; Ruby Ridge Standoff.

FURTHER READING

Crothers, Lane. 2019. *Rage on the Right: The American Militia Movement from Ruby Ridge to the Trump Presidency.* 2nd ed. Lanham, MD: Rowman & Littlefield.

Levin, Sam. 2020. "White Supremacists and Militias Have Infiltrated Police across US, Report Says." *The Guardian*, August 27, 2020. https://www.theguardian.com/us-news/2020/aug/27/white-supremacists-militias-infiltrate-us-police-report

McAleenan, Kevin, and Thomas K. Plofchan III. 2020. "Domestic Terror Is a Rising Threat." *Washington Post*, October 12, 2020.

Quinn, Melissa. 2020. "Feds Bust Alleged Plot to Kidnap Michigan Governor Gretchen Whitmer." CBS News, October 9, 2020. https://www.cbsnews.com/news/gretchen-whitmer-michigan-governor-fbi-kidnapping-plot/

Montana Freemen Siege

March 26–June 13, 1996

In 1996, near the town of Jordan, Montana, two dozen individuals from an anti-government group belonging to the Christian Patriot movement, the Montana Freemen, engaged in an armed standoff with federal authorities. The siege peacefully ended after eighty-one days when the Montana Freemen finally surrendered.

Throughout the early 1990s, in Garfield County, Montana, Richard Clark, a rancher, whose 960-acre wheat farm had been threatened with foreclosure, became involved with a group who called themselves "Freemen" and belonged to the Christian Patriot movement led by LeRoy M. Schweitzer. The group claimed to be "sovereign citizens" and that the government no longer had authority over their persons or property. They called Clark's ranch "Justus Township," and after it was sold at auction on April 14, 1994, the Clarks refused eviction from their property.

Schweitzer and his followers were engaged in Posse Comitatus–type activities. This type of tactic, often referred to as "paper terrorism," consists of filing bogus property liens and fake tax forms, harassing public officials through lawsuits against institutions and officials, and producing counterfeit checks and money orders. The Freemen also offered financial and legal help to outside people and taught them how to produce fake money orders. According to the FBI, the Freemen fraud schemes exceeded $2 million.

In December 1995, a dozen Freemen were charged with conspiracy, mail fraud, and threatening the life of a federal judge. On March 25, 1996, the FBI arrested two members of the group, LeRoy M. Schweitzer and Daniel E. Petersen Jr., outside the Clark ranch. The FBI had arrest warrants for other members, prompting twenty-one Freemen (including men, women, and children) to barricade themselves in the ranch that was soon surrounded by over 100 FBI agents.

The resultant siege occurred a few years after two other notorious, prolonged armed standoffs, the 1992 Ruby Ridge siege in Idaho and the 1993 Branch Davidian siege in Waco, Texas. Given that both ended in bloodshed, the FBI's Critical

Incident Response Group (CIRG) opted not to launch an assault on the ranch. Instead, it was persistent in conducting negotiations that involved forty-five different third-party intermediaries, including state legislators, religious studies experts, and members of other Christian Patriot movements. The negotiations lasted for eighty-one days; then, on June 13, 1996, the siege peacefully ended with the Freemen finally surrendering without firing a shot—a bloodless ending unlike those in 1992 and 1993 that inspired the 1995 terrorist bombing of the Oklahoma City Federal Building.

Since the siege, several Freemen have been convicted for multiple crimes, including conspiracy, bank fraud, false claims to the IRS, and firearms violations. Richard Clark received a twelve-year sentence, Daniel E. Peterson a fifteen-year sentence, and LeRoy M. Schweitzer a twenty-two-year sentence, the latter dying in prison in 2011. Even while in prison, however, some Freemen continued to harass officials and pursue other political activities.

Gwenola Ricordeau

See also: Armed Militias; Domestic Terrorist Groups; Ruby Ridge Standoff.

FURTHER READING

Barkun, Michael. 1997. *Religion and the Racist Right: The Origins of the Christian Identity Movement.* Chapel Hill: University of North Carolina Press.

Jakes, Dale, Connie Jakes, and Clint Richmond. 1998. *False Prophets: The Firsthand Account of a Husband-Wife Team Working for the FBI and Living in Deepest Cover with the Montana Freemen.* Garden City, MI: Dove Books.

Wessinger, Catherine. 1999. "Religious Studies Scholars, FBI Agents, and the Montana Freemen Standoff." *Nova Religio: Journal of Alternative and Emergent Religions* 3 (1): 36–44.

Munich Olympics Terrorist Attack

September 5, 1972

The 1972 Munich massacre significantly changed counterterrorism in several ways: the necessity of improving counterterrorism preparations to respond to transnational terrorism (attacks far from the homeland of the terrorists) and for subsequent large public events; the significant increase in Israeli operations; changing perceptions of terrorism in the West; and a recognition of the power of live media.

In the early morning of September 5, during the 1972 Olympic Games in Munich, West Germany, eight members of the Palestinian terrorist organization Black September entered the Olympic Village, killed two members of the Israeli team, and took nine other Israeli athletes hostage. Threatening to kill their captives, they demanded the release of over 200 Palestinians and the eponymous founders of the Baader-Meinhof Group from Israeli and West German prisons as well as safe transport. International television crews gathered for the Olympics presented the crisis to the world. The terrorists eventually accepted a German offer of allowing them to fly to Tunisia, where they would then release the Israelis.

A poorly designed rescue attempt at the airfield resulted in a prolonged firefight and led to the terrorists killing all hostages, the deaths of five terrorists and a policeman, and the capture of the three remaining terrorists. A subsequent hijacking of a Lufthansa flight the following month resulted in their release by the Germans in exchange for the airliner's passengers. Israeli operatives later killed a number of those involved in the Munich attack as part of their vigorous response, Operation Wrath of God.

The Munich massacre continues to serve as a casebook study in how not to prepare for terrorism. German authorities did not develop extensive security precautions for the 1972 games (in part because of their desire to overcome the militaristic image from the Nazi-led 1936 Olympics). The leadership of their ad hoc crisis committee included only one experienced operational leader as well as two politicians. Police, disguised as cabin crew on the airplane the terrorists were to board, left their posts, fearing for their own lives. Those assigned as snipers at the airfield lacked proper training as well as equipment (i.e., proper rifles, night vision accessories, and communications devices).

The snipers were also outmanned. The police thought there were only five terrorists, but when they discovered their mistake, they had no way of informing the five snipers, who also never received detailed operational guidance. Because of West Germany's postwar constitution, better-trained military units were prohibited from engaging in nonwartime operations and could not assist the police. Armored personnel carriers needed for the firefight experienced two significant delays: they were not prepared in advance, and normal traffic flowing to the airport was not diverted. Such internationally broadcast errors have compelled the development of extensive counterterrorism planning for major events.

Israel's strategic response to the murders included a dramatic increase in assassinations. The country now became increasingly concerned about attacks against Jews outside Israel and had to develop more effective intelligence gathering.

Because of the many television crews in Munich for the Olympics, events received instant global coverage with an estimated audience of almost one billion in over 100 countries. (Live broadcasts also warned terrorists of the movements of German police preparing an attack in the Olympic Village.) Counterterrorist planning has subsequently recognized the dangerous possibility of media's rapid transformation of an attack into a worldwide phenomenon with live reporting, thereby significantly increasing the publicity value of attacks.

The extensive media coverage contributed to an increased global awareness of Palestinian political aspirations. However, the event's culmination in the athletes' murders did not lead to sympathy for the cause but to international condemnation and increased counterterrorist planning.

Helena M. Hansson and David Keck

See also: Evolution of Terrorism; Media, Changing Roles in the Terrorist Era.

FURTHER READING

Daoud, Abu. 1999. *Palestine: From Jerusalem to Munich.* Paris: Anne Carriere Editions.

Klein, Aaron J. 2005. *Striking Back: The 1972 Munich Olympics Massacre and Israel's Deadly Response*. New York: Random House.

Reeve, Simon. 2000. *One Day in September: The Full Story of the 1972 Munich Olympics Massacre and the Israeli Revenge Operation "Wrath of God."* New York: Arcade Publishing.

Muslim American Community and Homeland Security

HISTORICAL PRESENCE

After Christianity and Judaism, Islam is the third-largest religion in the United States. As Islam is a religion and not a nationality or ethnicity, it is composed of people from many countries and ethnicities—much like the followers of Christianity and other religions. A Muslim is a person who follows the teachings of Islam.

Though not part of the mainstream curriculum taught in schools from kindergarten through university, Muslim communities have been part of the American experience since the Revolutionary War. The majority of seventeenth- and eighteenth-century Muslims in America were African slaves that brought the faith of Islam to America. Slaves not forced to convert to Christianity kept their faith. After Independence, American Muslims continued to serve in and support the government, the military, and business efforts.

In terms of homeland security, Muslims have and continue to serve in the military, work in public safety careers, and serve as elected officials. The narrative pairing national security and Muslims, framed within the events of September 11, 2001, disregards the many contributions of Americans that practice Islam.

ISLAMOPHOBIA

The late twentieth and early twenty-first centuries in the United States portrayed the followers of Islam, Muslims, with a broad brush of mistrust and intolerance largely in response to the 9/11 terrorist attacks by al-Qaeda. The subsequent military actions in Iraq and Afghanistan added to this fear and mistrust.

Adding to a long history of American intolerance to immigrants that pose a threat to the perceived fabric of a Eurocentric culture, in 2017, President Trump issued Executive Order 13769, Protecting the Nation from Foreign Terrorist Entry into the United States, to ban travelers from seven predominantly Muslim countries from entering the United States. Detractors immediately attacked the executive order. In 2018, after revisions, the U.S. Supreme Court, in *Doe et al. v. Donald Trump*, upheld the provisions of the so-called Muslim ban. The ruling affected not only people wishing to immigrate to the United States but also to the Muslim communities across the nation as populist national and white supremacist groups targeted American Muslims as not being American.

Signs of Islamophobia were criminal acts carried out against mosques in addition to efforts to restrict the construction of mosques—houses of worship—throughout the United States. At the time of this writing, California, Washington,

Texas, Florida, Virginia, Pennsylvania, New York, Ohio, and Michigan have experienced anti-mosque incidents since 2005. Six states reported no incidents, while the remaining states reported from one to ten incidents—a sign of how integrated the Muslim community is across the country.

Meanwhile, and more disturbing still, the University of Maryland's START program has reported that white supremacists have killed more Americans than Muslim extremists since 9/11.

MUSLIMS IN CONGRESS

Although the United States professes to be a secular nation, the deep Christian faith of the general public has questioned inclusion of non-Protestants elected to public office. Though Article 6 of the U.S. Constitution stipulates there is no religious test for office, popular dissent contrasts with the nature of the article. A significant test of Article 6 came to light when people questioned whether President John F. Kennedy, as a Catholic, would be subservient to the Pope.

Mirroring the fears of a counter-faith entering the political offices of the nation was the election of Keith Ellison, an African American from Minnesota, in 2006 as the first Muslim congressperson. When swearing into office, Ellison used Thomas Jefferson's copy of the Holy Quran instead of the Holy Bible, which created a controversy about the faith of elected officials affecting their ability to carry out the duties of office. Again, in conflict with the Constitution, religious faith entered American politics.

Interestingly, Thomas Jefferson's consideration of the Muslim community as part of the United States is evident in his contribution to the Virginia Statute for Religious Freedom: "Our civil rights have no dependence on our religious opinions." According to Jefferson's notes, he based this phrase on John Locke by penning, "He says neither Pagan nor Mahometan (Muslim) nor Jew ought to be executed from the civil rights of the commonwealth because of his religion."

The second Muslim elected to Congress was Representative Andre Carson in 2008. Carson, an African American, converted to Islam in the 1990s. Carson also used the Holy Quran to swear into office. In 2019, Congresswoman Rashida Tlaib from Michigan, a Palestinian American, used a personal copy of the Holy Quran to swear into office. Also, in 2019, Congresswoman Ilhan Omar from Minnesota, a Muslim woman of Somali descent who became the first naturalized Muslim woman of African descent to hold office in Minnesota, used a commemorative copy of the Holy Quran when swearing in at a private ceremony for family members.

Though American media elects to concentrate on the race of the individual and the book used to swear in Muslim officials to elected office, the significance of serving Muslim officials reveals the diversity of Islam as part of the American experience.

ETHNICITY OF MUSLIMS

The population of Muslims in the United States is composed of many ethnicities. According to the U.S. Department of State, the composition of Muslims by broad ethnic composition is South Asians at 34 percent, Arabs at 25 percent, African Americans at 25 percent, and other ethnicities comprising 15 percent.

MUSLIM ORGANIZATIONS

The Council on American-Islamic Relations (CAIR) is one of the largest Muslim organizations in the United States. CAIR aims to advocate for Muslims in the United States and further social justice issues as they relate to Islam. Although its first office opened in Washington, DC, in 1994, CAIR traces its roots to Los Angeles. Many of its founders were active members of the Islamic Center of Southern California in the 1980s and 1990s. CAIR based its offices in Washington, DC, after expanding its reach and associations with Muslims across the country. CAIR holds sway with many domestic and international organizations stemming from a focus on lobbying its interests. The organization is controversial for its characterization as a supporter of Hamas and other terrorist organizations. Several CAIR directors and founding members came under scrutiny for allegedly helping to further the goals of Hamas and other terrorist organizations, a claim they strongly deny. CAIR's more notable advocates include Representative Ilhan Omar, who was criticized for supporting and speaking at recent CAIR events.

The Islamic Society of North America (ISNA), also with roots in Los Angeles, is an organization that traces its roots back to the consolidation of several Muslim student organizations, the largest being the Muslim Students Association of the U.S. and Canada. With a primary goal of providing a common platform for presenting Islam and supporting Muslim communities, the ISNA focuses on social outreach and improving relations with other religious communities and civic organizations. Unlike CAIR, the ISNA focuses less on governmental lobbying efforts and more on grassroots associations with local communities and organizations.

Not all Muslim organizations are homogeneous. The American Islamic Forum for Democracy (AIFD), led by Dr. M. Zuhdi Jasser, is critical of many mainstream Muslim organizations. Jasser, a former medical officer in the navy, stresses the primary importance of being an American.

There are many other Muslim organizations in the United States that focus on the interests of Muslim people. Some of them are the Islamic Circle of North America (ICNA), the Fiqh Council of North America (FCNA), the Holy Land Foundation for Relief and Development Charity, the American Islamic Congress (AIC), and the Islamic Supreme Council of America (ISCA).

Elsewhere, the Islamic Association of Palestine (AIAP), headquartered in Texas, closed after being associated with raising money for Hamas. Operating since 1981, the organization disbanded in 2004 because of strong ties to the Holy Land Foundation for Relief and Development and several American organizations established to serve as fronts for Hamas.

The Nation of Islam (NOI) stands apart from other Muslim organizations. Founded in 1930 by Wallace Fard Muhammad, the NOI concentrates on issues to improve the spiritual, mental, social, and economic condition of African Americans. Considered a racist, anti-Semitic, and anti-LGBT organization, it has a history of controversy. Notable leaders from the NOI are Elijah Muhammad, Louis Farrakhan, and Malcom X, though Malcom X eventually left the NOI.

MAJOR MUSLIM COMMUNITIES

There are several Muslim "little towns" in the United States. These towns host cultural restaurants, cafés, hookah lounges, ethnic markets, and cultural centers as well as mosques, which are considered to be the heart of these towns. The oldest Muslim communities are located in New York and New Jersey, as immigrants arriving in the United States via Ellis Island tended to settle close by. One of the largest Muslim communities in the United States today is located in Dearborn, Michigan, where the Arab-American National Museum is located. Another example of a little town is in Anaheim, California, where the Little Arabia District is located. This district is not only home to a large Muslim community but also a host of stores, restaurants, and supermarkets catering to Muslims and Arab Americans.

Like other religions in the United States, Islam has different sects within the religion. In the case of Islam, there are three primary sects: Sunni, Shia and Sufism.

Sunni Muslims are largely considered to be the more moderate mainstream Muslims and have largely integrated well into the United States while still holding on to their cultural identity. As the largest sect in Islam, this sect traditionally holds the most sway in both academia and theology in the largely Muslim countries of the Middle East and Asia.

Shia Muslims are a much smaller sect and are traditionally limited to Iran and surrounding areas bordering Iran. Shia mark their divergence from mainstream Sunnis after the death of Islam's Prophet Muhammad. At this point, there was an internal disagreement as to whether the direct descendants of Muhammad or the nascent caliphate should rule. It was at this point that the primary split in Islam occurred. Shia adhere to a strict belief that only the direct descendants of Muhammad, which they have meticulously documented, have the divine authority to speak on behalf of the Muslim world. It is this ideology that drives much of the animosity between Iran and Saudi Arabia, as Iran feels it would be a better steward of the religion and should have direct control of Mecca, the Muslim world's primary holy site.

Sufism, the smallest sect in Islam, has a disputed and murky history, although many scholars agree that it was practiced shortly after the inception of Islam. Sufism is thought of as a more mystical tradition that involves traditional Muslim practices as well as more spiritual practices such as dance and meditation. Over time, the sect has grown smaller, as it is frowned upon by much of the Muslim world.

MUSLIMS AND HOMELAND SECURITY

In 2015, the secretary of homeland security, Jeh C. Johnson, made a statement that government actions must include outreach to Muslim communities. However, the deep-seated fears of Muslims called for the Department of Homeland Security to continue to monitor Sunni Muslim immigrants on a long-term basis. While pursuing this practice, government organizations have been accused of seeking Muslims to essentially serve as spies on their own communities.

Tarek Azmy and Ygnacio "Nash" Flores

See also: Anti-Muslim Attacks; Domestic Terrorism, White Supremacists.

FURTHER READING

American Civil Liberties Union. 2020. "Nationwide Anti-Mosque Activity." https://www.aclu.org/issues/national-security/discriminatory-profiling/nationwide-anti-mosque-activity

Doe et al. v. Donald Trump, Case No. 6:18-cv-01073-TC (D. Or. Aug. 24, 2018).

Levitt, Matthew. 2007. *Hamas: Politics, Charity, and Terrorism in the Service of Jihad.* Washington, DC: Washington Institute for Near East Policy.

Mullins, Lisa, and Lynn Jolicoeur. 2017. "'I Am Not the Catholic Candidate for President': How Faith Shaped JFK and His 1960 Campaign." WBUR, May 25, 2017. https://www.wbur.org/news/2017/05/25/kennedy-catholicism-presidential-campaign

National Consortium for the Study of Terrorism and Responses to Terrorism (START). 2020. "Global Terrorism Overview: Terrorism in 2019." College Park: University of Maryland. https://www.start.umd.edu/pubs/START_GTD_GlobalTerrorismOverview2019_July2020.pdf

Porter, Tom. 2018. "Muslim Men in America Should Be Continuously Monitored, Says Department of Homeland Security." *Newsweek*, February 6, 2018. https://www.newsweek.com/department-homeland-security-recommends-continuous-monitoring-muslims-800199

Southern Poverty Law Center. 2020. "Nation of Islam." https://www.splcenter.org/fighting-hate/extremist-files/group/nation-islam

Spellberg, Denise A. 2018. "Why Jefferson's Vision Of American Islam Matters Today." *The Conversation*, June 7, 2018. https://theconversation.com/why-jeffersons-vision-of-american-islam-matters-today-97915

N

National Security Act of 1947

The National Security Act of 1947 brought about an expansive restructuring of American government as well as its national security, national defense, and intelligence operations and infrastructure. The act (Public Law 80-253) realigned the roles, structures, and activities of U.S. military services and created two new executive branch agencies to adapt to the realities of post–World War II international geopolitics and the challenges of the emerging Cold War era.

The act was introduced in Congress in March 1947; signed into law by President Harry S. Truman on July 26, 1947; and took effect on September 18, 1947, concurrent with James Forrestal's Senate confirmation as the nation's first secretary of defense.

The act renamed the Department of War as the Department of the Army, created the United States Air Force (formerly the Army Air Corps) under a new Department of the Air Force, and subsumed these departments as well as the existing Department of the Navy under a new cabinet-level entity designated as the National Military Establishment (NME). The secretary of defense position was created to manage, direct, and oversee the National Military Establishment. The act was amended in 1949 to redesignate the National Military Establishment as the Department of Defense and to expand the powers and authority of the secretary of defense. The National Security Act of 1947 also formally established the U.S. Marine Corps as a separate service branch operating under the Department of the Navy, and it formally established the structure of the Joint Chiefs of Staff.

The act established the National Security Council as an executive branch agency with the mandate to advise the president on national security and related foreign policy matters, to harmonize national security policies and activities, and to coordinate the activities of the service branches (army, navy, air force and marine corps), the Central Intelligence Agency (CIA), and other federal agencies in regard to national defense priorities, policies, and operations.

The act also created a National Security Resources Board to advise the president on matters related to industrial and economic preparedness and the resources necessary for national defense. The National Security Resources Board was eliminated in 1953 when its responsibilities were transferred to the Department of Defense.

In addition, the act established the CIA under the executive branch as the nation's first peacetime intelligence agency and created the position of director of central intelligence to head the agency. Following the 1945 dissolution of the Office of Special Services (OSS) that had operated under the aegis of the Joint Chiefs of Staff to conduct intelligence, counterintelligence, and espionage operations during World War II, some OSS functions were divided among the State Department and War Department. In 1946, President Truman created the interim Central Intelligence Group (CIG) prior to the establishment of the CIA. As its name implies, the CIA assumed primary responsibility for the nation's intelligence, counterintelligence, and espionage functions.

The roles and infrastructure prescribed for the Department of Defense by the 1947 act were substantially modified in 1986 with the passage of the Goldwater-Nichols Act, which streamlined the command structure of the Department of Defense to reduce interservice boundaries, facilitate joint operations, and simplify the operational chain of command over military forces. The chain of command now runs from the president as commander in chief to the secretary of defense to regional combatant commanders. The Joint Chiefs of Staff are primarily relegated to an advisory role.

The National Security Act of 1947 remained the most extensive restructuring of government agencies and functions in American history until the Homeland Security Act of 2002 created or moved twenty-two agencies and offices from various departments to create the Department of Homeland Security.

Vincent E. Henry

See also: Central Intelligence Agency; Director of National Intelligence.

FURTHER READING

Congressional Research Service. 2017. *The National Security Council: Background and Issues for Congress.* Washington, DC: Congressional Research Service. https://www.hsdl.org/?view&did=801051

National Security Act of 1947, Pub. L. 80-253, 61 Stat. 495 (1947). https://www.dni.gov/index.php/ic-legal-reference-book/national-security-act-of-1947

Stevenson, Charles A. 2008a. "The Story behind the National Security Act of 1947." *Military Review* 88 (3): 13–20. https://www.hsdl.org/?view&did=486185

Stevenson, Charles A. 2008b. "Underlying Assumptions of the National Security Act of 1947." *Joint Forces Quarterly* 1st Quarter (48): 129–133. https://ndupress.ndu.edu/portals/68/Documents/jfq/jfq-48.pdf

National Security Agency

Before the July 30, 1916, explosion at the munitions plant at Black Tom Island, New Jersey—eventually traced to German sabotage at a time when the United States was officially neutral during World War I—the country had no peacetime agency dedicated to protecting it from such attacks nor statutes addressing peacetime spying by foreign states. That changed with the passage of the Espionage Act of 1917 and, with the United States now at war with Germany, the creation of the Cipher Bureau on April 28 of that year. Its lineal descendants were ended in 1929, only to be resurrected during World War II in the form of the Signal Intelligence Service (SIS), reorganized after the war as the Army Security Agency (ASA).

The National Security Agency (NSA), an ASA successor, was born covertly in a different war when, in his latter days in office, President Truman issued an

October 24, 1952, memorandum calling for its establishment in the Department of Defense (established 1949), with at least a three-star general as its director and a civilian as deputy director.

The emerging Cold War made the acquisition of foreign intelligence and protection of American secrets all the more important, and at the outset, the NSA's primary charge was *signals intelligence* (SIGINT), that is, intelligence acquired by monitoring communications between individuals and, more generally, electronic signals—the latter having subsequently expanded greatly from radio and television to various forms of Internet trafficking, bulk data storage operations, threats to cybersecurity, etc. The NSA's operations to protect national security information systems have expanded accordingly to include coordinating communications intelligence throughout the government, serving as the country's official cryptologic agency, venturing into the social media world, and engaging in counterintelligence in aid of the national defense. In the process, its number of employees and budget, though both classified, have likewise increased.

Its physical presence has also expanded from its Fort Meade, Maryland, headquarters to facilities in other states, such as Colorado, Georgia, Hawaii, and Utah. Most satellite sites focus on specialized areas—for example, data operations in Georgia and cryptology in Texas—and most strive for the same invisibility as the NSA's headquarters. The 2013 revelation that Edward Snowden had connections with its operations center in Hawaii thus generated unwelcomed publicity.

By the time of Snowden's revelations, however, NSA had already received substantial notoriety, particularly the 1976 Church Committee's findings of its routine interception of the international communications of activists opposed to the Vietnam War. Still, Snowden's disclosure of the NSA's widespread spying on both American citizens and the leaders of allies brought new concerns about its reach. One result was that the reauthorization of the 2001 Patriot Act in the 2015 USA FREEDOM Act included a curtailment of its prior ability to access and control bulk data collections.

Joseph R. Rudolph Jr.

See also: Counterterrorism and the George W. Bush Administration; Foreign Intelligence Surveillance Court; National Security Letters Controversy; USA PATRIOT Act of 2001.

FURTHER READING

Aid, Matthew M. 2009. *The Secret Sentry: The Untold History of the National Security Agency*. London, UK: Bloomsbury Press.

BBC News. 2014. "Edward Snowden: Leaks That Exposed US Spy Programme." January 14, 2014. https://www.bbc.com/news/world-us-canada-23123964

Byman, Daniel, and Benjamin Wittes. 2014. "Reforming the NSA: How to Spy after Snowden." *Foreign Affairs* 93 (3): 127–138.

Gravis, Olivia. 2020. "National Security Agency Warns That VPNs Could Be Vulnerable to Attacks." CBS News, July 2, 2020. https://www.cbsnews.com/news/national-security-agency-warns-that-vpns-could-be-susceptible-to-cyberattacks/

Zegart, Amy Beth. 1996. *In Whose Interest? The Making of American National Security Agencies*. Stanford, CA: Stanford University Press.

National Security Letters Controversy

National Security Letters (NSL) are administrative subpoenas authorized under various statutes, including the Stored Communications Act, the Fair Credit Reporting Act, and the Right to Financial Privacy Act, among others. NSLs are used to gather information for national security purposes and may be issued without judicial review or approval. These instruments are used to request non-content information, including transactional records such as dialed telephone numbers, IP addresses used, and websites visited. National Security Letters also typically include a nondisclosure clause that prohibits recipients from disclosing receipt of the request for information. In many instances, inclusion of the nondisclosure clause does require review and authorization by the director of the Federal Bureau of Investigation (FBI) and certification that disclosure would pose a danger to counterterrorism or counterintelligence investigations, pose a danger to national security, put an individual's life or safety at risk, or interfere with diplomatic relations.

Passage of the USA PATRIOT Act of 2001 changed several provisions of NSL use, raising concerns about the constitutionality of the new use provisions. Besides expanding the use of NSLs, the USA PATRIOT Act replaced language requiring the FBI director's approval for nondisclosure clauses, transferring approval authority to special agents in charge at FBI field offices. Penalties were also added for violating nondisclosure clauses where none had existed before, and earlier issuance standards were relaxed, with probable cause no longer required.

Critics pointed to three principal aspects of NSLs and their use in arguing their unconstitutionality: relevance, nondisclosure, and lack of judicial review. By allowing issuance of NSLs to seek information "relevant" to an authorized national security investigation, critics charged the probable cause standard had been abandoned, putting NSL recipients' Fourth Amendment rights against unreasonable search and seizure in jeopardy. Further, critics charged that the nondisclosure clause, with penalties for violation, effectively became a gag order that imperiled First Amendment rights to free speech. Finally, the lack of judicial oversight, to critics, reinforced the threat to both First and Fourth Amendment rights by eliminating necessary checks against unwarranted and excessive government power.

One of the noteworthy NSL-related cases illustrates critics' concerns and government actions to address those concerns. In *Doe v. Ashcroft*, an NSL recipient, later revealed as Nicholas Merrill, the founder of an Internet access company, contended an NSL he received represented an unconstitutional exercise of government power by preventing him from informing his attorney and by forcing him to deceive family members lest he violate the nondisclosure clause. A lower court ruled in favor of Merrill, finding the application of the NSL violated Merrill's First Amendment rights through unjustified prior restraint and content-based restriction on free speech and by effectively barring judicial challenge. That ruling, however, was vacated in 2008 by the Second Circuit Court of Appeals, which ruled that the USA PATRIOT Improvement and Reauthorization Act of 2005, which had been enacted as the original suit was being heard, had addressed the issues raised by providing a mechanism by which the nondisclosure clause could be challenged in federal court. The 2005 amendments to the USA PATRIOT Act also increased oversight by mandating semiannual reporting of NSL issuance and use to Congress, alleviating some of the concerns over NSL abuse.

Subsequent U.S. Supreme Court rulings have also held that the type of information sought through NSLs carry no reasonable expectation of privacy, further challenging arguments against their use. The court held that the non-content information sought through NSLs is information that is already freely and voluntarily provided to third parties, such as telephone companies and Internet service providers, and, as such, carries no expectation of privacy for the individual in question. Despite court rulings, some critics still question the relevancy standard as well as the appropriateness of the nondisclosure clause.

Daniel S. Gressang IV

See also: Counterterrorism, the Courts, and the Constitution; Intelligence Community, Adjustments to the Post-9/11 World; USA PATRIOT Act of 2001.

FURTHER READING

American Civil Liberties Union. n.d. "National Security Letters." https://www.aclu.org/other/national-security-letters

Electronic Frontier Foundation. n.d. "National Security Letters." https://www.eff.org/issues/national-security-letters/faq

Lawfare (blog). n.d. "National Security Letters." https://www.lawfareblog.com/topic/national-security-letters

Office of the Inspector General, U.S. Department of Justice. 2014. *A Review of the Federal Bureau of Investigation's Use of National Security Letters: Assessment of Progress in Implementing Recommendations and Examination of Use in 2007 through 2009.* Washington, DC: DOJ. https://oig.justice.gov/reports/2014/s1408.pdf

Office of the Inspector General, U.S. Department of Justice. 2016. *A Review of the Federal Bureau of Investigation's Use of National Security Letters.* Washington, DC: USDOJ. https://oig.justice.gov/reports/2016/NSL-2007.pdf

Waśko-Owsiejczuk, Ewelina. 2015. "National Security Letters—A Controversial FBI Tool to Fight Terrorism." *Internal Security* 7 (2): 71–90.

New Terrorism

As a political strategy or tactic distinguishable by its explicit targeting of noncombatants, terrorism has never been a static force. Initially a device used by those seeking to overthrow those holding political power and later a state tool for controlling the governed, the ends and means of terrorism have altered in tune with the opportunities provided by changing times, events, and technologies. During the last half century, experts studying terrorism have concluded that in both degree and type, the changes in terrorist activities have been sufficiently different from the face terrorism presented in the mid-twentieth century to warrant being designated *New Terrorism.*

TRANSNATIONAL TERRORISM: THE PRECURSOR

Dating the origins of this shifting narrative, which Jeffrey Kaplan has characterized as a fifth wave of terrorism ("Tribalism") beginning as late as the first decade of the twenty-first century, is not easy. Still, the attack by Black September terrorists from the Middle East on Israeli athletes at the 1972 Olympics in Munich, in retrospect, appears as a major point of transition. Previously, whether committed by outsiders bent on shaping policies or seizing political control, or by the state as a tool of control, terrorism mostly resided locally. During the 1960s, however, states sponsoring terrorist activists began hosting training camps in which Palestinian recruits met with radicalized others from such distant points as Japan, were instructed in the tools of terrorism, and developed connections that would later enable joint ventures. The Black September members at Munich were graduates of those camps, many meeting one another for the first time when getting their instructions on the eve of the Olympics, and presumably received their weapons from East Germans.

FROM MUNICH TO 9/11 TO TODAY: DEFINING THE "NEWNESS"

New Terrorism involves far more than a deed committed at a venue distant from the homeland of the terrorists. In his core text, *Understanding Terrorism*, Gus Martin summarizes many of its basic components: (1) an organizational shift from tightly controlled hierarchal models to loose networks of horizontally linked local cells and/or lone wolf activists; (2) a shift from publicity-seeking missions usually involving low casualties to fewer attacks with a high impact and designed to produce high body counts; (3) a related effort to acquire weapons of mass destruction; (4) goals more concerned with religion than national self-determination; and (5) the ever-growing use of the Internet for not just communication but as a means of recruiting and radicalizing terrorists, planning terrorist assaults, and publicizing the results. Other changes have followed, as heightened security throughout the Western world has reduced the prospects for future big budget successes of the 9/11 variety and as the war on terror has denied both al-Qaeda and the Islamic State (IS) protected homelands for plotting such organizational attacks. The result is that international terrorism is no less menacing today than in the past, just different in its New Terrorism guise in the areas discussed in the following sections.

Globalized Reach

The 9/11 attack turned Munich inside out. Munich was a localized terrorist organization attacking its target on a different continent. In 2001, al-Qaeda was a globally organized entity with a safe base in Afghanistan using a cell in Hamburg to plan an attack on localized targets. Without that camp and without the Internet, al-Qaeda's fortunes would have faded even more after 9/11 and the subsequent destruction of its base in Afghanistan. The Internet, however, provided al-Qaeda with a cyber presence, enabling a radicalization of new converts on distant continents and a means of continued communication with its regional namesakes, like its affiliated cells in Yemen. Others, like IS, have followed on that path, finding a virtual identity on the Internet even when losing territory in the war on terror and successfully encouraging small cell and lone-wolf terrorism abroad by those radicalized by their Internet messaging. Nor have the groups defining themselves in religious terms had a monopoly in exploiting the Internet to their advantage. White supremacists, antigay, and anti-foreigner groups from the United States to Europe to Australia and New Zealand have likewise bonded, feeding off one another's zeal to the point of undertaking their own lone-wolf terrorist attacks.

An Expanded and Increasingly Less Expensive Terrorist Toolbox

Those attacks, in turn, have changed with the times. The attacks in the West by suicide bombers that were so prevalent in the first five years of the new millennium—for example, the 2004 bombings of the commuter trains in Madrid and the 2005 attack on London's transit system—have been supplemented if not eclipsed by car bombs, roadside explosive devices, and both planned and impulse-driven vehicle attacks. The latter, perhaps in particular, have acquired a growing presence given the ease with which the "weapon" can be acquired, legally or otherwise, and the fact that they require little skill or resources to execute. It is estimated that the London attacks, for example, required several thousands of dollars in capital and cost the lives of 4 "soldiers" in taking the lives of 52 people. The attack by the truck driver who struck in Nice on Bastille Day did result in his eventual death in a shootout with police, but not until he had killed 86 and injured more than 450 more at the cost of zero euros. Others, motivated by a variety of hatreds and armed only with knives and axes, have likewise contributed with low costs and little skill to the recent death toll of terrorist victims in the United States, much of Western Europe, Canada, Australia, and New Zealand.

Such spontaneous acts have the advantage of being particularly hard to detect and prevent. Alternately, more casualties are likely to ensue in well-planned vehicle attacks where the perpetrator selects an event where the crowd is likely to be large and densely packed and there is little room to escape.

Beyond these tactics lie new threat sources, like Westerners returning home after volunteer service on behalf of IS, as well as new terrorist tools of the high-tech variety falling into the cyberwarfare category. There is also the threat posed by more conventional tools, for example, suicide bombs. As the "underwear bomber" aboard a Northwest/Delta flight over Detroit on Christmas Day 2009 demonstrated, even in failing in his mission, these bombs could be secreted in unconventional ways.

Target Repositioning

Changing times have also produced a significant change in the type of action encouraged by terrorist groups. As noted, at the outset of the new century, terrorist groups focused on dramatic terrorist acts. No plan envisioned anything to rival the destruction of the Twin Towers of the World Trade Center in New York and attack on the Pentagon on September 11, 2001, but such ambitious schemes as the simultaneous downing of a large number of passenger jets bound for the United States were frequently thwarted by the heightened vigilance of Western intelligence services after that attack.

In a like manner, although there is no evidence to suggest that terrorist organizations previously seeking weapons of mass destruction have abandoned their goals, the emphasis has clearly shifted to achieving a large number of small triumphs, and in this theater, suicide bombers can still be highly effective. To be sure, the devastating effect that COVID-19 has had in Europe and North America may set into motion a new search for bioterrorist weapons. On the other hand, it may not in light of COVID-19's demonstrated capacity to go global and threaten a terrorist's cherished habitat wherever it may be. Meanwhile, the lure of chemical and dirty bombs remains the same, given the difficulty of any terrorist group actually developing an atomic bomb and no evidence of any current nuclear power plants inclined to donate a nuclear bomb to a terrorist group.

Here, too, unfortunately, we live in an ever-changing world affecting the strategy, tactics, and level of threat presented by international terrorist groups in the contemporary world.

Joseph R. Rudolph Jr.

See also: Christmas Day "Underwear Bomber," Umar Farouk Abdulmutallab; Evolution of Terrorism; Internet as a Virtual School for Terrorism.

FURTHER READING

Davis, Jessica. 2017. *Women in Modern Terrorism: From Liberation Wars to Global Jihad and the Islamic State.* Lanham, MD: Rowman & Littlefield.

Gurski, Phil. 2016. *The Threat from Within: Recognizing Al Qaeda–Inspired Radicalization and Terrorism in the West.* Lanham, MD: Rowman & Littlefield.

Gurski, Phil. 2017. *Western Foreign Fighters: The Threat to Homeland and International Security.* Lanham, MD: Rowman & Littlefield.

Hartleb, Florian. 2020. *Lone Wolves: The New Terrorism of Right Wing Single Actors.* New York: Springer.

Kaplan, Jeffrey. 2007. "The Fifth Wave: The New Tribalism?" *Terrorism and Political Violence* 19 (4): 545–570.

Martin, Gus. 2020. *Understanding Terrorism: Challenges, Perspectives, and Issues.* 7th ed. Los Angeles: SAGE.

Miller, Vincent, and Keith J. Hayward. 2019. "'I Did My Bit': Terrorism Tarde and the Vehicle Ramming Attack as an Imitative Event." *British Journal of Criminology* 59 (1): 1–23. Accessed May 28, 2020. https://doi.org/10.1093/bjc/azy017

O

Oklahoma City Federal Building Bombing

April 19, 1995

Timed to mark the second anniversary of the deadly outcome of the federal siege of the Branch Davidian compound in Waco, Texas, the 9:01 a.m. truck bombing of the Alfred P. Murrah Federal Building in Oklahoma City, Oklahoma, on April 19, 1995, remains the deadliest act of homegrown terrorism ever committed in the United States.

Estimates of damage following the blast put the number dead at 168, including babies and children in the building's day care center; another 600 injured; and more than 300 buildings affected in a sixteen-block radius from the site of the detonation. To these numbers can be added the indirect victims: the 250 children who lost a parent and the thousands across the city who lost a friend or partner.

The blast resulted from the detonation of a 4,800-pound compound of mostly ammonium nitrate fertilizer and liquid nitromethane akin to the one Arab terrorists used in the 1993 bombing of the World Trade Center. The target was chosen because it housed numerous federal agencies, including those present at Waco.

Within days of the attack, the indicted perpetrators, Timothy McVeigh and Terry Nichols, were in custody, charged with conspiracy to use a weapon of mass destruction, murder, and involuntary manslaughter. McVeigh, who had planned the bombing as early as the previous December, rented the truck, and constructed the bomb, was a decorated Gulf War veteran with long-standing anti-government orientations and a history of being a well-armed survivalist. Those inclinations intensified following his postwar failure to qualify for the Green Berets and both the government's 1992 standoff with survivalists at Ruby Ridge, Idaho, and the outcome at Waco, where eighty-two members of the Branch Davidians perished. Convicted of capital crimes by a federal jury on August 14, 1997, after numerous appeals, McVeigh was executed on January 11, 2001.

As for Terry Nichols, McVeigh had met him in the army and had maintained a long acquaintanceship with him prior to the Oklahoma City bombing. Their shared belief in the government as a threat to an individual's constitutional rights appears to have sustained the relationship. Unlike in McVeigh's case, neither the federal nor the state juries trying Nichols found a direct enough involvement between him and either the acquisition of the explosive materials or execution of the attack to sustain a death sentence. Accordingly, Nichols was only convicted of the conspiracy and manslaughter charges and received a life sentence he continues to serve in a federal prison.

The investigation conducted by federal and state authorities into the bombing also uncovered two others tangentially involved: Michael Fortier, an Arizona hardware store employee who had watched McVeigh demonstrate with soup cans how he planned to organize the explosives to best destroy the building, and Fortier's wife, Lori. In a plea bargain arrangement guaranteeing a shorter sentence and the nonprosecution of his wife, Michael Fortier pleaded guilty to failing to notify authorities of the plot, lying to federal agents after the attack, and helping to finance the attack. He eventually served less than eleven years before his release in 2006.

Meanwhile, having demonstrated that government targets are not immune to homegrown terrorist attacks—a previous rarity—the bombing quickly led to new anti-terror legislation and major efforts to protect existing and future federal buildings from would-be terrorists. The horror of the images following the attack likely also dampened the latter's enthusiasm for violent acts for at least the remainder of the century. Ironically, however, among the politically alienated, the attack spawned a host of conspiracy theories blaming the attack on such diverse actors as the FBI and federal government in general (to disarm Americans) and then First Lady Hillary Clinton (to divert attention from her indictment in an Arkansas real estate deal). It also produced an immediate surge in the number of people joining fringe anti-government groups.

Joseph R. Rudolph Jr.

See also: Armed Militias; Counterterrorism and the Clinton Administration.

FURTHER READING

Irving, Clive. 1995. *In Their Name: Dedicated to the Brave and the Innocent, Oklahoma City, 1995.* Official Commemorative Volume. New York: Penguin Random House.

Lou, Michael, and Dan Herbeck. 2001. *American Terrorist: Timothy McVeigh and the Oklahoma City Bombing.* New York: Harper Collings.

Southern Poverty Law Center. 200. "10 Years Later, OKC Bombing Figure Walks Free." April 19, 2006. Accessed January 14, 2020. https://www.splcenter.org/fighting-hate/intelligence-report/2006/10-years-later-okc-bombing-figure-walks-free

Wright, Stuart A. 2007. *Patriots, Politics, and the Oklahoma City Bombing.* New York: Cambridge University Press.

Orlando Pulse Nightclub Shooting

June 12, 2016

Early in the morning of June 12, 2016, an active shooter killed forty-nine people and injured another fifty-three at the Pulse, an Orlando, Florida, nightclub whose clientele included members of the lesbian, gay, bisexual, transgender, and queer (LGBTQ+) community. The incident was classified as a terrorist attack based on the stated motives of the shooter, Omar Mir Seddique Mateen, and demonstrated the importance of training in tactical trauma care. It also led to criticisms of counterintelligence operations directed toward identifying terrorism suspects. Until the 2017 shooting at the Harvest Music Festival in Las Vegas, this remained the deadliest mass shooting in U.S. history.

At approximately 2:02 a.m., the shooter, armed with a semiautomatic rifle and a handgun, entered the nightclub and began his attack. Law enforcement responded quickly. At 2:08, the first police contact team entered the building, followed by a second team at 2:10. However, by then, the shooter had barricaded himself in a restroom with hostages.

As police began rescue activities, evacuating the injured and survivors, providing emergency trauma care, and transporting the wounded to hospitals, law enforcement strategized on how to respond to the hostage situation. Meanwhile, the shooter called a local media outlet and the 911 center to claim responsibility for the incident. Then, until approximately 3:19, the shooter had several phone conversations with a police hostage negotiator, in which he announced that he had placed high-powered explosives in nearby vehicles and explosive vests in his possession. The siege ended at 5:15, thirteen minutes after the police used explosives to breach the exterior wall of the building at several points, including near and in the restroom where the shooter had barricaded himself. After an exchange of gunfire, the police killed the shooter. A search of the area failed to detect the explosives claimed by the shooter.

What is known about Mateen comes from his own statements and information introduced by federal prosecutors during a trial of his widow, who was charged with, but later acquitted of, aiding and abetting and obstruction of justice. In his telephone calls, the shooter had stated that he committed the act for the Islamic State (IS) in retaliation for events that had occurred in Afghanistan, Iraq, and Syria. He also expressed allegiance to IS and referenced a sense of identification with the perpetrators of the 2013 Boston Marathon bombing. Federal authorities later alleged that the shooter had been radicalized online and that the Pulse was selected after the shooter had been deterred from another potential target due to police presence. It was also revealed that the Federal Bureau of Investigation (FBI) had twice investigated the shooter and found no basis for further action.

In the aftermath of the nightclub shooting, a review of the response found that 84 percent of the people who were rescued alive by responders survived. This was attributed to rapid medical response and to having police trained in field tactical care. Nevertheless, there was also much criticism of local counterintelligence efforts and questions as to why the shooter had not received greater scrutiny in the wake of two FBI investigations. Similar concerns, though not pertaining to terrorism, were raised about the FBI's handling of tips prior to the 2018 shooting at Marjory Stoneman Douglas High School in Parkland, Florida, given the importance that intelligence gathering and analysis can play in early warning and prevention of terrorist and active shooter situations.

Stephen Owen

See also: Active Shooter Scenarios; Fort Hood Shooting; Manhattan, New York City Bombing; San Bernardino Attack.

FURTHER READING

Kirby, Jen. 2016. "Did the FBI Miss the Warning Signs for the Orlando Gunman?" *New York*, June 14, 2016. http://nymag.com/intelligencer/2016/06/did-the-fbi-miss-warning-signs-around-mateen.html

Straub, Frank, Jack Cambria, Jane Castor, Ben Gorban, Brett Meade, David Waltemeyer, and Jennifer Zeunik. 2017. *Rescue, Response, and Resilience: A Critical Incident Review of the Orlando Public Safety Response to the Attack on the Pulse Nightclub*. Washington, DC: Office of Community Oriented Policing Services.

Zapotosky, Matt, and Mark Berman. 2016. "Orlando Gunman Who Pledged Loyalty to ISIS Was 'Homegrown' Extremist Radicalized Online, Obama Says." *Washington Post*, June 13, 2016. https://www.washingtonpost.com/news/post-nation/wp/2016/06/13/police-orlando-gunman-was-cool-and-calm-during-hostage-standoff

P

Pan Am Flight 103 (Lockerbie) Bombing

December 21, 1988

The bombing of Pan American World Airways Flight 103 occurred on December 21, 1988, over the Scottish town of Lockerbie when a bomb detonated aboard the midair flight to New York. All 243 passengers and the crew of 16 aboard the Boeing 747 perished as well as 11 people in the town of Lockerbie when portions of the fuselage crashed into a residential neighborhood. The passengers came from twenty-one different countries; 179 were American citizens.

The clue trail initially led investigators to suspect Iran as the agent behind the blast because the majority of the fatalities were American and the USS *Vincennes* had downed an Iranian commercial airliner earlier that year. Next, a cell of the terrorist organization the Popular Front for the Liberation of Palestine–General Command (PFLP-GC) became the investigators' focus because the plastic explosive SEMTEX caused the blast, and the PFLP-GC frequently employed it in its attacks. In the end, the discovery of a printed circuit board near the crash site ultimately led forensic investigators to a family-owned business in Malta, who said a Libyan, later identified as Abdelbaset Ali al-Megrahi, was the person who purchased the clothing found wrapped around the radio containing the SEMTEX.

On November 13, 1991, following a three-year investigation that included the Federal Bureau of Investigation (FBI), interviews of 15,000 people, and the examination of 180,000 pieces of evidence, Libyan intelligence agents al-Megrahi and Al Amin Khalifa Fhimah were charged with 270 counts of murder and attempted murder and for violation of the Aviation Security Act of 1982.

Libyan leader Muammar Gaddafi initially refused to hand over the accused persons, arguing that the Montreal Convention 1999, governing deaths and injuries aboard an aircraft, authorized Libya to try the suspects itself. In response to Gaddafi's refusal to extradite al-Megrahi and Fhimah, the UN Security Council imposed economic sanctions on Libya. As sanctions began to cripple Libya's economy, Gaddafi reached an agreement for a trial to take place on neutral territory under Scottish law. The High Court of Justiciary Order 1998 provided the legal framework for the trial to take place in the Netherlands.

The trial began on May 3, 2000, before three Scottish judges. The court announced its verdict on January 31, 2001. Based largely on eyewitness accounts and extensive forensic evidence, the court convicted al-Megrahi but found Fhimah not guilty. The court sentenced al-Megrahi to a minimum of twenty years before being eligible for parole. Following an appeal by al-Megrahi, who maintained his innocence, and the court's rejection of it, al-Megrahi was jailed at a maximum-security prison in

Glasgow before being transferred to Greenock Prison in 2005. The government of Scotland released al-Megrahi from the prison on August 20, 2009, on compassionate grounds, given his diagnosis of terminal prostate cancer.

Keith A. Leitich

See also: Gaddafi (Qaddafi), Muammar; State Terrorism; Transportation Security.

FURTHER READING

Bassiouni, M. Cherif. 2004. "Terrorism: The Persistent Dilemma of Legitimacy." *Case Western Reserve Journal of International Law* 36 (2–3): 295–306.

Connelly, Clare. 2001. "The Lockerbie Trial: Justice and Victims." *Syracuse Journal of International Law and Governance* 29 (1): 44–50.

Emerson, Steven, and Brian Duffy. 1990. *The Fall of Pan Am 103: Inside the Lockerbie Investigation.* London: Futura Publications.

Gerson, Allan, and Jerry Adler. 2001. *The Price of Terror: One Bomb, One Plane, 270 Lives: The History-Making Struggle for Justice after Pan Am 103.* 1st ed. New York: HarperCollins.

Loftus, Elizabeth F. 2013. "Eyewitness Testimony in the Lockerbie Bombing Case." *Memory* 21 (5): 584–590.

Malik, Omar. 1999. "Aviation Security before and after Lockerbie." In *Aviation Terrorism and Security*, edited by Paul Wilkinson and Brian M. Jenkins, 112–133. London and Portland, OR: Frank Cass.

Martenczuk, B. 1999. "The Security Council, the International Court and Judicial Review: What Lessons from Lockerbie?" *European Journal of International Law* 10 (3): 517–547.

Wallis, Rodney. 2001. *Lockerbie: The Story and the Lessons.* Westport, CT: Praeger.

Pipe Bomber Attacks, Lucas John "Luke" Helder

1982–

Although Lucas John "Luke" Helder's manifesto, published in his college newspaper, spoke of the necessity of "dismissing" people from the living, he was probably the least homicidal homegrown terrorist who has gained a media moniker thus far in the twenty-first century. Helder turned twenty-one on May 5, 2002, as he drove across Colorado on his more than 3,000-mile journey. He planted eighteen pipe bombs and anti-government notes in mailboxes in five different states, but he failed to arm the last dozen devices after the first batch injured six, including four mail carriers.

Helder's résumé is as short as his career as a terrorist. Born in 1981 in Pine Island, Minnesota, a small community near Rochester and about fifty miles south of Minneapolis, Helder was an outwardly normal high school student—to the point of being in a grunge band and having a minor encounter with the law involving marijuana. It was as a junior with considerable shop skills, majoring in industrial arts at the University of Wisconsin–Stout, that his growing beliefs that government controls people's lives and that a better world exists on an astral plane spurred him to build his bombs packed with BBs and nails.

To draw maximum media attention to his concerns, Helder planned to use the bombs to create a connect-the-dots smiley face in the center of a U.S. map. The first sixteen bombs were thus arranged in circles of eight to be the eyes, the right one bridging the border between Illinois and Iowa and the left one in Nebraska. The arc of the mouth got no farther than the bombs planted in Colorado and northern Texas before Helder was stopped following a forty-mile high-speed car chase in Nevada and talked out of killing himself with the shotgun he was carrying for that purpose.

Helder's arrest was the result of tips to law enforcement agencies by both his father and a college roommate, both of whom became concerned for his welfare once it was evident that the reason he had given for being away from school was false. Nearly two years later, in April 2004, a federal judge ruled that Helder was incompetent to stand trial on the multiple counts against him in several states, and he was remanded to the Federal Medical Center facility in Rochester, Minnesota. After a 2013 reevaluation of his condition, Luke Helder remains in that facility.

Joseph R. Rudolph Jr.

See also: Homegrown Terrorism; Psychology of Terrorists; Sociology of Terrorism.

FURTHER READING

ABC News. 2006. "Helder Said to Be Mapping Smiley Face." January 7, 2006. https://abcnews.go.com/US/story?id=91668

Janofsky, Michael, with Jodi Wilgoren. 2002. "Bomb Suspect Gave Few Hints of Violent Plan." *New York Times*, May 9, 2002. https://www.nytimes.com/2002/05/09/us/bomb-suspect-gave-few-hints-of-violent-plan.html

McDermott, Tricia. 2002. "Mailbox Bomb Suspect Charged." CBS News, May 3, 2002. https://www.cbsnews.com/news/mailbox-bomb-suspect-charged/

Reaves, Reaves. 2002. "Person of the Week: Lucas Helder." *Time*, May 9, 2002. http://content.time.com/time/nation/article/0,8599,236525,00.html

Pittsburgh Synagogue Shooting

October 27, 2018

Anti-Semitism has a long history in the United States and so does violence against American Jews, which is easily chronicled from the days of the Ku Klux Klan through to the lone-wolf terrorists of today. The attack by forty-six-year-old Robert Gregory Bowers on the Tree of Life Synagogue in the heart of Pittsburgh, Pennsylvania, on October 27, 2018, represents the most violent of these attacks to date—but it is not the most recent.

The assailant, except for being considerably older than the murderers in such other recent mass killings as that at the Emmanuel African Methodist Episcopal Church in Charleston, South Carolina, and the Walmart killings in El Paso, Texas, fit a similar profile. Described as a "loner" by acquaintances who knew him, Bowers was the product of an unstable upbringing (a broken home and a father who committed suicide when Bowers was six), a high school dropout, and a frequent visitor and contributor to websites attracting anti-Jewish, anti-immigrant, and white supremacist groups and individuals on the extreme right. He also left no doubts as to his motive, shouting, "All Jews must die," during the twenty minutes he fired into the congregation, killing eleven and injuring another eight before eventually surrendering to the police.

Bowers's action also fit into the "New Terrorism" global pattern of lone-wolf extremists who seek out soft targets like religious gatherings to maximize civilian casualties in a single act. Within a year of Bowers's attack, lone gunmen had killed three in a synagogue in Halle, Germany (October 2019); twenty-three at the Walmart in El Paso (August 2019); and fifty-one at a mosque in Christchurch, New Zealand, the latter shooter livestreaming his killing spree over the Internet.

Bowers's act prompted yet another discussion of whether such hate acts qualify as *domestic terrorism*, the U.S. attorney in Pittsburgh maintaining that there would have to be evidence that the shooter was trying to violently propagate an ideology for it to do so.

The murders also led to a series of steps intended to ameliorate such future occurrences, not the least of which involved the City of Pittsburgh enacting stricter gun control laws (struck down the following year because state law precludes Pennsylvania cities from regulating firearms) and some worshippers at synagogues now going armed.

For his act, Robert Bowers, at this writing (early August 2020), awaits trial on numerous charges, represented by Judy Clarke, a court-appointed attorney previously appointed to serve as counsel to Dylann Roof, the Charleston church shooter. Meanwhile, on April 27, 2019, nineteen-year-old John Timothy Earnest fired a series of shots in the Chabad of Poway synagogue in Southern California, killing one and injuring three before his rifle malfunctioned.

Joseph R. Rudolph Jr.

See also: Charleston Church Massacre; El Paso Walmart Shooting; Homegrown Terrorism.

FURTHER READING

Amend, Alex. 2018. "Analyzing a Terrorist's Social Media Manifesto: The Pittsburgh Synagogue Shooter's Posts on Gab." Southern Poverty Law Center, October 28, 2018. Accessed July 20, 2020. https://www.splcenter.org/hatewatch/2018/10/28/analyzing-terrorists-social-media-manifesto-pittsburgh-synagogue-shooters-posts-gab

Chavez, Nicole, Emanuella Grinberg, and Eliott C. McLaughlin. 2018. "Pittsburgh Synagogue Gunman Said He Wanted All Jews to Die, Criminal Complaint Says." CNN, updated October 31, 2018. https://cnnphilippines.com/world/2018/10/29/pittsburgh-synagogue-gunman-jews-die.html

Fattal, Isabel. 2018. "A Brief History of Anti-Semitic Violence in America." *The Atlantic*, October 28, 2018. https://www.theatlantic.com/politics/archive/2018/10/brief-history-anti-semitic-violence-america/574228/

Pengelly, Martin, Lois Beckett, and Mike Elk. 2018. "Pittsburgh Synagogue Shooting: Suspect Robert Bowers Charged with 11 Counts of Murder." *The Guardian*, October 28, 2018. https://www.theguardian.com/us-news/2018/oct/27/pittsburgh-synagogue-shooting

Police Officers as Terrorist Targets

It is generally accepted that terror activity is designed to harm, confuse, and mislead the citizens so that they will lose confidence in the government. Opinions about overreaction by the government are usually most observable when involving law enforcement agencies at the local, county, and state levels. Other government overreaction may also be alleged to be taking place by intelligence, investigative, and prosecutorial professionals; however, it is the "boots on the ground" that are the most visible and the direct providers of what some may view as excessive behavior, which makes them primary targets for violence. To paraphrase Egon Bittner, a former chair of the Sociology Department at Brandeis University who is widely celebrated for his work on the relationship between the police and society: "The police are a mechanism for the distribution of situationally justified force in society," and among the city dwellers' repertoire for solving problems is calling the cops because "the police do that which must be done and no one else is ready, willing or available to do it."

One need only go back fifty years to provide illustration of terror activity against police. The National Advisory Committee on Criminal Justice Standard and Goals Report of the Task Force on Disorders and Terrorism in 1976 reported that the Black Liberation Army (BLA) was founded in 1971 and responsible for multiple police officer assassinations, including four New York Police Department (NYPD) members in 1971 and 1972. The BLA also engaged in bank and armored car robberies to finance their cause.

The NYPD responded in part at the time by assigning the responsibility for investigations of organized attacks on police to a particular Detective Bureau unit, the Major Case Squad of the Special Investigation Division. This was done even though the FBI was, and is, the lead agency countering terrorism in the United States. An additional bureaucratic change came about in 1979 with the establishment of the NYPD/FBI Joint Bank Robbery Task Force (JBRTF) in response to a spike in bank and armored car robberies, often a fundraising tactic of terrorist groups.

In 1980, the FBI and NYPD officially pooled resources again and established the first Joint Terrorism Task Force (JTTF) in the country. One of the explanations for this new investigative and response model was the success of the JBRTF. Another was the investigative work that had been accomplished by both agencies in their responses to the terrorist Weather Underground's accidental bombing of a townhouse in Greenwich Village in 1970 and other situations.

Another terror attack example involved the killing of a New Jersey State Police trooper in 1981 when he approached two members of the radical environmental group the United Freedom Front during a routine traffic stop. This group also robbed banks to finance their activities and bombed energy sites to publicize their cause.

The terrorist attacks on September 11, 2001, are the starkest illustration of terrorism designed to frighten, intimidate, and cause doubt in the ability of the government to protect its citizens. It is also the date of the largest number of police officers killed by terrorists: seventy-two police officers died that day, including thirty-seven from the Port Authority Police Department, twenty-three from the NYPD, and an off-duty police officer who was a passenger on United Airlines Flight 93, which crashed in Pennsylvania after the passengers attempted to regain control of the plane, having become aware of what had already happened in New York City and at the Pentagon.

Fast-forward to the 2020s and levels of civil unrest not experienced since the 1960s and 1970s. Many legitimate demonstrations and protests are taking place, but agitators from the right and left ends of the political spectrum are instigating violent interactions with their counterparts and with the police. It is too soon to attribute recent shootings of police in Los Angeles, Louisville, and elsewhere to terrorist activity; however, whether by an organized group, an inspired lone wolf, or an individual experiencing emotional or psychological problems, police officers are dying, and citizens are less safe.

Annually, the FBI reports on law enforcement officers killed and assaulted in the line of duty (LEOKAs). In 2019, forty-eight officers died as a result of felonious acts, and two of those were the result of ambush. In 2020, forty-six officers were feloniously killed. Eight of these were ambushed, and two others were killed without having committed any known provocative acts on their part.

It is not always possible to attribute motivation for assaultive behavior against lawful authority. In 1976, Frederick Hacker identified a trilogy of motivations for such behavior: criminals, crusaders, or crazies. He further opined that there could well be a mixture of the motivations in a particular individual or group. To this, J. S. Gibbs noted in 2011 that insofar as the use of force against the police is a struggle between those that the government puts forth to maintain judicious social control and those who strive for a different world, "The police are attractive symbolic and strategic targets, and they were victimized in over 12% of terrorist attacks worldwide since 1970."

Robert J. Louden

See also: Domestic Terrorist Groups; Targeted Assassinations.

FURTHER READING

Bittner, Egon. 1975. *The Functions of Police in Modern Society.* Lanham, MD: Jason Aronson.

Creely, Edwin. n.d. "The Idea of Terrorism." Monash University.

Crossman, Ashley. 2019. "Definition of Social Control." ThoughtCo., October 13, 2019. www.thoughtco.com/social-control-3026587

Daley, Robert. 1973. *Target Blue: An Insider's View of the NYPD.* New York: Delacorte.

FBI. n.d. "2019 Law Enforcement Officers Killed & Assaulted." Accessed May 4, 2020. https://ucr.fbi.gov/leoka/2019

FBI website. n.d. www.fbi.gov

Ganor, Boaz. 2010. "Is One Man's Terrorist Another Man's Freedom Fighter?" International Institute for Counter Terrorism, January 1, 2010. http://www.ict.org.il/Article.aspx?ID=1123

Gibbs, Jennifer. 2011. *The Relationship between Legitimacy, Terrorist Attacks and Police.* Unpublished PhD diss., University of Maryland.

Hacker, Frederick. 1976. *Criminals, Crusaders or Crazies: Terror and Terrorism in Our Time.* New York: Norton.

Louden, Robert. 2005. "Policing Post-9/11." *Fordham Urban Law Journal* 32 (4): 757–765.

Manning, Peter. 2013. "The Work of Egon Bittner." *Ethnographic Studies* 13: 51–66. https://doi.org/10.5449/idslu-001091487

National Advisory Committee on Criminal Justice Standards and Goals. 1976. *Disorders and Terrorism: Report of the Task Force on Disorders and Terrorism.* Washington, DC: U.S. Government Printing Office.

Officer Down Memorial Page. 2020. www.odmp.org

Profiling

Terrorism dates at least as far back as the first century AD, when the Roman Empire utilized terrorist tactics to overthrow rivaling dictators. France's Reign of Terror, during the latter years of the eighteenth century, demonstrated a modern application of terrorism with planned assassinations and beheadings of opposing members of the state. History is relevant in developing a definition of terrorism because how one perceives it will dictate how law enforcement profiles terrorists as opposed to profiling common criminals.

The Federal Bureau of Investigation (FBI), on its What We Investigate website, defines *international terrorism* as acts "perpetrated by individuals and/or groups inspired by or associated with designated foreign terrorist organizations or nations." The same source defines *domestic terrorism* as activity "perpetrated by individuals and/or groups inspired by or associated with primarily U.S. based movements that espouse extremist ideologies of a political, religious, social, racial, or environmental nature." The derivative profile sees the terrorist as likely to be well trained, organized, idealistic, and highly motivated. In contrast, the common criminal is not usually well trained, is opportunistic, and, in most cases, will flee from law enforcement. A terrorist will also avoid apprehension by blending into his or her surroundings until the last possible moment prior to a planned attack. In addition, terrorists are usually non-state actors, having denounced their state(s), which they vehemently oppose for various reasons, or state-sponsored actors acting at the behest of their governments.

Similar to criminal profiling, knowing why terrorists commit acts of violence is key to preventing future attacks. Successful investigative strategies in profiling identify prominent personality traits and behavioral characteristics of suspected or known terrorists and their affiliated groups by applying baseline phases of information gathering. Conducting a thorough analysis of all crime scene findings, such as crime scene photographs, autopsy reports, eyewitness statements, and police reports, is ground zero of any terrorist attack investigation. Additionally, confidence in knowing whether a terrorist is acting in a rogue-like manner or as a member of a much larger cell can assist profilers in identifying a modus operandi or method of committing an attack.

Such knowledge is essential to profiling because having insight into how a terrorist or terrorist group plans to espouse an attack speaks to the psychological or sociological states of the actors, thereby providing additional tools for prevention, linkage, and apprehension. Linkage aids in apprehension by aligning characteristics of a terrorist attack and its terrorist actor(s) to both past attacks and current threats. This technique is also very useful for profiling criminals, such as serial killers and arsonists. These characteristics may include but not be limited to financial behaviors, unique bomb-making signatures, language use, handwriting style, and word choices.

The reception of terrorist profiling varies significantly by agency policy, demographic makeup of a given population, and operational practice. Contemporary U.S. legal jurisprudence condemns targeted profiling that could be considered racially motivated; however, profiling social media dossiers, suspicious facial expressions or body language, and an actor's geographical origin are widely used by law enforcement agencies across the United States and the world with aplomb in the efforts to thwart attacks and apprehend terrorists. Meanwhile, sociopolitical groups and civil liberties defenders counter profiling based on race, ethnicity, and nationality with legislation and the influence of public discomfort.

Pamela K. Mertens

See also: Homegrown Terrorism; Psychology of Terrorists; Recruiting Terrorists; Sociology of Terrorism.

FURTHER READING

FBI. 2018. "What We Investigate: Terrorism." August 1, 2018. Accessed September 8, 2018. https://www.fbi.gov/investigate/terrorism

Hudson, Rex. A., and Marilyn L. Majeska. 2013. *The Sociology and Psychology of Terrorism: Who Becomes a Terrorist and Why? A Report.* Washington, DC: CreateSpace Independent Publishing Platform.

Laquer, Walter. 1999. *The New Terrorism: Fanaticism and the Arms of Mass Destruction.* New York: Oxford University Press.

Phillips, Brian J. 2018. "Terrorist Tactics by Criminal Organizations: The Mexican Case in Context." *Perspectives on Terrorism* 12 (1): 46–63. Accessed September 17, 2018. http://www.jstor.org/stable/26343745

Record, Jeffrey. 2003. *Bounding the Global War on Terrorism.* Carlisle, PA: Strategic Studies Institute. Accessed September 5, 2017. https://man.fas.org/eprint/record.pdf

Strang, Kenneth David, and Maximiliano E. Korstanje. 2018. "Comparing the Socio-Political Ethics of Fighting Terrorism with Extreme Self-Defense in USA: An Exploratory Insight." *International Journal of Risk and Contingency Management* 7 (1): 1–19. https://doi.org/10.4018/IJRCM.2018010101

Protect America Act of 2007

The Protect America Act (PAA) of 2007, Public Law 110-55, amended the Foreign Intelligence Surveillance Act (FISA) of 1978 by making substantive changes that eased the government's ability to address gaps in foreign intelligence collection. Citing continued substantial threats to the United States from terrorism, the government presented PAA as a necessary mechanism for protecting the country by addressing technical developments since the passage of FISA almost thirty years earlier. Introduced in the Senate by Mitch McConnell (R-KY), the act passed the Senate by a 60–28 vote, passed the House of Representatives by a 227–183 vote, and was signed into law by George W. Bush on August 5, 2007.

The act amended FISA in several ways. One such provision removed the requirement that intelligence agencies obtain a warrant for collecting intelligence information against foreign intelligence targets outside the United States. Warrant requirements under FISA were replaced with a series of internal government control mechanisms, coupled with certification by an appropriate national security official, thus allowing more robust collection against foreign intelligence targets. Further, this provision allowed for the intercept of communications, without a court order, if a foreign entity communicated with someone in the United States and that communication involved terrorism or foreign intelligence. By allowing for the possibility of warrantless collection involving U.S. citizens in some circumstances, critics of the law maintained the act opened the door to domestic spying by violating the Fourth Amendment prohibition against unreasonable search.

The definition of *electronic surveillance* was also clarified under the act. Under FISA, the definition of electronic surveillance was carefully constructed yet quite complex and had been overtaken by changes in communications technologies in the three decades since FISA became law. The PAA addressed those changes, particularly with respect to Internet-based communications and disposable cell phones, in a way that eased the government's ability to gather foreign intelligence information. By revising the definition of electronic surveillance in a way that addressed technological advances, the act removed the need for the government to seek a warrant against relevant targets outside the United States. The act did not provide the government with an ability to target Americans in the United States under the guise of targeting an authorized foreign target (a process commonly referred to as *reverse targeting*) as some critics have charged.

Beyond the removal of FISA's warrant requirements for collection against foreign targets, one of the more controversial provisions of PAA was the inclusion of a mechanism by which communications providers could be compelled to cooperate with government information gathering requests. Under PAA, failure to provide information, facilities, or assistance as requested could result in a contempt of court citation. Critics feared this would allow the government to gather personally sensitive data, open domestic mail, or conduct physical searches of homes, businesses, or personal belongings, even though the act offered no such provisions.

The act also provided for oversight, including notification to the Foreign Intelligence Surveillance Court (FISC), of the internal government procedures through which the government would determine that authorized collection was, for foreign intelligence purposes, directed against foreign targets and did not constitute electronic surveillance requiring court approval. Additional oversight was provided through compliance reporting to the Intelligence and Judiciary Committees of Congress and by authorizing individuals and businesses receiving requests for assistance to challenge any such request in court.

The PAA carried a sunset provision that terminated the act after 180 days. It expired on February 17, 2008.

Daniel S. Gressang IV

See also: Counterterrorism and the George W. Bush Administration; Foreign Intelligence Surveillance Court; USA PATRIOT Act of 2001.

FURTHER READING

Bush, George W. 2007. "President's Radio Address." White House, Radio, July 28, 2007. https://georgewbush-whitehouse.archives.gov/news/releases/2007/07/print/20070728.html

Department of Justice. n.d. "Myth/Fact: Key Myths about FISA Elements in the Protect America Act." https://www.justice.gov/archive/ll/paa-dispelling-myths.html

McConnell, J. Michael. 2007. *House Judiciary Committee Hearing on the Foreign Intelligence Surveillance Act and Protect America Act: 18 September 2007: Statement for the Record of J. Michael McConnell, Director of National Intelligence.* House

Judiciary Committee, September 18, 2007. https://www.dni.gov/files/documents/Newsroom/Testimonies/20070918_testimony.pdf
Protect America Act of 2007, Pub. L. 110-55, 121 Stat. 552 (2007). https://www.congress.gov/bill/110th-congress/senate-bill/1927

Psychology of Terrorists

One of the more common themes in the literature on terrorism, and in the speeches and statements of government officials on terrorism, is the need to develop and implement effective tools for identifying those individuals and groups that are at risk of involvement in terrorism. This goal underlies many government efforts to counter violent extremism, shaping security policies and actions at various levels of government. Yet, it also begs the questions of who becomes a terrorist, and why individuals would resort to violence in pursuit of political, religious, or social goals. Answering these questions can offer insights that will allow for the effective application of countermeasures and preventative measures that can reduce the level of terrorism, guide development of deradicalization programs, and heighten national security. The questions are simple and straightforward, yet they mask a degree of complexity and uniqueness that have, so far, yielded few generalizable answers.

CONTRIBUTIONS FROM SOCIAL PSYCHOLOGY

Taken as a whole, the most common characteristic of terrorists is their normality. Social psychology offers some insights into questions of who becomes a terrorist and why by focusing attention on intergroup conflict and intergroup dynamics. Differences, and conflict, between people can be based on a variety of factors, including ethnicity, race, national origin, politics, and religion, among others. When those differences escalate into conflict, polarization between groups and subgroups, othering, and isolation may emerge and lead to the cultivation of extreme attitudes about and toward identifiable out-groups. With increasing and more frequent conflict between groups, groupthink may also emerge, creating the need for in-group consensus that overrides appropriateness in collective decision-making. Greater and more prevalent consensus, in turn, may lead to the transfer of personal responsibility, in both belief and action, from the individual to the group, allowing members and supporters to feel absolved of responsibility for violent acts they commit or that may be committed in their name.

Framing theory offers a perspective in which terrorist groups are understood to leverage and exploit polarization, othering, isolation, and similar factors in recruiting new members, in building and sustaining support in the larger society, and in justifying their violent actions to themselves and to the outside world. In doing so, terrorist groups develop, produce, and disseminate meaning by framing messages, in words and deeds, of intent, purpose, and justification in ways that are intended to resonate with the interests, beliefs, goals, and grievances of an identified audience. As that audience increasingly identifies with the message, more and more individuals will come to identify and support, if not join, the terrorist group.

The group's opponent, typically the government, can and often does exacerbate the growth and militancy of terrorist groups through a process of *co-radicalization*. In this process, the government's reaction to terrorist statements and activities emphasizes belligerence toward that group, further hardening the terrorists' militancy. The government, in turn, sees that growing militancy and escalates its own rhetorical and physical actions against the group, perpetrating a spiraling series of action and reaction that increases polarization, hardens attitudes, and increases the likelihood of continued escalating violence. The terrorist violence that results, as suggested by expected utility theory, is an outcome of the strategic choice to protect, defend, or extend some desired condition against an implacable and increasingly hostile government adversary.

CONTRIBUTIONS FROM INDIVIDUAL PSYCHOLOGY

As much as social psychology helps our understanding of terrorism, it offers little to explain why individuals choose to engage in terrorism. To the questions of *who* becomes a terrorist and *why*, individual psychology provides a venue for exploring causes and motivations. While there have been dozens of studies seeking individual-level answers over the last fifty years, the only clear answer that has emerged is that the decision to engage in terrorism is as unique and as complex as the individuals themselves. The only two persistent qualities of terrorists evident in these studies are the complexity and diversity of motives, reasons, and mechanisms. Each terrorist's path into violence is unique and nonlinear in that there exists no single cause, psychological factor, or path evident.

Pioneering studies of behavior by Stanley Milgram and Philip Zimbardo, American psychologists who researched and taught at Yale University and Stanford University, respectively, offer some insights into these questions. Milgram's experiments on the limits of authority and Zimbardo's on authoritarian roles demonstrated that some individuals can be induced or led, whether by authority figures or role, to conduct extreme acts of violence. While not all of Milgram's and Zimbardo's subjects were led in this way, the findings suggest that two factors of the power relationship dynamic may be critical for understanding terrorism: identification and dissociation. To be induced to commit violence, a person must identify with the ideas and members of a given group. For Milgram's subjects, this was identification with the authority figure of the experimenter, who directed actions and behaviors. For Zimbardo's subjects, identification was with the roles—jailer or inmate—and the expectations associated with each assigned role. The second factor, dissociation, requires individuals to cognitively separate themselves from an out-group, allowing them to sever expectations of affinity and empathy with the out-group.

MENTAL CONSIDERATIONS

Yet, for many of Milgram's and Zimbardo's subjects, identification and dissociation were insufficient to overcome the reluctance to mistreat others. For some researchers, that reluctance is explained by suggesting terrorists are irrational, if not psychopathic. This explanation seemed to offer a compelling answer to the question of why individuals would knowingly and willingly risk alienation from friends and family, incarceration, and death for causes that were doomed to fail. It also seemed to offer an equally compelling explanation for why some would willingly kill themselves, as suicide bombers, when the act guaranteed they would not live to realize any gains from their actions. Subsequent research has cast doubt on the irrational and psychopathic actor hypothesis, with numerous studies attesting to rational and strategic decision-making by lucid individuals. In the last few years, however, there have been some studies suggesting some terrorists may well suffer from one or more mental illnesses, leaving the question of psychopathology's role for further exploration.

IMPACT OF AUTHORITY

Other theories by American and European social scientists tie the decision to engage in terrorism to the interactive dynamic between authority and the individual. Scott Atran, for example, emphasizes both group dynamics and the close and intimate relationship between and within peer groups and families as critical factors. For many terrorists, initial entry into militancy and terrorism can be traced to friendship or kinship to someone who has already joined or affiliated with a terrorist group. These ties form a strong and resilient bond between individuals, where comradery and shared purpose can overcome reluctance. Whereas strong, persuasive authority figures have the power to create a shared identity, purpose, and goal, friendship and kinship ties offer the bridge that unites such leaders with potential followers.

However, there needs to be a distinction drawn between adoption of radical ideas and radical action. Most radical idea adopters never transition to radical action, and relatively few supporters of terrorist groups actually engage in violence themselves, leading McCauley and Moskalenko to suggest the two-pyramids model in which more prosaic mechanisms, like personal grievances, transition from small transgressions to more serious acts; love, status seeking, loss of social connections, hatred, and the desire for martyrdom may drive individuals to embrace and engage in terrorism. These individual mechanisms can, and often do, interact and overlap with group radicalization processes such as intergroup competition, polarization, and group isolation and marginalization to reinforce a need to find a sense of purpose and belonging.

Other theories emphasize a variety of personal factors that can lead or contribute to terrorism, although none offer a truly generalizable explanation. Particularly since the September 11, 2001, attacks, religion has been seen by some as a primary motivating factor for terrorism. The perception or belief that one's religion is besieged by oppressors can, according to some, create a sense of moral outrage that drives the desire to defend one's religion by any means necessary. This can then serve to create a hero/victim duality in which the terrorist is a hero for the sacrifice he willingly makes in pursuit of his cause while also being a victim of the perceived aggressor's attacks.

THE SEARCH FOR MEANING

Whether the motivating factor is religion, some other personal grievance, or a shared group grievance, some see terrorists as searching for meaning. In one study of 2,032 foreign fighters who sought affiliation with al-Qaeda and related groups, the recurring theme, according to Venhaus, was that they were all "looking for something. . . . They want to understand who they are, why they matter, and what their role in the world should be." This search for meaning addresses strong personal needs, providing structure, purpose, and context to what the individual may perceive as an otherwise fruitless existence. In a similar vein, Gurr suggested that those who engage in illicit violence may be driven, at least in part, by relative deprivation, the sense that one has, either by intent or circumstance, been unjustly deprived of some desired goal, status, recognition, or opportunity. When the sense of unjust denial reaches a critical point, relative deprivation theory suggests the decision to rebel may become more acceptable, making the individual more susceptible to radicalization and self-radicalization.

Theories concerning the psychology of terrorism vary greatly and address a wide variety of perspectives, including personal, group, community, sociopolitical, and ideological factors, with no theory adequately explaining the complexity and uniqueness of motivations underlying individual decisions to engage in terrorism. By the same token, theories of terrorist group behavior offer insights but are not yet capable of explaining all terrorist behaviors. Terrorism, and the decision to engage in it, is a highly individualized process unique to each participant and his or her perceptions and circumstances. The triggering events that lead radicalized individuals to transition to active participation are similarly unique in their effect on susceptible individuals. What we know about the psychology of terrorism has grown considerably over the last several decades, but we remain challenged to explain the psychology of terrorists and terrorist groups.

Daniel S. Gressang IV

See also: Profiling; Sociology of Terrorism.

FURTHER READING

Atran, Scott. 2010. *Talking to the Enemy: Violent Extremism, Sacred Values, and What It Means to Be Human.* London: Allen Lane.

Borum, Randy. 2012. "Radicalization into Violent Extremism I: A Review of Social Science Theories." *Journal of Strategic Security* 4 (4): 7–36.

Crenshaw, Martha. 1981. "The Causes of Terrorism." *Comparative Politics* 13 (4): 379–399.

Gurr, Ted Robert. 1970. *Why Men Rebel.* Princeton, NJ: Princeton University Press.

Horgan, John. 2017. "Psychology of Terrorism: Introduction to the Special Issue." *American Psychologist* 72 (3): 199–204.

Juergensmeyer, Mark. 2000. *Terror in the Mind of God: The Global Rise of Religious Violence.* Berkeley: University of California Press.

Koomen, Willem, and Joop van der Pligt. 2016. *The Psychology of Radicalization and Terrorism.* London: Routledge.

McCauley, Clark, and Sophia Moskalenko. 2011. *Friction: How Radicalization Happens to Them and Us.* Oxford, UK: Oxford University Press.

McCauley, Clark, and Sophia Moskalenko. 2017. "Understanding Political Radicalization: The Two Pyramid Model." *American Psychologist* 72 (3): 205–216.

Milgram, Stanley. 1974. *Obedience to Authority*. New York: Harper and Row.

Sageman, Marc. 2004. *Understanding Terrorist Networks*. Philadelphia: University of Pennsylvania Press.

Simon, Jeffrey D. 2013. *Lone Wolf Terrorism: Understanding the Growing Threat*. Amherst, NY: Prometheus Books.

Venhaus, John M. 2010. *Why Youth Join Al-Qaeda*. May 4, 2010. Washington, DC: United States Institute of Peace. https://www.usip.org/publications/2010/05/why-youth-join-al-qaeda

Zimbardo, Philip. 2007. *The Lucifer Effect: Understanding How Good People Turn Evil*. New York: Random House.

R

Rahman, Sheikh Omar Abdel

1938–2017

Omar Abdel Rahman was a blind Egyptian cleric and militant Islamist who was convicted of seditious conspiracy in a U.S. federal court in connection with a foiled terrorist plot against numerous landmark targets in New York City. Rahman, who was known within the United States as "the Blind Sheikh," was sentenced to life in federal prison, and he died in federal custody in February 2017.

Rahman was born in Egypt in 1938 and lost his eyesight as an infant. After memorizing the Quran (which he read in Braille), Rahman attended and earned a doctorate in Islamic theology from Egypt's Al-Azhar University, the oldest and most prestigious university in the Islamic world. A staunch opponent of Egypt's secular government under Gamal Abdel Nasser, Rahman became affiliated with two militant Islamist organizations, al-Jama'a al-Islamiyya and Egyptian Islamic Jihad, and he developed a close relationship with Egyptian Islamist Jihad leader Ayman al-Zawahiri. Al-Zawahiri became the leader of al-Qaeda following the 2011 death of Osama bin Laden.

Rahman was imprisoned in Egypt on suspicion of complicity in Egyptian Islamic Jihad's 1981 assassination of Egyptian president Anwar Sadat and was accused of conferring religious legitimacy on the assassination by issuing a fatwa calling for Sadat's death, but he was released without charges after several years. Upon his release, he traveled to Afghanistan to join Abdullah Azzam, al-Zawahiri, and bin Laden as a leader of the jihadist group Maktab al-Khadamat al-Mujahideen al-Arab (MAK). That organization was also known as the Afghan Services Bureau and raised funds to support the anti-Soviet war in Afghanistan through offices in several American cities, including in Brooklyn's Al Farooq Mosque where Rahman would later preach. Al-Zawahiri and bin Laden eventually founded al-Qaeda and absorbed MAK into it.

In 1990, Rahman was issued a tourist visa to enter the United States (despite being on a terrorist watch list), and he eventually obtained a Permanent Resident Card. When the U.S. government recognized its error and revoked Rahman's visa, he requested political asylum and was permitted to remain in the United States, where he traveled widely while preaching against it, raising funds for the Afghan mujahideen supported by the Afghan Services Bureau, and advocating jihad against the United States and the West.

Rahman became affiliated with three mosques in the New York City area, including the Al Farooq Mosque in Brooklyn, which included several Islamist extremists in their congregations, including El Sayyid Nosair (responsible for the assassination of Jewish Defense League founder Rabbi Meir Kahane) and Mahmud Abouhalima (later convicted for his role in the 1993 World Trade Center bombing). Based on his connection to those extremists and his past association with extremist groups, Rahman became the focus of an FBI investigation after the 1993 World Trade Center bombing. That investigation led to his arrest and eventual conviction on federal charges of seditious conspiracy in connection with the "Landmarks Plot" in New York City—a foiled plot to bomb the United Nations Building, the Holland and Lincoln Tunnels, a federal building, and the George Washington Bridge—as well as conspiracy to bomb a military base and conspiracy to assassinate Egyptian president Hosni Mubarak. He was sentenced to life in prison, serving that term in federal prison medical facilities in Minnesota and North Carolina. He died in the Butner, North Carolina, Federal Medical Center in February 2017.

Vincent E. Henry

See also: al-Qaeda; bin Laden, Osama; World Trade Center Attack.

FURTHER READING

Camarota, Stephen A. 2002. *The Open Door: How Militant Islamic Terrorists Entered and Remained in the United States, 1993–2001.* Washington, DC: Center for Immigration Studies. https://cis.org/Report/How-Militant-Islamic-Terrorists-Entered-and-Remained-United-States

Gerges, Fawaz. 2009. *The Far Enemy: Why Jihad Went Global.* 2nd ed. New York: Cambridge University Press.

Lance, Peter. 2004. *1,000 Years for Revenge: International Terrorism and the FBI.* New York: William Morrow.

Preston, Julia. 2017. "Omar Abdel-Rahman, Blind Cleric Found Guilty of Plot to Wage 'War or Urban Terrorism,' Dies at 78." *New York Times*, February 18, 2017. https://www.nytimes.com/2017/02/18/world/middleeast/omar-abdel-rahman-dead.html

Recruiting Terrorists

For terrorist groups, recruiting new members is a necessity. Active members who are incarcerated, incapacitated, expelled, or killed must be replaced if the group is to survive and maintain operational capability. The group must not only replace active members but also build a nonviolent support base that can provide funds, logistics, propaganda dissemination, and intelligence while also serving as a potential pool for replacing lost members. For many years, recruiting depended on face-to-face interaction, which limited the ability to recruit. Technology, however, has changed the recruiting process, making it faster and easier, providing terrorist groups unprecedented reach, and offering more security in vetting potential recruits. While the basic process remains unchanged, relying on personal connections and effective messaging, the opportunities brought about by technological innovation have fundamentally changed the recruiting process, opening the door to more recruits and also providing new opportunities to inspire others to act on their own.

TECHNOLOGY'S IMPACT

Technology, particularly the ubiquitous computer, smartphone, and tablet, has changed the face of terrorist recruiting. As computers became more widely available during the 1990s, terrorists began to leverage the Internet and the new opportunities it provided for fundraising, publicity, and propaganda. Stormfront, a white nationalist and white supremacist site that is generally considered one of the first extremist sites, was launched in November 1996. Two years later, there were fifteen websites associated with terrorist groups, and by 1999, the Internet had become the principal venue for terrorist propaganda, enabling more terrorist groups and their supporters to reach a wider audience. Just six years later, in 2005, there were an estimated 4,500 websites associated with or maintained by forty terrorist groups. While significantly expanding terrorist groups' recruiting and inspiration potential, these sites remained top-down and one-way in the transmission of propaganda and messaging.

With the advent of social media sites like Facebook, Twitter, and YouTube, the potential for web-based recruiting expanded considerably. Social media provides two-way communication and interaction between terrorist groups, their supporters, and the curious web surfer. Through the uses of forums and chat rooms, these groups have been able to both provide their messages and actively recruit and vet new aspirants, supporters, and members. Today, there are thousands of websites that can serve as gateways for recruitment and radicalization.

As social media use expanded, terrorists learned to diversify messaging, with many al-Qaeda and Islamic State in Iraq and the Levant (ISIL) associated sites launching English, French, German, and other languages in addition to Arabic, allowing them to reach a much larger and diverse audience. For example, there are over 600 pro–Islamic State sites in English today. The far right, including white nationalists and supremacists, also remain active on social media, with over 200 separate white supremacist channels on the Telegram messaging app alone, in addition to sites on other social media platforms.

The adoption of social media by terrorists has also allowed groups and their advocates to broaden the participatory parameters for both radicalization and recruiting, making entry and participation for interested individuals much easier. Anwar al-Awlaki, the U.S.-born propagandist for al-Qaeda in the Arabian Peninsula (AQAP), for example, established a social media presence that opened the door to direct communication between al-Awlaki and a worldwide audience. In creating, editing, and posting *Inspire*, AQAP's professionally produced e-magazine, al-Awlaki expanded opportunities for the direct transmission of ideology, intent, and operational knowledge, boosting support for AQAP and related groups as well as disseminating violent ideologies to unaffiliated, like-minded individuals typically referred to as "lone wolves."

While the Internet and social media themselves do not have the power to radicalize or recruit, both provide easily accessible mechanisms for the dissemination of propaganda and messaging that provides a foundation for recruitment activities. Both play a significant role, yet recruitment still requires secondary reinforcement from social, friendship, or family connections.

THE RECRUITMENT PROCESS

In general, the recruiting process has both push and pull components. The push components include active messaging by terrorists highlighting discrimination, oppression, injustice, and similar broadly defined grievances as a rationale for action. Grievances are blamed on the deliberate actions and policies of the terrorists' opponents, and their presentation is designed to create and encourage a sense of outrage or anger in message recipients. In doing so, the messaging creates a reason, a rationale, for supporting or joining the terrorist group by encouraging a sense of common cause, belonging, and shared purpose. These messages serve to create a sense of community, a network, often highlighting adventure and heroism while suggesting that by joining, one gains the ability to do something of value, not just for oneself but for a broader, more deserving community. The push and pull factors, in tandem, create the sense that there are problems that need to be solved, and by joining with the group, a new recruit can have a role in bringing about a worthwhile outcome.

ISIL videos and the dissemination strategies employed by the group offer an example of the push/pull tandem in messaging. Many ISIL videos targeted at Muslim audiences highlighted the valiant, determined young men, cheerfully sacrificing themselves for the benefit of the great Muslim *ummah* ("community"). Violence was explained as heroes fighting to right the wrongs done to Muslims by apostates and, especially, the West. At the same time, ISIL videos often seek to shame those Muslims who fail to "do their duty" in supporting the ISIL cause. The presentation of gender-specific roles, with men as the warriors seeking to avenge Islam and women as their loyal supporting partners, reinforce the message that all Muslims have been aggrieved and share a responsibility to contribute.

Interestingly, videos intended for Muslim audiences depicted the self-declared ISIL caliphate in largely peaceful terms, presenting something like a utopian vision, while those intended for Western audiences highlighted savagery and brutal violence. This narrowcasting—or tailoring messages to intended audiences—emphasized the dual push/pull factors for Muslim audiences while emphasizing threat and intimidation to its perceived opponents.

PROCESS MECHANICS

Online recruitment begins with a website where potential recruits are identified and subjected to a process of belief reinforcement. In using social media, terrorist groups generally create and maintain a presence that allows the group to engage targeted populations equitably. Access is generally unlimited, and posted messages take a variety of forms designed to appeal to a range of users and interests. Website and web page maintainers monitor use of the site to gauge the degree, frequency, and tone of user interaction with the site and its contents. Users who post negative or hostile replies and comments are either subjected to continuous messaging using different approaches or are simply ignored and abandoned. Those who engage positively with the site's content are identified and offered continuous positive reinforcement, often including some form of authoritative justification for group activities.

Those users identified as potential recruits are funneled into a phased incremental interaction designed to further strengthen the users' affinity for the group and its message. At this stage, interaction is likely with a disseminator, an associate of the group who acts as a go-between linking the user and group members or leaders. Disseminators will share statements and responses from group leaders directly to users, creating a sense of direct connection and personal attention being paid to the recruits by group leadership. The interactions are typically individualized based on cues provided by the user. As affinity grows between user and group, as evidenced by ongoing interactions, the group simultaneously vets the user to ensure the recruit is not in the employ of police or security services.

Once the terrorist group feels comfortable with the recruit, that individual will often be redirected to password-protected sites and forums such as Telegram, where recruitment can proceed more directly and expeditiously. The recruit's sense of alienation, social frustration, sense of inadequacy, and solitude are leveraged to shift the recruit's perspective to one of belonging. As indoctrination of the recruit continues, ties between the individual and the group strengthen, forming an ideological bond between the two that can be leveraged later. The redirection also serves to reinforce the belief that the recruit has joined a vibrant community of like-minded individuals pursuing a noble goal. The recruit is continuously exposed to reinforcing propaganda and messaging and receives online guidance and mentoring. From this point, the recruit can be activated, either as a member of the group or an inspired lone wolf.

RECENT TRENDS

Two recent trends in terrorist recruiting are noteworthy. Narrowcasting, or targeting selected demographics, is born of the idea that mass audiences for messaging no longer exist. For effective messaging and recruiting, efforts must be tailored to a targeted population on the basis of some actual or perceived characteristic or shared value. Overseas and diaspora communities, for example, are frequent targets for ethnic or religiously inspired groups like ISIL and al-Qaeda. Ethnic or racial groups are also frequently targeted, such as the narrowcasting by white supremacists. Most disturbing, however, is the deliberate targeting of children through the use of stories, activities, and cartoons, as has been seen from Hamas and the white supremacist World Church of the Creator's "Creator for Kids" pages.

A second noteworthy trend is a shift from recruiting for membership toward recruiting lone wolves, unaffiliated individuals who can be inspired to act independently of group direction or control. While calls for leaderless resistance, the essence of lone-wolf terrorism, are not new, the use of the Internet and social media have ensured the message is disseminated widely to multiple varied audiences, expanding the terrorists' ability to pursue their goals.

CONCLUSION

Terrorist recruiting has changed, but at the same time, it has remained fundamentally the same. The Internet and social media have expanded terrorists' ability to reach widely separated and diverse audiences, heightening the potential for reaching and influencing disaffected individuals who may be prone to the lure of terrorist messaging. The Internet provides near instantaneous message dissemination while cloaking its consumers in the anonymity of web presence. Through user interaction with terrorist and terrorist-supporting sites, terrorist groups can take advantage of individual needs to build a sense of mission and community, opening the door to recruitment for the terrorists' cause.

Daniel S. Gressang IV

See also: al-Awlaki, Anwar; Counterterrorism and the Obama Administration; Orlando Pulse Nightclub Shooting.

FURTHER READING

Barr, Andrew, and Alexandra Herfroy-Mischler. 2018. "ISIL's Execution Videos: Audience Segmentation and Terrorist Communication in the Digital Age." *Studies in Conflict and Terrorism* 41 (12): 946–967.

Bob, Clifford. 2005. *The Marketing of Rebellion: Insurgents, Media, and International Activism.* Cambridge, UK: Cambridge University Press.

Committee on Homeland Security and Governmental Affairs. 2016. *Jihad 2.0: Social Media in the Next Evolution of Terrorist Recruitment.* Washington, DC: U.S. Government Publishing Office. https://www.hsdl.org/?view&did=798565

Guhl, Jakob, and Jacob Davey. 2020. "A Safe Space to Hate: White Supremacist Mobilisation on Telegram." Institute for Strategic Dialogue. https://www.isdglobal.org/isd-publications/a-safe-space-to-hate-white-supremacist-mobilisation-on-telegram/

Hamm, Mark S. 2007. "Terrorist Recruitment in American Correctional Institutions: An Exploratory Study of Non-Traditional Faith Groups Final Report." National Institute of Justice. https://www.ncjrs.gov/pdffiles1/nij/grants/220957.pdf

Holbrook, Donald. 2019. "The Terrorism Information Environment: Analysing Terrorists' Selection of Ideological and Facilitative Media." *Terrorism and Political Violence* 33 (4): 697–719. https://doi.org/10.1080/09546553.2019.1583216

Jones, Edgar. 2017. "The Reception of Broadcast Terrorism: Recruitment and Radicalisation." *International Review of Psychiatry* 29 (4): 320–326.

Lakomy, Miron. 2019. "Let's Play a Video Game: *Jihadi* Propaganda in the World of Electronic Entertainment." *Studies in Conflict and Terrorism* 42 (4): 383–406.

Pearson, Elizabeth. 2018. "Online as the New Frontline: Affect, Gender, and ISIS-Take-Down on Social Media." *Studies in Conflict and Terrorism* 41 (11): 850–874.

Von Behr, Ines, Anaïs Reding, Charlie Edwards, and Luke Gribbon. 2013. *Radicalisation in the Digital Era: The Use of the Internet in 15 Cases of Terrorism and Extremism.* Cambridge, UK: RAND Europe. http://www.rand.org/content/dam/rand/pubs/research_reports/RR400/RR453/RAND_RR453.pdf

Waskiewicz, Todd. 2020. "Friend of a Friend Influence in Terrorist Social Networks." https://www.hsdl.org/?view&did=744909

Weimann, Gabriel. 2006. *Terror on the Internet: The New Arena, the New Challenges.* Washington, DC: United States Institute of Peace.

Weimann, Gabriel. 2015. *Terrorism in Cyberspace: The Next Generation.* Washington, DC: Woodrow Wilson Center Press.

Reign of Terror

1793–1794

The Reign of Terror was the period in postrevolutionary France when a tiny portion of the French population gained control of the state and used intimidation and political violence to sustain their rule until being swept out of power and, for the leaders, meeting a violent end themselves.

The English statesman Edmund Burke is widely credited with introducing the term *terrorism* in referring to the Reign of Terror (*regime de la terreur*), which was overseen by the prominent French lawyer and politician Maximilien Robespierre and the Committee of Public Safety in the name of preserving the ideals of the French Revolution that began on July 14, 1789. The importance of that era as a watershed in the evolution of terrorism, however, goes far beyond the vocabulary of violence.

In its origin, the dominant characteristics of terrorism were that it consisted of indiscriminate acts of violence and that it was conducted locally by people who were political "outs" seeking to achieve political power or other forms of personal gain, and such was the general nature of terrorism for more than a thousand years. In the aftermath of the French Revolution, Robespierre and his Committee of Public Safety made two significant contributions to terrorism as an evolving political force during the brief period between September 1793 and July 1794, when they controlled France.

Robespierre understood that the power of terrorism was not to be found in the act itself but in the psychological climate of insecurity that it can engender in the broader community. Thus, it did not so much matter who went to the guillotine. In a systematic use of random violence, what counted was that enough people would lose their heads that others would be intimidated from trying to topple the regime.

Robespierre's stint in power demonstrated that terrorism could be an effective state tool for maintaining control over the governed, at least for a while. Thus, under the auspices of the Committee for Public Safety that he commanded between September 5, 1793, and July 27, 1794, he and the perhaps 10,000 collaborators he had assembled from his followers throughout France were able to dominate a country of at least twenty-five million people.

States and terrorist organizations alike have subsequently followed in these channels, with repressive states relying on their secret police or sanctioned paramilitary groups to prolong their existence. Similarly, terrorist organizations pick targets likely to inspire the greatest possible fear in the larger communities. Meanwhile, counterterrorism organizations seek ways to prevent entities such as the Islamic State from recruiting in their countries the kind of followers that Robespierre found throughout France to enforce his rule.

Joseph R. Rudolph Jr.

See also: Evolution of Terrorism; Psychology of Terrorists; Sociology of Terrorism.

FURTHER READING

Andress, David. 2006. *The Terror: The Merciless War for Freedom in Revolutionary France*. New York: Farrar, Strauss, & Giroux.

Charles Rivers Editors. 2012. *Decisive Moments in History: The Reign of Terror*. Ann Arbor, MI: Charles River Editors Digital Publication.

Robespierre, Maximilien. 2007. *Robespierre: Virtue and Terror*. Edited by Jean Ducange and translated by John Howe. London: Verso.

Tackett, Timothy. 2015. *The Coming of Terror in the French Revolution.* Cambridge, MA: Belknap Press.

Returnees from Wars and Refugees as Terrorist Threats

The fear of a terrorist threat to the West, and to Western European countries in particular, from foreign terrorist fighters (FTFs)—that is, Muslim Europeans returning from foreign wars—has been present at least since Osama bin Laden founded al-Qaeda and summoned volunteers to fight the Russian army that invaded Afghanistan on December 24, 1979.

The ethnic civil wars in the Balkans, beginning less than three years after the 1989 Russian withdrawal from Afghanistan, kept those fears current, especially when news circulated of the atrocities committed by jihadists fighting on behalf of Bosnia's Muslim community. The struggle for independence of Kosovo's 90 percent Albanian Muslim province in Serbia then began almost immediately after the late 1995 settlement of the war in Bosnia, eventually leading to a successful 1999 NATO bombing campaign on behalf of the province's autonomy, keeping very much alive the fear that the return of Europe's volunteer jihadists from these wars would spike terrorist activity in Britain, France, and other Western European countries containing unassimilated second- and third-generation Muslim minorities disproportionately occupying the lower rungs of their socioeconomic ladders and already being courted by Islamic extremists.

In fact, when homegrown terrorism emerged in Britain in the early years of the twenty-first century, the perpetrators only occasionally came from lower socioeconomic groups or men seasoned in foreign wars. Rather, the terrorists tended to be young, middle-class, and motivated by a resentment that because of their origins, they were not being accorded proper respect by their host populations. For example, one of the quartet that carried out the 2004 bombings of London's mass transit system was a widely respected European soccer player, and the two men whose car rammed the Glasgow airport in 2007 were a British-born doctor of Iraqi descent and an engineer. Likewise, the lethal Madrid train bombings in 2005 did not involve Spanish-born Muslims but were carried out by a Moroccan group in suspected collaboration with non-Islamic Spaniards.

A decade later, the threat was back, different, real, and with two prongs as a result of the continued wars in the Syria-Iraq axis as well as in Asia (Myanmar) and Africa (Libya and Sudan). The principal thread was the familiar one. An estimated 5,000 Europeans volunteered to fight for the Islamic State in Iraq and Syria (ISIS) among the estimated 42,000 FTFs who went to Syria and Iraq. Of these, 30 percent are expected to try to return but different in nature from those fighting in the prior wars in Afghanistan and the Balkans. The appeal of ISIS was not to help Muslims elsewhere achieve self-government as much as a promise of brides, booty, and the chance to kill, including other Muslims who were not adhering to the "true faith." Moreover, once arrived, those for whom the call had appeal were often subjected to a thorough indoctrination process unknown in the prior wars on behalf of foreign Muslim peoples.

When ISIS later began to lose territory, what has been called a "terrorist diaspora" resulted, with the fighters going home or elsewhere. In addition to the Europeans who traveled to fight for ISIS representing a terrorist threat themselves, there is concern that with their combat experience they may also be dangerous as mentors to Europe's younger homegrown terrorists. Moreover, although returnees to date lag behind in terms of the number of attacks committed by local homegrown violent extremists (HVEs) within EU member states, they have been part of such infamous terrorist attacks as the 2016 bombings in Brussels' airport and metro station and the 2017 terrorists attacks in Paris. To cope with the danger they pose, Eurojust (the EU agency for judicial cooperation in criminal matters) has recommended they be prosecuted cumulatively for war crimes, genocide, murder, and crimes against humanity.

There is also a second threat emanating from the same region: the more than two million refugees who have fled to Europe from ISIS-controlled territories and the continued fighting elsewhere, the majority seeking asylum in the countries where they have settled. Beyond the danger that within these numbers may be terrorists posing as asylum seekers, there is the danger that these mostly unattached males, young and bitter over their losses, may be both a source of violent crime and a pool of potential recruits vulnerable to Internet radicalization if left idle.

Joseph R. Rudolph Jr.

See also: al-Qaeda; Islamic State, The; Recruiting Terrorists; War on Terror: Afghanistan and Pakistan.

FURTHER READING

Gurski, Phil. 2016. *The Threat from Within: Recognizing Al Qaeda–Inspired Radicalization and Terrorism in the West.* London: Rowman & Littlefield.

Gurski, Phil. 2017. *Western Foreign Fighters: The Threat to Homeland and International Security.* London: Rowman & Littlefield.

Middle East Monitor. 2020. "Eurojust Calls for Daesh Returnees to Be Charged with War Crimes." May 26, 2020. https://www.middleeastmonitor.com/20200526-eurojust-calls-for-daesh-returnees-to-be-charged-with-war-crimes/

Orr, Conrad E. 2017. "The Terrorist Diaspora, Its Returnees, and Disrupting the Rise of Homegrown Violent Extremists." *Small Wars Journal*, September 6, 2017. https://smallwarsjournal.com/jrnl/art/the-terrorist-diaspora-its-returnees-and-disrupting-the-rise-of-homegrown-violent-extremist

Ruby Ridge Standoff

August 21–31, 1992

Ruby Ridge is a small rock formation in far northern Idaho near Naples, where U.S. marshals tried to arrest survivalist Randy Weaver on August 21, 1992. Weaver had failed to appear in court to face a charge of selling two shotguns whose barrels were half an inch shorter than allowed by law to an undercover informant for the Bureau of Alcohol, Tobacco and Firearms (ATF). Weaver claimed never to have received the court notice at his mountain cabin, where he lived with his wife,

Vicki; a friend, Kevin Harris; four children, and a dog. When the marshals came upon Harris, Weaver, and his fourteen-year-old son, Sammy, one of them shot the dog, which prompted Sammy to fire back. An exchange of fire left Sammy and U.S. Marshal Michael Degan dead.

A standoff ensued, and an FBI hostage team joined the ATF. The next day, FBI sniper Lon Horiuchi wounded Weaver and Harris outside the cabin. As they attempted to get back inside, Horiuchi then inadvertently killed Vicki Weaver, who was holding the door open for them. Thus began an eleven-day siege that generated intense publicity and hundreds of spectators. It ended when a retired army colonel, Bo Gritz, who had considerable support throughout the mountain west, convinced Harris, Weaver, and his surviving children to surrender on August 31.

This controversial standoff generated a nationwide debate on the use of force by federal law enforcement. It is claimed by some to have catalyzed the birth of militia organizations such as the Montana Freemen and the sovereign citizen movement. It certainly encouraged narratives that the federal government was out to subvert the Second Amendment of the U.S. Constitution and to get people's guns by any means necessary.

Upon his later trial for many charges, including murder, Harris was acquitted of all charges in an Idaho court, and Weaver was only convicted of the original failure to appear and bail violation for the arms charges. The Weavers later won civil judgments against the government for excessive use of force and were awarded $3.1 million in damages, and Harris was awarded a $380,000 settlement in September 2000. A U.S. Senate panel accused the federal agencies of "substantial failures" in 1995 and noted parallels with an even larger disaster in 1993 in Waco, Texas, where four federal agents and seventy-six other people, including twenty-five children, died.

Today, the Ruby Ridge case is an exercise for FBI trainees on how not to do law enforcement in rural areas. It illustrates delicate balances in appropriate use of force and shows how hundreds of new, armed opponents can be generated by trying to arrest one minor scofflaw. Twenty-two years later, in 2014, another western family headed by Cliven Bundy of southeast Nevada attracted hundreds of armed supporters to drive off federal agents from the Bureau of Land Management (BLM) who were confiscating cattle from BLM land due to failure to pay grazing fees by the Bundy family.

The practical lesson from Ruby Ridge for efforts to combat terrorism worldwide is that excessive uses of force against citizens can increase the numbers who are willing to take up arms against governments and decrease the political legitimacy of law enforcement among millions of onlookers in the Internet age, where vivid images can quickly be available worldwide.

Michael Andregg

See also: Armed Militias; Montana Freemen Siege; Waco Standoff.

FURTHER READING

Britannica, Editors of Encyclopedia. 2021. "Ruby Ridge." *Encyclopedia Britannica*, May 6, 2021. https://www.britannica.com/event/Ruby-Ridge-incident

Goodman, Barak, dir. 2017. *American Experience*. Season 29, episode 5, "Ruby Ridge." Aired February 14, 2017, on PBS. http://www.pbs.org/wgbh/americanexperience/films/ruby-ridge/

History.com Editors. 2010. "Shootings at Ruby Ridge." History, February 9, 2010. https://www.history.com/this-day-in-history/incident-at-ruby-ridge

U.S. Department of Justice. 1994a. *Department of Justice Report Regarding Internal Investigation of Shootings at Ruby Ridge, Idaho, during Arrest of Randy Weaver*. https://www.scribd.com/document/17106356/DOJ-Report-on-the-Internal-Investigation-of-the-Shooting-at-Ruby-Ridge

U.S. Department of Justice. 1994b. *Report of the Ruby Ridge Task Force to the Office of Professional Responsibility of Investigation of Allegations of Improper Governmental Conduct in the Investigation, Apprehension and Prosecution of Randall C. Weaver and Kevin L. Harris*. June 10, 1994. https://www.justice.gov/sites/default/files/opr/legacy/2006/11/09/rubyreportcover_39.pdf

Rudolph, Eric Robert

1966–

Often referred to as the Centennial Olympic Park bomber because of the site of the most famous of his four attacks, which took place during his 18-month (August 1996–January 1998) run as a homegrown bomber, Eric Rudolph took the lives of 3, injured more than 150 others, and—as collateral damage—shattered the life of another.

Born in Florida on September 19, 1966, and only twenty-nine years old when his bomb detonated on July 27, 1996, at the Summer Olympic Games held in Atlanta, Eric Rudolph spent his teenage years with his mother in Nantahala, in western North Carolina's Macon County. A high school dropout, he joined the army after obtaining his GED and received specialized training in the Air Assault School at Fort Campbell, Kentucky, before being discharged in 1989 for marijuana use. By then, Rudolph was already forming what the head of the FBI office in Charlotte, North Carolina, later described as his own ideology, weaving together borrowed ideas with his own prejudices against the open practice of gay lifestyles and the "murder" of children by abortionists.

The latter beliefs provided his justification for his four bombings: the one in Atlanta to embarrass the United States for its policies condoning abortion and homosexual lifestyles, which led to 2 deaths and injured over 100; the January 29, 1998, bombing of the New Woman All Health Care Clinic in Birmingham, Alabama, which killed an off-duty police officer working as a security guard; and two bombings in Georgia in 1997 (an abortion clinic and a gay club) that collectively injured another fifty people. In the time between the Atlanta and Birmingham blasts, however, blame for the Centennial Olympic Park bombing had focused on Richard Jewell, a security guard at the park whose life was essentially ruined by government investigators and the media reporting of both that investigation and his personal life.

Jewell was not formally cleared of the crime until a captured Eric Rudolph confessed to it in 2003, but the Birmingham bombing both shelved ruminations about his guilt and led to Rudolph being placed on the FBI's Ten Most Wanted Fugitives list in May 1998, complete with a million-dollar reward offered for information leading to his arrest. Forensic evidence gathered in Birmingham was subsequently linked to the Olympic Park bombing. Meanwhile, a couple having coffee the morning of the Birmingham attack had observed Rudolph behaving suspiciously, followed him, noted his license plate number, and provided that information to investigating personnel.

Lone-wolf terrorists are invariably the most difficult to anticipate as well as capture, and Rudolph was no exception to this rule. Once sought, he retreated to the wooded mountains of western North Carolina that he knew, and for five years he eluded the combined forces of the local, state, and federal agents hunting him. His apprehension itself was a matter of luck: a rookie policeman, making his early morning rounds on May 31, 2003, spotted him foraging in a dumpster behind a grocery store in Murphy, North Carolina.

Charged on October 14, 2003, it was not until April 8, 2005, that it was announced that he had avoided execution by agreeing to plead guilty to the Birmingham and Atlanta bombings—but still insisting that abortion is murder, and force is justified to stop it.

Rudolph was sentenced on July 18, 2005, to four consecutive life sentences without possibility of parole. He remains in a federal maximum-security prison in Colorado.

Joseph R. Rudolph Jr.
(No relation to Eric Rudolph)

See also: Army of God; Centennial Olympic Park Bombing; Profiling.

FURTHER READING

Eastwood, Clint, dir. 2019. *Richard Jewell.* Burbank, CA: Warner Bros. Entertainment.

FBI. n.d. "Eric Rudolph: FBI Ten Most Wanted Fugitive." https://www.fbi.gov/history/famous-cases/eric-rudolph

NPR. 2005. "Full Text of Eric Rudolph's Confession." April 14, 2005. https://www.npr.org/templates/story/story.php?storyId=4600480

Rosenwald, Michael S. 2019. "The Furious Manhunt for Eric Rudolph, Who Almost Got Away with the Olympic Park Bombing." *Washington Post*, December13, 2019.

Rudolph, Eric Robert. *Between the Lines of Drift: Memoirs of a Militant.* http://www.armyofgod.com/EricRudolphBetweentheLines_.html

Vollers, Maryanne. 2006. *Lone Wolf: Eric Rudolph: Murder, Myth, and the Pursuit of an American Outlaw.* New York: Harper.

S

San Bernardino Attack

December 2, 2015

On December 2, 2015, fourteen persons were killed and another twenty-two were injured during an active shooter attack at the Inland Regional Center (IRC) in San Bernardino, California. The attack was classified by the Federal Bureau of Investigation (FBI) as a terrorist incident. Unlike most active assailant incidents, there were two perpetrators who fled before police arrived, both of whom were killed in a shootout later the same day.

The IRC facility is operated by a nonprofit organization that serves people with developmental disabilities. On the day of the attack, the San Bernardino County Environmental Health Department was using an IRC conference room for a training program. The attack was committed in this conference room and on the exterior of the building, with casualties at both locations. At 10:58 a.m., shooting began outside the building, and shortly thereafter, one masked shooter entered the conference room, followed by a second. In addition to their attack with firearms, the assailants left behind improvised explosive devices. Police officers began to arrive on the scene within six minutes of the shooting, but by that time, the assailants had fled in a black SUV. Witnesses at the scene identified a coworker as a possible suspect.

Law enforcement agencies released information about the SUV to the media and public and received several calls about possible sightings. One caller reported the license plate number of a suspicious vehicle, which was traced to a rental car company. The company reported that the vehicle had been rented to the suspect identified by witnesses. A team of police officers in unmarked cars responded to the suspect's address and observed an SUV leaving the property. At 3:09 p.m., following a brief pursuit, the SUV stopped on a public street, and its two occupants engaged police in a gunfight. Both occupants of the vehicle were killed, and two officers sustained injuries.

The incident was unusual in two ways. According to data from Advanced Law Enforcement Rapid Response Training (ALERRT) at Texas State University, based on an analysis of 347 known active assailant attacks from 2000 through 2019, 98 percent of incidents are committed by one attacker, and in only 12 percent of cases do offenders flee the scene prior to police arrival. The likelihood of a multiattacker incident in which the offenders flee the scene is a rare event, but one for which law enforcement agencies must be prepared.

Investigations by the FBI led them to conclude that the attack was an act of terrorism. Evidence indicated that the offenders, Syed Rizwan Farook, born in Chicago, and his Pakistan-born wife, Tashfeen Malik, had been radicalized as adherents to Islamic State ideologies. Intelligence gathering and threat assessment protocols must recognize that offenders may plan active assailant incidents as a form of terrorist attack. Likewise, investigative protocols must cue investigators to consider terrorism as a motive when active assailant incidents occur, which may require collaborative investigative efforts with federal agencies.

Identifying terrorism as the motive brought the case under the FBI's purview. One publicized aspect of the investigation was a dispute with Apple Inc., as the FBI sought the company's assistance in accessing information on a passcode-protected iPhone that belonged to one of the suspects. Apple challenged a court ruling ordering them to do so, but legal proceedings were dropped when the FBI was able to access the phone with assistance from an unspecified third party. As investigations continue to rely on evidence from electronic platforms, technologies permitting retrieval and analysis of such data will remain important while also potentially generating conflict between the values of privacy and security. The courts will likely become the arbiters of these disputes.

Stephen Owen

See also: Active Shooter Scenarios; Homegrown Terrorism; Recruiting Terrorists.

FURTHER READING

Advanced Law Enforcement Rapid Response Training. n.d. "ALERRT Active Attack Data." Accessed July 25, 2020. https://www.activeattackdata.org/allattacks.html

Braziel, Rick, Frank Straub, George Watson, and Rod Hoops. 2016. *Bringing Calm to Chaos: A Critical Incident Review of the San Bernardino Public Safety Response to the December 2, 2015, Terrorist Shooting Incident at the Inland Regional Center*. Washington, DC: Office of Community Oriented Policing Services. https://www.justice.gov/usao-cdca/file/891996/download

Nagourney, Adam, Salman Masood, and Michael Schmidt. 2015. "Killers Were Long Radicalized, F.B.I. Investigators Say." *New York Times*, December 7, 2015. https://www.nytimes.com/2015/12/08/us/fbi-says-san-bernardino-assailants-were-radicalized.html

September 11, 2001, Attack on America

The weaponizing of four hijacked airliners on September 11, 2001, to attack targets in New York City and Washington, DC, led to the single-deadliest terror attack in history. The subsequent political and military responses dramatically transformed American foreign policy and counterterrorism strategies. As noted at the time, the United States shifted from a secure 911 world, in which a simple phone call could bring whatever help was needed, to an uncertain 9/11 world—a world characterized by unpredictable violence and the need to develop new strategies for combating terrorism.

Planning for the attacks began as early as 1995, when Khalid Sheikh Mohammed (KSM) envisioned hijacking airplanes for direct attacks. When he and Osama bin Laden, the leader of the jihadist organization al-Qaeda, met in Afghanistan in 1996, they brought together ideological fervor, financial resources, and calculated planning. Bin Laden declared a fatwa against the United States, condemning it for supporting Israel, oppressing Muslims across the world, and stationing troops in Muslim lands. He also vigorously opposed any Arab government that cooperated with the United States, especially the Saudi leaders who permitted the sacrilege of allowing infidel troops on the holy peninsula of Arabia. The plotters hoped to humiliate the United States, compel an American withdrawal from the Middle East, and possibly initiate an apocalyptic struggle for Islam.

THE ATTACK

The four flights chosen by the attackers were, in order of their takeoff and crash times, American Airlines Flight 11, Boston to Los Angeles; United Airlines Flight 175, Boston to Los Angeles; American Airlines Flight 77, Washington, DC, to Los Angeles; and United Airlines Flight 93, Newark to San Francisco. The terrorists chose transcontinental flights because the planes would be carrying a large quantity of fuel.

Soon after their takeoffs, the nineteen terrorists, several of whom had received pilot training at American flight schools, used knives and box cutters to attack the crews and force their way into the cockpits. The targets for Flights 11 and 175 were the north and south towers of the World Trade Center (WTC), respectively. Both towers soon collapsed, killing over 2,000 occupants and first responders. The hijackers chose the WTC both for its literal and symbolic value as a center of American commercial power.

Flight 77 smashed into the Pentagon, a direct strike at the center of the U.S. military. Flight 93 was heading to Washington, DC. But by the time the hijackers had taken control of this flight, the passengers were aware of what had happened to other flights through cell phone conversations with family members. Consequently, the passengers rushed the cockpit, forcing a struggle that caused the hijackers to crash the plane near Shanksville, Pennsylvania. This courageous act most likely saved the U.S. Capitol from attack.

The total number of confirmed initial deaths of crews, passengers, civilian and military building occupants, and first responders was 2,974 (excluding the nineteen attackers), though the number has increased to 2, 977 because of subsequent deaths caused by exposure to hazardous particles and other injuries. Tracking those who survived the attacks as well as first responders who had worked amid the debris has led some to argue for including several thousand others who died years later from cancer or other illnesses in the total. Further, millions witnessed the attacks directly or watched on live television. This extraordinary media coverage helped promote al-Qaeda, and the violence also led to significant psychological trauma for many Americans.

FAILURES AND BREAKDOWNS PRIOR TO TAKEOFF

The attacks were daring, well funded, and well coordinated. They represented a transnational effort involving years of planning that was grounded in a powerful ideology capable of instilling a willingness to die for a cause. Despite extraordinary efforts by many on the day of the attacks, American counterterrorist plans and procedures were not prepared for events of this complexity and magnitude.

Relatively lax immigration standards allowed all but one of the terrorists to enter the country without difficulty. Another jihadist, Zacarias Moussaoui, had been arrested that August due to suspicious behavior during flight training, but the FBI did not investigate his activities extensively due to legal limitations and problems with intelligence sharing.

At the local level, airport screening proved inadequate, perhaps even incompetent. Several of the hijackers were flagged by the existing prescreening system, but this only meant that the airlines waited until they were confirmed aboard the planes before they loaded their checked bags. One hijacker was allowed to proceed despite not having any photo identification. Several carry-on bags set off alarms on x-ray machines, but the screeners (who were provided by private companies hired by the airlines) either just passed the bags on through other machines or waved metal detection wands over their bodies before allowing the attackers to proceed.

At the national level, military and civilian counterterrorist experts had considered the possibility of terrorists using a commercial jet as an attack vehicle, but their thinking focused on the delivery of a lethal payload stowed aboard the plane rather than the possibility of weaponizing the planes themselves. Strategic planning assumed that planes would not seek to hide themselves on approach to a target. Similarly, officials did not anticipate the fact that complicated chain-of-command communications would inhibit an effective real-time response.

Further, officials had not planned appropriately for a coordinated hijacking of multiple airplanes. Philippine authorities had prevented the 1995 Bojinka plot, also planned by KSM and also involving the destruction of multiple airliners, before it began. But whereas KSM learned from the mistakes of this plot as well as the 1993 WTC bombing (e.g., the unreliability of explosives), American intelligence seems not to have used the information gained from the Philippines adequately. In the months following the attacks, officials were criticized for failing to connect the dots and prevent the attack in advance. Critical pieces of information about al-Qaeda, a possible imminent attack, suspicious activities by individuals, and others were all known, but no one saw the complete picture. Diverse American intelligence agencies did not share information effectively (no one had all the dots), and even when relevant pictures emerged, accurate, actionable information was lacking.

DECISIVE PROBLEMS DURING THE ATTACKS

There were less than twenty-five minutes between the time when controllers in Boston were first aware of a hijacking and when the first plane crashed into the WTC. And the final crash took place less than an hour and twenty minutes after the first. Actions taken that morning underscored existing weaknesses for efficient responses to quickly developing terrorist attacks. Air traffic controllers, for example, struggled to track the actual locations of planes that had turned off their transponders.

As the planes made their ways to their targets, numerous communications took place involving American and United Airlines, local and national Federal Aviation Administration (FAA) controllers and officials, the North American Aerospace Defense Command (NORAD) and several military installations, and the White House. Establishing and confirming basic facts, such as how many planes were involved (there was concern that a Delta flight had also been targeted), took precious time. Officials depended on flight attendants and passengers calling the airlines and family members for critical information. Questions about formal authorizations and responsibilities also delayed responses. When the military finally scrambled jet fighters, it did not initially know where to send them. The unprecedented grounding of all nonemergency flights and the issuing of warnings to planes in the air was piecemeal, involving the airlines, local FAA officials, and then, finally, the FAA's national headquarters.

Communications problems likewise inhibited the work of many first responders in New York and may have contributed to some deaths; firefighters did not receive information about the police assessment of a likely tower collapse. Departments were using systems that could not communicate directly via radio with other departments, some communications infrastructure was destroyed in the attacks, and the sheer volume of transmissions overwhelmed some systems.

AMERICA RESPONDS: THE WAR ON TERROR

Following the attacks, Americans responded in numerous and decisive ways, including reforms to counterterrorist practices as well as new initiatives that transformed how the United States was to combat terrorism in the twenty-first century.

For many Americans, the flying of American flags and getting back to normal became pride-filled, community-building, patriotic statements. President George W. Bush encouraged Americans to not be overcome by terror and to go out shopping, just as before. Americans celebrated the return of baseball and football games after their initial cessation as a shared victory over terrorism.

On November 19, 2001, the Transportation Security Administration (TSA) was created by Congress, replacing private contractors at airports. New TSA protocols included greater restrictions on what passengers were allowed to bring aboard airplanes (e.g., no more small knives or box cutters), better screening procedures, and greater international, national, and local data sharing and analysis regarding potential terrorists. Limited commercial air traffic had resumed on September 13. Airplanes would come to have hardened cockpit doors, and crew training procedures for hijacking likewise evolved.

In the weeks after 9/11, President Bush created the Office of Homeland Security to develop and implement a nationwide strategy to prevent terrorist attacks. This office became the Department of Homeland Security on November 25, 2002, now the third-largest department in the cabinet, which oversees the work of the TSA, the Coast Guard, and the Secret Service, among others.

When Congress passed and President Bush signed the Authorization for the Use of Military Force (AUMF) on September 18, 2001, the American response shifted from immediate concerns about domestic safety to long-term changes in American foreign policy, military interventions, and counterterrorism strategies—collectively known as the *war on terror.*

On October 7, 2001, the United States and NATO allies attacked the Taliban in Afghanistan as punishment for their support of al-Qaeda, thus beginning what has been called America's longest war. The AUMF facilitated preemptive war, the doctrine that the United States would be justified in attacking targets before they had a chance to attack. It has been used to legitimate anti-terrorist military deployments in the Philippines, Yemen, Somalia, and other countries. A second AUMF in 2002 authorized the invasion of Iraq to prevent Saddam Hussein from using weapons of mass destruction.

On October 26, 2001, Congress passed the USA PATRIOT Act (or Patriot Act) to enhance surveillance capacities by law enforcement agencies, increase punishments for terroristic activities, broaden what constitutes such activities, and improve communications between intelligence and law enforcement agencies. Further enhancements to intelligence gathering, coordination, and communication received impetus from the recommendations of the National Commission on Terrorist Attacks upon the United States (the 9/11 Commission). Changes included the establishment of the National Counterterrorism Center as well as the passage of the Intelligence Reform and Terrorism Prevention Act of 2004 (IRTPA), which created the position of director of national intelligence (DNI).

CONTROVERSIES

Controversies about the attacks and the war on terror began almost immediately. Some began to use the intelligence term for unintended consequences, *blowback*, to characterize al-Qaeda's actions as an understandable response to American foreign policy. The Patriot Act raised significant questions about how to sustain political liberties while providing effective counterterrorism protection.

Similarly, critics have raised concerns about securing prisoners from the war on terror in the military base at Guantánamo Bay as well as the use of torture and extreme interrogation techniques to extract information, practices that have significantly delayed the trials of KSM and other plotters. Some lament the ways in which the AUMF appears to have become a way for presidents to take military action without congressional approval or oversight.

Some scholars in the field of critical terror studies argue that the politicized usage of 9/11 as a decisive before/after world-changing moment serves only to legitimate American militarism. Although Saudi Arabia strengthened its oversight of religious charities following the attacks to restrict this method of funding terrorists, some still question the country's possible involvement in aspects of the attacks. Finally, many first responders and their families have been outraged by Congress's delays in providing long-term medical care for those who labored in the debris and toxic materials following the attacks.

Victoria L. Gustafsson and David Keck

See also: al-Qaeda; bin Laden, Osama; Intelligence Community, Adjustments to the Post-9/11 World; War on Terror: Afghanistan and Pakistan.

FURTHER READING

Bolton, M. Kent. 2008. *U.S. National Security and Foreign Policymaking after 9/11*. Lanham, MD: Rowman & Littlefield.

Calhoun, Craig, Paul Price, and Ashley Timmer, eds. 2002. *Understanding September 11*. New York: The New Press.

Crotty, William, ed. 2004. *The Politics of Terror: The U.S. Response to 9/11*. Boston: Northeastern University Press.

Elias, Barbara, ed. 2006. *Complete Air-Ground Transcripts of Hijacked 9/11 Flight Recordings*. National Security Archive Electronic Briefing Book No. 196. August 11, 2006. Accessed August 1, 2020. https://nsarchive2.gwu.edu/NSAEBB/NSAEBB196/index.htm

National Commission on Terrorist Attacks upon the United States. 2004. *The 9/11 Commission Report*. Accessed August 1, 2020. https://9-11commission.gov/report/

Roy Rosenzweig Center for History and New Media and American Social History Project/Center for Media and Learning. 2020. *The September 11 Digital Archive*. Accessed August 1, 2020. https://911digitalarchive.org/

Wright, Lawrence. 2006. *The Looming Tower: Al-Qaeda and the Road to 9/11*. New York: Knopf.

Single-Issue Terrorism

Single-issue terrorism is a form of extremism that seeks specific change regarding one or a select few political or social matters. Members of such organizations mainly come from radical sectors of voting or lobbying movements that are unable to achieve reform through traditional democratic political processes. Single-issue terrorism differs from religious or ideological terrorism in three distinct ways. First, its scope of grievances is extremely limited; that is, these groups do not seek comprehensive political restructuring. Second, associations identified as single-issue terrorists are not isolated to one particular sector of the political spectrum. And third, single-issue terrorists rarely target government offices or political officials to achieve their ends; rather, institutions or businesses are the source of their protests. Due to the difficulty of defining its exact parameters, other titles have been assigned to these activities, such as *subrevolutionary terrorism*, *issue group militancy*, *direct action*, and *special-interest terrorism*.

Well-known single-issue terrorism variants include eco-radicalism and animal rights activism. The Earth Liberation Front (ELF), Earth First! (EF!), and Greenpeace represent the former, while the Animal Liberation Front (ALF), the Animal Rights Militia (ARM), the Band of Mercy, and a group called Justice Department exemplify the latter. Other interest groups identified as single-issue terror organizations include extreme anti-abortion activists, most notably the American-based Army of God, and a handful of early twentieth-century suffragette movements, such as the Women's Social Political Union (WSPU) of Great Britain.

Single-issue terrorists employ a variety of nonviolent tactics for achieving their aims. Many of these are not directed toward people but property. Civil disobedience and vandalism typify most of these methods. Eco-activists, for example, implement approaches that include *tree sitting* (where activists occupy timberlands with the intent of delaying or disrupting deforestation efforts) and *ecotage* (the sabotage of land clearing equipment used by developers or loggers). Animal rights activists similarly destroy equipment used by companies involved in live experimentation and liberate animals from scientific testing and agricultural facilities.

On occasion, however, some members from each of these movements do resort to physical violence. For instance, beyond vandalism and intimidation, the Army of God committed numerous acts of assault, attempted murder, and murder in their targeting of abortion clinicians during the 1980s. Likewise, some suffragettes of the WSPU moved from hunger strikes and breaking the windows of symbolic targets to political bombing campaigns and arson when their nonviolent approaches proved fruitless.

Because of their limited goals, if single-issue terrorists' demands are met—as was the case of the radical suffragette movements—most such groups would necessarily cease to exist.

Andrew Tompkins

See also: Army of God; Domestic Terrorist Groups; Earth Liberation Front.

FURTHER READING

Monaghan, Rachel. 2000. "Single-Issue Terrorism: A Neglected Phenomenon?" *Studies in Conflict & Terrorism* 23 (4): 255–265.

Price, Eric. 2014. "Bibliography on Single-Issue Terrorism." *Perspectives in Terrorism* 8 (6): 123–129.

Smith, G. Davidson. 1990. *Combating Terrorism.* London: Routledge Press.

Teichman, Jenny. 1989. "How to Define Terrorism." *Philosophy* 64 (250): 505–517.

Wilkinson, Paul. 1986. *Terrorism and the Liberal State.* London: Macmillan Publishing.

Snowden, Edward

1983–

In 2013, Edward Snowden was a contractor working for the U.S. National Security Agency (NSA) as a subject matter expert on technology and cybersecurity. He became notorious by leaking information to the media about a highly classified NSA project code-named Prism as well as a number of other classified documents dealing with NSA eavesdropping on foreign government leaders and other matters.

Snowden worked for the U.S. intelligence community (IC) for seven years, first at the Central Intelligence Agency (CIA) and later as an employee of Dell Technologies and then Booz Allen Hamilton, which contracted him to the NSA. After stealing classified material, Snowden traveled to Hong Kong in late May 2013, where he first met with journalists from *The Guardian* and shared top secret documents with them. *The Guardian* first published some of the Snowden leaks on June 5, 2013, and Snowden disclosed that he was the source of the leaks on June 9. On June 23, the United States filed espionage charges against Snowden and requested that Hong Kong authorities detain him for extradition, but he evaded capture and traveled to Moscow, where the Russian government granted him political asylum. He was granted permanent residence in Russia in late 2020.

Many consider Snowden to be a traitor, and the U.S. warrant for his arrest on charges of espionage and theft of government property is still in effect. However, others consider him a hero who blew the whistle on the NSA's illegal surveillance of Americans and U.S. allies. Snowden has received awards for courage, integrity, and public service, and he was named the top global thinker of 2013 by *Foreign Policy* magazine. Today, he works on methods of enforcing human rights through the application and development of new technologies.

Snowden justifies his actions by explaining that he does not want to live in a world where there is no personal privacy and therefore no room for intellectual exploration and creativity. He remains convinced that Project Prism, which the Obama administration shutdown in 2015 amid public objections and unfavorable court decisions, posed an existential threat to democracy. Project Prism data mined massive amounts of information collected from telecommunications and social media companies in search of hidden patterns that might indicate that an individual was planning or engaging in acts of terrorism. The project's pattern recognition software used metadata to attempt to identify likely terrorists. The term *metadata* is most commonly explained as being "data about the data." For example, metadata are the time and place of a phone call (or email), the originating phone number and the number called, and so forth, rather than the identities of the persons involved and the content of their communication.

Opponents of Project Prism's data mining activities charged that the use of metadata violates Americans' privacy rights because the project conducted data searches without a proper search warrant. Critics also charged that IC data mining creates a slippery slope that leads toward a total surveillance state in which any claim to the existence of individual privacy is a mirage.

In addition to disclosing Project Prism, U.S. intelligence officials believe that Snowden downloaded and stole approximately 1.5 million classified files containing various U.S. government emails and other documents disclosing sensitive sources and methods of the IC. Snowden continues to periodically release documents from this extensive collection. They have revealed that the IC routinely intercepts the classified communications of its allies. Additionally, other documents contain U.S. government communications that are highly critical of foreign leaders, which has harmed U.S. relations with its allies to varying degrees.

William J. Lahneman

See also: Central Intelligence Agency; Director of National Intelligence; Federal Bureau of Investigation; Information Sharing Environment; National Security Agency.

FURTHER READING

Greenwald, Glenn. 2015. *No Place to Hide: Edward Snowden, the NSA, and the U.S. Surveillance State.* New York: Picador.

Greenwald, Glenn, Ewen MacAskill, and Laura Poitras. "Edward Snowden: The Whistleblower behind the NSA Surveillance Revelations." *The Guardian*, June 11, 2013. https://www.theguardian.com/world/2013/jun/09/edward-snowden-nsa-whistleblower-surveillance

MacAskill, Ewen. 2019. "Snowden." September 13, 2019. https://www.theguardian.com/us-news/ng-interactive/2019/sep/13/edward-snowden-interview-whistleblowing-russia-ai-permanent-record

Snowden, Edward. 2019. *Permanent Record.* New York: Metropolitan Books, Macmillan Publishers.

Social Media and Terrorism

According to *Oxford English Dictionary*, *social media* is "websites and applications that enable users to create and share content or to participate in social networking." DataReportal, an independent think tank, released its 2021 report in October stating social media is being utilized by 4.55 million people around the globe. This equates to almost two-thirds of the world's population and also reflects a 9.9 percent increase from the previous report (October 2020). Why do these numbers matter? How does this relate to terrorism?

The field of terrorism is anything but stagnant. It is constantly growing, evolving, and learning from its historical past as well as maximizing the synergy of current events. A strong contributor to the evolution of terrorism recently is the utilization of social media by extremist organizations to showcase their acts of aggression, recruit new members, and continuously raise critical funds for their organizations. Although originally reluctant to embrace technology over the last several years, there has been a significant shift to maximize the reachability of the cyber highway.

The shift over the last few decades to an open platform communication tool where the terrorist organizations control their narrative is imperative, especially in terms of radicalization. Information no longer needs to be vetted for it to reach the public. Facebook, Twitter, YouTube, and many others have vastly changed how the world receives information. Once rudimentary and low budget, we continue to see many groups that have very visually engaging social media sites that showcase well-edited videos, live chats, and many other aspects that are engaging and attractive, especially to the younger population, both domestically and internationally.

SOCAL MEDIA, TERRORISM, AND INTERGOVERNMENTAL ORGANIZATIONS

Extremist groups are not the only ones utilizing social media. Intergovernmental organizations have worked diligently to educate law enforcement, share resources, and assist in identifying and prosecuting possible terrorists. This did not happen overnight. It was not until 2017 when the Soufan Group shared with the United States and the United Kingdom, among others, that since the Syrian conflict began, the Islamic State in Iraq and Syria (ISIS) had recruited over 40,000 soldiers from approximately 110 countries. This caused great alarm within the global community and helped expedite the need for a coalition approach.

For example, in 2018–2019, Interpol launched its first joint project with the United Nations Counter-Terrorism Centre (UNCCT), which created and oversaw workshops for investigators in four main areas:

1. Detecting terrorist-related activities online
2. Collecting electronic records

3. Requesting e-evidence across borders through police-to-police cooperation
4. Engaging with the private sector to advance investigations by law enforcement agencies

These trainings assisted in enhancing participants' operational picture of what is needed to address recruitment mechanisms, propaganda, and other tools used by extremist organizations online.

What is critical is for us to have a direct pulse on the communication mechanisms utilized by extremists, to continue to assist local governments to identify high-risk groups within their own communities, and to seek answers to the questions we currently have as well as the questions we should be focusing on in the ever-changing dynamics of our field. For example, we know historically that "orphan node" (a lone wolf in one geographical area) makes radicalization difficult for the "core group." Will that be the case in five years? Will it be the case if COVID-19 continues to change how we engage as a society? Continuing to be vigilant and question what we know is critical in addressing what many believe is a persistent crisis.

Rachel E. McGinnis

See also: Islamic State, The; Sociology of Terrorism.

FURTHER READING

DataReportal. 2022. "Digital 2022: The World's Favourite Social Media Platforms." https://datareportal.com/reports/digital-2022-favourite-social-platforms

Farwell, James P. 2014. "The Media Strategy of ISIS." *Survival* 56 (6): 49–55. https://doi.org/10.1080/00396338.2014.985436

Gartenstein-Ross, Daveed. 2015. *Jihad 2.0: Social Media in the Next Evolution of Terrorist Recruitment.* Washington, DC: U.S. Senate.

Interpol. 2021. "Analysing Social Media." https://www.interpol.int/en/Crimes/Terrorism/Analysing-social-media

Klausen, Jytte. 2015. "Tweeting the *Jihad*: Social Media Networks of Western Foreign Fighters in Syria and Iraq." *Studies in Conflict and Terrorism* 38 (1): 1–22. http://www.tandfonline.com/doi/pdf/10.1080/1057610X.2014.974948

National Institute of Justice. 2017. "The Role of Social Media in the Evolution of Al-Qaeda-Inspired Terrorism." September 5, 2017. https://nij.ojp.gov/topics/articles/role-social-media-evolution-al-qaeda-inspired-terrorism

Sociology of Terrorism

Explanations of terrorism are grounded within the basic elements of sociology: functionalism, symbolism, and conflict. Throughout history, each of these sociological concentrations consisted of significant and diverse elements influencing ideology and doctrine. These influences are present and often deeply rooted in diverse populations and how people interact with one another. Applying this well-founded sociological approach to understanding terrorism has allowed practitioners and academics to continue to develop the necessary mindsets needed in addressing these phenomena. Predicting the behavioral changes of any given population is a nearly impossible task. Awareness of individual and larger social behavioral changes, and how these changes expand in followers, is key to mitigating terrorism.

Structure and functionality of a population are perhaps the most tangible elements of societies. Norms, traditions, socioeconomic status, school systems, and institutions collectively provide a broad view of a population's structural function and ability to thrive. Consider your neighborhood or community. Your family and friends have proclaimed days of celebration with symbols of patriotism and Western culture. Labor Day picnics, fireworks on the Fourth of July, and family dinners on Thanksgiving Day are meaningful traditions and norms to most. This is not the case in all cultures. Rigid thinking and differing cultural beliefs can create a "cultural tightness" that often encourages like-minded others to participate in terrorist behavior. In this type of culture, its members celebrate extremism and violence as their norms and traditions. For decades, Palestinians and Israeli extremists have celebrated acts of terrorism against each other with music, dancing and brandishing weapons in the street, just as your family might celebrate a graduation or birthday, even calling them "hate fests."

In many societies, structural social layers, such as those previously mentioned, are intentionally limited to individuals in power with radical ideologies. For instance, gender inequality can drastically impact structure functionality by preventing women and homosexuals from participating in or holding any status at home or in the workplace. An extreme or radical society might celebrate the killing of certain groups in an effort to flatten the structure and maintain power. Socioeconomic differences exist as well. Your own high school more than likely consisted of a range of students: those with great family wealth, middle-class students, and students whose families struggled financially. This diversity can be expanded even further by classifying the education of your parents and siblings, the jobs they maintained, and the salaries they earned. Specific high school location, quality of teachers, modernization of technology, athletic programs, and parental involvement are all useful in evaluating a population's functionality.

At the time of this writing, the structural functionality of several metropolitan areas throughout the United States and globally are being challenged. Members of organizations like Antifaschistische Aktion (Antifa) and Black Lives Matter (BLM) have protested at city and federal buildings, rioted in the streets, occupied city blocks, and in extreme cases, committed acts of terrorism and homicide. Systemic racism in policing and accusations of economic inequality hampered the functionality of these locales. When individuals perceive that their needs are being ignored by those in power, conflict will most likely occur. Norms, traditions, institutions, and equality are replaced with deviant alternatives. Institutions that were once held in high regard by society become adversaries, and the oppressed often become the new oppressors. This behavior can have lasting effects on fragile social structures.

Individuals, communities, and collective societies all symbolize facets of their cultures. Baseball, apple pie, the Pledge of Allegiance, the Bible, marriage, family, parenthood—the list goes on and on of Western cultural symbols. People, concepts, and places have been assigned value while other symbols are scorned, such as infidelity, racism, suicide, and violent behavior. The demonization of others' beliefs and symbols while celebrating one's own, whether it be gods, flags, gender, or even something as simple or benign as a handshake, could invoke extremism within radical groups. All societies, cultures, and subcultures have symbols unique to their belief systems, and some symbols overlap with neighboring societies.

The interactions of the people within these societies help to create symbols of importance as well as unimportance. Consider, for example, that in Western culture, women are permitted to choose their sexual partners, wear clothes that bare a significant amount of their bodies, and make decisions concerning reproduction. These are all symbols of freedom and are not only defended but celebrated by women around the world. In direct conflict with these symbols of freedom are arranged marriages and the forced wearing of hijabs or burkas (head, chest, or full-body coverings). In India and surrounding countries, bride burning is symbolized as payment for families unable to present dowries in marriage. It is easy to imagine how these practices could create conflict with those who oppose such behavior. That these extreme symbols of purity and value might create a catalyst to terrorism is not a stretch of the imagination.

Words and actions create languages. In turn, these words are assigned meaning and value that may only appeal to those directly associated with their origination. To better understand this, take the language of texting as an example. With the use of acronyms, cultural jargon, and revised use or nonuse of punctuation, a language for sharing ideas digitally now exists. Texting or emailing in all capital letters implies screaming, while "lol" is translated to "laughing out loud." Emojis of smiley faces, hearts, and hand waves have all been assigned specifically clear meanings when communicating electronically. Many of these abbreviations have even evolved into spoken language. Earlier generations of letter writing with the expectation of excellent penmanship, grammar, and spelling also have meaning, that of a lost art, romance, or nostalgia.

Now that you understand symbolism and its place in social structures, it is important to understand how terrorism might manifest as a product of conflicts between what one society perceives as valued above all while another perceives it as meaningless. Rituals belonging to white supremacists, such as neo-Nazism, apartheid, homophobia, and anti-Semitism, exemplify extreme symbolic interactionism. These rituals are viewed as immoral and often legislated against by the general population in traditional Western cultures. In Russia, many of these rituals are not only condoned but legal. Although Russia shares the "Western" designation with the United States and Europe, Russia does not share the same symbolic ideology. These differences in social structures and symbolism are precursors for terroristic behaviors when members of societies perceive oppression or are forced to celebrate meaningless rituals or denounce the ones that they hold at high value.

Conflict was previously referred to many times for the simple reason that it is impossible to scrutinize any society without including it as a constant variable. Whatever the who, what, when, where, why, or how, the presence of conflict is embedded in all societies. Many of these conflicts embolden violent behavior, often leading to terroristic outcomes. Karl Marx's theory of conflict gave particular attention to social classes, capitalism, and what he considered a false consciousness—the disillusion that those who have amassed wealth have rightfully earned it. How social structures are created, by whom, the symbolism within subcultures, and whether these structures are actually functional can lay the foundations for not only radicalization but also the readiness of a society's members to carry out terroristic violence. Extreme social construction of any ideology can evolve into radicalization in an effort to either preserve a particular social structure or to force change.

Competition between groups over limited resources such oil, water, food, favorable climates, security, land, power, and weapons has been the root cause of terrorism around the world. Many regions experience these shortages or threats with overlapping, dysfunctional structures within their societies. The United States is not the only recipient of terrorism. As recently as the fall of 2019, more than half of the Saudi Arabian oil fields were attacked. These attacks by people believed to be Iranian terrorists forced oil prices to skyrocket for people around the globe who depend on the unproduced and undersupplied oil.

Intangible resources are favorable climates and power. Favorable climates have sound and functional structures that provide education, security, food, employment, equality, housing options, dependable transportation, and potential growth. So, what does the climate have to do with any of these things? When extreme climate changes occur, floods, storms, mudslides, and fires can deplete or completely eliminate resources for thousands of people. Power is exerted against those without the financial or physical ability to acquire scarce resources. Droughts occur, and agriculture suffers; crops yield small amounts or simply die. When education is not symbolized as a priority within certain demographics, technology and adequate housing will most likely be difficult to achieve. Chaos ensues within social structures such as these, and a disorganization or dysfunction begins to eat away at a society's functionality. Deprivation becomes the new normal, and the desire to have what others possess often leads to terroristic violence.

Religious and political conflicts are as old as time; recall the Crusades in 1096, when religious and hidden political agendas created several battles between Muslims, Christians, and Jews for well over 1,100 years. More recently, the violence continues between Israelis and Palestinians over whom should occupy the Holy Land. Terrorist attacks in Paris in 2015 left over 130 dead and several hundred wounded as a result of conflicting religious beliefs and secular retaliation. Islamic State terrorists attacked Paris in multiple locations, targeting what they deemed as the "center of prostitution and obscenity" and as retaliation for France's air strikes against Muslims in a caliphate.

Divides among socioeconomic classes, political groups, and subcultures are also responsible for breakdowns in social structures. Political subcultures like Antifa, BLM, white supremacists, pro-life or pro-choice advocates, and members of the LGBTQ community have either been recipients of or contributors to domestic terrorist violence in the United States and around the world. In early 2020, Antifa was officially designated as a terrorist organization by the U.S. Department of Homeland Security as a result of the group's recent violent attacks on peaceful protestors, the arson and destruction of federal buildings, choreographed attacks on law enforcement officers, and physical assaults of news journalists.

Socioeconomic challenges play a major role in terrorism. According to the *Global Terrorism Index*, in 2012, the top ten poorest countries also experience the greatest amount of terrorism. Absent or limited resources by one group are almost always controlled by another more powerful group. Poverty is indicative of inadequate leadership or governing, education may be unobtainable, and security or safety is unrealistic. Individuals or groups with low social status and a lack of assets are perceived as more susceptible to radicalization and extreme ideologies out of desperation. Desperation and what Marx referred to in his conflict theory as a "false conscious" are played upon by terrorists as a means to recruit and further their causes with expendable people who are willing to espouse violence. Unemployment and poverty appear to be directly related to terroristic activity, just as we see increases in traditional crimes in society. As former secretary of defense and U.S. marine, retired general John Mattis profoundly observed in 2013, "If you don't fund the State Department fully, then I need to buy more ammunition ultimately."

Structures exist within societies, providing functionality and, in essence, keeping the machine of everyday life running. How functional a society is and how prone it may be to terroristic ideology can be relatively or quantitatively measured. As previously pointed out, poverty appears to have a direct impact on terrorism and radical ideological development. Certain socioeconomic classes who perceive or legitimately experience a removal or lack of resources are primed for charismatic leadership, which may present itself as terroristic and radical figures. Concepts or items that societies symbolize and hold in high esteem will lessen or increase the vulnerability to radicalization if they are offered as favorable replacements. Terrorism is not random violent behavior. It is a product of human interactions between social structure layers, such as cultures, subcultures, religions, political groups, gender, race, wealth, and education. The list is endless. Terrorism greatly differs from other sociological phenomenon in that extremists refuse to utilize legitimate pathways for change but rather invoke fear in populations through violent, indiscriminate means.

Pamela K. Mertens

See also: Antifa; Domestic Terrorism, Anarchists; Homegrown Terrorism; Recruiting Terrorists.

FURTHER READING

Baroud, Ramzy. 2020. "Why Does Israel Celebrate Its Terrorists? Ben Uliel and the Murder of the Dawabsheh Family." *Dissident Voice*, May 25, 2020.

Gelfand, Michele J., Gary LaFree, Susan Fahey, and Emily Feinberg. 2013. "Culture and Extremism." *Special Issue: Uncertainty and Extremism, Journal of Social Issues* 69 (3): 495–517. https://doi.org/10.1111/josi.12026

Institute for Economics and Peace. 2012. *2012 Global Terrorism Index: Capturing the Impact of Terrorism from 2002–2011.* Wilmington, DE: Institute for Economics and Peace.

Marx, Karl. 2009. *A Contribution to the Critique of Political Economy.* Translated by S. W. Ryazanskaya. Moscow: Profess Publishers. Originally published in 1859.

OECD. 2017. *Terrorism, Corruption and the Exploitation of Natural Resources.* October 2017. http://www.oecd.org/corruption/Terrorism-Corruption-Criminal-Exploitation-Natural-Resources-2017.pdf

Pauwels, Lieven, and Nele Schils. 2014. "Differential Online Exposure to Extremist Content and Political Violence: Testing the Relative Strength of Social Learning and Competing Perspectives." *Terrorism and Political Violence* 28 (1): 1–29.

Quentin. 2018. "'If You Don't Fund the State Department Fully, Then I Need to Buy More Ammunition Ultimately' James N Mattis, United States—Secretary Of Defense." DVC Consultants, November 8, 2018. https://dvcconsultants.com/if-you-dont-fund-the-state-department-fully-then-i-need-to-buy-more-ammunition-ultimately-james-n-mattis-united-states-secretary-of-defens/

Reynolds, Larry T., and Nancy J. Herman-Kinney, eds. 2003. *Handbook of Symbolic Interactionalism*. Walnut Creek, CA: AltaMira Press.

State Terrorism

Discussions of *terrorism* and *terrorists* typically center on non-state actors' violence against the state and its citizens. Some experts, however, posit the existence of *state terrorism*. This phenomenon manifests itself in numerous ways, all of which fall under what R. Hrair Dekmejian, a professor of political science at the University of Southern California and a recognized expert on global terrorism, calls "macro-terrorism," or terrorism perpetrated by or on behalf of the state.

State terrorism takes many forms and can be used against international or domestic targets. International objectives may be achieved through state sponsorship (e.g., funding, equipping, training) of non-state terrorist groups. Often considered a form of proxy war, states such as Libya, Iran, and the United States have all sponsored terrorist groups in the past. Domestically, state terrorism can take the form of genocide (targeting a social, ethnic, or religious group), politicide (killing real or perceived political enemies), counterterrorism efforts, the use of paramilitaries, and repression (e.g., torture, intimidation, imprisonment).

The twenty-first century has already witnessed several state-sanctioned genocides, including the Darfur genocide (South Sudan, 2003–2004) and the ongoing Rohingya genocide (Myanmar, since 2016) and Uighur genocide (China, since 2017). Politicides in modern memory include the infamous Soviet gulag system, China's Cultural Revolution, and President Erdogan's crackdowns against Turkish citizens allegedly involved in the failed coup of July 2016 in Turkey.

Counterterrorism campaigns are also often classified as state terrorism due to overzealous and unduly harsh policies, for example, the counterterrorism strategies of Israel (against Palestinian terrorists) and Nigeria (against Boko Haram). Paramilitary groups, death squads, and other state and non-state actors may also be employed by the state to commit acts of terrorism against noncombatant populations. The use of death squads has characterized state terrorism under many Latin American and Middle Eastern regimes.

American policies toward state terrorism have been mixed. The United States has, in some cases, refused to take substantive action against state terrorism, as in its failure to respond to the genocides in Rwanda (1994), Darfur (2003–2004), Myanmar (since 2016), and China (since 2017). On the other hand, it has long relied on the U.S. State Department's list of state sponsors of terrorism, which now carries with it a set of sanctions, although these have proven fairly ineffective.

The United States has also taken military action against states practicing or sponsoring terrorism (i.e., its use of force in Libya, Iraq, and the former Yugoslavia). Additionally, the United States has sponsored proxy forces in Syria and Libya, and in January 2020, it conducted a drone strike that killed Major General Qasem Soleimani, who was the leader of Iran's vaunted Quds Force and had been responsible for repressing dissent in Iran and abetting similar campaigns in Syria, Lebanon, and elsewhere in working against U.S. regional interests.

Some critics argue that the United States has itself engaged in state terrorism, citing, for example, the extrajudicial killing of Anwar al-Awlaki, an American citizen, via a 2011 drone strike in Yemen. The use of torture against captured alleged transnational terrorists during the war on terror likewise came under sharp scrutiny, and some maintain that the measures adopted as part of the USA PATRIOT Act (2001) provide too much power to the federal government in surveilling and detaining its citizens. Such concerns reemerged due to government responses to the Black Lives Matter protests in Portland, Oregon, and other cities in 2020.

Benjamin V. Allison

See also: Abu Ghraib Scandal; Criminal Organization Terrorism; Enhanced Interrogation Debate; Reign of Terror.

FURTHER READING

Blakely, Ruth. 2007. "Bringing the State Back into Terrorism Studies." *European Political Science* 6 (3): 228–235.

Blakely, Ruth. 2011. *State Terrorism and Neoliberalism: The North in the South.* New York: Routledge.

Claridge, David. 1996. "State Terrorism? Applying a Definitional Model." *Terrorism and Political Violence* 8 (3): 47–63.

Dekmejian, R. Hrair. 2006. *Spectrum of Terror.* Washington, DC: CQ Press.

Gareau, Frederick H. 2010. *State Terrorism and the United States: From Counterinsurgency to the War on Terrorism.* Atlanta: Clarity Press.

Sproat, Peter Alan. 1997. "Can the State Commit Acts of Terrorism? An Opinion and Some Qualitative Replies to a Questionnaire." *Terrorism and Political Violence* 9 (4): 117–150.

Stohl, Michael. 2006. "The State as Terrorist: Insight and Implications." *Democracy and Security* 2 (1): 1–25.

T

Taliban

The Taliban, from the Pashto *talib*, meaning "religious student," were the product of the Soviet invasion of Afghanistan in 1978. The reaction of the radicalized descendants of the refugees from the conflict and the Afghans frustrated by the country's lawlessness grew into an Islamic fundamentalist movement and militia that eventually assumed control of Afghanistan following the internecine warfare in the wake of the Soviet withdrawal. Closely allied with al-Qaeda, the Taliban refused to cooperate with NATO and turn over the leadership of that organization after the September 11, 2001, attacks. That decision led to the Western intervention in Afghanistan, becoming the seminal event in the war on terror and the geopolitics of the early twenty-first century.

Soviet warfare in Afghanistan resulted in millions of refugees, many of whom migrated to Pakistan where a network of religious schools, primarily organized on a fundamentalist Salafi interpretation of Islam, provided them with humanitarian assistance and ideological indoctrination. In September 1994, Mullah Mohammad Omar mobilized the frustration among that demographic over the lack of a theocratic state governed by a strict interpretation of the Islamic law and founded the Taliban as a political party and a militant organization.

Buoyed by popular frustration with the ongoing warlord violence and lawlessness engulfing Afghanistan following the Soviet withdrawal, by 1996, the Taliban controlled most of the country and had declared themselves the government of the new Islamic Emirate of Afghanistan. Support from Pakistan was instrumental in their success, and Taliban rule was characterized by determined efforts to return to what the group considered pure Islam, resulting in widespread human right abuses and damage to Afghanistan's historical heritage.

Throughout this period, the Taliban also established a close relationship with Osama bin Laden, who considered Afghanistan to be the only true Islamic country in the Muslim world. This relationship culminated in the Taliban providing al-Qaeda a safe haven within Afghanistan, which the terrorist group used to plan and execute its attacks in the United States on September 11, 2001.

Following the 9/11 attacks, the U.S. government presented an ultimatum to the Taliban that included a demand to surrender the leaders of al-Qaeda to the United States. Upon its refusal, an American-led coalition initiated hostilities. The military effort by local anti-Taliban forces, colloquially known as the Northern Alliance, supported by the CIA, U.S. Special Forces, and U.S. air support, resulted in the overthrow of the Taliban by December 2001.

The surviving leadership proceeded to reestablish bases in Pakistan and from there reconstituted itself as an insurgency with the avowed intent to expel American forces and reclaim control of Afghanistan. Throughout the following two decades, the insurgency grew precipitously, supported by the Pashtu tribes of the disputed border region and the southern provinces of Afghanistan as well as the stratum of the Afghan population that was disenchanted with the ineffectiveness and corruption of the central government.

The financial and material underpinnings of the insurgency relied on significant involvement in drug trafficking and support by the Pakistani intelligence agency, the ISI. Pakistan strongly disputes the latter accusation. By 2019, the Taliban controlled territory encompassing 10.8 percent of the Afghan population, and the U.S. government was engaged in persistent attempts to bring them to the negotiating table.

That process culminated in a February 2020 agreement between the Trump administration and the Taliban in which the latter pledged that Afghan soil would never again be used to support a threat to the security of the United States, and the United States agreed to the phased withdrawal of all American troops from Afghanistan. The following year, the Biden administration honored the second part of that pact, agreeing to withdraw all military personnel by August 31, 2021. By that date, the Taliban already controlled Kabul and all but a few small zones in the country.

In sum, the Taliban's central role in succoring al-Qaeda in the prelude to the terrorist attacks of 9/11 made it an integral actor in the central event of the twenty-first century, its transformation into a highly effective insurgency that engaged U.S. forces in the longest war in American history.

Daniel Stotland

See also: al-Qaeda; September 11, 2001, Attack on America; War on Terror: Afghanistan and Pakistan.

FURTHER READING

Brown, Vahid, and Don Rassler. 2013. *Fountainhead of Jihad: The Haqqani Nexus, 1973–2012*. New York: Oxford University Press.

Coll, Steve. 2018. *Directorate S: The C.I.A. and America's Secret Wars in Afghanistan and Pakistan*. New York: Penguin Press.

Moj, Muhammad. 2015. *The Deoband Madrassah Movement: Countercultural Trends and Tendencies*. London: Anthem Press.

Rashid, Ahmed. 2000. *Taliban: Militant Islam, Oil and Fundamentalism in Central Asia*. New Haven, CT: Yale University Press.

Targeted Assassinations

Assassination has been a tool of terrorists and governments for millennia. It has been an act of terrorists and nation-states in warfare since the formal *state* was invented. The term *assassin* probably comes from a group of Islamic enthusiasts formed in 1090 CE (the Nizari Ismalilis) that specialized in targeted killings of opponents. Assassinations differ from ordinary murders or killings on battlefields by the implication that the target has some special political importance. One famous assassination was when a nineteen-year-old Serbian named Gavrilo Princip killed Archduke Franz Ferdinand of Austria in Sarajevo in 1914, leading to World War I, which killed almost a tenth of all males in Central Europe.

In theory, the United States is prohibited from employing assassination as a tool of foreign policy by an executive order (No. 12333, United States Intelligence Activities) signed by Ronald Reagan in 1981. However, this did not prevent hundreds of attempts to kill political people, such as Anwar al-Awlaki in Yemen on October 14, 2011, or Abu Musab al-Zarqawi in Iraq on June 7, 2006, using Hellfire missiles. The United States also tried to assassinate Cuba's president Fidel Castro at least eight times (CIA records), perhaps as many as twenty-eight times (Cuba's estimate), during the Cold War. The assassination of President John F. Kennedy in 1963 raised questions about the wisdom of targeting national leaders.

The Russian government refined assassination to high art. It was connected to the murders of Georgi Markov in London on September 11, 1978, using the biological poison ricin, and of Alexander Litvinenko, using polonium 210 on November 23, 2006. Russia is also alleged to have poisoned Sergie Skripal and his daughter Yulia with a very sophisticated Novichok nerve agent on March 4, 2018.

But no state has a more diversified record of assassinations than Israel. Its Mossad intelligence agency decided to use this as a common tool in its long-running covert war against Palestinian organizations, a host of Islamic terrorist groups, and other declared enemies, such as Iran. Mossad killed many Iranian nuclear scientists, for example, using ordinary pistols and limpet mines attached to cars to slow down nuclear weapons development in Iran. Years before, Mossad set out to avenge the murders of eleven Israeli athletes at the 1972 Olympics by killing most of the Palestinians who had been involved in those assassinations.

This history is described in riveting detail in Ronen Bergman's *Rise and Kill First* (2018). That book is noteworthy because it was informed and endorsed by many of Mossad's former directors. A comprehensive view of targeted assassinations requires recognition that thousands of "targeted killings" have also been committed by various Arab *mukhabarat* (secret police and intelligence groups) in their countries and against enemies abroad. This business of spies killing spies (or generals or presidents of enemy entities) has a long and very complex history, obscured by the secrecy that attends such events.

Therefore, this section ends with downsides of such tactics revealed by this history. First, sometimes innocent people are killed because they are near the bomb or were incorrectly identified as targets, such as Ahmed Bouchikhi, killed by Mossad in Lillehammer, Norway, on July 21, 1973. Killing innocents has terrible public relations consequences. Second, if you kill able leaders of enemy groups, they may be replaced by less intelligent but more brutal others who push hatred harder and make peace negotiations impossible. Third, if one country adopts assassination as a tool of statecraft, its enemies may reply in kind, resulting in killings on both sides.

So, prudent leaders are warned about the perils of assassination, and all need special protection today from terrorists and many other rivals.

Michael Andregg

See also: al-Awlaki, Anwar; Domestic Terrorism, Anarchists; Psychology of Terrorists; State Terrorism.

FURTHER READING

Bergman, Ronan. 2018. *Rise and Kill First: The Secret History of Israel's Targeted Assassinations*. New York: Random House.

Cockburn, Alexander. 2009. "The CIA and a Long History of Assassinations." *The Week*, July 24, 2009. http://www.theweek.co.uk/politics/21051/cia-and-long-history-assassinations

Emerson Kent.com. 2018. "Assassinations in History—Chronologically." http://www.emersonkent.com/assassinations_in_history_chronologically.htm

Kahana, Ephraim. 2006. *Historical Dictionary of Israeli Intelligence*. Lanham, MD: Scarecrow Press.

Perliger, Arie. 2015. "The Causes and Impact of Political Assassinations." *CTC Sentinel* 8 (1): 11–14. https://ctc.usma.edu/the-causes-and-impact-of-political-assassinations/

Terrorism

Although having existed for centuries, in the last few decades, terrorism has become a global threat to the stability of governments and to the safety and security of citizens worldwide. Complicating both understanding terrorism and the issue of how to respond to and combat it is the fact that there is no international agreement or consensus on what terrorism is. Even within the United States, the State Department, the Department of Defense, and the Federal Bureau of Investigation offer slightly different definitions of it.

IDENTIFYING TERRORISTS

Despite this confusion and lack of international consensus on defining *terrorism*, it is still possible to identify some of its common features. First, terrorism is the threat of violence or the use of violence to achieve a political goal. Terrorists thus deliberately choose their targets with the expectation to further their political goals or objectives, unlike criminals who also commit acts of violence but have no political agenda and instead are motivated purely out of financial considerations. To be sure, terrorists also require money to operate, but for terrorists, money is a means to an end, not the end.

In addition, terrorists see themselves positively, as noble and virtuous, because they are allegedly fighting injustice and oppression, while they regard criminals negatively as the murderers and thieves that they are. Terrorist groups have, however, been known to engage in the counterfeiting of currency, engaging in various kinds of fraud, and growing and selling narcotics to fund their terrorist activities.

What makes terrorism seem morally wrong and arguably evil is that terrorists deliberately target civilians, who are by definition almost always unarmed and according to the laws of war known as the Geneva Conventions are considered noncombatants, meaning they cannot be lawfully attacked. Terrorists, however, often target civilians because they are not only easy targets but—perhaps more importantly—attacking them is likely to generate more attention and publicity than targeting government, police, and military personnel.

Moreover, because terrorists commit violence to promote a political agenda, they seek to instill fear into their enemy, and nothing provokes more fear than killing civilians in public places, such as airports, cafés and restaurants, hospitals, stores, and places of worship. By attacking civilians, terrorists aim to not only raise awareness of their cause but also to pressure the governments of the citizens to change their policies or accede to their demands, which could range from releasing jailed prisoners of the terrorist group to changing policies related to the cause or grievance the terrorist group is promoting or fighting. As such, terrorism is a form of blackmail.

BROAD TYPOLOGIES

There are two broad forms of terrorism: state terrorism committed by a state or government and non-state terrorism committed by a group or individual not part of a government. Support for terrorism can be covert (so as to enjoy plausible deniability) or overt or public, without any attempt to conceal a government's support for terrorism. Support or sponsorship of terrorism can include political support, providing financial or military assistance or training, or offering sanctuary. Political support would involve publicly endorsing or praising the actions and causes of a terrorist group, for example, Iran publicly defending or praising acts of violence by Hamas or Hezbollah against Israel as resistance against Israeli occupation and oppression. Iran also provides funds and weapons to Hamas and Hezbollah, has trained Hezbollah fighters, and is accused of providing sanctuary for Hezbollah in Iran.

Historically, terrorism has been committed by both states and non-state actors. Most dictatorships engage in some form of terrorism to suppress dissent and strike fear among the people, thereby reducing the risk of opposition and rebellion. Infamous examples of state terrorism include the "Great Purge" of the 1930s in the Soviet Union under Joseph Stalin; the Cultural Revolution under Mao Zedong in China; Idi Amin of Uganda's genocide against rival tribes; and the Rwandan genocide in 1994 of the Tutsi minority and dissenting Hutus.

In the last few decades, however, terrorism has become more often associated with non-state groups. Examples of such groups include the Islamic State (IS) and its affiliates; al-Qaeda and its affiliates; Hamas in the Gaza Strip; the Taliban in Afghanistan and Pakistan; Boko Haram in Nigeria; Hezbollah in Lebanon; Abu Sayyaf in the Philippines; ETA in the Basque region of Spain; and the FARC (Revolutionary Armed Forces of Colombia) in Colombia. These and many other groups may cross international boundaries to commit, plan, or fund terrorist acts. This has made international terrorism by non-state groups an important security issue for many countries around the world.

Perhaps the oldest example of a non-state terrorist group still around is the Ku Klux Klan (KKK). Founded in 1866 by former Confederate military officers, it very quickly began threatening and killing the freedmen—the newly freed slaves—to preserve white supremacy and fight any attempt at establishing racial equality in the South. So successful was the KKK in promoting its goals, in 1876, the U.S. government abandoned what became known as Reconstruction—the ten-year effort (1866–1876) to modernize the South's slave-based economy and promote racial equality in the South between whites and Blacks, almost all three million of whom had been slaves until 1865.

CONTEMPORARY TERRORISM

Terrorism today is most often associated with groups that engage in political violence against states and their citizens, usually to overthrow a government, or at the very least to change policies. For example, the attacks of September 11, 2001, by al-Qaeda were allegedly in retaliation for U.S. "crimes" in the Middle East and against Muslims and were designed to pressure or possibly force the U.S. government to change its foreign policy in the Middle East—namely, its support for Israel and Arab dictatorial states, particularly Saudi Arabia—and to close U.S. military bases in the region.

Setting aside lone-wolf terrorists, homegrown and otherwise, and the actions of domestic terrorist groups—both of which are treated elsewhere in this volume—more recent examples of (internationalized) terrorism include the actions by IS as it conquered vast parts of Iraq and Syria in 2014 and 2015 that have involved public broadcasting of it shooting, beheading, drowning, crushing by tanks, and burning alive dozens of hostages (including American, European, and Japanese journalists and aid workers) and at least hundreds of captured Iraqi and Syrian soldiers. Starting in 2013, but picking up pace as it started losing territory in 2015 to American and allied air strikes, IS also launched terrorist attacks around the world, from Australia to Turkey, killing thousands. These included the November 2015 terrorist bombings and shootings that killed 130 people in Paris; the June 2016 murder of 49 people at the Pulse nightclub in Orlando, Florida; the 86 people who died in Nice on Bastille Day 2016 when a truck was driven into the crowd; the April 2017 suicide bombings in two Egyptian churches the killed 46 people; and the May 2017 slaying of 22 people at a concert in Manchester, England, by a suicide bomber.

It is important to note that in the mind of the perpetrators, terrorism is not illogical or irrational but rather purposive, designed to achieve some political goal. In this sense, terrorism is rational, albeit not in the psychological sense of the word (rational as in having reason or understanding); instead, according to rational choice theory, the actions are designed to maximize stated objectives or goals. In short, if actions undertaken by terrorists further their goals or elicit the desired response, they are deemed rational. The March 2004 al-Qaeda bombings of Madrid commuter trains that killed 191 people and injured over 1,000 provides an example. The bombings occurred three days before parliamentary elections, suggesting al-Qaeda hoped to influence the result and possibly punish Prime Minister Jose Aznar for his support of President George W. Bush's 2003 invasion of Iraq and for having deployed some 1,300 Spanish troops in Iraq. Although it is not clear whether Aznar's Popular Party lost the election for these reasons, al-Qaeda's action was rational in that the attacks weakened the incumbent party, and the newly elected prime minister, Jose Zapatero, removed Spain's troops from Iraq.

Similarly, the Palestinian terrorist group Hamas (an Arabic acronym for "Islamic Resistance Movement") has yet to achieve its goal of destroying Israel, which it views as an illegal nation occupying Arab land, and in its place establishing an Islamic government in Palestine. However, it arguably did derail the 1993 Oslo Accords between Israel and the Palestine Liberation Organization (PLO) that called for a future Palestinian state. The series of suicide bombings by Hamas in the mid-1990s inside Israel primarily targeting buses, restaurants, and stores killed hundreds of Israelis, predictably soured Israeli public opinion on continued peace talks with the PLO, and caused the narrow election defeat of the Labor Party that had negotiated the Oslo Accords. The right-wing Likud Party was elected, and its candidate for prime minister, Benjamin Netanyahu, openly questioned the wisdom of the Oslo Accords and the idea of a future Palestinian state existing alongside Israel. Subsequently, the Oslo Accords have remained stalled.

Terrorism can also be inspired by secular (nonreligious) ideologies such as communism, nationalism/ethnic grievances, fascism, neofascism/neo-Nazism, environmentalism, animal rights activism, anarchism, racism, and other forms of prejudice or other ideological influences. Additionally, it can be motivated by religion, whether Christian, Jewish, Islamic, or other faiths, including obscure cults and sects. It is also possible that terrorism can be a mixture of both secular and religious motivations; for example, groups such as the KKK and American neofascists/neo-Nazis that espouse hatred toward a particular group, namely, Jews or people of color, also use motives from Christian narratives to justify their views and actions.

It is important to note that there is much international controversy and dispute over whether actions performed by a particular group even constitute terrorism. For this reason, the international community and many states are unable to agree on what terrorism is. The reason for this confusion and controversy associated with the definition of *terrorism* is political: some regard terrorism as acts of self-defense against oppression and injustice. Yasser Arafat, the late chairman of the PLO, said this before the United Nations in 1974:

> The difference between the revolutionary and the terrorist lies in the reason for which each fights. For whoever stands by a just cause and fights for the freedom and liberation of his land from the invaders, the settlers and the colonialists cannot possibly be called terrorist, otherwise the American people in their struggle for liberation from the British colonialists would have been terrorists; the European resistance against the Nazis would be terrorism, the struggle of the Asian, African and Latin American peoples would also be terrorism, and many of you who are in this Assembly hall were considered terrorists.

With similar thinking, Osama bin Laden justified the attacks of September 11, 2001, that killed almost 3,000 mostly American civilians on the basis that since the American people elect their leaders, they are ultimately responsible for the country's unjust and evil policies in the Middle East and against Muslims.

Finally, and further complicating the debate around international terrorism, there is the fact that terrorism and actions considered by others to be terrorism are often the tools of the weak or the weaker party in a political or military conflict or struggle. This is why, as noted at the outset, terrorists and those so labeled deliberately target civilians; they are an easier group to attack, and such attacks also generate far more attention and publicity not only for the victims but also, more importantly, for the terrorists and their cause than if they only attacked soldiers and police.

Stefan Brooks

See also: al-Qaeda; Hamas; Islamic State, The; Madrid Train Bombings and the War on Terror; Reign of Terror.

FURTHER READING

Hoffman, Bruce. 2017. *Inside Terrorism*. New York: Columbia University Press.
Horgman, John. 2014. *The Psychology of Terrorism*. New York: Routledge Press.
Law, Randall. 2016. *Terrorism: A History*. Cambridge, UK: Policy Press.
Martin, Gus. 2017. *Understanding Terrorism: Challenges, Perspectives, and Issues*. Thousand Oaks, CA: SAGE Publications.

Times Square Bombing Attempt

May 1, 2010

On the early evening of May 1, 2010, an attempted vehicle-borne improvised explosive device (VBIED) bombing of Times Square in New York City was averted when the device failed to fully detonate and alert passersby, who observed smoke emanating from the vehicle, notified NYPD officers. Bomb Squad technicians responded and rendered the device safe before an explosion could take place.

The explosive device, which consisted of a pressure cooker bomb, gunpowder, propane gas canisters, several hundred pounds of urea-based fertilizer, fireworks, and several gallons of gasoline, was secreted in a 1993 Nissan sports utility vehicle. Forensic analysis of the vehicle and motor vehicle registration records determined Faisal Shahzad had fraudulently purchased it two weeks earlier. A thirty-year-old Pakistani-born financial analyst who immigrated to the United States on a student visa in 1997, Shahzad became a naturalized American citizen in 2009.

Experiencing financial difficulties, around 1996, Shahzad became increasingly religious and critical of U.S. foreign policy toward the Middle East. His increased religiosity led to the dissolution of his arranged marriage and estrangement from friends and acquaintances.

After being identified as a suspect, on May 3, Shahzad was placed on the no-fly list maintained by the FBI's Terrorist Screening Center (TSC) to prevent him from fleeing the country. Eluding an FBI surveillance team, that same day, he made the cash purchase at JFK International Airport of an Emirates Airlines flight to Dubai, with a connecting flight to Pakistan. Airline employees neglected to check the no-fly list, enabling Shahzad to board the flight. Shortly before departure, however, a flight manifest check by the U.S. Customs and Border Protection's National Targeting Center (NTC) discovered Shahzad was aboard, and the plane was recalled to the gate minutes before takeoff.

Post-arrest investigations revealed that Shahzad had traveled to Pakistan several times and spent time in a terrorist training camp in Waziristan, where he received bomb-making training from the Taliban- and al-Qaeda-affiliated Tehrik-e-Taliban Pakistan (TTP) terrorists. He also informed investigators that he had received $12,000 in funding from a Taliban contact in Pakistan and that he would have attempted a second bombing if still free. On May 2, TTP posted an online video claiming responsibility for the attempted bombing on a jihadist website.

Shahzad was indicted by a federal grand jury on June 10, 2010, and eleven days later, he pleaded guilty to ten federal crimes, including attempted use of a weapon of mass destruction, attempted act of terrorism transcending national boundaries, and conspiracy to commit an act of terrorism transcending national boundaries. He is currently serving a life sentence at the federal supermax prison in Florence, Colorado.

Because the Times Square area in the city's Theater District is heavily trafficked with tourists and pedestrians, if the explosive device had actually detonated, the number of casualties, dead and injured, would likely have been in the hundreds, perhaps thousands. Additionally, glass falling from shattered windows in the surrounding skyscrapers would have rained down on pedestrians over an area of several blocks.

Vincent E. Henry

See also: Foreign Terrorist Groups at War with the United States; Homeland Security; Recruiting Terrorists.

FURTHER READING

Elliott, Andrea. 2010. "For Times Sq. Suspect, Long Roots of Discontent." *New York Times*, May 15, 2010. https://www.nytimes.com/2010/05/16/nyregion/16suspect.html

New York Police Department. 2010. *NYPD SHIELD Assessment: Times Square Car Bomb Arrest.* May 4, 2010. New York: New York Police Department Counterterrorism Bureau.

Shane, Scott. 2010. "Lapses Allowed Suspect to Board Plane." *New York Times*, May 4, 2010. https://www.nytimes.com/2010/05/05/nyregion/05plane.html

U.S. Attorney, Southern District of New York. 2010. "Faisal Shahzad Sentenced in Manhattan Federal Court to Life in Prison for Attempted Car Bombing in Times Square." October 10, 2010. https://www.justice.gov/archive/usao/nys/pressreleases/October10/shahzadfaisalsentencingpr.pdf

U.S. Department of Justice. 2010. "Faisal Shahzad Pleads Guilty in Manhattan Federal Court to 10 Federal Crimes Arising from Attempted Car Bombing in Times Square." June 21, 2010. https://www.justice.gov/opa/pr/faisal-shahzad-pleads-guilty-manhattan-federal-court-10-federal-crimes-arising-attempted-car

Transportation Security

The al-Qaeda terrorist organization used commercial airliners as weapons of mass destruction to execute their attacks on September 11, 2001. The commercial airline industry is part of the Aviation subsector of the Transportation sector of the United States' critical infrastructure (CI). Other elements of the Transportation sector, including ships, trains, pipelines, buses, trucks, and even personal automobiles, have proven to be not only frequent targets but also popular instruments of terrorist attacks.

The prominent role that the Transportation sector plays in terrorist operations is due to several factors. First, the sector is vast and widely distributed, which makes providing security for all aspects of the sector impractical. Second, many features of the sector, such as the airliners used in the 9/11 attacks, the ability for large trucks to hold a considerable amount of explosives, and the kinetic energy in a rapidly moving vehicle, lend themselves to direct use as weapons of mass destruction. Third, the elements of the sector that transport persons, such as airliners, trains, buses, and ships, present ideal targets for a bombing or other violent attack because they concentrate many people in a small space while offering limited means of egress. Fourth, all subsectors of the Transportation sector rely on important nodes that concentrate people (e.g., airports, train stations), which make them attractive targets. Fifth, other Transportation sector nodes concentrate the nation's commerce (e.g., major port facilities, trucking transshipment terminals, pipelines), and significant damage to these facilities can disrupt the country's economy. Sixth, destruction or disruption of Transportation sector assets, systems, and networks can produce cascading casualties to other CI sectors due to the fact that virtually all of the other sectors depend on the Transportation sector for their continued operations.

The Transportation sector is divided into the following subsectors:

- Aviation—includes aircraft, airports, air traffic control and navigation functions in three main areas of operation: commercial passenger airline operations, air cargo companies, and civil aviation. There are approximately 19,700 airports in the United States, 500 of which offer commercial service.
- Maritime—consists of 95,000 miles of coastline, 261 ports, and more than 25,000 miles of navigable waterways traveled by commercial and privately owned ships and other watercraft of a wide range of displacements.
- Freight Rail—includes approximately 1.33 million freight cars in service on 140,000 miles of active rail track and key intermodal facilities.
- Highway and Motor Carrier—includes bridges, major tunnels, trucks carrying hazardous material, other commercial freight vehicles, motor coaches, school buses, and related intermodal facilities, such as transshipment terminals.
- Pipeline—includes over 2.5 million miles of pipelines that transport almost all natural gas and more than half of all hazardous liquids, including crude and refined petroleum.
- Mass Transit—includes transit buses, trolleybuses, monorails, heavy rail (subways), light rail, passenger rail, commuter rail, and van pool/rideshare accounting for over 10.3 billion passenger trips per year.

A large number of public and private entities own and are responsible for the performance of the Transportation sector's assets, systems, and networks, which exist in the physical, cyber, and human dimensions. Accordingly, providing security for the Transportation sector involves the coordination of many actors. Moreover, each subsector is unique in many ways. For instance, while maritime, air, and ground transport must smoothly interface with each other at transshipment points, moving goods by sea requires different knowledge, equipment, and skill sets than moving the same goods by air, train, truck, or pipeline. Accordingly, while all subsectors utilize risk analysis to prioritize which assets, systems, and networks receive the greatest levels of security, the security measures employed vary considerably from one subsector to another. All transposition subsectors employ a system of layered defenses that require a terrorist to successfully overcome several security measures to gain access to and successfully attack their target.

For example, the maritime shipping industry uses large standardized cargo containers as a principal means of transporting non-bulk cargos (these are extremely space-efficient, weatherproof, and can be readily transferred to truck semitrailers and railroad cars or stored at transshipment points). Terrorists and criminals view containers as an attractive means for smuggling illegal weapons and other contraband. Containers can also be used for transporting and detonating a large explosive device. One defense against this threat is the Container Security Initiative (CSI), which is managed by U.S. Customs and Border Protection (CBP), an agency within the Department of Homeland Security (DHS), and involves the cooperation of many international public and private partners. CSI is an intelligence-driven program that identifies high-risk containers for inspection by CBP officers. Other aspects of this layered defense include the DHS's Secure Freight Initiative and the Customs Trade Partnership against Terrorism (C-TPAT). These programs are in addition to upgraded construction features for new containers that make them more tamperproof, improved container locking devices, real-time tracking of each container, and a range of independent security measures taken by individual ships, maritime terminals, port authorities, and the U.S. Coast Guard.

As another example, the commercial air passenger industry employs a different set of security measures for its layered defense. Passengers are prescreened when they buy their tickets. The Federal Bureau of Investigation's (FBI) Terrorist Screening Center maintains the Terrorist Screening Database of known or suspected terrorists. DHS's Transportation Security Administration (TSA) uses this list to identify and, if necessary, detain suspicious persons scheduled to board commercial aircraft. After arriving at the airport, passengers' tickets and identities are verified, and they must pass through a TSA security checkpoint before gaining entry into the airport's secure area. TSA officers use a number of security measures to provide a layered defense at checkpoints. Any suspicious persons identified through these security checks are taken to a secure area for further questioning and inspection. TSA also coordinates safety standards with security organizations at foreign airports that serve as the last point of departure for the United States to ensure that stringent security standards are met.

Checked baggage is subjected to inspections before being permitted to be loaded onto the aircraft, and baggage is removed and reinspected if the person who checked the bag fails to check in at the gate and board the aircraft. Carry-on baggage is inspected separately using various methods, and any object that can be used as a weapon is confiscated. The amount of liquids that passengers can bring through the security checkpoint is limited to reduce the probability that passengers will smuggle explosives aboard the aircraft.

In addition to measures focused on each traveler, airport security personnel use a variety of techniques to identify suspicious travelers, including the analysis of security camera outputs using gait recognition software (to identify a person who might be hiding a heavy object or wearing a bomb vest) and facial recognition software (to identify individuals on watch lists).

Should terrorists successfully evade these layered defense measures, each aircraft is designed and operated to minimize the chance of a successful terrorist attack. These measures include reinforced and locked cockpit doors, the use of plastic rather than metal eating utensils, and special counterterrorist training for all flight crews. Also, any flight may include armed U.S. air marshals posing as passengers. Pilots can also elect to be armed after accomplishing the relevant training.

The TSA is the U.S. government entity responsible for the security of all aspects of U.S. air, sea, and ground transportation. However, over 90 percent of the TSA's annual budget is devoted to its aviation security mission because of the high risks posed by terrorist attacks to this Transportation subsector. In addition to the airport security measures listed above, TSA is responsible for the following programs that aim to reduce the risk of terrorist attacks to the Aviation subsector. The TSA Secure Flight Program conducts passenger watch list matching for 100 percent of covered U.S. aircraft operator and foreign air carrier flights into, out of, and within the United States. The TSA PreCheck program, the Global Entry Trusted Traveler Network, the NEXUS program, and the SENTRI program prescreen individuals and allow those who pass a background check to use expedited lanes at U.S. airports and when crossing international borders. The Visa Waiver Program (VWP) is administered by the DHS in consultation with the State Department and allows citizens of thirty-eight countries to travel to the United States for up to ninety days without a visa and grants reciprocal privileges to American citizens traveling to program member countries. The VWP uses a risk-based, multilayered approach to detect and prevent terrorists from traveling to the United States.

In addition to security measures that protect the different parts of the Transportation sector, another series of layered defenses indirectly protect against threats to this sector by identifying and detaining terrorists before they can commit attacks. For instance, the U.S. government devotes considerable resources to identifying and intercepting terrorists before they enter the country. DHS organizations concerned with border security, immigration, cyberattacks, and the smuggling of weapons, including WMDs, fall into this category. They include the CBP, the TSA, the Cybersecurity and Infrastructure Security Agency (CISA), U.S. Citizenship and Immigration Services (USCIS), the U.S. Coast Guard, U.S. Immigration and Customs Enforcement (ICE), and the U.S. Secret Service. In addition, the intelligence community (IC), elements of the Department of Defense responsible for maritime and air domain awareness programs, the FBI, the State Department, and law enforcement organizations at all levels of government have counterterrorism missions, as do all private companies that own critical infrastructure.

William J. Lahneman

See also: Critical Infrastructure as a Terrorist Target; Department of Homeland Security; Director of National Intelligence; Federal Bureau of Investigation, Directorate of Intelligence; Intelligence Community, Adjustments to the Post-9/11 World; Intelligence Fusion Centers; Profiling.

FURTHER READING

U.S. Customs and Border Protection. 2019. "CSI: Container Security Initiative." Accessed September 25, 2020. https://www.cbp.gov/border-security/ports-entry/cargo-security/csi/csi-brief

U.S. Customs and Border Protection. 2020. "CTPAT: Customs Trade Partnership against Terrorism." Accessed September 25, 2020. https://www.cbp.gov/border-security/ports-entry/cargo-security/ctpat

U.S. Department of Homeland Security. 2019. "Transportation Security." Accessed September 24, 2020. https://www.dhs.gov/topic/transportation-security

U.S. Department of Homeland Security and U.S. Department of Transportation. 2015. *Transportation Systems Sector-Specific Plan.* Washington, DC: U.S. Department of Homeland Security and U.S. Department of Transportation. Accessed September 24, 2020. https://www.cisa.gov/sites/default/files/publications/nipp-ssp-transportation-systems-2015-508.pdf

U

Unabomber Attacks, Theodore John "Ted" Kaczynski

1942–

By almost any standard, Theodore "Ted" Kaczynski stands out even in the United States' long and assorted list of lone-wolf terrorists. He was a mathematical genius who entered Harvard University at sixteen and became the youngest assistant professor of mathematics in the history of the University of California at Berkeley. He was also an elusive terrorist at the top of the FBI's most wanted list for more than fifteen years, who focused his anger on neither racial or ethnic groups nor government policy but on the technological and industrial world in which he grudgingly lived. In the end, it was his desire to share his image with the public that led to his capture.

Kaczynski's terrorist bent was apparently shaped by two broad currents. The son of Polish parents growing up during the turbulent years of desegregation in a non-Polish, ethnically mixed Chicago neighborhood, his efforts to fit in were undone by his brilliance and father's willingness to allow him to skip grades. Consequently, he found himself smaller than his classmates and subject to bullying. The bullying continued when he entered Harvard at sixteen, smaller and notably less affluent than most classmates.

The loner lifestyle gradually emerging out of these experiences found an ideological outlet in literature depicting the impersonal, evil nature of industrial societies to which Kaczynski was exposed at Harvard. Eventually, the ideology triumphed over his commitment to theoretical mathematics. After two years at Berkeley, following his PhD at the University of Michigan, he left academia and eventually settled in 1971 outside of Lincoln, Montana, where he built a primitive cabin without water or electricity and taught himself survival skills.

Seven years later, as civilization encroached upon his Montana lifestyle in the form of an aggressive timber industry, Kaczynski began his bombing career, initially targeting Northwestern University (May 1978 and May 1979) and an American Airlines flight out of Chicago (November 1979). Given the similarity of the bombs, the FBI merged the files under UNABOM, for University and Airline Bomber, from which the "Unabomber" designation emerged.

Kaczynski later explained that his turn to violence was necessary to attract the public's attention to the industrial revolution's costs in terms of individual freedom, and from 1978 until his apprehension in 1995, his efforts to start a revolution against technology's steady growth involved sixteen mailed or delivered bombs, claiming three lives and injuring more than a score. Significantly, the first fatality involved a computer store owner and only occurred seven years into Kaczynski's campaign. As time passed, however, his bombs became more sophisticated, and the last two (December 1994 and April 1995) each succeeded in killing their intended victims—the last a timber industry lobbyist.

In the interim, Kaczynski worked on his 35,000-word manifesto, *Industrial Society and Its Future*, and in 1995, he offered it to numerous magazine and newspaper sources; he especially coveted its publication in the *New York Times* and *Washington Post*. Both initially demurred, but on the possibility it might lead to the Unabomber's capture, Attorney General Janet Reno gave the green light to both papers. Eventually, Kaczynski's brother David read the piece, saw parallels in his brother's writing style, hired a private investigator to look further into whether Ted could be the Unabomber, and convinced the FBI to search his brother's cabin, where the evidence of his guilt was conclusive.

Kaczynski was arrested on April 3, 1996, and swiftly indicted on ten counts of transporting explosives and three counts of murder. He refused to follow his public defender's advice to plead insanity to avoid the death penalty, but he was eventually able to get it off the table by pleading guilty to all charges (January 22, 1998).

Kaczynski continues to serve eight life sentences without the possibility of parole while corresponding widely with less homicidal critics of our industrial and postindustrial technological age.

Joseph R. Rudolph Jr.

See also: Domestic Terrorist Groups; Pipe Bomber Attacks, Lucas John "Luke" Helder; Psychology of Terrorists.

FURTHER READING

Chase, Alston. 2000. "Harvard and the Making of the Unabomber." *The Atlantic*, June 2000. Accessed June 8, 2020. https://www.theatlantic.com/magazine/archive/2000/06/harvard-and-the-making-of-the-unabomber/378239/

Kaczynski, Theodore J. 2019. *Technological Slavery*. Vol. 1. Revised and expanded ed. Scottsdale, AZ: Fitch & Madison Publishers.

Pruitt, Sarah. 2018. "Why It Took 17 Years to Catch the Unabomber." History, October 25, 2018. Accessed June 9, 2020. https://www.history.com/news/unabomber-letter-bombs-investigation-arrest

United States Embassy and Consulate Attacks

United States embassies and consulates are the official representatives of the United States overseas. Ensuring safe operation of these diplomatic missions is critical to international relations, but American diplomatic facilities have been targets of violence for decades. A variety of motivations drive these events, and security measures have grown significantly in recent years.

After World War II, the United States expanded its international presence and assumed a global leadership role. Inevitably, other foreign actors did not always agree with U.S. values, positions, or actions. Unable or unwilling to carry out acts of violence inside the United States, many targeted American diplomatic missions. In the 1970s, this violence increased but remained small in scale. Most attacks were perpetrated by left-wing revolutionaries, such as the Japanese Red Army or Peru's Shining Path guerrillas.

The 1980s saw a shift in motivations as Islamists carried out more attacks on U.S. diplomatic posts, with the 1979 seizure of the U.S. embassy in Tehran, Iran, being a watershed moment in diplomatic security. Large-scale attacks on U.S. posts in Beirut, Lebanon, in 1983 and 1984 resulted in over 80 deaths and hundreds of injuries. On August 7, 1998, simultaneous truck bomb detonations destroyed U.S. embassies in Nairobi, Kenya, and Dar es Salaam, Tanzania, killing over 200. Although these strikes were directed against American targets, the vast majority of victims were local citizens passing on crowded streets. Some had legitimate purposes to be near the embassies, such as applying for visas. Islamist extremists justified these deaths by claiming they were necessary to achieve broader ends or by labeling some of the victims as Muslims who had abandoned their religion ("apostates").

On September 11, 2012, terrorists struck the U.S. diplomatic mission in Benghazi, Libya, during a visit by the U.S. ambassador to Libya, John Christopher Stevens. The terrorists then moved on to attack a CIA annex nearby. Ambassador Stevens and three other American personnel were killed.

Countering the terrorist threat to diplomatic establishments is complex and multilayered. The baseline level of security has been raised since Benghazi, but each post maintains its own security plan based on the threat level, capabilities of the host, and size of the post. Any state hosting diplomats from other countries is responsible for their protection. Attacks on, or evacuations of, embassies can have severe diplomatic repercussions between the states involved. Typically, the outer ring of security is provided by the host government through their police, military, or contract security personnel. Guards on the facility's perimeter are local citizens hired by the embassy, known as the local guard force. The U.S. Marine Corps Security Guard detachment (MSG) will be found within the buildings. Their primary role is not, contrary to popular belief, protecting personnel or facilities but to protect classified material by preventing unauthorized access to sensitive information and destroying classified material if the post is overrun by attackers. Their role in overall security operations has, however, increased in recent years.

All of these efforts are planned and supervised by the U.S. State Department's Diplomatic Security Service (DSS). Security planning is intelligence driven, and DSS collaborates with the host nation and other U.S. intelligence agencies to keep the security posture current. In the post-Benghazi environment, diplomatic personnel undergo much more rigorous security training, the physical security of posts has been augmented, and contingency plans have been modernized. Preventing or deterring future attacks against U.S. diplomatic posts is an evolving, ongoing process.

*James T. Barry**

See also: Benghazi; Foreign Terrorist Groups at War with the United States.

---

* Mr. Barry served the FBI for twenty-two years, retiring as a supervisory special agent with global assignments. Much of his career was spent in the WMD arena. Any opinions expressed in this article are those of the writer and not the official position of the FBI.

FURTHER READING

Birdzell, Billy. 2013. "Embassy Security: The Strategic Context." USNI News, February 5, 2013. https://news.usni.org/2012/09/18/embassy-security-strategic-context

Burns, William J., and Thomas Nides. "Benghazi: The Attack and the Lessons Learned." U.S. Department of State, December 20, 2012. https://2009-2017.state.gov/s/d/former/burns/remarks/2012/202309.htm

Congressional Research Service. 2014a. *Securing U.S. Diplomatic Facilities and Personnel Abroad: Background and Policy Issues.* July 30, 2014. https://crsreports.congress.gov/product/pdf/R/R42834

Congressional Research Service. 2014b. *Securing U.S. Diplomatic Facilities and Personnel Abroad: Legislative and Executive Branch Initiatives.* December 23, 2014. https://crsreports.congress.gov/product/pdf/R/R43195

U.S. Department of State, Bureau of Diplomatic Security. 2014. *Significant Attacks against U.S. Diplomatic Facilities and Personnel 1998–2013.* Washington, DC: U.S. Department of State, Bureau of Diplomatic Security. https://2009-2017.state.gov/documents/organization/225846.pdf

United States Senate Bombing

November 7, 1983

The United States Senate bombing was the third and most destructive bombing in a series of politically motivated attacks perpetrated by the Armed Resistance Unit against the U.S. government in 1983. No one was injured in any of the bombings; however, they highlighted the need for increased focus on domestic terrorist groups.

Late on the evening of November 7, 1983, the U.S. Capitol switchboard received a call warning of a bomb placed in the U.S. Capitol building. Minutes later, at 10:58 p.m., a violent explosion rocked the second floor of the building's north wing. The blast caused no structural harm but damaged furniture, walls, and artwork, including a painting of Daniel Webster. The attack led to several enhanced security measures in the Capitol that are still utilized, including the closing of certain areas to the public, metal detectors at the building's entrance, and a staff identification card system.

The Armed Resistance Unit took credit for the bombing in a prerecorded phone call received minutes before the attack and in a typed letter received by National Public Radio the day afterward. The group claimed the attack was in retaliation for the United States' imperialist and exploitative military aggression in Lebanon, Grenada, El Salvador, and Nicaragua. In May 1988, six unit members were arrested and charged with the bombing as well the bombings at Fort McNair and the Washington Navy Yard: Laura Whitehorn, Linda Evans, Marilyn Buck, Susan Rosenberg, Timothy Blunk, and Alan Berkman. A seventh member, Elizabeth Duke, remains a fugitive to this day.

The six members all received lengthy prison terms for their involvement in the attacks and for possession of illegal weaponry. Alan Berkman was paroled after serving eight years of his ten-year sentence. Laura Whitehorn was sentenced to twenty years and served over fourteen before her release in 1999. Linda Evans, who was already serving a thirty-five-year sentence for illegal weapons charges, received two concurrent five-year sentences. Marilyn Buck served thirty-three years of an eighty-year sentence before passing away in 2010. Timothy Blunk and Susan Rosenberg were sentenced together and received the maximum sentence of fifty-eight years.

The Armed Resistance Unit, also known as the May 19 Communist Organization (M19CO), was a far-left domestic terrorist organization that began as an offshoot of the radical left terrorist Weather Underground Organization (WUO) after many of its members were arrested in November 1977. The remaining members of the WUO banded together to form the M19CO, naming the group in honor of Malcolm X and Ho Chi Minh's birthday.

Unlike many terrorist organizations, M19CO often operated in conjunction with other radical left groups with mutual interests. Composed mostly of white middle-class women, M19CO also joined forces with the Black Liberation Army (BLA) to accomplish their mutual goal of a socialist revolution in the United States, allowing M19CO to adopt a division of labor wherein they handled the dissemination of propaganda and many logistical aspects while the BLA carried out much of the violence. In addition to freeing prisoners of allied groups, the M19CO typically robbed American institutions to finance its politically motivated terrorist attacks in the name of women's liberation, Black liberation, and anti-imperialism. This collaborative nature of radical left terrorist organizations prompted the Reagan administration to reopen old investigations of several far-left organizations.

Jeffrey Neuman

See also: Domestic Terrorism, the Vietnam Era; Domestic Terrorist Groups; United States Embassy and Consulate Attacks.

FURTHER READING

GlobalSecurity.org. n.d. "May 19th Communist Organization (M19CO)." Accessed July 20, 2019. https://www.globalsecurity.org/military/world/para/m19co.htm

Greene, Harold H. "United States v. Whitehorn, 710 F. Supp. 803 (D.D.C. 1989)." Justia US Law. Accessed July 19, 2019. https://law.justia.com/cases/federal/district-courts/FSupp/710/803/1462627/

Hansen, Susan. 1990. "Ex-Baltimorean Sentenced in Bombings." *Baltimore Sun*, December 6, 1990. https://www.baltimoresun.com/news/bs-xpm-1990-12-07-1990341060-story.html

Hevesi, Dennis. 2009. "Alan Berkman, 63, Activist Doctor, Dies." *New York Times*, June 14, 2009. https://www.nytimes.com/2009/06/15/nyregion/15berkman.html

Lambert, Laura. 2011. "May 19 Communist Organization." In *The SAGE Encyclopedia of Terrorism*, edited by Gus Martin, 380. Thousand Oaks, CA: SAGE Publications. https://doi.org/10.4135/9781412980173.n258

Mintz, John. 1983. "Small Explosion Damages Building at the Navy Yard." *Washington Post*, August 19, 1983. https://www.washingtonpost.com/archive/local/1983/08/19/small-explosion-damages-building-at-the-navy-yard/0fe4496c-448e-4f65-8459-e282251f4bb7

U.S. Senate. "Bomb Explodes in Capitol." November 7, 1983. Accessed July 6, 2019. https://www.senate.gov/artandhistory/history/minute/bomb_explodes_in_capitol.htm

Unmanned Aerial Systems

Even before the Wright brothers' first flight, owning the high ground and the skies has been a central goal for militaries. Unmanned aerial systems (UAS) or unmanned aerial vehicles (UAVs), commonly known as *drones*, have become an integral part of the U.S. military strategy for combating global terrorism, playing an important role in some of the most famous and infamous military operations since the terrorist attacks on September 11, 2001. Used for many different tasks, including surveillance and targeted strikes, UAVs are often operated from command centers from thousands of miles away. Because of the distance between the operator and the theater of operation, the use of UAVs allows for much less risk to U.S. troops.

The original use for UAVs was for surveillance of military targets, for example, Israel's early use of this technology to monitor the activities of Palestinians who might attack that country. The United States has expanded the surveillance use of drones and weaponized them during the war on terror. Two advantages of UAVs are that (1) they are able to remain airborne much longer over or near a target than traditional aircraft, and (2) there is less risk to personnel than that posed by special operations forces on the ground. Of note, drone surveillance allowed the U.S. military to find and confirm the locations of both Osama bin Laden and Anwar al-Awlaki.

The use of this technology for surveillance has led to controversy over potential domestic surveillance use. *Signature strikes*, in which drone strikes are ordered because a crowd meets certain characteristics, became another source of concern in both the George W. Bush and Barack Obama presidential administrations. The Bush administration conducted about 50 targeted strikes, while President Obama signed off on over 400 during his administration in an effort to limit the U.S. military footprint and casualties in the targeted regions. President Trump authorized nearly 250 drone strikes in the first two years of his administration, a rate much higher than either of his predecessors.

There is often an ethical question raised regarding the use of drones by the U.S. government that centers on whether drone strikes on certain groups or individuals are morally permissible or tactically sound if they have the potential to incur civilian casualties and thereby result in increased radicalization of the bereaved and others. Supporters of the use of drones counter that their use can have some ethical advantages, including a higher rate of precision and more discrimination in the time and manner of the strike than manned aircraft would afford. Moreover, these strikes must pass through a staunch level of analysis and bureaucracy before they are approved, and their effectiveness is not in question. Since the United States has been carrying out targeted strikes, it estimates that more than 3,000 terrorists have been killed, including 50 or more upper-level leaders and commanders in al-Qaeda, the Islamic State, and other terror organizations.

Finally, although UAVs are governed by the same rules as any other weapon under the Laws of Armed Conflict (LOAC), questions have been raised over whether this type of surveillance and targeted strikes is constitutional. Much debate, for example, concerns the lethal overseas drone strike on Anwar al-Awlaki, a U.S. citizen who became an extremely radicalized al-Qaeda recruiter, including whether his constitutional right to due process was violated. Despite his citizenship, the Obama administration argued he had waived his rights when he became radicalized and was considered a combatant under the LOAC.

Brett M. Gould and Tobias T. Gibson

See also: al-Awlaki, Anwar; War on Terror, The; War on Terror: Afghanistan and Pakistan.

FURTHER READING

Ackerman, Spencer. 2018. "Trump Ramped Up Drone Strikes in America's Shadow Wars." *Daily Beast*, November 25, 2018. https://www.thedailybeast.com/trump-ramped-up-drone-strikes-in-americas-shadow-wars

American Civil Liberties Union. 2011. *Protecting Privacy from Aerial Surveillance: Recommendations for Government Use of Drone Aircraft*. New York: ACLU. www.aclu.org/report/protecting-privacy-aerial-surveillance-recommendations-government-use-drone-aircraft

Blom, John David. 2010. *Unmanned Aerial Systems: A Historical Perspective*. Occasional Paper 37. Fort Leavenworth, KS: Combat Studies Institute Press. www.armyupress.army.mil/Portals/7/combat-studies-institute/csi-books/OP37.pdf

Byman, Daniel L. 2013. "Why Drones Work: The Case for Washington's Weapon of Choice." Brookings, June 17, 2013. www.brookings.edu/articles/why-drones-work-the-case-for-washingtons-weapon-of-choice/

Jurecic, Quinta. 2016. "Obama's Term-End Thoughts on Targeted Killing." Lawfare, October 17, 2016. www.lawfareblog.com/obamas-term-end-thoughts-targeted-killing

McCurley, T. Mark, with Kevin Maurer. 2015. *Hunter Killer: The True Story of the Drone Mission That Killed Anwar al-Awlaki*. New York: Dutton.

Sehrawat, Vivek. 2017. "Legal Status of Drones under LOAC and International Law." *Penn State Journal of Law & International Affairs* 5 (1): 164–206. https://elibrary.law.psu.edu/jlia/vol5/iss1/7

USA PATRIOT Act of 2001

The USA PATRIOT Act of 2001 (or Patriot Act) was the name given to federal legislation following the terrorist attacks of September 11, 2001. The act, formally titled Uniting and Strengthening America Providing Appropriate Tools Required to Intercept and Obstruct Terrorism, enhanced the power of the federal government to protect domestic security, conduct investigations, and capture terrorist suspects. Specifically, the act outlined ten titles as a means for the government to deter and punish terrorists. These measures included, but were not limited to, enhanced surveillance procedures, wiretapping, countering money laundering, immigration probes, information sharing between federal law enforcement and intelligence agencies, and strengthening criminal laws against terrorism.

The Patriot Act made significant changes to federal law by amending statutes and guidelines. Under the Patriot Act, the National Security Act of 1947 is amended by having the director of central intelligence (DCI) tasked with establishing requirements and priorities for foreign intelligence collected under the Foreign Intelligence Surveillance Act (FISA) of 1978. It also required the DCI to provide assistance to the U.S. attorney general (AG) to ensure that information derived from electronic surveillance or physical searches would be disseminated for foreign intelligence purposes.

Furthermore, the act facilitated the government's collection of data from a wider variety of sources without the strict evidentiary standards for court approval. These sources included electronic messages, telephone conversations, credit reports, education/medical/library records, business communication, and banking activity. In doing so, the Patriot Act amended the Computer Fraud and Abuse Act (CFAA), the Electronic Communications Privacy Act, the Family Education Rights and Privacy Act (FERPA), the Federal Rules of Criminal Procedure, the Health Insurance Portability and Accountability Act (HIPAA), federal wiretap laws, immigration laws, and money laundering laws. In understanding the ephemeral need for such regulations, the Patriot Act also set forth sunsetting provisions on many of the procedures.

Republican representative James F. Sensenbrenner Jr. (WI-9) introduced the bill to the 107th Congress as House Resolution 3162 on October 23, 2001, exactly six weeks after the terrorist attacks of September 11, 2001. Republican representative Michael G. Oxley (OH-4) cosponsored the bill. The House passed the act 357–66 on October 24, 2001, and it passed in the Senate 98–1 on October 25, 2001. The lone dissenter in the Senate was Democrat Russ Feingold (WI). On October 26, 2001, the Patriot Act was signed by President George W. Bush and became Public Law 107-56.

CONTROVERSIES

The Patriot Act animated the security versus liberty dialectic by exposing the monumental power of the government to investigate terrorist activity in the wake of 9/11 and generating prolonged litigation by civil rights and liberties organizations. Passed a mere forty-five days after the events of 9/11, the Patriot Act swiftly empowered the federal government by expanding the authority to monitor the activities of American citizens. At the time, the urgency of investigating terrorist activity and uncovering cells that displayed a "clear and present danger" to national security, as well as the demand for flexibility with regard to new technology, trumped civil rights and privacy concerns. Yet, despite the act's sunset clauses, the details of the legislation and the alacrity by which they were implemented alarmed privacy advocates and civil rights and liberties organizations.

Due to the extraordinary weight of the sections on enhanced surveillance procedures and the removal of obstacles to investigating terrorism, the act itself has been most challenged on the grounds that it violates the First, Fourth, and Fifth Amendment rights outlined in the U.S. Constitution. Notably, Section 206, which granted roving surveillance authority on targets who thwart FISA, and Section 215, which granted the Federal Bureau of Investigation (FBI) permission to apply to the Foreign Intelligence Surveillance Court (FISC), have been subject to intense scrutiny. Section 505, which expanded the FBI's authority to issue National Security Letters (NSLs), has also been the subject of litigation and debate.

NOTABLE LITIGATION

There have been numerous lawsuits regarding the constitutionality of the Patriot Act; the most salient showcase the law's ambiguities and the government's liberal interpretation of the legislation. The American Civil Liberties Union (ACLU), which serves to defend the constitutional rights of U.S. citizens, has been at the forefront of many of the litigation efforts to control the power of the government outlined in the Patriot Act. The ACLU has filed Freedom of Information Act (FOIA) requests with the Department of Justice (DOJ) to seek information regarding the government's interpretation of the Patriot Act, legal procedures, and the scope of programs that authorize enhanced surveillance on U.S. citizens. Many of the ACLU's efforts have concentrated on Sections 206, 215, and 505. Consequently, these sections have prompted several modifications to the law as it has come up for renewal.

In a 2003 lawsuit, *Muslim Community Association of Ann Arbor v. Ashcroft*, the ACLU contended that Section 215 of the act, which granted warrantless and suspicion-less collection of phone records and metadata, violated the First Amendment rights of the plaintiffs. The ACLU withdrew its lawsuit in 2006 due to a revision in the law upon its renewal.

In 2004, an Internet service provider (ISP) filed suit against the FBI's use of NSLs to obtain information, arguing it violated the First, Fourth, and Fifth Amendment rights of its clientele. In *Doe v. Ashcroft*, a district court found the NSLs issued by the FBI to be unconstitutional and stayed a prohibition against the FBI using NSLs.

In 2005, the ACLU filed *Doe v. Gonzales*, which challenged the FBI's use of NSLs to demand library records without court approval, and they challenged the mandate that the librarians could not disclose the existence of the NSLs. A district court ruling struck down the FBI's demands and the nondisclosure clauses regarding the NSLs. After a request to vacate the stay by a federal appeals court, U.S. Supreme Court justice Ruth Bader Ginsburg weighed in on the matter and rejected the request. In 2006, the FBI abandoned its demand for the records and lifted the gag order on the librarians, thereby nullifying the case.

In *Holder v. Humanitarian Law Project*, the ACLU argued that the expressive component of humanitarian aid is a right under the First Amendment, even if that aid results in legal advocacy and training to designated terrorist organizations. In 2010, the U.S. Supreme Court ruled in favor of AG Eric Holder, upholding the provisions of the Patriot Act in 6–3 ruling. The court determined that it is a crime to provide material support to any group designated a foreign terrorist organization by the AG of the United States.

In 2013, Edward Snowden, a contractor for the National Security Agency (NSA), leaked program information regarding the agency's copious metadata collection on U.S. citizens. The scope of the program prompted *ACLU v. Clapper*, by which the ACLU argued the NSA's collection programs violated the First and Fourth Amendment rights of U.S. citizens. In 2015, a U.S. federal appeals court ruled in favor of the ACLU, agreeing that the Patriot Act did not authorize metadata collection on U.S. citizens.

LONG-TERM EFFECTIVENESS

Supporters of the Patriot Act contended the law was instrumental in preventing more terrorist attacks on the U.S. homeland and that it enabled law enforcement personnel to root out existing terror cells. Nonetheless, the legislation has been heavily scrutinized by policy makers, academics, journalists, and civil rights organizations. The scrutiny led to disputes over the law's indelible impact on civil liberties and privacy. As the act has been renewed over the years, votes in both houses of Congress have become tighter, with progressively more lawmakers abandoning their initial support of its most intrusive sections.

At the end of 2005, sixteen provisions under the Patriot Act's enhanced surveillance procedures were set to expire under the sunset clauses. Legislation drafted in 2005 sought to make fourteen of the sixteen enhanced surveillance procedures permanent; however, it included civil liberties safeguards, greater congressional and judicial oversight, and renewed sunsetting provisions on Sections 206 and 215. In early 2006, Congress voted to renew the Patriot Act. The renewal included three bills: the USA PATRIOT Act Improvement and Reauthorization Act of 2005, the USA PATRIOT Act Additional Reauthorizing of Amendments Act of 2006, and the Combat Methamphetamine Act of 2005. Senator Russ Feingold (D-WI) filibustered on the grounds that the legislation did not do enough to protect civil liberties, but the Senate voted to end his filibuster. The bill subsequently passed in the House 280–138 and in the Senate 89–10. On March 9, 2006, President George W. Bush signed the renewal of the USA PATRIOT Act, and the legislation became Public Laws 109-177 and 109-178.

In 2011, President Barack Obama signed a four-year extension of Patriot Act, which passed in the House of Representatives 250–153 and in the Senate 72–23. In 2015, during the second Obama administration, the act officially expired. In lieu of the Patriot Act, the 114th Congress passed the USA FREEDOM (Uniting and Strengthening America by Fulfilling Rights and Ensuring Effective Discipline over Monitoring) Act. The House approved the legislation 338–88, and it passed in the Senate 67–32. President Obama signed the legislation on June 2, 2015, making it Public Law 114-23. The act restored most of the provisions of the Patriot Act but largely due to the public backlash after Snowden's revelations, it reformed the government's metadata collection of phone records on American citizens.

In 2020, the House of Representatives passed the renewal of the USA FREEDOM Reauthorization Act 278–136. The bill passed in the Senate 80–16. The act includes amendments to the provisions related to intelligence gathering under FISA.

Diane M. Zorri

See also: Foreign Intelligence Surveillance Act of 1978; Intelligence Community, Adjustments to the Post-9/11 World; Internet Surveillance.

FURTHER READING

Bush, George W. n.d. "USA PATRIOT Act." White House Archives. Accessed May 29, 2020. https://georgewbush-whitehouse.archives.gov/infocus/patriotact/

Etzioni, Amitai. 2005. *How Patriotic Is the Patriot Act? Freedom versus Security in the Age of Terrorism*. New York: Routledge.

Howell, Beryl A. 2004. "Seven Weeks: The Making of the USA PATRIOT Act." *George Washington Law Review* 72 (6): 1145–1205.

McCarthy, Michael T. 2002. "Recent Developments: USA PATRIOT ACT." *Harvard Journal on Legislation* 39: 435–453.

Office of the Inspector General, U.S. Department of Justice. 2016. "A Review of the FBI's Use of Section 215 Orders for Business Records in 2012 through 2014." September 2016. Accessed June 10, 2020. https://oig.justice.gov/reports/2016/o1604.pdf

Raab, Christopher P. 2006. "Fighting Terrorism in an Electronic Age: Does the PATRIOT Act Unduly Compromise Civil Liberties." *Duke Law and Technology Review* 2: 3–33.

Soma, John T., et al. 2005. "Balance of Privacy vs. Security: A Historical Perspective of the USA PATRIOT Act." *Rutgers Computer & Technology Law Journal* 31 (2): 285–327.

Stolberg, Sheryl G. 2006. "Senate Passes Legislation to Renew Patriot Act." *New York Times*, March 3, 2006. Accessed May 30, 2020. https://www.nytimes.com/2006/03/03/politics/senate-passes-legislation-to-renew-patriot-act.html

Uniting and Strengthening America Providing Appropriate Tools Required to Intercept and Obstruct Terrorism (USA PATRIOT ACT) Act of 2001, H.R. 3162, 107th Congress (2001). Congress.gov. Accessed May 29, 2020. https://www.congress.gov/bill/107th-congress/house-bill/3162

USA FREEDOM Act of 2015, H.R. 2048, 114th Congress (2015). Congress.gov. Accessed June 10, 2020. https://www.congress.gov/bill/114th-congress/house-bill/2048

USA FREEDOM Reauthorization Act of 2020, H.R. 6172, 116th Congress (2020). Congress.gov. Accessed June 10, 2020. https://www.congress.gov/bill/116th-congress/house-bill/6172

USA PATRIOT Improvement and Reauthorization Act of 2005, H.R. 3199, 109th Congress (2005). Congress.gov. Accessed June 10, 2020. https://www.congress.gov/bill/109th-congress/house-bill/3199

Yeh, Brian T., and Charles Doyle. 2006. "USA PATRIOT Improvement and Reauthorization Act of 2005: A Legal Analysis." Congressional Research Service, December 21, 2006. Accessed June 3, 2020. https://fas.org/sgp/crs/intel/RL33332.pdf

Zusman, Lynne K., and Neil S. Helfand. 2004. "USA Patriot Act (2001)." In *Major Acts of Congress*, Vol. 3, edited by Brian K. Landsberg, 256–260. New York: Macmillan.

USS *Cole* Attack

October 12, 2000

The USS *Cole* is an active-duty U.S. Navy warship that was attacked by Islamic terrorists in 2000. The *Cole* was being refueled in Aden harbor, Yemen, when it was attacked by suicide bombers onboard a smaller vessel. The terror organization al-Qaeda took responsibility for the attack, which was the deadliest action against a U.S. Navy ship since the Iraqi attack on the USS *Stark* in 1987.

The $1 billion, 8,300-ton, USS *Cole* (DDG-67) is an Arleigh Burke–class Aegis-equipped guided missile destroyer that was commissioned on June 8, 1996. The ship, homeported at Naval Station Norfolk, Virginia, was named after U.S. Marine sergeant Darrell S. Cole, who was killed in action on Iwo Jima during World War II. On the morning of October 12, 2000, the *Cole*, under the command of Commander Kirk Lippold, was conducting a routine refueling operation during its ongoing Middle East deployment.

At approximately 11:18 a.m., local time, a small fiberglass boat laden with explosives and carrying two men approached the port side of the *Cole* and exploded. The investigation later established that the crew of the *Cole* believed the boat to be a local harbor garbage skiff and allowed it to come alongside. It was estimated that 400–700 pounds of the explosive C4 was used to construct the vessel-born suicide bomb. The explosion ripped a forty-by-sixty-foot hole in the port side of the ship's hull just under the ship's galley, causing the deaths of several sailors who were eating lunch. The blast killed seventeen American sailors and the two suicide bombers, injured an additional thirty-nine others, and seriously damaged the ship. The crew of the *Cole* kept the ship afloat in Aden until it was placed aboard a Dutch salvage vessel and shipped to Pascagoula, Mississippi, for rebuilding and repair in December 2000.

The Federal Bureau of Investigation (FBI), working with the Navy Criminal Investigative Service (NCIS), arrived in Aden days after the attack and soon established that the bombing had been conducted by members of the al-Qaeda terror organization. Nine months prior to the successful attack on the *Cole*, Osama bin Laden had approved a similar vessel-born bomb plan to use against the U.S. Navy destroyer USS *The Sullivans* while in port at Aden. That attack was aborted when the suicide boat was overloaded with explosives and sank. Three months before the attacks of September 11, 2001, an al-Qaeda recruiting video was publicly released that featured Osama bin Laden bragging about the effectiveness of the attack on the *Cole* and encouraging similar ones in the future.

In November 2011, Abd al-Rahim al-Nashiri, a Saudi Arabian citizen of Yemeni descent, was formally arraigned on terror charges, including organizing and planning the bombing of the *Cole*. On September 29, 2004, al-Nashiri had previously been sentenced to death in absentia by a Yemeni court for his role in planning the USS *Cole* bombing. Captured by the U.S. military in 2002, al-Nashiri is one of three high-value detainees who have been publicly acknowledged by the U.S. government to have been subjected to waterboarding and other enhanced interrogation techniques. Al-Nashiri had long been suspected of being a key player in al-Qaeda and has been housed at the U.S. military detention center in Guantánamo Bay, Cuba, since 2006.

John R. Capra

See also: al-Qaeda; bin Laden, Osama; Counterterrorism and the Clinton Administration; Foreign Terrorist Groups at War with the United States.

FURTHER READING

Burnett, Betty. 2005. *The Attack on the USS Cole in Yemen on October 12, 2000*. New York: Rosen Publishing Group.

Lippold, Kirk S. 2012. *Front Burner: Al Qaeda's Attack on the USS* Cole. New York: PublicAffairs.

Perl, Raphael, and Ronald O'Rourke. 2001. "Terrorist Attack on USS Cole: Background and Issues for Congress." January 30, 2001. Washington, DC: Library of Congress and Congressional Research Service. https://nsarchive2.gwu.edu//NSAEBB/NSAEBB55/crs20010130.pdf

Rosenberg, Carol. 2017. "Emotionally Drained Crew Kept USS Cole Afloat while FBI Collected Bombing Evidence." *Miami Herald*, March 14, 2017. https://www.miamiherald.com/news/nation-world/world/americas/guantanamo/article138308948.html

V

Virginia Tech Shooting

April 16, 2007

On April 16, 2007, thirty-two persons were killed and another seventeen were injured during an active shooter attack on the campus of Virginia Tech in Blacksburg, Virginia. The motives of the shooter, Seung Hui Cho, remain unclear. In the aftermath of the incident, college campuses sought to improve emergency preparedness protocols.

Two separate shootings comprised the incident. The weapons for both incidents were two semiautomatic handguns. The first, at approximately 7:15 a.m., occurred in the West Ambler Johnston residential hall. It is unclear how the shooter gained access to the building, but after entering, he shot a student inside her room and a resident adviser, who had gone to the room to investigate upon hearing noises. Law enforcement and emergency medical services responded, as the initial report was that sounds were consistent with someone having fallen from a lofted bed. Upon discovering the gunshot victims, both of whom were later pronounced dead, the incident was initially treated as a possible domestic disturbance, until the second shooting occurred and the cases were linked. Controversy later emerged about whether mass notifications to the campus community should have been sent earlier (they were distributed at approximately 9:30 a.m.) and whether classes should have been canceled after the first shooting (they were not).

The second shooting began at approximately 9:40 a.m. in Norris Hall, a classroom building. After chaining and padlocking the public doors to the building, the shooter entered and shot students and faculty in five classrooms and the hallway on the second floor of the building. Police responded rapidly, already being on alert after the first incident. After breaching a locked maintenance door that was unchained, police contact teams entered the building. The Blacksburg Police Department and the Virginia Tech Police Department trained together and frequently collaborated, a practice credited for their rapid deployment and effective teamwork in responding to the shootings. As the police arrived, the shooter shot and killed himself. Until the 2016 shooting at the Orlando Pulse nightclub, this remained the deadliest mass shooting in U.S. history.

The shooter was born in Korea in 1984 and moved to the United States with his family in 1992. In childhood, he was diagnosed with social anxiety, depression, and selective mutism, for which treatment and social support were provided. As a student at Virginia Tech, numerous faculty had concerns about his behavior in class. He engaged in stalking and cyberstalking of female students, and he was referred for a temporary mental health detention order in which he was briefly hospitalized and found to pose an imminent danger to himself. The motives for the shooting remain unknown, but at some point between the first and second incidents, the shooter mailed a manifesto and videos to a national media outlet, in which he expressed anger at the world, perceptions of mistreatment by society, a desire to avenge others who had been poorly treated, and a desire for fame as a result of his actions.

In the aftermath of the Virginia Tech shooting, institutions examined protocols for security and preparedness. This included physical security, such as installation of door hardware that prevents chaining and that allows classroom doors to be locked from the inside; development or refinement of emergency plans; and increased attention to technologies and policies for mass notification systems to alert campus communities of potential dangers. In addition, focus was placed on developing threat assessment processes, allowing behaviors of concern to be reported and reviewed by a team trained to identify threatening or dangerous behavioral patterns and to recommend interventions. Attention also focused on federal academic and medical record privacy laws and exceptions to them that would allow risk factors to better be identified in hopes of preventing future incidents.

Stephen Owen

See also: Active Shooter Scenarios; Columbine Attack; Hard and Soft Targets; Profiling.

FURTHER READING

Fox, James Alan, and Jenna Savage. 2009. "Mass Murder Goes to College: An Examination of Changes on College Campuses Following Virginia Tech." *American Behavioral Scientist* 52 (10): 1465–1485.

Leavitt, Michael O., Alberto R. Gonzales, and Margaret Spellings. 2007. *Report to the President on Issues Raised by the Virginia Tech Tragedy.* Washington, DC: Department of Health and Human Services, Department of Justice, and Department of Education. https://www.justice.gov/archive/opa/pr/2007/June/vt_report_061307.pdf

TriData Division, System Planning Corporation. 2009. *Mass Shootings at Virginia Tech: Addendum to the Report of the Review Panel.* Arlington, VA: TriData Division, System Planning Corporation. https://scholar.lib.vt.edu/prevail/docs/April16ReportRev20100106.pdf

W

Waco Standoff

February 28–April 19, 1993

The compound of the Branch Davidian religious cult, located near Waco, Texas, was the scene of a fifty-one-day siege in 1993 that began on February 28 when agents from the Bureau of Alcohol, Tobacco and Firearms (ATF) attempted to serve search and arrest warrants based on a yearlong investigation into federal firearms violations. During the initial encounter, four ATF agents were killed, and an additional twenty agents were wounded. An unknown number of suspects within the compound were killed, and others, including their leader, David Koresh, were wounded. Although negotiations were somewhat successful during the siege, the event ended in the deaths of more than seventy additional individuals inside the compound on April 19.

During the standoff, thirty-five individuals were negotiated out, including twenty-one children. Two additional people who breached the perimeters and entered the compound subsequently exited safely. Numerous other Koresh sympathizers tried to join him but were repelled by the surrounding authorities. In an internal memorandum dated March 22, 1993, the FBI negotiating team stated that "the long-term prospect for a peaceful resolution remains good." As it turned out, no Davidian members were negotiated out after March 23. An individual who attempted to enter the compound is reported to have later been involved in the bombing of the Oklahoma City Federal Building on April 19, 1995, exactly two years after the horrific ending of the Waco standoff.

Alan Stone, a Harvard professor of psychiatry and law, conducted a review of the incident for the federal government and noted that "during the first phase of the FBI's engagement at Waco, a period of days, the agents on the ground proceeded with a strategy of conciliatory negotiation, which had the approval and understanding of the entire chain of command" (1993, 8). However, Stone also reported that a little more than a month into the siege the FBI first "took a more aggressive approach to negotiation" and later "gave up the process of negotiation" and concentrated "on tactical pressure alone" (10). Stone subsequently concluded that "the FBI command failed to give adequate consideration to their own behavioral science and negotiation experts" (p. I).

Nancy T. Ammerman, a scholar of the sociology of religion at Boston University, observed that the advice of the FBI negotiators was not heeded in part because "there was an understandable desire among many agents in Waco to make Koresh and the Davidians pay for the harm they had caused. Arguments for patience and unconventional tactics fell on deaf ears" (1993, 4).

This incident illustrates that many people inside law enforcement, as well as academic advisers to incident reviews, believe that a strategy of formal negotiation may be useful in reducing violent outcomes. This incident also illustrated that a strategy of formal negotiation was not fully accepted within the law enforcement community and was often set aside in favor of more traditional tactics. Effective, if not actual, control of the situation was in the hands of the tactical element (SWAT team) or of an incident command structure that was apparently more oriented toward use of force than negotiation.

Robert J. Louden

See also: Hostage Negotiation; Montana Freemen Siege; Munich Olympics Terrorist Attack; Oklahoma City Federal Building Bombing; Ruby Ridge Standoff.

FURTHER READING

Ammerman, N. T. 1993. *Report to the Justice and Treasury Departments Recommendations of Experts for Improvements in Federal Law Enforcement after Waco.* Washington, DC: U.S. Department of Justice.

Edwards, J. C. 2001. "Self-Fulfilling Prophecy and Escalating Commitment: Fuel for the Waco Fire." *Journal of Applied Behavioral Sciences* 37 (3): 343–360.

Louden, R. J. 1993. "How Much Is Enough? How Much Is Too Much?" In *Recommendations of Experts for Improvements in Federal Law Enforcement after Waco.* Washington, DC: U.S. Department of Justice. https://www.ojp.gov/pdffiles1/Digitization/145688NCJRS.pdf

Louden, R. J. 1999. *The Structure and Procedures of Hostage/Crisis Negotiation Units in U.S. Police Organizations.* Unpublished doctoral dissertation, City University of New York.

Merari, A. 1993. "Report for the Departments of Justice and Treasury's Review Board of Barricade Events." In *Recommendations of Experts for Improvements in Federal Law Enforcement after Waco.* Washington, DC: U.S. Department of Justice. https://www.ojp.gov/pdffiles1/Digitization/145688NCJRS.pdf

O'Hara, P. 2012. *Why Law Enforcement Organizations Fail: Mapping the Organizational Fault Lines in Policing.* Durham, NC: Carolina Academic Press.

Stone, Alan A. 1993. *Report and Recommendations Concerning the Handling of Incidents such as the Branch Davidian Standoff in Waco, Texas.* Unpublished. Cambridge, MA.

Wall Street Bombing

September 16, 1920

On September 16, 1920, a bomb ripped through downtown Wall Street in New York City. The explosion, which originated from a single horse-drawn cart packed with 100 pounds of dynamite and several hundred pounds of cast-iron weights, exploded at the corner of Wall and Broad streets, directly across from the main headquarters of the J.P. Morgan Bank. The attack killed thirty-eight people and injured hundreds more. The driver was believed to have abandoned the small wagon after setting the device to explode, as no unidentified body was recovered among the other victims. To this day, this criminal act of terror remains unsolved, and no one has ever claimed responsibility.

Although the crime remains unsolved, investigators and historians, then and now, believe that the bombing was generally related to anti-capitalist, post–World War I social unrest carried out by various immigrant anarchist groups and often influenced by communist agitators. Initially, the Justice Department's Bureau of Investigation (the precursor to the Federal Bureau of Investigation) proceeded under the expectation that the blast was the result of an accident and not an act of terror. But the investigation soon concluded that the nature, method, and target of the attack likely made it the work of militant socialists or communists, in particular a group of Italian anarchists known as Galleanists, who had been responsible for a series of simultaneous bombings in nine U.S. cities the year before.

Although the Bureau of Investigation conducted exhaustive interviews with hundreds of people who had been within the vicinity of the attack, little hard evidence emerged as to the actual perpetrators. One promising lead consisted of some crude printed flyers that were found in the area in a post office box by a letter carrier before the blast occurred. They called for the release of political prisoners and were signed by a group calling itself the "American Anarchist Fighters." Regardless, even this development proved of limited value in actually disclosing the guilty, who never came forward to claim responsibility.

As horrible an act of violence as this attack was, it was of limited or no value in stemming the American system of capitalism that was being practiced on Wall Street in 1920, if that was indeed the motivation. By late the same day of the bombing, as the board of governors of the New York Stock Exchange were meeting to vote to open trading the next morning, cleaning and repairs were already well underway. The criminal investigation was undoubtedly hindered by the destruction of evidence caused by this quick cleanup. However, the swift return to normal business operations the next day and the fact that the crime remains unsolved have all contributed to this early terror attack on U.S. soil sliding into history.

John R. Capra

See also: Domestic Terrorism, Anarchists; Haymarket Affair.

FURTHER READING

Barron, James. "After 1920 Blast, the Opposite of 'Never Forget'; No Memorials on Wall St. for Attack That Killed 30." *New York Times*, September 17, 2003. Retrieved June 30, 2020. https://www.nytimes.com/2003/09/17/nyregion/after-1920-blast-opposite-never-forget-no-memorials-wall-st-for-attack-that.html

Gage, Beverly. 2009. *The Day Wall Street Exploded: A Story of America in Its First Age of Terror*. New York: Oxford University Press.

McCormick, Charles H. 2005. *Hopeless Cases: The Hunt for the Red Scare Terrorist Bombers*. New York: University Press of America.

Murray, Robert K. 1955. *Red Scare: A Study in National Hysteria, 1919–1920*. Minneapolis: University of Minnesota Press.

Neville, John F. 2004. *Twentieth-Century Cause Cèlébre: Sacco, Vanzetti, and the Press, 1920–1927*. Westport, CT: Praeger.

Watson, Bruce. 2007. *Sacco and Vanzetti: The Men, the Murders, and the Judgment of Mankind*. New York: Viking Press.

War on Terror, The

The term *war on terror* refers to the international military campaign launched by the United States and allied governments in the aftermath of the September 11, 2001, attack by al-Qaeda on the United States. It was coined by President George W. Bush in an impromptu interview on September 16 and was fleshed out in his address to a joint session of Congress on September 20.

The "war" metaphor in reference to a major government undertaking against a generally defined evil had long been a part of the vocabulary of politics in the United States—for example, Lyndon Johnson's war on poverty and Richard Nixon's war on drugs. President Reagan came close to using it in 1984 in seeking more funding to combat the guerrilla Muslim fighters in Afghanistan when he spoke of a "war against terrorism." The shift in nouns to a "war on terror" simultaneously meant a broader range of non-state targets (initially al-Qaeda bases in Afghanistan) as well as the states tendering aid to terrorists and terrorist organizations (initially Afghanistan's Taliban government). It also denoted the beginning of, in Bush's words to Congress, "a lengthy campaign, unlike any other we have seen. .. [including] dramatic strikes, visible on TV, and covert operations, secret even in success."

Distinct from the wide support that enveloped the United States' first action in the war, the destruction of al-Qaeda's camp in Afghanistan and removal of the Taliban government from power, the term was criticized from the outset for its vague and open-ended nature, as in "who" would qualify as the enemy and by what criteria. The failure to find the alleged weapons of mass destruction following the invasion of Iraq in the name of the war on terror intensified that criticism, as did the collateral damage (the displacement of tens of thousands of civilians and the hundreds of civilians killed by drone attacks on terrorist targets) resulting from the growing list of military activities subsumed under the banner.

Finally, given the vague definition of the war's targets and its unspecified duration, there was broad criticism of the war for allowing a few thousand Muslim extremists to hijack U.S. foreign policy and dissipating the military's strength by luring it into fighting in scores of countries, often on behalf of regimes crying "terrorist threats" while abusing their own citizens' rights.

All such criticism led President Obama, in the process of reducing troop levels in Afghanistan and withdrawing troops from Iraq, to declare that what had become "the global war on terror" was over in May 2013. The rise of the Islamic State in Iraq and Syria (ISIS) in the latter days of his presidency, however, caused Obama to reverse course and launch a renewed buildup of forces in Afghanistan and energetic use of targeted killings against al-Qaeda and ISIS operatives and affiliated organizations in Iraq, Syria, and elsewhere under a variety of "operation" names in lieu of "the war on terror." Secret intelligence and low-grade warfare missions also continued under the auspices of the U.S. Special Forces Command, by some estimates in over 130 countries during his presidency.

Nor did the war on terror's targeted killing that began with George W. Bush's presidency end when the "America First" Trump administration took office in 2017, as witnessed by its relaxing of the rules governing drone strikes in September of that year and the targeted drone strike that killed Qasem Soleimani, a high-ranking Iranian military officer accused of orchestrating attacks on U.S. forces in Iraq, at the Baghdad airport in early January 2020.

Joseph R. Rudolph Jr.

See also: Intelligence Community, Adjustments to the Post-9/11 World; September 11, 2001, Attack on America; War on Terror: Afghanistan and Pakistan; War on Terror: Somalia and Sudan.

FURTHER READING

Birkenstein, Jeff. 2010. *Reframing 9/11: Film, Popular Culture and the "War on Terror."* New York: Continuum.

Clarke, Richard A. 2004. *Against All Enemies: Inside America's War on Terror.* New York: Free Press.

Duffy, Helen. 2015. *The "War on Terror" and the Framework of International Law.* Cambridge, UK: Cambridge University Press.

Losey, Stephen. 2020. "Your Air Force 19 Years into War on Terror, Overstretched AFSOC at a Crossroads." *Air Force Times*, September 14, 2020. https://www.airforcetimes.com/news/your-air-force/2020/09/14/19-years-into-war-on-terror-overstretched-afsoc-at-a-crossroads/

Polumbo, Brad. 2020. "New Report Finds 'War on Terror' Has Forced 37 Million People to Flee Their Homes." Foundation for Economic Education, September 9, 2020. https://fee.org/articles/new-report-finds-war-on-terror-has-forced-37-million-people-to-flee-their-homes/

War on Terror: Afghanistan and Pakistan

The United States has prosecuted its war on terror globally, but the central battlefield has been in Afghanistan and Pakistan. Following the September 11, 2001, terrorist attacks, the United States sought to punish the attacks' perpetrators, al-Qaeda, and eliminate their safe haven in Afghanistan. The resulting military campaign began in October 2001 and met with rapid initial success as it overthrew the Taliban regime, but then it transformed into a larger and more complex counterinsurgency. The United States grew to depend on neighboring Pakistan for counterterrorism cooperation and especially for the sustainment of military forces in Afghanistan. The war in Afghanistan dragged on inconclusively, while a new insurgency began to destabilize nuclear-armed Pakistan. In an attempt to break the stalemate, the United States "surged" its military presence in Afghanistan, temporarily, and then withdrew most combat forces by 2014. Relations with Pakistan, meanwhile, steadily deteriorated, as it became clear that Pakistan's policies, especially its covert support to the Taliban, were working against U.S. interests. With no prospect of counterinsurgency success, and with the rise of other national security priorities elsewhere, the United States signed a peace agreement with the Taliban in 2020 and ended its military presence with a chaotic withdrawal in August 2021.

THE FALL AND RISE OF THE TALIBAN

Two weeks after the September 11 attacks, a CIA team landed in Afghanistan. Two weeks after that, the United States began its aerial bombing campaign against the Taliban regime. The United States coerced Pakistan's president, Pervez Musharraf, to support its operations, which he publicly pledged to do. On the ground, CIA and Special Operations soldiers linked up with local Northern Alliance fighters, who for years had been losing a civil war against the Taliban. With the support of U.S. money, arms, advice, and air strikes, the Northern Alliance went on the offensive, quickly taking every major city in turn as the Taliban regime crumbled.

To replace the Taliban, the United Nations organized a process to establish a new government. Based on the Bonn Agreement, this process developed a constitution and new institutions for a strong central government in Kabul. Meanwhile, U.S. and coalition forces still had to mop up remnants of the Taliban and al-Qaeda. They pursued Osama bin Laden and other key al-Qaeda leaders to Tora Bora, in the mountains on the Afghanistan-Pakistan border, in December 2001. The al-Qaeda fighters, however, escaped over the border. Over the next few months, hundreds of other militants, including members of other terrorist groups, like the Islamic Movement of Uzbekistan, who had previously found safe haven in Afghanistan, fled into Pakistan. The Taliban also fled and established several new bases in Pakistan, with the senior leadership concentrated in Quetta and Peshawar.

With the Taliban ousted, the U.S. military preferred to maintain its light footprint. As the looming war in Iraq diverted scarce military resources, the United States chose not to build a robust peacekeeping force in Afghanistan. Instead, security and postwar reconstruction was left to coalition forces in the International Security Assistance Force (ISAF), which came under the command of NATO in 2003 and expanded its presence across the country in 2004–2006. But the new Afghan government was still too weak to effectively provide security and governance. The Taliban, having regrouped in its Pakistani safe haven, began to rise again, especially in Afghanistan's rural areas, which were largely beyond the reach of the government and international coalition. In 2006, violence began to rise sharply. The insurgency against the fledgling Afghan government was taking hold.

Meanwhile, in Pakistan, a different violent uprising was taking hold. In July 2007, the Pakistan Army assaulted the Lal Masjid (Red Mosque) in Islamabad, home to an increasingly radical group of Islamist militants. Following the assault, outraged militants launched a wave of suicide attacks across the country. Several groups, which had earlier enjoyed close contact and support of the Pakistani government's Inter-Services Intelligence (ISI), now claimed that President Musharraf's support for the U.S. war effort in Afghanistan had betrayed Pakistan and its Islamic values. Calling for an Islamic revolution, they declared war on the Pakistani state.

The core of the budding insurgency was composed of Pashtun tribal militants. In the preceding years, they had lent support to various elements of the Afghan Taliban, especially the Haqqani network. By the end of 2007, several of these tribal militants had joined together in the Tehrik-e Taliban Pakistan (TTP), a Pakistani Taliban federation united in its opposition to both the NATO campaign in Afghanistan and the Pakistani state.

The Pashtun tribes had perennially battled the Pakistani state, but now they were reinforced and radicalized by al-Qaeda. In the years since their escape from

Afghanistan, al-Qaeda's mostly Arab leaders had insinuated themselves among the tribal militants, securing local protection in exchange for money, ideological guidance, and operational advice. The TTP insurgency was also joined in its anti-state turn by Punjabi extremists—groups that had previously been focused on targeting either sectarian minorities or India. This coalescing movement against the Pakistani state was thus composed of increasingly amalgamated networks of militants sharing resources, information, and members.

The Pakistan Army responded with unprecedented offensives in the northwest, beginning with Swat in late 2007. Such operations continued for the next decade. The new Pakistani insurgency also threatened to go global. The TTP sponsored at least one plot against the U.S. homeland in 2010. The war in Afghanistan had spilled over into Pakistan in a potentially even more dangerous form.

SURGE AND STALEMATE

In Afghanistan, the Taliban insurgency continued to gather momentum. ISAF lacked the force density or reconstruction resources necessary to keep the Taliban at bay, and the insurgents began exercising shadow governance and seized outright control of some districts. Violence rates kept rising. In response, in 2009, the United States ordered a "surge," with a sharp increase in U.S. and coalition military forces, civilian staff, and investment. This escalation emulated an earlier surge in Iraq, which had contributed to security improvements there in 2007–2008. Troop levels in Afghanistan increased from about 30,000 in early 2009 to over 100,000 in 2010–2011. Most of the new forces were positioned near Afghanistan's most important economic centers—and the Taliban's heartland—in the south.

Some in the U.S. government advocated maintaining a light footprint. They argued that a small but highly capable U.S. presence, with particular emphasis on air power, intelligence, and special operations forces, should stay focused on the counterterrorism mission against al-Qaeda, the original reason for the Afghanistan war. Instead, Washington chose to augment forces to support a new "population-centric" counterinsurgency campaign, which would provide much broader types of support to the Afghan government.

In the larger counterinsurgency, U.S. and ISAF forces would suppress the Taliban and help the Afghan government improve its capacity to provide security, governance, reconstruction, and development assistance. Major operations were designed to have ISAF "clear" towns of Taliban and then have Afghan security forces "hold" the town with a persistent presence and "build" new services and governance. The largest such operation, known as Operation Moshtarak, sought to clear the southern town of Marjah, beginning in February 2010. As with most such operations, the clear phase was executed very effectively, temporarily pushing out the local Taliban presence, but the hold and build phases were undermined by weaknesses in the Afghan government.

The government was primed to introduce vital services rapidly; however, it remained corrupt and inept. In Marjah and around the country, coalition forces could provide local security and build new infrastructure, but those gains were always localized and temporary. The Taliban, through strong community links, the provision of effective judicial services, and ruthless intimidation, maintained a level of influence sufficient to reassert control as soon as coalition forces handed over security to Afghan forces.

Despite added resources and planning, the surge could not paper over the Afghan government's fundamental lack of legitimacy. Afghan government, army, and police officials had high rates of illiteracy, corruption, drug use, and sexual predation. More broadly, the United States and ISAF often had to strike an uncomfortable balance, partnering with warlords and senior officials who were complicit in corruption and other illegal activity but were relatively effective bulwarks against the Taliban. Local leaders, primarily motivated by local community disputes, would often switch allegiances between the government and the insurgency. Indeed, much of the insurgency was grounded in unrelated local conflicts; the coalition rarely understood and often inflamed them. Meanwhile, the coalition's development projects injected enormous sums of money—much of it wasted through mismanagement and corruption—which artificially inflated the local economy and empowered some warlords, with their extensive patronage networks, over others.

Periodically, the uneasy relationship between the coalition and its Afghan partners would break down. President Karzai grew hostile to the coalition's military operations and especially their toll in civilian casualties. At the local level, the Taliban infiltrated security forces and launched a spate of "green-on-blue" attacks on coalition forces to sow distrust among the counterinsurgent forces.

U.S. relations with Pakistan also began to break down. The United States began more aggressively using unmanned drones to attack al-Qaeda, the Haqqani network, and associated militant targets in northwest Pakistan. These strikes were tactically effective; the al-Qaeda leadership cadre was under severe pressure, focused on survival and replacing losses rather than plotting terrorist attacks. But the drone attacks also exposed the growing distrust between the erstwhile partners, with Pakistan frustrated by breaches of its sovereignty and the United States frustrated by the apparent tolerance of terrorist safe havens.

A series of incidents fueled these suspicions, including the arrest of a CIA contractor for killing two locals in Lahore. They peaked in May 2011, when U.S. forces launched a secret, unilateral strike to kill Osama bin Laden in Abbottabad, a small army town. As bilateral relations soured, Pakistan denied ISAF the ability to use its roads for resupplying forces in Afghanistan. Both sides grudgingly returned to working together, but finding bin Laden in Pakistan, the subsequent rupture in relations, and concerns over a mounting insurgency in a nuclear state convinced many in Washington that Pakistan's policies were working against U.S. interests.

The war in Afghanistan became a stalemate. U.S. and NATO forces began handing over security responsibility to Afghan forces and transitioned from active counterinsurgency to an advisory role. The U.S. government had publicly announced that the surge troops would be withdrawn by 2012 and combat operations would cease in 2014. The Taliban could thus patiently wait for the counterinsurgency campaign to conclude and were ready to fill the vacuum as coalition troops gradually vacated.

Recognizing that its military leverage was declining, the United States explored other options. It experimented with arming local militias to supplement official Afghan security forces in a program known as Village Stability Operations, and it tested the potential for reconciliation talks with the Taliban, engaging in several diplomatic probes beginning in 2011. None of these concepts bore fruit before counterinsurgency operations ended in 2014.

ENDING THE "FOREVER WAR"

In 2015, the ISAF mission transitioned to Operation Resolute Support, with a much-reduced force presence. This NATO-led force was primarily tasked with a "train, advise, and assist" mission to improve the capabilities of Afghan security forces. A smaller U.S. force also remained for direct counterterrorism operations. As the militant threat continued to metastasize, so too did the focus of these counterterrorism operations. They increasingly targeted the Islamic State in Khorasan (ISK), an offshoot of the Iraqi group, which emerged in Afghanistan in 2014. ISK drew the ire of the Taliban and al-Qaeda by challenging them for resources and relevance and reintroduced a brutal transnational dimension to the terrorism threat in Afghanistan. By 2017, it had become the primary focus of U.S. counterterrorism strikes, and in some cases, the United States even provided air support to Taliban forces fighting ISK.

Having abandoned the counterinsurgency mission, the United States began seeking an end to its campaign. Washington's objective was to negotiate a settlement with the Taliban, and the United States and Taliban restarted direct talks in 2018. To pressure the Taliban into talks, the United States also slightly increased its force presence in Afghanistan and loosened its rules of engagement so that U.S. troops and aircraft could apply more military pressure. The United States also sought to ratchet up diplomatic pressure on the Taliban's Pakistani hosts by cutting military aid. Washington remained publicly wedded to a "conditions-based" strategy, although in reality there was no political appetite for continuing the "forever war."

In February 2020, the United States signed a peace agreement with Taliban leaders in Doha, Qatar. Many of the accord's operative conditions were secret, although the United States reportedly pledged to withdraw entirely from Afghanistan in return for a Taliban pledge to not support transnational terrorism. The Afghan government was not party to the agreement. As U.S. forces began withdrawing, the Taliban renewed a countrywide offensive against Afghan national security forces, which suffered heavy casualties. The United States pledged continued support to Kabul and anticipated that the Afghan government could, with ongoing international aid, remain standing for several months or years after the U.S. military withdrawal.

In 2021, President Biden renewed the U.S. commitment to withdrawal. He recognized that after two decades of inconclusive war, the United States was unwilling to pay the political or material costs to defeat the Taliban, and he sought to commit the United States to the higher strategic priority of managing the great-power competition against China. The United States calculated that it could continue some counterterrorism operations against Afghanistan-based terrorists with forces based elsewhere in the region, although the viability of such "over the horizon" counterterrorism remains unclear.

On the ground, the Taliban steadily gained increasing control across most of Afghanistan's rural districts. With unperturbed support from Pakistan and high tactical cohesion, the Taliban was militarily superior to Afghan forces that had dwindling U.S. support. The Taliban encircled provincial capitals, seized control of lucrative border crossings, and as the apparently inevitable victor, cut deals with district leaders to gain control quickly and relatively bloodlessly. In August 2021, it took control of provincial capitals across the country in a matter of days. President Ghani fled the country, and the Afghan state collapsed without implementing any transition; the Taliban took control of Kabul and quickly announced a new emirate government.

The Taliban that has returned to power twenty years after its ouster appears to be unreformed, with brutal, uncompromising enforcement of its political control and no incentive to break ties with al-Qaeda. In the years since the initial U.S. invasion, the terrorist and militant ecosystem in Afghanistan and Pakistan has evolved considerably but remains at least as dangerous. Al-Qaeda's senior leadership remains active, and its ideology has fueled a potentially more dangerous new insurgency in Pakistan. The region now suffers the Islamic State, itself an outgrowth of the U.S. invasion of Iraq. And with the United States again estranged from Pakistan, its influence there has been dwarfed by China, and the Pakistan security establishment has been buoyed by the ultimate success of its policy supporting the Taliban. U.S. strategies for managing these threats have also evolved but show no clear path to a lasting peace for the region or security for Americans.

Arzan Tarapore

See also: al-Qaeda; bin Laden, Osama; Counterterrorism and the George W. Bush Administration.

FURTHER READING

Abbas, Hassan. 2009. "Defining the Punjabi Taliban Network." *CTC Sentinel* 2 (4). https://ctc.usma.edu/defining-the-punjabi-taliban-network/

Chandrasekaran, Rajiv. 2012. *Little America: The War within the War for Afghanistan.* New York: Alfred A. Knopf.

Coll, Steve. 2018. *Directorate S: The CIA and America's Secret Wars in Afghanistan and Pakistan.* New York: Penguin Press.

Council on Foreign Relations. 2018. "The U.S. War in Afghanistan, 1999–2021." https://www.cfr.org/timeline/us-war-afghanistan

Farrell, Theo. 2018. *Unwinnable: Britain's War in Afghanistan, 2001–2014.* London: Random House.

Gall, Carlotta. 2015. *The Wrong Enemy: America in Afghanistan, 2001–2014.* Boston, MA: Mariner Books.

Nicholson, John W. 2017. "Department of Defense Press Briefing by General Nicholson via Teleconference from Kabul, Afghanistan." U.S. Department of Defense, November 28, 2017. https://www.defense.gov/News/Transcripts/Transcript-View

/Article/1382901/department-of-defense-press-briefing-by-general-nicholson-via-teleconference-fr/

Zucchino, David. 2021. "Collapse and Conquest: The Taliban Strategy That Seized Afghanistan." *New York Times*, August 18, 2021. https://www.nytimes.com/2021/08/18/world/asia/taliban-victory-strategy-afghanistan.html

War on Terror: Somalia and Sudan

U.S. concerns about terrorism in the Horn of Africa can be traced back to August 1998, when al-Qaeda attacked the American embassies in Dar es Salaam and Nairobi. Washington accused Sudan of collusion in these attacks. Three years later, following the September 11, 2001, attacks, the Bush administration considered executing military strikes against the fundamental terrorist group in East Africa, al-Shabaab, given its ties to al-Qaeda, but the operation was abandoned for want of sufficient intelligence.

U.S. COUNTERTERRORISM EFFORTS IN SOMALIA

Renewed American interest in combating terrorism in Somalia came two years later, in 2003, and the U.S. Central Intelligence Agency (CIA) has had ad hoc bases there ever since. Senior leaders of al-Shabaab insist that they do not share al-Qaeda's objective of waging global jihad but instead have a regional focus, namely, uniting the Somali-inhabited regions of neighboring countries, especially Kenya and Ethiopia. Still, the group has been implicated in plots to attack civilian aircraft, and it enjoys a close enough relationship with al-Qaeda in the Arabian Peninsula (AQAP) for the United States to consider it a threat to American security.

The group has also proved its capability to conduct complicated terrorist attacks, such as its attack on Westgate Mall in Nairobi, Kenya, in 2013, which resulted in the deaths of about seventy people. Concern also exists over its ties to Iran, one of the few countries that has colluded in funding the group. According to UN monitors, Iran has also acted as a transit point for the illegal Somali charcoal exports that provide al-Shabaab with millions of dollars annually.

Iran was not, however, directly implicated in the group's daring assault on American forces stationed at a Kenyan airbase on January 5, 2020, which killed three Americans and destroyed six aircraft, some used by U.S. Armed Forces for reconnaissance missions inside Somalia. Still, the attack came after the United States assassinated Qasem Soleimani, the head of the elite Quds Force wing of Iran's Islamic Revolutionary Guard Corps (IRGC), which caused speculation that al-Shabaab's attack may have been coordinated with Iran as revenge for Soleimani's killing.

The U.S. effort against the group has focused on two strategies. The first strategy is indirect: assisting the African Union forces seeking to uproot the group with military supervisors. These forces have been able to drive al-Shabaab militants from most of the Somali capital of Mogadishu; however, it continues to enjoy a presence in Mogadishu's suburbs and in central and southern Somalia.

The second strategy is the targeted killing of al-Shabaab's senior leaders through drone attacks. In 2011, Barack Obama became the first American president to authorize the use of these strikes against al-Shabaab, and President Trump depended more heavily on such targeted killing than his predecessor. Indeed, Trump altered the rules of engagement by abolishing the need for proof that the target was an *imminent* threat, thus allowing attacks to be conducted on a more frequent basis to assassinate high-profile terrorist leaders. In addition, Trump delegated the decision to carry on these lethal attacks to the U.S. Army field commander; consequently, Somalia became one of the regions where the new rules of engagement were first applied, with the U.S. Army conducting thirty-five strikes in 2017, compared to fourteen strikes in 2016 and eleven in 2015.

Meanwhile a major obstacle to American efforts to counter al-Shabaab in Somalia remains the inability of the Somali National Army to retake and secure towns from al-Shabaab control without foreign backing. The Somali army is still dependent on the 22,000-strong African Union Mission in Somalia (AMISOM) multinational force, which has been battling the group for at least a decade. However, AMISOM started to withdraw its troops in October 2019 and was expected to complete its withdrawal by December 2021, but the mandate of the forces was extended and replaced by AU Transition Mission in Somalia (ATMIS), which should be operation in Somalia until the end of 2024, after which the Somali forces will be fully responsible for fighting the group.

U.S. COUNTERTERRORISM EFFORTS IN SUDAN

Sudan was added to the U.S. state sponsors of terrorism (SST) list in August 1993 due to the Sudanese government harboring and supporting a large number of both Sunni and Shia terrorist organizations; for example, the Lebanese Hezbollah, Egypt's al Gama'at al-Islamiyya, and Iranian-backed extremist groups.

Sudan also harbored Osama bin Laden from 1991 until 1996; however, he was not implicated in any high-profile attacks against American interests during this period. He only became considered a threat to American interests after al-Qaeda's attack on American embassies in Tanzania and Kenya in 1998, when Sudan itself was accused by the United States of colluding in the attacks.

Sudan has also utilized terrorism against its regional enemies, as evident in the assassination attempt on the Egyptian president in Addis Ababa on June 26, 1995, with elements of Sudanese intelligence providing logistical and financial support to the al-Qaeda operatives who conducted the attack. Subsequently, in January 1996, the UN Security Council passed Resolution 1044 requesting of the government in Khartoum, Sudan's capital, the extradition to Ethiopia of the three persons suspected of participating in the assassination attempt. The government was also asked to end its assistance, support, and facilitation of terrorist activities, including the provision of shelter and sanctuary to terrorist elements.

Elsewhere, between 1992 and 1996, several al-Qaeda leaders met with an Iranian official in Khartoum to arrange an agreement between al-Qaeda, the National Islamic Front of Sudan, the Iranian Revolutionary Guard, and the Lebanese

Hezbollah. Sudan's leader at the time, Hassan al-Turabi, was instrumental in the formation of this alliance, as he succeeded in persuading al-Qaeda and the Shiite groups (Hezbollah and the Iranian Revolutionary Guards Corps) to put aside their differences to fight their common enemies: the United States and Israel. Under this agreement, both Iran and Hezbollah would provide al-Qaeda with expertise in bomb making and launching terrorist attacks.

On August 20, 1998, as a part of Operation Infinite Reach in response to the attack on the American embassies in East Africa, the United States fired Tomahawk missiles at the El-Shifa pharmaceutical plant located in Khartoum, which, according to American officials, was producing chemical warfare–related weapons and was linked to bin Laden's terrorist network. Inspection of the facility after the attack found inconclusive evidence that the plant was used in such a way.

U.S.-Sudanese relations did not improve over the following decade, as Sudan was known to be acting as an important channel for the transfer of weapons from Iran to Hamas in the Gaza Strip. In January 2009, the United States warned Sudan to desist from this smuggling of Iranian weapons just before Israel launched its Cast Lead offensive against the Gaza Strip. The Israeli Air Force reportedly carried out at least two secret strikes in Sudan as well in January and February 2009. For its part, Sudan denied being involved in any transfer of Iranian weapons to Gaza and labeled Israel's accusations to the contrary as an effort to smear Sudan's reputation to thwart Sudan's efforts to be removed from the State Department's state sponsors of terrorism list.

As a point of fact, in the aftermath of the 9/11 attacks on the United States, Sudan did cooperate with Washington against al-Qaeda, fearing reprisals from the United States, especially after the United States invaded Afghanistan and toppled the Taliban regime that had harbored al-Qaeda there. In 2005, Sudan tried to utilize that cooperation with the United States against the terrorist organization to remove its name from the aforementioned list of state sponsors of terrorism but without much success due to concerns over the Sudanese army's implication in war crimes in Darfur.

More recently, in 2016, Sudan severed its quarter-century alliance with Iran in favor of the Saudis and tried to eradicate the Iranian presence within the country. In return, the Saudis provided Sudan with much-needed financial aid to support the economy in the face of a collapsing currency and rising unemployment. The relationship with Iran proved to be a burden for Khartoum, especially as it did not receive financial aid from Iran. Sudan has even participated in the Saudi military efforts to contain the Houthis, the Iranian proxies, in Yemen since 2015.

After the removal of Sudanese president Omar al-Bashir due to revolts in April 2019, Khartoum renewed its efforts to be removed from the state sponsors of terrorism list. In February 2020, Sudan agreed to a key condition set by the United States for Sudan's deletion from the list, as it accepted to compensate the families of seventeen U.S. sailors who died when al-Qaeda bombed the USS *Cole* off the coast of Yemen in 2000. The United States held Sudan responsible for the attack, as the two suicide bombers involved were trained in the country. In addition, a preliminary agreement was reached in May 2020 to compensate those who died in al-Qaeda's attack on U.S. embassies in East Africa in 1998. This agreement, if accepted by the U.S. Congress, would take the country a step closer to its removal from that list, thus ending Sudan's economic isolation.

Lastly, Sudan has also started to improve its relations with Israel in a further attempt to be removed from the list. In early February 2020, a meeting was arranged between Sudan's leader, Abdel Fattah al-Burhan, and Israeli prime minister Benjamin Netanyahu in Uganda, with the aim of normalizing relations between the two countries.

In short, Sudan is actively enhancing its efforts to sever its relations with terrorist organizations and hopes to be exempted from American sanctions in return. The situation in Somalia, however, remains turbulent, as the Somali government is incapable of fighting al-Shabaab by itself.

Shady Abdelwahab Mansour

See also: al-Qaeda; United States Embassy and Consulate Attacks; War on Terror: Afghanistan and Pakistan.

FURTHER READING

Abdelaziz, Khalid. 2016. "As Economy Crumbles, Sudan Ditches Iran for Saudi Patronage." Reuters, January 12, 2016. https://reut.rs/3hB03PS

BBC News. 2020. "USS Cole Bombing: Sudan Agrees to Compensate Families." February 13, 2020. https://bbc.in/2Az6TVx

Black, Ian. "'Israeli Attack' on Sudanese Arms Factory Offers Glimpse of Secret War." *The Guardian*, October 25, 2012. https://bit.ly/3fzHfii

Daniels, Matthew.2019. "Assessing the Goals of U.S. Counterterrorism Efforts in Somalia." *Small Wars Journal*, September 5, 2019. https://bit.ly/2N1pHzm

The Economist. 2020. "An Attack on American Forces in Kenya Raises Questions and Concerns." January 11, 2020. https://econ.st/30Oryzp

Gikandi, Halima. 2020. "The State Dept. Is Nearing a Deal over 1998 Terrorism Victims. But Can Sudan Pay It?" *The World*, May 25, 2020. https://bit.ly/2YDhfLU

Hastert, Paul. 2007. "Al Qaeda and Iran: Friends or Foes, or Somewhere in Between?" *Studies in Conflict & Terrorism* 30(4): 327–336. https://doi.org/10.1080/10576100701200132

Hudson, Cameron. 2020. "Removing Sudan's Terrorism Designation: Proceeding with Caution." Atlantic Council, March 16, 2020. https://bit.ly/3ht8RY5

Institute for Security Studies. March 29, 2022. https://bit.ly/3aldl40

Jean, Celia, trans. 2020. "Sudan's Leader: Israel to Help Remove Us from US List of Terrorism Supporters." *Jerusalem Post*, February 14, 2020. https://bit.ly/2zAMNJM

Levitt, Matthew. 2011. "U.S. Court Ruling Links Iran to Al-Qaeda." *Iran Primer*, December 13, 2011. https://bit.ly/2UPGjhs

Lobel, Jules. 1999. "The Use of Force to Respond to Terrorist Attacks: The Bombing of Sudan and Afghanistan." *Yale Journal of International Law* 24: 537.

Nichols, Michelle. 2018. "Iran Is New Transit Point for Somali Charcoal in Illicit Trade Taxed by Militants: U.N. Report." Reuters, October 9, 2018. https://reut.rs/2Y23ZkX

Nzwili, Fredrick. 2013. "After Westgate Mall Attack: Al Shabab Penetrates even to Kenya High Schools." *Christian Science Monitor*, October 18, 2013. https://bit.ly/3d541wz

Okiror, Samuel. 2017. "Countdown to AMISOM Withdrawal: Is Somalia Ready?" *New Humanitarian*, February 28, 2017. https://bit.ly/3hxwizx

Oxford Analytica. 2016. "Al-Shabaab's Threat to Somalia's Capital Will Persist." *Expert Briefing*, September 2, 2016. https://bit.ly/3hrEm4R

Quaranto, Peter J. 2008. "United States Counter-Terrorism in Somalia." Institute for Security Studies, May 2008. https://bit.ly/2MYIw5U

Sharfi, Mohammed Hussain. 2018. "Sudan and the Assassination Attempt on President Mubarak in June 1995: A Cornerstone in Ideological Reverse." *Journal of Eastern African Studies* 12 (3): 454.

Tchie, Andrew. 2020. "Sudan's Quest to Come Off the US Terror List." IISS, February 28, 2020. https://bit.ly/3d6ckbx

Vito, Caitlin. 2018. "Shifting US Counter-Terrorism Strategy Plays Out in the Horn of Africa." IISS, June 13, 2018. https://bit.ly/30LnW1k

Weak and Failed States

Weak and failed states generally refer to political entities that cannot support the basic needs of the population and are characterized by low levels of governance, in addition to extreme violence, corruption, and poverty. Former U.S. ambassador to the United Nations in Geneva Gerald Helman and Steven Ratner of the Council of Foreign Relations—noted as the first to use the term formally—examined the proliferation of failed states within the lens of the increase of newly independent countries after the end of World War II and the decline of foreign aid to those nations at the end of the Cold War. Central governments in these states often lack fundamental authority over all regions, and their governments are generally unable to participate in the international community. Weak institutions and internal violence within them exacerbate responses to humanitarian issues, resulting in instability and insurgencies, which can lead to the diffusion of refugees into neighboring regions.

The Fund for Peace publishes a yearly *Fragile States Index* as a quantitative measure of weak and failed states. This ranking is based on a combination of economic, political, social, and cohesion indicators. Factors considered include threats to the state, such as terrorism; the legitimacy of the state; economic decline; and demographic pressures. The 2020 index ranked Yemen, Somalia, South Sudan, Syria, and the Democratic Republic of Congo as the top fragile states.

Many researchers have contested both the definition of *weak and failed states* and the measures used to classify them. Despite this, a wide array of research highlights the linkages between weak and failed states and terrorism. James Piazza, a professor of political science at Penn State, concluded that states that exhibited indications of failure were more likely to host terrorists that commit transnational attacks and are targeted by transnational terrorists. Peter Tikuisis found that weak states were far more likely to experience terrorist attacks resulting in fatalities than other states, particularly those weak states with displaced populations, uneven economic development, groups with grievances for perceived wrongs, and internal security forces that operate irregularly.

The research highlights that one factor alone, such as economic decline, does not create the necessary conditions for terrorism. Edward Newman, who focuses on security studies at the University of Leeds, concluded that while weak and failed states may be an "enabling factor" for terrorist groups to form and operate, many terrorist groups have formed within strong states as well. Justin George, a professor of economics at the University of Texas, Dallas, found conditions of disorder in failed states create operational limitations to a terrorist group's ability to carry out cross-border terrorist attacks and impede external terrorist groups from forming bases and attacking targets within these nations, making targeting by domestic groups more likely in failed states. Given these findings, the mitigation of the conditions leading to fragility within a nation may result in increased terrorist activity, making counterterrorism strategies vital in rebuilding.

Dawn M. Wozneak

See also: Hezbollah; Islamic State, The; Taliban.

FURTHER READING

Fund for Peace. 2020. *Fragile States Index Annual Report 2020*. Washington, DC: Fund for Peace. https://fragilestatesindex.org/wp-content/uploads/2020/05/fsi2020-report.pdf

George, Justin. 2018. "State Failure and Transnational Terrorism: An Empirical Analysis." *Journal of Conflict Resolution* 62 (3): 471–495.

Helman, Gerald B., and Steven R. Ratner. 1992. "Saving Failed States." *Foreign Policy* 89: 3–20.

Newman, Edward. 2007. "Weak States, State Failure, and Terrorism." *Terrorism and Political Violence* 19 (4): 463–488.

Piazza, James A. 2008. "Incubators of Terror: Do Failed and Failing States Promote Transnational Terrorism?" *International Studies Quarterly* 52 (3): 469–488.

Rotberg, Robert I. 2002. "The New Nature of Nation-State Failure." *Washington Quarterly* 25 (3): 83–96.

Tikuisis, Peter. 2009. "On the Relationship between Weak States and Terrorism." *Behavioral Sciences of Terrorism and Political Aggression* 1 (1): 66–79.

Weaponizing the Internet

Over the past forty years, the world has witnessed a rapid growth of the Internet of Things (IoT). The IoT is the interconnection of objects that are embedded with hardware that enables them to send and receive data through an Internet connection. Computers, televisions, cell phones, and "smart" devices are part of the IoT. Although these devices produce clear user benefits, risks accompany the interconnection of devices. People, organizations, and nations all utilize the IoT to collect information, disrupt communications, and destroy infrastructures by any means possible.

There are untold ways to weaponize the Internet, depending on the target, goal, and tools that the attacker possesses. The type of attacker and the tools they use can be broken down into three levels: scammers, hacktivists, and state-sponsored hacktivists.

Scammers focus on small, quick monetary gain through phishing, a form of fraud in which an attacker masquerades as a reputable entity or person in email or other communication channels. Spam emails and malicious content emails containing viruses and spyware are examples of scammer activity pursued for financial gain. Neither poses a direct challenge to the homeland's national security, and the damage of both can be prevented through awareness training.

Hacktivists typically have a broader goal with a narrower scope than that of scammers. Hacktivism is a type of political activism that is mainly carried out through a cyber domain. Hacktivists are less driven by a monetary reward and more focused on igniting political change by attacking their target(s). In addition to the tools used by scammers, hacktivists also employ denial-of-service software, which overloads a website or server to stop its functioning; virtual privacy networks (VPNs), which enable the sending and receiving of data across public networks as if directly connected to the private network; and network mapping software, which identifies all devices connected to a network and the least secure openings in that network for access.

State-sponsored hacktivists (SSHs) weaponize the IoT to produce *political effects* similar to those traditionally achieved by a conventional use of force by states at a far lower cost compared to traditional military attacks. SSHs use the same set of tools and methodologies as hacktivists; however, funded by governments, SSHs possess more funding, technology, and skilled staff, which leads to more efficient and effective operations. The United States, North Korea, China, Russia, and other major nations utilize SSHs alongside their standard national cyber operational forces.

LACK OF CONSENSUS IN INTERNATIONAL LAW

The lack of international agreement related to acceptable uses of, and limits to, weaponizing the Internet results from inadequate international law standards on this subject. Attempts to reach consensus through the United Nations have failed. However, many nations, including the United States, have started to create law and policy by applying the standards found in the Law of Armed Conflict (LOAC). For example, in the 2012 National Defense Authorization Act (NDAA), Congress allowed the Department of Defense, with presidential direction, to conduct offensive, not merely defensive, cyber operations within the confines provided by LOAC and the War Powers Resolution. Similarly, in cyber operations, the United States often depends on "secret law," where there is an established but unpublished legal authority or precedent on a particular issue, thus compounding the problem of having no clear legal standard for international cyber conflicts.

Andrew Broyhill, Brett M. Gould, and Tobias T. Gibson

See also: al-Awlaki, Anwar; Cyberattacks; Cybersecurity.

FURTHER READING

Donohue, L. K. 2016. *The Future of Foreign Intelligence: Privacy and Surveillance in a Digital Age.* New York: Oxford University Press.

Goodman, Marc. 2016. *Future Crimes: Inside the Digital Underground and the Battle for Our Connected World.* New York: Anchor Books.

Kaplan, F. M. 2017. *Dark Territory: The Secret History of Cyber War.* New York: Simon & Schuster Paperbacks.

Lucas, George R. 2017. *State-Sponsored Hacktivism and "Soft War" Civil American* 2, Article 2. Society of Philosophers in America. https://www.philosophersinamerica.com/2017/05/25/state-sponsored-hacktivism-and-soft-war/

Sauter, Molly. 2014. *The Coming Swarm: DDOS Actions, Hacktivism, and Civil Disobedience on the Internet.* New York: Bloomsbury Publishing USA. http://oddletters.com/files/2014/04/Sauter-The-Coming-Swarm-CC-Copy.pdf

Theohary, Catherine A., and John W. Rollins. 2015. *Cyberwarfare and Cyberterrorism: In Brief.* Washington, DC: Congressional Research Service.

Weapons of Mass Destruction (WMDs)

Weapons of mass destruction (WMDs) have three major types: nuclear, biological, and chemical. Some people think that this range should be expanded to include electromagnetic pulse weapons (EMP), radioactive dirty bombs, recent developments like cyberwarfare, and sophisticated information operations. By any definition, all WMDs are characterized by the potential to cause large numbers of casualties without distinction between combatants and civilians. The prospect of terrorists acquiring such weapons has renewed interest in them and in defenses against WMDs deployed by either states or terrorists.

Nuclear weapons cause the most general destruction because they can destroy structures as well as people. They were used twice in war, over Hiroshima, Japan, on August 6, 1945, and over Nagasaki, Japan, on August 9, 1945. These were relatively primitive, small atom bombs compared to modern hydrogen or thermonuclear bombs that can be 1,000 times more powerful. Those two weapons each destroyed the city and about 200,000 citizens, when long-term radiation effects are included. Global warhead inventories peaked in 1986 at over 70,000 nuclear warheads, but they have since declined to about 15,000 held by 9 countries: Russia, the United States, China, France, Great Britain, Israel, India, Pakistan, and North Korea. The *Bulletin of the Atomic Scientists* is a periodical founded by scientists who actually built the first nuclear weapons. Its website has great details on global nuclear weapons inventories and issues.

Biological weapons have a longer history, as medieval warriors sometimes threw plague-infected corpses into besieged cities, and some American colonists shared smallpox-infected blankets with local Indians with the goal of reducing their populations. The Soviet Union (and to a lesser degree the United States) developed "cocktails" of mixed smallpox and anthrax agents complete with delivery systems. The United States also used some biological weapons to attack Cuban agriculture during Operation Mongoose in the Cold War. This superpower rivalry frightened the world so much that comprehensive arms control legislation (both international and national) prohibited further development, production, or stockpiling of biological weapons by nations in 1975.

Modern genetic engineering techniques raise even more fearsome possibilities of designer germs enabled to resist medicines and infect all people. Perhaps the worst nightmare of biological weapons is that they can reproduce themselves. Therefore, a disease organism that might infect everyone could, in theory, grow from the point of attack to damage the entire world. Despite such nightmare scenarios, biological weapons have actually killed fewer people in the last century than either nuclear or chemical weapons.

Chemical weapons became infamous during World War I, when mustard gas and other relatively primitive but deadly weapons were used by both sides during trench warfare in Europe. These gases were very efficient at killing or maiming a large number of troops, but if the wind suddenly changed direction, clouds of deadly gas could turn back to kill the troops who deployed the gas. Indiscriminate deaths of civilians were also unintended but common effects. In World War II, Germans also used chemical agents to kill some millions of Jews, Gypsies, and other victims in concentration/extermination camps. This unpredictability, persistent lethality, and inability to stop the spread of effects on battlefields contributed to attempts to ban both chemical and biological weapons after World War II.

Despite the essentially total ban on chemical weapons in international law (Chemical Weapons Convention of April 29, 1997) and the presence of very sophisticated control institutions like the Organization for the Prohibition of Chemical Weapons (OPCW), some modern "nerve agents" have been used in recent years to assassinate Kim Jong-nam (the half-brother of North Korea's leader) in Malaysia in 2017 and in assassination attempts by Russia. The Organization for the Prohibition of Chemical Weapons (OPCW) maintains the most comprehensive collection of open-source education resources in the world on chemical weapons.

Terrorist groups have expressed considerable interest in WMDs. Therefore, better control of WMDs before terrorists can build or buy any is a top priority for counterterrorism today.

Michael Andregg

See also: Anthrax Attacks of 2001; Biological Weapons; Electromagnetic Pulse; New Terrorism.

FURTHER READING

Cirincione, Joseph, John B. Wolfsthal, and Miriam Rajkumar. 2005. *Deadly Arsenals: Nuclear, Biological and Chemical Threats.* 2nd ed. Washington, DC: Carnegie Endowment for International Peace.

Wright, Susan. 2002. *Biological Warfare and Disarmament: New Problems/New Perspectives.* Lanham, MD: Rowman & Littlefield.

Organization for the Prohibition of Chemical Weapons (OPCW) at https://www.opcw.org / maintains the most comprehensive collection of open-source education resources in the world on chemical weapons.

Note: The *Bulletin of the Atomic Scientists* is a periodical founded by scientists who actually built the first nuclear weapons. Its website has great details on global nuclear weapons inventories and issues at http://thebulletin.org. Their "Nuclear Notebook" at http://thebulletin.org/nuclear-notebook-multimedia is of special value.

World Trade Center Attack

February 26, 1993

Transnational (i.e., extra-continental) terrorism's arrival on the world stage is generally dated from October 1972, when Arab terrorists journeyed to Munich and attacked the Israeli athletes participating in the Olympic Games there. It arrived in the United States a little after noon on February 26, 1993, when terrorists from the Middle East tried to bring down the Twin Towers of the World Trade Center (WTC) by toppling the north tower into the other.

The explosive device was a gas-enhanced bomb weighing approximately 1,300 pounds, parked in a rented Ryder Ford van on a ramp linking the two towers in the WTC's underground garage. In the mid-1980s, a government agency had warned that the garages were vulnerable to terrorism, but the recommendation for eliminating public parking in them was rejected.

The bomb itself, whose explosion killed six people and injured more than a thousand, was the handiwork of Ramzi Ahmed Yousef, an explosives expert and Kuwaiti native. He arrived in the United States from Pakistan in September of the previous year, after being trained in an al-Qaeda camp in Afghanistan, a fact that only became known several years later. Once in the United States, he immediately began planning the attack. His coconspirators, the majority recruited from among the followers of the "Blind Sheikh," Omar Abdel Rahman, would eventually include Mohammad Salameh (who rented the van), Eyad Ismoil (the driver of the van), Mahmud Abouhalima, Nidal A. Ayyad, Ahmed Ajaj, and Abdul Rahman Yasin.

Four of these seven—Abouhalima, Salameh, Ayyad, and Ajaj—were arrested in short order. The plate containing the van's vehicle identification number (VIN) was located amid the blast's debris, and the rental dealership identified Salameh, who had reported the van stolen. Salameh was consequently arrested on March 4 when he returned to the rental agency to retrieve his deposit. A search of his apartment and investigation into his associates eventually led to other arrests, and in March of the following year, all four were convicted of their roles in the explosion and given life sentences.

In the meantime, Yousef, Ismoil, and Yasin were able to flee the United States; however, once Yousef's central role in the bombing became known, the U.S. Department of State offered a $2 million reward for information leading to his arrest. Based on an informant's lead, that arrest occurred in Pakistan on February 7, 1995, the same year in which Ismoil was arrested in Jordan. Both were subsequently extradited to the United States, and, in November 1997, both received life sentences for their roles in the bombing. Yasin, who fled to Iraq after being questioned by the FBI, disappeared from there following the American invasion of that country in March 2003 and remains at large.

Two principals in the investigation but unindicted for the bombing were Yousef's uncle, Khalid Sheikh Mohammed, who provided minor funding for the venture and was later thought of as an architect of the 9/11 attack on the WTC, and the Blind Sheikh. The investigation into the latter's affairs, however, revealed plans for terrorist attacks across the United States, and he was eventually tried and convicted on other charges. Meanwhile, the 1993 attack led to new evacuation procedures that are widely credited with having saved lives in the 2001 attack on the WTC.

Joseph R. Rudolph Jr.

See also: Counterterrorism and the Clinton Administration; Munich Olympics Terrorist Attack; September 11, 2001, Attack on America.

FURTHER READING

Bureau of Diplomatic Security, U.S. Department of State. "1993 World Trade Center Bombing." DDS Articles, February 21, 2019. https://www.state.gov/1993-world-trade-center-bombing

Dwyer, Jim, Deidre Murphy, Peg Tyre, and David Kocieniewski. 1997. *Two Seconds under the World: Terror Comes to America—The Conspiracy behind the World Trade Center Bombing.* New York: Crown Publishing.

Greenspan, Jesse. 2018. "Remembering the 1993 World Trade Center Bombing." History, September 1, 2018. https://www.history.com/news/remembering-the-1993-world-trade-center-bombing

PRIMARY DOCUMENTS

Internment of Americans of Japanese Heritage during World War II, 1942

Executive Order No 9066, Relocation of Japanese during World War II, February 19, 1942

U.S. citizens have long been proud of their rights and liberties. Yet, the new country was less than a decade old when President John Adams in 1798 signed into law the four bills collectively known as the Alien and Sedition Acts. These bills infringed on the liberty of citizens and impeded the pathway of immigrants seeking full citizenship. Three of these bills—the Naturalization Act, which lengthened the residency requirement for citizenship from five to fourteen years; the Alien Friends Act, which permitted the incarceration or deportation of those deemed dangerous to the country's security; and the Sedition Act, which criminalized the making of false statements critical of the government—were either repealed or allowed to lapse by 1802.

The fourth law signed by Adams, the Alien Enemy Act of 1798, permits the president to imprison and deport "aliens"—liberally defined to include American citizens who originated from a hostile country during wartime—and is still on the books in a recodified form as part of U.S. Code Title 50, War and National Defense. Cited as the authority for President Franklin D. Roosevelt's issuance of Executive Order 9066, the Alien Enemy Act also served as the basis for the World War II imprisonment of those deemed to be suspected agents of Japan, Germany, and Italy. Authorization for these actions came from Presidential Proclamations 2525, 2526, and 2527, respectively, issued in the immediate aftermath of the Japanese attack on Pearl Harbor. In 1948, the U.S. Supreme Court, ruling in Ludecke v. Watkins *(335 U.S. 160), widened the applicability of the Alien Enemy Act by allowing the detainment of "enemy aliens" beyond the duration of hostilities and until the signing of a treaty between the United States and the former adversary.*

Meanwhile, World War I resulted in the passage of two new laws—the Espionage and Sedition Acts of 1917–1918—that infringed on the freedoms of speech and press guaranteed in the First Amendment of the U.S. Constitution. The Espionage Act of 1917 focused on prohibiting individuals from verbally expressing or publishing statements that could impede the U.S. war efforts. The more controversial Sedition Act extended this curtailment of First Amendment freedoms to the uttering or writing of anything critical of the U.S. involvement in World War I. Both acts were upheld by the Supreme Court in the 1919 case of Schenck v. United States *(249 U.S. 47) on the reasoning that acts such as openly opposing conscription during war can constitute a "clear and present danger" to the country's wartime security.*

Although portions of the Espionage Act continue to be a part of U.S. law, the federal government repealed the more controversial Sedition Act in 1921. By then, however, federal authorities had convicted approximately 1,000 individuals under the acts for inhibiting the war effort or criticizing the government and the Constitution in a disloyal or profane fashion.

Nonetheless, Executive Order 9066, which was promulgated on February 9, 1942, and authorized the forced detention and dispersal of Japanese Americans from their West Coast homes to relocation centers built by the military across the country, constitutes the greatest incursion on U.S. civil rights during wartime. Issued shortly after a March 2 military order imposing a tight curfew on the movements of Japanese Americans living within forty miles of the West Coast, Executive Order 9066 eventually resulted in the coerced relocation of more than 110,000 people of Japanese descent, over 60 percent of whom were U.S. citizens.

To these numbers can be added residents of German and Italian ancestry who were directly affected by post–Pearl Harbor security measures. In January 1942, the Department of Justice required both groups to register in post offices, be fingerprinted and photographed, and issued identification cards to be carried at all times. Mass relocation of these peoples, however, was rejected given the hundreds of thousands of Americans of Italian and German descent. Hence, internment overwhelmingly involved German and Italian nationals rather than American citizens. In all, slightly more than 10,000 Germans and slightly fewer than 2,000 Italians were detained at least temporarily as enemy aliens, with proportionately few housed in the Department of Justice's relocation centers throughout the war.

Constitutional questions involving the federal government's actions in imprisoning residents for seditious utterances during World War I only reached the Supreme Court after the conclusion of that war. By contrast, the Supreme Court heard several cases involving the detention of those of Japanese ancestry while World War II was still in progress. The most significant of these were Hirabayashi v. United States *(320 U.S. 81) in 1943, which sustained the government's right to impose a curfew law*, and Korematsu v. United States *(323 U.S. 214), which in 1944 upheld the forced relocation of those of Japanese ancestry. In both cases, the Supreme Court explicitly noted that distinctions based on race would normally be highly suspect; the* Hirabayashi *decision used the phrase "odious to a free people" to describe such measures. In both cases, however, a majority of justices upheld the government's internment actions against people of Japanese descent, being unwilling "by availing ourselves of the calm perspective of hindsight—now to say that at the time these actions were unjustified" (*Korematsu*). Facilitating that conclusion, Justice Black wrote for the majority in* Korematsu, *was the fact that "five thousand American citizens of Japanese ancestry refused to swear unqualified allegiance to the United States and to renounce allegiance to the Japanese Emperor and several thousand evacuees requested repatriation to Japan."*

Although neither the federal government nor a state government has ever apologized to German Americans for the policies targeting them during the World War II, in 2010, the California State Legislature passed a resolution apologizing to its Italian community for their wartime treatment. During the early 1980s, a federal Commission on Wartime Relocation and Internment of Civilians (which convened 1980–1983) had recommended that the U.S. government do the same for Japanese Americans and pay reparations to those whose lives were disrupted by the "racial prejudice, wartime hysteria, and failure of political leadership" that led to their internment. In 1988, President Reagan signed a congressional bill that did both. Thirty years later, in 2018, the Supreme Court took the opportunity to apologize as well in the case of Trump, President of the United States, et al. v. Hawaii, et al., *in which a dissenting opinion used the* Korematsu *decision in support of its stance. Responding for the majority, Chief Justice John Roberts stated that the dissent's reference to* Korematsu *"affords this Court the opportunity to make express what is already obvious*: Korematsu *was gravely wrong the day it was decided, has been overruled in the court of history, and—to be clear—has no place in law under the Constitution" (323 U. S., at 248).*

Executive Order No. 9066
The President
Executive Order
Authorizing the Secretary of War to Prescribe Military Areas

Whereas the successful prosecution of the war requires every possible protection against espionage and against sabotage to national-defense material, national-defense premises, and national-defense utilities as defined in Section 4, Act of April 20, 1918, 40 Stat. 533, as amended by the Act of November 30, 1940, 54 Stat. 1220, and the Act of August 21, 1941, 55 stat. 655 (U.S.C., Title 50, Sec. 104):

Now, therefore, by virtue of the authority vested in me as President of the United States and Commander in Chief of the Army and Navy, I hereby authorize and direct the Secretary of War, and the Military Commanders whom he may from time to time designate, whenever he or any designated Commander deems such action necessary or desirable, to prescribe military areas in such places and of such extent as he or the appropriate Military commander may determine, from which any or all persons may be excluded and with respect to which, the right of any person to enter, remain in, or leave shall be subject to whatever restrictions the Secretary of War or the appropriate Military Commander may impose in his discretion. The Secretary of War is hereby authorized to provide for residents of any such area who are excluded therefrom, such transportation, food, shelter and other accommodations as may be necessary, in the judgment of the Secretary of War or the said Military Commander, and until other arrangements are made, to accomplish the purposes of this order. The designation of military areas in any region or locality shall supersede designations of prohibited and restricted areas by the Attorney General under the proclamations of December 7 and 8, 1941, and shall supersede the responsibility and authority of the Attorney General under the said Proclamations in respect to such prohibited and restricted areas.

I hereby further authorize and direct the Secretary of War and the said Military Commanders to take such other steps as he or the appropriate Military Commander may deem advisable to enforce compliance with the restrictions applicable to each Military area hereinabove authorized to be designated, including the use of Federal troops and other Federal agencies, with authority to accept assistance of state and local agencies.

I further here by authorize and direct all Executive Departments, independent establishments and other Federal Agencies, to assist the Secretary of War or the said Military commanders in carrying out this Executive Order, including the furnishing of medical aid, hospitalization, food, clothing, transportation, use of land, shelter, and other supplies, equipment, utilities, facilities, and services.

This order shall not be construed as modifying or limiting in any way the authority heretofore granted under Executive Order No. 8972, dated December 12, 1941, not shall it be construed as limiting or modifying the duty and responsibility of the Federal Bureau of Investigation, with respect to the investigation of alleged acts of sabotage or the duty and responsibility of the Attorney General and the Department of Justice under the Proclamations of December 7 and 8, 1941, prescribing regulations for the conduct and control of alien enemies, except as such duty and responsibility is superseded by the designation of military areas hereunder.

Franklin D. Roosevelt
The White House, January 18, 1942

Source: Executive Order 9066, February 19, 1942. General Records of the United States Government; Record Group 11; National Archives.

Griswold v. Connecticut and the Right to Privacy, 1965

Griswold v. Connecticut *(381 U.S. 479), June 7, 1965*

U.S. law enforcement agencies, including those charged with counterterrorism duties, function under a Bill of Rights system that limits their operations to a far greater extent than the restrictions that their counterparts face in other Western democracies. Under the protections provided by the First Amendment, for example, white supremacists are entitled to hold public meetings and indulge in hate speech so long as it falls short of provoking immediate public harm. The Second Amendment enables their members, excepting those with criminal records or a history of mental illness, to purchase firearms—firearms that many states allow owners to carry openly while demonstrating. The rights enumerated in the Bill of Rights are explicit, though also subject to changes in meaning and application over time. "Freedom of assembly" means the right to meet freely without arbitrary interference by government, "freedom of speech" means the right to speak freely, and so forth. Not so is the derivative "right to privacy," which was "found" in the U.S. Constitution by the U.S. Supreme Court in Griswold v. Connecticut. *From the outset, this right posed three major questions or issues with implications for U.S. intelligence and counterespionage and counterterrorism agencies.*

The first issue concerned the degree to which government agencies may have already been invading the zones of privacy protected from governmental infringement when the court decided Griswold. *The answer came within a decade, when newspaper revelations of spying on American civilians by U.S. military and intelligence agencies and covert assassination plots by the CIA against foreign governments led to the 1975 creation of the U.S. Senate Select Committee to Study Governmental Operations with Respect to Intelligence Activities.*

More commonly known as the Church Committee, after its chairman, Senator Frank Church of Idaho, the committee carried out exhaustive investigations of the CIA, National Security Agency (NSA), FBI, and Internal Revenue Service (IRS).

Investigators found that major telecommunications companies had regularly shared private customer information with the NSA for more than a quarter century and that the CIA and FBI had been secretly opening the mail of American citizens for years prior to the termination of the program in 1973.

Drawing a firm line against such activities, however, was difficult given the problem of reconciling the right to privacy with the legitimate need of intelligence services to collect domestic intelligence to protect American society from hostile foreign agents within. The Griswold *decision, after all, came amid the Cold War's most dangerous days, less than three years after the 1962 Cuban Missile Crisis brought the United States and Soviet Union to the edge of a thermonuclear war.*

The policy response came a decade later, in 1978, during the détente era between the superpowers and two years after the Church Committee tendered its findings in April 1976. The Foreign Intelligence Surveillance Court (FISC) was established to review governmental applications for surveillance and related activities pertaining to the collection of foreign intelligence inside the United States. With respect to non-foreign intelligence surveillance, Katz v. United States *(1967), which was decided two years after* Griswold, *remains the foundation case. As a result of the court's ruling in* Katz, *the wiretapping, eavesdropping, and other information gathering techniques on private citizens that were previously common subsequent to* Griswold *must now obtain (ordinary) court-issued probable cause warrants to satisfy Fourth Amendment requirements of legality.*

Meanwhile, the third issue remains and looms ever larger in our age of soaring electronic communications: how broad is the right to privacy, and what does it cover today? The answer still essentially lies in the twofold test suggested by Justice John Marshall Harlan II in his concurring opinion in Katz v. United States. *To invoke the claim of Fourth Amendment protection against government action, an individual must demonstrate that he or she believed himself or herself to have been operating in a protected zone and that society might agree that such an expectation would be reasonable. Unfortunately, determining whether there is a "reasonable expectation of privacy" often comes down to expensive judicial litigation on a case-by-case basis.*

Mr. Justice Douglas delivered the Opinion of the Court, reversing the lower court opinion upholding Connecticut's anti-contraception law. In addition to Justice Douglas's opinion, three other Justices filed three separate concurring opinions. Two Justices, Black and Steward, dissented in separate opinions.

Mr. Justice Douglas

Coming to the merits, we are met with a wide range of questions that implicate the Due Process Clause of the Fourteenth Amendment. . . . We do not sit as a super-legislature to determine the wisdom, need, and propriety of laws that touch economic problems, business affairs, or social conditions. This law, however, operates directly on an intimate relation of husband and wife and their physician's role in one aspect of that relation.

The association of people is not mentioned in the Constitution nor in the Bill of Rights. The right to educate a child in a school of the parents' choice—whether public or private or parochial—is also not mentioned. Nor is the right to study any particular subject or any foreign language. Yet the First Amendment has been construed to include certain of those rights.

By *Pierce v. Society of Sisters, supra*, the right to educate one's children as one chooses is made applicable to the States by the force of the First and Fourteenth Amendments. By *Meyer v. Nebraska, supra*, the same dignity is given the right to study the German language in a private school. In other words, the State may not, consistently with the spirit of the First Amendment, contract the spectrum of available knowledge. The right of freedom of speech and press includes not only the right to utter or to print, but the right to distribute, the right to receive, the right to read (*Martin v. Struthers*, 319 U.S. 141, 143) and freedom of inquiry, freedom of thought, and freedom to teach. . . . Without those peripheral rights, the specific rights would be less secure. And so we reaffirm the principle of the *Pierce* and the *Meyer* cases.

In *NAACP v. Alabama*, 357 U.S. 449, 462 we protected the "freedom to associate and privacy in one's associations," noting that freedom of association was a peripheral First Amendment right. Disclosure of membership lists of a constitutionally valid association, we held, was invalid

> as entailing the likelihood of a substantial restraint upon the exercise by petitioner's members of their right to freedom of association.

Ibid. In other words, the First Amendment has a penumbra where privacy is protected from governmental intrusion. In like context, we have protected forms of "association" that are not political in the customary sense, but pertain to the social, legal, and economic benefit of the members.

Those cases involved more than the "right of assembly"—a right that extends to all, irrespective of their race or ideology. *De Jonge v. Oregon*, 299 U.S. 353. The right of "association," like the right of belief (*Board of Education v. Barnette*, 319 U.S. 624), is more than the right to attend a meeting; it includes the right to express one's attitudes or philosophies by membership in a group or by affiliation with it or by other lawful means. Association in that context is a form of expression of opinion, and, while it is not expressly included in the First Amendment, its existence is necessary in making the express guarantees fully meaningful.

The foregoing cases suggest that specific guarantees in the Bill of Rights have penumbras, formed by emanations from those guarantees that help give them life and substance. *See Poe v. Ullman*, 367 U.S. 497, 516–522 (dissenting opinion). Various guarantees create zones of privacy. The right of association contained in the penumbra of the First Amendment is one, as we have seen. The Third Amendment, in its prohibition against the quartering of soldiers "in any house" in time of peace without the consent of the owner, is another facet of that privacy. The Fourth Amendment explicitly affirms the "right of the people to be secure in their persons, houses, papers, and effects, against unreasonable searches and seizures." The Fifth Amendment, in its Self-Incrimination Clause, enables the citizen to create a zone of privacy which government may not force him to surrender to his detriment. The Ninth Amendment provides: "The enumeration in the Constitution, of certain rights, shall not be construed to deny or disparage others retained by the people."

We recently referred in *Mapp v. Ohio*, 367 U.S. 643, 656, to the Fourth Amendment as creating a "right to privacy, no less important than any other right carefully an particularly reserved to the people."

We have had many controversies over these penumbral rights of "privacy and repose." . . . These cases bear witness that the right of privacy which presses for recognition here is a legitimate one.

The present case, then, concerns a relationship lying within the zone of privacy created by several fundamental constitutional guarantees. And it concerns a law which, in forbidding the use of contraceptives, rather than regulating their manufacture or sale, seeks to achieve its goals by means having a maximum destructive impact upon that relationship. Such a law cannot stand in light of the familiar principle, so often applied by this Court, that a

> governmental purpose to control or prevent activities constitutionally subject to state regulation may not be achieved by means which sweep unnecessarily broadly and thereby invade the area of protected freedoms.

NAACP v. Alabama, 377 U.S. 288, 307. Would we allow the police to search the sacred precincts of marital bedrooms for telltale signs of the use of contraceptives? The very idea is repulsive to the notions of privacy surrounding the marriage relationship.

Reversed. (pp. 482–487)

Justice Black, Dissenting

Speech is one thing; conduct and physical activities are quite another. *See, e.g., Cox v. Louisiana*, 379 U.S. 536, 554–555; . . . The two defendants here were active participants in an organization which gave physical examinations to women, advised them what kind of contraceptive devices or medicines would most likely be satisfactory for them, and then supplied the devices themselves, all for a graduated scale of fees, based on the family income. Thus, these defendants admittedly engaged with others in a planned course of conduct to help people violate the Connecticut law. Merely because some speech was used in carrying on that conduct—just as, in ordinary life, some speech accompanies most kinds of conduct—we are not, in my view, justified in holding that the First Amendment forbids the State to punish their conduct. Strongly as I desire to protect all First Amendment freedoms, I am unable to stretch the Amendment so as to afford protection to the conduct of these defendants in violating the Connecticut law.

The Court talks about a constitutional "right of privacy" as though there is some constitutional provision or provisions forbidding any law ever to be passed which might abridge the "privacy" of individuals. But there is not. There are, of course, guarantees in certain specific constitutional provisions which are designed in part to protect privacy at certain times and places with respect to certain activities. Such, for example, is the Fourth Amendment's guarantee against "unreasonable searches and seizures." But I think it belittles that Amendment to talk about it as though it protects nothing but "privacy." To treat it that way is to give it a niggardly interpretation, not the kind of liberal reading I think any Bill of Rights provision should be given. . . .

One of the most effective ways of diluting or expanding a constitutionally guaranteed right is to substitute for the crucial word or words of a constitutional guarantee another word or words, more or less flexible and more or less restricted in meaning. This fact is well illustrated by the use of the term "right of privacy" as a comprehensive substitute for the Fourth Amendment's guarantee against "unreasonable searches and seizures." "Privacy" is a broad, abstract and ambiguous concept which can easily be shrunken in meaning but which can also, on the other hand, easily be interpreted as a constitutional ban against many things other than searches and seizures. . . . (pp. 507–510)

Source: Justice Douglas's majority opinion and Justice Black's dissent, *Griswold v. Connecticut* (381 U.S. 479), June 7, 1965.

Church Committee Condemns Excessive Government Surveillance of Americans, 1976

Church Committee Report on Intelligence Activities and the Rights of Americans, *U.S. Senate, April 14, 1976*

The difficulty of balancing the twin quests for liberty and security in the United States is as old as the constitutional system itself. In the 1790s, for instance, conflict raged between the Federalists supporting the Alien and Sedition Acts and those perceiving them as unconstitutional and even subject to nullification by the states (per the Virginia and Kentucky Resolutions).

A century later, the task became even more difficult, with the rise of the "national security state" in response to two World Wars and the Cold War on the one hand and the U.S. Supreme Court's decision in Griswold v. Connecticut *recognizing a constitutional right to privacy on the other. The tensions between these goals was cast in stark relief in 1971 with Daniel Ellsberg's disclosures of government lying and spying by the Johnson administration during the Vietnam War. Ellsberg's documents, released as* The Pentagon Papers *and printed in the* New York Times, *led to a flurry of congressional investigatory hearings to identify the actors carrying out surveillance of American citizens and the scope of their activity. The most extensive of these oversight inquiries was that of the Select Committee to Study Government Operations with Respect to Intelligence Activities chaired by Senator Frank Church of Idaho. In 1976, it tendered its final report in multiple volumes. Book II (excerpted below) specifically focuses on abuses of the constitutional rights of domestic citizens.*

INTELLIGENCE ACTIVITIES AND THE RIGHTS OF AMERICANS

BOOK II

I. INTRODUCTION AND SUMMARY

. . .

The critical question before the Committee was to determine how the fundamental liberties of the people can be maintained in the course of the Government's effort to protect their security. . . . We reject the view that the traditional American principles of justice and fair play have no place in our struggle against the enemies of freedom. Moreover, our investigation has established that the targets of intelligence activity have ranged far beyond persons who could properly be characterized as enemies of freedom and have extended to a wide array of citizens engaging in lawful activity. [1]

. . .

C. Summary of the Main Problems

. . .

. . . Too many people have been spied upon by too many Government agencies and to [*sic*] much information has been collected. The Government has often undertaken the secret surveillance of citizens on the basis of their political beliefs, even when those beliefs posed no threat of violence or illegal acts on behalf of a hostile foreign power. The Government, operating primarily through secret informants, but also using other intrusive techniques such as wiretaps, microphone "bugs", surreptitious mail opening, and break-ins, has swept in vast amounts of information about the personal lives, views, and associations of American citizens. Investigations of groups deemed potentially dangerous—and even of groups suspected of associating with potentially dangerous organizations—have continued for decades, despite the fact that those groups did not engage in unlawful activity. Groups and individuals have been harassed and disrupted because of their political views and their lifestyles. . . . Unsavory and vicious tactics have been employed—including anonymous attempts to break up marriages, disrupt meetings, ostracize persons from their professions, and provoke target groups into rivalries that might result in deaths. Intelligence agencies have served the political and personal objectives of presidents and other high officials. While the agencies often committed excesses in response to pressure from high officials in the Executive branch and Congress, they also occasionally initiated improper activities and then concealed them from officials whom they had a duty to inform. . . . [5]

3. Covert Action and the Use of Illegal or Improper Means

(a) Covert Action.—Apart from uncovering excesses in the collection of intelligence, our investigation has disclosed covert actions directed against Americans, and the use of illegal and improper surveillance techniques to gather information. For example:

(i) The FBI's COINTELPRO—counterintelligence program—was designed to "disrupt" groups and "neutralize" individuals deemed to be threats to domestic security. The FBI resorted to counterintelligence tactics in part because its chief officials believed that the existing law could not control the activities of certain dissident groups, and that court decisions had tied the hands of the intelligence community. Whatever opinion one holds about the policies of the targeted groups, many of the tactics employed by the FBI were indisputably degrading to a free society. COINTELPRO tactics included:

–Anonymously attacking the political beliefs of targets in order to induce their employers to fire them;
–Anonymously mailing letters to the spouses of intelligence targets for the purpose of destroying their marriages;
–Obtaining from IRS the tax returns of a target and then attempting to provoke an IRS investigation for the express purpose of deterring a protest leader from attending the Democratic National Convention;
–Falsely and anonymously labeling as Government informants members of groups known to be violent, thereby exposing the falsely labelled member to expulsion or physicial [*sic*] attack; . . . [10]

6. The Adverse Impact of Improper Intelligence Activity

. . .

(b) Media Manipulation.—The FBI has attempted covertly to influence the public's perception of persons and organizations by disseminating derogatory information to the press, either anonymously or through "friendly" news contacts. . . .The Bureau also attempted to influence media reporting which would have any impact on the public image of the FBI. Examples include:

–Planting a series of derogatory articles about Martin Luther King, Jr., and the Poor People's Campaign. . . . [15–16]

(e) Preventing the Free Exchange of Ideas. Speakers, teachers, writers, and publications themselves were targets of the FBI's counterintelligence program. The FBIs efforts to interfere with the free exchange of ideas included:

–Anonymously attempting to prevent an alleged "Communist front" group from holding a forum on a midwest campus, and then investigating the judge who ordered that the meeting be allowed to proceed.
–Using another "confidential source" in a foundation which contributed to a local college to apply pressure on the school to fire an activist professor. . . . [17]

II. THE GROWTH OF DOMESTIC INTELLIGENCE: 1936 TO 1976

A. Summary

1. The Lesson: History Repeats Itself

During and after the First World War, intelligence agencies, including the predecessor of the FBI, engaged in repressive activity. A new Attorney General, Harlan Fiske Stone, sought to stop the investigation of "political or other opinions." This restraint was embodied only in an executive pronouncement, however. No statutes were passed to prevent the kind of improper activity which had been exposed. Thereafter, as this narrative will show, the abuses returned in a new form.

2.The Pattern: Broadening Through Time

Since the re-establishment of federal domestic intelligence programs in 1936, there has been a steady increase in the government's capability and willingness to pry into, and even disrupt, the political activities and personal lives of the people. The last forty years have witnessed a relentless expansion of domestic intelligence activity beyond investigation of criminal conduct toward the collection of political intelligence and the launching of secret offensive actions against Americans. . . . [21]

3. Three Periods of Growth for Domestic Intelligence

. . .

a. 1936–1945

By presidential directive—rather than statute—the FBI and military intelligence agencies were authorized to conduct domestic intelligence investigations. These investigations included a vaguely defined mission to collect intelligence about "subversive activities" which were sometimes unrelated to law enforcement. Wartime exigencies encouraged the unregulated use of intrusive intelligence techniques; and the FBI began to resist supervision by the Attorney General.

b. 1946–1963

Cold War fears and dangers nurtured the domestic intelligence programs of the FBI and military, and they became permanent features of government. Congress deferred to the executive branch in the oversight of these programs. . . . The scope of investigations of "subversion" widened greatly. Under the cloak of secrecy, the FBI instituted its COINTELPRO operations to "disrupt" and "neutralize" "subversives". The National Security Agency, the FBI, and the CIA re-instituted intrusive wartime surveillance techniques in contravention of law.

c. 1964–1976

Intelligence techniques which previously had been concentrated upon foreign threats and domestic groups said to be under Communist influence were applied with increasing intensity to a wide range of domestic activity by American citizens. . . . [22]

[Elaborating Segments]

4. Domestic Covert Action

a. COINTELPRO

The FBI's initiation of COINTELPRO operations against the Ku Klux Klan, "Black Nationalists" and the "New Left" brought to bear upon a wide range of domestic groups the techniques previously developed to combat Communists and persons who happened to associate with them.

The start of each program coincided with significant national events. The Klan program followed the widely-publicized disappearance in 1964 of three civil rights workers in Mississippi. The "Black Nationalist" program was authorized in the aftermath of the Newark and Detroit riots in 1967. The "New Left" program developed shortly after student disruption of the Columbia University campus in the spring of 1968.

These programs were not directed at obtaining evidence for use in possible criminal prosecutions arising out of those events. Rather, they were secret programs—"under no circumstances" to be "made known outside the Bureau." . . . [86]

(3) "New Left" COINTELPRO.—The most vaguely defined and haphazard of the COINTELPRO operations was that initiated against the "New Left" in May 1968. It was justified to the FBI Director by his subordinates on the basis of the following considerations:

> The nation was "undergoing an era of disruption and violence" which was "caused to a large extent" by individuals "generally connected with the New Left."
>
> Some of these "activists" were urging "revolution" and calling for "the defeat of the United States in Vietnam. . . ."

Consequently, the COINTELPRO was intended to "expose, disrupt, and otherwise neutralize" the activities of "this group" and "persons connected with it." The lack of any clear definition of "New Left" meant, as an FBI supervisor testified, that "legitimate" and nonviolent antiwar groups were targeted because they were "lending aid and comfort" to more disruptive groups. [88]

5. Foreign Intelligence and Domestic Dissent

In the late 1960's, CIA and NSA, acting in response to presidential pressure, turned their technological capacity and great resources toward spying on certain Americans. The initial impetus was to determine whether the antiwar movement—and to a lesser extent the "black power" movement—were controlled by foreigners. Despite evidence that there was no significant foreign influence, the intelligence gathering which culminated in CIA's "Operation CHAOS" followed the general pattern of broadening in scope and intensity. . . . [96]

(2) Operation CHAOS.—. . .Under White House pressure, the CIA developed its own program—Operation CHAOS[,] . . . although CIA officials recognized from the outset that it had "definite domestic counterintelligence aspects.

The first CHAOS instructions to CIA station chiefs in August 1967 described the need for "keeping tabs on radical students and U.S. Negro expatriates as well as travelers passing through certain select areas abroad." [99–100]

III. FINDINGS

. . .

A. VIOLATING AND IGNORING THE LAW

Major Findings

The Committee finds that the domestic activities of the intelligence community at times violated specific statutory prohibitions and infringed the constitutional rights of American citizens. The legal questions involved in intelligence programs were often not considered. On other occasions, they were intentionally disregarded in the belief that because the programs served the "national security" the law did not apply. . . . The Committee finds that the most serious breaches of duty were those of senior officials, who were responsible for controlling intelligence activities and generally failed to assure compliance with the law. . . . [137]

D. USING COVERT ACTION TO DISRUPT AND DISCREDIT DOMESTIC GROUPS

Major Findings

The Committee finds that covert action programs have been used to disrupt the lawful political activities of individual Americans and groups and to discredit them, using dangerous and degrading tactics which are abhorrent in a free and decent society.

Subfindings

(a) Although the claimed purposes of these action programs were to protect the national security and to prevent violence, many of the victims were concededly nonviolent, were not controlled by a foreign power, and posed no threat to the national security.

(b) The acts taken interfered with the First Amendment rights of citizens. They were explicitly intended to deter citizens from joining groups, "neutralize" those who were already members, and prevent or inhibit the expression of ideas.

(d) The sustained use of such tactics by the FBI in an attempt to destroy Dr. Martin Luther King, Jr., violated the law and fundamental human decency. . . . [211]

E. POLITICAL ABUSE OF INTELLIGENCE INFORMATION

Major Findings

. . .

The Committee finds that information has been collected and disseminated in order to serve the purely political interests of an intelligence agency or the administration, and to influence social policy and political action.

Subfindings

(a) White House officials have requested and obtained politically useful information from the FBI, including information on the activities of political opponents or critics.

(b)Neither the FBI nor the recipients differentiated in these cases between national security or law enforcement information and purely political intelligence.

(c) The FBI has also volunteered information to Presidents and their staffs, without having been asked for it, sometimes apparently to curry favor with the current administration. Similarly, the FBI has assembled intelligence on its critics and on political figures it believed might influence public attitudes or Congressional support. . . . [225]

G. DEFICIENCIES IN CONTROL AND ACCOUNTABILITY

. . .

Subfindings

(a) Presidents have given intelligence agencies firm orders to collect information concerning "subversive activities" of American citizens, but have failed until recently to define the limits of domestic intelligence, to provide safeguards for the rights of American citizens, or to coordinate and control the ever-expanding intelligence efforts by an increasing number of agencies. . . . [265]

(g) The weakness of the system of accountability and control can be seen in the fact that many illegal or abusive domestic intelligence operations were terminated only after they had been exposed or threatened with exposure by Congress or the news media. . . . [266]

IV. CONCLUSIONS AND RECOMMENDATIONS

A. Conclusions

. . .

Recommendation 1.—There is no inherent constitutional authority for the President or any intelligence agency to violate the law.

ii. United States Foreign and Military Agencies Should Be Precluded from Domestic Security Activities

. . . Past abuses also make it necessary that the Central Intelligence Agency, the National Security Agency, the Defense Intelligence Agency, and the military departments be precluded expressly, except as specifically provided herein, from investigative activity which is conducted within the United States. . . . [297]

Recommendation 92—The Committee believes that criminal penalties should apply, where appropriate, to willful and knowing violations of statutes enacted pursuant to the Domestic Intelligence Recommendations.

Recommendation 93.—Congress should either repeal the Smith Act (18 U.S.C. 2385) and the Voorhis Act (18 U.S.C. 2386), which on their face appear to authorize investigation of "mere advocacy" of a political ideology, or amend those statutes so that domestic security investigations are only directed at conduct which might serve as the basis for a constitutional criminal prosecution, under Supreme Court decisions interpreting these and related statutes.

Source: Select Committee to Study Governmental Operations with respect to Intelligence Activities. *Intelligence Activities and the Rights of Americans*. Book II, *Final Report*. U.S. Senate, April 26, 1976. Washington, DC: GPO, 1976. https://www.intelligence.senate.gov/sites/default/files/94755_II.pdf.

President Reagan Responds to the Hijacking of TWA Flight 847, 1985

President Ronald Reagan's Press Conference following the Hijacking of TWA Flight 847 and Murder of the U.S. Navy Diver On Board, June 18, 1985

By the time that President Ronald Reagan began his second term in office in January 1985, terrorism was no stranger to U.S. foreign policy in general or Beirut, Lebanon, in particular. Intervention in the Lebanon Civil War by the United States and its NATO allies had led to a Hezbollah suicide bombing of the U.S. Embassy in Beirut on April 18, 1983. The attack killed seventeen Americans and nearly fifty other innocent people, most of them Lebanese.

Six months later, with the Western peacekeeping presence being increasingly perceived as favoring the Christian factions in the Lebanese Civil War, Shiite suicide bombers simultaneously attacked two barracks housing American marines and French military personnel. The blasts killed 241 Americans soldiers, 58 French paratroopers, 5 French civilians, and 2 Lebanese.

In response to the bombing of the marine barracks in Beirut, President Reagan proclaimed that

> *If terrorism and intimidation succeed, it'll be a devastating blow to the peace process and to Israel's search for genuine security. It won't just be Lebanon sentenced to a future of chaos. . . . What of Western Europe and Japan's dependence on Middle East oil for the energy to fuel their industries? The Middle East is, as I've said, vital to our national security and economic well-being.*

Nonetheless, the following February, President Reagan ordered the withdrawal of what had been a force of 1,600 U.S. troops in Lebanon, indirectly handing the extremist Muslin factions a victory. Whether that withdrawal further emboldened Middle Eastern terrorist groups to escalate attacks against American targets remains debatable.

Another favorite tactic of terrorist groups during the 1960s, 1970s, and 1980s was the hijacking of commercial planes. Hijacking of American airliners began in 1961 when a domestic U.S. flight to Key West, Florida, was diverted to Cuba, and occurrences soared thereafter to over 130 hijacking and hijacking attempts in the 1960–1980 period. One of the most infamous of these hijackings was the seizure by terrorists of TWA Flight 847 in June 1985 and the subsequent brutal killing of a U.S. Navy service member on board after the flight bound for Rome was diverted to Beirut.

The hijackers' avowed purpose in seizing TWA Flight 847 was the release of approximately 700 Shiites in custody in Israel; however, once the flight landed in Beirut, several passengers were beaten, even as negotiations were inaugurated. Eventually, the hijackers murdered navy diver Robert Stethem and threw his body from the aircraft onto the runway. The following is the statement Reagan issued after learning of Stethem's death.

Other passengers, including Americans, remained as hostages for more than a week after Reagan's statement. During this period, they were repeatedly moved by the terrorists to thwart any rescue plans. They were finally released after some of their captors' kidnapping demands were met.

The President. I have a statement. One hour ago the body of a young American hero Navy diver, Robert Dean Stethem, was returned to his native soil in a coffin after being beaten and shot at pointblank range.

His murder and the fate of the other American hostages still being held in Beirut underscore an inescapable fact: The United States is tonight a nation being attacked by international terrorists who wantonly kill and who seize our innocent citizens as their prisoners.

In response to this situation, I am directing that the following steps be taken. I have directed the Secretary of Transportation, in cooperation with the Secretary of State, to explore immediately an expansion of our armed sky marshal program aboard international flights of U.S. air carriers for better protection of passengers.

I have directed the Secretary of State to issue an immediate travel advisory for U.S. citizens traveling through the Athens International Airport warning them of dangers.

This warning shall remain in effect until the Greek Government has improved the security situation there and until it has demonstrated a willingness to comply with the security provisions of the U.S.-Greek civil aviation agreement and the Tokyo, Montreal, and Hague conventions regarding prosecution and punishment of air pirates.

I've asked for a full explanation of the events surrounding the takeover of the aircraft in Athens. I have appealed through the Department of Transportation and the Federal Aviation Administration for all U.S. air carriers to review the wisdom of continuing any flights into Athens until the security situation there improves.

And further, I have asked Secretaries Shultz and Dole to report to me on whether we should terminate the service of foreign air carriers whose governments do not honor appropriate international conventions or provide adequate security at their airports.

I'm calling upon all allied and friendly governments to redouble their efforts to improve airport security and take other measures to prevent the hijacking of aircraft.

I will also be asking them to take steps to prevent travel to places where lawlessness is rampant and innocent passengers are unprotected. And I'm urging that no American enter any Middle Eastern country that does not publicly condemn and disassociate itself from this atrocity and call for the immediate safe release of our citizens.

Let me further make it plain to the assassins in Beirut and their accomplices, wherever they may be, that America will never make concessions to terrorists—to do so would only invite more terrorism—nor will we ask nor pressure any other government to do so. Once we head down that path there would be no end to it, no end to the suffering of innocent people, no end to the bloody ransom all civilized nations must pay.

This act of terrorism is a stain on Lebanon and particularly on those Lebanese in whose name it has been done. Those in Lebanon who commit these acts damage their country and their cause, and we hold them accountable.

I call upon those holding our people to release them without condition. I call upon the leaders of Lebanon, political and religious, to meet their responsibilities and to do all that is necessary to end this crime now in the name of the God they worship. And I call on other governments to speak out and use their influence as well.

This attack is an attack on all citizens of the world who seek to live free from the fear and scourge of terrorism. My thoughts and prayers are, as are those of all Americans, with the prisoners now being held in Lebanon and with their families.

Let me conclude by stating the obvious: We're in the midst of a dangerous and volatile situation. Before taking your questions, I must stress that speculation tonight over what steps we might or might not take in hypothetical circumstances can only lead terrorists to work harder. Consequently, there are many questions to which I should not and cannot respond. I think I have, in this statement, covered virtually all the points that I can safely discuss, and I'm sure that you would understand the reason for that.

Source: Reagan, Ronald. Statement on Trans World Airlines Hijacking Incident. President's Press Conference, June 18, 1985. Ronald Reagan Library. https://www.reaganlibrary.gov/research/speeches/61885c.

President Clinton's Remarks following the Oklahoma City Terrorist Bombing, 1995

President William J. Clinton's Statement following the Bombing of the Alfred P. Murrah Federal Building in Oklahoma City, April 19, 1995

The events of September 11, 2001, largely shaped and dominated security thinking during much of the following decade. Long-standing concerns with domestic terrorist organizations were set aside or de-emphasized to focus resources on combating hostile terrorist organizations abroad and the homeland security threats they might pose on American soil. Yet, the prior decade, and perhaps especially the tenure of the Clinton administration, brimmed with terrorist activity that affected the lives and interests of U.S. citizens at home and abroad and exposed serious divisions and tensions in American society.

Hardly a month after President Clinton took the oath of office in January 1993, international terrorists launched a ground-based bombing attack on the World Trade Center on February 26. Two days later, federal and Texas law personnel, supported by components of the U.S. military, commenced the nearly two-month-long siege of the ranch headquartering the Branch Davidians religious sect near Waco, Texas, that eventually ended in the deaths of nearly eighty people. The tragedy in Waco spurred two white American males to bomb the Alfred P. Murrah Federal Building in Oklahoma City, Oklahoma, on April 19, 1995. That event still holds the infamous record for being the greatest mass murder terrorist attack ever carried out on American soil by American citizens.

Six months later, the pendulum swung back to New York and international terrorism with the October conviction of the Egyptian Sheikh Omar Abdel Rahman ("the Blind Sheikh") for conspiring with the perpetrators of the attack on the World Trade Center two years earlier. In 1996, another homegrown terrorist, Eric

Rudolph, detonated a bomb at the Summer Olympics in Atlanta, Georgia, and Osama bin Laden published the first of his two declarations of war on the United States. The seriousness of that threat was driven home twice before the end of Clinton's second term in the form of two attacks: an August 1998 attack by an al-Qaeda affiliate on two U.S. embassies in East Africa and the October 2000 bombing of the USS Cole *while it was refueling in the Aden harbor in Yemen.*

The terrorist attack on the Alfred P. Murrah Federal Building remains the most infamous of the incidents of terrorism that took place during the Clinton presidency. President Clinton delivered a short but pointed address to the American people about the Oklahoma City bombing the evening of the attack. He eulogized the 168 victims of that blast, including nearly a score of babies and children, in a memorial ceremony in Oklahoma City four days later. At that time, any mention of terrorism was limited to two brief sentences: that we had a "duty to purge ourselves of the dark forces, which gave rise to this evil. They are forces that threaten our common peace, our freedom, our way of life." In the immediate aftermath, his address—in its entirety below—was a call for action to defend the United States against violent extremism.

Much of that action came in the form of immediate efforts to safeguard federal buildings across the country and in the passage of the Anti-Terrorism and Effective Death Penalty Act of 1996 excerpted elsewhere in this volume. Among its various provisions, that act limited the ability of federal courts to provide relief in instances of alleged habeas corpus violations by state and local authorities pursing terrorist investigations.

The perpetrators of the bombing, Timothy McVeigh and Terry Nichols, were both in custody within two days of the explosion. A partial identity plate on the truck used in the attack quickly led investigators to a Ryder rental agency in Kansas and the subsequent identification of McVeigh as the man who had rented it under an assumed name. Indeed, McVeigh was already in jail by then; he was arrested within ninety minutes of the blast for driving a car without a license plate and carrying an unregistered firearm. For his part, Nichols turned himself in upon learning he was wanted for questioning. He was charged when a subsequent search of his house revealed evidence of his involvement in the attack.

Both McVeigh and Nichols faced trials in federal and state courts, and both were convicted of a wide assortment of felony charges, including conspiracy, murder, and using a weapon of mass destruction. McVeigh was executed on January 11, 2001. Nichols escaped the death penalty when the juries in his trials failed to find direct evidence of his involvement in the acquisition of the explosives and the execution of the bombing. He continues to serve a life sentence based on conspiracy and manslaughter charges.

For Immediate Release April 19, 1995

STATEMENT BY THE PRESIDENT

The Briefing Room
5:30 P.M. EDT

THE PRESIDENT: The bombing in Oklahoma City was an attack on innocent children and defenseless citizens. It was an act of cowardice, and it was evil. The United States will not tolerate it. And I will not allow the people of this country to be intimidated by evil cowards.

I have met with our team, which we assembled to deal with this bombing. And I have determined to take the following steps to assure the strongest response to this situation:

First, I have deployed a crisis management team under the leadership of the FBI, working with the Department of Justice, the Bureau of Alcohol, Tobacco and Firearms, military and local authorities. We are sending the world's finest investigators to solve these murders.

Second, I have declared an emergency in Oklahoma City. And at my direction, James Lee Witt, the Director of the Federal Emergency Management Agency, is now on his way there to make sure we do everything we can to help the people of Oklahoma deal with the tragedy.

Third, we are taking every precaution to reassure and to protect people who work in or live near other federal facilities.

Let there be no room for doubt—we will find the people who did this. When we do, justice will be swift, certain and severe. These people are killers, and they must be treated like killers.

Finally, let me say that I ask all Americans tonight to pray—to pray for the people who have lost their lives, to pray for the families and the friends of the dead and the wounded, to pray for the people of Oklahoma City.

May God's grace be with them. Meanwhile, we will be about our work.

Thank you.

Source: Clinton, Bill. Remarks on the Oklahoma City Bombing, April 19, 1995. *Public Papers of the Presidents of the United States: William J. Clinton, 1995.* Book I, *January 1–June 30, 1995.* Washington, DC: GPO, 1996, 662.

Congress Passes the Antiterrorism and Effective Death Penalty Act, 1996

Antiterrorism and Effective Death Penalty Act of 1996, Public Law 104-132, April 24, 1996

Prior to the 1995 Oklahoma City anti-government terrorist bombing that claimed 168 lives and injured hundreds more, terrorist acts in the United States were prosecuted within the criminal justice system. For example, authorities charged antiabortion activists who killed doctors who provided abortion services with murder, not terrorism. PETA activists who invaded the animal testing labs of cosmetic firms received sentences for destruction of private property, not terrorism.

The primary reason for this approach lay in the activity of the terrorists themselves. Prior to the Oklahoma City bombing, and excluding anarchist assassinations of public figures, American terrorists very rarely attacked the institutions of the U.S. government itself. At its height, the Ku Klux Klan engaged in a violent and often murderous terror campaign against immigrant Jews and Catholics as well as Blacks in the post–Civil War South, but it never bombed the Congress for its immigration policies or its role in the passage of the Thirteenth and Fourteenth Amendments. And the Army of God did not try to kill the U.S. Supreme Court justices who affirmed a woman's right to an abortion during the first trimester of pregnancy in the landmark 1973 case of Roe v. Wade.

The events in Oklahoma City, however, pushed the U.S. government toward enacting the specifically anti-terrorist legislation that European countries combating separatist groups or urban terrorists had enacted long before. Alarmed and disturbed by the Oklahoma City bombing, Congress passed and President Clinton signed into law the Antiterrorism and Effective Death Penalty Act of 1996.

This act gave authorities new powers to investigate possible threats to the United States. However, civil liberties opponents were able to turn aside several proposed features, including enhanced wiretapping authority for investigators. Those tools would have to await until 9/11 and the subsequent passage of the 2001 USA PATRIOT Act. Meanwhile, one part of the 1996 act—Title I's limits of prolonged appeals resting on habeas corpus grounds—drew considerable attack until it was unanimously sustained by the Supreme Court in Felker v. Turpin *two months after the act's passage.*

The following are excerpts from the act that explicitly focus on terrorism. In many instances, as indicated below, the act involved amending previous criminal statutes and immigration laws to reflect the threat posed by terrorist activity. Even so, the excerpts provide only a snapshot of the act's reach. Readers are therefore encouraged to use the link below to explore other sections, such as Section 706 on the Mandatory Penalty for Transferring an Explosive Material Knowing That It Will Be Used to Commit a Crime of Violence and Section 721, which extends criminal jurisdiction "over certain terrorism offenses overseas," including aircraft piracy.

An Act

To deter terrorism, provide justice for victims, provide for an effective death penalty, and for other purposes.

. . .

TITLE I—HABEAS CORPUS REFORM

SEC. 101. FILING DEADLINES.

Section 2244 of title 28, United States Code, is amended by adding at the end the following new subsection:

"(d)(1) A 1-year period of limitation shall apply to an application for a writ of habeas corpus by a person in custody pursuant to the judgment of a State court. . . ."

. . .

SEC. 102. APPEAL.

"(b) There shall be no right of appeal from a final order in a proceeding to test the validity of a warrant to remove to another district or place for commitment or trial a person charged with a criminal offense against the United States, or to test the validity of such person's detention pending removal proceedings."

. . .

SEC. 104. SECTION 2254 AMENDMENTS.

Section 2254 of title 28, United States Code, is amended—

(1) by amending subsection (b) to read as follows:

"(b)(1) An application for a writ of habeas corpus on behalf of a person in custody pursuant to the judgment of a State court shall not be granted unless it appears that—

"(A) the applicant has exhausted the remedies available in the courts of the State; or

"(B)(i) there is an absence of available State corrective process; or

"(ii) circumstances exist that render such process ineffective to protect the rights of the applicant.

"(2) An application for a writ of habeas corpus may be denied on the merits, notwithstanding the failure of the applicant to exhaust the remedies available in the courts of the State."

. . .

TITLE II—JUSTICE FOR VICTIMS

. . .

"Sec. 3663A. Mandatory restitution to victims of certain crimes

"(a)(1) Notwithstanding any other provision of law, when sentencing a defendant convicted of an offense described in subsection (c), the court shall order, in addition to, or . . . in lieu of, any other penalty authorized by law, that the defendant make restitution to the victim of the offense or, if the victim is deceased, to the victim's estate.

"(2) For the purposes of this section, the term 'victim' means a person directly and proximately harmed as a result of the commission of an offense for which restitution may be ordered including, in the case of an offense that involves as an element a scheme, conspiracy, or pattern of criminal activity, any person directly harmed by the defendant's criminal conduct in the course of the scheme, conspiracy, or pattern. In the case of a victim who is under 18 years of age, incompetent, incapacitated, or deceased, the legal guardian of the victim or representative of the victim's estate, . . . but in no event shall the defendant be named as such representative or guardian."

. . .

SEC. 232. VICTIMS OF TERRORISM ACT.

(a) Authority To Provide Assistance and Compensation to Victims of Terrorism.—The Victims of Crime Act of 1984 (42 U.S.C. 10601 et seq.*) is amended by inserting after section 1404A the following new section:*

"SEC. 1404B. COMPENSATION AND ASSISTANCE TO VICTIMS OF TERRORISM OR MASS VIOLENCE.

"(a) Victims of Acts of Terrorism Outside the United States.—The Director may make supplemental grants . . . to provide compensation and assistance to the residents of such States who, while outside of the territorial boundaries of the United States, are victims of a terrorist act or mass violence and are not persons eligible for compensation under title VIII of the Omnibus Diplomatic Security and Antiterrorism Act of 1986.

"(b) Victims of Terrorism Within the United States.—The Director may make supplemental grants . . . to States for eligible crime victim compensation and assistance programs to provide emergency relief, including crisis response efforts, assistance, training, and technical assistance, for the benefit of victims of terrorist acts or mass violence occurring within the United States. . . ."

. . .

TITLE III—INTERNATIONAL TERRORISM PROHIBITIONS

Subtitle A—Prohibition on International Terrorist Fundraising

SEC. 301. FINDINGS AND PURPOSE.

(a) Findings.—The Congress finds that—

(1) international terrorism is a serious and deadly problem that threatens the vital interests of the United States;

(2) the Constitution confers upon Congress the power to punish crimes against the law of nations and to carry out the treaty obligations of the United States, and therefore Congress may by law impose penalties relating to the provision of material support to foreign organizations engaged in terrorist activity;

(3) the power of the United States over immigration and naturalization permits the exclusion from the United States of persons belonging to international terrorist organizations;

(4) international terrorism affects the interstate and foreign commerce of the United States by harming international trade and market stability, and limiting international travel by United States citizens as well as foreign visitors to the United States;

(5) international cooperation is required for an effective response to terrorism, as demonstrated by the numerous multilateral conventions in force providing universal prosecutive jurisdiction over persons involved in a variety of terrorist acts.

(6) some foreign terrorist organizations, acting through affiliated groups or individuals, raise significant funds within the United States, or use the United States as a conduit for the receipt of funds raised in other nations; and

(7) foreign organizations that engage in terrorist activity are so tainted by their criminal conduct that any contribution to such an organization facilitates that conduct.

(b) Purpose.—The purpose of this subtitle is to provide the Federal Government the fullest possible basis, consistent with the Constitution, to prevent persons within the United States, or subject to the jurisdiction of the United States, from providing material support or resources to foreign organizations that engage in terrorist activities.

SEC. 302. DESIGNATION OF FOREIGN TERRORIST ORGANIZATIONS.

(a) In General.—Chapter 2 of title II of the Immigration and Nationality Act (8 U.S.C. 1181 et seq.) is amended by adding at the end the following:

"SEC. 219. DESIGNATION OF FOREIGN TERRORIST ORGANIZATIONS.

"(a) Designation.—

"(1) In general.—The Secretary is authorized to designate an organization as a foreign terrorist organization in accordance with this subsection if the Secretary finds that—

"(A) the organization is a foreign organization;

"(B) the organization engages in terrorist activity (as defined in section 212(a)(3)(B)); and

"(C) the terrorist activity of the organization threatens the security of United States nationals or the national security of the United States."

"(2) Procedure—

. . .

"(C) Freezing of assets.—Upon notification under paragraph (2), the Secretary of the Treasury may require United States financial institutions possessing or controlling any assets of any foreign organization included in the notification to block all financial transactions involving those assets until further directive from either the Secretary of the Treasury, Act of Congress, or order of court."

. . .

TITLE VII—CRIMINAL LAW MODIFICATIONS TO COUNTER TERRORISM

Subtitle A—Crimes and Penalties

SEC. 701. INCREASED PENALTY FOR CONSPIRACIES INVOLVING EXPLOSIVES.

Section 844 of title 18, United States Code, is amended by adding at the end the following new subsection:

"(n) Except as otherwise provided in this section, a person who conspires to commit any offense defined in this chapter shall be subject to the same penalties (other than the penalty of death) as the penalties prescribed for the offense the commission of which was the object of the conspiracy."

SEC. 702. ACTS OF TERRORISM TRANSCENDING NATIONAL BOUNDARIES.

(a) Offense.—Chapter 113B of title 18, United States Code, relating to terrorism, is amended by inserting after section 2332a the following new section:

"Sec. 2332b. Acts of terrorism transcending national boundaries

. . .

(c) Penalties.—

"(1) Penalties.—Whoever violates this section shall be punished—

"(A) for a killing, or if death results to any person from any other conduct prohibited by this section, by death, or by imprisonment for any term of years or for life;

"(B) for kidnapping, by imprisonment for any term of years or for life;

"(C) for maiming, by imprisonment for not more than 35 years;

"(D) for assault with a dangerous weapon or assault resulting in serious bodily injury, by imprisonment for not more than 30 years;

"(E) for destroying or damaging any structure, conveyance, or other real or personal property, by imprisonment for not more than 25 years;

"(F) for attempting or conspiring to commit an offense, for any term of years up to the maximum punishment that would have applied had the offense been completed; and

"(G) for threatening to commit an offense under this section, by imprisonment for not more than 10 years.

"(2) Consecutive sentence.—Notwithstanding any other provision of law, the court shall not place on probation any person convicted of a violation of this section; nor shall the term of imprisonment imposed under this section run concurrently with any other term of imprisonment."

. . .

SEC. 705. INCREASED PENALTIES FOR CERTAIN TERRORISM CRIMES.

. . .

(b) Penalty for Carrying Weapons or Explosives on an Aircraft.—Section 46505 of title 49, United States Code, is amended—

(1) in subsection (b), by striking "one year" and inserting "10 years"; and

(2) in subsection (c), by striking "5" and inserting "15."

Source: Antiterrorism and Effective Death Penalty Act of 1996. Pub. L. No. 104-132, 110 Stat. 1214 (April 24, 1996). Washington, DC: GPO, 1996. https://www.congress.gov/104/plaws/publ132/PLAW-104publ132.pdf.

Osama bin Laden Declares Jihad against America, 1996

Osama bin Laden's 1996 Declaration of Jihad against the Americans Occupying the Land of the Two Holiest Islamic Sites

Although not a document that originated in the United States—and given little attention when it was first issued—it is difficult to imagine an international missive more relevant to the U.S. efforts to combat terrorism and protect the homeland than the declaration of war on the United States that Osama bin Laden initially released in 1996.

The document, issued as an authoritative ruling on a point of Islamic law (a fatwa*), is a wordy, often repetitive polemic, which may account for why it generated little direct reaction at the time. Cut to its core, however, and it contained three arguments that, even under the circumstances of the time, should not have been taken lightly.*

First, there was the call for a unity of effort against the United States and its allies in Saudi Arabia and beyond. A similar call for a jihad against the Soviets in Afghanistan following its invasion of Afghanistan in 1979 drew recruits from afar, and the resultant conflict ended badly for the Soviet leaders.

Second, the declaration paints a portrait of a U.S. military easily intimidated, based on the U.S. withdrawal from both Beirut (1983) and Somalia (1993–1994) following the heavily publicized loss of American soldiers on those fronts.

Finally, although the message is about the U.S. presence, broadly defined, in the most holy cities of Islam, Medina and Mecca, bin Laden's statement emphasizes the need to fight the Americans through unconventional means. The fatwa's menacing message acquired greater credibility soon thereafter with the embassy attacks in East Africa two years later and the attack on the USS Cole *in the Aden harbor in the last days of the Clinton administration. As early as 1998, President Clinton considered plans to assassinate bin Laden, but he ultimately never approved such a strike. Instead, his administration left stern warnings for the incoming George W. Bush administration that Osama bin Laden seemed intent on attacking the United States. That warning, however, did not even generate a presidential briefing session until less than a month before the 9/11 attacks on New York and Washington, DC.*

Declaration of Jihad Against the Americans Occupying the Land of the Two Holiest Sites. (Expel the infidels from the Arab Peninsula). A message from Usamah Bin Muhammad Bin Ladin Unto his Muslim brethren all over the world generally and the Arabian Peninsula specifically.

Praise be to Allah, we seek His help and ask for His pardon. We take refuge in Allah from our wrongs and bad deeds. Whom ever Allah has guided will not be misled, and who ever has been misled, will never be guided. I bear witness that there is no God but Allah, no associate with Him and I bear witness that Muhammad is His servant and Messenger.

Peace and Prayers be upon His servant and messenger who said: "The people are close to an all encompassing punishment from Allah if they see the oppressor and fail to restrain him". Here thereafter: It is not concealed from you that the people of Islam had suffered from aggression, iniquity and injustice imposed on them by the Jewish-Christian alliance and their collaborators to the extent that the Muslims' blood became the cheapest and their wealth and assets looted by the hands of the enemies. Their blood was spilled in Palestine and Iraq. The horrifying pictures of the massacre of Qana, in Lebanon are still fresh in our memory. Massacres took place in Tajikistan, Burma, Kashmir, Assam, Philippine, Fattani, Ugadin, Somalia, Eritrea, Chechnya and in Bosnia Herzegovina. Massacring Muslims that sent shivers in the body and shook the conscience. All of that happened and the world watched and heard, and not only did not respond to these atrocities, but also with a clear conspiracy between America and its allies prevented the weaklings from acquiring arms to defend themselves by using the United Nations as a cover. Muslims became aware that they were the main targets of the Jewish-Crusader alliance of aggression. The false propaganda regarding human rights have vanished under the tribulations and massacres that were committed against Muslims everywhere. This last aggression was the worst catastrophe that was inflicted upon the Moslems since the death of the Prophet. That is, the occupation of the land of the two holiest sites, Islam's own 2 grounds, the cradle of Islam, source of the Prophet's mission, site of the Ka'bah, [that] was launched by the Christian army of the Americans and their allies.

Today, from the same shelters in Afghanistan, we are working to lift off the injustice that was inflected upon the nation by the Jewish-Crusaders alliance, especially after their occupation of the Prophet's land, praise and peace be upon him, and their desecration of land of the two holiest sites. We ask Allah to grant us victory. He is the defender and the almighty. . . . Through its course of actions, the regime has ripped apart its legitimacy the most important being:

1—Suspension of Islamic laws, and replacing it with statuary laws and embarking upon bloody confrontation with devoted scholars and righteous youths. We do not justify anyone above God.

2—Failure of the regime to protect the country, and allowing the enemy of Crusaders American forces to occupy the land years present the main reason for our disaster in every aspect, especially economically.

The right thing to do in this prevailing situation is what the scholars decided, like what sheikh [Ibn Tamimah] may Allah bless his soul; said: "all Muslims should join forces to drive back the infidelity, which controls the Islamic world". Putting up with minimum harm for the sake of driving back the biggest harm, which is the great infidelity. Driving back the American occupier enemy is the most essential duty after faith. There is nothing more important than that, as the scholars have determined, and what sheikh [Ibn Tamimah] have mentioned: if there is more than one duty to be carried out, then the most important one should receive priority. Clearly after Belief there is no more important duty than pushing the American enemy out of the Holy land. . . . If it is not possible to push back the enemy except by a collective movement of the Muslim people, then there it is a duty of the Muslims to ignore the minor differences among themselves. The ill effect of ignoring these differences, at a given period of time, is much less than the ill effect of the occupation of the Muslims' land by the main infidels. . . . Moreover, there is a wealth of fighting Mujahideen available in Yemen ready to fight for God's cause.

The King has violated the prophet's command by allowing the crusaders to be in the Arab Peninsula. The Prophet said on his deathbed. . . . It is out of date and no longer acceptable to claim that the presence of the crusaders is a necessity and only a temporary measure to protect the land of the two holiest sites, especially when the civil and military infrastructures of Iraq were savagely destroyed showing the depth of the Jewish-Crusaders' hatred of the Muslims and their children, and the rejection of the idea of replacing the crusaders forces by an Islamic force composed of the sons of other Muslim countries. . . . After the Islamic world condemned the presence of the Crusaders in the land of the two holiest sites, The King said that: "the issue is simple, the American and their allied forces will leave in few months". Today it has been seven years since their arrival, and the regime is unable expel them out of the country.

It must be obvious to you that, due to the imbalance of power between our armed forces and the enemy forces a suitable means of fighting must be adopted, such as using fast moving forces operating in total secrecy. In other words to initiate guerilla warfare, were the sons of the nation, and not the military forces, take part in it. As you know, it is wise at this stage to exclude the armed forces from a traditional warfare with the Crusader enemy forces, except for daring and intensive operations, which can be executed by some members of the armed forces, meaning, without the interference of regular forces with its traditional formation. shedding the Muslims blood. The Mujahideen, your brothers and sons, request that you support them in every possible way by supplying them with the necessary information, material and arms. . . . The regime is fully responsible for what has been happening to this country. However the occupying American enemy is the principal cause of this situation. Therefore efforts should be concentrated on destroying, fighting and killing the enemy until, by the Grace of Allah, it is completely defeated.

Few days ago the news agencies had reported that the Defense Secretary of the Crusading Americans saying, "the explosion in Riyadh and Al-Khobar had taught him one lesson, and that is not to withdraw when attacked by cowardly terrorist". We say to the Secretary that his talk can induce a grieving mother to laughter, and shows the fears that had enshrined you all. Where was this false courage of yours when the explosion in Beirut took place in 1983. You were turned into scattered bits and pieces in all directions. And where was this false courage of yours when two explosions made you leave Aden in less than 24 hours? But your most disgraceful case was in Somalia, where after vigorous propaganda that lasted few months, regarding the power of America and its post cold war leadership of the new world order; you moved tens of thousands of international force, including twenty eight thousand American soldiers into Somalia. However, when dozens of your troops were killed in minor battles, and one American pilot was dragged in the streets of Mogadishu, you left the area defeated, carrying 14 [of] your dead in disappointment and humiliation. Clinton appeared in front of the whole world threatening and promising revenge. But these threats were merely a preparation for withdrawal. God has dishonored you when you withdrew, and it clearly showed your weaknesses and powerlessness.

The most honorable death is to die for the sake of God; like those four heroes who set off the explosives that killed the Americans in Riyadh.

Source: bin Laden, Osama. Declaration of Jihad against the Americans Occupying the Land of the Two Holiest Islamic Sites, 1996. Combating Terrorism Center at West Point. https://ctc.usma.edu/wp-content/uploads/2013/10/Declaration-of-Jihad-against-the-Americans-Occupying-the-Land-of-the-Two-Holiest-Sites-Translation.pdf.

Secretary of State Albright Issues Terrorism Warning, 1999

Secretary of State Madeleine Albright's Senate Testimony on the Danger Posed by Terrorism to American Personnel and the World Order, February 4, 1999

By the time Clinton administration secretary of state Madeleine Albright addressed the Senate Subcommittee on Appropriations on February 4, 1999, to seek more funding for the protection of U.S. diplomatic personnel abroad, whatever doubts the Clinton administration may have initially had about the seriousness of al-Qaeda's threats against American interests had been vanquished by the nearly simultaneous attacks by an al-Qaeda affiliate on two U.S. embassies in Africa on August 7, 1998. These coordinated attacks claimed the lives of more than 200 people and intensified the administration's consideration of an assassination operation targeting al-Qaeda leader Osama bin Laden.

Against this backdrop, Secretary Albright's testimony provides both a succinct summary of what the Clinton administration was trying to do at the time to protect its personnel abroad and an implicit but clear rebuke of uncooperative nations in what after 9/11 would become known as the U.S. "war on terror" abroad.

Good morning, Mr. Chairman and members of the Subcommittee. I welcome this opportunity to testify concerning U.S. efforts to counter the forces of international terror. As you know, the President has designated the Department of State as the lead agency for coordination of our counterterrorism policy and operations abroad, while the FBI is the lead agency for countering terrorism in the United States.

The Threat

. . .

Last August, I had the sad honor of bringing back to U.S. soil the bodies of Americans who perished in the embassy bombing in Kenya. . . . They were casualties . . . of a new kind of confrontation that looms as a new century is about to begin.

In this struggle, our adversaries are likely to avoid traditional battlefield situations because there, American dominance is well established. They may resort, instead, to weapons of mass destruction and the cowardly instruments of sabotage and hidden bombs. As we know from explosions over the past decade in Africa, the Khobar apartment complex, the World Trade Center and Pan Am 103, these unconventional threats endanger both Americans and others around the world.

Accordingly, we must be vigilant in protecting against the terrorist triple threat posed, first, by the handful of countries that actively sponsor terrorism; second, by long-active terrorist organizations; and third, by loosely affiliated extremists such as, among others, Osama bin Laden, who has urged his followers to kill Americans when and wherever they can.

Our strategy must be long-term. . . . The advance of technology has given us new means to counter terrorists. But it has also enabled terrorists to develop more powerful weapons and to travel, communicate, recruit, and raise funds on a global basis.

Fighting Back

Following the embassy attacks last August, President Clinton ordered military strikes to disrupt terrorist operations and deter new bombings.

The message he conveyed is that, in this battle, we will not simply sit back and wait. We will take the offensive. We will do all we can to limit terrorist movements, block terrorist funds and prevent terrorist acts.

For example, we place the highest priority on measures to prevent weapons of mass destruction from falling into the wrong hands. This imperative is on our agenda with virtually every nation and figures in almost every major meeting I have.

We constantly exchange information with friendly governments concerning terrorist activities and movements, thereby preventing attacks and facilitating arrests.

We work with other agencies and other countries to strengthen screening procedures and increase intelligence sharing on visa applications.

We are expanding our Anti-terrorism Training Assistance Program, which has already instructed more than 20,000 law enforcement officers from more than 90 countries, in subjects such as airport security, bomb detection, maritime security, VIP protection, hostage rescue and crisis management.

We are engaged, through the State Department–chaired Technical Suport [*sic*] Working Group, in a vigorous research and development program to improve our ability to detect explosives, counter weapons of mass destruction, protect against cyber sabotage and provide physical security.

We are making use of the Terrorism Information Rewards program to encourage persons to come forward with information to prevent acts of terrorism and apprehend those who commit them.

We impose economic sanctions against state sponsors of terror. Currently, the seven governments on this list are Cuba, Iran, Iraq, Libya, North Korea, Sudan and Syria.

And both domestically and internationally, we are working to strengthen the rule of law.

The Rule of Law

At home, we have changed our statutes to block the financial assets of terrorist groups, prevent them from raising funds in the United States, and allow us to bar foreigners who support such groups.

Around the world, we couple law enforcement with diplomacy in order to bring suspected terrorists before the bar of justice.

Law enforcement success often depends upon international cooperation. That cooperation has been extraordinary in some cases.

[But] I cannot leave the subject of bringing terrorists to justice without highlighting the tragic case of justice delayed with respect to the bombing more than a decade ago of Pan Am flight 103. As Senators know, we have challenged the Government of Libya to meet its pledge to deliver the two suspects in that case for trial in the Netherlands under Scottish law. This approach has been approved by the

Security Council and is supported by Arab and African regional organizations. It is an approach that is reasonable and fair and that has been on the table now for more than six months.

I would like to take this opportunity once again to urge Libya to deliver the suspects for trial and thereby gain suspension of the UN sanctions.

Attached to my testimony is a chart showing the extent to which countries have ratified eleven international antiterrorism conventions. Our goal is to obtain universal adherence to these treaties. Our purpose is to weave a web of law, power, intelligence, and political will that will entrap terrorists and deny them the mobility and sustenance they need to operate.

It is right for nations to bring terrorists to justice and those who do so should be recognized and rewarded appropriately.

It is wrong to finance terrorist groups, whether or not specific contributions are for terrorist purposes. It is cowardly to give terrorist groups money in return for not being targeted. It is irresponsible simply to look the other way when terrorists come within one's jurisdiction. And it fools no one to pretend that terrorist groups are something they are not.

In this connection, I was very disappointed that Germany failed to make good on the recent opportunity to prosecute Abdullah Ocalan, leader of the terrorist PKK; and that Italy and Turkey were unable to find an alternative way to ensure he was brought to justice. Instead of determination, this opportunity was greeted with handwringing and vacillation. Ocalan has left Italy and his current whereabouts are unknown. We call upon any nation into whose jurisdiction Ocalan comes to cooperate in ensuring that he stands trial for his alleged crimes.

Diplomatic Force Protection.

The measures we take to provide physical protection for our diplomatic personnel overseas play a major role in our strategy for countering terror. I know this subject is a matter of great interest to the Subcommittee. And certainly, nothing is of more urgent concern to me.

In the aftermath of the embassy bombings last August, I established Accountability Review Boards, chaired by Admiral William Crowe, to investigate and recommend improved security systems and procedures.

In both cases, the terrorists were prevented from penetrating the perimeter of the post. In neither case, did U.S. employees or members of the military breach their duty.

The Boards did, however, identify what they termed "a collective failure" by the Executive and Legislative branches of our government over the past decade "to provide adequate resources to reduce the vulnerability of U.S. diplomatic missions."

. . .

According to the report, "We must undertake a comprehensive and long-term strategy . . . including sustained funding for enhanced security measures, for long-term costs for increased security personnel and for a capital building program based on an assessment of requirements to meet the new range of global terrorist threats."

. . .

I wish to stress, Mr. Chairman, that our request for support is not special pleading. American embassies include a broad range of U.S. Government employees and their families. They host a constant flow of U.S. citizens who turn to our people for help on everything from business advice to travel tips to emergency medical aid. They are open to foreign nationals who wish to come to our country as tourists or students or for commercial reasons. And as the casualty list for the Africa bombings illustrates so starkly, many of our embassy employees are locally hired.

Under international law, the host country is responsible for protecting diplomatic missions. We hold every nation to that standard, and will assist, where we can, those who need and want help in fulfilling that duty. In an age of advanced technology and suicide bombers, no one can guarantee perfect security. But our embassies represent America. They should not be easy targets for anyone. We owe our people and all who use or visit our facilities the best security possible.

As I noted at the time I received Admiral Crowe's report, the Department is already implementing, or studying the best way to implement, a significant number of its recommendations.

I cannot detail in public everything that we are doing, often in partnership with others, to prevent and prepare for potential terrorist strikes.

I am able to say, however, that we will continue to implement additional physical protection measures as rapidly as we can.

We are improving our programs for dealing with vehicle-bomb attacks, such as those experienced in Africa.

We see the need for additional crisis management training and have begun such a project at the Foreign Service Institute.

We . . . need a modern plane to replace the specially-configured aircraft used to deploy the Foreign Emergency Support Team (FEST) that we dispatch overseas when there is a major terrorist incident. The current aircraft is 36 years old and was delayed while en route to Nairobi last August by the need to make repairs. This is not acceptable.

. . .

Conclusion

. . .

Over the past six years, on too many occasions, the President has had the job of comforting the loved ones of those murdered and maimed by terrorists. I know from my own experience—it is an impossible task. After the last hand has been held, and the last words of condolence offered, all you can really do is vow that everything within your power will be done to prevent similar tragedies.

. . .

Mr. Chairman, I have quoted New Hampshire's Daniel Webster to you before. I do so again in closing my testimony this morning. "God grants liberty," said Webster, "only to those who love it, and are always ready to guard and defend it."

To that, I say "Amen," and thank you again for the opportunity to testify before you today.

Source: Albright, Madeleine K. "Testimony before the Senate Appropriations Subcommittee on Commerce, State, the Judiciary and Related Agencies, February 4, 1999, Washington, DC." Avalon Project. https://avalon.law.yale.edu/20th_century/t_0006.asp.

American Intelligence Agencies Warn Bush White House about Bin Laden, 2001

"Bin Laden Determined to Strike in US," Presidential Daily Briefing Paper, August 6, 2001

Just as the September 11, 2001, attacks on the United States by al-Qaeda jihadists constitute a pivotal moment in contemporary U.S. counterterrorism history, no recounting of that moment would be complete without including the notorious "Bin Laden Determined to Strike in US" intelligence memo that was presented to President George W. Bush a month before the attack.

The origins of bin Laden's grievances with the United States can be debated. The conventional explanation lies in the government of Saudi Arabia's decision to permit the deployment of American troops in the country following Saddam Hussein's August 2, 1990, invasion of Kuwait and their continued presence in "the land of the two Holiest Sites," as bin Laden framed it in his 1996 declaration of war on the United States.

The presence of American business and culture in Saudi Arabia had already spread widely. It had gained its first foothold when an exploratory well owned and operated by Standard Oil of California (SOCAL) discovered oil in what was to prove to be the world's largest oil field on March 3, 1938. Despite the subsequent efforts of the country's governmental and, especially, religious authorities to contain that influence to the Western compounds and facilities in the nation's oil-producing regions, like an oil slick, it gradually oozed into Saudi society. In 1993, for example, McDonald's opened the first of its fast food restaurants in Saudi Arabia (as of early 2020, more than 160 McDonald's outlets were operating across the country).

Oddly, the Clinton administration gave little credence to bin Laden's 1996 declaration when initially issued, despite the fact that as early as April 1995, a State Department report had noted the growing efforts of international terrorists to develop logistical support networks in the United States by linking up with domestic criminal organizations. Moreover, nearly two months earlier, a truck bomb, attributed a decade later to Hezbollah and Iran, had taken the lives of nineteen Americans living in a housing complex in Khobar, Saudi Arabia.

It was only after the 1998 attacks on American Embassies in Nairobi, Kenya, and Dar es Salaam, Tanzania, which collectively killed 224 (including 12 Americans) and injured more than 4,000, that the Clinton administration's stance changed. Thirteen days after the attacks, American cruise missiles attacked al-Qaeda bases in Afghanistan and a pharmaceutical plant in Sudan suspected of producing chemical weapons, and over the following two years, on at least two occasions, the administration considered assassinating bin Laden but abandoned the plans because of the likelihood of collateral civilian deaths.

The October 19, 2000, attack on the USS Cole *guided missile ship while refueling in Yemen, which took the lives of seventeen American shipmen, provided additional reasons for concern. This attack, which took place less than three months before Clinton's second term ended, led his administration to leave somber warnings about bin Laden's commitment to attacking the U.S. homeland for the incoming George W. Bush administration. Unfortunately, given what was to ensue, the Bush administration was as slow in appreciating the gravity of that warning as the Clinton administration had been in responding to bin Laden's declaration of war.*

Also dismissed or overlooked by the Bush administration was the specific danger that hijacked airliners could serve as "flying bombs" to attach domestic targets in the United States. After the 9/11 attacks, both President Bush and Vice President Cheney proclaimed that they had never considered the possibility. But as early as 1995, the investigation and subsequent trial of Sheik Omar Adel Rahman for conspiracy in the 1993 bombing of the World Trade Center disclosed plans to hijack as many as fifty planes to attack historical and strategic targets across the United States. Indeed, even the specific targets of 9/11 (the World Trade Center and Pentagon) were the subjects of NORAD (North American Aerospace Defense Command) and Department of Defense exercises involving airliners being used as attack missiles conducted during the two years preceding the September 11, 2001, attacks.

Some of the heaviest criticism of the Bush administration in the weeks and months following September 11, however, came from the revelation that Bush had been given a presidential briefing on August 6, 2001, thirty-five days before the deadly terrorist attack that was bluntly titled "Bin Ladin Determined to Strike in US." This document was declassified and made available to the American public on April 10, 2004.

Bin Ladin Determined to Strike in US

Clandestine, foreign government, and media reports indicate Bin Ladin since 1997 has wanted to conduct terrorist attacks in the US. Bin Ladin implied in US television interviews in 1997 and 1998 that his followers would follow the example of World Trade Center bomber Ramzi Yousef and "bring the fighting to America."

After US missile strikes on his base in Afghanistan in 1998, Bin Ladin told followers he wanted to retaliate in Washington, according to a [redacted] service.

An Egyptian Islamic Jihad (EIJ) operative told an [redacted] service at the same time that Bin Ladin was planning to exploit the operative's access to the US to mount a terrorist strike.

The millennium plotting in Canada in 1999 may have been part of Bin Ladin's first serious attempt to implement a terrorist strike in the US. Convicted plotter Ahmed Ressam has told the FBI that he conceived the idea to attack Los Angeles International Airport himself, but that Bin Ladin lieutenant Abu Zubaydah encouraged him and helped facilitate the operation. Ressam also said that in 1998 Abu Zubaydah was planning his own US attack.

Ressam says Bin Ladin was aware of the Los Angeles operation.

Although Bin Ladin has not succeeded, his attacks against the US Embassies in Kenya and Tanzania in 1998 demonstrate that he prepares operations years in advance and is not deterred by setbacks. Bin Ladin associates surveilled our Embassies in Nairobi and Dar es Salaam as early as 1993, and some members of the Nairobi cell planning the bombings were arrested and deported in 1997.

Al-Qa'ida members—including some who are US citizens—have resided in or traveled to the US for years, and the group apparently maintains a support structure that could aid attacks. Two al-Qa'ida members found guilty in the conspiracy to bomb our Embassies in East Africa were US citizens, and a senior EIJ member lived in California in the mid-1990s.

A clandestine source said in 1998 that a Bin Ladin cell in New York was recruiting Muslim-American youth for attacks.

We have not been able to corroborate some of the more sensational threat reporting, such as that from a [redacted] service in 1998 saying that Bin Ladin wanted to hijack a US aircraft to gain the release of "Blind Shaykh" 'Umar 'Abd al-Rahman and other US-held extremists.

Nevertheless, FBI information since that time indicates patterns of suspicious activity in this country consistent with preparations for hijackings or other types of attacks, including recent surveillance of federal buildings in New York.

The FBI is conducting approximately 70 full field investigations throughout the US that it considers Bin Ladin-related. CIA and the FBI are investigating a call to our Embassy in the UAE in May saying that a group of Bin Ladin supporters was in the US planning attacks with explosives.

Source: Central Intelligence Agency. "Bin Ladin Determined to Strike in US." President's Daily Brief, August 6, 2001. Declassified and approved for release, April 10, 2004. https://nsarchive2.gwu.edu/NSAEBB/NSAEBB116/pdb8-6-2001.pdf.

President Bush Addresses Congress and the Nation following 9/11 Attacks, 2001

President George W. Bush's Address to the Congress following the September 11 Attacks on the World Trade Center and the Pentagon, September 20, 2001

Delivered nine days after the 9/11 attacks on New York and Washington, DC, President Bush's nationally televised remarks to a joint session of the Congress constituted the most awaited address by an American president to the American people since President Roosevelt's address sixty years before, the day after the Pearl Harbor attack on the homeland by Imperial Japan on December 7, 1941.

Much of the speech is noteworthy in the degree to which it foreshadows Bush administration actions to come. Afghanistan's Taliban government receives a clear ultimatum: deliver the terrorists hiding in their country quickly or suffer the consequences. The consequences arrive only seventeen days later with the October 7 invasion of Afghanistan and the United States' subsequent success in driving the Taliban from power, closing the al-Qaeda safe haven in Afghanistan, and dismantling its organizational base there.

The address likewise stresses the need to accept an America with greater security concerns at home and law enforcement agencies with enhanced power. The Office of Homeland Security is born that night, and less than three weeks later, on October 26, President Bush signed the USA PATRIOT Act, which included many controversial national security and surveillance components that were assailed by critics as threats to American civil liberties.

Equally remarkable is the mix of candor and compassion in the speech. Bush warns that the "war on terror" announced in the address and formally inaugurated with the invasion of Afghanistan will be a long one that will probably result in the loss of American lives. At the same time, President Bush draws a firm line between the radical terrorists who attacked the United States and the vast millions of Muslims in the United States and around the world who practice a peaceful religion, who are not part of the war on terror, and who are entitled to respect.

The "kinder gentler" world for which President Bush's father had wished following the collapse of the Soviet Union only a decade before was over, and it fell on his son to deliver the news to the American nation.

Address to a Joint Session of Congress and the American People

United States Capitol
Washington, D.C.
9:00 P.M. EDT

THE PRESIDENT: Mr. Speaker, Mr. President Pro Tempore, members of Congress, and fellow Americans:

In the normal course of events, Presidents come to this chamber to report on the state of the Union. Tonight, no such report is needed. It has already been delivered by the American people.

. . .

Tonight we are a country awakened to danger and called to defend freedom. Our grief has turned to anger, and anger to resolution. Whether we bring our enemies to justice, or bring justice to our enemies, justice will be done. (Applause.)

. . .

On September the 11th, enemies of freedom committed an act of war against our country. Americans have known wars—but for the past 136 years, they have been wars on foreign soil, except for one Sunday in 1941. Americans have known the casualties of war—but not at the center of a great city on a peaceful morning. Americans have known surprise attacks—but never before on thousands of civilians. All of this was brought upon us in a single day—and night fell on a different world, a world where freedom itself is under attack.

Americans have many questions tonight. Americans are asking: Who attacked our country? The evidence we have gathered all points to a collection of loosely affiliated terrorist organizations known as al Qaeda. They are the same murderers indicted for bombing American embassies in Tanzania and Kenya, and responsible for bombing the USS *Cole*.

Al Qaeda is to terror what the mafia is to crime. But its goal is not making money; its goal is remaking the world—and imposing its radical beliefs on people everywhere.

The terrorists practice a fringe form of Islamic extremism that has been rejected by Muslim scholars and the vast majority of Muslim clerics—a fringe movement that perverts the peaceful teachings of Islam. The terrorists' directive commands them to kill Christians and Jews, to kill all Americans, and make no distinction among military and civilians, including women and children.

This group and its leader—a person named Osama bin Laden—are linked to many other organizations in different countries, including the Egyptian Islamic Jihad and the Islamic Movement of Uzbekistan. There are thousands of these terrorists in more than 60 countries. They are recruited from their own nations and neighborhoods and brought to camps in places like Afghanistan, where they are trained in the tactics of terror.

Afghanistan's people have been brutalized—many are starving and many have fled. Women are not allowed to attend school. You can be jailed for owning a television. Religion can be practiced only as their leaders dictate. A man can be jailed in Afghanistan if his beard is not long enough.

The United States respects the people of Afghanistan—after all, we are currently its largest source of humanitarian aid—but we condemn the Taliban regime. (Applause.) It is not only repressing its own people, it is threatening people everywhere by sponsoring and sheltering and supplying terrorists. By aiding and abetting murder, the Taliban regime is committing murder.

And tonight, the United States of America makes the following demands on the Taliban: Deliver to United States authorities all the leaders of al Qaeda who hide in your land. (Applause.) Release all foreign nationals, including American citizens, you have unjustly imprisoned. Protect foreign journalists, diplomats and aid workers in your country. Close immediately and permanently every terrorist training camp in Afghanistan, and hand over every terrorist, and every person in their support structure, to appropriate authorities. (Applause.) Give the United States full access to terrorist training camps, so we can make sure they are no longer operating.

These demands are not open to negotiation or discussion. (Applause.) The Taliban must act, and act immediately. They will hand over the terrorists, or they will share in their fate.

I also want to speak tonight directly to Muslims throughout the world. We respect your faith. It's practiced freely by many millions of Americans, and by millions more in countries that America counts as friends. Its teachings are good and peaceful, and those who commit evil in the name of Allah blaspheme the name of Allah. (Applause.) The terrorists are traitors to their own faith, trying, in effect, to hijack Islam itself. The enemy of America is not our many Muslim friends; it is not our many Arab friends. Our enemy is a radical network of terrorists, and every government that supports them. (Applause.)

Our war on terror begins with al Qaeda, but it does not end there. It will not end until every terrorist group of global reach has been found, stopped and defeated. (Applause.)

. . .

Americans are asking: How will we fight and win this war? We will direct every resource at our command—every means of diplomacy, every tool of intelligence, every instrument of law enforcement, every financial influence, and every necessary weapon of war—to the disruption and to the defeat of the global terror network.

This war will not be like the war against Iraq a decade ago, with a decisive liberation of territory and a swift conclusion. It will not look like the air war above Kosovo two years ago, where no ground troops were used and not a single American was lost in combat.

Our response involves far more than instant retaliation and isolated strikes. Americans should not expect one battle, but a lengthy campaign, unlike any other we have ever seen. It may include dramatic strikes, visible on TV, and covert operations, secret even in success. We will starve terrorists of funding, turn them one against another, drive them from place to place, until there is no refuge or no rest. And we will pursue nations that provide aid or safe haven to terrorism. Every nation, in every region, now has a decision to make. Either you are with us, or you are with the terrorists. (Applause.) From this day forward, any nation that continues to harbor or support terrorism will be regarded by the United States as a hostile regime.

Our nation has been put on notice: We are not immune from attack. We will take defensive measures against terrorism to protect Americans. Today, dozens of federal departments and agencies, as well as state and local governments, have responsibilities affecting homeland security. These efforts must be coordinated at the highest level. So tonight I announce the creation of a Cabinet-level position reporting directly to me—the Office of Homeland Security.

And tonight I also announce a distinguished American to lead this effort, to strengthen American security: a military veteran, an effective governor, a true patriot, a trusted friend—Pennsylvania's Tom Ridge. (Applause.) He will lead, oversee and coordinate a comprehensive national strategy to safeguard our country against terrorism, and respond to any attacks that may come.

These measures are essential. But the only way to defeat terrorism as a threat to our way of life is to stop it, eliminate it, and destroy it where it grows. (Applause.)

. . .

I ask you to uphold the values of America, and remember why so many have come here. We are in a fight for our principles, and our first responsibility is to live by them. No one should be singled out for unfair treatment or unkind words because of their ethnic background or religious faith. (Applause.)

. . .

I ask for your patience, with the delays and inconveniences that may accompany tighter security; and for your patience in what will be a long struggle.

. . .

Tonight, we face new and sudden national challenges. We will come together to improve air safety, to dramatically expand the number of air marshals on domestic flights, and take new measures to prevent hijacking. We will come together to promote stability and keep our airlines flying, with direct assistance during this emergency. (Applause.)

We will come together to give law enforcement the additional tools it needs to track down terror here at home. (Applause.) We will come together to strengthen our intelligence capabilities to know the plans of terrorists before they act, and find them before they strike. (Applause.)

We will come together to take active steps that strengthen America's economy, and put our people back to work.

It is my hope that in the months and years ahead, life will return almost to normal. We'll go back to our lives and routines, and that is good. Even grief recedes with time and grace. But our resolve must not pass.

. . .

The course of this conflict is not known, yet its outcome is certain. Freedom and fear, justice and cruelty, have always been at war, and we know that God is not neutral between them. (Applause.)

Fellow citizens, we'll meet violence with patient justice—assured of the rightness of our cause, and confident of the victories to come. In all that lies before us, may God grant us wisdom, and may He watch over the United States of America.

Thank you.

Source: Bush, George W. "Address to a Joint Session of Congress and the American People." September 20, 2001. https://georgewbush-whitehouse.archives.gov/news/releases/2001/09/20010920-8.html.

Congress Passes the Patriot Act, 2001

Uniting and Strengthening America by Providing Appropriate Tools Required to Intercept and Obstruct Terrorism Act (USA PATRIOT Act) of 2001, Enacted October 26, 2001

Political scientists frequently speak of "policy windows"—moments in time when events make it possible to enact policies that were previously foreclosed. The 1973 Arab embargo on oil shipments to countries supporting Israel, for example, caused the Congress to exempt oil drilling in Alaska from the more rigid requirements of the 1969 National Environmental Policy Act, which had previously blocked the development of Alaskan oil reserves. So it was with many of the counterterrorism measures in the USA PATRIOT Act (or Patriot Act), which was passed in less than seven weeks following the September 11, 2001, terrorist attacks on the United States. The Patriot Act provided national security and law enforcement agencies with expanded domestic criminal investigatory tools long sought but denied as recently as 1996, when the Antiterrorism and Effective Death Penalty Act was passed in the wake of the 1995 bombing of the Oklahoma City Federal Building.

Not surprisingly, many of the controversial provisions in the Patriot Act were criticized for being hastily drafted and enacted into law. Such was especially true given the Patriot Act's reach, with provisions authorizing the interception of "wire, oral and electronic communications relating to terrorism" (Section 201); aid to law enforcement bodies (Section 222); verification of identity (Section 326);

monitoring of foreign students (Section 416); development of cyber forensic capacities (Section 816); and temporarily delaying the submission to Congress of intelligence reports and intelligence-related matters (Section 904).

The following excerpted provisions included in the Patriot Act were among the ones most troubling to civil liberties advocates. Even here, space precludes a full representation. Treated only briefly or omitted, respectively, are portions of Section 412, which authorizes the mandatory detention of aliens whom "the Attorney General has reasonable grounds to believe" are engaged in activity endangering national security, and Section 507, which enables the attorney general to seek the court-ordered release of the records of an educational institution or agency that may be relevant to investigating international or domestic terrorism. Also omitted is Section 805, which amended existing law to prohibit material assistance to any organization designated as terrorist in nature by the secretary of state, even if that aid is designed to aid only the peaceful activities of the organization. It was that provision that led to the Holder v. Humanitarian Law Project *case (2010), in which the U.S. Supreme Court rejected the plaintiff's claim that the prohibition violated the First Amendment freedom of association provisions, holding instead that such funds could free up resources for the organization's terrorist activities and could therefore be prohibited on national security grounds.*

This excerpt focuses on Sections 213, which permits authorities to delay notifying the affected parties that a search warrant had been executed against them, and Section 215, which allows the collection of phone metadata from communication suppliers without a court warrant. Indeed, the latter has remained the most controversial part of the act, pertaining as it does to surveillance authorized through the secret proceedings of the Foreign Intelligence Surveillance Court (FISC) established in 1978. Such searches were successfully challenged on Fourth Amendment unreasonable search and seizure grounds in an Oregon federal district court case in 2007, Brandon Mayfield, et al. v. United States of America. *Two years later, however, the court of appeals for the region reversed that judgment on the grounds that the plaintiffs lacked adequate standing to challenge the act.*

In short, controversy has been an integral part of the Patriot Act since its passage. Some provisions were intended to remain in effect for only four years, but it was renewed in 2006 and 2011. It expired in 2015 but was resurrected in the USA FREEDOM Act of that year, although the reach of Section 215 was scaled back in that legislation. The drama continued in 2019 when a last-minute amendment to a stopgap funding measure prolonged the warrantless data collection provision of the Patriot Act until March 15, 2020. Two months later, on May 14, the Patriot Act was reauthorized again, but without that provision.

Public Law 107-56
107th Congress

An Act

To deter and punish terrorist acts in the United States and around the world, to enhance law enforcement investigatory tools, and for other purposes.

. . .

TITLE I—ENHANCING DOMESTIC SECURITY AGAINST TERRORISM

. . .

SEC. 102. Sense of Congress Condemning Discrimination against Arab and Muslim Americans.

(a) FINDINGS.—Congress makes the following findings:

(1) Arab Americans, Muslim Americans, and Americans from South Asia play a vital role in our Nation and are entitled to nothing less than the full rights of every American.

(2) The acts of violence that have been taken against Arab and Muslim Americans since the September 11, 2001, attacks against the United States should be and are condemned by all Americans who value freedom.

(3) The concept of individual responsibility for wrongdoing is sacrosanct in American society, and applies equally to all religious, racial, and ethnic groups.

(4) When American citizens commit acts of violence against those who are, or are perceived to be, of Arab or Muslim descent, they should be punished to the full extent of the law.

(5) Muslim Americans have become so fearful of harassment that many Muslim women are changing the way they dress to avoid becoming targets.

(6) Many Arab Americans and Muslim Americans have acted heroically during the attacks on the United States.

(b) SENSE OF CONGRESS.—It is the sense of Congress that—

(1) the civil rights and civil liberties of all Americans, including Arab Americans, Muslim Americans, and Americans from South Asia, must be protected, and that every effort must be taken to preserve their safety;

(2) any acts of violence or discrimination against any Americans be condemned; and

(3) the Nation is called upon to recognize the patriotism of fellow citizens from all ethnic, racial, and religious backgrounds.

. . .

TITLE II—ENHANCED SURVEILLANCE PROCEDURES

. . .

SEC. 213. AUTHORITY FOR DELAYING NOTICE OF THE EXECUTION OF A WARRANT.

Section 3103a of title 18, United States Code, is amended . . . by adding at the end the following:

"(b) DELAY.—With respect to the issuance of any warrant or court order under this section, or any other rule of law, to search for and seize any property or material that constitutes evidence of a criminal offense in violation of the laws of the

United States, any notice required, or that may be required, to be given may be delayed if—

"(1) the court finds reasonable cause to believe that providing immediate notification of the execution of the warrant may have an adverse result (as defined in section 2705);

"(2) the warrant prohibits the seizure of any tangible property, any wire or electronic communication (as defined in section 2510), or, except as expressly provided in chapter 121, any stored wire or electronic information, except where the court finds reasonable necessity for the seizure; and

"(3) the warrant provides for the giving of such notice within a reasonable period of its execution, which period may thereafter be extended by the court for good cause shown."

. . .

SEC. 215. ACCESS TO RECORDS AND OTHER ITEMS UNDER THE FOREIGN INTELLIGENCE SURVEILLANCE ACT.

Title V of the Foreign Intelligence Surveillance Act of 1978 (50 U.S.C. 1861 et seq.) is amended by striking sections 501 through 503 and inserting the following:

"SEC. 501. ACCESS TO CERTAIN BUSINESS RECORDS FOR FOREIGN INTELLIGENCE AND INTERNATIONAL TERRORISM INVESTIGATIONS.

"(a)(1) The Director of the Federal Bureau of Investigation or a designee of the Director (whose rank shall be no lower than Assistant Special Agent in Charge) may make an application for an order requiring the production of any tangible things (including books, records, papers, documents, and other items) for an investigation to protect against international terrorism or clandestine intelligence activities, provided that such investigation of a United States person is not conducted solely upon the basis of activities protected by the first amendment to the Constitution.

"(2) An investigation conducted under this section shall—

"(A) be conducted under guidelines approved by the Attorney General under Executive Order 12333 (or a successor order); and

"(B) not be conducted of a United States person solely upon the basis of activities protected by the first amendment to the Constitution of the United States.

"(b) Each application under this section—. . .

(2) shall specify that the records concerned are sought for an authorized investigation conducted in accordance with subsection (a)(2) to obtain foreign intelligence information not concerning a United States person or to protect against international terrorism or clandestine intelligence activities.

"(c)(1) Upon an application made pursuant to this section, the judge shall enter an ex parte order as requested, or as modified, approving the release of records if the judge finds that the application meets the requirements of this section.

"(2) An order under this subsection shall not disclose that it is issued for purposes of an investigation described in subsection (a).

"(d) No person shall disclose to any other person (other than those persons necessary to produce the tangible things under this section) that the Federal Bureau of Investigation has sought or obtained tangible things under this section.

. . .

"SEC. 502. CONGRESSIONAL OVERSIGHT.

"(a) On a semiannual basis, the Attorney General shall fully inform the Permanent Select Committee on Intelligence of the House of Representatives and the Select Committee on Intelligence of the Senate concerning all requests for the production of tangible things under section 402.

"(b) On a semiannual basis, the Attorney General shall provide to the Committees on the Judiciary of the House of Representatives and the Senate a report setting forth with respect to the preceding 6-month period—

"(1) the total number of applications made for orders approving requests for the production of tangible things under section 402; and

"(2) the total number of such orders either granted, modified, or denied."

. . .

TITLE IV—PROTECTING THE BORDER

. . .

SEC. 412. MANDATORY DETENTION OF SUSPECTED TERRORISTS; HABEAS CORPUS; JUDICIAL REVIEW.

(a) IN GENERAL.—The Immigration and Nationality Act (8 U.S.C. 1101 et seq.) is amended by inserting after section 236 the following:

"MANDATORY DETENTION OF SUSPECTED TERRORISTS; HABEAS CORPUS; JUDICIAL REVIEW

"SEC. 236A. (a) DETENTION OF TERRORIST ALIENS.—

"(1) CUSTODY.—The Attorney General shall take into custody any alien who is certified under paragraph (3).

"(2) RELEASE.—Except as provided in paragraphs (5) and (6), the Attorney General shall maintain custody of such an alien until the alien is removed from the United States. Except as provided in paragraph (6), such custody shall be maintained irrespective of any relief from removal for which the alien may be eligible, or any relief from removal granted the alien, until the Attorney General determines that the alien is no longer an alien who may be certified under paragraph (3). If the alien is finally determined not to be removable, detention pursuant to this subsection shall terminate.

. . .

TITLE VIII—STRENGTHENING THE CRIMINAL LAWS AGAINST TERRORISM

. . .

SEC. 802. DEFINITION OF DOMESTIC TERRORISM.

(a) DOMESTIC TERRORISM DEFINED.—Section 2331 of title 18, United States Code, is amended—

(1) in paragraph (1)(B)(iii), by striking "by assassination or kidnapping" and inserting "by mass destruction, assassination, or kidnapping";

(3) in paragraph (4), by striking the period at the end and inserting "; and"; and

(4) by adding at the end the following:

"(5) the term 'domestic terrorism' means activities that—

"(A) involve acts dangerous to human life that are a violation of the criminal laws of the United States or of any State;

"(B) appear to be intended—

"(i) to intimidate or coerce a civilian population;

"(ii) to influence the policy of a government by intimidation or coercion; or

"(iii) to affect the conduct of a government by mass destruction, assassination, or kidnapping; and

"(C) occur primarily within the territorial jurisdiction of the United States."

Source: Uniting and Strengthening America by Providing Appropriate Tools Required to Intercept and Obstruct Terrorism (USA PATRIOT ACT) Act of 2001, Pub. L. No. 107-56, 115 Stat. 272 (2001–2002). Enacted October 26, 2001. https://www.congress.gov/107/plaws/publ56/PLAW-107publ56.pdf.

Final Report of the 9/11 Commission, 2004

Final Report of the National Commission on Terrorist Attacks on the United States *(The 9/11 Commission): Executive Summary, July 22, 2004*

The September 11, 2001, attack on the United States by the nineteen al-Qaeda operatives resulted in crisis decision-making and swift action. Al-Qaeda's base of military operations in Afghanistan was destroyed less than a month later, and the Taliban government in Kabul that had permitted the base to exist was dislodged from power shortly thereafter. Then came the hard tasks of identifying and correcting the deficiencies in the U.S. intelligence agencies that had allowed the attack to occur to reduce the country's vulnerability to such future attacks.

Toward achieving those goals, in November 2002, the Congress and Bush administration collaborated in the establishment of a bipartisan commission to study the 9/11 attacks and recommend such future action as might be required to make the country safer. After months of interviewing more than a thousand people spread across ten countries and sifting through hours of video footage and volumes of documents, the 9/11 Commission tendered its report in the summer of 2004.

Much of that report was devoted to specific recommendations—for example, the need to tighten port security. The executive summary touched on a few of these; however, after reviewing the factors that enabled the terrorists to succeed on 9/11, the heart of the document was devoted to the restructuring of the country's security services, which the commission deemed necessary to secure the homeland in the long term. The core of the commission's recommendations are now a part of the U.S. homeland security and counterterrorist systems.

A NATION TRANSFORMED

At 8:45 on the morning of September 11, 2001, the United States became a nation transformed.

More than 2,600 people died at the World Trade Center, 125 died at the Pentagon, 256 died on the four planes. The death toll surpassed that of Pearl Harbor in December 1941.

This immeasurable pain was inflicted by 19 young Arabs acting at the behest of Islamist extremists headquartered in distant Afghanistan. Some had been in the United States for more than a year, mixing with the rest of the population. Though four had training as pilots, most were not well educated. Most spoke English poorly; some hardly at all. [1–2]

. . .

A Shock, Not a Surprise

The 9/11 attacks were a shock, but they should not have come as a surprise. Islamist extremists had given plenty of warnings that they meant to kill Americans indiscriminately and in large numbers. Although Usama Bin Ladin himself would not emerge as a signal threat until the late 1990s, the threat of Islamist terrorism grew over the decade. [2]

. . .

GENERAL FINDINGS

Since the plotters were flexible and resourceful, we cannot know whether any single step or series of steps would have defeated them. What we can say with confidence is that none of the measures adopted by the U.S. government from 1998 to 2001 disturbed or even delayed the progress of the al Qaeda plot. Across the government, there were failures of imagination, policy, capabilities, and management.

Imagination

The most important failure was one of imagination. We do not believe leaders understood the gravity of the threat.

As late as September 4, 2001, Richard Clarke, the White House staffer long responsible for counterterrorism policy coordination, asserted that the government had not yet made up its mind how to answer the question: "Is al Qida a big deal?"

A week later came the answer. [9]

. . .

Problems within the Intelligence Community

The intelligence community struggled throughout the 1990s and up to 9/11 to collect intelligence on and analyze the phenomenon of transnational terrorism. The combination of an overwhelming number of priorities, flat budget an outmoded structure, and bureaucratic rivalries resulted in an insufficient response to this new challenge.

While there were many reports on Bin Laden and his growing al Qaeda organization, there was no comprehensive review of what the intelligence community knew and what it did not know, and what that means. There was no National Intelligence Estimate on terrorism between 1995 and 9/11. [12]

. . .

Problems in the FBI

From the time of the first World Trade Center attack in 1993, FBI and Department of Justice leadership . . . became increasingly concerned about the terrorist threat from Islamist extremists to U.S. interests, both at home and abroad. . . . The FBI's approach to investigations was case specific, decentralized, and geared toward prosecution. [13]

. . .

Permeable Borders and Immigration Controls

There were opportunities for intelligence and law enforcement to exploit al Qaeda's travel vulnerabilities. Considered collectively, the 9/11 hijackers

- included known al Qaeda operatives who could have been watchlisted;
- presented passports manipulated in a fraudulent manner;
- presented passports with suspicious indicators of extremism;
- made detectable false statements on visa applications;
- made false statements to border officials to gain entry into the United States; and
- violated immigration laws while in the United States.

Neither the State Department's consular officers nor the Immigration and Naturalization Service's inspectors and agents were ever considered full partners in a national counterterrorism effort. Protecting borders was not a national security issue before 9/11.

Permeable Aviation Security

Hijackers studied publicly available materials on the aviation security system and used items that had less metal content than a handgun and were most likely permissible. Once on board, the hijackers were faced with aircraft personnel who were trained to be nonconfrontational in the event of a hijacking. [13–14]

. . .

An Improvised Homeland Defense

. . .

At more senior levels, communication was poor. Senior military and FAA leaders had no effective communication with each other. The chain of command did not function well. The President could not reach some senior officials. The Secretary of Defense did not enter the chain of command until the morning's key events were over. Air National Guard units with different rules of engagement were scrambled without the knowledge of the President, NORAD, or the National Military Command Center. [14–15]

. . .

Congress

The Congress, like the executive branch, responded slowly to the rise of transnational terrorism as a threat to national security, The legislative branch adjusted little and did not restructure itself to address changing threats. Its attention to terrorism was episodic and splintered across several committees.

So long as oversight is undermined by current congressional rules and resolutions, we believe the American people will not get the security they want and need. . . . [15–16]

Are We Safer?

. . .

The problem is that al Qaeda represents an ideological movement not a finite group of people. It initiates and inspires, even if it no longer directs. In this way, it has transformed itself into a decentralized force. Bin Ladin may be limited in his ability to organize major attacks from his hideouts. Yet killing or capturing him, while extremely important, would not end terror. His message of inspiration to a new generation of terrorists would continue.

Because of offensive actions against al Qaeda since 9/11, and defensive actions to improve homeland security we believe we are safer today. But we are not safe. . . . [16]

. . .

WHAT TO DO: A GLOBAL STRATEGY

The enemy is not just "terrorism." It is the threat posed specifically by Islamist terrorism, by bin Ladin and others who draw on a long tradition of extreme intolerance within a minority strain of Islam that does not distinguish politics from religion, and distorts both.

Our strategy must match our means to two ends: dismantling the al Qaeda network, and in the long term, prevailing over the ideology that contributes to Islamist terrorism.

. . .

We propose a strategy with three dimensions: (1) attack terrorists and their organizations, (2) prevent the continued growth of Islamist terrorism, and (3) protect against and prepare for terrorist attacks.

Attack Terrorists and Their Organizations

- Root out sanctuaries. The U.S. government should identify and prioritize actual or potential terrorist sanctuaries and have realistic country or regional strategies for each, utilizing every element of national power and reaching out to countries that can help us. [17]

. . .

Prevent the Continued Growth of Islamist Terrorism

. . .

- Where Muslim governments, even those who are friends, do not offer opportunity, reject the rule of law, or tolerate differences, then the United States needs to stand for a better future.

. . .

- Expect less from trying to dry up terrorist money and more from following the money for intelligence, as a tool to hunt terrorists, understand their networks, and disrupt their operations. [18–19]

Protect against and Prepare for Terrorist Attacks

- Target terrorist travel, an intelligence and security strategy that the 9/11 story showed could be at least as powerful as the effort devoted to terrorist finance.
- Quickly complete a biometric entry-exit system, one that also speeds qualified travelers.
- Develop strategies for neglected parts of our transportation security system. Since 9/11, about 90 percent of this nation's $5 billion annual investment in transportation security has gone to aviation, to fight the last war.
- In aviation, prevent arguments about a new computerized profiling system from delaying vital improvement in the "no-fly" and "automatic selectee" lists.
- Underscore that as government power necessarily expands in certain ways, the burden of retaining such power remains on the executive to demonstrate the value of such powers and ensure adequate supervision of how they are used, including a new board to oversee the implementation of the guidelines needed for gathering and sharing information in these new security systems.
- Make homeland security funding contingent on the adoption of an incident command system to strengthen teamwork in a crisis, including a regional approach. . . . [19–20]

HOW TO DO IT? A DIFFERENT WAY OF ORGANIZING GOVERNMENT

The strategy we have recommended is elaborate, even as presented here very briefly. To implement it will require a government better organized than the one that exists today, with its national security institutions designed half a century ago to win the Cold War. Americans should not settle for incremental, ad hoc adjustments to a system created a generation ago for a world that no longer exists.

We call for unity of effort in five areas, beginning with unity of effort on the challenge of counterterrorism itself:

- unifying strategic intelligence and operational-planning against Islamist terrorists across the foreign-domestic divide with a National Counterterrorism Center;
- unifying the intelligence community with a new National Intelligence Director;
- unifying the many participants in the counterterrorism effort and their knowledge in a network-based information sharing system that transcends traditional governmental boundaries;
- unifying and strengthening congressional oversight to improve quality and accountability; and
- strengthening the FBI and homeland defenders. [20–21]

Unity of Effort: A National Counterterrorism Center

The 9/11 story teaches the value of integrating strategic intelligence from all sources into joint operational planning—with *both* dimensions spanning the foreign-domestic divide.

- In some ways, since 9/11, joint work has gotten better. The effort of fighting terrorism has flooded over many of the usual agency boundaries because of its sheer quantity and energy. Attitudes have changed. But the problems of coordination have multiplied.
- Breaking the older mode of organization stovepiped in purely executive agencies, we propose a National Counterterrorism Center (NCTC) that would borrow the joint, unified command concept adopted in the 1980s by the American military in a civilian agency, combining the joint intelligence function alongside the operations work.
- The NCTC would build on the existing Terrorist Threat Integration Center and would replace it and other terrorism "fusion centers" within the government.

. . .

- The NCTC should be a policymaking body. Its operations and planning should follow the policy direction of the president and the National Security Council. [21–22]

Unity of Effort: A National Intelligence Director

Since long before 9/11—and continuing to this day—the intelligence community is not organized well for joint intelligence work. It does not employ common standards and practices in reporting intelligence or in training experts overseas and at home. The expensive national capabilities for collecting intelligence have divided management. The structures are too complex and too secret.

- The community's head—the Director of Central Intelligence—has at least three jobs: running the CIA, coordinating a 15-agency confederation; and being the intelligence analyst-in-chief to the president. No one person can do all these things.
- A new National Intelligence Director should be established with two main jobs: (1) to oversee national intelligence centers that combine experts from all the collection disciplines against common targets—like counterterrorism or nuclear proliferation; and (2) to oversee the agencies that contribute to the national intelligence program, a task that includes setting common standards for personnel and information technology.
- This National Intelligence Director (NID) should be located in the Executive Office of the President and report directly to the president, yet be confirmed by the Senate.

. . .

- Secrecy stifles oversight, accountability, and information sharing. Unfortunately, all the current organizational incentives encourage overclassification.

This balance should change; and as a start, open information should be provided about the overall size of agency intelligence budgets.

Unity of Effort: Sharing Information.

The U.S. government has access to a vast amount of information. But it has a weak system for processing and using what it has. The system of "need to know" should be replaced by a system of "need to share." [24]

. . .

Unity of Effort: Congress

. . .

- Congress should create a single, principal point of oversight and review for homeland security. There should be one permanent standing committee for homeland security in each chamber. . . . [25]

Unity of Effort: Organizing America's Defenses in the United States

. . .

- We propose the establishment of a specialized and integrated national security workforce at the FBI, consisting of agents, analysts, linguists, and surveillance specialists who are recruited, trained, rewarded, and retained to ensure the development of an institutional culture imbued with a deep expertise in intelligence and national security. [26]

Source: *The 9/11 Commission Report: Final Report of the National Commission on Terrorist Attacks upon the United States. Executive Summary*. National Archives and Records Administration. Washington, DC: GPO, 2004. https://www.9-11commission.gov/report/911Report_Exec.pdf.

President Bush Mandates Increased Sharing of Terrorism Intelligence, 2005

Executive Order 13388: Further Strengthening the Sharing of Terrorism Information to Protect Americans, October 25, 2005

Executive Order 13388 is foremost concerned with implementing the directive in Section 1016 of the Intelligence Reform and Terrorism Prevention Act passed in December 2004. In its turn, the section on "Information Sharing" was a direct response to the recommendations of the 9/11 Commission, whose final report tendered in July 2004 urged moving away from "the need to know" system of intelligence hoarding that it uncovered to a "need to share" system" for all federal intelligence, security, and law enforcement agencies in the United States.

The following documents are (1) excerpts from the 9/11 Commission's final report urging reforms in how U.S. intelligence and law enforcement communities work with one another and (2) Executive Order 13388, which was signed by President Bush on October 25, 2005.

HOW TO DO IT? A DIFFERENT WAY OF ORGANIZING THE GOVERNMENT

13.3 UNITY OF EFFORT IN SHARING INFORMATION

Information Sharing

. . . The biggest impediment to all-source analysis—to a greater likelihood of connecting the dots—is the human or systemic resistance to sharing information.

The U.S. government has access to a vast amount of information. When databases not usually thought of as "intelligence," such as customs or immigration information, are included, the storehouse is immense. But the U.S. government has a weak system for processing and using what it has. . . .

In the 9/11 story, for example, we sometimes see examples of information that could be accessed—like the undistributed NSA information that would have helped identify Nawaf al Hazmi in January 2000. But someone had to ask for it. In that case, no one did. Or . . . the information is distributed, but in a compartmented channel. Or the information is available, and someone does ask, but it cannot be shared.

What all these stories have in common is a system that requires a demonstrated "need to know" before sharing. This approach assumes it is possible to know, in advance, who will need to use the information. Such a system implicitly assumes that the risk of inadvertent disclosure outweighs the benefits of wider sharing. Those Cold War assumptions are no longer appropriate. The culture of agencies feeling they own the information they gathered at taxpayer expense must be replaced by a culture in which the agencies instead feel they have a duty to the information—to repay the taxpayers' investment by making that information available.

. . . [S]ecurity concerns need to be weighed against the costs. Current security requirements nurture overclassification and excessive compartmentation of information among agencies. Each agency's incentive structure opposes sharing, with risks (criminal, civil, and internal administrative sanctions) but few rewards for sharing information. No one has to pay the long-term costs of overclassifying information, though these costs—even in literal financial terms—are substantial. There are no punishments for not sharing information. Agencies uphold a "need-to-know" culture of information protection rather than promoting a "need-to-share" culture of integration.[15]

Recommendation: Information procedures should provide incentives for sharing, to restore a better balance between security and shared knowledge.

. . . The logical objection is that sources and methods may vary greatly in different locations. We therefore propose that when a report is first created, its data be separated from the sources and methods by which they are obtained. The report should begin with the information in its most shareable, but still meaningful, form.

We propose that information be shared horizontally, across new networks that transcend individual agencies. . . .

- . . . Agencies would still have their own databases, but those databases would be searchable across agency lines. In this system, secrets are protected through the design of the network and an "information rights management" approach that controls access to the data, not access to the whole network. An outstanding conceptual framework for this kind of "trusted information network" has been developed by a task force of leading professionals in national security, information technology, and law assembled by the Markle Foundation. Its report has been widely discussed throughout the U.S. government, but has not yet been converted into action.[17]

Recommendation: The president should lead the government-wide effort to bring the major national security institutions into the information revolution. He should coordinate the resolution of the legal, policy, and technical issues across agencies to create a "trusted information network."

- No one agency can do it alone. . . .
- Only presidential leadership can develop government-wide concepts and standards. Currently, no one is doing this job. Backed by the Office of Management and Budget, a new National Intelligence Director empowered to set common standards for information use throughout the community, and a secretary of homeland security who helps extend the system to public agencies and relevant private-sector databases, a government-wide initiative can succeed.
- White House leadership is also needed because the policy and legal issues are harder than the technical ones. The necessary technology already exists. What does not are the rules for acquiring, accessing, sharing, and using the vast stores of public and private data that may be available. . . .

****

Executive Order 13388, October 25, 2005

Further Strengthening the Sharing of Terrorism Information to Protect Americans

By the authority vested in me as President by the Constitution and the laws of the United States of America, including section 1016 of the Intelligence Reform and Terrorism Prevention Act of 2004 (Public Law 108-458), and in order to further strengthen the effective conduct of United States counterterrorism activities and protect the territory, people, and interests of the United States of America, including against terrorist attacks, it is hereby ordered as follows:

Section 1. Policy. To the maximum extent consistent with applicable law, agencies shall, in the design and use of information systems and in the dissemination of information among agencies:

(a) give the highest priority to (i) the detection, prevention, disruption, preemption, and mitigation of the effects of terrorist activities against the territory, people, and interests of the United States of America; (ii) the interchange of terrorism information among agencies; (iii) the interchange of terrorism information between agencies and appropriate authorities of State, local, and tribal governments, and between agencies and appropriate private sector entities; and (iv) the protection of the ability of agencies to acquire additional such information; and

(b) protect the freedom, information privacy, and other legal rights of Americans in the conduct of activities implementing subsection (a).

Sec. 2. Duties of Heads of Agencies Possessing or Acquiring Terrorism Information. To implement the policy set forth in section 1 of this order, the head of each agency that possesses or acquires terrorism information:

(a) shall promptly give access to the terrorism information to the head of each other agency that has counterterrorism functions, and provide the terrorism information to each such agency, unless otherwise directed by the President, and consistent with (i) the statutory responsibilities of the agencies providing and receiving the information; (ii) any guidance issued by the Attorney General to fulfill the policy set forth in subsection 1(b) of this order; and (iii) other applicable law, including sections 102A(g) and (i) of the National Security Act of 1947, section 1016 of the Intelligence Reform and Terrorism Prevention Act of 2004 (including any policies, procedures, guidelines, rules, and standards issued pursuant thereto), . . . and

(b) shall cooperate in and facilitate production of reports based on terrorism information with contents and formats that permit dissemination that maximizes the utility of the information in protecting the territory, people, and interests of the United States.

Sec. 3. Preparing Terrorism Information for Maximum Distribution. To assist in expeditious and effective implementation by agencies of the policy set forth in section 1 of this order, the common standards for the sharing of terrorism information established pursuant to section 3 of Executive Order 13356 of August 27, 2004, shall be used, as appropriate, in carrying out section 1016 of the Intelligence Reform and Terrorism Prevention Act of 2004.

Sec. 4. Requirements for Collection of Terrorism Information Inside the United States. To assist in expeditious and effective implementation by agencies of the policy set forth in section 1 of this order, the recommendations regarding the establishment of executive branch-wide collection and sharing requirements, procedures, and guidelines for terrorism information collected within the United States made pursuant to section 4 of Executive Order 13356 shall be used, as appropriate, in carrying out section 1016 of the Intelligence Reform and Terrorism Prevention Act of 2004.

Sec. 5. Establishment and Functions of Information Sharing Council.

(a) Consistent with section 1016(g) of the Intelligence Reform and Terrorism Prevention Act of 2004, there is hereby established an Information

Sharing Council (Council), chaired by the Program Manager to whom section 1016 of such Act refers, and composed exclusively of designees of: the Secretaries of State, the Treasury, Defense, Commerce, Energy, and Homeland Security; the Attorney General; the Director of National Intelligence; the Director of the Central Intelligence Agency; the Director of the Office of Management and Budget; the Director of the Federal Bureau of Investigation; the Director of the National Counterterrorism Center; and such other heads of departments or agencies as the Director of National Intelligence may designate.

(b) The mission of the Council is to (i) provide advice and information concerning the establishment of an interoperable terrorism information sharing environment to facilitate automated sharing of terrorism information among appropriate agencies to implement the policy set forth in section 1 of this order; and (ii) perform the duties set forth in section 1016(g) of the Intelligence Reform and Terrorism Prevention Act of 2004.

(c) To assist in expeditious and effective implementation by agencies of the policy set forth in section 1 of this order, the plan for establishment of a proposed interoperable terrorism information sharing environment reported under section 5(c) of Executive Order 13356 shall be used, as appropriate, in carrying out section 1016 of the Intelligence Reform and Terrorism Prevention Act of 2004.

Sec. 6. Definitions. As used in this order:

(a) the term "agency" has the meaning set forth for the term "executive agency" in section 105 of title 5, United States Code, together with the Department of Homeland Security, but includes the Postal Rate Commission and the United States Postal Service and excludes the Government Accountability Office; and

(b) the term "terrorism information" has the meaning set forth for such term in section 1016(a)(4) of the Intelligence Reform and Terrorism Prevention Act of 2004.

Sec. 7. General Provisions.

(a) This order:

(i) shall be implemented in a manner consistent with applicable law, including Federal law protecting the information privacy and other legal rights of Americans, and subject to the availability of appropriations;

(ii) shall be implemented in a manner consistent with the authority of the principal officers of agencies as heads of their respective agencies, including under section 199 of the Revised Statutes (22 U.S.C. 2651), section 201 of the Department of Energy Organization Act (42 U.S.C. 7131), section 103 of the National Security Act of 1947 (50 U.S.C. 403-3), section 102(a) of the Homeland Security Act of 2002 (6 U.S.C. 112(a)), and sections 301 of title 5, 113(b) and 162(b) of title 10, 1501 of title 15, 503 of title 28, and 301(b) of title 31, United States Code;

(iii) shall be implemented consistent with the Presidential Memorandum of June 2, 2005, on "Strengthening Information Sharing, Access, and Integration Organizational, Management, and Policy Development Structures for Creating the Terrorism Information Sharing Environment;"

(iv) shall not be construed to impair or otherwise affect the functions of the Director of the Office of Management and Budget relating to budget, administrative, and legislative proposals; and

(v) shall be implemented in a manner consistent with section 102A of the National Security Act of 1947.

(b) This order is intended only to improve the internal management of the Federal Government and is not intended to, and does not, create any rights or benefits, substantive or procedural, enforceable at law or in equity by a party against the United States, its departments, agencies, instrumentalities, or entities, its officers, employees, or agents, or any other person.

Sec. 8. Amendments and Revocation.

(a) Executive Order 13311 of July 29, 2003, is amended:

(i) by striking "Director of Central Intelligence" each place it appears and inserting in lieu thereof in each such place "Director of National Intelligence"; and

(ii) by striking "103(c)(7)" and inserting in lieu thereof "102A(i)(1)".

(b) Executive Order 13356 of August 27, 2004, is hereby revoked.

George W. Bush
The White House,
October 25, 2005.

Sources: *The 9/11 Commission Report: Final Report of the National Commission on Terrorist Attacks upon the United States*. Section 13.3, pp. 416–420. https://fas.org/irp/offdocs/911comm-sec13.pdf; Executive Order 13388: Further Strengthening the Sharing of Terrorist Information to Protect Americans, October 25, 2005. https://georgewbush-whitehouse.archives.gov/news/releases/2005/10/print/20051025-5.html.

President Obama Announces the Death of bin Laden, 2011

President Barack Obama Addresses the Nation after U.S. Forces Kill Osama bin Laden, May 2, 2011

The death of Osama bin Laden at the hands of U.S. Navy SEALs carrying out Operation Neptune Spear on May 2, 2011, (local Pakistan time) marked the end of the largest global manhunt in U.S. history.

The search for bin Laden, the al-Qaeda leader who was the architect of the September 11, 2001, attacks on New York and Washington, DC, began almost immediately after investigators failed to find his body following the post-9/11 destruction of an al-Qaeda training camp in Afghanistan by U.S. military strikes.

U.S. intelligence officials were finally able to track bin Laden down after the 2007 identification of a courier believed to be in contact with bin Laden and the 2010 linking of that courier to a suspiciously fortified compound in Abbottabad, a town in northwestern Pakistan.

The SEALs, who carried out their mission following months of U.S. monitoring of the compound, launched the operation from a site in Afghanistan without informing Pakistani authorities. The operation reportedly lasted less than forty minutes and ended with the SEALs killing bin Laden. President Obama's subsequent address to the nation, in which he discussed both the raid and the pending disposal of bin Laden's body at sea, occurred less than eight hours after the president received word that bin Laden was dead.

News of bin Laden's death was not only well received by the nation as a whole but doubtless provided some measure of closure to the survivors of the attacks and the families and friends of those who lost their lives on 9/11. The Obama administration listed the successful operation to bring down bin Laden as among its most notable accomplishments in Obama's successful reelection campaign in 2012. However, the fact that it took approximately nine years before U.S. intelligence services were able to find bin Laden was seen by many observers as an indication that U.S. global intelligence gathering resources needed to be further shored up and expanded.

THE PRESIDENT: Good evening. Tonight, I can report to the American people and to the world that the United States has conducted an operation that killed Osama bin Laden, the leader of al Qaeda, and a terrorist who's responsible for the murder of thousands of innocent men, women, and children.

It was nearly 10 years ago that a bright September day was darkened by the worst attack on the American people in our history. The images of 9/11 are seared into our national memory—hijacked planes cutting through a cloudless September sky; the Twin Towers collapsing to the ground; black smoke billowing up from the Pentagon; the wreckage of Flight 93 in Shanksville, Pennsylvania, where the actions of heroic citizens saved even more heartbreak and destruction.

And yet we know that the worst images are those that were unseen to the world. The empty seat at the dinner table. Children who were forced to grow up without their mother or their father. Parents who would never know the feeling of their child's embrace. Nearly 3,000 citizens taken from us, leaving a gaping hole in our hearts.

On September 11, 2001, in our time of grief, the American people came together. We offered our neighbors a hand, and we offered the wounded our blood. We reaffirmed our ties to each other, and our love of community and country. On that day, no matter where we came from, what God we prayed to, or what race or ethnicity we were, we were united as one American family.

We were also united in our resolve to protect our nation and to bring those who committed this vicious attack to justice. We quickly learned that the 9/11 attacks were carried out by al Qaeda—an organization headed by Osama bin Laden, which had openly declared war on the United States and was committed to killing innocents in our country and around the globe. And so we went to war against al Qaeda to protect our citizens, our friends, and our allies.

Over the last 10 years, thanks to the tireless and heroic work of our military and our counterterrorism professionals, we've made great strides in that effort. We've disrupted terrorist attacks and strengthened our homeland defense. In Afghanistan, we removed the Taliban government, which had given bin Laden and al Qaeda safe haven and support. And around the globe, we worked with our friends and allies to capture or kill scores of al Qaeda terrorists, including several who were a part of the 9/11 plot.

Yet Osama bin Laden avoided capture and escaped across the Afghan border into Pakistan. Meanwhile, al Qaeda continued to operate from along that border and operate through its affiliates across the world.

And so shortly after taking office, I directed Leon Panetta, the director of the CIA, to make the killing or capture of bin Laden the top priority of our war against al Qaeda, even as we continued our broader efforts to disrupt, dismantle, and defeat his network.

Then, last August, after years of painstaking work by our intelligence community, I was briefed on a possible lead to bin Laden. It was far from certain, and it took many months to run this thread to ground. I met repeatedly with my national security team as we developed more information about the possibility that we had located bin Laden hiding within a compound deep inside of Pakistan. And finally, last week, I determined that we had enough intelligence to take action, and authorized an operation to get Osama bin Laden and bring him to justice.

Today, at my direction, the United States launched a targeted operation against that compound in Abbottabad, Pakistan. A small team of Americans carried out the operation with extraordinary courage and capability. No Americans were harmed. They took care to avoid civilian casualties. After a firefight, they killed Osama bin Laden and took custody of his body.

For over two decades, bin Laden has been al Qaeda's leader and symbol, and has continued to plot attacks against our country and our friends and allies. The death of bin Laden marks the most significant achievement to date in our nation's effort to defeat al Qaeda.

Yet his death does not mark the end of our effort. There's no doubt that al Qaeda will continue to pursue attacks against us. We must—and we will—remain vigilant at home and abroad.

As we do, we must also reaffirm that the United States is not—and never will be—at war with Islam. I've made clear, just as President Bush did shortly after 9/11, that our war is not against Islam. Bin Laden was not a Muslim leader; he was a mass murderer of Muslims. Indeed, al Qaeda has slaughtered scores of Muslims in many countries, including our own. So his demise should be welcomed by all who believe in peace and human dignity.

Over the years, I've repeatedly made clear that we would take action within Pakistan if we knew where bin Laden was. That is what we've done. But it's important to note that our counterterrorism cooperation with Pakistan helped lead us to bin Laden and the compound where he was hiding. Indeed, bin Laden had declared war against Pakistan as well, and ordered attacks against the Pakistani people.

Tonight, I called President Zardari, and my team has also spoken with their Pakistani counterparts. They agree that this is a good and historic day for both of our nations. And going forward, it is essential that Pakistan continue to join us in the fight against al Qaeda and its affiliates.

The American people did not choose this fight. It came to our shores, and started with the senseless slaughter of our citizens. After nearly 10 years of service, struggle, and sacrifice, we know well the costs of war. These efforts weigh on me every time I, as Commander-in-Chief, have to sign a letter to a family that has lost a loved one, or look into the eyes of a service member who's been gravely wounded.

So Americans understand the costs of war. Yet as a country, we will never tolerate our security being threatened, nor stand idly by when our people have been killed. We will be relentless in defense of our citizens and our friends and allies. We will be true to the values that make us who we are. And on nights like this one, we can say to those families who have lost loved ones to al Qaeda's terror: Justice has been done.

Tonight, we give thanks to the countless intelligence and counterterrorism professionals who've worked tirelessly to achieve this outcome. The American people do not see their work, nor know their names. But tonight, they feel the satisfaction of their work and the result of their pursuit of justice.

We give thanks for the men who carried out this operation, for they exemplify the professionalism, patriotism, and unparalleled courage of those who serve our country. And they are part of a generation that has borne the heaviest share of the burden since that September day.

Finally, let me say to the families who lost loved ones on 9/11 that we have never forgotten your loss, nor wavered in our commitment to see that we do whatever it takes to prevent another attack on our shores.

And tonight, let us think back to the sense of unity that prevailed on 9/11. I know that it has, at times, frayed. Yet today's achievement is a testament to the greatness of our country and the determination of the American people.

The cause of securing our country is not complete. But tonight, we are once again reminded that America can do whatever we set our mind to. That is the story of our history, whether it's the pursuit of prosperity for our people, or the struggle for equality for all our citizens; our commitment to stand up for our values abroad, and our sacrifices to make the world a safer place.

Let us remember that we can do these things not just because of wealth or power, but because of who we are: one nation, under God, indivisible, with liberty and justice for all.

Thank you. May God bless you. And may God bless the United States of America.

Source: Obama, Barack. "Osama bin Laden Dead." The White House, May 2, 2011. https://obamawhitehouse.archives.gov/blog/2011/05/02/osama-bin-laden-dead.

Secretary of State Clinton Responds to Congressional Questions about Benghazi, 2013 and 2015

Secretary of State Hillary Rodham Clinton's 2013 Testimony before the House Foreign Affairs Committee, January 23, 2013 and October 22, 2015, Testimony before the House Committee on Benghazi, Inquiring into the 2012 Death of American Diplomats in Benghazi, Libya.

When Libyans in the Benghazi area of eastern Libya rose up against dictatorial ruler Muammar Gaddafi in February 2011 during the pro-democracy Arab Spring, the United States covertly supported the rebels. Chris Stevens, later named the U.S. ambassador to Libya, became the Department of State's principal liaison officer with the growing opposition. The United States, however, provided little direct military support for the rebels beyond the initial firing of a volley of Tomahawk missiles at Libyan forces. Rather, as part of President Obama's "leadership from behind" approach to international engagements, military units from other NATO member states provided the air support for the anti-Gaddafi rebels, operating under a United Nations resolution seeking to establish a cease-fire on the ground. NATO's enforcement of a no-fly zone and bombing campaign in Libya enabled the rebels to topple the Gaddafi government. Officially, the civil war ended on October 23, 2011, with the rebels in control of the country's capital, Tripoli. Gaddafi himself died trying to escape the country.

The fact that NATO lacked ground forces when the fighting ended, however, left NATO—and the United States—without any direct ability to halt Libya's slide into chaos as various groups contended for control in the power vacuum created by the Gaddafi government's collapse. That slide was particularly apparent in Benghazi, where the United States had transformed a building complex thought to have been the home of its wartime CIA operatives into a consulate. In addition to attacks on that compound in April and June 2012, the escalating number of attacks by Islamic extremists against foreign entities in Benghazi included a May attack on the Red Cross headquarters office, a June assassination attempt on the visiting British ambassador, and an assault on the Tunisian consulate that same month,

Ambassador Stevens journeyed to Benghazi that September to assess the growing strength of radical Islamic groups in eastern Libya. Shortly thereafter, he and three other Americans were killed in an attack on the facility by radical Islamists on the eleventh anniversary of the September 11, 2001, al-Qaeda attack on the United States.

The attack came less than two months before the 2012 presidential election in the United States. The Republican Party quickly attacked President Obama and Secretary of State Clinton for failing to protect American personnel in Benghazi. Partisan rhetoric remained strong when Secretary Clinton appeared before the House Foreign Affairs Committee three days after the inauguration of President Obama's second term. It had greatly intensified by the time she appeared before the House Select Committee on Benghazi two years later, when she was already pursuing the Democratic Party's 2016 presidential nomination.

Secretary Clinton's 2015 testimony stretched more than nine hours. In the excerpt below, the representatives questioning Clinton are Tammy Duckworth (D-IL) and Jim Jordan (R-OH).

Excerpts of Secretary Clinton's Opening Remarks before the House Foreign Affairs Committee, January 23, 2013.

Any clear-eyed examination of this matter must begin with this sobering fact: . . . Since 1977, 65 American diplomatic personnel have been killed by terrorists. In addition to those who have been killed, we know what happened in Tehran with hostages being taken in 1979, our Embassy and Marine barracks bombed in Beirut in 1983, Khobar Towers in Saudi Arabia in 1996, our embassies in East Africa in 1998, consulate staff murdered in Jeddah, Saudi Arabia in 2004, the Khost attack in Afghanistan in 2009, and too many others.

But I also want to stress the list of attacks that were foiled, crises averted, and lives saved is even longer. We should never forget that the security professionals get it right more than 99 percent of the time, against difficult odds, because the terrorists only need to get it right once.

. . .

Now you may recall, at this same time period [as the Benghazi attacks], we were also seeing violent attacks on our embassies in Cairo, Sana'a, Tunis, and Khartoum, as well as large protests outside many other posts, from India to Indonesia, where thousands of our diplomats serve. So I immediately ordered a review of our security posture around the world, with particular scrutiny for high-threat posts. . . . Benghazi did not happen in a vacuum. The Arab revolutions have scrambled power dynamics and shattered security forces across the region. Instability in Mali has created an expanding safe haven for terrorists who look to extend their influence and plot further attacks of the kind we just saw last week in Algeria.

Excerpts from Secretary Clinton's Testimony before the House Committee on Benghazi, October 22, 2015. [Opening Remarks]

What happened in Benghazi has been scrutinized by a non-partisan hard-hitting Accountability Review Board, seven prior congressional investigations, multiple news organizations and, of course, our law enforcement and intelligence agencies. So today, I would like to share three observations about how we can learn from this tragedy and move forward as a nation.

First, America must lead in a dangerous world, and our diplomats must continue representing us in dangerous places. The State Department sends people to more than 270 posts in 170 countries around the world. [Ambassador] Chris Stevens understood that diplomats must operate in many places where our soldiers do not, where there are no other boots on the ground and safety is far from guaranteed. In fact, he volunteered for just those assignments. . . . We have learned the hard way when America is absent, especially from unstable places, there are consequences. Extremism take root, aggressors seek to fill the vacuum and security everywhere is threatened, including here at home.

[Protecting Personnel in Unsafe Environments]

[DUCKWORTH] . . . As a member of the Armed Services Committee, which also looked at the Benghazi attack, I'm concerned that the interagency cooperation between State and DOD was not sufficient in the weeks and months leading up to the September 11, 2012 attacks. For example, . . . if we had conducted any joint interagency planning and training exercises, this may have actually helped State and DOD to identify and fix existing vulnerabilities in the temporary mission facility in Benghazi.

CLINTON: . . . It's very challenging to get military assets into countries that don't want them there. And in fact, that has been a constant issue that we have worked, between the State Department and the Department of Defense. The Libyans made it very clear from the very beginning they did not want any American military or any foreign military at all in their country.

. . .

You know, historically, the only presence at some of our facilities has been Marines. And as you know well, Marines were there not for the purpose of personnel protection. They were there to destroy classified material and equipment. And so part of the challenge that we have faced inn [*sic*] some of these hot-spot, dangerous areas is how we get more of a presence. And after Benghazi, we were able to get Marines deployed to Tripoli.

. . .

I wanted to point out that even when we try to get it right, which we do try, sometimes there are unintended consequences and there is an example out of this tragedy. Coming out of previous assessments of attacks on facilities, we now have safe havens, safe rooms in facilities, particularly residences. The diplomatic security officers were able to get both Chris and Sean into that safe room.

Of course, the idea behind the safe room, why security experts advocated for them, was to protect our—our civilians, our diplomats from attacks like the one that was occurring. The attackers used diesel fuel to set the compound on fire. And the safe room was anything but safe. I'm sure the committee members know that neither Chris Stevens nor Sean Smith died from injuries directly inflicted by the attackers. They both died of smoke inhalation.

. . .

[DUCKWORTH:] So I want to look at the State Department's policy of awarding local guard contracts using an—a very inflexible contract vehicle known as the Lowest Priced Technically Acceptable, or LPTA, vehicle. . . . When life and limb are at risk, such as when buying body armor for our troops overseas or barriers for our embassies, I don't know that Lowest Priced Technically Acceptable is the right vehicle.

So, can you discuss a little bit, why is it that the State Department appears to have awarded local guard contracts in Libya using this contracting method?

CLINTON: Congresswoman, . . . I think the State Department, like much of the rest of the government, often feels under pressure to go to the lowest price, whether or not that lowest price is the best contract.

And we had a lot of challenges, not just in Libya, but in many places around the world, trying to work to find the right contractors to provide static security for a lot of our posts and facilities, to find more kinetic contractors who could be the front line of defense, since we—as we discussed earlier, we're stationed in so many places where there were not American military that could be called and quickly respond.

And the other problem, as you pointed out, is that if the host country doesn't have any real resources, it's hard to know how much they can produce. That night, I was calling the president of Libya and demanding that he find any friendly militia, any friendly anybody, to show up and to support us.

When our reinforcements, the security reinforcements from Tripoli landed, a militia showed up and in fact kept them there until they had a big enough group to accompany them to the CIA annex. So it's a very unpredictable and even erratic process. And it starts with in many instances the lowest price. And I don't think that's always the best way to get a contract for security.

[JORDAN:] At 10:08, on the night of the attack, you released this statement, "Some have sought to justify the vicious behavior as a response to inflammatory material posted on the Internet."

At 10:08, with no evidence, at 10:08, before the attack is over, at 10:08, when Tyrone Woods and Glen Doherty are still on the roof of the annex, fighting for their lives, the official statement of the State Department blames a video.

Why?

CLINTON: During the day on September 11th, as you did mention, Congressman, there was a very large protest against our embassy in Cairo. Protesters breached the walls. They tore down the American flag. And it was of grave concern to us because the inflammatory video had been shown on Egyptian television, which has a broader reach than just inside Egypt.

And, in fact, during the course of that week, we had many attacks that were all about the video. We had people breaching the walls of our embassies in Tunis, in Khartoum; we had people, thankfully not Americans, dying at protests. But that's what was going on, Congressman.

. . ..

CLINTON: . . . Several of you have raised the video and have dismissed the importance of the video. And I think that is unfortunate, because there's no doubt, and as I said earlier, even the person we have now arrested as being one of the ringleaders of the attack on our compound in Benghazi, is reputed to have used the video as a way to gather up the attackers that attacked our compound. So, I think it's important. These are complex issues, Mr. Congressman. And I think it's important that we look at the totality of what was going on.

Source: Clinton, Hillary. Testimony before the House Foreign Affairs Committee, January 23, 2013. https://2009-2017.state.gov/secretary/20092013clinton/rm/2013/01/203192.htm; Clinton, Hillary. Testimony before the House Select Committee on Benghazi, House Select Committee, October 22, 2015.

Obama Administration Report on Balancing Civil Liberties and National Security, 2013

Report and Recommendations of the President's Review Group on Intelligence and Communications Technologies, Liberty and Security in a Changing World, *December 12, 2013*

This 2013 Report of the President's Review Group on Intelligence and Communications Technology *is widely and properly acknowledged to have provided an informative and much-needed examination of U.S. anti-terrorist and intelligence gathering policies and practices. The review, however, stemmed less from the desire of government agencies for new directives than from the government's need to respond to Edward Snowden's disclosures of U.S. spying on both its own citizens and the governments of U.S. Allies in the U.S. war on terror.*

Snowden's revelations first begin appearing on the front pages of newspapers in June 2013. The review group was assembled and formally appointed within two months, and its lengthy (over 300 pages) report—complete with forty-six thoughtful recommendations on protecting national security while protecting the civil liberties and privacy of Americans—was tendered before Christmas of the same year.

Therein, the committee recommends policy changes it describes as necessary to maintain the trust of our allies and citizens alike; handle the bulk data collection being harvested from phone calls and private sector data collection giants; increase the efficiency of intergovernmental information sharing; minimize future leaks of the Snowden variety; and better protect the privacy of Americans. The excerpts here indicate the range of its concerns and findings and provide a snapshot of its substantive recommendations. The 2015 USA FREEDOM Act enacted many of those recommendations into law.

LIBERTY AND SECURITY IN A CHANGING WORLD

Preface

The United States must pursue multiple and often competing goals at home and abroad. In facing these challenges, the United States must take into account the full range of interests and values that it is pursuing, and it must communicate these goals to the American public and to key international audiences. These goals include:

Protecting The Nation Against Threats to Our National Security.

. . .

Promoting Other National Security and Foreign Policy Interests.

. . .

Protecting the Right to Privacy. The right to privacy is essential to a free and self-governing society. The rise of modern technologies makes it all the more important that democratic nations respect people's fundamental right to privacy, which is a defining part of individual security and personal liberty.

Protecting Democracy, Civil Liberties, and the Rule of Law. . . . Excessive surveillance and unjustified secrecy can threaten civil liberties, public trust, and the core processes of democratic self-government. All parts of the government, including those that protect our national security, must be subject to the rule of law.

Promoting Prosperity, Security, and Openness in a Networked World. . . . For this reason, the United States must continue to establish and strengthen international norms of Internet freedom and security.

Protecting Strategic Alliances. . . . The collection of intelligence should be undertaken in a way that recognizes the importance of cooperative relationships with other nations and that respects the legitimate privacy interests and the dignity of those outside our borders. . . . [10–13]

Executive Summary

. . .

Principles

. . .

1. *The United States Government must protect, at once, two different forms of security: national security and personal privacy.*

In the American tradition, the word "security" has had multiple meanings. In contemporary parlance, it often refers to national security or homeland security. . . . At the same time, the idea of security refers to a quite different and equally fundamental value, captured in the Fourth Amendment to the United States Constitution:

2. *The central task is one of risk management; multiple risks are involved, and all of them must be considered.*

. . . In addition to reducing risks to national security, public officials must consider four other risks:

- Risks to privacy;
- Risks to freedom and civil liberties, on the Internet and elsewhere;
- Risks to our relationships with other nations; and
- Risks to trade and commerce, including international commerce.

3. *The idea of "balancing" has an important element of truth, but it is also inadequate and misleading.*

. . . But some safeguards are not subject to balancing at all. In a free society, public officials should never engage in surveillance in order to punish their political enemies; to restrict freedom of speech or religion; to suppress legitimate criticism and dissent; . . . or to benefit or burden members of groups defined in terms of religion, ethnicity, race, and gender.

4. *The government should base its decisions on a careful analysis of consequences, including both benefits and costs (to the extent feasible).*

. . . Surveillance decisions should depend (to the extent feasible) on a careful assessment of the anticipated consequences, including the full range of relevant risks. Such decisions should also be subject to continuing scrutiny, including retrospective analysis, to ensure that any errors are corrected. . . .[14–16]

Surveillance of US Persons

. . .

We recommend important restrictions on the ability of the Foreign Intelligence Surveillance Court (FISC) to compel third parties (such as telephone service providers) to disclose private information to the government. We endorse similar restrictions on the issuance of National Security Letters (by which the Federal Bureau of Investigation now compels individuals and organizations to turn over certain otherwise private records), recommending prior judicial review except in emergencies, where time is of the essence.

We recommend concrete steps to promote transparency and accountability, and thus to promote public trust, which is essential in this domain. . . . [18]

Surveillance of Non-US Persons

Any programs that allow surveillance of such persons even outside the United States should satisfy six separate constraints. They:

1) must be authorized by duly enacted laws or properly authorized executive orders;
2) must be directed *exclusively* at protecting national security interests of the United States or our allies;
3) must *not* be directed at illicit or illegitimate ends, such as . . . obtaining commercial gain for domestic industries;
4) must not target any non-United States person based solely on that person's political views or religious convictions;
5) must not disseminate information about non-United States persons if the information is not relevant to protecting the national security of the United States or our allies; and
6) must be subject to careful oversight and to the highest degree of transparency consistent with protecting the national security of the United States and our allies. [19]

Organizational Reform

We recommend a series of organizational changes. With respect to the National Security Agency (NSA), we believe that the Director should be a Senate-confirmed position, with civilians eligible to hold that position;

We favor a newly chartered, strengthened, independent Civil Liberties and Privacy Protection Board (CLPP Board) to replace the Privacy and Civil Liberties Oversight Board (PCLOB). The CLPP Board should have broad authority to review government activity relating to foreign intelligence and counterterrorism whenever that activity has implications for civil liberties and privacy. . . . [21]

. . .

Protecting What We Do Collect

We recommend a series of steps to reduce the risks associated with "insider threats." A governing principle is plain: Classified information should be shared only with those who genuinely need to know. . . . [23]

. . .

Recommendations

Chapter I

Principles [43]

[See summary above]

Chapter II

Lessons of History [53]

Many of the rules governing the actions of the Intelligence Community were amended in the wake of the attacks of September 11. Predictably, and quite properly, they were amended to give the Intelligence Community much broader authority to take action to ensure that the United States could prevent similar attacks in the future. But because we were acting in a moment of crisis, there was always the risk that the new rules—and the new authorities granted to the Intelligence Community—might have gone too far.

It is now time to step back and take stock. With the benefit of experience . . . we conclude that some of the authorities that were expanded or created in the aftermath of September 11 unduly sacrifice fundamental interests in individual liberty, personal privacy, and democratic governance. . . . [76–77]

Chapter III

Reforming Foreign Intelligence Surveillance Directed at United States Persons [79]

. . .

The central issue concerns the authority of the government in general, and the Intelligence Community in particular, to require third parties, such as telephone and Internet companies, to turn over their business records to the government. Because the data contained in those records can reveal significant information about the private lives of United States persons, it is essential to think carefully about the circumstances in which the government should have access to those records. [79]

. . .

Recommendation 1

We recommend that [Patriot Act] section 215 should be amended to authorize the Foreign Intelligence Surveillance Court to [compel] . . . a third party to disclose otherwise private information about particular individuals only if:

(1) it finds that the government has reasonable grounds to believe that the particular information sought is relevant to an authorized investigation intended

to protect "against international terrorism or clandestine intelligence activities" and

(2) . . . the order is reasonable in focus, scope, and breadth. [86]

. . .

Recommendation 4

We recommend that, as a general rule, and without senior policy review, the government should not be permitted to collect and store all mass, undigested, non-public personal information about individuals to enable future queries and data-mining for foreign intelligence purposes. Any program involving government collection or storage of such data must be narrowly tailored to serve an important government interest. [108]

. . .

At the very least, we should always be prepared to question claims that secrecy is necessary. That conclusion needs to be demonstrated rather than merely assumed. When it is possible to promote transparency without appreciably sacrificing important competing interests, we should err on the side of transparency. [128]

. . .

Chapter IV

Reforming Foreign Intelligence Surveillance Directed at Non-United States Persons [130]

. . .

Recommendation 13

We recommend that, in [authorizing] . . . the surveillance of non-United States persons who are outside the United States, in addition to the safeguards and oversight mechanisms already in place, the US Government should reaffirm that such surveillance:

(1) must be authorized by duly enacted laws or properly authorized executive orders;

(2) must be directed exclusively at the national security of the United States or our allies; [151]

. . .

Chapter V

Determining What Intelligence Should Be Collected and How

. . .

Intelligence collection is not an end in itself. Intelligence collection should not occur because it is possible, but only because it is necessary. [163]

. . .

Recommendation 19

We recommend that decisions to engage in surveillance of foreign leaders should consider the following criteria:

(1) Is there a need to engage in such surveillance in order to assess significant threats to our national security?

(2) Is the other nation one with whom we share values and interests, with whom we have a cooperative relationship, and whose leaders we should accord a high degree of respect and deference?

(3) Is there a reason to believe that the foreign leader may be being duplicitous in dealing with senior US officials or is attempting to hide information relevant to national security concerns from the US?

(4) Are there other collection means or collection targets that could reliably reveal the needed information?

(5) What would be the negative effects if the leader became aware of the US collection, or if citizens of the relevant nation became so aware? [170–171]

. . .

Recommendation 20

We recommend that the US Government should examine the feasibility of creating software that would allow the National Security Agency and other intelligence agencies more easily to conduct targeted information acquisition rather than bulk-data collection. [173–174]

. . .

Chapter VI

Organizational Reform in Light of Changing Communications Technology [177]

. . .

Recommendation 22

We recommend that:

(1) the Director of the National Security Agency should be a Senate-confirmed position;

(2) civilians should be eligible to hold that position; and

(3) the President should give serious consideration to making the next Director of the National Security Agency a civilian. [188]

. . .

Recommendation 26

We recommend the creation of a privacy and civil liberties policy official located both in the National Security Staff and the Office of Management and Budget. [194]

. . .

Recommendation 27
We recommend that:

(1) The charter of the Privacy and Civil Liberties Oversight Board [PCLOB] should be modified to create a new and strengthened agency, the Civil Liberties and Privacy Protection Board [CLPP], that can oversee Intelligence Community activities for foreign intelligence purposes, rather than only for counterterrorism purposes; . . . [195]

. . .

Oversight should match the scope of the activity being reviewed. Having the new CLPP Board oversee "foreign intelligence" rather than "anti-terrorism" would match the scope of FISA. . . . [197]

. . .

Chapter VII

Global Communications Technology: Promoting Prosperity, Security, and Openness in a Networked World [209]

. . .

Recommendation 29

We recommend that, regarding encryption, the US Government should:

(1) fully support and not undermine efforts to create encryption standards;
(2) not in any way subvert, undermine, weaken, or make vulnerable generally available commercial software; and
(3) increase the use of encryption and urge US companies to do so, in order to better protect data in transit, at rest, in the cloud, and in other storage. [216]

. . .

Chapter VIII

Protecting What We Do Collect [233]

. . .

Recommendation 38
We recommend that the vetting of personnel for access to classified information should be ongoing, rather than periodic. A standard of Personnel Continuous Monitoring should be adopted, incorporating data from Insider Threat programs and from commercially available sources, to note such things as changes in credit ratings or any arrests or court proceedings.

Recommendation 39
We recommend that security clearances should be more highly differentiated, including the creation of "administrative access" clearances that allow for support and information technology personnel to have the access they need without granting them unnecessary access to substantive policy or intelligence material. [234]

. . .

The security clearance system should be designed to have an extremely low false-positive rate (granting or continuing a clearance when one should have been denied). . . . The nature and degree of vetting procedures should be adjusted periodically and more closely tied to the sensitivity of the information to which access is granted. [235]

. . .

About five million people now have active security clearances granted by some arm of the US Government, of which almost 1.5 million have Top Secret clearance. Although we do not have the capability to determine if those numbers are excessive, they certainly seem high. We believe that an interagency committee, representing not just the Intelligence Community, should review in detail why so many personnel require clearances and examine whether there are ways to reduce the total. . . . [243]

. . .

Recommendation 41

We recommend that the "need-to-share" or "need-to-know" models should be replaced with a Work-Related Access model, which would ensure that all personnel whose role requires access to specific information have such access, without making the data more generally available to cleared personnel who are merely interested. [245]

Source: Review Group on Intelligence and Communications Technologies. *Liberty And Security in a Changing World: Report and Recommendations of the President's Review Group on Intelligence and Communications Technologies*. Defense Technical Information Center, December 12, 2013. https://apps.dtic.mil/dtic/tr/fulltext/u2/a597577.pdf.

FBI Director Comey on Technology, Privacy, and Counterterrorism, 2014

FBI Director James B. Comey's Address before the Brooking Institution, "Going Dark: Are Technology, Privacy, and Public Safety on a Collision Course?" Washington, DC, October 16, 2014

Edward Snowden's revelations of secret government surveillance of private citizens created mistrust of government intentions and fear of surveillance within the public. Congress responded by passing the 2015 USA FREEDOM Act, which imposed new limits on the government's ability to collect telecommunications metadata.

This address by Federal Bureau of Investigation (FBI) director James Comey came in the midst of this movement toward limiting the government's information gathering capacities. To Comey, whose ten-year term as FBI director received Senate confirmation by a 93–1 vote only a year before, it was already time "to suggest that the post-Snowden pendulum has swung too far in one direction." According to Comey, technological change in general, along with the growing encryption of public records offered by private sector actors as a "marketing pitch," would "have very serious consequences for law enforcement and national security agencies at all levels" if left unchecked.

Proposals for reconciling technological change with security needs continue to be debated, even as terrorist groups like ISIS experiment with ever more sophisticated means of keeping their plans "dark" until implemented. Still continuing as well is the quest for a mutually agreed upon basis for government–private sector cooperation in enhancing the authorized access of security agencies to metadata telecommunication files in the name of homeland security.

I wanted to meet with you to talk in a serious way about the impact of emerging technology on public safety. . . . There are a lot of misconceptions in the public eye about what we in the government collect and the capabilities we have for collecting information.

My goal today isn't to tell people what to do. My goal is to urge our fellow citizens to participate in a conversation as a country about where we are, and where we want to be, with respect to the authority of law enforcement.

The Challenge of Going Dark

Technology has forever changed the world we live in. We're online, in one way or another, all day long. Our phones and computers have become reflections of our personalities, our interests, and our identities. They hold much that is important to us.

And with that comes a desire to protect our privacy and our data—you want to share your lives with the people you choose. I sure do. But the FBI has a sworn duty to keep every American safe from crime and terrorism, and technology has become the tool of choice for some very dangerous people.

Unfortunately, the law hasn't kept pace with technology, and this disconnect has created a significant public safety problem. We call it "Going Dark," and what it means is this: Those charged with protecting our people aren't always able to access the evidence we need to prosecute crime and prevent terrorism even with lawful authority. We have the legal authority to intercept and access communications and information pursuant to court order, but we often lack the technical ability to do so.

We face two overlapping challenges. The first concerns real-time court-ordered interception of what we call "data in motion," such as phone calls, e-mail, and live chat sessions. The second challenge concerns court-ordered access to data stored on our devices, such as e-mail, text messages, photos, and videos—or what we call "data at rest." And both . . . are increasingly encrypted.

Let's talk about court-ordered interception first, and then we'll talk about challenges posed by different means of encryption.

In the past, conducting electronic surveillance was more straightforward. We identified a target phone being used by a bad guy, with a single carrier. We obtained a court order for a wiretap, and, under the supervision of a judge, we collected the evidence we needed for prosecution.

Today, there are countless providers, countless networks, and countless means of communicating. We have laptops, smartphones, and tablets. We take them to work and to school, from the soccer field to Starbucks, over many networks, using any number of apps. And so do those conspiring to harm us. They use the same devices, the same networks, and the same apps to make plans, to target victims, and to cover up what they're doing. And that makes it tough for us to keep up.

If a suspected criminal is in his car, and he switches from cellular coverage to Wi-Fi, we may be out of luck. If he switches from one app to another, or from cellular voice service to a voice or messaging app, we may lose him. We may not have the capability to quickly switch lawful surveillance between devices, methods, and networks. The bad guys know this; they're taking advantage of it every day.

In the wake of the Snowden disclosures, . . . some believe that the FBI has these phenomenal capabilities to access any information at any time—that we can get what we want, when we want it, by flipping some sort of switch. It may be true in the movies or on TV. It is simply not the case in real life.

Current law governing the interception of communications requires telecommunication carriers and broadband providers to build interception capabilities into their networks for court-ordered surveillance. But that law, the Communications Assistance for Law Enforcement Act, or CALEA, was enacted 20 years ago—a lifetime in the Internet age. And it doesn't cover new means of communication. Thousands of companies provide some form of communication service, and most are not required by statute to provide lawful intercept capabilities to law enforcement.

What this means is that an order from a judge to monitor a suspect's communication may amount to nothing more than a piece of paper. Some companies fail to comply with the court order. Some can't comply, because they have not developed interception capabilities. Other providers want to provide assistance, but they have to build interception capabilities, and that takes time and money.

The issue is whether companies not currently subject to the Communications Assistance for Law Enforcement Act should be required to build lawful intercept capabilities for law enforcement. We aren't seeking to expand our authority to intercept communications. We are struggling to keep up with changing technology and to maintain our ability to actually collect the communications we are authorized to intercept.

And if the challenges of real-time interception threaten to leave us in the dark, encryption threatens to lead all of us to a very dark place.

Encryption is nothing new. But the challenge to law enforcement and national security officials is markedly worse, with recent default encryption settings and encrypted devices and networks—all designed to increase security and privacy.

With Apple's new operating system, the information stored on many iPhones and other Apple devices will be encrypted by default. Shortly after Apple's announcement, Google announced plans to follow suit with its Android operating system. This means the companies themselves won't be able to unlock phones, laptops, and tablets to reveal photos, documents, e-mail, and recordings stored within.

Both companies are run by good people, responding to what they perceive is a market demand. But the place they are leading us is one we shouldn't go to without careful thought and debate as a country.

Correcting Misconceptions

There is a misconception that building a lawful intercept solution into a system requires a so-called "back door," one that foreign adversaries and hackers may try to exploit.

But that isn't true. We aren't seeking a back-door approach. We want to use the front door, with clarity and transparency, and with clear guidance provided by law. We are completely comfortable with court orders and legal process—front doors that provide the evidence and information we need to investigate crime and prevent terrorist attacks.

Cyber adversaries will exploit any vulnerability they find. But it makes more sense to address any security risks by developing intercept solutions during the design phase, rather than resorting to a patchwork solution when law enforcement comes knocking after the fact. And with sophisticated encryption, there might be no solution, leaving the government at a dead end—all in the name of privacy and network security.

Another misperception is that we can somehow guess the password or break into the phone with a so-called "brute force" attack. Even a supercomputer would have difficulty with today's high-level encryption, and some devices have a setting whereby the encryption key is erased if someone makes too many attempts to break the password, meaning no one can access that data.

Finally, a reasonable person might also ask, "Can't you just compel the owner of the phone to produce the password?" Likely, no. And even if we could compel them as a legal matter, if we had a child predator in custody, and he could choose to sit quietly through a 30-day contempt sentence for refusing to comply with a court order to produce his password, or he could risk a 30-year sentence for production and distribution of child pornography, which do you think he would choose?

With Going Dark, those of us in law enforcement and public safety have a major fear of missing out—missing out on predators who exploit the most vulnerable among us. . . .Missing out on violent criminals who target our communities . . . missing out on a terrorist cell using social media to recruit, plan, and execute an attack.

My Thoughts

I'm deeply concerned about this, as both a law enforcement officer and a citizen. I understand some of this thinking in a post-Snowden world, but I believe it is mostly based on a failure to understand why we in law enforcement do what we do and how we do it.

. . .

There will come a day—and it comes every day in this business—where it will matter a great deal to innocent people that we in law enforcement can't access certain types of data or information, even with legal authorization. We have to have these discussions now.

. . .

The people of the FBI are sworn to protect both security and liberty. It isn't a question of conflict. We must care deeply about protecting liberty through due process of law, while also safeguarding the citizens we serve—in every investigation.

Where Do We Go from Here?

We need to fix this problem. It is long past time.

We need assistance and cooperation from companies to comply with lawful court orders, so that criminals around the world cannot seek safe haven for lawless conduct. We need to find common ground. We care about the same things. I said it because I meant it. These companies are run by good people. And we know an adversarial posture won't take any of us very far down the road.

We understand the private sector's need to remain competitive in the global marketplace. And it isn't our intent to stifle innovation or undermine U.S. companies. But we have to find a way to help these companies understand what we need, why we need it, and how they can help, while still protecting privacy rights and providing network security and innovation. We need our private sector partners to take a step back, to pause, and to consider changing course.

We also need a regulatory or legislative fix to create a level playing field, so that all communication service providers are held to the same standard and so that those of us in law enforcement, national security, and public safety can continue to do the job you have entrusted us to do, in the way you would want us to.

Perhaps most importantly, we need to make sure the American public understands the work we do and the means by which we do it.

Source: Comey, James B. "Going Dark: Are Technology, Privacy, and Public Safety on a Collision Course?" Federal Bureau of Investigation, October 16, 2014. https://www.fbi.gov/news/speeches/going-dark-are-technology-privacy-and-public-safety-on-a-collision-course.

Congress Passes the USA FREEDOM Act, 2015

USA FREEDOM Act is Enacted by U.S. 114th Congress, 1st Session, June 2, 2015

Also known as the Uniting and Strengthening America by Fulfilling Rights and Ensuring Effective Discipline over Monitoring Act of 2015, the USA FREEDOM Act (or Freedom Act) was passed on June 2 of that year. Passage came approximately nineteen months after it was introduced in the previous Congress and two years after Edward Snowden revealed the degree to which the U.S. government was spying on the electronic communications of its citizens. The bill also became law one day after the expiration of the USA PATRIOT Act (or Patriot Act), restoring many of that law's provisions in a modified form, at least in part because of the fervor caused by those revelations. For the greater part, however, the surveillance portions of the Patriot Act, passed hurriedly in the aftermath of the 9/11 attacks on the World Trade Center and Pentagon, had been controversial from the outset and were authorized for only four years in that act.

As the longer title suggests, the Freedom Act's general focus was on enhancing the monitoring of intelligence agencies' online surveillance activities to protect the privacy and civil liberties of Americans. It did so by limiting the former's ability to collect and store electronic metadata on American citizens' business, computer, Internet, telephone, and other personal records. In part as a response to the

2013 recommendations of the President's Review Group on Intelligence and Communications Technologies, Foreign Intelligence Surveillance Court (FISA) procedures related to business records were reformed and the bulk collection of metadata by the National Security Agency (NSA) was terminated (although phone companies continued to have permission to do so, and NSA still had options for seeking access to that data).

Elsewhere, the act focuses on reporting requirements concerning the proceedings of FISA's largely secret warrant-granting procedures, creates panels to protect the public's privacy from unjustifiable violation, limits the government's ability to prevent the targets of its inquiries from disclosing that fact, and—in the interest of transparency—expands the obligation of government entities to report to the Congress the number of requests heard and granted by FISA.

At the same time, the act was not entirely devoted to restricting government intelligence gathering and counterterrorism operations. The definition of an "agent of a foreign power" was broadened, the roving electronic surveillance provisions of the Patriot Act pertaining to suspected foreign terrorists were extended in the act's penultimate Article (Title VII), and—independent from the Patriot Act's extension—the final portion of the act defines a variety of activities involving radioactive materials as terrorism.

Even with respect to that most controversial part of the original Patriot Act, Section 215, authorizing the collection of business records, the Freedom Act added subsections enabling the collection of "call detail records" (CDRs) of both terrorist suspects and their contacts covering long periods of time, even as it curtailed the government's bulk metadata gathering authority. That section, however, was due to expire at the end of March 2020, with the rest of the Patriot Act, barring the permanent extension of the act that the Trump administration was seeking in mid-March. Then, however, the coronavirus could no longer be ignored, and at least temporarily, the Freedom Act became one of the legislative casualties as the Congress and administration became focused on a far greater and immediate threat to homeland security than international terrorism.

Public Law 114-23
114th Congress

An Act

To reform the authorities of the Federal Government to require the production of certain business records, conduct electronic surveillance, use pen registers and trap and trace devices, and use other forms of information gathering for foreign intelligence, counterterrorism, and criminal purposes, and for other purposes.

. . .

TITLE II—FISA PEN REGISTER AND TRAP AND TRACE DEVICE REFORM

SEC. 201. PROHIBITION ON BULK COLLECTION.

. . .

(b) Definition.—Section 401 (50 U.S.C. 1841) is amended by adding at the end the following new paragraph:

"(4)(A) The term 'specific selection term'—

"(i) is a term that specifically identifies a person, account, address, or personal device, or any other specific identifier; and

"(ii) is used to limit, to the greatest extent reasonably practicable, the scope of information sought, consistent with the purpose for seeking the use of the pen register or trap and trace device.

"(B) A specific selection term under subparagraph (A) does not include an identifier that does not limit, to the greatest extent reasonably practicable, the scope of information sought, consistent with the purpose for seeking the use of the pen register or trap and trace device, such as an identifier that—

"(i) identifies an electronic communication service provider (as that term is defined in section 701) . . . ; or

"(ii) identifies a broad geographic region, including the United States, a city, a county, a State, a zip code, or an area code.

"(D) Nothing in this paragraph shall be construed to preclude the use of multiple terms or identifiers to meet the requirements of subparagraph (A).".

. . .

TITLE IV—FOREIGN INTELLIGENCE SURVEILLANCE COURT REFORMS

SEC. 401. APPOINTMENT OF AMICUS CURIAE.

Section 103 (50 U.S.C. 1803) is amended by adding at the end the following new subsections:

"(i) Amicus Curiae.—

"(1) Designation.—The presiding judges of the courts established under subsections (a) and (b) shall, not later than 180 days after the enactment of this subsection, jointly designate not fewer than 5 individuals to be eligible to serve as amicus curiae, who shall serve pursuant to rules the presiding judges may establish. In designating such individuals, the presiding judges may consider individuals recommended by any source, including members of the Privacy and Civil Liberties Oversight Board, the judges determine appropriate.

"(2) Authorization.—A court established under subsection (a) or (b), consistent with the requirement of subsection (c) and any other statutory requirement that the court act expeditiously or within a stated time—

"(A) shall appoint an individual who has been designated under paragraph (1) to serve as amicus curiae to assist such court in the consideration of any application for an order or review that, in the opinion of the court, presents a novel interpretation of the law, unless the court issues a finding that such appointment is not appropriate.

"(3) Qualifications of amicus curiae.—

"(A) Expertise.—Individuals designated under paragraph (1) shall be persons who possess expertise in privacy and civil liberties, intelligence collection, communications technology, or any other area that may lend legal or technical expertise to a court established under subsection (a) or (b).

"(4) Duties.—If a court established under subsection (a) or (b) appoints an amicus curiae under paragraph (2)(A), the amicus curiae shall provide to the court, as appropriate—

"(A) legal arguments that advance the protection of individual privacy and civil liberties;

"(B) information related to intelligence collection or communications technology. . . ."

. . .

SEC. 402. DECLASSIFICATION OF DECISIONS, ORDERS, AND OPINIONS

. . .

"(a) Declassification Required.—Subject to subsection (b), the Director of National Intelligence, in consultation with the Attorney General, shall conduct a declassification review of each decision, order, or opinion issued by the Foreign Intelligence Surveillance Court or the Foreign Intelligence Surveillance Court of Review (as defined in section 601(e)) that includes a significant construction or interpretation of any provision of law, including any novel or significant construction or interpretation of the term 'specific selection term', and, consistent with that review, make publicly available to the greatest extent practicable each such decision, order, or opinion."

. . .

TITLE V—NATIONAL SECURITY LETTER REFORM

. . .

SEC. 502. LIMITATIONS ON DISCLOSURE OF NATIONAL SECURITY LETTERS.

(a) Counterintelligence Access to Telephone Toll and Transactional Records.—Section 2709 of title 18, United States Code, is amended by striking subsection (c) and inserting the following new subsection:

"(c) Prohibition of Certain Disclosure.—

"(1) Prohibition.—

"(A) In general.—If a certification is issued under subparagraph (B) and notice of the right to judicial review under subsection (d) is provided, no wire or electronic communication service provider that receives a request under subsection (b), or officer, employee, or agent thereof, shall disclose to any person that the Federal Bureau of Investigation has sought or obtained access to information or records under this section.

"(B) Certification.—The requirements of subparagraph (A) shall apply if the Director of the Federal Bureau of Investigation, or a designee of the Director whose rank shall be no lower than Deputy Assistant Director at Bureau headquarters or a Special Agent in Charge of a Bureau field office, certifies that the absence of a prohibition of disclosure under this subsection may result in—

"(i) a danger to the national security of the United States;

"(ii) interference with a criminal, counterterrorism, or counterintelligence investigation;

"(iii) interference with diplomatic relations; or

"(iv) danger to the life or physical safety of any person.

"(2) Exception.—

"(A) In general—A wire or electronic communication service provider that receives a request under subsection (b), or officer, employee, or agent thereof, may disclose information otherwise subject to any applicable nondisclosure requirement to—

"(i) those persons to whom disclosure is necessary in order to comply with the request;

"(ii) an attorney in order to obtain legal advice or assistance regarding the request; or

"(iii) other persons as permitted by the Director of the Federal Bureau of Investigation or the designee of the Director."

. . .

TITLE VI—FISA TRANSPARENCY AND REPORTING REQUIREMENTS

. . .

"SEC. 603. ANNUAL REPORTS.

"(a) Report by Director of the Administrative Office of the United States Courts.—

"(1) Report required.—The Director of the Administrative Office of the United States Courts shall annually submit to the Permanent Select Committee on Intelligence and the Committee on the Judiciary of the House of Representatives and the Select Committee on Intelligence and the Committee on the Judiciary of the Senate, subject to a declassification review by the Attorney General and the Director of National Intelligence, a report that includes—

"(A) the number of applications or certifications for orders submitted under each of [authorizing] sections . . . ;

"(B) the number of such orders granted under each of those sections;

"(C) the number of orders modified under each of those sections;

"(D) the number of applications or certifications denied under each of those sections;

"(E) the number of appointments of an individual to serve as amicus curiae under section 103, including the name of each individual appointed to serve as amicus curiae; and

"(F) the number of findings issued under section 103(i) that such appointment is not appropriate and the text of any such findings."

. . .

TITLE VII—ENHANCED NATIONAL SECURITY PROVISIONS

SEC. 701. EMERGENCIES INVOLVING NON-UNITED STATES PERSONS.

. . .

"(f)(1) Notwithstanding any other provision of this Act, the lawfully authorized targeting of a non-United States person previously believed to be located outside the United States for the acquisition of foreign intelligence information may continue for a period not to exceed 72 hours from the time that the non-United States person is reasonably believed to be located inside the United States and the acquisition is subject to this title or to title III of this Act, provided that the head of an element of the intelligence community—

"(A) reasonably determines that a lapse in the targeting of such non-United States person poses a threat of death or serious bodily harm to any person;

"(B) promptly notifies the Attorney General of a determination under subparagraph (A); and

"(C) requests, as soon as practicable, the employment of emergency electronic surveillance under subsection (e) or the employment of an emergency physical search pursuant to section 304(e), as warranted."

. . .

SEC. 704. INCREASE IN PENALTIES FOR MATERIAL SUPPORT OF FOREIGN TERRORIST ORGANIZATIONS.

Section 2339B(a)(1) of title 18, United States Code, is amended by striking "15 years" and inserting "20 years".

. . .

TITLE VIII—SAFETY OF MARITIME NAVIGATION AND NUCLEAR TERRORISM CONVENTIONS IMPLEMENTATION

Subtitle B—Prevention of Nuclear Terrorism

. . .

SEC. 811. NEW SECTION 2332I OF TITLE 18, UNITED STATES CODE.

"(a) Offences

(1) In general.—Whoever knowingly and unlawfully—

"(A) possesses radioactive material or makes or possesses a device—

"(i) with the intent to cause death or serious bodily injury; or

"(ii) with the intent to cause substantial damage to property or the environment; or

"(B) uses in any way radioactive material or a device, or uses or damages or interferes with the operation of a nuclear facility in a manner that causes the release of or increases the risk of the release of radioactive material, or causes radioactive contamination or exposure to radiation—

"(i) with the intent to cause death or serious bodily injury or with the knowledge that such act is likely to cause death or serious bodily injury;

"(ii) with the intent to cause substantial damage to property or the environment or with the knowledge that such act is likely to cause substantial damage to property or the environment; or "(iii) with the intent to compel a person, an international organization or a country to do or refrain from doing an act,

shall be punished as prescribed in subsection (c)

. . .

"(c) Penalties.—Whoever violates this section shall be fined not more than $2,000,000 and shall be imprisoned for any term of years or for life.

"(d) Nonapplicability.—This section does not apply to—

"(1) the activities of armed forces during an armed conflict, as those terms are understood under the law of war, which are governed by that law; or

"(2) activities undertaken by military forces of a state in the exercise of their official duties."

Source: Uniting and Strengthening America by Fulfilling Rights and Ensuring Effective Discipline over Monitoring Act of 2015. Pub. L. No. 114-23, 129 Stat. 268 (June 2, 2015). https://www.congress.gov/114/plaws/publ23/PLAW-114publ23.pdf.

President Trump Declares Travel Ban on Visitors from Islamic Countries, 2017

Presidential Proclamation 9645, "Enhancing Vetting Capabilities and Processes for Detecting Attempted Entry into the United States by Terrorists or Other Public Safety Threats," September 24, 2017

Presidential Proclamation 9645 was the Trump administration's first successful effort to limit, by executive order, access to the United States by travelers originating in areas containing groups the administration deemed likely to pose a security threat to the U.S. homeland.

This proclamation was not the Trump's administration's first effort in that realm, however. The first originated in candidate Donald Trump's campaign for his party's presidential nomination and subsequent general election campaign. Control of illegal immigration and the dangers that illegal immigrants allegedly posed to public safety were major themes in Trump's campaign. He promised that, if elected, his administration would erect a wall along the border with Mexico to protect against illegal immigrants from the south and tighten entry to the United States from dangerous people otherwise seeking to enter the country.

Another major focus of candidate Trump's rhetoric focused on the threat of "Muslim" terrorism. That rhetoric escalated following the deadly June 12, 2016, terrorist attack on a nightclub in Orlando. Two days later, he delivered a speech at New Hampshire's St. Anselm College that was criticized for impugning the loyalty of Muslim American citizens. Trump's opponents asserted that postelection policies his administration embraced that were predicated on such assumptions would be constitutionally suspect under First Amendment provisions.

Following Trump's 2016 election victory, he issued an executive order limiting entry of persons from only Muslim countries. This executive order, however, quickly ran into formidable legal challenges.

District and circuit courts in the liberal-progressive and conservative parts of the country tend to be reflections of local political cultures, as represented in the Congress by their state's senators. It also means that conservative actions like President Trump's efforts to curb immigration from Muslim states are most likely to result in adverse outcomes in the country's more progressive regions when challenged on constitutional grounds. So it was with Trump's first effort to use his executive authority to limit access to the United States by travelers from predominantly Islamic states.

The language of the executive orders implied that the operative criterion in imposing the new limits on immigration from the Middle Eastern and North African regions was their Muslim religion. Early challenges to those orders were sustained at the district and appellate levels, often in part on the basis of candidate and President-elect Trump's anti-Muslim rhetoric. These courts found that Trump's executive order violated the "establishment" and "free exercise of religion" clauses in the First Amendment.

In response, Presidential Proclamation 9645's provisions were crafted so that they did not reflect an explicit anti-Muslim bias. Instead, the proclamation's language emphasized national security, asserting that the safety of Americans was the operative criteria in admitting or delaying the admission of visa applicants. Nonetheless, its journey to the U.S. Supreme Court followed much the same trek as its predecessors. Hawaii's government almost immediately and successfully challenged it in a federal district court on constitutional grounds as a violation of the First Amendment, and that decision was shortly thereafter upheld in the Ninth Circuit Court of Appeals, which represents the westernmost portion of the country, including the West Coast states, which contained over fifty "sanctuary cities" and "sanctuary counties" at the time of the challenge.

In Executive Order 13780 of March 6, 2017 (Protecting the Nation from Foreign Terrorist Entry into the United States), on the recommendations of the Secretary of Homeland Security and the Attorney General, I ordered a worldwide review of whether, and if so what, additional information would be needed from each foreign country to assess adequately whether their nationals seeking to enter the United States pose a security or safety threat. This was the first such review of its kind in United States history. As part of the review, the Secretary of Homeland Security established global requirements for information sharing in support of immigration screening and vetting. The Secretary of Homeland Security developed a comprehensive set of criteria and applied it to the information-sharing practices, policies, and capabilities of foreign governments. The Secretary of State thereafter engaged with the countries reviewed in an effort to address deficiencies and achieve improvements. In many instances, those efforts produced positive results. By obtaining additional information and formal commitments from foreign governments, the United States Government has improved its capacity and ability to assess whether foreign nationals attempting to enter the United States pose a security or safety threat. Our Nation is safer as a result of this work.

Despite those efforts, the Secretary of Homeland Security, in consultation with the Secretary of State and the Attorney General, has determined that a small number of countries—out of nearly 200 evaluated—remain deficient at this time with respect to their identity-management and information-sharing capabilities, protocols, and practices. In some cases, these countries also have a significant terrorist presence within their territory.

As President, I must act to protect the security and interests of the United States and its people. I am committed to our ongoing efforts to engage those countries willing to cooperate, improve information-sharing and identity-management protocols and procedures, and address both terrorism-related and public-safety risks. Some of the countries with remaining inadequacies face significant challenges. Others have made strides to improve their protocols and procedures, and I commend them for these efforts. But until they satisfactorily address the identified inadequacies, I have determined, on the basis of recommendations from the Secretary of Homeland Security and other members of my Cabinet, to impose certain conditional restrictions and limitations, as set forth more fully below, on entry into the United States of nationals of the countries identified in section 2 of this proclamation.

NOW, THEREFORE, I, DONALD J. TRUMP, by the authority vested in me by the Constitution and the laws of the United States of America, including sections 212(f) and 215(a) of the Immigration and Nationality Act . . . and section 301 of title 3, United States Code, hereby find that, absent the measures set forth in this proclamation, the immigrant and nonimmigrant entry into the United States of persons described in section 2 of this proclamation would be detrimental to the interests of the United States, and that their entry should be subject to certain restrictions, limitations, and exceptions. I therefore hereby proclaim the following:

Section 1. *Policy and Purpose.* (a) It is the policy of the United States to protect its citizens from terrorist attacks and other public-safety threats. Screening and vetting protocols and procedures associated with visa adjudications and other immigration processes play a critical role in implementing that policy. They enhance our ability to detect foreign nationals who may commit, aid, or support acts of terrorism, or otherwise pose a safety threat, and they aid our efforts to prevent such individuals from entering the United States.

. . .

(c) Section 2(a) of Executive Order 13780 directed a "worldwide review to identify whether, and if so what, additional information will be needed from each foreign country to adjudicate an application by a national of that country for a visa, admission, or other benefit under the INA (adjudications) in order to determine that the individual is not a security or public-safety threat." That review culminated in a report submitted to the President by the Secretary of Homeland Security on July 9, 2017. In that review, the Secretary of Homeland Security, in consultation with the Secretary of State and the Director of National Intelligence, developed a baseline for the kinds of information required from foreign governments to support the United States Government's ability to confirm the identity of individuals seeking entry into the United States.

(i) *Identity-management information.* The United States expects foreign governments to provide the information needed to determine whether individuals seeking benefits under the immigration laws are who they claim to be. . . . The criteria assessed in this category include whether the country issues electronic passports embedded with data to enable confirmation of identity, reports lost and stolen passports to appropriate entities, and makes available upon request identity-related information not included in its passports.

(ii) *National security and public-safety information.* The United States expects foreign governments to provide information about whether persons who seek entry to this country pose national security or public-safety risks. The criteria assessed in this category include whether the country makes available, directly or indirectly, known or suspected terrorist and criminal-history information upon request, . . . whether the country impedes the United States Government's receipt of information about passengers and crew traveling to the United States.

(iii) *National security and public-safety risk assessment.* The national security and public-safety risk assessment category focuses on national security risk indicators. The criteria assessed in this category include whether the country is a known or potential terrorist safe haven, ... whether it regularly fails to receive its nationals subject to final orders of removal from the United States.

. . .

(g) The Secretary of Homeland Security assesses that the following countries continue to have "inadequate" identity-management protocols, information-sharing practices, and risk factors, with respect to the baseline described in subsection (c) of this section, such that entry restrictions and limitations are recommended: Chad, Iran, Libya, North Korea, Syria, Venezuela, and Yemen. The Secretary of Homeland Security also assesses that Iraq did not meet the baseline, but that entry restrictions and limitations under a Presidential proclamation are not warranted. The Secretary of Homeland Security recommends, however, that nationals of Iraq who seek to enter the United States be subject to additional scrutiny to determine if they pose risks to the national security or public safety of the United States. In reaching these conclusions, the Secretary of Homeland Security considered the close cooperative relationship between the United States and the democratically elected government of Iraq, the strong United States diplomatic presence in Iraq, the significant presence of United States forces in Iraq, and Iraq's commitment to combating the Islamic State of Iraq and Syria (ISIS).

. . .

(i) In evaluating the recommendations of the Secretary of Homeland Security and in determining what restrictions to impose for each country, I consulted with appropriate Assistants to the President and members of the Cabinet, including the Secretaries of State, Defense, and Homeland Security, and the Attorney General. I considered several factors, including each country's capacity, ability, and willingness to cooperate with our identity-management and information-sharing policies and each country's risk factors, such as whether it has a significant terrorist presence within its territory. I also considered foreign policy, national security, and counterterrorism goals.

(ii) After reviewing the Secretary of Homeland Security's report of September 15, 2017, and accounting for the foreign policy, national security, and counterterrorism objectives of the United States, I have determined to restrict and limit the entry of nationals of 7 countries found to be "inadequate" with respect to the baseline described in subsection (c) of this section: Chad, Iran, Libya, North Korea, Syria, Venezuela, and Yemen. These restrictions distinguish between the entry of immigrants and nonimmigrants. Persons admitted on immigrant visas become lawful permanent residents of the United States. Such persons may present national security or public-safety concerns that may be distinct from those admitted as nonimmigrants. . . . And although immigrants generally receive more extensive vetting than nonimmigrants, such vetting is less reliable when the country from which someone seeks to emigrate exhibits significant gaps in its identity-management or information-sharing policies, or presents risks to the national security of the United States. For all but one of those 7 countries, therefore, I am restricting the entry of all immigrants.

[There follows a country-by-country breakdown of the specific reasons for denying entry to those immigrants and of exceptions available under certain circumstances.]

. . .

IN WITNESS WHEREOF, I have hereunto set my hand this twenty-fourth day of September, in the year of our Lord two thousand seventeen, and of the Independence of the United States of America the two hundred and forty-second.

Donald J. Trump

Source: Presidential Proclamation 9645, " Enhancing Vetting Capabilities and Processes for Detecting Attempted Entry into the United States by Terrorists or Other Public Safety Threats," September 24, 2017. https://www.federalregister.gov/documents/2017/09/27/2017-20899/enhancing-vetting-capabilities-and-processes-for-detecting-attempted-entry-into-the-united-states-by.

Supreme Court Rules in Favor of Trump Administration Travel Ban in *Trump v. Hawaii*, 2018

Majority Opinion of the Court in Trump, President of the United States, et al. v. Hawaii et al. *(585 U.S. [June 26] 2018)*

The principal takeaway from the U.S. Supreme Court's majority opinion in this landmark case upholding the September 24, 2017, presidential proclamation pertaining to would-be terrorists seeking to enter the United States is that wherever an executive order seemingly involves religious criteria, it will be subjected to a strict scrutiny test in which the government bears the burden of proof. It is a test rarely adopted by the high court, where normal practice requires those attacking a law to prove its unconstitutionality, and a test usually reserved for laws treading on the free speech, press, and assembly portions of the First Amendment.

This presumed validity of laws passed by Congress and state legislatures has long been a cornerstone of the code of judicial self-restraint that the Supreme Court adopted decades ago to police itself as a nonelected entity in exercising its power to declare unconstitutional the acts of democratically elected bodies. Thus, for example, although the constitutional power to tax is tied to the power to spend, the Supreme Court has often upheld taxes designed instead to regulate behavior (like high taxes on cigarettes) as long as the laws read as revenue-enhancing measures.

Likewise, Supreme Court decisions have long sustained executive orders in the areas of foreign and military policy based on the inherent powers doctrine, which holds that authority over these areas was never in the hands of the colonies. Instead, it passed directly from the Crown into the hands of first the Continental Congress and then the federal government with the ratification of the U.S. Constitution. Moreover, unlike the delegated powers conferred on the Congress by the states, in Article I of the Constitution, the executive branch enjoys considerable authority in crafting diplomatic and military policies. "In this vast external realm, with its important, complicated, delicate, and manifold problems, the President alone has the power to speak or listen as a representative of the nation," as Justice George Sutherland stated in the Supreme Court's 7–1 majority opinion in United States v. Curtiss-Wright Export Corporation, et al., *299 U.S. 304 (1936).*

Yet. despite these traditions and legal precedents, and despite of the fact that the presidential proclamation before it had taken great care to specify security-focused, nonsectarian criteria in screening visa applicants seeking admission to the United States, the Supreme Court upheld the proclamation by only a narrow 5–4 majority. Two of the dissenting opinions were largely on procedural grounds; however, Justices Ginsburg and Sotomayor stood fast in maintaining that the action violated the religious neutrality requirement of the First Amendment using a national security argument to mask its overt discrimination against Muslims.

ON WRIT OF CERTIORARI TO THE UNITED STATES COURT OF APPEALS FOR THE NINTH CIRCUIT [June 26, 2018]

CHIEF JUSTICE ROBERTS delivered the opinion of the Court.

Under the Immigration and Nationality Act, foreign nationals seeking entry into the United States undergo a vetting process to ensure that they satisfy the numerous requirements for admission. The Act also vests the President with authority to restrict the entry of aliens whenever he finds that their entry "would be detrimental to the interests of the United States." 8 U. S. C. §1182(f). Relying on that delegation, the President concluded that it was necessary to impose entry restrictions on nationals of countries that do not share adequate information for an informed entry determination, or that otherwise present national security risks. Presidential Proclamation No. 9645, 82 Fed. Reg. 45161 (2017) (Proclamation). The plaintiffs in this litigation, respondents here, challenged the application of those entry restrictions to certain aliens abroad. We now decide whether the President had authority under the Act to issue the Proclamation, and whether the entry policy violates the Establishment Clause of the First Amendment.

. . .

The Proclamation described how foreign states were selected for inclusion based on the review undertaken pursuant to EO–2. As part of that review, the Department of Homeland Security (DHS), in consultation with the State Department and several intelligence agencies, developed a "baseline" for the information required from foreign governments to confirm the identity of individuals seeking entry into the United States, and to determine whether those individuals pose a security threat. §1(c). The baseline included three components. The first, "identity-management information," focused on whether a foreign government ensures the integrity of travel documents by issuing electronic passports, reporting lost or stolen passports, and making available additional identity related information. Second, the agencies considered the extent to which the country discloses information on criminal history and suspected terrorist links, provides travel document exemplars, and facilitates the U.S. Government's receipt of information about airline passengers and crews traveling to the United States. Finally, the agencies weighed various indicators of national security risk, including whether the foreign state is a known or potential terrorist safe haven and whether it regularly declines to receive returning nationals following final orders of removal from the United States. *Ibid.*

. . .

Like its predecessors, the Proclamation makes clear that its "conditional restrictions" will remain in force only so long as necessary to "address" the identified "inadequacies and risks" within the covered nations. Proclamation Preamble, and §1(h); see *ibid.* (explaining that the aim is to "relax[] or remove[]" the entry restrictions "as soon as possible"). To that end, the Proclamation establishes an ongoing process to engage covered nations and assess every 180 days whether the entry restrictions should be modified or terminated. §§4(a), (b). Indeed, after the initial review period, the President determined that Chad had made sufficient improvements to its identity management protocols, and he accordingly lifted the entry suspension on its nationals. See Proclamation No. 9723, 83 Fed. Reg. 15937. Finally, the Proclamation properly identifies a "class of aliens"—nationals of select countries—whose entry is suspended.

. . .

IV

A

We now turn to plaintiffs' claim that the Proclamation was issued for the unconstitutional purpose of excluding Muslims.

. . .

B

. . .Plaintiffs believe that the Proclamation violates this prohibition by singling out Muslims for disfavored treatment. The entry suspension, they contend, operates as a "religious gerrymander," in part because most of the countries covered by the Proclamation have Muslim-majority populations.

At the heart of plaintiffs' case is a series of statements by the President and his advisers casting doubt on the official objective of the Proclamation. For example, while a candidate on the campaign trail, the President published a "Statement on Preventing Muslim Immigration" that called for a "total and complete shutdown of Muslims entering the United States until our country's representatives can figure out what is going on."

. . .

Plaintiffs argue that this President's words strike at fundamental standards of respect and tolerance, in violation of our constitutional tradition. But the issue before us is not whether to denounce the statements. It is instead the significance of those statements in reviewing a Presidential directive, neutral on its face, addressing a matter within the core of executive responsibility. In doing so, we must consider not only the statements of a particular President, but also the authority of the Presidency itself. The case before us differs in numerous respects from the conventional Establishment Clause claim. Unlike the typical suit involving religious displays or school prayer, plaintiffs seek to invalidate a national security directive regulating the entry of aliens abroad. Their claim accordingly raises a number of delicate issues regarding the scope of the constitutional right and the manner of proof. The Proclamation, moreover, is facially neutral toward religion. Plaintiffs therefore ask the Court to probe the sincerity of the stated justifications for the policy by reference to extrinsic statements—many of which were made before the President took the oath of office.

C

For more than a century, this Court has recognized that the admission and exclusion of foreign nationals is a "fundamental sovereign attribute exercised by the Government's political departments largely immune from judicial control." *Fiallo v. Bell*, 430 U. S. 787, 792 (1977); see *Harisiades v. Shaughnessy*, 342 U. S. 580, 588–589 (1952) ("[A]ny policy toward aliens is vitally and intricately interwoven with contemporaneous policies in regard to the conduct of foreign relations [and] the war power."). Because decisions in these matters may implicate "relations with foreign powers," or involve "classifications defined in the light of changing political and economic circumstances," such judgments "are frequently of a character more appropriate to either the Legislature or the Executive." *Mathews v. Diaz*, 426 U. S. 67, 81 (1976).

Nonetheless, although foreign nationals seeking admission have no constitutional right to entry, this Court has engaged in a circumscribed judicial inquiry when the denial of a visa allegedly burdens the constitutional rights of a U.S. citizen. In *Kleindienst v. Mandel*, the Attorney General denied admission to a Belgian journalist and self-described "revolutionary Marxist," Ernest Mandel, who had been invited to speak at a conference at Stanford University. 408 U. S., at 756–757. The professors who wished to hear Mandel speak challenged that decision under the First Amendment, and we acknowledged that their constitutional "right to receive information" was implicated. *Id.*, at 764–765. But we limited our review to whether the Executive gave a "facially legitimate and bona fide" reason for its action. *Id.*, at 769. Given the authority of the political branches over admission, we held that "when the Executive exercises this [delegated] power negatively on the basis of a facially legitimate and bona fide reason, the courts will neither look behind the exercise of that discretion, nor test it by balancing its justification" against the asserted constitutional interests of U. S. citizens. *Id.*, at 770.

. . .

Mandel's narrow standard of review "has particular force" in admission and immigration cases that overlap with "the area of national security." Din, 576 U. S., at ___ (KENNEDY, J., concurring in judgment) (slip op., at 3).

. . .

The upshot of our cases in this context is clear: "Any rule of constitutional law that would inhibit the flexibility" of the President "to respond to changing world conditions should be adopted only with the greatest caution," and our inquiry into matters of entry and national security is highly constrained. *Mathews*, 426 U. S., at 81–82. We need not define the precise contours of that inquiry in this case. A conventional application of *Mandel*, asking only whether the policy is facially legitimate and bona fide, would put an end to our review. But the Government has suggested that it may be appropriate here for the inquiry to extend beyond the facial neutrality of the order. . . . For our purposes today, we assume that we may look behind the face of the Proclamation to the extent of applying rational basis review. That standard of review considers whether the entry policy is plausibly related to the Government's stated objective to protect the country and improve vetting processes. See *Railroad Retirement Bd. v. Fritz*, 449 U. S. 166, 179 (1980). As a result, we may consider plaintiffs' extrinsic evidence, but will uphold the policy so long as it can reasonably be understood to result from a justification independent of unconstitutional grounds.

D

. . .

The Proclamation is expressly premised on legitimate purposes: preventing entry of nationals who cannot be adequately vetted and inducing other nations to improve their practices. The text says nothing about religion. Plaintiffs and the dissent nonetheless emphasize that five of the seven nations currently included in the Proclamation have Muslim-majority populations. Yet that fact alone does not support an inference of religious hostility, given that the policy covers just 8% of the world's Muslim population and is limited to countries that were previously designated by Congress or prior administrations as posing national security risks.

. . .

More fundamentally, plaintiffs and the dissent challenge the entry suspension based on their perception of its effectiveness and wisdom. They suggest that the policy is overbroad and does little to serve national security interests. But we cannot substitute our own assessment for the Executive's predictive judgments on such matters, all of which "are delicate, complex, and involve large elements of prophecy." *Chicago & Southern Air Lines, Inc. v. Waterman S. S. Corp.*, 333 U. S. 103, 111 (1948).

. . .

Three additional features of the entry policy support the Government's claim of a legitimate national security interest. First, since the President introduced entry restrictions in January 2017, three Muslim-majority countries—Iraq, Sudan, and Chad—have been removed from the list of covered countries.

Second, for those countries that remain subject to entry restrictions, the Proclamation includes significant exceptions for various categories of foreign nationals.

Third, the Proclamation creates a waiver program open to all covered foreign nationals seeking entry as immigrants or nonimmigrants. According to the Proclamation, consular officers are to consider in each admissibility determination whether the alien demonstrates that (1) denying entry would cause undue hardship; (2) entry would not pose a threat to public safety; and (3) entry would be in the interest of the United States.

. . .

V

Because plaintiffs have not shown that they are likely to succeed on the merits of their claims, we reverse the grant of the preliminary injunction as an abuse of discretion. *Winter v. Natural Resources Defense Council, Inc.*, 555 U. S. 7, 32 (2008).

The judgment of the Court of Appeals is reversed, and the case is remanded for further proceedings consistent with this opinion. It is so ordered.

Source: Supreme Court Majority Opinion, *Trump, President of the United States, et al. vs. Hawaii, et al.* (585 U.S. [June 26] 2018). Decided June 26, 2018. https://www.supremecourt.gov/opinions/17pdf/17-965_h315.pdf.

Remarks by Senator Mitt Romney following the Capitol Riot, 2021

Public Statement Delivered on January 6, 2021

In the aftermath of the shocking riot carried out by a mob of Trump supporters at the U.S. Capitol on January 6, 2021, Republican senator Mitt Romney of Utah, who had been his party's presidential standard-bearer in the 2012 election, excoriated President Trump for playing a leading role in sparking the violence. The following is a statement issued by Romney as the Senate prepared to reconvene to certify Democrat Joe Biden's victory in the November 2020 presidential election.

We gather today due to a selfish man's injured pride and the outrage of his supporters whom he has deliberately misinformed for the past two months and stirred to action this very morning. What happened here today was an insurrection, incited by the President of the United States. Those who choose to continue to support his dangerous gambit by objecting to the results of a legitimate, democratic election will forever be seen as being complicit in an unprecedented attack against our democracy. They will be remembered for their role in this shameful episode in American history. That will be their legacy.

The objectors have claimed they are doing so on behalf of the voters. Have an audit, they say, to satisfy the many people who believe that the election was stolen. Please! No Congressional led audit will ever convince those voters, particularly when the President will continue to claim that the election was stolen. The best way we can show respect for the voters who are upset is by telling them the truth. That is the burden, and the duty, of leadership. The truth is that President-elect Biden won this election. President Trump lost. Scores of courts, the President's own Attorney General, and state election officials both Republican and Democrat have reached this unequivocal decision.

We must not be intimidated or prevented from fulfilling our constitutional duty. We must continue with the count of Electoral College votes. In light of today's sad circumstances, I ask my colleagues: Do we weigh our own political fortunes more heavily than we weigh the strength of our Republic, the strength of our democracy, and the cause of freedom? What is the weight of personal acclaim compared to the weight of conscience?

Leader McConnell said that the vote today is the most important in his 40 plus years of public service. That is not because this vote reveals something about the election; it is because this vote reveals something about ourselves. I urge my colleagues to move forward with completing the electoral count, to refrain from further objections, and to unanimously affirm the legitimacy of the presidential election.

Source: Romney, Mitt. "Romney Condemns Insurrection at U.S. Capitol." January 6, 2021. https://www.romney.senate.gov/romney-condemns-insurrection-us-capitol.

FBI Director Wray Tells America That Capitol Riot Was "Not an Isolated Event," 2021

Statement to the Senate Judiciary Committee, March 2, 2021

On March 2, 2021, about eight weeks after a violent riot had been carried out by supporters of President Trump against the U.S. Capitol to overthrow the legitimate election results from the November 2020 presidential election, the Senate Judiciary Committee held a hearing to address the issue of domestic terrorism. The most prominent individual to testify at the hearing was Christopher Wray, the director of the Federal Bureau of Investigation (FBI). The following is a portion of Wray's opening statement at that hearing, in which he discusses the threat that violent right-wing extremist groups pose to the country's safety and national security.

I am honored to be here, representing the men and women of the FBI. Our people—nearly 37,000 of them—are the heart of the Bureau. I am proud of their service and their commitment to our mission. Every day, they tackle their jobs with perseverance, professionalism, and integrity—sometimes at the greatest of costs.

Despite the many challenges our FBI workforce has faced, I am immensely proud of their dedication to protecting the American people and upholding the Constitution. Our country has faced unimaginable challenges this past year. Yet, through it all, whether it was coming to the aid of our partners during the Capitol siege and committing all of our resources to ensuring that those involved in that brutal assault on our democracy are brought to justice, the proliferation of terroristic hate moving at the speed of social media, abhorrent hate crimes, COVID-19 related fraud and misinformation, the increasing threat of cyber intrusions and state-sponsored economic espionage, malign foreign influence and interference, the scourge of opioid trafficking and abuse, or human trafficking and crimes against children, the women and men of the FBI have unwaveringly stood at the ready and taken it upon themselves to tackle any and all challenges thrown their way.

Capitol Violence

First and foremost, I want to assure you, your staff, and the American people that the FBI has deployed every single tool at our disposal and our full arsenal of investigative resources to aggressively pursue those involved in the heinous violence and criminal activity that occurred on January 6, 2021. We are working closely with our federal, state, and local law enforcement partners, as well as private sector partners, to identify those responsible for the violence and destruction of property at the U.S. Capitol building who showed blatant and appalling disregard for our institutions of government and the orderly administration of the democratic process.

Our agents, analysts, and professional staff have been working non-stop with federal prosecutors to gather and preserve evidence, share intelligence, and identify and bring charges against those who participated in the siege of the U.S. Capitol. As we have said consistently, we do not and will not tolerate violent extremists who use the guise of First Amendment–protected activity to wreak havoc and incite violence. Thus far, our investigators have identified hundreds of individuals involved in the siege of the Capitol Complex and already charged well over 300 of them. Many of those identifications are the result of the over 200,000 digital media tips we have received from the public. Members of the public who have any information related to the siege should continue to provide tips, information, and videos of illegal activity at tips.fbi.gov or by calling 1-800-CALL-FBI.

Overall, the FBI assesses that the January 6 siege of the Capitol Complex demonstrates a willingness by some to use violence against the government in furtherance of their political and social goals. This ideologically motivated violence underscores the symbolic nature of the National Capital Region and the willingness of domestic violent extremists to travel to events in this area and violently engage law enforcement and their perceived adversaries. The American people should rest assured that we will continue to work to hold accountable those individuals who participated in the violent breach of the Capitol on January 6, and any others who attempt to use violence and destruction to intimidate, coerce, or influence the American people or affect the conduct of our government.

Top Terrorism Threats

As has been stated multiple times in the past, preventing terrorist attacks, in all forms, remains the FBI's top priority. The nature of the threat posed by terrorism—both international terrorism (IT) and domestic terrorism (DT)—continues to evolve.

The most significant threat to our homeland is posed by lone actors who often radicalize online and seek out soft targets to attack with easily accessible weapons. We see these individualized threats manifested within both domestic violent extremists (DVEs) and homegrown violent extremists (HVEs). Although they have different ideologies, they both typically radicalize and mobilize to violence on their own and are both located primarily in the United States. Individuals who commit violent criminal acts in furtherance of ideological goals stemming from domestic influences—some of which include racial or ethnic bias, or strong anti-government or anti-authority sentiments—are described as DVEs, whereas HVEs are individuals inspired primarily by achieving global jihad, but not receiving individualized direction from Foreign Terrorist Organizations (FTOs).

Domestic and homegrown violent extremists are often motivated and inspired by a mix of sociopolitical, ideological, and personal grievances against their targets, and more recently have focused on accessible targets to include civilians, law enforcement and the military, symbols or members of the U.S. government, houses of worship, retail locations, and mass public gatherings. Selecting these types of soft targets, in addition to the insular nature of their radicalization and mobilization to violence and limited discussions with others, challenges law enforcement to detect and disrupt the activities of lone actors before they occur.

The top threat we face from DVEs continues to be those we identify as racially or ethnically motivated violent extremists (RMVEs), specifically those who advocate for the superiority of the white race, and who were the primary source of ideologically motivated lethal incidents of violence in 2018 and 2019. It is important to note that we have recently seen an increase in lethal DVE attacks perpetrated by anti-government or anti-authority violent extremists, specifically militia violent extremists and anarchist violent extremists. Anti-government or anti-authority violent extremists were responsible for three of the four lethal DVE attacks in 2020. Also, in 2020, we saw the first lethal attack committed by an anarchist violent extremist in over 20 years.

Consistent with our mission, the FBI does not investigate First Amendment–protected speech or association, peaceful protests, or political activity. The FBI holds sacred the rights of individuals to peacefully exercise their First Amendment freedoms. Non-violent protests are signs of a healthy democracy, not an ailing one. Regardless of their specific ideology, the FBI will aggressively pursue those who seek to hijack legitimate First Amendment–protected activity by engaging in violent criminal activity such as the breach, destruction of property, and violent assaults on law enforcement officers that we witnessed on January 6 and during lawful protests throughout the U.S. during the summer of 2020. In other words, we will actively pursue the opening of FBI investigations when an individual uses, or threatens the use of, force, violence, or coercion, in violation of federal law and in the furtherance of a political or social ideological goal.

Source: Wray, Christopher. Opening Statement. *Oversight of the Federal Bureau of Investigation: the January 6 Insurrection, Domestic Terrorism, and Other Threats*. U.S. Senate Judiciary Committee hearing, March 2, 2021. https://www.fbi.gov/news/testimony/oversight-of-the-federal-bureau-of-investigation-the-january-6-insurrection-domestic-terrorism-and-other-threats.

About the Editors and Contributors

EDITORS

Joseph R. Rudolph Jr., PhD (University of Virginia), is a professor of political science at Towson University (Baltimore, Maryland). He has served as a Fulbright appointee to Czechoslovakia (1991–1992) and Kosovo (2011–2012), has published in the field of ethnic and nationalist politics for more than thirty years, and has frequently participated in the democratization operations of the Organization for Security and Cooperation in Europe (OSCE). His work on terrorism dates from the violent separatist movements in late twentieth-century Western Europe and the urban terrorist activity in Germany and Italy in the late 1970s. Most recently, he compiled, edited, and authored the lead essay in the section on "The State, Society, and Ethnopolitics" in *The Palgrave Handbook of Ethnicity* (Steven Ratuva, general editor, 2019).

William J. Lahneman is professor and chair of the Department of Security Studies and International Affairs at Embry-Riddle Aeronautical University in Daytona Beach, Florida. He holds a PhD in international relations from the Johns Hopkins University's School of Advanced International Studies (SAIS), an MA in national security affairs from the Naval Postgraduate School, and a BS from the U.S. Naval Academy, Annapolis, Maryland. A 2019 Fulbright Scholar (Rey Juan Carlos University, Madrid, Spain), his research interests include homeland security, the future of intelligence analysis, and international conflict resolution. His major publications are listed at https://works.bepress.com/william_lahneman/. He is a former commander in the U.S. Navy, with specializations in nuclear propulsion, international negotiations, and strategic planning.

CONTRIBUTORS

Benjamin V. Allison is a graduate student specializing in twentieth- and twenty-first-century American foreign policy and the coauthor with Samuel S. Stanton Jr. of *Understanding Violence in Ideological and Theological Insurgencies* (forthcoming).

Michael Andregg received a PhD in genetics from the University of California, Davis, and then did research and taught for thirty-five years at the University of Minnesota and University of St. Thomas.

Tarek Azmy received his BS and MS in criminal justice from the California State University, Long Beach. His more than quarter of a century work in law enforcement in Southern California has included serving on the FBI's Counterterrorism Task Force and a wide range of other assignments primarily focusing on counterterrorism and aviation security.

James T. Barry served in the FBI for twenty-two years, retiring as a supervisory special agent. As an FBI hazardous materials technician, he was involved in recovery efforts at the Pentagon site on 9/11 and was part of the AMERITHRAX investigation for over one year. He also represented the FBI in several nations around the globe. He holds a BA in international studies and MA in public administration.

Eliza Bechtold is a qualified lawyer and former ACLU attorney. She is currently a PhD candidate and part-time tutor at Durham Law School. Her degrees include a BA in legal studies from Scripps College; a JD from the University of California, Hastings College of the Law; and an LLM in public international law from the London School of Economics and Political Science.

Stefan Brooks, PhD, is an associate professor of homeland security at Rabdan Academy in Abu Dhabi, the United Arab Emirates, and a senior lecturer for Norwich University. He has published articles on U.S. foreign policy, Middle East politics, Russian politics, and terrorism. He is the coeditor of *Post-Soviet Conflicts* and the author of the chapter "Russian Foreign Policy under President Putin."

Andrew Broyhill is a senior undergraduate student at Westminster College in Fulton, Missouri, majoring in security studies with emphases in cyber and national security. He served as a panelist at the Citadel's Intelligence and Cybersecurity Conference in 2018, where he presented research findings on hacktivism and national security.

John M. Callahan is the dean of the School of Graduate and Professional Studies at New England College. He received his PhD from Old Dominion University in 2015, with a focus on U.S. foreign policy and national security decision-making. He has worked for the U.S. State Department and the intelligence community and served in the Department of Defense as a public affairs planner for homeland security events.

John R. "Jack" Capra received his BS from Florida State University, a JD from St. Thomas University College of Law, and an MBA from City University. A PhD candidate in forensic psychology, Capra served twenty-two years in the Navy Judge Advocate General's Corps, including tours of duty in the Middle East, Guantánamo Bay, Europe, and Africa. During his first tour in Iraq, he was awarded the Purple Heart and Combat Action Ribbon. He is currently the general counsel at Northwest Florida State College.

J. Philip Craiger, PhD, CISSP, is a professor of cybersecurity in the Department of Security Studies and International Affairs at Embry-Riddle Aeronautical University. His research interests include applied cyber forensics, aviation cybersecurity, and small unmanned aerial systems cybersecurity. He has over 130 published journal articles, book chapters, and conference presentations and serves as a coprincipal investigator of the NSF-funded National Cybersecurity Training and Education Center.

Braden Eisenbeis is a student at Westminster University in Fulton, Missouri, and the coauthor of "Armed Militias" in this volume.

Kyle Feeley is a former Marine Corps officer and is currently serving in the law enforcement community. He has a master's degree in homeland security management from Towson University.

Ygnacio "Nash" Flores is a retired navy lieutenant commander and former senior chief. After the military, he was the dean of Public Safety and Business before assuming a faculty position at Rio Hondo College. He holds, among other degrees, a doctorate from the University of Southern California, an MPS-HS from Pennsylvania State University, and a BSCJ from National University. He is the author of *The Pedagogy of Violent Extremism* and numerous book chapters on homeland security.

Jakob R. Gibson is a student at Westminster University in Fulton, Missouri, and the coauthor of "Enhanced Interrogation Debate" in this volume.

Tobias T. Gibson is the John Langton Professor of Legal Studies and Political Science and the Security Studies Program chair at Westminster College in Missouri. In addition, he is an instructor and subject matter expert for the Texas A & M Homeland Security graduate program. His recent work has appeared in the *National Security Law Journal* and the second edition of *Homeland Security: Foundations in Law and Policy.*

Brett M. Gould is currently a student at Westminster College, where he majors in security studies. He is active on campus, including being a member of the college's honors program and a tutor for the Security Studies program.

Daniel S. Gressang IV is an assistant professor of security studies and international affairs at Embry-Riddle Aeronautical University. Previously, he spent thirty-one years with the National Security Agency. He holds an AB and MA, both in political science, from the University of Alabama; a Master of Science of strategic intelligence (MSSI) from the National Defense Intelligence College, and a PhD in government and politics from the University of Maryland.

Amy E. Grubb is associate professor of security studies and international affairs at Embry-Riddle Aeronautical University in Daytona Beach, Florida. She holds a PhD from the University of California, Irvine; an MPIA from the University of California, San Diego; and a BA from Dartmouth College. Her research focuses on political violence and micro-level security processes. Her publications include an article in *Security Studies* and chapters in various edited volumes.

Victoria L. Gustafsson received her Bachelor of Science in human factors psychology from Embry-Riddle Aeronautical University in Daytona Beach, Florida, where she is currently pursuing a Master of Science in human factors. She is helping to lead the university's 9/11 Project, focusing on how aviation has evolved in the twenty years following 9/11.

Helena M. Hansson received her MS in human factors psychology from Embry-Riddle Aeronautical University in Daytona Beach, Florida, where she was a member of the women's soccer team. She has coauthored articles on sports, games, and religion, and she served as a teaching assistant for a course on Religion, Conflict, and Peace.

Vincent E. Henry, CPP, PhD, is professor at Long Island University's Homeland Security and Terrorism Institute and was founding director of the Homeland Security Management Institute. A twenty-one-year veteran of the NYPD and the first American police officer to be named a Fulbright Scholar, Vincent has had uniformed, plainclothes, supervisory, and management positions and was a first responder to the 9/11 World Trade Center terrorist attacks. His publications include *Death Work: Police Trauma and the Psychology of Survival* (2003).

Jonathan B. Hensley, JD, PhD, is a lecturer in political science at Towson University. He teaches courses on the American legal system, judicial politics, and U.S. constitutional law. His current research focuses on the activity of organized interest groups in the judicial system, in particular, the legal agendas of religiously affiliated groups. Before beginning graduate studies in political science, Dr. Hensley was an attorney in private practice for seven years.

Jeffrey Kaplan is a professor and author who has written about radical politics for decades. He is currently teaching in Saudi Arabia at the King Fahd Defense College. Retired from the University of Wisconsin–Oshkosh, his most recent book is entitled *Radical Religion and Violence: Theory and Case Studies.*

David Keck serves as chaplain at Embry-Riddle Aeronautical University, where he teaches a course on Religion, Conflict, and Peace. A medieval and Reformation historian by training, with a BA from Yale and PhD from Harvard, he is the author of three books, including *Angels and Angelology in the Middle Ages*. An ordained Presbyterian minister, he received his MDiv from Duke Divinity School.

Gary C. Kessler, PhD, CISSP, is president of Gary Kessler Associates, a consulting, research, and training company located in Ormond Beach, Florida. He has been in the information security and education fields for more than forty years and is currently a professor of cybersecurity in the Security Studies & International Affairs Department at Embry-Riddle University following stints elsewhere, including the U.S. Coast Guard Academy. His research interests focus on maritime cybersecurity, digital forensics, and cybersecurity management and policy.

Stacy Kowtko completed her master's in American history at Eastern Washington University and is ABD in modern U.S. history through Washington State University. She has been teaching undergraduate and graduate courses in United States, Middle East, and World history for over two decades. Her area of specialization is Early North American History.

Diana LaBoy has a master's degree in integrated homeland security management from Towson University. Her background includes serving as a crisis management lead supporting forty-seven sites around the globe for a multinational corporation.

Keith A. Leitich received an MA in political science from Arkansas State University and has taught political science at Pierce College and North Seattle College. He has contributed to *The War on Terror Encyclopedia: From the Rise of Al-Qaeda to 9/11 and Beyond* and *U.S. Conflicts in the 21st Century: Afghanistan War, Iraq War, and the War on Terror*. He is also the coauthor of *The History of Myanmar*.

Robert J. Louden long served as the chief hostage negotiator for the New York Police Department before retiring and is now professor emeritus at Georgian Court University, whose Criminal Justice and Homeland Security program he directed from 2005 to 2015. Some of his many contributions to his profession are listed as further reading on his "Hostage Negotiation" entry in this volume.

Shady Abdelwahab Mansour serves as executive editor in chief of Trending Events, a periodical published by FARAS (Future for Advanced Research and Studies) and head of the security studies unit in the Abu Dhabi think tank, after previously working at the Information Decision and Support Center, the Egyptian cabinet's think tank. His research interests focus on regional security and conflict management. His most recent work is "The Wedge Strategy: How Saudi Arabia Is Attempting to Influence the Syrian Conflict," in D.K. Khatib (ed.), *The Syrian Crisis* (2020).

Don Mason has over twenty years of higher education experience as well as twenty years of law enforcement experience working in custody, patrol, and special assignments as a supervisor and manager. The author of numerous articles on public safety, he has previously worked in the police academy as a recruit training officer and taught classes in administration of justice, corrections, and emergency preparedness at Compton College, El Camino College, Rio Hondo College, and California State University, Los Angeles.

Rachel E. McGinnis is an interdisciplinary scholar focusing on the fields of conflict science, sexual violence, and mass atrocities and is currently the director of the Peace and Conflict Studies program at the Rochester Institute of Technology Kosovo and Embry-Riddle University in Florida. She holds a PhD in conflict analysis and resolution from Nova Southeastern University and has developed courses on the Politics of Genocide, Globalization and the Nation-State, and the Troubles: Conflict in Northern Ireland. Her recent focus in teaching was Cultural Images of War and Terror, Global Exiles, and Human Rights.

Pamela K. Mertens has over twenty-seven years of combined experience in the U.S. military, homeland security, criminal justice, conflict resolution and emergency management fields. She is a former U.S. Marine and Navy Reservist who received her doctorate in conflict analysis and resolution from Nova Southeastern University. Her past teaching includes such diverse appointments as Cherokee Nation, Oklahoma. She is currently the department chair of Criminal Justice and Forensics at Keiser University–Flagship in South Florida.

Elisabeth Hope Murray, PhD, is the president of the International Network of Genocide Scholars and associate professor of security studies and international affairs at Embry-Riddle Aeronautical University. Her work focuses on ideology, macro-level violence, gender security, genocide, environmental insecurity, and the process of radicalization in genocidal states. Her publications include *Disrupting Pathways to Genocide* (2015) and *Environments of Security* (American Meteorological Society, November 2019).

Jeffrey Neuman completed his Bachelor of Science in political science at Towson University. He is currently pursuing his juris doctorate at the University of Baltimore Law School and hopes to one day work in the field of public interest law.

Stephen Owen is a professor of criminal justice at Radford University in Virginia. He holds a Master of Arts and Doctor of Philosophy in political science from the University of Missouri–St. Louis. His work has focused on such diverse subjects as emergency management, criminal justice education, and LGBTQ+ issues in criminal justice. He coauthored the introductory criminal justice textbook *Foundations of Criminal Justice* and has been recognized with his university's Distinguished Creative Scholar and college's Distinguished Teaching Awards.

Ann Phillips, JD, is an associate professor of homeland security at Embry-Riddle Aeronautical University. Previously, she worked for over twenty years with the Department of Legal Affairs, Office of the Attorney General for the State of Florida, in the Criminal Appeals Division, handling criminal appeal cases at all levels within state and federal courts. Board certified in criminal appellate practice, her research interests include constitutional issues, particularly those related to the Fourth and Fifth Amendments.

Mackenzie Rice is pursuing a graduate degree in the Master of Global Affairs program at the Munk School of Global Affairs and Public Policy at the University of Toronto, having completed her summer internship working with UNICEF in Nairobi. Her focus is on refugee resettlement processes and the protection of refugees under international law.

Tracy E. Rickman has spent thirty-eight years as a professional firefighter, educator, and coordinator of a regional fire academy and homeland security training center in Santa Fe Springs, California. His doctor of public administration, experience in the public and private sectors, and eight years of active-duty military service in the U.S. Air Force have provided insights into real-world challenges tied to public safety. He currently teaches at California State University, Los Angeles; California Baptist University, Riverside; and at three Southern California community colleges.

Gwenola Ricordeau received her PhD in social sciences from the University of Paris–IV (Sorbonne, France). She is an assistant professor of criminal justice at the California State University, Chico, and has devoted most of her research to gender identities and sexuality in prison. She has also conducted research in the Philippines on marriage migrations and women in politics.

Brian K. Simpkins is a faculty member within the Homeland Security program at Eastern Kentucky University, focusing on critical infrastructure protection, homeland security technologies, and intelligence and national security. He holds a Doctor of Education as well as graduate and undergraduate degrees in criminal justice and a graduate certificate in intelligence and national security. He is currently pursuing a PhD in criminal justice at the University of Louisville.

Daniel Stotland studied history at the University of Toronto and completed his doctorate at the University of Maryland. He specializes in twentieth-century Russian history. Currently, he is an associate professor of social sciences at Embry-Riddle Aeronautical University.

Arzan Tarapore is the South Asia research scholar at the Shorenstein Asia–Pacific Research Center at Stanford University and a senior nonresident fellow at the National Bureau of Asian Research. He holds a PhD in war studies from King's College London and previously served for thirteen years in the Australian Defense Department.

Brooke Thompson is currently an ROTC cadet at Westminster College in Missouri, the fifth generation of her family to serve in the military. Her future plans include graduate work in security studies and then a career in the military.

Andrew Tompkins, MPS, PhD, is a recent graduate of Drew University, where he received his doctorate in the history of American intelligence. His particular fields of study include human intelligence, military intelligence, and the intersection between intelligence operations and foreign policy making, especially during the mid-twentieth century.

Dawn M. Wozneak is a senior analyst producing geopolitical analyses related to international security threats, and she holds a doctorate in public safety. She has offered college courses related to intelligence education for law enforcement agencies engaged in counterterrorism initiatives globally. Previously, she served as an intelligence analyst and sworn law enforcement officer within U.S. law enforcement agencies at the local and federal levels.

Diane M. Zorri is a professor of security studies and international affairs at Embry-Riddle Aeronautical University and a nonresident senior fellow for Joint Special Operations University. A U.S. Air Force Academy, Naval Postgraduate School and George Mason University graduate, she completed A1-B2 coursework in Italian at the *Universita per Stranieri* in Perugia. During the Iraq War, she served in the Multi-National Force–Iraq in Baghdad, managing over 400 bilingual, bicultural advisers to the U.S. State Department and Department of Defense.

Index

Page numbers in **bold** indicate the location of main entries.